Restless
Visionaries

Published with the assistance of the V. Ray Cardozier Fund, an endowment created to support publication of scholarly books

Restless Visionaries

The Social Roots
of Antebellum Reform
in Alabama and Michigan

JOHN W. QUIST

LOUISIANA STATE UNIVERSITY PRESS   *Baton Rouge*

Copyright © 1998 by Louisiana State University Press
Manufactured in the United States of America
First printing

07 06 05 04 03 02 01 00 99 98   5 4 3 2 1

Designer: Michele Myatt Quinn
Typeface: Adobe Caslon
Typesetter: Wilsted & Taylor Publishing Services
Printer and binder: Edwards Brothers, Inc.

Library of Congress Cataloging-in-Publication Data
Quist, John W., 1960–
   Restless visionaries : the social roots of antebellum reform in
Alabama and Michigan / John W. Quist.
      p.   cm.
   Includes bibliographical references and index.
   ISBN 0-8071-2133-9 (alk. paper)
      1. Social reformers—Alabama—Tuscaloosa County—History—19th
century.   2. Social reformers—Michigan—Washtenaw County—
History—19th century.   I. Title.
   HN79.A42T876   1997
303.48′4′0976184—dc21   97-43640
                                                               CIP

The paper in this book meets the guidelines for permanence and durability of the Committee
on Production Guidelines for Book Longevity of the Council on Library Resources.♾

for Anne

Contents

Acknowledgments / ix

Introduction / 1

1 Slaveholding Operatives of the Benevolent Empire / 19

2 Occasionally Overwhelmed by Abolitionists:
Benevolence in Washtenaw County / 103

3 Toward the Sober Slaveholder: Temperance in Tuscaloosa
County / 155

4 Prohibition Attempted and Refuted: The Temperance
Movement in Washtenaw County / 235

5 Colonization, Plantation Missions, and the Limits of
Southern Reform / 303

6 The Personification of Principle: The Crusade Against
Slavery in Washtenaw County / 354

Conclusion / 462

Appendix: Tables 1–34 / 471

Bibliography / 517

Index / 547

ACKNOWLEDGMENTS

It is with pleasure that I acknowledge the numerous debts I have accumulated as this project has grown.

I have been greatly assisted by many residents of Washtenaw and Tuscaloosa Counties who kindly opened to me the records of their municipalities and churches, supplied friendly conversation, and sometimes provided refreshments as well. I am also beholden to the staffs of several libraries and archival institutions who, in doing their jobs well, made my work as a researcher easier and more enjoyable. These include the Michigan Historical Collections at the University of Michigan's Bentley Library (especially Nancy Bartlett and Karen Mason); the University of Alabama Special Collections (especially Gunetta Rich, Clark Center, and Joe Moudry); the Alabama Department of Archives and History (especially Edwin C. Bridges, Mimi Jones, Mike Breedlove, Rickie Brunner, and Debbie Pendleton); the Samford University Special Collections, Birmingham, Alabama (especially Elizabeth Wells); the William L. Clements Library, University of Michigan (especially Rob Cox); the Library of Michigan (especially Randy Riley); the Auburn University archives; the Burton Historical Collections, Detroit Public Library; the University of Michigan interlibrary loan office; the State Archives of Michigan; the archives of the American Bible Society, New York City; the Lafayette College Library, Easton, Pennsylvania; the National Archives; and the Library of Congress.

I must thank Jon Atkins, Andy Hoag, Daniel Walker Howe, Guy Hubbs, Bil Kerrigan, Marc Kruman, Gerry Leonard, Charles Loucks, John R. McKivigan, Richard Nation, Dale Prentis, Anne Huish Quist, Johanna Shields, Cara Shelly, Mitchell Snay, James Brewer Stewart, Kevin Thornton, Michael Watson, and Mayer Zald for reading portions of this work and offering insightful—and sometimes spirited—commentary. Professors Shields and Stewart have also extended crucial moral support, for which I am appreciative.

I have also benefited from the advice, encouragement, and friendship of Richard H. Abbott, Keith Arbour, Ben Brown, Chris Chamberlin, Ronald Delph, Eric Duskin, Stephen Grossbart, Mark Higbee, Sue Juster, David H. Kelly, Gerald Linderman, Ken Lockridge, Joseph Manzione, Rich Newman, Paul Pruitt, Bryn Roberts, Alfred Skerpan, Jim Topetzes, Mike Vorenberg, Ronald G. Walters, and John Wills. I will always be indebted to D. Michael Quinn, whose example as a scholar and receptiveness to my undergraduate work inspired me to pursue history further. Robert C. Kenzer and Marvin S. Hill also encouraged me as an undergraduate, and Bob has continued to serve me as a sounding board. I owe much to my colleagues at Eastern Michigan University, D'Youville College, and Shippensburg University for sustaining my academic career.

Research funding from the University of Michigan's Horace H. Rackham School of Graduate Studies and D'Youville College furnished important support for this work. Merrill and Cynthia Clark, and Mark and Linda Johnson, obliged me with accommodations and hospitality during two research trips.

Maris Vinovskis first suggested that I study Michigan but wisely urged me to limit this study to only two counties, rather than the four counties in four states that I was originally considering. Lawrence Frederick Kohl provided me with a thorough critique of the manuscript, has extended first-rate professional advice, and tutored me in Tuscaloosa's modern culinary delights. This study originated—in a much simpler form—as a seminar paper that I wrote for Shaw Livermore. I have profited from his prompt comments on each of these chapters in their earliest drafts, as well as from his supportive criticism and our lively discussions.

The staff at LSU Press has been first-rate. Executive Editor John Easterly shepherded the manuscript through the Press's editorial review process. Gerry Anders expertly and carefully copy-edited the entire manuscript and helped transform it into a book; he also found numerous mistakes and grammatical lapses that I thought had long since been purged.

I have been most fortunate to have enjoyed the involvement of J. Mills Thornton III with this project. Mills has charted me through the waters of antebellum and present-day Alabama. His diligent and meticulous reading of every chapter has saved me from many errors. He persuaded me to broaden the scope of this study yet helped me resist the temptation to examine every piece of data that *might* be relevant. Mills assembled his graduate students to critique one another's work, and in the process taught us the value of an intellectual community. Further, both he and his wife, Brenda Booth Thornton, generously accommodated and tolerated me during my research trips to Alabama. And foremost, he has been a firm believer in this study from its commencement to its conclusion.

Parts of chapters 1 and 6 appeared previously in the *Journal of Southern History* and the *Journal of the Early Republic,* respectively. My thanks to John B. Boles, Evelyn Thomas Nolen, John Lauritz Larson, and Michael A. Morrison for their editorial expertise and for their permission to republish portions of those articles.

Finally, I must mention the importance of my family concerning this project. I have been positively influenced in many ways by my parents and grandparents. My daughters, Johanna and Lauren, have reminded me of life's more important things. Most significant, though, has been the warm support and love that I have received for many years from my wife, Anne. Whatever the merits of this work, without her its preliminary research would have never been conducted. Although words insufficiently express the depth of my gratitude, "thanks" will have to do for now.

RESTLESS
VISIONARIES

Introduction

In the decades preceding the Civil War, the United States was swept by a reform impulse that was expressed in diverse ways. Among other things, crusaders endeavored to eliminate alcohol consumption, circulate Bibles and religious tracts, promote both secular and Sunday schools, establish prisons and asylums, and ameliorate or abolish slavery; some of the more renowned but less widespread causes included communitarian socialism, women's suffrage, and the peace movement. This plethora of efforts that resonated throughout the land has long fascinated historians, who have tried to explain why these efforts captured the imagination of so many Americans.

Since many of the most prominent reformers of these years demonstrated a deep commitment to evangelical religion, scholars have often described reform as religiously inspired. Indeed, the changing Protestant theology of the early nineteenth century caused many Americans to look at their social environment differently. The first quarter of the century witnessed a dramatic reorientation of Calvinism, involving both the rejection of determinism and the acceptance of the belief that sin is the result of the voluntary, selfish, and conscious actions of individuals. People were no longer considered to be helpless and depraved by nature. Instead, they were recognized as free agents and potential doers of good who could attain perfection and salvation through spiritual regeneration. Social evils could therefore be eliminated by making people aware of society's shortcomings and concurrently preaching the gospel to them. Reformers believed that as people became cognizant of the facts, they would quickly change their own lives and thus bring about social change. Some evangelicals were additionally inspired by the belief that their efforts were part of a holy eschatology that would eventually result in the millennial reign of Christ. This evangelical fervor created a sense of immediacy that turned previously genteel protests into crusades.[1]

People who espoused reform, however, were not necessarily committed to evangelical Protestantism. Many Americans viewed their nation's increased wealth, technological innovations, improved transportation, rapid urbanization, industrialization, growing agricultural production, and settlement of the frontier as positive achievements. The prospect of bettering the material comfort of all Americans, coupled with the belief that American society was young and expanding, contributed to a deep sense of optimism regarding the country's future. Some Americans also believed that the destiny of other nations was linked to American progress, and many were certain that their system of government was the means by which to lift the world out of ignorance, poverty, strife, and tyranny. With these goals in mind, reform became an essential component of human progress—a means by which Americans might remove social impediments to their promising future. For example, since the growth of markets placed a premium upon written communication, the growth of common schools was seen as a means whereby a larger portion of society could partake of the nation's expanding wealth; similarly, the regimentation of the industrial workplace and the drive toward efficiency made tippling on the job unthinkable. Those enamored of free labor saw slavery not only as a mockery of their own work, but also as an inefficient means of production, certain to hinder material growth and progress. And for many evangelicals, these attitudes respecting economic development converged neatly with their post-millennialist beliefs.[2]

All of this represented a positive view of humanity, affirming that people had the power to direct their lives and change society. But a darker side of reform existed as well. Optimism is seldom separable from uncertainty, and some Americans were not sure whether their nation's course would lead upward or downward. Many were doubtful about where material change would take America; were vexed by the personal and social dislocations that would re-

1. John L. Thomas, "Romantic Reform in America, 1815–1865," *American Quarterly*, XVII (Winter 1965), 656–81; Ronald G. Walters, *American Reformers, 1815–1860* (Rev. ed.; New York, 1997); George M. Thomas, *Revivalism and Cultural Change: Christianity, Nation Building, and the Market in the Nineteenth-Century United States* (Chicago, 1989).

2. Douglas T. Miller, *The Birth of Modern America, 1820–1850* (New York, 1970); Walters, *American Reformers.*

sult from this irreversible transformation of society; feared that the expanding market would create a nation of money-grubbing individualists who would seek their own well-being above that of their fellow citizens; wondered whether the impersonal forces of the marketplace, expanding government, and business institutions would undermine individual liberty and initiative; and were troubled that the prosperity of the rising generation might cause Americans to reject God and his ministers. Consequently, the rhetoric of pre–Civil War reform reiterated not only the hope of reshaping the world according to the vision of evangelical Protestants and their allies, but also expressed the fear that social change might become unmanageable.[3]

General treatments of reform, such as those by Alice Felt Tyler, C. S. Griffin, Ronald G. Walters, and Robert H. Abzug, have primarily described the activities of the most articulate and prominent activists. There have also been numerous studies of the separate movements, with much scholarly attention directed toward abolition and temperance. Many of these works are biographically oriented and center on the formation of national societies and the internal debates that often raged regarding the societies' platforms and methods. Others consider reform as an intellectual, rather than as a social, movement. In recent decades, however, scholars have investigated more closely the reform rank and file—as well as those whom the reformers hoped to reform—and have examined the functioning of these voluntary associations within community settings. Such studies, though, have concentrated mostly on the Northeast, particularly that region's larger cities.[4] Although the degree of ur-

---

3. For further development of some of these themes, see Mark Y. Hanley, *Beyond a Christian Commonwealth: The Protestant Quarrel with the American Republic, 1830–1860* (Chapel Hill, 1994).

4. General treatments: Alice Felt Tyler, *Freedom's Ferment: Phases of American Social History from the Colonial Period to the Outbreak of the Civil War* (Minneapolis, 1944); C. S. Griffin, *The Ferment of Reform, 1830–1860* (New York, 1967); Walters, *American Reformers;* Robert H. Abzug, *Cosmos Crumbling: American Reform and the Religious Imagination* (New York, 1994); Steven Mintz, *Moralists and Modernizers: America's Pre–Civil War Reformers* (Baltimore, 1995). Community studies and other works focused on the Northeast: Whitney Cross, *The Burned-Over District: The Social and Intellectual History of Enthusiastic Religion in Western New York, 1800–1850* (Ithaca, 1950); Carroll Smith Rosenberg, *Religion and the Rise of the American City: The New York City Mission Movement, 1812–1870* (Ithaca, 1971); Paul E. Johnson, *A Shopkeepers' Millennium: Society and Revivals in Rochester, New York, 1815–1837* (New York, 1978); Mary P. Ryan, *Cradle of the Middle Class: The Family in Oneida County, New York, 1790–1865* (Cambridge, Eng., 1981); Nancy

banization and industrialization in New England and New York pointed the direction that the rest of the nation would follow, it was by no means the norm for the rest of America at this time. For example, in 1820 a mere 7 percent of Americans lived in towns with a population of 2,500 or more, and by 1860 this figure had risen to only 20 percent. Even though this urban growth was exceptional, most Americans continued to live in rural settings or small villages on the eve of the Civil War.[5] Nor was reform in the Northeast typical: some radical manifestations that flourished there were less conspicuous in the rest of America. In the Old Northwest, abolitionism did not fragment as it did in Massachusetts, and radical reforms, such as women's rights and the peace movement, were scarcely present.

In order to understand how deeply and extensively the climate of reform penetrated into the lives of most Americans, one must study reform as most Americans observed and experienced it—that is, as it functioned in the villages and countryside. In this study, I compare reform in two separate counties that were mostly rural yet also had at least one large community that served as the commercial and political center. In each county, I principally investigate those causes that developed into large voluntary associations—namely, evangelical benevolence, temperance, colonization, and abolition. And by examining reform during the four decades prior to the Civil War, I track the changes and continuities that occurred with respect to the religious, social, and political constituencies of reform, and note the development of the means and mes-

---

A. Hewitt, *Women's Activism and Social Change: Rochester, New York, 1822–1872* (Ithaca, 1984); Sean Wilentz, *Chants Democratic: New York City and the Rise of the American Working Class, 1788–1850* (New York, 1984); Curtis D. Johnson, *Islands of Holiness: Rural Religion in Upstate New York, 1790–1860* (Ithaca, 1989); Lori D. Ginzberg, *Women and the Work of Benevolence: Morality, Politics, and Class in the Nineteenth-Century United States* (New Haven, 1990); Teresa Anne Murphy, *Ten Hours' Labor: Religion, Reform, and Gender in Early New England* (Ithaca, 1991). See also the following anthologies: Henry Steele Commager, ed., *The Era of Reform, 1830–1860* (Princeton, 1960); Lorman Ratner, ed., *Pre–Civil War Reform: The Variety of Principles and Programs* (Englewood Cliffs, N.J., 1967); David Brion Davis, ed., *Ante-Bellum Reform* (New York, 1967); Louis Filler, ed., *Abolition and Social Justice in the Era of Reform* (New York, 1972); Walter Hugins, ed., *The Reform Impulse, 1825–1850* (New York, 1972).

5. *Historical Statistics of the United States: Colonial Times to 1970* (Washington, D.C., 1975), 12. The figure of 2,500 is often used to distinguish "urban" from "rural" population centers. In 1820, 90.5 percent of the northern (nonslaveholding) states' population and 95.5 percent of the southern (slaveholding) states' population were rural; these figures declined to 79.7 percent and 91.4 percent in 1850, and 74.1 percent and 89.5 percent in 1860. *Ibid.,* 24–37.

sage of reformers. In both counties, reformers generally became disillusioned with moral suasion, and many subsequently embraced political agitation. In the end, some were forced to recognize that the elimination of vice and the attainment of human perfection were not as imminent as initially anticipated.

In three chapters of this study, I survey the organizational activity and culture of reform in one county in the Old Northwest—Washtenaw County, Michigan—and there discover a community earnestly engaged in many reform efforts of the day, but nevertheless lacking the multitudinous fragmentations of reform that were found in the Northeast. The other three chapters examine reform in Tuscaloosa County, Alabama. Although scholars have probed the politics, social structure, and economies of both sections, reform in the South has not yet been investigated sufficiently. Indeed, some scholars have suggested that southern reform was hindered because those who held power refused to allow the circulation of new ideas among slaves and nonslaveholding whites, lest the fragile social control of the slaveholding aristocracy be shattered and its members lose their power. The fear of slave revolts was undoubtedly responsible for stifling abolitionism in the South, but some students have also used this thesis to explain the purported dearth of southern enthusiasm for temperance and for the evangelical societies of the benevolent empire. On a similar note, some scholars have maintained that these movements were held subversive because of their association with ultraism in the North, and that this connection caused reform in general to be esteemed as too radical for the conservative South.[6]

6. Joseph R. Gusfield, *Symbolic Crusade: Status Politics and the American Temperance Movement* (Urbana, Ill., 1963), 54, notes that the "identification with antislavery was strong enough to stifle completely the organization of the temperance movement in the South." On the other hand, Ian Tyrrell, "Drink and Temperance in the Antebellum South: An Overview and Interpretation," *Journal of Southern History,* XLVIII (November 1982), 485–510, explains that although antislavery did not completely smother the crusade in the South, temperance was not as widespread there as in the North. Bertram Wyatt-Brown, "The Antimission Movement in the Jacksonian South: A Study in Regional Folk Culture," *Journal of Southern History,* XXXVI (November 1970), 501–29, may overemphasize the influence of the Antimission Baptists—and thus opposition to evangelical benevolence—in the antebellum South. Other works suggesting that reform in the South was hindered include John W. Kuykendall, *Southern Enterprize: The Work of National Evangelical Societies in the Antebellum South* (Westport, Conn., 1982), 76–79, 107–109; James M. McPherson, *Ordeal by Fire: The Civil War and Reconstruction* (New York, 1992), 15–22, 26; John Ashworth, *"Agrarians" and "Aristocrats": Party Political Ideology in the United States, 1837–1846* (1983; rpr. Cambridge, Eng., 1987), 179, 199; Peter Kolchin, *American Slavery, 1619–1877*

These considerations are at the heart of an old historiographical debate regarding the similarities and differences of the culture and politics in the antebellum North and South. Though recognizing that neither section was homogeneous, one school of thought maintains that the differences between the North and South were so great by the mid-nineteenth century that the United States was a nation consisting of two culturally conflicting civilizations. For some of these scholars, the North was based upon a market economy and rapid industrialization; northerners were acquisitive yet enjoyed an open and democratic society. White southerners, on the other hand, were slower paced yet rabidly militant; their society was closed, dominated by agriculture, and governed by a slaveholding aristocracy that successfully used the concept of white supremacy to link its class interests with the fears of the nonslaveholding population. Other scholars, however, argue that slavery's impact upon the social, cultural, political, and economic life in the South—at least among whites—has been overemphasized. They also point out that although the industrial capacity of the North greatly exceeded that of the South, urban industrialization was the exception rather than the rule for the vast majority of Americans, and both sections were largely agricultural. Furthermore, they explain, the politics in both North and South were grounded upon similar ideologies, suffrage for all white males, and a vigorous two-party system—at least during the time of the Whigs.[7]

(New York, 1993), 184–89; Mary Beth Norton *et al.*, *A People and a Nation: A History of the United States* (4th ed.; Boston, 1994), 374. Carl F. Kaestle, *Pillars of the Republic: Common Schools and American Society, 1780–1860* (New York, 1983), 206, contends that the "fear of incendiary publications and revolutionary ideas among slaves made some planters nervous about the free circulation of dissenting ideas anywhere in southern society."

7. Among those authors arguing for a distinctive South, see Ulrich B. Phillips, *Life and Labor in the Old South* (Boston, 1929); Frank L. Owsley, "The Irrepressible Conflict," in Twelve Southerners, *I'll Take My Stand: The South and the Agrarian Tradition* (New York, 1930), 61–91; Arthur C. Cole, *The Irrepressible Conflict: 1850–1865* (New York, 1934), 1–78; W. J. Cash, *The Mind of the South* (New York, 1941); Eugene D. Genovese, *The Political Economy of Slavery: Studies in the Economy of the Slave South* (1965; rpr. New York, 1967), 13–36; Forrest McDonald and Grady McWhiney, "The South from Self-Sufficiency to Peonage: An Interpretation," *American Historical Review*, LXXXV (December 1980), 1095–1118; James M. McPherson, "Antebellum Southern Exceptionalism: A New Look at an Old Question," *Civil War History*, XXIX (September 1983), 230–44; William H. Pease and Jane H. Pease, *The Web of Progress: Private Values and Public Styles in Boston and Charleston, 1828–1843* (New York, 1985); Elizabeth Fox-Genovese, *Within the Plantation Household: Black and White Women of the Old South* (Chapel Hill, 1988); Jane H. Pease and William H. Pease, *Ladies, Women, and Wenches: Choice and Constraint in Antebellum Charleston and Boston* (Chapel Hill, 1990); and Kolchin, *American Slavery*. Those arguing that the differ-

In this study, we shall see that white southerners generally responded affirmatively to the less radical reform movements, and many believed that the elimination of major social ills was attainable. Naturally, white Tuscaloosans feared abolitionism and were convinced that its promulgation would result in race war. Their hostility to this cause spilled over to colonization, leading them to receive it coldly. Whites did not, however, deem temperance and evangelical benevolence to be tainted by abolitionism, and devotees of these causes were frequently as active in Tuscaloosa as were their Washtenaw counterparts. It is true that the presence of chattel slavery in Tuscaloosa County—almost half of the county's population in 1860 were slaves and the overwhelming majority of identifiable reformers in Tuscaloosa County were themselves slaveholders— meant that slaves were occasionally the objects of white benevolence, and therefore added dimensions to reform that were not encountered in the North. Nevertheless, despite the presence of slavery and the fear among southern whites of northern abolitionists, I argue that a largely similar climate of reform existed in both Tuscaloosa and Washtenaw Counties.

Before proceeding further into this study, it will be necessary to describe

ences between the North and South have been overemphasized include Fletcher M. Green, "Democracy in the Old South," *Journal of Southern History,* XII (February 1946), 2–23; Charles G. Sellers Jr., "The Travail of Slavery," 40–71, and Thomas Govan, "Americans Below the Potomac," 19–39, both in *The Southerner as American,* ed. Charles G. Sellers Jr. (Chapel Hill, 1960); J. Steven Knight Jr., "Discontent, Disunity, and Dissent in the Antebellum South: Virginia as a Test Case, 1844–1846," *Virginia Magazine of History and Biography,* LXXXI (October 1973), 437–56; Leonard P. Curry, "Urbanization and Urbanism in the Old South: A Comparative View," *Journal of Southern History,* XL (February 1974), 43–60; David M. Potter, *The Impending Crisis, 1848–1861* (New York, 1976), 8–14, 27–50; Edward Pessen, "How Different from Each Other Were the Antebellum North and South?" *American Historical Review,* LXXXV (December 1980), 1119–49; Suzanne Lebsock, *The Free Women of Petersburg: Status and Culture in a Southern Town, 1784–1860* (New York, 1984); James Oakes, *Slavery and Freedom: An Interpretation of the Old South* (New York, 1990); R. Don Higginbotham, "The Martial Spirit in the Antebellum South: Some Further Speculations in a National Context," *Journal of Southern History,* LVIII (February 1992), 3–26; T. Lloyd Benson, "Entrepreneurialism in Late Antebellum Indiana and Mississippi" (Paper presented to the eighty-sixth annual meeting of the Organization of American Historians, Anaheim, Calif., April 16, 1993); and Frederick A. Bode, "The Formation of Evangelical Communities in Middle Georgia: Twiggs County, 1820–1861," *Journal of Southern History,* LX (November 1994), 711–48. See also Carl N. Degler, *Place over Time: The Continuity of Southern Distinctiveness* (Baton Rouge, 1977). An extensive review of the literature may be found in Drew Gilpin Faust, "The Peculiar South Revisited: White Society, Culture, and Politics in the Antebellum Period, 1800–1860," in *Interpreting Southern History: Historiographical Essays in Honor of Sanford W. Higginbotham,* ed. John B. Boles and Evelyn Thomas Nolen (Baton Rouge, 1987), 78–119.

briefly the counties under consideration. Settled by whites—mostly upstate
New Yorkers—in 1823, Washtenaw County experienced rapid growth during
the 1830s, expanding from a population of 4,042 in 1830 to 23,571 in 1840, to
28,567 in 1850, and to 35,686 in 1860. Tuscaloosa County was settled beginning
in 1816 by whites and blacks, primarily southerners—Carolinians, Virginians,
Georgians, and Tennesseans. Except in the years immediately following its
initial settlement, its growth was not as dramatic as Washtenaw County's, but
the population did increase steadily, from 8,229 in 1820, to 13,646 in 1830, to
16,583 in 1840, to 18,056 in 1850, and to 23,200 in 1860.[8] The most notable distinction between the two counties was their racial composition. Washtenaw
County was almost entirely white—in 1850, only 231 of its inhabitants (or 0.8
percent of the population) were black—but a significant portion of Tuscaloosa
County's residents were African American, with slaves constituting 28 percent
of the total population in 1820 and almost 44 percent in 1860.[9] Most of the major slaveholdings in Tuscaloosa County were south of the town of Tuscaloosa,
where the rich alluvial soils of the Black Warrior River and its tributaries made
large-scale production of corn and cotton profitable. Much of the remainder of
the county is hilly, and in the nineteenth century was not suitable for extensive
agriculture. Just north of the black belt, Tuscaloosa County had fewer large
plantations than did counties to the immediate south. Nevertheless, between
one-fourth and two-fifths of Tuscaloosa County's free households were slaveholding, and the percentage of the population that was slave generally ranked
near the middle among Alabama's counties (Tables 1 and 2). The society and
economy of Tuscaloosa County thus contained plantation-ascendant regions
that one would expect to find in the state's black belt to the south, as well as sections dominated by small slaveholders and nonslaveholding whites, which
were typical of the mountain region of northeastern and north-central Ala-

---

8. *A Compendium of the Ninth Census* (Washington, D.C., 1872), 24–25, 60–61.

9. Although there were very few free African Americans in the county prior to emancipation,
the 1850 published federal census count of eight is surely an underrepresentation; eighteen blacks
and mulattoes can be identified on the free population schedule of the manuscript census. See
J. D. B. De Bow, *The Seventh Census of the United States: 1850* (Washington, D.C., 1853), 421; population schedule of the 1850 census, Tuscaloosa County, Alabama, in ADAH. Additional information may be gleaned from James B. Sellers, "Free Negroes of Tuscaloosa County Before the
Thirteenth Amendment," *Alabama Review*, XXIII (April 1970), 110–27, and Robert L. Glynn,
"How Firm a Foundation": A History of the First Black Church in Tuscaloosa County, Alabama (Tuscaloosa, 1976), 7–10.

bama.[10] Although the term "representative" cannot be applied to this or any other county in Alabama, antebellum Tuscaloosa County was in many respects a cross-section of the state.

Despite the differences between Tuscaloosa and Washtenaw Counties in racial makeup and the status of their respective labor forces, there were important similarities as well. Although dwarfed in comparison with Detroit—Michigan's largest city had a population of 21,019 in 1850 and 45,619 in 1860—Ann Arbor was the state's second largest community prior to the 1850s, boasting an 1850 population of 4,868, while Ypsilanti's 3,051 residents placed it in the eighth spot. During the 1850s, Grand Rapids, Adrian, and Kalamazoo overtook Ann Arbor, but according to the 1860 census, Ann Arbor and Ypsilanti, with populations of 5,097 and 3,955, still ranked fifth and eighth among Michigan's population centers.[11] Both Ann Arbor and Ypsilanti served as market entrepôts for locally produced agricultural goods, and the preoccupation of these towns' newspapers with agricultural news indicates the importance of farming to the urban sector of Washtenaw County's economy. Similarly, the town of Tuscaloosa was among Alabama's largest communities. Located at the head of navigation on the Black Warrior River, it was an important trading center and provided access for the shipment of cotton to Mobile. A commercial nexus for central Alabama, the town—contemporaries called it a city—grew in population from 1,949 in 1840 to 3,983 in 1860, when it was exceeded in the state only by Mobile (29,258) and Montgomery (8,843).

10. Louis Friedman Herzberg, "Negro Slavery in Tuscaloosa County, Alabama, 1818–1865" (M. A. thesis, University of Alabama, 1955), 3–5; Basil Manly to J. D. Averell, February 16, 1841, in Basil Manly Diary No. 2, pp. 284–88, Manly Family Papers, W. S. Hoole Special Collections Library, University of Alabama [hereinafter cited as Hoole Special Collections]. For a description of Alabama's geography and its relation to the state's nineteenth-century economy, see Peter Kolchin, *First Freedom: The Responses of Alabama's Blacks to Emancipation and Reconstruction* (Westport, Conn., 1972), 12–14, and Frank L. Owsley and Harriet C. Owsley, "The Economic Basis of Society in the Late Ante-Bellum South," *Journal of Southern History,* VI (February 1940), 30–37.

11. De Bow, *Seventh Census,* 887–96; *Population of the United States in 1860: Compiled from the Original Returns of the Eighth Census* (Washington, D.C., 1864), 236–47. The 1850 and 1860 population figures for Ann Arbor and Ypsilanti are the totals of the villages and the rural townships of the same names. Although the 1850 federal census enumerator failed to distinguish between Ann Arbor township's rural and urban population, a contemporary who reviewed the manuscript calculated that 4,025 lived in the village proper. *Michigan Argus,* August 21, 1850. *Statistics of the State of Michigan, Compiled from the Census of 1860, Taken by Authority of the United States* (Lansing, 1861), inaccurately differentiates between the rural and village populations of many townships.

Also noteworthy is the fact that both Ann Arbor and Tuscaloosa were centers of education. Ann Arbor was selected as the home of the University of Michigan in 1837, and the institution began holding classes in 1841. The University of Alabama was located one mile east of the town of Tuscaloosa and opened in 1831. In neither of these communities, however, did the presence of the university loom as large in the mid-nineteenth century as in the twentieth. The University of Michigan began with only seven students; eleven years later, enrollment had grown to 222. It increased considerably during the remainder of the decade: to 460 in 1857 and to 674 in 1860. The student body at the University of Alabama was even smaller. The school had 94 students when it opened in 1831, but in the following thirty years enrollment never exceeded 158, and actually dipped to 38 in 1838.[12]

Both Ann Arbor and Tuscaloosa also vied to be their states' capitals. Tuscaloosa actually held that position from 1826 to 1847, in part because it was the most centrally located site in Alabama, given the transportation constraints of the era. For at least three months of the year, Tuscaloosa was accessible to southern Alabama through the Black Warrior, Tombigbee, and Alabama Rivers, the latter of which flowed into the Gulf of Mexico at Mobile. Though travel on the Black Warrior River north of the falls at Tuscaloosa was infeasi-

---

12. *Compendium of the Enumeration of the Inhabitants and Statistics of the United States, as Obtained at the Department of State, from the Returns of the Sixth Census* (Washington, D.C., 1841), 54; *Population of the United States in 1860*, 9; Howard H. Peckham, *The Making of the University of Michigan* (Ann Arbor, 1967), 22, 38, 47; James B. Sellers, *History of the University of Alabama* (University, Ala., 1953), 581. Local histories of Washtenaw County include *History of Washtenaw County, Michigan; Together with Sketches of Its Cities, Villages, and Townships, Educational, Religious, Civil, Military, and Political History; Portraits of Prominent Persons, and Biographies of Representative Citizens* (Chicago, 1881); *Portrait and Biographical Album of Washtenaw County, Michigan* (Chicago, 1891); Samuel W. Beakes, *Past and Present of Washtenaw County, Michigan* (Chicago, 1906); Harvey C. Colburn, *The Story of Ypsilanti* (Ypsilanti, 1923); Jonathan Marwil, *A History of Ann Arbor* (Ann Arbor, 1987); Ruth Bordin, *Washtenaw County: An Illustrated History* (Northridge, Calif., 1988). For Tuscaloosa County, see Archibald Bruce McEachlin, *The History of Tuscaloosa, 1816–1880* (1880; rpr. University, Ala., 1977); Morris Raymond Boucher, "Factors in the History of Tuscaloosa, Alabama, 1816–1846" (M. A. thesis, University of Alabama, 1947); Herzberg, "Negro Slavery in Tuscaloosa County"; Matthew William Clinton, *Tuscaloosa, Alabama: Its Early Days, 1816–1865* (Tuscaloosa, 1958); James B. Sellers, *The First Methodist Church of Tuscaloosa, Alabama, 1818–1968* (Tuscaloosa, 1968); G. Ward Hubbs, *Tuscaloosa: Portrait of an Alabama County* (Northridge, Calif., 1987). The literature is discussed in James F. Doster, "Tuscaloosa Historians," *Alabama Review*, XXVII (April 1974), 83–100.

ble, the Huntsville Road also passed through Tuscaloosa, providing access to the Tennessee Valley. The town's accessibility also brought a considerable amount of trade and visitors. Meanwhile, Ann Arbor failed in its bid to be state capital, losing out to the frontier settlement of Lansing in 1847.[13]

Politically, both counties were inclined toward Whiggery in states where, during most of the period in question, Democrats generally prevailed. The town of Tuscaloosa was strongly Whig and usually returned at least six-tenths of its ballots for that party. The county was not politically monolithic, however, and some rural beats were even more thoroughly Democratic. Accordingly, countywide election results were sometimes close although generally the Whigs won. Tuscaloosa Whigs outpolled the Democrats in the presidential contests of 1840, 1848, and 1852, as did the party's successor in Alabama, the American Party, in 1856. The county's Democrats prevailed only in 1836 and 1844. During these twenty years, the Whig Party and its successor secured 54.0 percent of Tuscaloosans' presidential ballots. In contrast, the Whig Party and the American Party obtained only 42.2 percent of the state's presidential votes from 1836 to 1856, and lost to the Democrats in each of these contests.

In Michigan, elections were more closely contested. Although Michigan Whigs were victorious only in the presidential contest of 1840—and the gubernatorial race of 1839—the electoral picture in the Wolverine State was complicated from 1841 to 1853 by the existence of the antislavery Liberty and Free Soil Parties, which drew most heavily from the Whigs, making the Whigs less competitive. Although in presidential contests Washtenaw Whigs were ascendant only in 1840, Democrats never obtained a majority of the county's presidential returns after 1836. Between 1836 and 1852, Democrats obtained 47.3 percent of the county's presidential votes, Whigs 44.2 percent, and the Liberty and Free Soil Parties, 8.5 percent; in 1844, 1848, and 1852, when these antislavery parties were strongest, the breakdown was Democrats 45.8 percent, Whigs 42.1 percent, and Liberty/Free Soil 12.1 percent. (The complex political realignment of the 1850s does not permit us to label the Republican Party as the Whigs' successor in Michigan as was true of the American Party in Alabama.) Statewide, Democrats were slightly more successful, gaining 49.2 percent of

13. Hubbs, *Tuscaloosa*, 19–27; Willis F. Dunbar and George S. May, *Michigan: A History of the Wolverine State* (Rev. ed.; Grand Rapids, 1980), 281–82; Marwil, *Ann Arbor*, 13. The Washtenaw County village of Dexter was also a contender to be state capital; Dunbar and May, *Michigan*, 281.

the presidential ballots from 1836 to 1852, Whigs 42.5 percent, and Liberty/Free Soil 8.3 percent; between 1844 and 1852, Democrats obtained 49.3 percent, Whigs 40.3 percent, and Liberty/Free Soil 10.5 percent.[14]

As with most Alabamians, church-affiliated Tuscaloosans were generally evangelical Protestants—primarily Baptists, Methodists, and to a lesser extent, Presbyterians. Washtenaw County was likewise dominated by evangelical Protestants but had proportionately fewer Baptists, and virtually none of the Antimission Baptists. Although scarce in Tuscaloosa County, Antimission Baptists were more plentiful in the less heavily settled counties of Alabama and vigorously opposed all reform efforts. Meanwhile, Congregationalists—entirely absent from Tuscaloosa County—were a leading force in Washtenaw's reform networks. Presbyterians constituted a similar percentage of the religious population in both places, but virtually all of Washtenaw's Presbyterians were New School Presbyterians, whereas after 1837, Tuscaloosa Presbyterians were divided between the less socially active Old School and Cumberland Presbyterians. Finally, the presence of Catholics, Lutherans, Universalists, and antislavery sects such as Wesleyan Methodists and Free Will Baptists contributed to a more diverse religious fabric in Washtenaw County (Tables 3 and 4).[15]

14. W. Dean Burnham, *Presidential Ballots, 1836–1892* (Baltimore, 1955), 260, 274, 514, 532. Michigan's Liberty Party returns for 1840, not included by Burnham but incorporated in the figures cited in the text, may be found in *Michigan State Journal*, November 17, 1840. For the returns of other antebellum elections in Michigan, see Ronald P. Formisano, *The Birth of Mass Political Parties: Michigan, 1827–1861* (Princeton, 1971), 24. See also Ypsilanti *Sentinel*, June 30, 1847, which describes Washtenaw County as "the staunchest whig county in the state." On the political character of Tuscaloosa County, see J. Mills Thornton III, *Politics and Power in a Slave Society: Alabama, 1800–1860* (Baton Rouge, 1978), 41–42; Thomas B. Alexander *et al.*, "Who Were the Alabama Whigs?" *Alabama Review*, XVI (January 1963), 17; *Flag of the Union*, November 23, 1836, August 9, 1837, August 15, 1838, August 7, 1839, August 11, 1841, August 16, 1843; and *Independent Monitor*, May 29, 1841, August 17, 1842, August 14, 1844, August 6, 1845, August 10, 1847, November 10, 1848, August 14, 1851, August 6, 1857.

15. Church-affiliation estimates for Michigan and Alabama during the antebellum period are sketchy. Comparing church membership across denominational lines is problematic, since denominations had different standards for membership. Using denominational records at the synod, association, circuit, or other level above the local congregation to establish the number of members within a particular county is sometimes complicated by the difficulty of linking a particular congregation to the county where its members resided and worshiped, especially in cases where the original congregation no longer exists and was not named after the place in which it was located. In some cases congregations now defunct were named after their locale, but the asso-

Of course, these two counties were not clones of each other, nor need they have been in order for this study to be conducted. They were not selected as the result of a careful examination of all the hundreds of American counties in existence during the antebellum years. Both, however, offered an abundance of sources—although it must be noted that the surviving sources come mostly from the more populous centers of each county, principally the towns of Tuscaloosa, Ann Arbor, and to a lesser extent, Ypsilanti. Consequently, the rural dimensions of reform in both places are sometimes understated. Naturally, the conclusions which I offer in this study ought to be regarded as most appropriate for similar-sized American communities and less apt for the country's remote rural sectors or large cities.

What follows is a largely topical examination of reform in both counties. Chapter 1 discusses the operations of Bible, tract, and Sunday-school societies in Tuscaloosa County. These organizations sought to do more than simply promote the Protestant gospel, which they believed would provide people with the means of salvation. They also aimed to have America become a Protestant republic and promoted a strict code of morality, which they expected would

---

ciation between the name and place has passed from memory. Useful approximations come from the U.S. censuses of 1850 and 1860, although they provide only the numbers of church buildings and the seating within these structures. These figures permit easy comparison with statewide numbers and account for minor denominations. These censuses, however, are not impeccable. In addition to overcounting the seats at Tuscaloosa's Episcopal church in 1850—the 1850 census claimed 800 seats, whereas the 1860 census reported only 300 seats for the same building—both censuses fail to note the existence of Tuscaloosa's Catholics, who constructed a building in 1845 proximate to the Protestant churches in the town of Tuscaloosa; according to a local historian, at least 100 Catholics lived in Tuscaloosa by this time. De Bow, *Seventh Census,* 435; *Statistics of the United States (Including Mortality, Property, & c.) in 1860: Compiled from the . . . Eighth Census* (Washington, D.C., 1866), 352, 354; Clinton, *Tuscaloosa: Early Days,* 117–18. As for Antimission Baptists, one scholar has estimated that there were 20,000 in Alabama in 1855; Lewy Dorman, *Party Politics in Alabama from 1850 through 1860* (Wetumpka, Ala., 1935), 110.

Walter Brownlow Posey arrived at estimates of church membership for Alabama in 1860 by applying the ratio between seating accommodations and church membership in 1890—the first year the census included membership data—to the figures on seating provided in the 1860 census. Posey proposed that 45.7 percent of Alabama's church members in 1860 were Methodists, followed by Baptists (36.8 percent), Presbyterians (6.5 percent), Catholics (5.5 percent), Episcopalians (2.7 percent), Cumberland Presbyterians (1.8 percent), and Disciples of Christ (1.0 percent). Posey, *Frontier Mission: A History of Religion West of the Southern Appalachians to 1861* (Lexington, Ky., 1966), 417–18. See also J. Wayne Flynt, "Alabama," in Samuel S. Hill, ed., *Religion in the Southern States: A Historical Study* (Macon, Ga., 1983), 5–26.

eliminate from Americans those behaviors that evangelicals were certain caused poverty and misery. Further, the larger world view of these proponents of benevolent activities was town-centered. They deemed the rural quarters of Alabama that were devoid of evangelical institutions to be economically underdeveloped, and deplored the spiritual and economic insularity of these regions. They were more likely to own slaves than the white population at large, but they were not members of an idle planter class who despised urban life; rather, they were professionals in their occupations who were usually closely connected with towns and cities. And although some scholars have proposed that the circulation of Bibles and tracts and the promotion of Sunday schools was occasionally hindered in the South because of fears of abolitionist contamination, little if any such animosity was present in Tuscaloosa County.

Due to the greater combined proportion of Presbyterians and Congregationalists in Washtenaw County, benevolent activity there, which is considered in chapter 2, was more pervasive than it was in Tuscaloosa County. Further, because of its closer proximity to the northeastern homes of most agents of the national benevolent societies, Michigan received many more of these emissaries than did Alabama. Numbers aside, the message delivered by these agents was much the same in both places. Benevolent societies in Washtenaw County, however, had to meet a challenge unknown to their Tuscaloosa counterparts: the agitation of abolitionists who denounced these bodies' willingness to accept contributions from slaveholders and disinclination to condemn slavery. As a consequence of their frustration with mainstream benevolence, abolitionists often formed their own benevolent societies.

Tuscaloosa's temperance partisans, the subject of chapter 3, initially found some of their fellow residents openly hostile to their message. Beginning in 1829, when Tuscaloosa's first temperance society was formed, opponents ridiculed the cause and charged that its proponents sought to impose a monolithic moral code upon all Americans and, eventually, to unite church and state. Though this debate was sometimes shrill, it eventually quieted, and by the mid-1830s temperance was transformed from a controversial issue into a component of the dominant social paradigm. The early temperance movement in Tuscaloosa was mostly an elite-dominated effort that relied upon moral suasion only and condemned hard liquor but tolerated wine. By the late 1830s, however, temperance advocates embraced total abstinence from all intoxicants and agitated for laws to end the sale of liquor. After the legislature failed to abolish the licensing of liquor sales, temperance devotees returned to moral suasion and embraced two national temperance groups, the Washingtonians and the Sons of Temperance. By the late 1840s, temperance activists were again trying—unsuccessfully—to abolish the legal sale of alcohol by raising liquor-license fees to a prohibitive level in Tuscaloosa and the cross-river village of Northport, and through petitioning the legislature to enact a local-option "Alabama Law." And as with Tuscaloosa's benevolence crusaders, temperance advocates were more likely to own slaves than was the population at large. Further, their largely commercial and professional occupations and their greater willingness to send their children to school suggest that they identified with the growth of the American market economy.

Temperance in Washtenaw will be discussed in chapter 4. As with Tuscaloosa County, Washtenaw temperance commenced among elites and was a cyclical phenomenon, with sequential periods of enthusiasm and moribundity. In both counties, temperance shifted from the vilification of only hard liquor to total abstinence, followed the similar pattern from moral suasion to legal suasion, and then repeated this latter course. Whereas political victories were generally denied to Alabama's temperance partisans, Michigan's enthusiasts obtained a local-option law in 1845 and several statewide prohibitory laws during the 1850s. But even though the majority of voters during the 1840s and 1850s were won over to prohibition, all laws on this issue proved to be unenforceable, and accordingly failed to eliminate liquor from Michigan. As in Washtenaw's benevolent causes—and in contrast to Alabama's temperance crusade, which was dominated by slaveholders—abolitionists were disproportionately represented in Washtenaw's temperance ranks, and often encouraged temperance devotees to adopt more radical measures.

In the fifth chapter, I argue that, analogous to the more tolerant attitude that Tuscaloosans held for religious skepticism and drinking during the 1820s, white residents of the town were also less fearful of abolitionists and slave revolts then than later. The pivotal events responsible for the transition were the Nat Turner slave revolt in 1831 and the contemporaneous emergence of immediate abolitionism in the North. During the abolitionist mail controversy in 1835, many Tuscaloosans—including a number who were active in benevolence and temperance—staged a public protest and pledged to confiscate any abolitionist literature sent to their community. This increased hostility to abolition also caused whites to treat colonization with greater suspicion. As a result, colonization publicists shifted their stated goals from seeking to separate the black and white races to explaining that their only objective was to promote the emigration of free African Americans to Liberia. And although a few of Tuscaloosa's white-oriented benevolence and temperance efforts were also directed toward the county's slave population, the most notable white evangelical cause aimed toward African Americans was the so-called mission to the slaves, or plantation mission. Notwithstanding this cause's implicit acceptance of the spiritual equality of blacks and whites, the plantation mission explicitly strove not to be subversive of slavery, as white preachers continually reminded their audiences of the biblical injunction for slaves to obey their masters.

Abolition in Washtenaw County is the focus of chapter 6. As did temperance, abolition evolved from a movement committed to moral suasion to one that embraced political measures—in this case, the Liberty Party. Later, the antislavery message was diluted as the Liberty Party was absorbed by the Free Soil Party. Free Soilers were in turn engulfed by the Republican Party— which largely protested the extension of slavery into the federal territories and showed far less concern for the plight of the enslaved. Even after the creation of the Liberty Party, however, antislavery agitation continued to extend beyond political party activity. A handful of nonresistance-oriented Garrisonian abolitionists rejected antislavery political parties and were particularly active during the 1850s. And similar to their actions in Washtenaw County's temperance and benevolence movements, local women also organized their own antislavery societies. But antislavery activity was often most intense within the evangelical faiths, where abolitionists labored to have their churches pronounce slavery a sin and withhold fellowship from slaveholders. Frustrated by the response of some ecclesiastics, a few abolitionists formed their own churches, with antislavery principles as a part of their creed.

Finally, I must say something about the structure and arrangement of chapters. Some readers may be disappointed that there is not more attention devoted to the reform activities of women, and may judge that the short segments within several of the chapters on women's activism amount to the "ghettoization" of women's history. As I explain in the text, sources pointing to female participation in reform from these two counties are scarce. Accordingly, the separate treatment of women in antebellum reform permits us to focus on efforts that were almost always underreported in most of the male-created sources of the time.

I have also chosen to address benevolence, temperance, and abolition, in that order, because many antebellum activists' engagement in reform progressed in that sequence.[16] In each instance, I discuss the Tuscaloosa case first. This may puzzle some readers, who feel that Washtenaw County would serve as a better base of comparison, reform in the North having been better studied. Several considerations persuaded me to begin with Tuscaloosa County. The Alabama county was settled earlier than Washtenaw County, and benevolence and temperance activity began there earlier than in Washtenaw; in chapters 1 and 3 we shall see glimpses of life in Tuscaloosa prior to the commencement of reform. But most important, reform in the South—particularly in a community setting—has been greatly understudied and misunderstood. Accordingly, by examining reform movements in Tuscaloosa County first, it is my hope to shed greater light on southern reform on its own terms.

16. Abzug, *Cosmos Crumbling.*

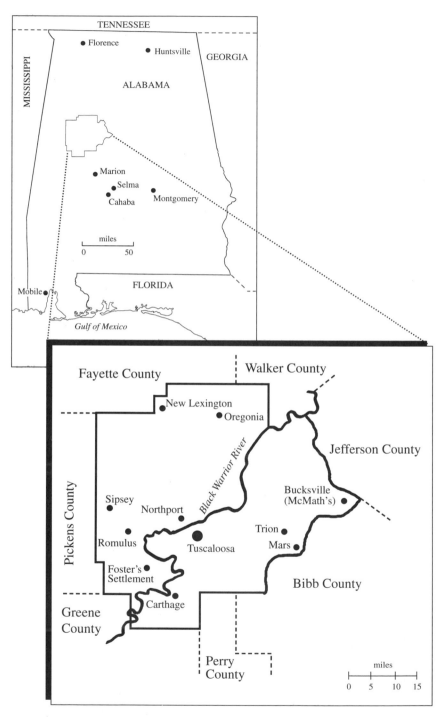

Tuscaloosa County, Alabama

I

Slaveholding Operatives
of the Benevolent Empire

In this chapter we will examine antebellum Tuscaloosa's experience with Sunday schools, Bible societies, and tract societies; their cyclical rise and fall; and their objectives, both religious and secular. As evangelical associations, they endeavored to promote the Protestant gospel, which they believed would bring salvation. But they had an agenda that extended beyond saving individual souls. They sought to have America become a Protestant republic and believed that their exertions would effect a profound moral transformation in American society: vice would be subdued, poverty eliminated, industrious and sober habits adopted, and a strict code of morality embraced. Since, in their view, unbridled passions prevented people from attaining their full human potential, devotees of these enterprises perceived their efforts as liberating for individuals and believed that they provided a progressive course for American society.

Much has been written about the operations of the national and regional benevolent societies in the antebellum North, but less is known about these enterprises in the South. Because northern abolitionists also advocated other reforms, some white southerners, despite their Protestantism, considered such endeavors as temperance and evangelical benevolence to be dangerous Yankee importations. Modern historians, however, have either exaggerated the animosity of southern whites toward evangelical benevolence or ignored the subject altogether. The neglect of antebellum southern benevolence is perhaps best illustrated by the conclusions of the scholar who wrote that evangelical benevolence—as well as "a host of organizations with a cluster of religious, moral, and social concerns"—"must be seen primarily as a Northern phenomenon."[1]

A serious treatment of the operation of southern benevolence is provided by John Kuykendall in *Southern Enterprize: The Work of National Benevolent Societies in the Antebellum South;* however, scholars need to know still more about the subject, particularly about the experience of activists and recipients on the local level. It is true that some Alabamians initially displayed hostility toward the emergence of these societies, but by the mid-1830s opposition to evangelical benevolence was generally restricted to Antimission Baptists, whose pro-

1. Gregory H. Singleton, "Protestant Voluntary Organizations and the Shaping of Victorian America," *American Quarterly,* XXVII (December 1975), 549. The following important works on the benevolent empire generally do not treat its southern dimensions in depth: Charles C. Cole Jr., *The Social Ideas of the Northern Evangelists, 1826–1860* (New York, 1954); John R. Bodo, *The Protestant Clergy and Public Issues, 1812–1848* (Princeton, 1954); Clifford S. Griffin, *Their Brothers' Keepers: Moral Stewardship in the United States, 1800–1865* (New Brunswick, N.J., 1960); Charles I. Foster, *An Errand of Mercy: The Evangelical United Front, 1790–1837* (Chapel Hill, 1960); W. David Lewis, "The Reformer as Conservative: Protestant Counter-Subversion in the Early Republic," in *The Development of an American Culture,* ed. Stanley Coben and Lorman Ratner (Englewood Cliffs, N.J., 1970); Rosenberg, *Religion and the Rise of the American City;* Paul Boyer, *Urban Masses and Moral Order in America, 1820–1920* (Cambridge, Mass., 1978); Anne Boylan, *Sunday School: The Formation of an American Institution, 1790–1880* (New Haven, 1988); Diana Hochstedt Butler, "The Church and American Destiny: Evangelical Episcopalians and Voluntary Societies in Antebellum America," *Religion and American Culture,* IV (Summer 1994), 193–219; Karl Eric Valois, "To Revolutionize the World: The American Tract Society and the Regeneration of the Republic" (Ph.D. dissertation, University of Connecticut, 1994); Peter J. Wosh, *Spreading the Word: The Bible Business in Nineteenth-Century America* (Ithaca, 1994); Paul Nord, "Religious Reading and Readers in Antebellum America," *Journal of the Early Republic,* XV (Summer 1995), 241–72. The most important work on antebellum benevolence and the South is Kuykendall, *Southern Enterprize.* Also worthy of note is Janet Duitsman Cornelius, *"When I Can Read My Title Clear": Literacy, Slavery, and Religion in the Antebellum South* (Columbia, S. C., 1991), 109–16, 125–28, which analyzes the interaction between national benevolent societies and southern slaves. Barbara L. Bellows, *Benevolence Among Slaveholders: Assisting the Poor in Charleston, 1670–1860* (Baton Rouge, 1993), 31–38; Daniel Dupre, "Barbecues and Pledges: Electioneering and the Rise of Democratic Politics in Antebellum Alabama," *Journal of Southern History,* LX (August 1994), 485–86, briefly discuss the operation of southern evangelical benevolence on the local level. Although he does not examine the operations of the national benevolent associations, a study by Frederick A. Bode, "A Common Sphere: White Evangelicals and Gender in Antebellum Georgia," *Georgia Historical Quarterly,* LXXIX (Winter, 1995), provides a serious treatment of southern benevolence. Laurie F. Maffly-Kipp, *Religion and Society in Frontier California* (New Haven, 1994), 13–37, considers the national benevolent societies in another understudied region.

test was based upon theological concerns, not sectional animosities. Notwithstanding slavery's integration into Tuscaloosa's economy and society, and despite the unequivocal hostility of many whites to abolitionists, white Tuscaloosans rarely excoriated these northern-managed national benevolent societies, nor the regional and denominational benevolent associations dominated by southerners. Ultimately, the vigor of benevolence in Tuscaloosa County had more to do with the health of the economy than with the peculiarities of slave society.

This chapter will also focus on the characteristics and beliefs of those who were involved in such benevolent undertakings. The majority of Sabbath-school teachers and other proponents of benevolence were members of the Whig Party, and their world view was also highly compatible with Whig ideology. For example, they typically depicted portions of Alabama that were "destitute"—a word frequently used by contemporary Protestant activists to denote the absence of Bibles, evangelical institutions, or both—as also being economically backward. Rather than praising the independence of a strong-willed yeomanry, these advocates lamented the economic and spiritual isolation of rural dwellers. Many supporters of benevolence in Tuscaloosa County were socially prominent, and as a group they were more likely to be slave owners than was the white population at large. But these devotees were not leisured planters who scorned urban life; rather, they were primarily professionals who maintained close ties to towns and cities. While benevolence was not incompatible with the presence of slavery, slaves were seldom the targeted population of these societies, since the success of Sabbath schools and, particularly, tract and Bible societies depended upon literacy, which was illegal for slaves. Some whites did endeavor through these benevolent means to promote the evangelical gospel among Alabama's slaves; these efforts are considered further in chapter 5. Here, it will be argued that despite important differences between the two societies, the objectives of most benevolent organizations in the South were similar to those in the North.

During the decade following its settlement by whites and blacks, visitors and residents described Tuscaloosa as a community freshly cut from the frontier, and a few insisted it was a place that stood in need of the evangelical gospel. In 1821 a visitor from Connecticut, William Ely, found his refined tastes unsettled by this hastily built village "of 6 to 800 souls." He despised the egalitarian mores of white Tuscaloosans: they were "more Mobocratic than I have anywhere else met with," as people of all classes mixed "promiscuously . . .

without reserve or embarrassment." In Ely's mind, proper social deference was not followed: "Gross, excessive profanity is very prevalent, & appears to be indulged without restraint before their Preachers Magistrates & other peace officers, & indeed many of those Officers themselves are guilty of it." Tuscaloosans were also indolent, as they spent too much time "lounging about Taverns, Stores, tipling [*sic*] and gambling houses, or in making & attending horse races, cockfights, . . . shooting at a Mark, hunting or fishing." Ely also reported crime to be extensive in Tuscaloosa, and that the "guilty commonly escape the Penalty of the Laws." At the core of the town's problems—and in Ely's mind the cause of Tuscaloosa's loathsome behaviors—was the absence of "enough of a religious or moral Principle in the Body politic to cause the Laws to be put in execution." Although there were "many Methodists & Baptists who pretend to preach and teach," their impact on community mores was negligible. Emblematic of Tuscaloosa's moral problems was the condition of those denominations' meetinghouses, which were "mean uncomfortable Places generally left open for hogs & c. to enter at pleasure."[2]

The homesick Yankee Ely was not alone in being distraught about Tuscaloosa's irreligious ways. In 1824 a writer to a Tuscaloosa newspaper lamented that the town's inadequate church facilities had "materially contributed . . . to produce a lukewarmness in some, and a disregard in others for the cause of religion." But "Religiosus" realized that some of his fellow residents disliked the religion preached in these hovels at least as much as the buildings themselves, as he prefaced his appeal for contributions for the improvement of the Methodist meetinghouse with the remark that his request would be considered "dry, uninteresting, and disgusting to many of your readers."[3]

Not only did Tuscaloosa have strong irreligious undercurrents during its first decade, but skepticism and anticlericalism also operated there without significant opposition. Both skepticism and deism had been widely embraced by southern planters of the Revolutionary generation and continued to enjoy a

2. William H. Ely to Clarissa May Davis, June 2, 1821, in W. Stanley Hoole, ed., "Elyton, Alabama, and the Connecticut Asylum: The Letters of William H. Ely, 1820–1821," *Alabama Review*, III (January 1950), 64–68. For other descriptions of the roughhewn nature of early Tuscaloosa, see *American Mirror*, April 27, 1824; Theodore Dwight Weld, *American Slavery As It Is: Testimony of a Thousand Witnesses* (New York, 1839) 194; Anson West, *A History of Methodism in Alabama* (Nashville, 1893), 126; Clinton, *Tuscaloosa*, 29–30.

3. *American Mirror*, June 26, 1824. See also J. Wayne Flynt, "Alabama," in *Religion in the Southern States: A Historical Study*, ed. Samuel S. Hill (Macon, Ga., 1983), 5–6.

following in the South during the first few decades of the nineteenth century.[4] Such views—or at least toleration of them—occasionally found their way into the town's newspapers. For example, "Little Faith" was incredulous of miracle health cures through prayer and faith. Writing in 1824 of a highly publicized healing of a Washington woman's paralysis, Little Faith pointed to a rational, naturalistic explanation for her recovery rather than identifying it as the work of God; her case was not the first time that the "prognostications of Doctors and nurses have failed." Adding that "most sick people are prayed for," yet very few enjoy such a rapid recovery, Little Faith was convinced that the case demonstrated only natural causes and good luck: "According to the best statistical account there are at this time, six hundred and thirty two millions of inhabitants in the world, most of whom have frequently been sick; and is it strange, that out of so many cases there should be one sudden recovery?"[5] Further, the scorn that evangelicals held for Thomas Paine was not shared by Thomas Davenport, the editor of the *American Mirror,* who reported that "several persons have been punished in England for selling Paine's Age of Reason," adding contemptuously, "What an age we live in."[6]

Of course, not everyone in Tuscaloosa was pleased with these conditions. Evangelicals in particular combatted irreligion and disorderly ways with revivals, benevolent organizations, and temperance societies; eventually, they succeeded in establishing moral hegemony over Tuscaloosa. Although this study will focus on temperance and benevolence, a few remarks on revivalism are appropriate. Perry Miller underlined the significance of revivals in nineteenth-century America when he wrote that they were the "central mode of this culture's search for national identity. . . . In fact, the dominant theme in America from 1800 to 1860 is the inevitable persistence of the revival technique. . . . We can hardly understand Emerson, Thoreau, Whitman, Melville, unless we comprehend that for them this was the one clearly given truth of their society." While the success of the revival required people who were receptive to the gos-

4. Albert Post, *Popular Freethought in America, 1825–1850* (New York, 1943), 16–33; Clement Eaton, *The Freedom-of-Thought Struggle in the Old South* (Rev. ed.; New York, 1964), 10–18, 300–316; Niels Henry Sonne, *Liberal Kentucky, 1780–1828* (New York, 1939); E. Brooks Holifield, *The Gentlemen Theologians: American Theology and Southern Culture, 1795–1860* (Durham, North Carolina, 1978), 50–57; Henry F. May, *The Enlightenment in America* (New York, 1976), 327–36.

5. *American Mirror,* May 8, 1824. The writer did not go so far as to disavow a belief in God or in miracles, but he remained skeptical of both.

6. *Ibid.,* August 28, 1824.

pel message, that receptiveness was skillfully cultivated by preachers who were master orators. In a nation of voluntary churches, ministers, like politicians, had to turn to the people for support; they had to speak to the real concerns of both the faithful and the unchurched. And if the revivalists' message had particular resonance among people who had been raised in a religious atmosphere, it may also have found a welcome audience among settlers lacking a religious background but distressed by their new surroundings. The confusion of newly settled Tuscaloosa must have been troubling to many people who came from well-ordered, established communities. Nor did high geographical mobility affect only those who relocated; people who remained in Tuscaloosa over decades found themselves with different neighbors almost continuously. (Of course, high mobility in itself suggests that much of the population held expectations that were unfulfilled.) Most southerners simply accepted these tense and unstable circumstances, while others found release in liquor, violent sports, and other hedonistic behavior. Some, however, obtained solace in religion.[7] And the principal means of recruiting new members into the evangelical churches during the nineteenth century was through camp meetings and revivals.[8]

In many respects, camp meetings and revivals served a social function similar to that of frontier hedonism: they were vivid, often thrilling experiences

7. Perry Miller, *The Life of the Mind in America from the Revolution to the Civil War* (New York, 1965), 7; Timothy L. Smith, *Revivalism and Social Reform in Mid-Nineteenth-Century America* (New York, 1957), 36–40; Dickson D. Bruce Jr., *And They All Sang Hallelujah: Plain-Folk Camp-Meeting Religion, 1800–1845* (Knoxville, Tenn., 1974), 34; Charles A. Johnson, *The Frontier Camp Meeting: Religion's Harvest Time* (Dallas, 1955); and John B. Boles, "Evangelical Protestantism in the Old South: From Religious Dissent to Cultural Dominance," in *Religion in the Old South*, ed. Charles Reagan Wilson (Jackson, Miss., 1985), 13–34. Southern whites who owned few or no slaves were extraordinarily mobile during the antebellum years, often staying in one place for a few years before moving to a new land which they hoped would provide them with a better life. One highly mobile southerner, Gideon Lincecum, had already moved six times in his twenty-five years before briefly settling in Tuscaloosa in the late 1810s, after which he removed to Mississippi, and later to Texas. "Autobiography of Gideon Lincecum," *Publications of the Mississippi Historical Society*, VIII (1904), 443–519. See also the 1836 remarks of Henry Watson of neighboring Greene County in James Oakes, *The Ruling Race: A History of American Slaveholders* (New York, 1982), 79.

8. In Tuscaloosa County, evangelicals usually designated as a "camp meeting" any protracted, out-of-doors, religious meeting aimed at converting sinners to Christ, whereas "revivals" were held in churches—although "revival" was often used to describe any protracted religious activity, regardless of where it was held.

that momentarily enabled the participant to ignore life's frustrations. This is not to say that revivals were nothing more than social events providing an emotional release; most people who converted undoubtedly hoped for salvation and a better life after death. But an important consequence of revivals was that they, and their sponsoring evangelical faiths, assisted antebellum Americans to resolve the strains and instabilities of life, and provided a set of alternative goals that, though difficult, were more easily attainable for most southerners than social or economic stability. Further, revivals provided a framework that made the changes in society comprehensible. New settlement, high geographical mobility, and the expansion of the market assuredly challenged the ways in which people viewed the world. Many Americans who, in their confusion, blurred religious and social tensions together may have found resolution in the revival.[9]

At the heart of revivalistic conversion was a rejection of the things of the world. Revivalists denounced vice continually, and the convert found worldly pursuits—namely drunkenness, dancing, fighting, gambling, profanity, and secular amusements such as circus and theater attendance—systematically invalidated. These vices, according to Dickson D. Bruce Jr., "took on symbolic as well as practical value." By classifying "such common vices as taboo," new converts

> were enabled to make their rejection of the world a concrete act as well as an intellectual belief. It would have done them little good to have forbidden activities in which they could not have possibly participated, but in focusing upon the most popular frontier recreations they were able to demonstrate the force of their beliefs in their daily lives. What they were in fact rejecting was of far greater breadth and far less specificity than frontier fun because, as they proclaimed in their songs, salvation had meant a release from the whole world and not merely the sort of marginal reform which would have been effected by moderation in all things.[10]

9. Bruce, *And They All Sang*, 7, 35, 130; Donald G. Mathews, "The Second Great Awakening as an Organizing Process, 1780–1830: An Hypothesis," *American Quarterly*, XXI (Spring 1969), 34–35.

10. Bruce, *And They All Sang*, 89, 126. See also Christopher Waldrep, "The Making of a Border State Society: James McReady, the Great Revival, and the Prosecution of Profanity in Kentucky," *American Historical Review*, XCIX (June 1994), 767–84. Regarding the denunciation of vice by Tuscaloosa evangelicals, see John W. Quist, "Social and Moral Reform in the Old North

The "Great Revival" began in Kentucky in 1797 and spread throughout the country; revivals continued for several decades throughout the United States, often occurring in cycles of enthusiasm followed by relative quiet. Revivalism peaked in Tuscaloosa from the late 1830s to the mid-1840s, but spiritual rumblings had commenced there in the early 1820s, and they continued at least through the 1850s. The primary sources do not provide a complete reckoning of all the revivals that occurred in Tuscaloosa during the antebellum years, but the evidence indicates that they had an extensive effect. Writing in the 1890s, Anson West noted that the Hopewell Methodist Society, located about eighteen miles east of the town of Tuscaloosa, "was organized in 1821 or 1822" and that during its first decade, "there was a large Camp-ground there at which large congregations assembled and great spiritual harvests were reaped." The Purity Methodist Society, twelve miles southwest of Tuscaloosa, was the site of a "most remarkable revival" in 1826, with "nearly one hundred conversions." Other Methodist-led revivals occurred in rural Tuscaloosa County in 1827 and 1828.[11] In August 1831, a four-day meeting was held at Tuscaloosa's Methodist meetinghouse, and in the fall of that year, camp meetings were the rage in Tuscaloosa's environs. Presbyterians had planned a camp meeting in Greene County, and interdenominational camp meetings were scheduled for Tuscaloosa County and the neighboring counties of Fayette, Jefferson, and Greene. Cumberland Presbyterians were particularly active in October 1835, holding three camp meetings in rural Tuscaloosa County that month.[12]

Unfortunately, existing church records do not permit us to determine who joined the evangelical faiths. By the late 1830s, however, revivals were receiving unprecedented endorsements from Tuscaloosa newspaper editors, who increasingly embraced them as a cause that created better citizens. In particular, editors and town boosters welcomed the self-discipline that revivalists and the evangelical faiths insisted on converts' incorporating into their lives. Although

and the Old South: Washtenaw County, Michigan, and Tuscaloosa County, Alabama, 1820–1860" (Ph.D. dissertation, University of Michigan, 1992), 47–69.

11. West, *Methodism in Alabama*, 159–60, 162, 302; Tuscaloosa *Chronicle*, August 2, 1828.

12. *Alabama State Intelligencer*, August 6, 1831, September 17, 1831; *Spirit of the Age*, August 8, 1832; William H. Williams to ASSU, August 28, 1834, in ASSU Papers, Special Collections, Samford University, Birmingham, Alabama (microfilm); *Alabama Intelligencer and State Rights Expositor*, October 3, 10, 1835; *Flag of the Union*, October 10, 1835. A series of revivals also swept through the Tennessee Valley during the late 1820s and early 1830s. Dupre, "Barbecues and Pledges," 479–512.

the drive toward self-control has been most often associated with the Whig agenda, Tuscaloosa's Democrats also celebrated the consequences of the revival. In November 1838, Samuel A. Hale, editor of the Democratic *Flag of the Union,* announced to his readers that Tuscaloosa "for the last five or six weeks has been the scene of a very unusual and highly interesting religious excitement" and that the protracted meetings held in the Presbyterian, Methodist, and Baptist churches "have been attended with very gratifying success." Although these revivals apparently were ignored by numerous citizens—whom Hale denounced for their excessive preoccupation "in the petty and perplexing cares of life"—the editor reported that "a degree of seriousness still pervades our population." Believers, he wrote, "will rejoice" at the conversions to Christ, while "every good citizen will be glad that any have been reformed."[13]

This latter comment suggests the profound impact that revivalism had upon Tuscaloosa's collective comportment. As the evangelical faiths grew, and as they sought the elimination of vice among their adherents, untamed behavior in Tuscaloosa became increasingly unacceptable. In a similar vein, Stephen F. Miller, the editor of the Whig *Independent Monitor,* praised an 1841 revival. Although he considered himself "unworthy . . . to unite in these stirring exercises, and too frail or timid to seek the pure relations with our Creator," he nevertheless was pleased to see "numbers of our respected fellow-beings bend at the altar in agony and rise in triumph," and he applauded the social good that he believed was wrought by the revival: "We entreat the smiles of Heaven to favor the occasion still more and more, until its glorious results shall be seen and felt throughout the whole community." The *Flag of the Union* also reported on this Methodist-led revival and proclaimed it to be "more extensive in its operations . . . than any similar scene we have ever witnessed in our city. We hope the good work will continue to progress and spread its gracious influences over the entire circle of our young population."[14]

Other observers concurred that numerous Tuscaloosans were absorbed by revivals. Basil Manly, whose lengthy tenure (1837–1855) as president of the University of Alabama never removed him far from his career as a Baptist minister, reported in 1839 that "many revivals are now actually progressing, and the public mind seems rife for it. Any sort of a preacher gets a hearing." Two years later,

13. Lawrence Frederick Kohl, *The Politics of Individualism: Politics and the American Character in the Jacksonian Era* (New York, 1989), 69–78, 148–57; *Flag of the Union,* November 21, 1838.

14. *Independent Monitor,* March 5, 1841; *Flag of the Union,* March 3, 1841.

Manly wrote to his wife that a Methodist camp meeting was proceeding eight
or nine miles southeast of Tuscaloosa: "Yesterday nearly every thing from Tuscaloosa went there."[15]

Revivals continued in Tuscaloosa throughout the 1840s. Every autumn,
when revivals in Tuscaloosa (and the South) were most commonly held, the
town's newspapers not only printed announcements regarding planned camp
meetings, but also provided editorial endorsement of these events. In 1842 both
the Democratic *Flag of the Union* and the Whig *Independent Monitor* praised
the effects of a prolonged Methodist revival, a subsequent series of Baptist protracted meetings, and revivals in Tennessee and neighboring Greene and Perry
Counties. The Methodist camp meetings resulted in the conversion of forty-
four whites—including "some of our prominent citizens"—and forty-eight
African Americans. Encouraged by the "serious and inquiring spirit in the
community," the Methodist clergy continued their efforts with protracted
meetings at the Methodist meetinghouse, converting another thirty-five or
forty. Tuscaloosans were more "deeply and universally agitated" with respect to
religion than the editor of the *Flag* had heretofore seen: "Almost every other
topic of conversation has, for a time, been laid aside, or merged in the general
discussion of this truly solemn and interesting subject."[16]

Revivals continued during the following two years, and an even greater outpouring of spirit occurred in 1845. Half a century later, Anson West, in his *History of Methodism in Alabama*, pointed to the 1845 revival's sweeping effect upon
Tuscaloosa: it "was a moral revolution."[17] Contemporaries were likewise daz-
zled by its impact. The revival began rather slowly. Several days of preaching
produced inauspicious results. Basil Manly, who preached at the camp meeting
a few days after it commenced, wrote that initially the assembly was "very
cold." On the day after Manly's sermon, though, the Reverend John Christian
Keener of Tuscaloosa's Methodist Episcopal Church appeared at the camp
meeting immediately after the funeral of one of his children. Keener's "forcible
and soul-stirring effort" created a "sudden gust of excitement" in the assembly.
The consequent revival lasted more than three weeks and ended only when

15. Basil Manly to Rev. J. L. Reynolds, August 27, 1839, Basil Manly to Sarah Manly, October
4, 1841, both in Manly Family Papers.

16. *Independent Monitor*, October 5, 12, 19, 1842, November 23, 1842; *Flag of the Union*, October
19, 1842.

17. *Flag of the Union*, September 13, 1843; Basil Manly to Basil Manly Jr., August 7, 1844, in
Manly Family Papers; West, *History of Methodism in Alabama*, 568.

Keener's health and voice failed. About 150 were converted, slightly more than a hundred of them joining the Methodists. Newspapers announced that the revival exceeded all previous efforts in Tuscaloosa, and even Basil Manly, generally more restrained in his judgments than the town's editors, wrote to his son that he had "never seen such excitement in these parts." The *Monitor* claimed that the impact of the revival extended beyond the accession of members into the churches:

> Deep and solemn feelings pervade the community. The hearts of the people have been troubled. This is no temporary excitement. Religion is the theme of almost every tongue. It has taken hold upon the young men. A large number of them have made an open profession, and cast the world behind. Gay and fashionable young ladies have embraced religion, and instead of the amusements in which they once delighted, their joy is in the hopes of heaven. Indeed, all classes, the young, the middle aged, seem resolved upon a new life, improving their time and opportunities so as to die happily.

The *Monitor* report concluded that the "moral foundations of Tuskaloosa have been shaken, and long will the good work display its fruits."[18]

Perhaps the impact of revivalism in Tuscaloosa can also be measured by the rising opposition to those behaviors and organizations to which evangelicals objected. For example, after Tuscaloosa's antigambling crusade of the early 1830s, local prosecutions against gambling increased significantly during the mid-1830s as this vice became disreputable among respectable citizens. Similarly, during the mid-1820s Tuscaloosans welcomed troupes of stage actors to their community, but by 1829 thespians reported that vocal opposition by evangelicals to theatrical performances resulted in fewer people attending. Further,

18. *Independent Monitor,* August 20, 1845, September 10, 17, 24, October 1, 1845; Basil Manly to Basil Manly Jr., September 25, 1845, in Manly Family Papers. A series of Baptist protracted meetings, which commenced in the summer of 1845, continued after the Keener-led revival. Basil Manly to Basil Manly Jr., November 5, 1845, in Manly Family Papers. After this zenith of revivalism in Tuscaloosa, evangelical enthusiasm continued to affect the county, and existing records show that considerable revival activity also occurred in rural churches. By the 1850s, though, revivals seem to have lost much of their spontaneity and became standardized; church congregations usually held protracted meetings once a year, and agreed months in advance upon a specific time to hold them. Revivals are mentioned in the minutes of the following churches: Big Creek Baptist Church, and Dunn Creek's Baptist Church (photocopies in Hoole Special Collections); First Baptist Church of Tuscaloosa (originals at Tuscaloosa First Baptist Church).

although Antimasonry was never a substantial political movement in Alabama, evangelical opposition to Masonry brought about the closing of many Masonic lodges in the state and caused Tuscaloosa's Rising Virtue Lodge to become moribund during the early 1830s.[19] And as we shall see in chapter 3, alcohol consumption in Alabama decreased significantly following the emergence of Alabama's temperance crusade in 1829.

The advance of revivalism occurred simultaneously with the expansion of the market in Alabama. Many of Alabama's early small farmers took an increasingly greater portion of their output and sold it for goods that they did not produce themselves, while planters—and those aspiring to enter this class— usually emphasized the production of a single cash crop, such as cotton, and likewise sold it with the aim of increasing their wealth in both land and slaves. In towns such as Tuscaloosa, farmers sold their surplus to merchants who in turn sent it to distant markets—trade that was facilitated by Tuscaloosa's position as the commercial gateway linking north and south Alabama, and as the state capital after 1826. But whether one grew surplus crops or sold goods to the farmers, success in the market was often based upon self-discipline: it was necessary to put aside pleasures of the moment in order to realize long-term objectives. And since the evangelical commitment stressed self-discipline, the simultaneous growths of evangelicalism and the market were undoubtedly mutually reinforcing. Moreover, just as a market of petty producers could not subsist under the authoritarianism of traditional society, so the evangelical commitment had little to do with religious authority. It was a highly individualistic affair that was accepted voluntarily. In the words of Daniel Walker Howe, its adherents took "charge of their own lives and identities."[20] Nineteenth-century revivalism affirmed that the individual was answerable for his or her salvation; it was the responsibility of the individual to turn his or her heart to God and plead for grace. Arminianism, which influenced Baptists and Presbyterians as well as Methodists, made far greater sense to antebellum Americans who celebrated the achievements of the individual than did Calvinism, which, many people concluded, simply taught that salvation was entirely up to a God who capriciously saved some and condemned everyone else to damnation.[21]

19. Quist, "Social and Moral Reform," 47–69.

20. Daniel Walker Howe, "Religion and Politics in the Antebellum North," in *Religion and American Politics: From the Colonial Period to the 1980s*, ed. Mark A. Noll (New York, 1990), 128.

21. George Thomas, *Revivalism and Cultural Change*, 8.

Beyond this intellectual accord was considerable behavioral compatibility as well. Of course, for many people, virtue was and is its own reward. But the Christian who shunned the sins of dancing, gambling, fighting, and drunkenness found abstinence to be complementary with sound market behavior, be he or she a merchant, small producer, or laborer. Honesty and the avoidance of strong drink and gambling made one more efficient and assisted one in accumulating capital, while frivolous activities, such as dancing and the theater, were a waste of time. These connections were recognized by contemporaries. Thus Stephen Miller of the *Monitor* applauded the results of the great 1845 revival in Tuscaloosa: "The consolations of Christianity have banished worldly pleasures. Men of business, who have experienced a change of heart, rejoice to find that religion does not interfere with their just pursuits. It calls forth new industry, and steadier, higher aims."[22]

For the most part, the spread of self-discipline was probably an unintended consequence of revivalism and the expansion of the market. Nevertheless, proponents of temperance and the benevolent empire were explicit in expressing their desire to fashion the social order on this basis. They recognized that American society was changing so rapidly that the older forms of social discipline, based upon deference and the strong external controls of family, neighbors, and community, were quickly becoming obsolete. In search of techniques of social discipline that were appropriate for the dynamic and democratic society in which they lived, many antebellum reformers concluded that the social order could be maintained only through the widespread regeneration of individuals. And because many benevolence and temperance leaders were self-made people who utilized evangelical self-discipline in their upward struggle, they saw no reason that such methods could not similarly uplift society.[23]

Concurrent with the spread of revivals was the emergence of benevolent activity in Tuscaloosa. Perhaps as a way to expand their influence, evangelicals founded the Baptist Missionary Society of Tuscaloosa County in the early summer of 1824. The society sought to promote foreign and domestic missionary activity and to assist in the education of young men called to the ministry. The genesis of the Female Baptist Missionary Society of Tuscaloosa followed shortly; that its organizational meeting featured a sermon by the town's Methodist minister, the Reverend Robert L. Kennon, suggests that the efforts of

22. *Independent Monitor,* September 17, 1845.
23. Boylan, *Sunday School,* 65–68.

these two societies were interdenominational.[24] Sabbatarians organized at this time in neighboring Greene County; a "meeting of the Merchants of the town of Erie" resolved not to "receive or forward property" on Sunday and to "use our exertions" to see that local blue laws were enforced.[25] These societies proved ephemeral, and since there was no opposition expressed to them in the *American Mirror,* it is safe to assume that during the mid-1820s they posed no threat to the still raucous mores of Tuscaloosa.

More permanent were the efforts of the Alabama Bible Society, formed in 1824 in Cahaba—the state capital at the time—as an auxiliary of the New York–based American Bible Society. One of the aims of the Alabama Bible Society was to provide every white family in the state with a copy of the Scriptures. In order to ascertain the extent of this task, the corresponding secretary of the Alabama Bible Society requested that the assessors and tax collectors in each county ask households whether they had a Bible. Although only a few of the state's revenue collectors acceded to the society's request, Tuscaloosa County tax collector James Knox was among those who did. Despite receiving the request after he had begun collecting the county's taxes, Knox nevertheless found 529 families with Bibles and 234 without; he believed that as many as 400 of the 1,300 families in the county did not have the Good Book. The state society estimated that nearly half of the families in Alabama lacked a Bible, and its leaders concluded that persons who had previously supposed the society's work unnecessary would now see their mistake: "Surely the friends of good order— of good government—of sound religion, will unite their prayers and offerings in this work. Let the wants of 7000 families, containing the future hope of the government and the church, chide the past indifference of some, and stimulate the labors of us all." The Alabama Bible Society emphasized that this enterprise was not sectarian: "It is the common cause of the patriot and the Christian. . . . Peace, order, industry, and happiness are among the happy fruits of its general influence upon society. Nothing else is adequate to restrain those passions which produce so much misery and mischief in the world." The Bible

24. *American Mirror,* July 10, 31, August 7, 1824.

25. *Ibid.,* May 29, 1824. It is not known if Tuscaloosa enacted blue laws during the 1820s, as such records are not extant. Several 1820 Montgomery ordinances, however, prohibited commercial activity, participation in sports, and all forms of entertainment on Sundays. Clanton W. Williams, ed., "Extracts from the Records of the City of Montgomery, Alabama, 1820–1821," *Alabama Review,* I (April 1948), 136–37. If such laws were on the books in Tuscaloosa, it does not appear that they were enforced.

crusade preached more than conversion of those unmoved by evangelical Protestantism. The crusaders were convinced that neglect of the Scriptures would result in a society governed by chaos. To inhibit base impulses, encourage self-control, and promote a peaceful and well-ordered republic, it was necessary to place the Bible in the hands of as many people as possible.[26]

Upon becoming the state capital in 1826, Tuscaloosa was the natural site for the annual December meetings of the Alabama Bible Society. In 1827, the society ordered 100 Bibles and 75 Testaments; these were to be sold at the Tuscaloosa drugstore of Dr. Samuel Mills Meek, who was also a physician and a Methodist minister. The Scriptures were sold at a low cost—and free to those who could not afford them. At about this time the state society reported that it had distributed 1,100 Bibles and Testaments throughout Alabama during the past year and noted that the state had seven auxiliary societies. The Madison County Bible Society was highly successful in circulating the Bible; after canvassing Huntsville, members of this auxiliary discovered only seven families to be without Scriptures. "How does Tuscaloosa stand in this respect," wondered the editor of the Tuscaloosa *Chronicle.* "May there not be 7 × 7."[27] The rural portions of Alabama, where the vast majority of the population lived, were less fully supplied. Despite some success in the towns, and notwithstanding the ambitious rhetoric that Bible partisans uttered annually at the Alabama Bible Society meetings, during the late 1820s and early 1830s evangelicals were clearly unable to provide Bibles to all of Alabama's white families.

Judging from the annual reports of the Alabama Bible Society, sustained enthusiasm for the cause in the Cotton State was difficult to maintain throughout these years. The same was true for the Tuscaloosa auxiliary. In October 1830, activists held a public meeting in Tuscaloosa to arrive at a plan for supplying all the scripturally destitute families in the county. Those present at

---

26. ABS *Annual Report,* IX (1825), 65–66, X (1826), 78–79; see also *American Mirror,* August 28, 1824. Regarding the development of the ABS, see Wosh, *Spreading the Word.* Naturally, the successful circulation of religious literature was dependent upon adult literacy. White literacy in Alabama during the 1820s is not known; according to the 1850 federal census, 33,757 of the state's 178,116 adults over nineteen years old (19.0 percent) were unable to read and write, while in Tuscaloosa, 1,133 of the county's 5,213 white adults (21.7 percent) were illiterate. De Bow, *Seventh Census,* xxii, 414–16, 428.

27. Tuscaloosa *Chronicle,* December 15, 1827, December 8, 1828; *Alabama State Intelligencer,* December 18, 1829, January 8, 1831; William H. Williams to ASSU, December 23, 1830, in ASSU Papers; ABS, *Annual Report,* XII (1828), 25; Tuscaloosa *Chronicle,* August 30, 1828.

the meeting divided the county into five beats, and in each beat they appointed two people to make "the necessary inquiries"—that is, to determine which local families lacked a copy of the Scriptures. The hope was that by early 1831 "the amount of destitute families in this county" could "be laid before her pious and humane citizens." The objective was not soon realized, and distribution of Bibles in Tuscaloosa and elsewhere did not proceed as well as proponents had hoped. The Alabama Bible Society reported to the national body that the greatest impediments were a lack of people to circulate books and the absence of a full-time agent who would travel the state and remind evangelicals of the importance of the Bible endeavor. In Tuscaloosa, a recommitment drive commenced in February 1837, with a meeting at the Methodist Church to reorganize the local auxiliary of the American Bible Society (this auxiliary, incidentally, bore the same name as the statewide body). The society's previous goal of supplying all of Tuscaloosa County's scripturally destitute families was restated. This time, however, their outreach centered on the rising generation: the aim was now to supply a Bible to all white children under fifteen years old who could read. The group also proposed to form a new Bible repository in Tuscaloosa, and they set a goal of raising $500 within thirty days to assist in its creation. The repository was established by July under the custody of Alfred Battle, the auxiliary's treasurer.[28]

These actions notwithstanding, Tuscaloosa's Bible repository was short-lived. The nationwide depression commencing in 1837 greatly hindered the ability of all benevolent societies to raise money and especially impeded Bible and tract societies from circulating their publications. The deadened economy, coupled with the resignation of the national society's agent for Alabama, Mississippi, and western Tennessee, brought the Alabama Bible Society to a standstill: the American Bible Society's *Annual Report* for 1839 simply stated, "In Alabama nothing of note is to be recorded in relation to the past year." Contributions to the national society plummeted and did not rise again until economic recovery commenced in the mid-1840s.[29] But the American Bible Society and its Alabama auxiliaries then rebounded strongly, with the national organization's new agent, John Kain, organizing new auxiliaries and revitalizing older ones—including the Tuscaloosa-based Alabama Bible Society, which was formally reorganized in December 1844.

28. *Alabama State Intelligencer,* January 8, 1831; ABS *Annual Report,* XIV (1830), 41, XV (1831), 42–43; *Flag of the Union,* February 24, July 26, 1837.

29. Kuykendall, *Southern Enterprize,* 100–102; ABS *Annual Report,* XXIII (1839), 34.

As in previous forays of Bible circulation in the state, this new society aimed to "supply every family in Alabama, if practicable, with a copy of the Holy Scriptures." It did not want for prestige or credibility, for it attracted some of Tuscaloosa's leading citizens, many of whom were also connected to the state's major Protestant denominations. At an organizational meeting, Justice Henry W. Collier of the Alabama Supreme Court, who was a Methodist and future Democratic governor, was selected president of the Alabama Bible Society; Democrats Lincoln Clark, a legislator and a Presbyterian, and Joseph Phelan, a Methodist who had served as clerk of the Alabama House of Representatives and later as secretary of the state senate, were chosen to be secretaries; Philip L. Sink, a merchant, Sunday-school promoter, and temperance supporter, was elected treasurer; prayers were offered by the Episcopal bishop of Alabama, Nicholas Hamner Cobb, and by University of Alabama president Basil Manly, a Baptist. Among the speakers at this meeting, Collier delivered the most otherworldly message: "If the Bible was read with the same solicitude to learn the truth and submit to its guidance, as we read the political and commercial intelligence of the day, many who are now upon earth might live to see the full development of the millennial era." Such millenarian rhetoric, however, was not common among Bible advocates in Alabama. More typical were the remarks of the other speakers on this occasion, who explained that the wide circulation of the Bible would not only convert its readers to Christianity, but would also advance the public good. Agent Kain expressed his fervent desire that a "cause so calculated to improve society, and to spread peace and good will among men not be permitted to languish." Isaac Croom, a Whig member of the Alabama House of Representatives from Greene County, proclaimed "the benefits to mankind which resulted from a knowledge of the Bible. Wherever that blessed book was read, it elevated the morals of the people and made them better in all the relations of life, social and political." State senator Samuel C. Oliver of Montgomery County, also a Whig, similarly praised the Bible's influence in "moralizing the people and rendering them submissive to the laws, and [making] them happy members of the community." According to Oliver, one could see the consequences of disbelief in the Bible by merely studying the French Revolution, where atheism abounded with lawlessness.[30]

---

30. *Independent Monitor,* December 18, 1844, December 25, 1844. Apparently a meeting of the Alabama Bible Society scheduled for December 1842 inspired no residual activity. *Flag of the Union,* November 30, 1842.

As these Bible proponents understood their world, religion and the belief in God were important in keeping society orderly, law-abiding, and peaceable.

Within a few years of this meeting, Alabama's economy began to rebound from the depression, and from then until secession, enthusiasts consistently sent large sums of money to the national society. By 1862, Alabamians donated more than $7,700 to the headquarters of the American Bible Society and remitted almost $63,000 for Bibles to be sold and given away in Alabama. During these years, the Tuscaloosa-based Alabama Bible Society—renamed the Tuscaloosa Bible Society in 1854—sent more than $5,000 to the national society in donations and remittances. With this stronger financial backing, Bible supporters further attempted to penetrate the remote areas of the state. In 1846 agent Kain devoted himself to providing books "in places where Auxiliary Societies could not be sustained," while the Tuscaloosa society employed a temporary agent "who spends a part of his time in making collections in the more wealthy counties, and a part in making distributions in the poor and mountainous counties." Meanwhile, Philip L. Sink sold Bibles at his Tuscaloosa store "at New-York cost"—that is, he added no shipping or selling fees to the price—and supplied volumes to the poor at no charge.

In subsequent years, Alabama's Bible proponents generally sent the national society optimistic reports that recounted the labors of a handful of agents who circulated books among the state's scripturally destitute and also organized new auxiliary societies. The number of societies increased more than fivefold from 1842 to 1849, and by the mid-1850s nearly seventy local auxiliaries of the American Bible Society had been established in Alabama. So successful were these societies—as well as Bible societies auxiliary to Alabama's Baptist churches—that, according to data collected by agents of the American Tract Society in the 1850s, over 90 percent of Alabama's white families who were approached by American Tract Society colporteurs possessed copies of the Scriptures in their homes.[31]

31. Quist, "Social and Moral Reform," 85–96, 548–52; ABS *Annual Report*, XXX (1846), 54–55; *Independent Monitor*, February 18, 1846. Of course, the data collected from the American Tract Society must be taken with caution, as many colporteurs may have labored in portions of the state in which the population was well-supplied with Bibles. It is also possible that some Alabamians simply told tract society agents that they owned a Bible, hoping to rid themselves quickly of an intrusive nuisance. But the large percentage of Alabama's surveyed families who reported possessing Bibles indicates that the benevolent empire was largely successful in circulating its publications among the state's white population.

Despite these successes, by the mid-1850s growing sectionalism sometimes resulted in white southerners' treating the American Bible Society with suspicion, although there is no recorded expression of hostility in Tuscaloosa County. The amount of money that Alabama auxiliaries of the American Bible Society collectively forwarded to the national body remained consistent until 1860, but after 1858 the vast majority of the state's auxiliaries no longer sent remittances to the New York headquarters. Contemporary figures released by the national society likewise indicate that most auxiliaries in the southern states were no longer active by 1859.[32]

In addition to the support it received from political leaders, the efforts of the American Bible Society were also embraced by the different evangelical Protestant churches in Alabama. A resolution of the Presbyterian Synod of Alabama proclaimed that if all Christians would unite in supporting the American Bible Society "with the zeal which its importance demands, the time is not far distant, when the Bible might be placed in every family in the face of the earth." The synod's leaders called on members to labor toward the more immediate goal of forming auxiliary societies in every county, and "by personal efforts to discover and supply" every "destitute family in this State"; they also encouraged ministers to take collections for the Bible cause and to preach at least one sermon a year on the virtues of the American Bible Society.[33] The Alabama Conference of the Methodist Episcopal Church, South, expressed its "undiminished confidence in the American Bible Society" and invited "its authorized Agents to visit our several fields of labor, and for the sale and distribution of the sacred volume, and for the collection of funds to promote the interests of the cause."[34]

Although Alabama's Baptists initially embraced the American Bible Soci-

32. Quist, "Social and Moral Reform," 548–50, 552; Wosh, *Spreading the Word*, 204, 209–11. Compare the conclusions of Nord, "Religious Reading and Readers," 258.

33. Records of the Synod of Alabama, 1837–1849, January 21, 1843 (p. 40), typescript in ADAH. The Alabama Synod was more favorable to the efforts of the American Bible Society than some other Old School Presbyterians in the South. See Kuykendall, *Southern Enterprize,* 106.

34. *Minutes of the Alabama Conference of the M. E. Church, South, Held at Talladega, Ala., December 13th, 1854, Together with the Annual Sermon, Preached Before the Conference by A. M. Mitchell, D. D.* (Montgomery, 1855), 8–9. See also *Minutes of the Alabama Conference of the Methodist Episcopal Church, South, Held in Eutaw, Alabama, December 5, 1855, Together with the Annual Sermon, Preached Before the Conference by Phil P. Heely, D. D.* (Montgomery, 1856), 9; ABS *Annual Report,* XXXVI (1852), 90.

ety, they eventually withdrew their support and formed their own denominational Bible concern—demonstrating that the benevolent crusade was not restricted to the operations of national interdenominational societies. As early as 1829, the Alabama Baptist State Convention resolved that "Bible Societies, Tract Societies, Sabbath Schools, and all such institutions" were "calculated to advance the interest of the Redeemer's Kingdom among men," and it recommended that Baptists give them "liberal support." Five years later, Robert S. Foster, corresponding secretary both of the Baptist State Convention of Alabama and of the Grant's Creek Sunday School in Tuscaloosa County, was more specific when he praised the cooperation of the American Bible Society and the American Tract Society in Burma: "They exhibit that catholic and fraternal disposition to co-operate in every evangelical enterprise, which brightly betokens the coming of the Messiah's kingdom."[35] But in November of 1836, a number of Alabama Baptists, aggrieved over certain policies of the American Bible Society, formed the Alabama Baptist Bible Society. These Baptists particularly deplored the national society's decision no longer to aid the printing of Bibles "in the vernacular languages of the heathen" with the Greek verb *baptizo* specifically translated to mean "immerse." In compliance with a directive of the Baptist Board of Foreign Missions, the Alabama Baptists formed a new society that would circulate a "pure undisguised Bible to the heathens."[36] The formation of the Alabama Baptist Bible Society meant that the Cotton State was graced with two Bible societies. Because of its strong denominational base of support, the Baptist society—whose meetings occurred yearly at the state Baptist convention—did not suffer as greatly during cycles of apathy as did the Alabama Bible Society.

Tuscaloosans were particularly active in founding the Alabama Baptist Bible Society. John L. Dagg, a national vice-president of the American and For-

35. *Minutes of the Sixth Anniversary of the Alabama Baptist State Convention* (Montgomery, 1829), 3; *Minutes of the Eleventh Anniversary of the Baptist State Convention, in Alabama, Held at Salem Meeting House, Near Greensborough* (Tuscaloosa, 1834), 7–11. Claiborne resident the Reverend J. A. Randalson, who was clerk of the Alabama Baptist State Convention from 1823 to 1824, also served as corresponding secretary of the Alabama Bible Society from 1824 to 1825. Thomas McAdory Owen, *History of Alabama and Dictionary of Alabama Biography* (4 vols.; Chicago, 1921), IV, 1408; ABS *Annual Report*, IX (1825), 128.

36. *Minutes of the Thirteenth Anniversary of the Alabama Baptist State Convention, Held at Fellowship Meeting House, Wilcox County, Alabama. Commencing on Saturday, November 12th, 1836* (Tuscaloosa, 1836), 15.

eign Bible Society and principal of Tuscaloosa's Alabama Female Athenaeum, was president of the new society, and Robert Foster was its treasurer; A. J. Holcombe, a secretary to the Alabama State Baptist Convention and a member of the Tuscaloosa Temperance Society's corresponding committee, was also a secretary of the Alabama Baptist Bible Society. Directors of the Alabama Baptist Bible Society included John A. Hodges, a teacher in the Tuscaloosa Union Sunday School and later a superintendent at the Buck's Creek Sunday school in rural Tuscaloosa County; James Foster, superintendent of the Grant's Creek Sunday School; James H. DeVotie, Tuscaloosa town's Baptist pastor, president of the Alabama Female Athenaeum, and a member of the executive committee of the Tuscaloosa Temperance Society; and Joseph Lacy, a merchant and active Whig who had taught in the Tuscaloosa Union Sunday School, served as a secretary of the Tuscaloosa Baptist Sunday School, and was elected a vice-president of the Tuscaloosa Young Men's Total Abstinence Society.[37] In subsequent years, other officers of the Alabama Baptist Bible Society hailed from Tuscaloosa.[38]

Following a June 1853 address by the Reverend John D. Williams, an agent for the Alabama Baptist Bible Society, twenty-three Tuscaloosa Baptists—ten of them female—formed the Tuskaloosa Baptist Bible Society. Money col-

37. On Dagg: *Ibid.*, 15; *Alabama Baptist* (Marion), June 17, November 4, 1843. On Holcombe: *Flag of the Union*, December 6, 1837, August 29, 1838. On Hodges: Minutes of the Teachers' Association of the Tuscaloosa Union Sunday School, February 11, 1833, in possession of the First Presbyterian Church of Tuscaloosa; Thomas W. Cox to ASSU, November 30, 1834, ASSU Papers. On Foster: William H. Williams to Frederick W. Porter, January 31, 1832, Thomas W. Cox to ASSU, November 30, 1834, both ASSU Papers. On DeVotie: *Flag of the Union*, October 9, 1837, October 2, 16, 1839. On Lacy: Minutes of the Teachers' Association of the Tuscaloosa Union Sunday School, March 25, 1833; *Flag of the Union*, August 23, 1837, August 28, 1839; *Independent Monitor*, June 6, 1840, and William H. Williams to ASSU, June 1, 1834, in ASSU Papers. Hosea Holcombe, a vice-president of the Alabama Baptist Bible Society, had been a pastor of Tuscaloosa town's Baptist Church from 1824 to 1827; Luther Quentin Porch, *History of the First Baptist Church, Tuscaloosa, Alabama, 1818–1968* (Tuscaloosa, 1968), 129.

38. *Minutes of the Sixteenth Anniversary of the Baptist State Convention of Alabama; Held at Oakmulgee Meeting House, Perry County, commencing on Saturday, Nov. 9, 1839* (Tuscaloosa, 1839), 13–16; *Minutes of the Seventeenth Anniversary of the Baptist State Convention of Alabama, Held at Salem, Greene County, Alabama* (Tuscaloosa, 1840), 10; *Minutes of the Eighteenth Anniversary of the Baptist State Convention, of Alabama* (N.p., 1841[?]), 23; *Minutes of the Thirty-first Anniversary of the Alabama Baptist State Convention, held at Marion, Perry County* (Marion, 1854), 30; *Minutes of the Thirty-fourth Anniversary of the Alabama Baptist State Convention, held at Marion* (Tuskegee, 1857), 29.

lected by this body was to be sent to the Tuskaloosa Association Bible Society, which was organized three months later when delegates from the Mt. Moriah, Philadelphia, and Tuskaloosa Baptist Bible Societies gathered for the association's first annual meeting. The objective of this body and its auxiliaries was similar to that of other Bible societies in Alabama during the 1850s: they sought to raise "funds for the support of Bible operations in the southern fields—home and foreign." They were also greatly concerned about the scripturally destitute and resolved "that any person not able to purchase a Bible, who shall apply shall be furnished gratuitously." The greater Tuscaloosa Association endorsed these actions and in 1854 passed a resolution that "earnestly recommend[ed] that each church which is a member of this body . . . organize a Bible Society, to be auxiliary to the Bible Society of this Association."[39]

A year after its organization, the Alabama Baptist Bible Society became an auxiliary of the Baptist-governed American and Foreign Bible Society. The Alabama society explained that its purpose was not to proselyte souls to the Baptist faith; rather, its "sole object" was to "aid in disseminating the sacred scriptures among all people, in the most current versions which can be obtained"—which, of course, meant circulating translations that supported the Baptist contention that baptism ought to be performed only by immersion. In the early 1840s, however, America's Baptists became increasingly divided over slavery. As will be discussed more fully in chapter 5, Alabama's Baptists in 1840 voted to withhold all contributions from the American Baptist Board of Foreign Missions and the American and Foreign Bible Society "until the officers and managers of these institutions satisfy us, that they are not connected, either directly or indirectly, with these anti-slavery proceedings." Four years later, Tuscaloosa's delegates to the state Baptist convention questioned the propriety of sending money to Baptist benevolent and missionary operations headquartered in the North as these societies frequently condemned slavery. Things came to a head two years afterward, when the Alabama Baptist Bible Society severed its ties to the American and Foreign Bible Society and became an auxiliary of the Southern Baptist Convention. But denominationalism, as well as slavery, continued to play an important role in the benevolent operations that were supported by Alabama's Baptists. Even though the American

39. Minutes of the Tuscaloosa Baptist Church, June 19, 1853 (p. 130); *Minutes of the Twenty-First Annual Session of the Tuskaloosa Baptist Association* (Tuscaloosa, 1853), 6–7, 8; *Minutes of the Twenty-Fifth Annual Session of the Tuskaloosa Baptist Association* (Tuscaloosa, 1857), 9; *Minutes of the Twenty-Second Annual Session of the Tuskaloosa Baptist Association* (Tuscaloosa, 1854), 5, 7.

Bible Society's position on slavery remained unobjectionable to most white southerners, Alabama's Baptists continued to reject offers of cooperation with the national body in both 1852 and 1856, and cited the persistent disagreement over the translation of *baptizo* as the chief stumbling block.[40]

The agenda of the American Tract Society—also headquartered in New York—was closely related to that of the American Bible Society. Like those who advocated the distribution of Bibles, the promoters of tracts were greatly alarmed at the extent of religious ignorance and indifference among Americans. Similarly, tract enthusiasts believed that their crusade would not only convert sinners to Christ, but would also persuade people to embrace self-discipline and moral lives. The enterprise had a certain advantage over the Bible cause, as the Bible was difficult for many people to comprehend when it was removed from a liturgical context, or obscure for those who lacked a religious background. Tracts, on the other hand, could be tailored for people of almost any occupation, class, or age.

Also like their Bible-society counterparts, supporters of the circulation of tracts were convinced during the 1820s and early 1830s that Alabama suffered greatly from a lack of religious knowledge. As the national tract society's *Annual Report* lamented, "Perhaps no state in the union has such extraordinary claims upon the American Tract Society." Indeed, one tract advocate estimated that in some portions of Alabama, one-half to two-thirds of the people

40. *Minutes of the Fourteenth Anniversary of the Baptist State Convention of Alabama, held at Enon Meeting House, Madison County* (Tuscaloosa, 1837), 14; *Minutes of the Seventeenth Anniversary of the Baptist State Convention of Alabama*, 4–6; *Journal of the Proceedings of the Baptist State Convention in Alabama at its Twentieth Anniversary at Marion, Perry County, Commencing on Saturday, November 16, 1844* (N.p., 1844[?]), 2; *Minutes of the Twenty-first Anniversary of the Alabama Baptist State Convention* (N.p., 1845[?]), 23; *Minutes of the Twenty-second Anniversary of the Alabama Baptist State Convention, Marion, Perry County, November 14–17, 1846* (N.p., 1846[?]), 21; *Alabama Baptist* (Marion), November 20, 1846; Robert Andrew Baker, *Relations Between Northern and Southern Baptists* ([Fort Worth, Texas], 1948), 72–87; William Wright Barnes, *The Southern Baptist Convention, 1845–1953* (Nashville, 1954), 12–42; Mary B. Putnam, *The Baptists and Slavery, 1840–1845* (Ann Arbor, 1913); Porch, *History of the First Baptist Church*, 21–23; Posey, *Frontier Mission*, 363–71; Griffin, *Their Brothers' Keepers*, 181–82; Kuykendall, *Southern Enterprize*, 134–36; *Minutes of the Thirty-third Annual Session of the Alabama Baptist Association, Held in the Providence Church, Dallas Co., Ala., October 8th to 11th, 1852* (Montgomery, 1852), 9; *South Western Baptist*, March 20, 1856.

were "wholly destitute of the Bible," and that many of these were without "any Christian privileges whatever." The American Tract Society reasoned that, since evangelicals had not responded to this spiritual dearth by sending Bibles to every "destitute" family in the land, the best solution was the dissemination of tracts. Concerned Tuscaloosans responded by forming an auxiliary of the American Tract Society in 1829, appointed J. B. Cook as the auxiliary's treasurer, and remitted $150 to the national society to purchase tracts for local distribution. By 1833, Connecticut native David Woodruff, a Tuscaloosa bookseller, active Presbyterian, and later mayor of the town, had become the most important local leader of this benevolent enterprise. In 1835 the national society provided the Tuscaloosa auxiliary with 15,000 pages of tracts, gratis, for local distribution. This auxiliary functioned through 1839, by which time its members had purchased almost $300 worth of tracts from the parent society.[41]

Possibly more than any other benevolent organization, the American Tract Society was prostrated by the national depression that began in 1837. Previously, the society had relied upon auxiliaries to raise money and dispense tracts. By the early 1840s, however, few of the auxiliaries sent money to New York, and in the Mississippi Valley—the region of America that most concerned tract officials—auxiliaries were almost entirely defunct. To compensate for the lack of local support, the national society after 1842 turned to the colportage system, hiring young men (usually theological students, devoted laity, or ministers) at $150 to $200 a year to promote the evangelical agenda. Combining the methods of itinerant preacher and peddler, the colporteurs sold the society's books and tracts or provided them free to the impoverished. In addition, these agents encouraged their contacts to pray, attend church, live abstemious lives, convert to evangelical Protestantism, and send their children to Sunday school. Thus, despite the economic recovery that was underway by the mid-1840s, the Alabama auxiliaries of the American Tract Society had no real function and did not rebound like those of the American Bible Society. Most of the tract activity in Tuscaloosa County—as in the rest of America— continued to be conducted by colporteurs, who both circulated tracts among the unchurched and solicited funds from the converted. For example, W. Carey Crane, an agent for the national society, collected contributions dur-

---

41. *Alabama State Intelligencer,* May 17, 1829; American Tract Society [hereinafter cited as ATS] (New York), *Annual Report,* IV (1829), 26, V (1830), 75, VIII (1833), 94, X (1835), 28, XXXIII (1838), 169, XIV (1839), 144, XX (1845), 155. See also Boyers, *Urban Masses,* 22–33.

ing a visit to Tuscaloosa in early 1844, and W. L. Chase of the Newton Theological Seminary of Massachusetts "performed a brief agency in Tuscaloosa County" later that year.[42]

Local evangelicals also served as colporteurs. Chase was succeeded by the Reverend Reuben Dodson, a Baptist minister in rural Tuscaloosa County. Willis Burns, a minister and missionary for the Tuscaloosa Baptist Association, also devoted some of his time to working as an American Tract Society colporteur. In 1849, Burns reported to the national society that he had spent eight months canvassing Tuscaloosa and Shelby Counties. His report provides a glimpse into the work of a colporteur; during the eight months, Burns visited only 224 families, indicating that his was a part-time endeavor. He found 99 families who were "Rom. Catholics or fatal errorists," 70 families "habitually neglecting evan. preach'g," and 37 families without Bibles. Burns's responsibilities as an agent required that he strive to correct these ills. He succeeded in conversing or praying with 178 of the households that he visited, sold 947 volumes and gave away 484 volumes of the society's publications, held 35 "public or prayer meetings," and distributed 44 Bibles. Colporteurs were energetic and widespread, and, in the years under study, as many as one-fourth of Alabama's white families were confronted by agents of the American Tract Society.[43]

There were other tract enterprises that operated in Tuscaloosa. In 1831, the Methodists formed a society auxiliary to the New York–based Tract Society of the Methodist Episcopal Church. Although many of the seventy-five male and female members of the auxiliary were Methodists, at least twenty-one were not, indicating that it was open to all friends of the tract cause. Membership was conferred upon payment of a year's dues, fifty cents. Convinced that "the circulation of Religious Tracts would improve the Moral and Religious condition of the community," the auxiliary encouraged members to provide religious literature to "the destitute, gratuitously." Another tract organization in Tuscaloosa was the Benevolent Society of the University of Alabama, formed in 1844 after a number of students at the university converted and

42. Griffin, *Their Brothers' Keepers*, 90–92; Kuykendall, *Southern Enterprize*, 112–14, 126; (Marion) *Alabama Baptist*, March 16, 1844, February 22, 1845; ATS (New York), *Annual Report*, XX (1845), 64. See also *ibid.*, XXIV (1849), 125, XXVI (1851), 33. The work of colporteurs is richly described in Nord, "Religious Reading and Readers."

43. ATS (New York), *Annual Report*, XX (1845), 64; XXIV (1849), 60; *South Western Baptist* (Marion, Ala.), October 9, 1850, October 8, 1851; Quist, "Social and Moral Reform," 552. See also the endorsement of the ATS in the *Independent Monitor*, May 25, 1842.

joined evangelical churches during their school vacation that year. This society
held Sunday-evening prayer meetings that one writer claimed were "attended
by a majority of the students." The most important function of this body,
however, was its effort to effect "the moral improvement of the less fortunate"
through the circulation of tracts; members of the society collected money and
contributed their own funds to this end. The extent to which the students actually distributed tracts among the "less fortunate" is not known; however, a
lengthy letter from R. S. Cook, secretary of the American Tract Society, in
which he thanked the Benevolent Society for its "liberal donation" to one of
the national society's agents, suggests that the young men delegated to the
American Tract Society the task of diffusing "the Gospel of Jesus Christ . . .
among the masses." In Tuscaloosa, observers praised the society for its positive
influences upon the community. One man, "not a professor of religion," hoped
that the effects of the Benevolent Society would "obtain abroad a better character" for the university, while the *Independent Monitor* concluded that if similar societies were established at all of America's colleges, "the salutary influence
on public morals, would be vast. A new era would spring up through such instrumentality."[44]

Until 1857, Alabama's Baptists heartily approved of the American Tract Society. The Alabama State Baptist Convention praised the society in a series of
resolutions it passed in 1844, and two years later the *Alabama Baptist* sanctioned
the society as "one of the most useful of modern benevolent organizations. It is
supported by all evangelical denominations, and is doing incalculable good." A
further endorsement occurred in 1846. At the same meeting in which the Alabama Baptist Bible Society announced that its ties with the Baptist-sponsored
American and Foreign Bible Society had been dissolved because of disagreements over slavery, the Baptist Bible group also reported that it had furnished
J. F. Herrick, a colporteur of the American Tract Society, with Bibles to provide for "the destitute in the counties in which he has travelled." Clearly, these
white Alabamians did not consider the American Tract Society to be tainted
by abolitionism during the 1840s. But in 1857, when the national organization
approved a report that permitted the American Tract Society to publish tracts
condemning moral evils and vices arising from slavery—although not slavery

44. James B. Sellers, *The First Methodist Church,* 47–48, 311; *Independent Monitor,* November
12, 1845, October 22, 1845; *Alabama Baptist* (Marion), February 22, 1845 (see also October 15, 1845);
Basil Manly to Basil Manly Jr., October 20, 1845, in Manly Family Papers; *State Journal and Flag
of the Union,* October 9, 1846.

itself—and later that year published a tract entitled *The Duties of Masters,* many white southerners were indignant. Basil Manly, at the time serving as Baptist minister in Charleston, South Carolina, was among those outraged. He complained that the American Tract Society refused to express unequivocally that it intended to follow "the policy hitherto pursued by them" regarding slavery, and he urged other Baptists in the South not to cooperate with the society "so long as the present suspicious attitude is maintained." Ever the sectionalist, Manly was naturally insulted by any suggestions from northerners on how white southerners ought to manage their "domestic institutions." Southern protest against the *Duties of Masters* became so intense that the society's officers decided not to distribute the copies they had printed, and the organization's policy regarding slavery reverted to its previous position.[45] Nevertheless, as strongly as Manly and other white southerners protested the ATS's policy regarding slavery, they did not question the practice of circulating tracts.

Activists in the Bible and tract causes were found generally among the elite, and their numbers were relatively small, in Tuscaloosa County and elsewhere. In all, the names of forty-seven Tuscaloosans—seven of them women—could be identified from various sources as having either attended a meeting of, served as a local officer of, or contributed money to the American Tract Society, the American Bible Society, or one of their auxiliaries before 1860. Some thirty-three of these enthusiasts were linked to other reform efforts. At least twenty-three members of this group participated in the antebellum Sabbath-school movement, eighteen participated in the temperance crusade, fourteen were colonizationists, three contributed to Tuscaloosa's Female Benevolent Society, and one each was active promoting Sabbatarianism and common schools. A few hearty individuals displayed a penchant for activism, as ten supported temperance, colonization, and the Bible and/or tract causes, and seven endorsed these three reforms as well as Sabbath schools.[46]

Thirty-nine of these Bible and tract enthusiasts were traced to a church, of whom the largest portion (23, or 59.0 percent) were Presbyterians, followed by

45. *Journal of the Proceedings of the Baptist State Convention in Alabama at its Twentieth Anniversary,* 4; *Alabama Baptist* (Marion), December 18, November 20, 1846; *South Western Baptist* (Tuskegee, Ala.), June 18, 1857; Griffin, *Their Brothers' Keepers,* 161–97; Kuykendall, *Southern Enterprize,* 136–38; Valois, "To Revolutionize the World," 326–34.

46. So closely linked together were Alabama's early Bible and temperance societies that state meetings were held on successive days in January 1833. *State Rights Expositor and Spirit of the Age,* December 22, 1832.

Methodists (10, or 25.6 percent), and Baptists and Episcopalians (3, or 7.7 percent, each).[47] As we shall see later, sectarian opponents of the benevolent empire sometimes based their hostility on what they felt was the excessive influence of Presbyterians in the national bodies. Clearly, the national societies and their local auxiliaries received their greatest support from Tuscaloosans of this faith. It is unlikely that many white Tuscaloosans suspected that local supporters of these national societies were clandestine abolitionists, since devotees were mostly southern-born, and many were slaveholders of local significance.[48] The slaveholding status could be determined for thirty-five advocates of benevolence; twenty-seven were slaveholders according to either the 1830, 1840, or 1850 census, and their holdings for these years averaged 20.3, 16.8, and 23.8 slaves, respectively.[49]

Of the thirty-six whose principal occupations could be ascertained, twenty-seven (75.0 percent) were professionals (including two women whose husbands fell into this category), seven (19.4 percent) were engaged in commerce, and two (5.6 percent) were farmers or planters. This occupational breakdown suggests that although many benevolence proponents possessed moderate-to-large slaveholdings, their economic world extended beyond the plantation. They were dual careerists who maintained close ties to the more

47. Tuscaloosa church affiliations were obtained from Tuscaloosa newspapers and the following sources: Records of the First Baptist Church of Tuscaloosa, Records of the First Presbyterian Church of Tuscaloosa, Records of the St. John's Catholic Church (Tuscaloosa), Records of Christ Episcopal Church, Tuscaloosa, all of which remain in the possession of their respective congregations; the published minutes of the Tuscaloosa Baptist Association and the Alabama Baptist State Convention; and Sellers, *First Methodist Church*.

48. Of the twenty-six with identifiable places of birth, nineteen (73.0 percent) were born in the South.

49. There were 11, 20, and 15 promoters of Bibles and tracts who owned slaves according to the 1830, 1840, and 1850 censuses, respectively; their median slaveholdings for these years were 17, 7, and 8. A number of large slaveholders served as officers of Tuscaloosa's benevolence auxiliaries. These included Alfred Battle, who owned 34 slaves in 1830, 96 in 1840, and 134 in 1850, and served as vice-president of the Alabama Bible Society in 1837, and treasurer from 1838 to 1845; Henry W. Collier, president of the Alabama Bible Society in 1837 and 1844, and of the Tuscaloosa Bible Society from 1854 to 1855, owned 88 slaves in 1850; the Rev. Robert M. Cunningham, pastor of the First Presbyterian Church, Tuscaloosa, and vice-president of the Alabama Bible Society in 1831, possessed 22 slaves in 1830; while Alexander Perry Hogan, corresponding secretary of the Tuscaloosa Bible Society from 1856 until secession, owned 17 slaves in 1850. Regarding Battle, see *Flag of the Union*, February 24, 1837, July 26, 1837; ABS *Annual Report*, XXIII (1838), 135; XXIX (1845), 145; James Sellers, *First Methodist Church*, 73. On the other subjects, see the sources cited in n. 50.

cosmopolitan life of villages and towns. In the rural America of the early to mid-nineteenth century, such places were the centers of culture and the entrepôts of commerce.[50]

While the Philadelphia-based American Sunday School Union (ASSU) and the larger Sabbath-school movement shared the same ultimate goals as the Bible and tract campaigns, the methods of the two groups were different. In theory, at least, it was possible that a small area could be supplied with sufficient tracts and Bibles, and that local evangelicals could then feel that their objective had been attained. In reality, however, volunteer colporteurs could become overwhelmed by the task of providing publications to so many people,

50. A number of Tuscaloosans involved in the circulation of Bibles and tracts held prominent positions in society. Additionally, Tuscaloosa's advocates of benevolence often consisted of several noteworthy Alabamians whose political responsibilities required their presence at the state capital. These individuals included Governors Israel Pickens, John Murphy, Gabriel Moore, and Henry Collier, each of whom served as president of the Alabama Bible Society (Collier was also president of the Alabama State Temperance Society during the 1830s, the Alabama Total Abstinence Society in 1843, the Alabama State Agricultural Society in 1842, and a national vice-president of the American Colonization Society); Alabama Supreme Court Justices Henry Hitchcock, John White, and John J. Ormond (the latter of whom was also a national vice-president of the American Colonization Society); legislators James G. Birney, Benjamin B. Fontaine, Lincoln Clark, Samuel C. Oliver, Isaac Croom, and Dr. George Phillips; Samuel Pickens, state auditor in 1819; Episcopal Bishop Nicholas Hamner Cobb and University of Alabama president Basil Manly, both of whom also supported temperance and colonization; Tuscaloosa merchant and future mayor David Woodruff; Joseph Phelan, clerk of the Alabama House of Representatives, later secretary of the state senate, and vice-president of Tuscaloosa's Young Men's Total Abstinence Society; Methodist Episcopal minister and temperance and colonization activist Robert L. Kennon; Samuel Mills Meek served as vice-president of the Tuscaloosa Society for the Promotion of Temperance in 1829, president of the Tuscaloosa Temperance Society from 1831 to at least 1835, treasurer of the Alabama State Temperance Society in 1831, and an officer in the state colonization society and in 1835 was a candidate for the state senate. ABS *Annual Report,* VIII (1824), 189; XII (1828), 95; *Alabama State Intelligencer,* January 1, 1830, January 8, 1831. Biographical information on these subjects was gleaned from Tuscaloosa newspapers; volumes III and IV of Owen, *History of Alabama;* and William Garrett, *Reminiscences of Public Men in Alabama, for Thirty Years* (Atlanta, 1872). On the dual careers of slaveholders, see Oakes, *Ruling Race,* 57–65.

Because so many of these individuals were benevolent activists before the formation of the second party system, their linkages to political parties were less meaningful than was the case with the devotees of Sunday schools, discussed below. Of the 15 whose political party membership could be ascertained, 10 were Whigs and 5 were Democrats. See n. 70, and the related discussion in the text.

and individuals who found it difficult to set aside time to canvass their neighborhoods could lose interest in the cause. Then too, the circulation of publications could be hindered by an economic downturn, as happened during the depression that began in 1837.

Sabbath schools were less afflicted by these hindrances. Although they had their own publications, Sabbath-school promoters did not seek to saturate their communities with thousands of tracts and thus were not as adversely affected by a depressed economy. In contrast to Bible and tract distributors, the Sabbath-school teacher had a set time each week in which to perform his or her duties. Sabbath-school teaching in the antebellum United States was, however, more than a weekly obligation; according to Anne Boylan, it was a "keystone to a structured style of living centered on introspection and self-improvement" that facilitated the era's quest for mastery and enabled teachers to feel as though "they were living orderly, examined lives."[51] Further, these weekly classes fostered relationships between teachers and students that were undoubtedly instrumental to building a broader and more durable commitment to this cause than were the more impersonal encounters that occurred between the givers and receivers of religious publications. And finally, since children were continuously entering the age of Sabbath-school attendance, the work of their teachers was never complete—which probably facilitated the establishment of more stable institutions.

Although Sabbath schools often met in churches, their objectives, like those of the Bible and tract societies, extended beyond Protestant indoctrination. To be sure, one purpose of the schools was to socialize the children of churchgoing families into the religious community of their parents. But Sabbath-school partisans also sought to enroll unchurched children. Their special objects of concern were the children of the poor, and many antebellum Sabbath-school teachers canvassed their communities in search of youngsters who were not enrolled in a Sabbath school. Like the Bible and tract proponents, supporters of Sabbath schools believed that their enterprise—in conjunction with other benevolent efforts—would revolutionize American society. But unlike the Bible and tract causes, in which devotees supplied a morally indigent adult with something to read and expected that it would transform his or her life, the Sunday school provided the evangelical reformer with a child whose habits

51. Boylan, *Sunday School,* 101, 103.

were inchoate. Sabbath-school promoters hoped that children, after attending an hour or two of Sabbath school each week over a period of years, would not only embrace the evangelical Protestant faith, but would also pattern their lives according to the values of "self-control, delayed gratification, and self-improvement."[52]

While evangelicals in Alabama were troubled by the lack of churches and religious sentiment, others—particularly in the Northeast—shared their concerns. In Albany, New York, William H. Williams, a Presbyterian minister, wrote to the ASSU in 1830 that his mind had long been troubled by the "superior wants & urgent claims of the new settlements in the South & West," and the mere contributions of money to benevolent causes provided him no consolation. Convinced that there was no better means by which he could "effectively advance the interests of my Country & of the Redeemer's kingdom," Williams volunteered to serve as an agent for the ASSU—a full-time activist devoted to the creation and maintenance of Sunday schools. After receiving a positive response, he resigned his pastorate, departed Albany for Tuscaloosa—which became his base of operations—and preached the Sunday-school cause on his way, convinced as he was of the "peculiar adaptability" of Sunday schools to meet the "moral wants of the South."[53]

The inauguration of Sunday schools in Tuscaloosa County did not, however, result from the internal agonies of William H. Williams. The Grant's Creek Sunday School, located at Foster's, a rural settlement eleven miles southwest of the town of Tuscaloosa, was possibly the first Sabbath school organized in the county, opening in January 1828.[54] Writing fifteen months later, corresponding secretary Robert S. Foster explained to the ASSU that although the school's initial prospects had been gloomy, it had surpassed "our most sanguine expectations." Foster hoped that the ASSU would send a missionary to the area, as he believed that an agent could establish additional Sunday schools nearby. The united efforts of Sunday-school enthusiasts and the proponents of

52. *Ibid.,* 3. Regarding the objectives of Sunday schools, see *ibid.* and Boyer, *Urban Masses,* 34–53.

53. William H. Williams to ASSU, July 15, 1830, December 23, 1830, both in ASSU Papers.

54. According to local tradition, Grant's Creek Sunday School was the first Sabbath school in Alabama. Sunday schools were apparently well-established in the town of Tuscaloosa by July, 1828, however, when one writer argued that local Sunday schools were an inadequate substitute for free public schools. *Pioneers of Tuscaloosa Prior to 1830,* 6; Tuscaloosa *Chronicle,* July 19, 1828.

other benevolent causes would, according to Foster, transform humanity by assisting in "conquering the Kingdom of Satan, and erecting on the ruins the Kingdoms of the Great King of Zion."[55] A year later, Foster wrote to the national union that the Grant's Creek school's board of managers had formed another Sabbath school locally. Because of the regenerative qualities of the Grant's Creek Sunday School, the vicinity it served had been transformed from a spiritual desert, and after "a considerable revival of religion," sixty-four persons had joined the Baptist Church.[56]

Although Sunday schools had existed in the town of Tuscaloosa since at least 1828, they were limited in their operations prior to William Williams' arrival in late 1830. Before this time, the town's three Sunday schools "had scarcely more than a nominal existence, including in all perhaps 45 children." Possibly because of Tuscaloosa's position as the capital, which brought people to town from all over the state, Williams was "filled with anxiety to revive the S. Schools in this place." As an agent of the ASSU, he took the lead in the revitalization of Tuscaloosa's Sunday schools by delivering a public address on their importance and by commissioning friends of this cause to visit "almost every family" in town. Present at the reorganization of the Presbyterian-operated Sunday school were a number of state legislators. This school had quickly grown to about sixty children, and a resuscitated school connected with the Episcopal church now had about thirty students. Before long, Williams expected also to assist in the reorganization of the Methodist Sunday school. Despite his activism in promoting these three Sunday schools in Tuscaloosa town, only the Presbyterian school agreed to be an auxiliary of the ASSU, indicating that Williams' commitment to the cause transcended denominational boundaries. Local devotees of Sunday schools praised Williams' zeal. Thomas Manning, who taught in one of Tuscaloosa's academies and later in one of the town's Sunday schools, testified a few months after Williams' arrival that the New Yorker was "exerting a favourable influence" not only in Tuscaloosa, but also in the surrounding country: "From a school of about 25 scholars, he has built up one of above a hundred." Williams additionally conducted a flourishing Bible class and looked forward to meeting "clergymen and others from different parts of the state, who will be present at the anniversaries of the

55. Robert S. Foster to ASSU, April 19, 1829, in ASSU Papers. Anne Boylan, *Sunday School,* 60, concludes that millennial flourishes, such as the one that Foster provided to the ASSU, became less common as school organizers placed increasing stress upon steady practicality.

56. Robert S. Foster to ASSU, April 11, 1830, in ASSU Papers.

State Societies, Bible, Temperance, & Colonization. I hope then to form a So. Alabama S. S. Union."[57]

Manning and Williams worked together to build up the Sunday schools in the town of Tuscaloosa and organize them in the countryside. By January 1832 they had organized ten Sunday schools, principally affiliated with Baptist and Presbyterian congregations. Except in the winter months, these schools were reported to "have generally been in successful operation," and most of them had Sunday-school libraries. Williams informed the ASSU that these rural Sunday schools had caused "great interest & . . . much serious excitement regarding" religion in their communities, although "no special cases of conversion have been reported." The school in the town of Tuscaloosa, however, had "prospered beyond [the] wildest expectations of many of its Friends." Even during the winter, "we never had less than 30 and often more than 40 of our scholars present & that too in a house without fire." The evangelical supporters of the enterprise were most pleased, though, that nine teachers and three scholars had converted during the past six or eight months. One writer boasted, "There is scarcely a parent that has a child old enough, who does not send it to one or the other of these schools." At the Tuscaloosa Union Sunday School alone, there were twenty-two teachers and 154 students. A Sunday-school depository was established in Tuscaloosa at the bookstore of David Woodruff, who in addition to his activity with the American Tract Society— and later temperance—provided a 15-percent discount "to schools auxiliary to the American Sunday School Union." Five months later, Williams requested additional Sunday-school materials for Woodruff's bookstore, as "the demand I am happy to say is increasing." In fact, the demand was so high that one correspondent complained that the ASSU depositories in Alabama, and especially the one in Tuscaloosa, were lacking books. The Sunday-school cause advanced elsewhere in Alabama, and by late 1831 devotees had reportedly formed hundreds of schools. One single missionary was said to have established more than seventy, another agent had established nearly as many, and a volunteer agent was responsible for the creation of twenty schools.[58]

57. William H. Williams to ASSU, December 23, 1830, Thomas Manning to ASSU, March 17, 1831, both in ASSU Papers; Minutes of the Teachers' Association of the Tuscaloosa Union Sunday School, March 1, 1832, in possession of the Tuscaloosa First Presbyterian Church [hereinafter cited as Tuscaloosa SS Minutes]. Regarding the operation of Methodist Sunday schools in early Tuscaloosa, see James Sellers, *First Methodist Church*, 261–64.

58. William H. Williams to ASSU, January 31, 1832, March 24, 1832; Thomas Manning to

In January 1832, a number of Tuscaloosans formed the interdenominational
Tuscaloosa Sunday School Union, auxiliary to the ASSU, for Tuscaloosa "and
adjoining counties." The union was openly nonsectarian: its constitution entreated its teachers carefully to exclude "every book, and every subject of a political and sectarian character." The organization sought to promote the opening of new Sunday schools, to establish among existing schools "a regular
communication . . . by which improvements in teaching, and all other communications may be easily transmitted," to furnish impoverished schools with
books free of charge, to "obtain reports from the different auxiliary schools,"
and to "encourage each other in the education of the ignorant." The thirteen
officers chosen on this occasion were members of the Presbyterian, Methodist
Episcopal, Methodist Protestant, and Baptist denominations and included
citizens of high social standing, such as University of Alabama president Alva
Woods; future Alabama governor Henry W. Collier; James H. Dearing, president of the Tuscaloosa Female Academy, an officer of the Tuscaloosa Temperance Society, and later active in planning the Northeast and Southwest Alabama Railroad; Samuel M. Meek, a longtime president of the Tuscaloosa
Temperance Society and a candidate for the state legislature in 1835; and Benjamin Whitfield, later a president of the Tuscaloosa Horticultural Society.
The union also prescribed the roles for Sunday-school superintendents and
teachers. Superintendents were to "class the Scholars, and assign to the Teachers their respective classes, preserve order during the hours of school, [and] frequently examine and address the scholars upon the selected lesson." Teachers
were expected to "attend regularly and punctually at the appointed hours," visit
the absent members of their classes, and "carefully endeavor to engage [stu-
dents'] attention during the hours of recitation, and to interest and instruct
their minds by affectionate conversations and appropriate explanations and
addresses."[59]

ASSU, April 6, 1831, June 22, 1831; Thomas Maddin to ASSU, October 2, 1832, all in ASSU Papers; Tuscaloosa *Inquirer*, September 8, October 20, 1831; Tuscaloosa SS Minutes, April 1, 1832;
Alabama State Intelligencer, September 17, 1831. Boylan, *Sunday School*, 31, relies on published reports of the ASSU to arrive at much lower figures of Sabbath-school activity in the South. Although her conclusion may be correct, we shall see in this chapter that there were many Sabbath
schools in Alabama, that, albeit favorable towards the ASSU, were not officially aligned with the
national body.

59. *Spirit of the Age*, March 21, 1832. For biographical data on Dearing, see *State Rights Expositor and Spirit of the Age*, February 9, April 6, 1833, and *Independent Monitor*, July 15, 1853. On Meek,
see chap. 5 herein. On Whitfield, see *Independent Monitor*, May 6, 1858.

In 1833, Williams praised the Presbyterian-dominated Tuscaloosa Union Sunday School—the flagship institution of the Tuscaloosa Sunday School Union—in his correspondence to the ASSU: "Our Sabbath School is sustained & successful beyond my expectations." The last portion of each Sunday-school session was devoted to a fifteen-minute examination, to which parents were invited and which Williams believed promoted the "prosperity and usefulness of our Tuscaloosa School." Small children were taught to read at the school, and conversions continued among both teachers and students. But despite Williams' enthusiasm, his duties as pastor of the Tuscaloosa Presbyterian Church—a more remunerative responsibility that town Presbyterians had urged upon him after his arrival—prevented him from devoting his full energies to the Sunday-school cause. As a result, Williams and some other evangelical Tuscaloosans recommended Thomas W. Cox, the outgoing pastor of the Tuscaloosa Baptist Church, as the ASSU agent for Alabama. Cox labored zealously for the national union for about twelve months and established thirty Sunday schools in Jefferson, St. Clair, Blount, Shelby, Benton, and Tuscaloosa Counties. In 1835, Simpson Shepherd, a traveling agent for the ASSU, reported that Tuscaloosa's enthusiasm for Sabbath schools remained very strong. In his two sermons in the town, he collected $161 for the national union, and the Baptist and Presbyterian churches were filled to capacity: "All could not get seats. The Supreme Court is in Session, we had the Judges and the most distinguished Lawyers in the State." Also present were University of Alabama president Woods and a number of university faculty. Publicly, Williams also spoke optimistically of Sunday schools, proclaiming his "conviction that these institutions are gaining more fully the confidence and approbation of the wise and good of every party, and enlisting more generally the feelings and efforts of intelligent christians of every sect." But in his private correspondence to the ASSU, he was ambivalent: "The cause of Sabbath Schools in this region is more prosperous than any other [benevolent] department; tho' is unhappy [*sic*] saying much less than I would be glad to say."[60]

Sunday schools in Tuscaloosa were plagued by some problems that characterized much of Alabama, the South in general, and the rest of the United States. Basil Manly was a Baptist minister in Charleston, South Carolina,

60. William H. Williams to ASSU, January 26, April 4, 1833, Williams *et al.* to ASSU, June 1, 1834, Thomas W. Cox to ASSU, September 15, 30, 1834, April 15, June 30, September 23, 1835, Simpson Shepherd to ASSU, July 15, 1835, Williams to ASSU, April 28, 1835, all in ASSU Papers; *Flag of the Union*, March 12, 1836.

when he was solicited by the ASSU in 1833 for his views on Sunday schools in his vicinity. Manly expressed his conviction that Sunday schools would have a positive influence in the South and that a judicious plan for them might succeed, but he also pointed to obstacles that, in his opinion, were quite formidable: "a sparse population, the want of teachers suitably disposed and qualified, the diffusion [of] labours among ministers, and the want of any congregational arrangements among our churches for meeting at their places of worship on each successive Sabbath." Manly agreed with the ASSU that the promotion of Sunday schools required a "suitable agent among ourselves to carry this work on," but he was not optimistic of obtaining a southerner to do the job; for as he noted, the most important benevolent efforts among the Baptists in South Carolina were failing due to an inability to find worthy agents locally. Despite his keen interest in Sunday schools, Manly felt that his pastoral duties were foremost in importance, and he turned down an offer from the ASSU to be an agent.[61]

Benevolence-minded Tuscaloosans were already cynical regarding the prospects of Sunday schools when Williams arrived in town in late 1830. As Williams reported to the national society, "in this place, many difficulties have been encountered in advancing the SS cause resulting from past failures; a very respectable lawyer even expressing the opinion that the permanent prosperity of S. Schools in this country is impossible. Tis indeed the general complaint that to form schools is easy, but to maintain them impracticable." In the following years, Williams found that maintenance of Sunday schools was indeed difficult. Part of the problem arose from what he called the "evils of interruption." Many of the rural Sunday schools in Tuscaloosa County suspended operations during the winter, and even Williams' efforts could not overcome the elements. In the spring of 1833, he reported that only the Tuscaloosa Union Sunday School "and perhaps one other" of the dozen or so schools in the Tuscaloosa Sunday School Union had continued through the winter. Thomas Cox explained to the ASSU that travel during the winter was difficult, and that "most of the schools are in the country where the population is." As a result, "vary [sic] often the teachers and some of the scholars have to come several miles over bad roads and meet in vary open rooms so that it is allmost [sic] impossible to form new schools." During such climatic troughs, Cox's attention was directed toward "visiting, encouraging and keeping the minds of the min-

---

61. Basil Manly to ASSU, April 23, 1833, October 16, 1833, both in ASSU Papers.

isters and people for a more vigorous effort in the Spring by preaching, lecturing and discoursing on the importance of Sunday-Schools and by distributing the Societies publications."[62] Nevertheless, even committed agents such as Cox and Williams could not completely overcome the widespread apathy among both teachers and students that resulted from these seasonal hiatuses.

The effects of winter aside, it also appears that the enthusiasm for Sunday schools that Williams and others reported to the ASSU often turned to indifference when it became necessary to commit one's time to the cause. Williams, who was the corresponding secretary of the Tuscaloosa Sunday School Union, often had difficulty obtaining statistics from the union's auxiliary schools. Williams himself ran short of time. As a part-time volunteer agent for the ASSU, he had hoped to devote one Sunday a month to the formation and visitation of Sunday schools. The actual results, however, were often quite different. His pastorate over Tuscaloosa's Presbyterians and his assignment as stated clerk for the Tuscaloosa Presbytery left him with little time to visit and encourage the rural Sunday schools that he organized. This problem was recognized as early as March 1832, when the board of managers of the Tuscaloosa Sunday School Union resolved to have Williams "engage suitable persons to visit the schools already organized, and to organize new schools within our bounds." It does not appear that Williams found anybody to accept this responsibility. The lack of consistent encouragement may have contributed to the demise of many Sabbath schools; in his 1835 report, Williams acknowledged that "some of the schools reported last year are not now in operation." Recognizing that the Sunday-school union was unraveling, Williams and Cox visited and reorganized some of the schools in the spring of 1835. When family illnesses prevented Cox from traveling to other counties, he found that there was plenty to do in Tuscaloosa County, "as it is large and a quantity of labor is now needed to keep it up, and encourage the many schools already organized."[63]

---

62. William H. Williams to ASSU, December 23, 1830, April 4, 1833, Thomas W. Cox to ASSU, January 31, 1835 (see also Cox to ASSU, December 31, 1834), all in ASSU Papers. The volatility of Sunday schools in Alabama is suggested by the numbers of students reported in ASSU-affiliated schools. For 1826, 1827, 1828, and 1829, there were 352, 412, 723, and 1,558 students, respectively. There was no further report until 1838, when only 119 students were counted in Alabama's ASSU-affiliated schools. ASSU *Annual Report,* II (1826), 11, III (1827), 8, IV (1828), 8, V (1829), 6, XIV (1838), 24.

63. William H. Williams to ASSU, December 23, 1830, April 4, 1833, March 27, 1834, April

Unfortunately for the ASSU, maintaining committed, full-time agents in the field was a difficult task. Agents traveled from town to town almost continuously, and many passionate Sabbath-school devotees found this life inimical to raising a family. Recognizing the problem, the national body, like other benevolent organizations, was often forced to rely upon young ministerial trainees as agents. But the ASSU was often seen by other evangelicals as a Presbyterian organization, and since there were few Presbyterians in the South and few northern Presbyterians willing to move there, many ASSU agencies in the South—and indeed, the southern agencies of other national benevolent societies—remained unfilled. Some contemporaries believed that benevolent operations in the South were further hindered by the fact that many southerners favored people from their own section and held Yankee agents in suspicion.[64] Additionally, since ASSU salaries were meager, many agents, despite their passionate love of the cause, did not stay long in the job. For example, Thomas Cox resigned his pastorate over Tuscaloosa's Baptists to serve as the ASSU agent for Alabama, but his request for a $600 annual salary was answered with only $200, far less than he believed was necessary to sustain his family; he persisted as an ASSU agent for only a year before resigning because of insufficient income. Without an agent to encourage them, many Sunday schools that he organized faltered.

Apathy was evident among the teachers of the Tuscaloosa Union Sunday School as well. Teacher absenteeism was often a problem. In December 1832, the Sunday-school superintendent began keeping a list of teacher attendance; fifteen months later, the superintendent was empowered to dismiss any teacher

28, 1835, Thomas W. Cox to ASSU, November 15, 1834, all in ASSU Papers; *Spirit of the Age*, March 21, 1832.

64. Griffin, *Their Brothers' Keepers*, 95; William H. Williams to ASSU, June 1, 1834, in ASSU Papers; Kuykendall, *Southern Enterprize*, 71, 75; ASSU *Annual Report*, XIII (1837), 29, XXVI (1850), 32. Kuykendall further notes (38–40, 76–79) that some southern whites suspected Yankee benevolent agents of being clandestine abolitionists. Although white Tuscaloosans were greatly frightened by the threat of abolitionists in their midst, I have encountered no evidence that Tuscaloosa's proponents of benevolence were accused of abolitionism. Nor did the fact that a person or an institution was northern in origin necessarily strike pathological animosity into the breasts of Tuscaloosans. In addition to its affiliation with the Philadelphia-based ASSU, the Tuscaloosa Union Sunday School purchased for its library in 1841 a number "of the publications of the Massachusetts Sabbath School Society & the New England S. S. Union as are not published by the American SS Union." Tuscaloosa SS Minutes, January 28, 1841.

absent from the school two weeks in succession without a sufficient excuse. Recognizing the need to increase their enthusiasm and commitment, the teachers of the Tuscaloosa Union Sunday School pledged to attend a weekly meeting for prayer and study of the week's Sunday-school lesson. Teachers were required by the Sunday-school constitution to visit the homes of their absent scholars but had apparently grown lax in this duty, as an 1837 teachers' meeting determined that the "resolution requiring teachers to visit their absent scholars & report at the monthly meeting be revived." Those who consistently fulfilled their teaching assignments continued to be irritated at the absence of some of their colleagues, and as a result, the Sabbath-school faculty again resolved that the superintendent keep an attendance record of the teachers— which practice had apparently been suspended. Acknowledging that "much injury has been done to the [cause] by teachers absenting themselves or coming in late," the faculty further resolved "that the Secretary shall make out & keep a correct list or Roll of the Teachers." "Delinquents" would then be "called upon the succeeding sabbath for an excuse for thus absenting themselves." Moreover, "supernumery [*sic*]" teachers were appointed to "take charge of such classes as shall be without teachers." Indifference, though, was present not only on Sundays, but during the week when teachers' meetings were scheduled to be held. For example, at one meeting held at the house of P. L. Sink, "there being but few present the meeting was not organized" and "no business [was] done." Perhaps one reason teachers stayed away from meetings was that these sessions were often long and indecisive. Milford Woodruff, briefly the secretary of the Union Sunday School, noted that one teachers' meeting lasted 1 hour 45 minutes. Topics for discussion were noted by Woodruff, and were followed by comments such as "nothing definite was done," or "nothing decided in reference to it."[65]

   Tuscaloosa's Sabbath-school teachers left no reminiscences recounting what the work meant to them or why they volunteered to teach. Some information on the teachers, however, may be gleaned from the minutes of the Teachers' Association of the Tuscaloosa Union Sunday School, a Presbyterian-affiliated auxiliary of the ASSU. This record lists the names of 151 teachers who taught

65. Tuscaloosa SS Minutes, December 31, 1832, March 17, 1834, August 28, September 11, 1837, November 19, December 3, 10, 1839, March 17, 1847. The irregular attendance of teachers is also evident in the Minutes of the Grant's Creek Sunday School, in Samford University Library, Birmingham, Alabama (microfilm).

at the school between 1832 and 1848—of whom 73 (48.3 percent) were female.[66] Due to gaps in the minutes, though, this count is incomplete. The minutes often refer to teachers only by honorific—Mr., Miss, or Mrs.—and surname, and therefore precise identification is sometimes not possible. The minutes reveal that many of these volunteers taught only briefly. Many were young— more than half of the 65 whose age could be ascertained began teaching Sabbath school before they were thirty, and one-fourth were in their teens. The relative youth and brief tenure of the volunteers certainly contributed to instability in the teaching ranks.[67]

66. Tuscaloosa SS Minutes. The Union Sunday School's constitution, similar to that of the Tuscaloosa Sunday School Union, denounced sectarianism, and during the Union Sunday School's early years, its teachers met at least once at the local Baptist church (*Flag of the Union*, March 12, 1836; Tuscaloosa SS Minutes February 11, 1833). By the 1840s, however, the school became increasingly sectarian in its focus, and teachers were "earnestly recommend[ed]" to "adopt the use of the Westminster Catechism in their respective classes" immediately. Session Book No. 3 of the Tuscaloosa Presbyterian Church, July 6, 1842, located at Tuscaloosa First Presbyterian Church; Tuscaloosa SS Minutes January 28, 1841.

67. The ages of teachers who taught in the Tuscaloosa Union Sunday School between 1832 and 1848 are as follows:

Age when began teaching	Number	Percent
15–19	17	26.2
20–29	20	30.8
30–39	16	24.6
40–49	6	9.2
50–59	4	6.2
60–69	1	1.5
70–79	0	
80–89	1	1.5
Totals	65	100.0

The ages of only 43.3 percent of teachers could be determined from the 1830, 1840, or 1850 censuses and other biographical aids; those who could be identified were undoubtedly the most stable element of Tuscaloosa's white population. Several individuals who were not heads of household were linked to their father, mother, or spouse through the assistance of *Pioneers of Tuscaloosa County, Alabama Prior to 1830* (Tuscaloosa, 1981).

Although the place of birth of only 44 teachers could be ascertained, they, like the proponents of Bibles and tracts, were largely southern-born; 30 of the 44 (68.2 percent) were from the slaveholding states, whereas 9 (20.5 percent) were born in the North, and 5 (11.4 percent) were born outside the United States. Of the 61 teachers whose families' slaveholding status is available, 54 (88.5 percent) were listed in the 1830, 1840, and/or 1850 censuses as having lived in slaveholding families. Among these 54, they or their families averaged 8.5, 6.3, and 10.8 slaves for the three censuses, respectively. A number of teachers were themselves planters.[68] The occupational profile of these teachers is similar to that of the Bible and tract enthusiasts, in that the overwhelming majority (36 of 47, or 76.6 percent) came from households headed by professionals or shopkeepers/proprietors.[69] Although the political party affiliation of only 35 male teachers could be determined, it should come as no surprise that nearly two-thirds were Whigs; Whigs often recognized Sabbath schools to be complementary to their objective of having a society that embraced self-restraint, sound morals, and voluntary compliance with civil law. On the other hand, although some Democrats were strong supporters of evangelical religion and benevolence, members of this party were less inclined than Whigs to emphasize the social benefits of religion and the larger reform agenda. Whereas Whigs were likely to point to the ways in which Sabbath schools and other institutions sustained the social order by preparing citizens to participate in a free society, Democrats were more apt to argue that freedom itself was the best insurance against disorder. Democrats often maintained that a person's right to play a role, however small, in politics and government developed a commitment within that person to the community; they frequently rejected, as Lawrence

68. The 1830, 1840, and 1850 censuses, respectively, show 22, 31, and 29 teachers in slaveholding families, with median slaveholdings for these years being 3, 5, and 8. Planters included John A. Hodges, who owned 20 slaves in 1850; James Madison Dunlap, whose father owned 35 slaves in 1830, and who himself—along with his wife and fellow Sabbath school teacher Sarah H. Dunlap—owned 28 slaves in 1850; Hollis Coudy Kidder, who owned 18 slaves in 1840; the father of teachers James L. Childress and Susan W. Childress Read owned 40 slaves in 1830, while James owned 22 slaves himself in 1840.

69. The occupations of 33 male teachers, the occupation of 1 female teacher, the occupations of the husbands of 8 female teachers, and the occupations of the fathers of 5 female and male teachers (47 total) were obtained from the 1850 census, and were as follows: artisan, 2 (4.3 percent); clerk, 1 (2.1 percent); shopkeeper/proprietor, 9 (19.1 percent); farmer, 5 (10.6 percent); professional, 27 (57.4 percent); nothing listed on census, 2 (4.3 percent); other 1 (2.1 percent).

Frederick Kohl has argued, the idea that "restraints and controls were necessary, either for society or the individual."[70]

As was true of those who endorsed the increased circulation of Bibles and
tracts, a number of teachers either came from or would later enter the ranks of
the social and political elite.[71] Also worthy of note are the 41 teachers who were
linked to one or more other reformist undertakings. They included 22 temperance activists, 15 devotees of Bible or tract causes, 9 contributors to Tuscaloosa's
Female Benevolent Society, 7 colonizationists, 2 enthusiasts of common
schools, and 2 adherents of the local antigambling society that functioned dur-

70. Kohl, *Politics of Individualism*, 145–57; Rush Welter, *The Mind of America, 1820–1860*
(New York, 1975), 253–73; John Ashworth, *"Agrarians" and "Aristocrats,"* 194–205; Daniel Walker
Howe, *The Political Culture of the American Whigs* (Chicago, 1979), 36–37; Richard J. Carwardine,
Evangelicals and Politics in Antebellum America (New Haven, 1993), 35. Of the 35 male teachers
with an identifiable political affiliation, 22 were Whigs, and 13 were Democrats. Political affilia-
tion was generally determined from newspaper accounts of political activity in Tuscaloosa
County.

71. Teachers of local and statewide renown, active in the Democratic Party, and who taught
at the Tuscaloosa Union Sunday School included Lincoln Clark, secretary of the Alabama Bible
Society 1837–1844, a member of the corresponding committee of the Tuscaloosa Temperance Society 1838–1840, supporter of the American Colonization Society in 1846, president of Tuscaloosa's Union Sabbath School Missionary Society in 1846, a representative from Tuscaloosa in the
Alabama legislature during the 1840s and from 1851 to 1853 a member of the United States Congress from Iowa; Peter Martin, a director of the Alabama Bible Society in 1830 and 1831, Alabama
attorney general from 1831 to 1836, justice for Alabama's third circuit from 1836 to 1843, and member of the state House of Representatives in 1825 and 1844; Reuben Searcy, a contributor to the
ACS in 1846, state legislator in 1838, and appointee of Governor Joshua L. Martin in 1845 to examine the state bank; and Jones M. Withers, who belonged to two of Tuscaloosa's temperance
societies in 1839, had already served as secretary of the state senate, and would later become a director of the state bank, represent Mobile in the legislature, be elected that city's mayor, and attain the rank of major general in the Confederate army. Whigs included David Woodruff, who,
in addition to his previously mentioned positions, was a supporter of the ACS in 1846 and a leader
in the Sons of Temperance from at least 1849 to 1852; James B. Wallace, clerk of the Alabama Supreme Court for ten years, and elected to the state House of Representatives in 1851; Thomas M.
Peters, a teacher at the Union Sunday School until his graduation from the University of Alabama in 1834, who represented Lawrence County in the Alabama House in 1845 and the Alabama
Senate in 1847 and served as an Alabama Supreme Court justice from 1868 to 1874; and Sewell
Jones Leach, a temperance devotee during the 1830s and the proprietor of Tuscaloosa's foundry
during the 1850s. Biographical information on these subjects was obtained primarily from Tuscaloosa newspapers, from Vols. III and IV of Owen, *History of Alabama*, and from Garrett, *Reminiscences of Public Men in Alabama*.

ing the early 1830s. Three-fourths of the teachers identified as Democrats (9 of 12) were engaged in these other reform efforts, suggesting that they may have been more politically and socially compatible with the Whigs than with other members of their own party. During the late 1840s and 1850s, a number of Alabama's Democrats—the most notable of whom was Henry Collier—developed positions on banking, state aid to railroads, and public schools that were increasingly similar to those of the Whigs. It was probably this type of "Collier Democrat" who was attracted to benevolence.[72]

The most noteworthy Democrat to teach at the Tuscaloosa Union Sunday School was Joshua L. Martin, an antidebtor and antibanking Democrat who successfully campaigned as an independent for Alabama's governorship in 1845 after the Democrats nominated a candidate who favored both banks and debtor relief. But despite Martin's ultra-Democratic views on economic questions, his support of the American Colonization Society indicates his interest in the wider agenda of reform. Nevertheless, Martin's pro-Union politics during the 1850s distinguishes him from another Democrat, Richard T. Brumby, who also taught at the school. During the early 1830s Brumby edited the Tuscaloosa *State Rights Expositor and Spirit of the Age*, a nullificationist paper, and was afterward a University of Alabama professor until 1849. Later he became "a very hot secessionist" who in 1861 sold virtually all his possessions and invested the proceeds in Confederate bonds.[73] But the extent to which the

72. Thornton, *Politics and Power*, 47, 52, 182, 299–312, 323–29. In another study of politics in antebellum Alabama, a research team headed by Thomas B. Alexander found that younger political activists were more likely to be Democrats than Whigs: Thomas B. Alexander *et al.*, "The Basis of Alabama's Antebellum Two-Party System," *Alabama Review*, XIX (October 1966), 250–51. It is possible in this consistently Democratic state that politically ambitious young men who were ideologically inclined toward the Whigs may have supported the Democrats, and carried with them their Whiggish notions into the Democracy. Again, these were likely the sorts of Democrats who were also benevolence activists.

73. On Joshua L. Martin, see Thornton, *Politics and Power*, 49–50, 267; Owen, *History of Alabama*, IV, 1166; Garrett, *Reminiscences of Public Men in Alabama*, 168, 410–12; *African Repository*, XXII (April 1846), 136. Martin was elected governor in 1845 with the help of Whig votes. Despite Whig opposition to his economic positions, many Whigs hoped that Martin's election would permanently damage the state's Democratic party. Although Whigs were frustrated in this expectation, Martin also received Whig consideration during the early 1850s when that party preferred Martin's Unionist politics over the threat posed by the radical proponents of southern rights, the "fire-eaters." By 1856, however, Martin had returned to the Democratic fold, as he served that year as a delegate to the state's political convention. *Daily Alabama Journal* (Mont-

Whiggish proclivities of most of these individuals accorded with the characteristics of the other teachers in the Tuscaloosa Union Sunday School cannot
be known, since the names of most teachers could not be correlated with other
sources. Of course, most teachers who were identified were young, and if they
were typical, their youth and likely geographical mobility probably precluded
them from appearing in the census or any other records.[74]

A similar profile with respect to slaveholding and occupation emerges when
we examine promoters of Sabbath schools who were not affiliated with the
Tuscaloosa Union Sunday School. The names of 79 advocates (3 of whom were
women)—chiefly superintendents, teachers, speakers at public meetings sponsored by Sabbath schools, and officers of Sabbath school associations—were
obtained primarily from Tuscaloosa newspapers, church minutes, and the correspondence of ASSU agents with the national body. The slaveholding status
of 37 of these Sabbath-school partisans was available from the 1830, 1840, and/
or 1850 censuses, and of this group, 31 were slaveholders, with mean slaveholdings for these years of 14.8, 16.1, and 21.3, respectively.[75] Again, the occupational

---

gomery), April 17, 1851; Montgomery *Advertiser and State Gazette*, January 16, 1856. On Brumby,
see Owen, *History of Alabama*, III, 240.

74. The religious affiliation of 86 teachers (or 57.3 percent of those listed in the minutes of the
Teacher's Association) at the Tuscaloosa Union Sunday School was ascertained from Tuscaloosa's
church records. The school was principally a Presbyterian-run operation—despite its nonsectarian professions—and, expectedly, 74 teachers were Presbyterian church members, another 8
either presented children for baptism at the Presbyterian church or had parents who were members, 3 were identified in Tuscaloosa's Baptist church records, and 1 was listed in the Episcopalian
registry. Nevertheless, given that the records of the Presbyterian church list the names of virtually
all church members from 1820 through the Civil War, one may conclude from the substantial
number of teachers not found in the records that many of the teachers at the Union Sunday
School were unchurched and unconverted or that they left Tuscaloosa before formally joining a
church. Recognizing that many teachers were unconverted, Tuscaloosa's Presbyterians voted in
1851 to hold a "sessional prayer-meeting for the conversion of our youth" in the lecture room "at
sunrise every Sabbath morning," and asked "that the attention of the congregation, & especially
of the Sabbath School teachers, be called to this arrangement." The session's use of the term
"youth" could not refer to the Sabbath school students, as they were all children; undoubtedly, the
session hoped to encourage the conversion of the teachers. Tuscaloosa Presbyterian Church, Session Book No. 3, November 3, 1851, located at Tuscaloosa First Presbyterian Church, Tuscaloosa,
Alabama. See also ASSU *Annual Report*, XVII (1841), 22.

75. There were 18, 15, and 15 individuals living in slaveholding families according to the 1830,
1840, and 1850 censuses, respectively; the median slaveholdings for these years were 13, 9, and 17.
Inasmuch as these proponents were in many cases the leaders of their Sabbath school organiza-

profile heavily favored professionals (26 of the 41 whose occupations could be determined, or 63.4 percent), followed by farmers (8, or 19.5 percent), shop-keepers/proprietors (6, or 14.6 percent), and artisans (1, or 2.4 percent). The church affiliations of 54 could be determined, and were as follows: Baptists, 28 (51.9 percent); Methodists, 18 (18.5 percent); Episcopalians, 10 (18.5 percent); and Presbyterians, 2 (2.6 percent). Whigs were more numerous than Democrats; of the 17 individuals whose political party could be ascertained, 11 were Whig and 6 were Democrat.[76] And similar to the teachers in the Tuscaloosa Union Sunday School, 27 of these Sabbath-school enthusiasts were active in other reform efforts: 16 promoters of Bibles and tracts, 15 temperance activists, 9 colonizationists, 3 devotees of the common school, and 1 supporter each of Tuscaloosa's Female Benevolent Society and Young Men's Christian Association.

Having discussed the characteristics of many of the disciples of Sabbath schools, we can turn to the intended objects of their benevolence. Unlike the teachers, one of the students of the Tuscaloosa Union Sunday School left a reminiscence of the powerful impact that the school had upon him. George Little, who attended the school in the late 1840s, was a decade afterward a student at the University of Berlin. Although he usually attended church while he was in Europe, one Sunday he decided to go swimming at a lake instead:

---

tions, they were not as young as the teachers of the Tuscaloosa Union Sunday School. Quist, "Social and Moral Reform," 116.

76. On the sources of political identification, see n. 70 this chapter. Besides Henry W. Collier, Basil Manly, Benjamin B. Fontaine (who also supported temperance and colonization), and Samuel M. Meek, all mentioned earlier in connection with their activities in the Bible and tract causes, other members of the political and social elite who endorsed Tuscaloosa County's Sabbath schools included legislator and editor of the Democratic Tuscaloosa *Observer* Newbern Hobbs Browne; Alabama House of Representatives clerk and colonization supporter T. Nixon Van Dyke; legislator and state attorney general Constantine Perkins; and circuit court judge and delegate to the 1819 constitutional convention, Henry Minor, who also owned 29 slaves in 1830. Several other Sabbath-school devotees had significant slaveholdings. Daniel Jones Hargrove, superintendent of Fellowship Sunday School, twenty-six miles northwest of Tuscaloosa, held 19 slaves in 1830; James Foster, superintendent of the Grant's Creek Sunday School, owned 23 and 63 slaves in 1830 and 1840, respectively; John S. Caldwell, secretary of the Mt. Joy Sunday School, held 21 and 28 slaves in 1840 and 1850, respectively; Robert P. Blount, secretary of the Union Sabbath School Missionary Society of Tuscaloosa in 1846, owned 24 slaves in 1850; and William R. Colgin, who served on the Board of Managers of Tuscaloosa's Episcopal Sunday School in 1830, held 21 slaves in 1830 and 29 slaves in 1840. Biographical information on these subjects was mostly

I thought that I could easily swim across the lake and set out to do so, but when about half way across I began to give out, and felt that I was in danger of drowning. At this time . . . the events of my past life came up before me; I suddenly remembered that it was Sunday and there came before me a picture of the old Sunday School at Tuscaloosa where I had recited the Shorter Catechism, at the age of eight years, and where I was later librarian. I knew that if I drowned while in swimming on Sunday, Dr. [John B.] Read, the superintendent, would preach a sermon to the school and hold me up as a fearful example of Sabbath breaking. This thought spurred me on to more strenuous endeavors. I could not bear the thought of thus being read out in Sunday School, and I managed to reach the other shore.[77]

Although a number of children—such as Little—from privileged families attended the Tuscaloosa Union Sunday School, from the school's earliest years its promoters frequently directed their outreach toward the town's lower classes. In 1832, some Tuscaloosan evangelicals were alarmed that there were children who still were not receiving any Sabbath-school instruction. A committee of four male and four female teachers from the Tuscaloosa Union Sunday School was appointed in September to "ascertain what children in town are not going to any Sabbath School." They were to encourage these children to attend one of Tuscaloosa's Sunday schools, and to determine whether the children's absence ensued "from want of suitable clothing." The following month the committee reported that its members had enticed several children to attend their Sunday school and that clothing would be furnished for those whose lack of attire had discouraged them from participating. A few years later, in August 1837, the Sunday-school teachers hoped to revive their school by resorting to this familiar strategy and again appointed a committee of eight to canvass the town "for the purpose of obtaining new scholars & to promote the interest of the Sabbath School cause." This desire to provide religious instruction to the poor was once again manifest in 1860, when the Presbyterian church minutes reported that the Tuscaloosa congregation sponsored "a Sabbath school composed chiefly of the children of families connected with the factory here, which is sustained by members of this church chiefly, & which seems to be ac-

---

obtained from Tuscaloosa newspapers, from the 1830 and 1840 federal censuses, and from the slave schedule of the 1850 federal census.

77. George Little, *Memoirs of George Little* (Tuscaloosa, 1924), 27; Tuscaloosa SS Minutes, January 2, 1848.

complishing a great good among that class of poor." Unfortunately, the minutes do not specify the extent to which factory children actually participated in the school.[78]

Significantly, the Presbyterian Sabbath school for children of Tuscaloosa factory workers functioned separately from the school that Presbyterian children attended. This fact may explain, in part, why the efforts of the Tuscaloosa Union Sunday School to recruit the children of the poor may have been less than successful. Two registers of students are in the minutes of the Teachers' Association of the Tuscaloosa Union Sunday School. One list notes all 154 students who were enrolled in the school in 1832. Unfortunately, because the 1830 census enumerates only the name of the head of household, and merely the sexes and ages of his or her dependents, this list is of little utility. More useful is the roll of 456 absentees at the school between May 2, 1847, and April 23, 1848. The names of 113 individuals were established from this register—which, however, failed to distinguish between absent teachers and absent students. Census and other records suggest that at least 15 of these 113 were teachers and that 57 were students; the majority of the remaining 41 were probably students, but they could not be located in the census or other records. The students were born between 1833 and 1845, making them as young as two and as old as fifteen. The median year of birth was 1839, and nine-tenths of the students were born between 1835 and 1843.[79] Of these 57 students, 53 were born in the South, 51 of them in Alabama; the 4 nonsouthern children were from Indiana. Only 21 of the 57 students were female (36.8 percent). Of the 41 probable students whose names could not be corroborated in other records, 11 were male, 14 were female, and 16 could not be identified by sex, as they were listed only by first initial.

Although it can be contended that children of the Tuscaloosa Union Sunday School came from all social classes, in truth they were disproportionately from well-to-do backgrounds, as indicated by the occupations, wealth, and

78. Tuscaloosa SS Minutes, September 24, October 24, 1832, March 28, 1836, August 21, 1837 (see also July 28, 1834); Session Book No. 3 of the Tuscaloosa Presbyterian Church, April 1, 1860. In July 1860, a number of Tuscaloosans observed Independence Day by joining the students of this Presbyterian Sabbath school—the one for the children of the town's factory workers—for a picnic and speeches by local political and religious leaders. Basil Manly Diary No. 6, July 4, 1860, in Manly Family Papers.

79. Of the 57 students whose age was ascertained, 55 were located in the 1850 census, while 2 were found in Owen, *History of Alabama*, III, 243. Their average age in 1850 was 11.0, the median was 11, and the standard deviation was 2.9.

slaveholding status of their parents. As is evident from the following table, commercial and professional occupations were predominant and artisans were few among parents of Union Sunday School children:

Occupation of parent	Sunday-school children in households headed by this occupation	Percent
Artisan	5	8.8
Shopkeeper/proprietor	13	22.8
Farmer	8	14.0
Professional	20	35.1
Other	1	1.8
Female head of household	10	17.5
Totals	57	100.0

In contrast, the entire population of Tuscaloosa town's children who were born between 1833 and 1845 were far more likely to live in a household headed by an artisan and less likely to have a parent who was a professional or engaged in commerce:

Occupation of parent	Tuscaloosa town children in households headed by this occupation	Percent
Artisan	93	25.3
Shopkeeper/proprietor	34	9.2
Farmer	55	14.9
Professional	91	24.7
Laborer	4	1.1
None listed on census (males)	8	2.2
Other	13	3.5
Illegible	1	0.3
Female head of household	69	18.8
Totals	368	100.0

Not all of the Union Sunday School students who lived in female-headed households ought to be considered poor. Five of these children's mothers owned no property according to the 1850 census, but the other five had mothers whose real holdings were worth at least $4,000. And although there were a few children whose parent or parents held no realty in 1850, the majority of students lived in households with real estate holdings of at least $2,500 (mean $3,635, median $2,500):

Real property holding of parent ($)	Sunday-school children in households with this amount of property	Percent
0	15	27.3
1–999	10	18.2
1,000–2,499	1	1.2
2,500–4,999	14	26.1
5,000–9,999	9	16.4
10,000–25,000	6	10.9
Totals	55	100.1

In contrast, most of the children in this age group in Tuscaloosa lived in households in which the parent or parents owned less than $1,000 in real estate, and over two-thirds lived in households where the holding was less than $2,500 (mean $2,182, median $300):[80]

Real property holding of parent ($)	Tuscaloosa town children in households with this amount of property	Percent
0	156	42.4
1–999	49	13.3
1,000–2,499	41	11.1
2,500–4,999	54	14.6
5,000–9,999	40	10.9
10,000–25,000	28	7.6
Totals	368	99.9

80. For the entire town of Tuscaloosa, the mean real estate holding was $1,882, and the median was 0; only 141 of the town's 245 households in 1850 had children aged 5 to 17, inclusive, living

The lack of real estate, however, did not preclude a person from being a slaveholder. Of the 57 Union Sunday School children, slaveholding data were available for 54, of whom 46 came from slaveholding households.[81] Among the 52 for whom slaveholding data could be ascertained from the 1850 census, 44 (84.6 percent) came from slaveholding households. For these 44, the median slaveholding was 7 and the mean was 9.3. Among all the households in the town of Tuscaloosa, the extent of slaveholding was slightly less: as only 171 of the 245 households (69.8 percent) owned slaves, with a median of 6 and a mean of 10.2.[82]

As we have seen, the teachers of the Tuscaloosa Union Sunday School endeavored to open their classes to the children of the poor, even offering such children suitable clothing as an inducement to attend. Further, the children's social correlates show that they came from all of Tuscaloosa's occupational, slaveholding, and real-wealth groups. Perhaps those students from less prosperous backgrounds attended as a result of the teachers' outreach, or perhaps their parents personally identified with the well-to-do and wanted their children to be upwardly striving. But generally, the children of the poor did not flock to this school. Why the children of the middle and wealthy classes were disproportionately represented cannot be answered conclusively. One possibility is that the Union Sunday School was located in a part of town where most of the population was affluent. It is also likely that poor children may have perceived that they lived in a different cultural world from the one presented at Sunday school and thus felt unwelcome. At least some of the poor may have re-

---

therein. Real estate and occupational data were determined from the 1850 federal manuscript census for Tuscaloosa County. Regarding the boundaries of the town of Tuscaloosa, see n. 95.

81. The three for whom slaveholding data are unavailable were the children of James B. Wallace, a prominent Tuscaloosa attorney who, according to the 1850 census, owned $12,000 in real estate. It is possible that he owned no slaves but more likely that he was missed by the enumerator of the slave schedule (see n. 82), or that his slaves lived outside of Tuscaloosa County. See Herzberg, "Negro Slavery," 9–10.

82. Because the 1850 census lists the free and slave populations on different schedules, establishing the slaveholding status of an individual is at times tricky, and occasionally not possible. Sometimes, an individual whom one would expect to be a slaveholder would appear on the population schedule but not on the slave schedule. In spite of these problems, the households on both the population and slave schedules of the 1850 federal census were generally enumerated in the same order, and thus many individuals could reasonably be designated as nonslaveholders. Nevertheless, a more complete 1850 slave schedule would possibly yield even more slaveholders than are listed here and elsewhere in this volume.

sented what they felt was upper-class condescension, and some parents may have found the teachers' evangelistic efforts intrusive. Finally, establishing a separate Sabbath school for the children of factory workers, rather than incorporating them into the existing school, suggests that snobbishness may have been a component of Presbyterian benevolence.[83]

The intended audience of the Tuscaloosa Union Sunday School differed slightly from that of Alabama's other benevolent endeavors. Unlike some reformers elsewhere in America—in particular, the Northeast—Alabama's promoters of Bibles, tracts, and Sabbath schools did not generally designate their targeted population to be the urban poor, young people who had recently relocated from the farm to the city, the working class, or Catholic immigrants. The principal concern of the benevolent societies in Alabama was poor rural whites who were removed from religion and the advancing American civilization of transportation, commerce, technology, and education—although as we shall see in chapter 5, some white evangelicals labored to circulate the gospel among Alabama's slaves as well. Accordingly, enthusiasts of benevolence viewed those areas of the state with high rates of scriptural destitution to be economically and socially backward. Reporting to the American Bible Society in 1857, the Reverend Jonathan Lyons grieved over Alabama's Wiregrass counties, which he described as "the poorest and most destitute portion of the whole state. . . . The land is sandy and generally very poor. . . . Many of the people have been raised in the woods, without books of any kind, and also without any religious instruction. I have been informed by citizens of this country that there are men and women here who have never seen a minister of the Gospel." Lyons was certain that in Covington County, one-third of the population was without the Scriptures. Perhaps equally appalling for Lyons—and possibly, in his mind, both the cause and consequence of so many people living without an understanding of evangelical Protestantism—was that the "county town is made up of *seven families—all living in log cabins*."[84]

Of course, some of the people who lived in these rural and undeveloped

83. In contrast, Daniel Walker Howe, "The Evangelical Movement and Political Culture in the North During the Second Party System," *Journal of American History*, LXXVII (March 1991), 1222, suggests that the Sunday school effort in the northern states "transcended class lines."

84. ABS *Annual Report*, XLI (1857), 83. See also ASSU *Annual Report*, XXV (1849), 58–60; XXVI (1850), 19.

areas may have recognized the condescension of evangelicals holding these views and treated the visitors with hostility. Although some benevolent-society agents must certainly have been discouraged by such animosity, others labored diligently to find persons dissatisfied by their religious, social, and economic isolation. One colporteur of the Tuscaloosa-based Alabama Bible Society recounted an experience that occurred on Christmas, 1845, in a "poor smoky hovel" located in the remote corner "of a deep hollow":

> Approaching the door, I saw two miserably ragged females hurrying to and fro, to prepare for my reception. They concealed their persons with some difficulty. I entered slowly. There lay two sleeping babes. Here was squalid poverty. Their simple story was soon told. They had seen better things in other days. But in an evil hour they had married, one a poor sot, the other a lazy huntsman. They had been, one of them five, the other two years in this lonely spot; one of them had formerly been a Methodist, the other a Baptist; but since they settled in *that hollow*, they had not seen a minister of the Gospel. No Bible had greeted their sorrowing eyes; not a prayer had they heard! They both could read, they said, but could not buy a Bible. I drew two from my saddle-bags, gave one to the elder of them, and sat down to read from the other the fourteenth chapter of John. I sang a few verses, and fell upon my knees in prayer. When through, I gave the book to the lady—her eyes were filled with tears—she pressed it to her bosom, and shouted 'Glory to God, I have once more got the BOOK *that* TELLS *about* JESUS!'[85]

Like those who belonged to the Alabama Bible Society, the members of the Alabama Baptist Bible Society were greatly troubled that some people did not possess a copy of the Scriptures, and they similarly associated the lack with backwardness and unsophistication. The ABBS identified those portions of Alabama that were most destitute of the Scriptures as "sparsely settled" and places where "great poverty and ignorance prevails. Great labor is necessary to reach these out of the way places among the back country piny hills." After traveling for seven weeks through portions of Perry, Tuscaloosa, Walker, Fayette, and Pickens Counties as the society's colporteur, the Reverend Randolph

---

85. ABS *Annual Report,* XXX (1846), 55. One of the duties of the ABS agent in Alabama was to "collect funds in the more wealthy counties, more than is required for their supply, so that the poorer counties may receive supplies gratuitously"; *ibid.,* XXXI (1847), 54; (see similar sentiments in XXXIII [1849], 58–59).

Reddins was appalled at the "lamentable destitution" that, he asserted, was ubiquitous in the region. In addition to finding families without Bibles, Reddins encountered adults who had never *seen* a Bible. He related the dearth of Bibles in these counties to other social ills: "Intemperance prevails to an alarming extent in some portions of these counties. The people are without schools. There is a miserable destitution in all that is important to the well-being of souls."[86]

Bible enthusiasts aimed their benevolence toward what they considered the effects of poverty, and they associated their efforts with economic prosperity, which suggests their cosmopolitan outlook and their Whig, rather than Jacksonian, orientation. They might have agreed with Henry Adams' conviction that "bad roads meant bad morals." But as slaveholders, they would have certainly differed with the young Adams' conclusion that Virginia's bad roads were the natural consequence of slavery. Regardless, Alabama's Bible proponents shared with many northern and southern Whigs a hope that economic development could be channeled into "a vision of national progress that would be both moral and material. Society would become more prosperous and at the same time cleansed of its sins."[87]

Given the elite constituency of these benevolent organizations—particularly of the Bible and tract societies—it is tempting to conclude that the principal objective of benevolence activists was to manipulate the masses and to legitimate their own position in society. Such was the view of an earlier generation of scholars, perhaps best exemplified by the pathbreaking work of Clifford S. Griffin, who argued that the wealthy managers of the benevolent empire

86. *Alabama Baptist* (Marion), September 5, 1846; *Alabama Baptist Advocate,* April 6, 1849. The Tuscaloosa Baptist Association also endeavored to supply the repositories of poorer Sabbath schools in the Association with materials from its more affluent members. *Minutes of the Twenty-second Annual Session of the Tuscaloosa Baptist Association* (Tuscaloosa, 1854), 3.

87. Henry Adams, *The Education of Henry Adams* (Boston, 1918), 47; Howe, *Political Culture of American Whigs,* 9; Carwardine, *Evangelicals and Politics,* 58–59, 320–21. Thornton, *Politics and Power,* 52–53, suggests that Alabama Democrats made a more determined effort to appeal to small farmers and the poor than did the Whigs. Albeit the benevolence activists studied herein were not politicians campaigning for office, their descriptions of rural Alabama, noted in the text, can be seen as further evidence of the strong support for benevolence by Whig-minded people. Although an orthodox Democrat would not have congratulated these settlers for their poverty, he or she might well have celebrated the independence of these settlers, praised them for being closer to nature, and asserted that their lives were governed by common sense rather than irrelevant book learning.

feared that the tumultuous changes in America during the first half of the nineteenth century—including the "rise of the common man," the enlarging electorate, the growth of political parties, westward migration, the swelling of cities, the expansion of the working class, and immigration—would threaten their positions of privilege. Subsequent scholarship, though, has cast doubts upon this "social control" school of thought.[88] Although it cannot be said that disciples of benevolence advanced positions that endangered their status, in recent years a number of scholars have proposed that the secular dimension of the evangelical agenda—a distinction surely drawn by twentieth-century historians, because agents of benevolence probably did not compartmentalize their secular and religious objectives—was not merely to keep the masses in subjection, but rather to point the behavior of Americans toward greater participation in the growing market economy. Rather than social control, activists of the benevolent empire hoped to use their institutions to encourage self-control.[89] In this important respect, the agenda of Tuscaloosa's promoters of Bibles, tracts, and Sabbath schools paralleled northern efforts.

Enthusiasm for the changes stemming from the modernization of the economy and the era's technological advances appears frequently in the writings of benevolence devotees. The leaders of the Alabama Bible Society, for example, identified their cause with the course of human progress and reminded their supporters of the need to use "all the forces employed to develope [*sic*] the resources of the earth. The power that moves the steamboat, the rail car, must be here. If the men of the world go by steam, the men of the church must go by steam."[90] Further, as we have seen, proponents of benevolence were overwhelmingly in urban-oriented occupations—recall that 34 of the 36 (94.4 percent) advocates of Bibles and tracts held professional or commercial occupations, while 36 of the 47 (76.6 percent) Tuscaloosa Union Sunday School

88. Clifford S. Griffin, "Religious Benevolence as Social Control," *Mississippi Valley Historical Review*, XLIV (December 1957), 423; Griffin, *Their Brothers' Keepers*. For criticisms of this view, see Lois Banner, "Religious Benevolence as Social Control: A Critique of an Interpretation," *Journal of American History*, LX (June 1973), 23–41; Lawrence Frederick Kohl, "The Concept of Social Control and the History of Jacksonian America," *Journal of the Early Republic*, V (Spring 1985), 21–34; Howe, "The Evangelical Movement and Political Culture," 1217–22. For further bibliographic information, see Stuart M. Blumin, *The Emergence of the Middle Class: Social Experience in the American City, 1760–1900* (Cambridge, Eng., 1989), 193–94, 364–65.

89. Howe, "The Evangelical Movement and Political Culture," 1218–22; Howe, *Political Culture*, 300–301.

90. Montgomery *Advertiser*, March 11, 1857.

teachers came from households headed by a person with a commercial or professional occupation. These figures are even more compelling when compared with the occupations of the adult male heads of household in the town of Tuscaloosa in 1850, of whom only slightly more than a third were professionals or shopkeepers/proprietors:[91]

Occupation of male head of household	Number	Percent
Artisan	56	29.2
Clerk	6	3.1
Shopkeeper/proprietor	25	13.0
Farmer	29	15.1
Laborer	5	2.6
Professional	45	23.4
None listed on census	10	5.2
Other	14	7.3
Illegible	2	1.0
Totals	192	100.0

Not surprisingly, benevolence enjoyed strong support from Tuscaloosa's small community of industrialists.[92] But it is Alabama Supreme Court justice

91. Countywide, 72.1 percent of the 1,723 male heads of household were farmers in 1850, while 6.0 percent were professionals, 9.6 percent were artisans, and 2.8 percent were shopkeepers/ proprietors. The occupational data for both Tuscaloosa town and county were compiled from the 1850 manuscript census for Tuscaloosa County.

92. Washington Moody, an attorney who served as secretary of the Tuscaloosa Manufacturing Company—which produced cotton yarn—was also the recording secretary of the Alabama Central Sunday School Union in 1851, and twenty years earlier had been a contributor to the local Methodist tract society. *Flag of the Union,* May 24, 1837, August 15, 1838; *Independent Monitor,* June 19, 1851; James Sellers, *First Methodist Church,* 73, 311. Thomas Maxwell reminisced that the industrial potential of Tuscaloosa caught his attention during his initial visit in 1837. He eventually became a prosperous merchant, and maintained an interest in manufacturing. In 1848, Maxwell toured the textile plants in Graniteville, South Carolina, and wrote an enthusiastic report on them for a Tuscaloosa newspaper; included were suggestions for improving textile production in Tuscaloosa. In the late 1850s, Maxwell served as treasurer of the local auxiliary of the YMCA. This benevolent organization aimed to provide a wholesome environment and support network for young men recently relocated from rural to urban America. In Tuscaloosa, President Landon

and governor Henry Collier with whom we can draw the most explicit connections between benevolence and industrial manufacturing.

Collier, whose leadership of the Alabama Bible Society, Tuscaloosa Bible Society, and two state temperance organizations has already been noted, denied, as did some of his contemporaries, that manufacturing was incompatible with the society and economy of the antebellum South. In an 1846 speech before the Alabama Agricultural Society—of which he had also formerly served as president—Collier maintained that even though white southerners would remain "essentially an agricultural people" for years to come, more of the section's resources ought to be devoted to manufacturing. If the South failed to in-

---

C. Garland of the University of Alabama described the YMCA as a "humble auxiliary of the Christian church"; it sponsored a reading room and religious and secular lectures. Thomas Maxwell, "Mobile and Tuscaloosa, 1836–1837," *Alabama University Monthly*, I (February 1874), 56; James Robert Maxwell, *Autobiography of James Robert Maxwell of Tuskaloosa, Alabama* (New York, 1926), 66; *Independent Monitor*, July 27, 1848, November 25, 1858, February 26, 1859. Regarding the early YMCA, see also Boyer, *Urban Masses*, 108–20; *Independent Monitor*, February 6, March 19, April 30, October 8, 15, 1859, January 7, March 3, 10, September 1, 1860. Garland, a frequent speaker at the YMCA, was also a zealous promoter of the railroad, serving as president of the Northeast and Southwest Alabama Railroad during its planning stage, and authored numerous essays promoting this project. *Independent Monitor*, May 11, 1854; *Dallas Gazette* (Cahaba, Ala.), September 1, 1854.

Sewell Jones Leach, the co-proprietor of a manufacturing complex that eventually included a foundry, paper mill, plow factory, corn mill, wool carding facility, and a hat factory, was also, though an Episcopalian, a teacher in the Tuscaloosa Union Sunday School; *Crystal Fount*, June 6, 1851; *Independent Monitor*, April 21, 1853, December 14, 1854, October 15, 1857, June 18, 1859; Maxwell, *Autobiography*, 41–42; *State Journal and Flag of the Union*, March 20, 1846; Tuscaloosa SS Minutes, August 28, 1837, May 28, 1838.

Arthur F. Hopkins, an attorney who was also president of the Mobile and Ohio Railroad during the 1850s, had served as a director of the Alabama Bible Society during the early 1830s and president of the Alabama State Sabbath Convention in 1846; Garrett, *Reminiscences of Public Men in Alabama*, 377–80; *Alabama State Intelligencer*, January 1, 1830, January 3, 1831; *Independent Monitor*, June 3, 1846; Tuscaloosa Presbyterian Church, unpaginated communion roll, Session Book No. 2, August 3, 1844, January 1846.

Alfred Battle, a planter whose benevolent activities have already been cited in n. 49, was also an enthusiastic supporter of railroads. In 1853, he publicly favored a three-year property tax increase in order to finance the construction of a railroad through Tuscaloosa. Later in the decade, he played a prominent role in the Northeast and Southwest Alabama Railroad, again urging citizens to invest in the construction of this project and calling upon the South to manufacture its own iron for this purpose. *Independent Monitor*, July 15, 1853, May 7, 1857, April 30, 1859; Owen, *History of Alabama*, III, 112.

dustrialize, whites there would surrender profits to those "who are denouncing us with all bitterness, as slave breeders and relentless task masters." But Collier was even more concerned that the section's exclusive reliance upon agriculture was having a detrimental effect upon the population: "In a country where the facilities for living are as great as they are at the South, there are, and must continue to be thousands who, without any visible employment, live as an *incubus* upon the bosom of society."

Collier's visit to a manufacturing establishment in Cincinnati convinced him that in order to diminish indolence the South must expand its manufacturing: "No man can enter a well-regulated manufacturing establishment without being struck with the order and method prevailing there; and is apt to leave with a higher appreciation of the blessings of industry. Let manufacturing be extensively undertaken, agriculture and the mechanic arts will soon catch the impulse; neatness, comfort and elegance will be seen about the homestead, and among the household. Increasing wealth will flow in upon us, public morals will be diffused in proportion as we can induce the idle and profligate to labor." If manufacturing proliferated and these idlers were "reclaimed and reduced to work," Collier expected that their children would then "be reared up to habits of industry" and thus positively transform southern society: "I am solicitous for the moral and intellectual elevation of man wherever found, am desirous of seeing everyone industriously employed, as one of the most efficient means of promoting virtue and all its happy results. I have long been persuaded that instead of afflicting a curse, God really gave us a blessing when in our fallen state, he doomed us to ceaseless labor. A life of idleness is incompatible with the teachings of revelation." In Collier's mind, manufacturing and benevolence were complementary means of reaching the same end.[93]

Tuscaloosa County's partisans of Bibles, tracts, and Sabbath schools were also more likely than the rest of the population to send their children to secular schools. In the world of the expanding marketplace, schools were where children would best be taught the skills—literacy, arithmetic, abstemiousness, and punctuality—that contemporaries recognized to be essential to upward mobility. The parents' decision to have their children attend school, according to one scholar, "demonstrated their orientation toward the future and their aspirations for upward mobility by their readiness to sacrifice the short-term

---

93. *State Journal and Flag of the Union,* January 9, 1846. Collier's activism regarding benevolence, temperance, and other reform efforts are cited in nn. 49 and 50, this chapter.

earnings of their children in favor of education."[94] Not all parents enrolled their children in school, and school attendance was quite low in some portions of Alabama. Statewide, only a third of white children between the ages of five and nineteen attended school in 1850. In Tuscaloosa County, school attendance was virtually equal to the state mark, but in the town of Tuscaloosa it was much higher: nearly seven-tenths of white children attended school.[95] And among those families whose members circulated Bibles and tracts or taught Sabbath school, an even higher percentage of children attended school. Nearly nine-tenths of the children who lived in the households of teachers at the Tuscaloosa Union Sunday School attended secular school. Among the group of Sabbath-school devotees not affiliated with the Union Sunday School, and among the promoters of Bibles and tracts, the figures were only slightly lower.[96]

Activists of the benevolent empire had to do more, though, than simply utilize the age's technological advancements and embrace the expanding economy. According to members of the Alabama Bible Society, the success of human genius without a corresponding furtherance of evangelical Christianity

94. Richard D. Brown, *Modernization: The Transformation of American Life, 1600–1865* (New York, 1976), 138. Regarding the teaching of marketplace skills—among other things—in antebellum northern schools, see Kaestle, *Pillars of the Republic*, 62–70.

95. School attendance figures for Alabama (35.5 percent) and Tuscaloosa County (37.9 percent) were calculated from *Seventh Census*, 414, 427. The Tuscaloosa town figure was compiled from the population schedule of the 1850 federal manuscript census. Although the census enumerator did not specifically designate which residents lived in the town of Tuscaloosa, these statistics were obtained by counting all the households between numbers 176 and 420, inclusive. In this group were clustered mostly nonagrarian occupations; the households listed before and after this group were overwhelmingly agricultural. Of the 412 white individuals between five and nineteen in these 245 households, 285, or 69.2 percent, were listed in the 1850 census as having attended school in the past year. Further, among these 245 households, 1,128 free inhabitants—18 of whom were free blacks—were listed on the population schedule, and 1,748 slaves were enumerated within the 171 Tuscaloosa town households that were included on the slave schedule. In 1860, the free population of the town of Tuscaloosa was 1,589—which included 69 free blacks—and the slave population was 2,400. *Population of the United States in 1860*, 9.

96. School attendance for these groups are as follows: 66 of the 76 children (86.8 percent) between the ages of five and nineteen who lived in the households of teachers at the Tuscaloosa Union Sunday School—and who also shared the surname of the teacher—were listed on the 1850 federal census as having attended school within the past year; among the group of Sabbath school proponents not affiliated with the Union Sunday School, and among the promoters of Bibles and tracts, the figures were 31 of 38 (81.6 percent) and 41 of 48 (85.4 percent), respectively.

could spell disaster for humanity: "If the Christian Faith march not by the side, or lead the van of the tramp of nations, then the future is a cloudland, and they march steadily to an abyss which will swallow up and hide forever the glory and renown, the pride and pomp, the knowledge and art, which admitted no obligations to God, nor any debt to his Providence, nor any subjection to the mental forces of his grace." History had demonstrated that "nations may grow great and glorious, without a recognition of the one true God over all . . . but great and glorious they cannot continue." Additionally, "where a numerous population is found to exist, with a large destitution of the Bible among its families, there the foundations of all good society are being sapped." Not surprisingly, members of the benevolent empire believed that "All public morals—all good citizenship—all true progress—must be based on the knowledge of the Bible by the people."[97] As they saw things, their labors were vital both to preserving the American republic and to enabling it to attain its potential greatness.

Evangelicals believed that their programs provided society with necessary behavioral restraints, the absence of which would result in chaos. They pointed to the fact that objectionable behavior reigned in locales where their institutions were absent. They were especially saddened by the conditions in northeastern Alabama, which in the 1830s was a newly settled area. In that section there were a few schools, and some residents were sympathetic to evangelicals, but these forces alone were too weak, in the estimation of ASSU agent Thomas Cox, to prevent familiarity between the races. He lamented that the "Creek Indians and the white people all live intermixed," and regretted "to see the disapation caried on by the lower class of whites and Indians in drinking Sabbath breaking & c. which makes virtue to weep and humanity to shudder." Cox noted that Northport, across the Black Warrior River from his home in the town of Tuscaloosa, was likewise "a place of much disorder and Sabbath breaking; they have but little preaching." Although disheartened by these scenes, evangelicals remained certain that the proper application of benevolence could transform a community. Cox claimed that Northport had changed dramatically due to the "influence of a well-organized Sabbath School sustained by a few pious lay men"; he was overjoyed at how "good order has been restored and

---

97. Montgomery *Advertiser*, March 11, 1857. Regarding those Protestant ministers who felt great misgivings about the direction of American nationalism and about the country's material agenda, see Hanley, *Beyond A Christian Commonwealth*.

the whole face of society changes in such a manner that it is visible and notorious to every beholder." Robert S. Foster similarly asserted that Sabbath schools in the Tuscaloosa County settlement of Grant's Creek had been the impetus behind a "great improvement in the morals and society at large," and part of the reason behind the success of a revival.[98]

The supporters of the Sunday school advanced it as a mechanism that not only instructed children in the theological precepts of Protestantism, but also directed them into paths of virtue and self-mastery. Devotees of benevolence viewed a child's character as malleable and were convinced that both behavior and world view could be shaped according to the external forces placed upon them. As "W." wrote in a Tuscaloosa newspaper in 1831, "It is the peculiar excellence of Sabbath schools, that they redeem the mind from the thraldom of ignorance and superstition, and promote freedom, power, and correctness of thought." The Sunday school was praised by the Tuscaloosa-dominated leadership of the Central Alabama Sunday School Union two decades later because it "begins at the beginning—with the formative period of life and character; and applies the mould of a higher civilization and a better morality to man's plastic nature. . . . It is the true nursery of both men and means; and provides for that holy work in perpetuity."[99] Thomas Curtis, pastor of the Tuscaloosa Baptist Church, affirmed these positions and argued that changed times required more diligence on the part of evangelical Protestants. As a result of the spread of education within the past generation,

> character is forming earlier, as the mind is earlier developed. This we cannot stop if we would. . . . Shall then the character be left to form for good or for evil, without any suitable religious instruction to lead it right[?] This impetuous stream which you cannot resist, may be guided into channels of greatest utility, but then for this Sabbath Schools and Bible Classes will be needed, and these conducted with the greatest energy and wisdom; nor will it do for us to say, there were no Sabbath Schools fifty years ago, we will have nothing to do with these enterprises now. That were not to observe the signs of the times.[100]

98. Thomas W. Cox to ASSU, June 30, 1835, December 31, 1834; Robert S. Foster to ASSU April 11, 1830, all ASSU Papers. See also ASSU *Annual Report*, XXVI (1850), 19. Concerning the behavior of white settlers in the Old Southwest—and the contrast with the ways of whites who remained in the south-Atlantic-seaboard states—see Joan E. Cashin, *A Family Venture: Men and Women on the Southern Frontier* (Baltimore, 1991), 99–112.

99. *Alabama State Intelligencer*, September 10, 1831; *Independent Monitor*, June 19, 1851.

100. *Minutes of the Eleventh Annual Session of the Tuscaloosa Baptist Association Held at Gilgal Meeting-House, Tuscaloosa County, Alabama* (Tuscaloosa, 1843), 7. Similar views on Sabbath

Of course, the plasticity of human character furnished both opportunity and peril, and the possibility of failure certainly supplied evangelicals with some of their zeal.

Advocates of benevolence in Tuscaloosa claimed that economic gains would follow as their agenda succeeded. One of their foremost preoccupations was the circumstances of the poor. The widespread circulation of Bibles would, in the estimation of the Whig *Independent Monitor*, do much to eliminate poverty: "Persons who wish to do good with their money, cannot make a better investment than to purchase cheap Bibles for gratuitous distribution among their poor neighbors." Sabbath-school proponents praised their institution as useful for the poor, "for it is often the only school they have; and has raised many a forlorn child of indigence and misfortune to most desirable eminence in all good things." The Sunday school, argued its enthusiasts, taught the necessary behavioral qualities that prevented and corrected impecuniosity. According to the leaders of the Central Alabama Sunday School Union, the Sunday school thus was "better than the almshouse for the relief of human destitution and wretchedness; for it tends to prevent idleness, improvidence, and pauperism, which the other indirectly, but inevitably, fosters." It was also the least costly way to prevent crime, surpassing courts and penitentiaries, "for it strikes at the very root and cause of evil, and turns men from 'the ways of disobedience to the wisdom of the just.'" Of the thousands of persons taught in English Sunday schools over the years, asserted these Sunday-school leaders, not one had been found in a prison or become a beggar.[101]

Alabama Bible Society president and state governor Israel Pickens, speaking before the first annual meeting of the society in Cahaba in 1824, explained that the circulation of the Scriptures was done, in part, to improve the moral and temporal condition of humanity. But he and others involved in benevolent networks were also convinced that their endeavors advanced a stable social order: "To know that religious instruction is promotive of great temporal good, is

---

schools may be found in *Minutes of the Twenty-second Annual Session of the Tuscaloosa Baptist Association*, 3; *Minutes of the Twenty-fourth Annual Session of the Tuscaloosa Baptist Association* (Tuscaloosa, 1856), 3–4; *Minutes of the Sixteenth Anniversary of the Baptist State Convention of Alabama; Held at Oakmulgee Meeting House, Perry County, Commencing on Saturday, Nov. 9, 1839* (Tuscaloosa, 1839), 6; *Minutes of the Seventeenth Anniversary of the Baptist State Convention of Alabama, Held at Salem, Greene County, Alabama* (Tuscaloosa, 1840), 4; *South Western Baptist* (Marion, Ala.), March 31, 1852. See also the sermon delivered at Tuscaloosa's YMCA and reported in the *Independent Monitor*, February 26, 1859.

101. *Independent Monitor*, February 18, 1846, June 19, 1851.

itself a sufficient inducement for perseverance in the work. The lessons of pure morality which fill the pages of the volume we are engaged in distributing, are well directed to the maintenance of social order. The principles of fellowship and brotherly kindness it inculcates, tend to produce those friendly offices which endear man to his fellow man, and bind together the materials of society in the interesting relation of good neighborhood." Likewise, the Sunday school, in the opinion of Basil Manly, Henry W. Collier, and Columbus Franklin Sturgis, gave laws "their bond of support, and renders their adminis-tration easy, by leavening public opinion with the love of law and order: or as the rudeness of society may require, it grapples, silently, but effectively, with man's fierce and vicious nature—and rears a population that shall welcome the authority and administration of law."[102] Joshua H. Foster, a Baptist pastor in rural Tuscaloosa County and corresponding secretary of the Alabama Central Sunday School Union, agreed. Sunday schools provided society with an exem-plary "class of citizens thoroughly trained in the great principles, which consti-tute the ground-work of all correct moral and civil law, thus preventing crime, and operating as a conservative agent in promoting the perpetuity of our polit-ical institutions, amid all the discordant elements rapidly concentrating in our country."[103]

These individuals did not aver that the social order was maintained by coercion. Rather, they understood that the good society emerged when indi-viduals, without external constraint, subscribed to the principles of law and order.[104]

Partisans of benevolence also argued that the position of women in society was strengthened as evangelical publications proliferated. In the eyes of one man who enthusiastically endorsed the Bible cause, the success of benevolent efforts would only serve further to elevate "woman to her proper rank. In hea-then countries where the Bible was unknown, and where of course civilization

102. *Ibid.,* June 3, 1846 (a correspondent of the *Monitor* discovered Pickens' address more than twenty years after it was delivered and requested that the editor publish it), June 19, 1851.

103. *South Western Baptist* (Marion, Ala.), August 4, 1852. Similar views on the importance of Sabbath schools as tools to develop patriotism and political stability may be found *ibid.,* April 7, 1852, and *Minutes of the Twenty-first Annual Session of the Tuskaloosa Baptist Association* (Tusca-loosa, 1853), 14.

104. A conclusion for the antebellum North similar to the one posited here is found in Howe, "Evangelical Movement and Political Culture," 1220. See also Kohl, *Politics of Individualism,* 69–78, 146–57.

never dawned, woman . . . was degraded. Through the influence of the Bible, she had risen to her present exalted state—the companion and trusty friend of man." Unfortunately, the extent to which women participated in the benevolent campaigns outlined in this chapter, and the degree to which their views accorded with those of men who were active in these enterprises, cannot be fully known. As mentioned previously, almost one-half of the teachers in the Tuscaloosa Union Sunday School and the members of the Tuskaloosa Baptist Bible Society were women, as were one-fourth of the contributors to the Methodist Episcopal Tract Society Auxiliary, and seven of the Tuscaloosa contributors to the American Tract Society.[105] The participation of these women in benevolent operations—especially the high percentage of women teachers in the Sunday school—is probably a manifestation of women taking advantage of their narrower social opportunities, and their implicit acceptance of the evangelical conception of womanhood.[106]

Information on the activity of women in other benevolent movements is scarce, but scattered evidence from Tuscaloosa's newspapers demonstrates that Tuscaloosa's white women participated in a number of voluntary associations

105. *Independent Monitor,* December 18, 1844; ATS (New York) *Annual Report,* XI (1836), 138, XXXIII (1838), 198, XV (1840), 158, XVII (1842), 154. Among these seven female contributors to the ATS, I have included Mrs. Sarah C. Smith of Tuscaloosa, who in 1840 contributed $12 to the ATS Boston. While both the New York and Boston bodies supported agents throughout the United States, the Boston Society devoted most of its attention to New England. ATS (Boston), *Annual Report,* XXVII (1841), 77, XXIX (1843), 20; see the comment on this body in chap. 2, n. 20). On women's benevolent activity in another southern community—Petersburg, Virginia— see Lebsock, *Free Women of Petersburg,* 215–25.

106. Boylan, *Sunday School,* 102. There is some dispute regarding organized female benevolent activity in the antebellum South. Lebsock, in *Free Women of Petersburg,* 215–25, shows that the women of this Virginia city were energetic participants of religious auxiliaries and reform associations. Gail S. Murray, "Within the Bounds of Race and Class: Female Benevolence in the Old South," *South Carolina Magazine of History,* XCVI (January 1995), 54–70, looks at female charitable societies in five large southern cities. Murray draws clearer distinctions between the reform efforts of southern and northern women than does Lebsock and argues that female-sponsored poor relief in the South was more paternal and hierarchical than its northern counterpart. Lebsock's study has been discounted by Elizabeth Fox-Genovese, *Within the Plantation Household,* 70, who, along with Jean E. Friedman, *The Enclosed Garden: Women and Community in the Evangelical South* (Chapel Hill, 1985), xi-xiii, 6–7, 9, 19–20, 21, maintains that the rural character of southern society generally precluded the formation of female voluntary associations. Bode, "A Common Sphere," however, demonstrates a variety of ways that both rural and town-dwelling women actively contributed to the evangelical world.

during the antebellum years. Tuscaloosa's Female Baptist Missionary Society was organized in 1824 as male benevolence campaigns got under way in the town. In 1830, Tuscaloosa's women formed a Ladies' Benevolent Society. They were encouraged in this endeavor when the Episcopal rector, A. A. Muller, gave a public address on the subject. If this body was similar in its aims to a like-named society in Mobile, it sought to "ameliorate the condition of the sick and poor."[107] How long either of these Tuscaloosa associations lasted is unknown. The timing of their emergence, however, suggests that the development of women's reform efforts paralleled those of the men.

In antebellum Tuscaloosa, women's activities were less likely to be publicized than those of men. Male-edited newspapers generally reported only on male-dominated societies. It was rare for a woman's name to appear in a newspaper. On one of the few occasions that this occurred—in 1848, when the *Monitor* reported the presentation of a temperance banner by Miss Harriette Wallace on behalf of the "ladies of Tuscaloosa" to Captain John G. Barr, who represented Tuscaloosa's Sons of Temperance—the editor prefaced his celebratory remarks by noting that "to speak publicly of a lady, even to praise, is a matter of some delicacy." Contemporary social customs constrained women to be passive and discouraged them from being forward in public. Wallace expressed her agreement with this role of women when she explained that "it is man's prerogative to conceive and execute all great schemes for the improvement of the human race." Nevertheless, she did not believe that women should avoid activism, for "surely woman is not transcending her privilege, when she stands forth to encourage [man] in his onward struggles." In Wallace's mind, this relationship had a decidedly chivalric tone: "As the ladies of olden time bade their knights, when they sped forth on the crusade, so we bid you, 'on to glory.'"[108] Because of these constraints, the sentiments of female participants in Tuscaloosa's Bible, tract, and Sunday-school societies have generally not survived.

But newspapers did occasionally report on women's activities—at least enough, in conjunction with other sources, to demonstrate that Tuscaloosa's white women operated their own voluntary associations. For example, a "Ladies Fair" held in January 1839 raised a thousand dollars for the expansion of

107. *American Mirror*, July 31, 1824, August 7, 1824; *Alabama State Intelligencer*, July 2, 1830, July 17, 1829.

108. *Independent Monitor*, December 28, 1848, January 4, 1849.

the Presbyterian church building. (Significantly, no mention of this organization or of the money it raised for the congregation was ever made in the church minutes.)[109] In 1838 the *Flag of the Union* printed the constitution of the Tuscaloosa Maternal Association, whose members assembled every other Saturday evening and shared suggestions on the best ways "of bringing up our children in the nurture and admonition of the Lord." A female-operated free school for about thirty small children met at the Methodist church during the mid-1840s. The "Young Ladies" who conducted the school divided the work among themselves through weekly rotation and donated their efforts to "persons unable to incur the expense of tuition, or who may not be willing to send their children to other primary schools."[110] Unfortunately, existing sources do not tell us how long these associations survived. Exactly who these women were must also remain a mystery; no records of their organizations exist, nor did their names appear in the newspapers. If they came from the same social ranks as members of the other movements discussed in this chapter, they were from the middle and upper classes. But because of incomplete records, we cannot determine whether white women of the lower classes—let alone the handful of free blacks in Tuscaloosa—formed any voluntary associations of their own.

The records of Tuscaloosa's Female Benevolent Society, however, permit us to delve more deeply into one female association than would the few notices that the group received in the town's newspapers. Whether this was the same organization as the Ladies' Benevolent Society of 1830 is not clear, but the chronicles of the group demonstrate consistent activity from 1853 to 1867—longer than any similar but male-dominated voluntary association persisted in Tuscaloosa.[111]

The Female Benevolent Society enjoyed remarkable autonomy for its era, in that it was operated completely by women and was not affiliated with any other organization. The society raised money primarily among Tuscaloosa's middle-

---

109. *Ibid.*, January 23, 1839. Baptists, however, recounted in their church minutes that a similar fund-raising effort by the Baptist Female Sewing Society permitted Tuscaloosa's Baptists to improve their Sabbath-school library; the sources also suggest that the women in the sewing society controlled their own finances. Records of the First Baptist Church of Tuscaloosa, 1842–1867, September 12, 1853, January 12, 1857.

110. *Flag of the Union*, October 10, 1838; *Independent Monitor*, April 29, 1846.

111. The first entry in the record book of the Female Benevolent Society (October 24, 1853) notes "officers of last year reelected," demonstrating that the society's existence antedated 1853. The minutes of this organization are located in the Hoole Special Collections.

class and wealthy women and used it to dispense goods among the town's poor. Such societies appear to have existed in many cities and towns in antebellum America, in both the North and the South.[112] The Tuscaloosa society assisted twelve to twenty-one families per year between 1853 and 1861. Those assisted were the "worthy poor"—almost without exception, women who could not be held culpable for their impoverished condition. Alongside the names of the society's aid recipients occasionally appear such comments as "a feeble woman— drunken husband," "widow, with 5 children," "feeble and widow," or *very old woman.* Members of the society appointed a board of officers who considered the needs of potential recipients. After aid was bestowed, a visiting committee continued to "enquire into the character & condition of the persons assisted." The society offered assistance but could not provide complete support. A few recipients received direct cash payments, but most aid was in the form of goods and services. Occasionally, the minutes specifically note how the aid was provided: $3 was spent on *"shoes* for Mrs Alberts boys"; $2 for *"meat* and *meal* for Mrs Hinton, widow, 79 years"; $15 was "expended in paying the tuition of William McMillan"; $1.25 for "a load of wood Mrs Johnson"; $5 "for Mrs Reynolds *groceries*"; $4 "for house rent for Mrs Johnson."[113]

Tuscaloosa's white males praised the Female Benevolent Society, and several male voluntary associations contributed to it. The *Independent Monitor* proposed that affluent citizens "who may be disposed to contribute for the relief of the poor and destitute" make Christmas donations to the society, as "this Association is an admirable channel through which to do it." During the late 1850s, and especially in 1860 following the closure of a local factory in midwinter, affluent Tuscaloosans increasingly looked to the Female Benevolent Society to shoulder the burden of providing for the town's poor. Tuscaloosa's Young Men's Christian Association, the Sons of Malta, and the Odd Fellows provided gifts that increased the society's operating budget from the mid-1850s

112. Michael B. Katz, *In the Shadow of the Poorhouse: A Social History of Welfare in America* (New York, 1986), 64–66. See also Bellows, *Benevolence Among Slaveholders,* and Gail Murray, "Within the Bounds." Fox-Genovese, *Within the Plantation Household,* 81, contends, however, that there were fewer of these organizations in the South, as "southern society discouraged women from developing . . . networks, bonds, voluntary associations, mothers' clubs, [and] an ideology of domesticity"; see also 80, 413–14.

113. Minutes of the Female Benevolent Society February 13, 1858, February 23, 1858, December 30, 1861, January 23, 1860, March 3, 1856, February 2, 1857, December 3, 1855, February 3, 1858, January 29, 1858, November 26, 1858, June 23, 1859, July 15, 1859.

onward. In addition, when University of Alabama president Landon C. Garland presented a series of lectures in March 1860 that defended slavery, he donated the admission proceeds to the Benevolent Society. But despite the financial backing that Tuscaloosa's men provided to the society, there is no evidence to suggest that women surrendered the control of their organization.[114]

In all, 210 individuals contributed money to the Female Benevolent Society between 1853 and 1860, and 204 of them were women. Most contributors played only a passive role in the organization, doing nothing more than making an annual gift of one dollar (nearly all of the donations to the Benevolent Society were of this amount), but 34 of the 204 female contributors served as officers. They met several times per year, determined the needs and worthiness of potential aid recipients, and collected the money that kept their enterprise operating.

Almost three-fourths of the contributors—or "subscribers," as they were designated in the minutes—were identified on the 1850 and 1860 censuses and provide us with a significant demographic profile of the Female Benevolent Society. Virtually every subscriber lived within a few miles of the town of Tuscaloosa.[115] The majority did not head households; 110 subscribers were not listed as heads of household in either census, while 31 women and 5 men were heads of households in one or both censuses. Of the 110 contributors who were not listed as heads of household in either census, 93 were married females, 13 were females living with their parents, and 4 were female adults who did not appear to live with family members. Nine households had more than one contributor to the Female Benevolent Society. Contributors with discernible ages ranged from adolescents to the elderly, although most were born between 1811 and 1830 (median year of birth, 1820):

---

114. *Independent Monitor*, December 24, 1857 (see also January 21, 1858); Minutes of the Female Benevolent Society October 24, 1853, November 11, 1856, January 1, 1858, April 28, 1858, January 4, 1859, January 6, 1860, March 31, 1860, June [no precise date] 1860 (the disbursements of the Female Benevolent Society increased from $76.35 in 1856 to $303.45 during the first six months of 1860); *Independent Monitor*, April 1, 1858, January 7, 1860, March 3, 10, 1860; Quist, "Social and Moral Reform," 141–42. Compare the case of Petersburg, Virginia, where men encroached upon female voluntary associations—almsgiving bodies in particular—during these years. Lebsock, *Free Women of Petersburg*, 198, 226–36.

115. Contributors to the Female Benevolent Society included 33 found only in the 1850 census, 43 found only in the 1860 census, and 70 found in both censuses.

Year of birth	Age in 1860	Number	Percent
1841–1850	10–19	3	2.1
1831–1840	20–29	28	19.3
1821–1830	30–39	36	24.8
1811–1820	40–49	37	25.5
1801–1810	50–59	23	15.9
1791–1800	60–69	14	9.7
1781–1790	70–79	2	1.4
1771–1780	80–89	2	1.4
Totals		145	100.1

The vast majority, 122 of 146 (83.6 percent) with identifiable places of birth, were born in the South, the remainder having northern or foreign places of birth—15 (10.3 percent) and 8 (5.5 percent), respectively. This percentage of southern birth is higher than that among male heads of household in the town of Tuscaloosa (72.9 percent) but lower than the 93.4 percent for all male heads of household in Tuscaloosa County (see Table 5).

But perhaps more significantly, census data reveal the extent to which contributors to the Female Benevolent Society, like the members of other causes discussed in this chapter, came from the ranks of Tuscaloosa County's elite. For example, the occupations of male contributors and of the husbands or fathers of female contributors were as follows:

Occupation	Number	Percent
Artisan	8	6.7
Clerk	1	0.8
Shopkeeper/proprietor	20	16.8
Farmer	32	26.9
Laborer	1	0.8
Professional	51	42.9
Other	2	1.7
None listed on census	4	3.4
Totals	119	100.0

When compared with the occupational breakdown for Tuscaloosa town, contributors disproportionately came from households headed by males holding Tuscaloosa's most prestigious occupations—farmers (many being planters), professionals, and people engaged in commerce. Those contributors to the Female Benevolent Society who were found on the 1850 census were also among the wealthiest Tuscaloosans:

Real property ($) of contributor or head of household	Number	Percent
0	20	20.6
1–999	8	8.2
1,000–2,499	19	19.6
2,500–4,999	17	17.5
5,000–9,999	19	19.6
10,000 and over	14	14.4
Totals	97	99.9

The mean real-estate holding—including those who owned no property—was $5,222, and the median was $2,500. These figures are significantly larger than those for all Tuscaloosa County households, among which the median holding was $195 (mean $873), and for the town of Tuscaloosa, where median and mean for all households in 1850 were $0 and $1,640, respectively:

Real property ($) of head of household, Tuscaloosa town	Number	Percent
0	127	51.8
1–999	35	14.3
1,000–2,499	31	12.7
2,500–4,999	22	9.0
5,000–9,999	18	7.3
10,000 and over	12	4.9
Totals	245	100.0

Comparing these last two tables, one sees that not only did the Female Benevolent Society's contributors come disproportionately from the ranks of the wealthy, but it was also uncommon for a woman from a wealthy household to reject the society's requests for aid.[116]

A high percentage of Female Benevolent Society subscribers were slaveholders. The slaveholding status could be determined for 106 people from the 1830, 1840, and/or 1850 censuses, and of these individuals, 97 (91.5 percent) could be linked to slaveholding families. This percentage is remarkable given the fact that of the 1,897 Tuscaloosa County households listed in the 1850 census population schedule, only 671 (35.4 percent) owned slaves, and that in the town of Tuscaloosa, 171 of 245 households (69.8 percent) were slaveholding. The typical slaveholding among Benevolent Society contributors was also greater than it was among the white population at large. For example, among Tuscaloosa County slaveholders in 1850, the median holding was 6, the mean was 11.2, and 442 (65.9 percent) slaveholdings numbered 9 or fewer, while only 98 (14.6 percent) of the slaveholding households owned 20 or more slaves; in the town of Tuscaloosa, the median was also 6, the average 10.2, and 118 of the 171 (69.0 percent) held 9 or fewer slaves, while only 27 (15.8 percent) owned 20 or more. Among the 91 contributors identified in the 1850 census whose immediate families owned slaves, the holdings were much higher: the median was 10, the mean was 17.3, and only 39 (42.9 percent) owned fewer than 10 slaves, while 23 contributors (25.3 percent) came from households with 20 or more slaves. The fact that contributors to the Benevolent Society were among the wealthiest in Tuscaloosa should come as no surprise, since the well-to-do were the ones who could best afford to give money, even if the sum was only one dollar annually.

The Female Benevolent Society was dominated by religious women. Officers' meetings opened and closed with prayer, and informal networks among the officers existed in the town's churches.[117] The religious affiliations of 119 contributors could be ascertained from Tuscaloosa's church records:

116. Benevolent Society contributors from households with more than $5,000 of real property outnumbered the wealthy households in Tuscaloosa town because a few subscribers lived on the outskirts of the town of Tuscaloosa—which was the case with 29 of the 103 (28.2 percent) who were located on the 1850 census—and because some households had more than one member who contributed to the society.

117. Minutes of the Female Benevolent Society January 1, 1858, January 1, 1860. The Female Benevolent Society in Tuscaloosa was essentially operated from the top down. The society's records imply that the leadership was virtually self-perpetuating; that is, a core of activists continually reelected its members to the society's offices. The leaders were in turn responsible for solicit-

Religion	Number	Percent
Baptist	34	28.6
Catholic	2	1.7
Episcopal	7	5.9
Methodist	31	26.1
Presbyterian	45	37.8
Totals	119	100.1

The preponderance of Presbyterian supporters—among both contributors and the society's leadership—is significant, particularly since Tuscaloosa and Alabama Presbyterians were far fewer than either Baptists or Methodists.[118] Although Baptists, Methodists, and Episcopalians were not averse to creating their own denominational auxiliaries for promoting Bibles, tracts, and Sabbath schools, Presbyterians—locally, statewide, and nationally—were the strongest supporters of interdenominational benevolent societies. Quite possibly the nonsectarian pretensions of the Female Benevolent Society were less threatening to Presbyterians than to members of other denominations.

As we shall see in subsequent chapters, Presbyterians also supported the American Colonization Society and the early temperance movement with strength disproportionate to their numbers—although not to the extent to which Presbyterian women supported Tuscaloosa's Female Benevolent Society.

Some Tuscaloosans feared and loathed the benevolent empire. Nonevangelical Christians were naturally suspicious of religious crusades that they believed were aimed at them, and the anticlerical and irreligious likewise viewed these benevolent causes unfavorably. These Tuscaloosans—and others in the community—directed much of their spleen toward the incipient temperance movement of the late 1820s and early 1830s, but the devotees of benevolence

---

ing contributions from Tuscaloosa's women. Thus the Presbyterian-dominated leadership was probably the cause of a Presbyterian-dominated list of donors, rather than vice versa.

118. Of the 34 Benevolent Society officers listed in the society's minutes between 1853 and 1860, the religious affiliation of 23 could be determined from Tuscaloosa's church records. There were 12 Presbyterians, 6 Methodists, and 5 Baptists.

also received hostile barbs during these years. Significantly, opponents of both temperance and benevolence voiced their opposition only briefly. By the mid-1830s, these forces no longer enjoyed access to town newspapers, as evangelicals and devotees of moral order gained ascendancy in Tuscaloosa.

As early as 1824, when benevolent efforts in Tuscaloosa were in their infancy, one writer to the *American Mirror* derided William Crawford's presidential campaign, noting that Crawford appealed to the benevolent people who wished to take the gospel to the Indians.[119] The advent of significant benevolent activity in Tuscaloosa in the late 1820s, coupled with the steady growth of revivalism during the preceding half dozen years, may have created a critical mass of evangelical activity that caused some evangelicals to take courage and nonevangelicals to feel threatened.

In response to the expansion of benevolent organizations in Tuscaloosa, several authors submitted sarcastic essays to the town's newspapers. In May 1829, the *Alabama State Intelligencer* published a letter from "Tracks," who ridiculed the establishment of an American Tract Society auxiliary in "our very fortunate town": "For kindly condescending to send out their 'Little messengers of grace' even to poor benighted Alabama, I sincerely hope that they may be dutifully rewarded for their pious trouble. Ever hereafter, I would advise his Satanic Majesty, when he pays us a visit, to demean himself as becomes a gentleman, if he does not wish to create unpleasant feelings among us goodly folks; and to his usual good sense and politeness, I trust that will keep his cloven foot out of view, for he might meet with rather a *cold* reception." Tracks further castigated the American Tract Society officers for their exorbitant salaries and for using the "little dribblets of the 'widow's mite,' and the industrious and liberal poor" to build in New York "an edifice, equal in point of spaciousness and magnificence to our state house." These circumstances led Tracks to conclude that "'these little messengers of grace' are intended for our own good, yea, for all our *goods*."[120]

119. *American Mirror,* May 22, 1824. Crawford's ties to the benevolent empire included a national vice-presidency of the ACS. P. J. Staudenraus, *The African Colonization Movement, 1816–1865* (New York, 1961), 30, 52–53, 69, 174; Chase H. Mooney, *William H. Crawford, 1772–1834* (Lexington, 1974), 188–91.

120. *Alabama State Intelligencer,* May 17, 1829. More than two years later, the *Intelligencer* reprinted an article from the New York *Courier and Enquirer* that suggested money had been skimmed from the coffers of the ABS, as the society had collected $181,000 over the past four

Later, the *Intelligencer*'s editors ridiculed the age as an "era of reform, and we shall soon have no need of temperance and many other societies, which are becoming so numerous as to be a little burdensome to the wicked and profligate; so much so, that as a last resort, they will doubtless forsake their evil ways, and thereby lighten the labors of the philanthropists of the present day." While denouncing Henry Clay's "American System," the *Intelligencer* associated it with the burgeoning antislavery movement and "the scheme for stopping the transportation of the United States Mail, on the Christian Sabbath," all of which the editor traced "to the pious land of New England." The efforts of evangelicals to interfere with the secular world by shutting down the federal mail on Sunday were further blasted by the *Intelligencer* when it censured a sermon on the topic by the Reverend James Hillhouse of Greensboro—formerly the Presbyterian pastor of Tuscaloosa. According to the paper, Hillhouse's remarks were "characterized by the most bitter invectives and anathemas; and those in favor of the present system were denounced as INFIDELS AND EMISSARIES OF THE DEVIL! This is a little worse than we could have expected in this age of freedom and toleration—in the enlightened age of the NINETEENTH CENTURY."[121] In Huntsville, a newspaper reportedly claimed "that the Sabbath School Union and the Bible Society was formed to mislead the young minds and to cause them [to] believe that it would be right to [have] an established religion[,] to alter the Constitution and cause the people to wade in scenes of blood."[122]

Before long, supporters of benevolent enterprises counterattacked with equal vehemence. In August 1831, the *Intelligencer* republished an article from the Richmond *Whig* that was critical of Sunday schools and was endorsed by *Intelligencer* editor Thomas H. Wiley. Erasmus Walker, the editor of the rival

---

years, had given away $64,000 worth of Bibles during that time, yet was $34,000 in debt; *ibid.,* October 15, 1831.

121. *Ibid.,* August 28, 1829, January 26, 1831, April 6, 1831. Citizens in neighboring Greene County similarly objected to religious efforts to ban the transportation of the United States mail on Sunday, and resolved that "the advocates of that measure, are actuated by an inordinate *ambition,* by a *thirst for power,* and by a *disposition,* to UNITE CHURCH and STATE, a measure to be depricated [*sic*] as one of the greatest evils, to which a free country can be subjected"; *ibid.,* February 2, 1831.

122. Jacob Gibson Jr., to ASSU, September 14, 1831, ASSU Papers. For a brief summary of the opposition to the benevolent empire in Huntsville, see Betty Fladeland, *James Gillespie Birney: Slaveholder to Abolitionist* (Ithaca, 1955), 33–35.

Tuscaloosa Inquirer, believed that the piece unfairly degraded Tuscaloosa's Sunday schools and "should meet with rebuke of every man who has a just regard for the ordinary decencies of life, and much more of those who cherish a feeling of interest in the cause of religion and its benevolent institutions." Walker proclaimed the essay a libel upon the community and refused to "pollute our columns by extracts from it to show how unfit it may be" lest it "find its way to the family circle." Sunday schools were embraced by the entire community, asserted Walker, as "there is scarcely a parent that has a child old enough, who does not send it to one or the other of these schools." The *Intelligencer* article was an attack upon these people, and upon the young men and women who conducted the Sunday schools. Walker suggested that Wiley change his ways: "If the editor of the Intelligencer instead of indulging, amid the fumes of wine, his feelings of party animosity on the fourth of July last, had attended the Sunday School Celebration, he would have scarcely charged ministers with a want of patriotism. If he had witnessed attentively the interesting and impressive manner in which the principles of pure patriotism were instilled into the tender swelling hearts of an hundred little hearers, it might have greatly increased his sleader [*sic*] stock of the article."[123]

Of course, Wiley was unwilling to take such abuse passively and proposed that his rival's defense of Sabbath schools was motivated by self-promotion.[124] Nevertheless, not all of the *Intelligencer*'s readership was pleased with its anti-benevolent position. "W." (possibly ASSU agent William Williams) was more conciliatory than the *Inquirer,* as he doubted that Wiley desired to use his press to oppose "an institution so manifestly conducive to the intellectual, the moral and religious improvement of the community." Yet W. feared that the republication of the *Whig* article might possibly serve to "diminish the zeal of some, and to prejudice the minds of many, in regard to Sabbath School operations and efforts." Further, he denied that Sunday schools were "designed to subject

123. *Alabama State Intelligencer,* August 27, 1831, as quoted in Tuscaloosa *Inquirer,* September 8, 1831; Tuscaloosa *Inquirer,* September 8, 1831. Unfortunately for Walker, he failed to internalize the Sabbath school precepts he so zealously advocated, and was later caught pocketing funds belonging to the Bank of Alabama; Thornton, *Politics and Power,* 76.

124. *Alabama State Intelligencer,* September 10, 1831. Walker was briefly an editor of the *Intelligencer,* but sold his interest to Wiley in 1830. Personal and political disagreements later erupted, which were continued through editorial columns after Walker began publishing the *Inquirer.* Robert McKenzie, "Newspapers and Newspaper Men During Tuscaloosa's Capital Period, 1826–1846," *Alabama Historical Quarterly,* XLIV (Fall–Winter 1982), 193–94.

people to the dominion of the priesthood" or that they were sectarian enterprises. On the contrary, he maintained, the ASSU did not enjoin its schools to study catechisms or any book aside from the Bible, as its teachers aimed solely "to excite and assist the youthful mind to examine for itself the word of God."[125]

William Sayre of Montgomery was saddened by the continued opposition to benevolence. He wrote to James Birney in 1833 that the "party Politics in this region you are well aware, is not friendly enough to any enterprise of benevolence . . . indeed you may have seen in your own place [Huntsville], attacks on Missionary efforts, and in Tuscaloosa, a disclaimer, to every thing of that kind and kindred institutions." Sayre also echoed a charge made by the *Intelligencer* two years earlier, stating that he believed the disparagement of benevolence was the same as that expressed toward anything "which is not considered entirely southern." Two years later, "Sophitus" wrote that despite the "outstanding reports of Missionary Societies, who assure us that the advantages of the Christian divinity are preached and taught to all the nations of the world, by the holy bands of pilgrims emanating from their zeal in philanthropy," such efforts were mere "Quackery," as "but a slight attention to the modern travels proves to us that not more than one-half of all our race know that such a religion exists." But by this time, essays cynical toward benevolence had become scarce in Tuscaloosa newspapers. Concurrently, ASSU agent Cox reported to the national society that resistance to Sunday schools in Alabama had diminished. Unfortunately, it is difficult to specify conclusively the values that these opponents of reform espoused, and impossible to know who they were, since they wrote under pseudonyms. Although they were not necessarily nonbelievers in Christianity, their fear of evangelical ascendancy implies that they were skeptics, religious pluralists, or dissenters—views that were better tolerated, in the Old South, prior to the proliferation of revivals.[126]

125. *Alabama State Intelligencer,* September 10, 1831.
126. William Sayre to James Birney, August 7, 1833, in Dwight L. Dumond, ed., *Letters of James Gillespie Birney* [hereinafter cited as *Birney Letters*] (2 vols.; New York, 1938), I, 83; *Alabama Intelligencer and State Rights Expositor,* October 24, 1835 ("Sophitus" also labeled temperance as "quackery"); Thomas W. Cox to ASSU, November 30, 1834, in ASSU papers. Post, *Popular Freethought in America,* 16–33; Eaton, *Freedom-of-Thought Struggle,* 10–18, 300–16; Sonne, *Liberal Kentucky, passim.* For a discussion of religious "populists" who opposed the benevolent efforts of what they perceived to be an educated and respectable Calvinist establishment, see Nathan O. Hatch, *The Democratization of American Christianity* (New Haven, 1989), especially 170–79.

Although a few opponents raised eyebrows at benevolence by asserting that these causes were not indigenous to the South, this charge was not the central focus of their arguments, which instead were based largely on the condescending character of evangelicals. In addition to anticlerical complaints voiced against the benevolent empire, sectarian animosities often frustrated its devotees. Despite the nonsectarian proclamations of the national benevolent associations, many Methodists in particular felt that the Bible, tract, and Sunday-school societies were Presbyterian plots attired in interdenominational clothing. Not only did some Methodists fear Calvinist indoctrination, but they also suspected that Presbyterians, through these societies—in particular the ASSU—were bent on political power. Soon after arriving in Tuscaloosa, William Williams "rec'd the painful information" that some of the Methodist clergy in Alabama "had adopted the common infidel objections against the Union as a 'Money making institution,' 'tending to a union of church & state &c.'" Williams was further told that he was viewed with suspicion, being regarded by some as a "zealous young man, not fully initiated into the secret plans of those who were behind the scenes."[127]

When Williams and others formed the interdenominational Tuscaloosa Sunday School Union, he regretted that "our Methodist brethren do not enter cordially into our efforts." Williams believed that Robert L. Walker, Tuscaloosa's Methodist Episcopal pastor, was "an excellent, & truly pious man" who "for reasons not explained to me utterly declined cooperating with the American Union or with our County S. S. Union, consenting however to unite with us in the SS Concert, which we regularly observe."[128] The succeeding Methodist pastor in Tuscaloosa was even more hostile to the ASSU, although not to benevolent efforts conducted by his own denomination. Williams reported that this pastor

> openly denounces the Amer. S. S. Union, Tract Socy & even the Bible Socy as
> dangerous Presbyterian Plots & as one argument, asked why we agents & mis-

127. William H. Williams to ASSU, December 23, 1830, in ASSU Papers. See also the defense of the ASSU and denial that the Presbyterians were intent upon political domination in the letters by "W."—possibly authored by Williams—in the *Alabama State Intelligencer*, September 10, 17, 1831.

128. William H. Williams to ASSU, January 31, March 21, 1832, both in ASSU Papers. Little is known of the Sabbath school concert, save that it was a monthly interdenominational meeting of Tuscaloosa's evangelicals. See Elvina S. Searcy Diary, November 9, 1835, James T. Searcy Papers, ADAH.

sionaries were all Presbyterians, stating that they in many instances had abused & misrepresented other denominations. When I replied that the Union were [*sic*] desirous to engage missionaries of other denominations, & that I had been specially requested to find suitable men Methodists or Baptists, he admitted candidly & fully that Methodists would not & ought not to engage in behalf of the Union, being pledged as he asserted to their own Book concern.[129]

The following year, an ASSU agent traveling through Tuscaloosa appealed for funds at the Baptist and Presbyterian churches, but not the Methodist church. A decade later, however, any animosity seems to have subsided, as Tuscaloosa's Methodists in 1846 eagerly joined with local Baptists and Presbyterians to form the Union Sabbath School Missionary Society. The society was a cooperative effort in which "the pecuniary contributions of each Sabbath School are kept distinct, and under its own control—so that there are, in fact, three societies confederated for certain specified objects"; these "objects" were an annual meeting on the fourth of July and quarterly meetings held during a "convenient part of the Lord's day."[130]

In 1851, Alabama's Methodist governor, Henry Collier, joined with Basil Manly and Greensboro Female Seminary president Columbus Franklin Sturgis, both Baptists, to form the presiding quorum of the Central Alabama Sunday School Union. The society heartily endorsed the publications of the ASSU because they were "suited to the tastes and acquirements—to the general cast and quality of mind of our youthful population."[131] This increased willingness

129. William H. Williams to ASSU, March 27, 1834, in ASSU Papers. Fear of Presbyterian influence in Tuscaloosa extended beyond benevolent efforts into the affairs of the University of Alabama: "One of the trustees Mr. [David] Hubbard, has already started the favorite cry of presbyterian influence & I am sorry, my dear Sir, to say that I know it to be encouraged by our Head [University of Alabama president Alva Woods, a Baptist]." Henry Tutwiler to James Birney, January 26, 1833, James Gillespie Birney Papers, William L. Clements Library, University of Michigan.

130. Simpson Shepherd to ASSU, July 15, 1835, in ASSU Papers; *Independent Monitor,* July 1, 8, 14, August 11, 1846. After the Methodist schism of 1844, southern Methodists avoided the publications of the northern Methodist Book Concern and temporarily relied upon the ASSU to supply their denominational Sunday schools. Many southern Methodists afterwards spoke with high regard of the ASSU. Kuykendall, *Southern Enterprize,* 124.

131. *Independent Monitor,* June 19, 1851. The Montgomery *Daily Alabama Journal* (June 20, 1851) welcomed the establishment of this association: "We are glad to see that in the midst of political oscillations, convulsions of governments, turmoil and strife, the cause of Sabbath reform, morality and the church is not forgotten." The editor of the *South Western Baptist,* July 31, 1850,

of Methodists to cooperate in interdenominational efforts probably stemmed from Methodism's shift from an insurgent religious movement into the Protestant mainstream. Early Methodists and other opponents of the Calvinist establishment viewed themselves as "self-consciously provincial, fiercely independent, and culturally marginal." Such a self-portrait must have eroded considerably by the time that one of their own was elected governor of Alabama.[132]

Baptists in Tuscaloosa were generally favorable to Sunday schools. William Williams' first impression of Baptist sentiments in this regard was positive. He encountered several Baptists who were "very zealous in behalf of the Amer Union," although he heard rumors of one who had preached against it. As noted previously, a number of Tuscaloosa Baptists played an active role in ASSU activities, and several Baptist-run Sabbath schools in Tuscaloosa County were affiliated with the ASSU. Additionally, Tuscaloosa's Baptists strongly endorsed the Union Sabbath School Missionary Society, as they were convinced that such interdenominational endeavors could foster "the principle of systematic benevolence on the part of the youth" and "bids fair to promote, in some degree the cause of Christian Union." During the 1850s, the town's Baptists placed an even greater stress on Sunday schools and spent over $150 for the establishment of a Sabbath-school library. Furthermore, the Alabama Baptist Convention and most of its constituent associations, including the Tuscaloosa Baptist Association, avidly promoted Sunday schools, along with the circulation of Bibles and tracts, as a means of bringing religion to the numerous rural Alabamians who lived beyond convenient access to a church. In 1842 a committee of the Alabama Baptist State Convention urged that "some systematic measures be adopted . . . by which Sabbath Schools may be established in every church and neighborhood in the state." Willis Burns, appointed by the Tuscaloosa Baptist Association's committee on destitution to "seek out destitute neighborhoods and establish preaching places," spent 1850 trying to take religion to the rural churchless through preaching, Bible and

---

however, was skeptical of such interdenominational efforts, as he had "not generally found such measures [to] be successful." This Sabbath-school union—which was sometimes also referred to as the Alabama Central Sunday School Union—was successful as antebellum voluntary associations went, in that it was still in existence over three years later. *South Western Baptist* (Marion, Ala.), April 21, August 4, 1852; *Independent Monitor*, December 14, 1854.

132. Hatch, *Democratization of American Christianity*, 170–71, 193, 201–206; Roger Robins, "Vernacular American Landscape: Methodists, Camp Meetings, and Social Respectability," *Religion and American Culture*, IV (Summer 1994), 165–91.

tract distribution, visitation, and organizing Sunday schools. The association also endeavored to support the growth of Sabbath schools through the establishment of a Sunday-school depository in Tuscaloosa, and later requested that every minister in the association "do all he can to aid in the establishment and support of Sabbath Schools and prayer meetings" as a means to remedy the "great coldness and want of spirituality" in many congregations. During the 1850s high-ranking Alabama Baptists not only promoted their own denominational schools, but they continued to praise the ASSU. In 1854, the editor of the *Southwestern Baptist* was "sorry to learn that the American Sunday School Union is straitened for funds. This should not be. A cause so excellent should never be allowed to halt for want of means."[133]

In spite of this strong Baptist support of Sunday schools and other benevolent activities, the most persistent opponents of these enterprises in Alabama were a faction often designated as Antimission Baptists. Also known as Hardshell or Primitive Baptists, they generally inhabited remote corners of the South, although Antimission enclaves existed in the North too. Fiercely committed to congregational worship, many of these Baptists felt threatened by national evangelical societies—headquartered in Philadelphia or Manhattan—that seemed to endow religion with a commercial spirit and a centralized framework. Antimission Baptists feared that benevolent associations would destroy the republican character of their churches, as benevolent causes governed from afar could appeal directly to church members for aid, without the active encouragement of the minister or the Baptist Association to which they belonged. Primitive Baptists in many respects were similar to orthodox Jacksonians; their sectarian fears of benevolent societies mirrored the Democratic concern about a national bank. As Bertram Wyatt-Brown has noted, Hardshells were frightened that through these societies, "community control would

133. Williams to ASSU, December 23, 1830; *Minutes of the Nineteenth Anniversary of the Baptist State Convention of Alabama* (N.p., 1842[?]), 6; Records of the First Baptist Church of Tuscaloosa, 1842–1867, n.d. [July or August 1846], 37; Basil Manly to Jane Cameron May 1, 1851, in Manly Family Papers; Records of the First Baptist Church of Tuscaloosa, 1842–1867, September 12, 1853, p. 132, January 15, 1854, p. 137, February 15, 1858, p. 212, October 15, 1860, p. 252; *Minutes of the Eighteenth Annual Session of the Tuscaloosa Baptist Association* (Tuscaloosa, 1850), 14. See also *South Western Baptist* (Marion, Ala.), October 21, 1853; *Minutes of the Twenty-first Annual Session of the Tuscaloosa Baptist Association* (Tuscaloosa, 1853), 7; *Minutes of the Twenty-second Annual Session of the Tuscaloosa Baptist Association* (Tuscaloosa, 1854), 4–5; *Minutes of the Twenty-fourth Annual Session of the Tuscaloosa Baptist Association* (Tuscaloosa, 1856), 3; *South Western Baptist* (Marion, Ala.) November 9, 1854.

diminish, while alien, unreachable powers in distant cities imposed a new tyranny. [Antimission Baptists] had deep forebodings that a new aristocracy was
emerging in America, one that was subverting religious action to a spirit of
commercial, northern imperialism."[134]

Among ASSU agents who labored in parts of Alabama where Antimis-
sionism was dominant, it often seemed as though few, if any, Baptists endorsed
their work. Thomas Manning believed that the Baptists were "the greatest opposers" to the ASSU, and noted that the "apostolic Baptists" opposed benevolent efforts of all kinds.[135] Another agent, Thomas Maddin, similarly claimed
that the entire religious community, with the exception of the Baptists, endorsed the Sunday schools. Reuben Dodson, a Baptist minister in rural Tuscaloosa County, lamented neighboring Fayette County's extraordinary "destitution of efficient preaching; where the greater part of the Baptists oppose all the
benevolent operations of the day."[136]

Antimission Baptists were strongest in the poorest and most rural sectors of
Alabama. As Tuscaloosa was Alabama's third largest city (after Mobile and
Montgomery), the site of the state capital from 1826 to 1847, and the home of
the University of Alabama, much of Tuscaloosa County had a degree of urban-
ity that muted the Hardshell appeal. In the remote corners of the county, however, the Antimission Baptists held some sway. Although Primitive and Missionary Baptists often formed separate congregations and associations, thus
virtually functioning as different denominations, often individuals of both in-
clinations worshiped side by side. For example, in 1837 it was reported that the
churches of the Tuscaloosa Association were "divided in sentiment on benevolent operations." A few years later at the Big Creek Baptist Church in rural

134. T. Scott Miyakawa, *Protestants and Pioneers: Individualism and Conformity on the American Frontier* (Chicago, 1964), 144–58; Posey, *Frontier Religion*, 59–64; Kuykendall, *Southern Enterprize*, 43–46, 83–84, 109; Byron Cecil Lambert, "The Rise of the Anti-mission Baptists: Sources
and Leaders, 1800–1840" (Ph.D. dissertation, University of Chicago, 1957); Wyatt-Brown, "Antimission Movement in the Jacksonian South," 510. For a discussion of the literature, see Richard F.
Nation, "Primitive Baptists and the Anti-Missionary Movement" (Seminar Paper, University of
Michigan, 1990). Although precise figures are unavailable, one scholar has estimated that there
were 20,000 Primitive Baptists in Alabama in 1855. Dorman, *Party Politics in Alabama*, 110.

135. Thomas Manning to ASSU, March 17, 1831, in ASSU Papers; one group of Antimission
Baptists claimed apostolic descent; Posey, *Frontier Religion*, 63.

136. Thomas Maddin to ASSU, May 30, 1832, in ASSU Papers; *Minutes of the Seventeenth
Annual Session of the Tuscaloosa Baptist Association, held at the Mt. Moriah Meeting-House, Bibb Co.,
Ala.* (Tuscaloosa, 1849), 22–23.

Tuscaloosa County, one member voiced his reservations about benevolent efforts and proposed that the following resolution be made a part of the church's rules of decorum: "The church shall not become a member of any benevolent or missionary society only by a unanimous vote, and this Article shall not be repealed until the consideration of a second conference." Following "a few debates" the resolution was tabled until the next meeting. After a month of thinking things over, the church reconsidered the proposed article and unanimously agreed to table it permanently.[137]

Occasionally, however, Antimission strength was more pronounced. In 1835 a prospectus appeared in Tuscaloosa's newspapers announcing the publication of *The Disciple,* which would "carefully avoid any interference in politics, and will countenance none of the y'clept benevolent societies of the day," and would consider only "the undefiled, unmixed religion of Christ a subject of importance, meriting its undivided attention." It does not appear that *The Disciple* was ever published, but the extent of Antimission influence in Tuscaloosa County can also be ascertained from the example of Colin Finnell. Finnell was an early advocate of benevolence—in 1824 he was the corresponding secretary of the Baptist Missionary Society of Tuscaloosa County. Twenty years later, however, at the annual meeting of the Tuscaloosa Baptist Association, he opposed a resolution that called for a missionary sermon and the collection of money for foreign missions at the next yearly meeting. According to Basil Manly, Finnell feared that the resolution would harm the feelings of "precious brethren" if it passed—although Finnell felt no animus against missions himself and told Manly that he would rejoice in the measure if no one in the association took offense.[138] The following year, a Hardshell resolution rejecting the

---

137. *Minutes of the Fourteenth Anniversary of the Baptist State Convention of Alabama,* 7; Big Creek Baptist Church Minutes, April 8, 1843, in Hoole Special Collections (photostat). On August 9, 1856, the Big Creek church appointed two members as "a committee to take up a collection for domestic mission." See also *South Western Baptist* (Marion, Ala.), October 29, 1851; Charles E. Boyd, *At Liberty on Bear Creek, 1835–1985: A 150th Anniversary of Liberty Baptist Church, Hagler, Alabama* (Birmingham, 1984), 38.

138. *Flag of the Union,* October 24, 1835; *American Mirror,* July 10, 1824; Basil Manly to Basil Manly Jr., September 23, 1844, in Manly Family Papers. Basil Manly, a devoted advocate of Baptist missions, expressed his anti-Hardshell sentiments on this occasion: "I know that it is now 30 years since the subject was first generally agitated in this country—& that it is time every body had made up his mind. If they were really an anti-mission body, better say so and let the discordant elements of which we are composed work themselves into more congenial Associations." Manly then recounted a speech made at the Association by a young man from Pickens County:

annual missionary sermon was narrowly passed by the Tuscaloosa Baptist Association, twenty-seven to twenty-three, while many delegates were not present. Taken by surprise, the anti-Hardshell forces gathered their delegates and shortly afterward overturned the resolution by adding an article to the association's constitution "making the Asso^n to the fullest extent a missionary body"; the vote was fifty-one to nineteen.[139]

Recognizing the hostility of some Baptists, a number of Tuscaloosa's leading Sunday-school advocates from the three evangelical denominations recommended Thomas Cox as a full-time ASSU agent in 1834. William Williams praised Cox as "much needed in our state, & on account of the great number of Baptists, in some degree prejudiced against benevolent operations, [he] would be especially useful." Furthermore, Cox was said to have many acquaintances who could be enlisted in the cause: "As a Baptist & as a Southern man he would encounter less prejudice than many others." Williams attributed Cox's success as Alabama's ASSU agent to the fact that he possessed "the confidence of his own denomination, which is the most numerous in this portion of the state." Thus Cox could "successfully meet their objections & remove their indifference in regard to the cause of Sabbath Schools."[140]

During the antebellum years, white evangelical Tuscaloosans used Bible societies, tract societies, and Sunday schools—in addition to revivals—to combat vice and irreligion, and to reshape their community and country. Although activists in the benevolent empire were principally concerned with religious indoctrination, they also aimed to establish a more orderly society—a hoped-for society that was, incidentally, congruent with the vision of the American Whigs. Far from being viewed as a threat to the peculiar institution, proponents of benevolence overwhelmingly came from the ranks of slaveholders.

"He said that the missionaries harrass [*sic*] us with the cry of nations perishing without the Gospel, but that none had ventured to name one that was destitute: That God is every where, Jesus every where, and where Jesus is the gospel is preached in its purity and men can be saved. That there is no nation without the Gospel—&c. &c. I could scarcely believe the testimony of my senses; that a man 21 years cd. live in this good year of 1844, in the white settlements, & know no better. Such was the fact."

139. Basil Manly to Basil Manly Jr., September 25, 1845, in Manly Family Papers.

140. William H. Williams *et al.* to ASSU, June 1, 1834; Williams to ASSU, August 28, 1834, April 28, 1835, all ASSU Papers.

While opposition to evangelical benevolence did rear its head, for the most part such hostility was sectarian, coming initially from the Methodists and, more strongly—in the remote corners of Alabama, at least—from Antimission Baptists. But our examination of evangelical benevolence during the antebellum years is not yet complete. In the following chapter, we shall pursue this phenomenon in Washtenaw County, Michigan, and in the process will note the similarities and peculiarities of benevolence in both places.

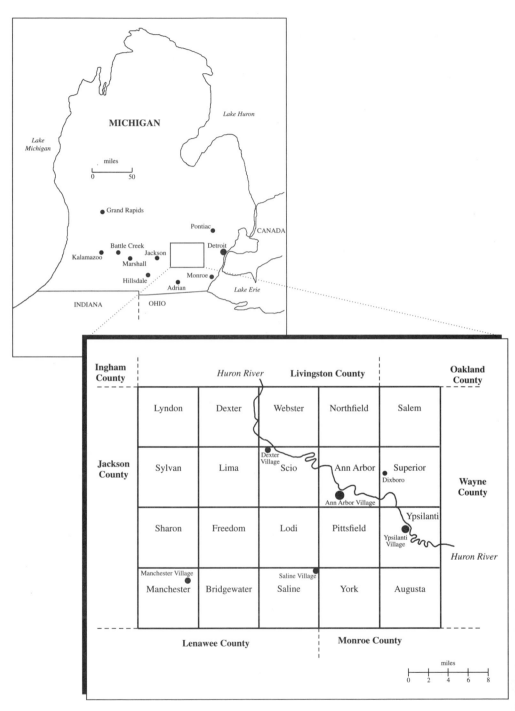

Washtenaw County, Michigan

2

Occasionally Overwhelmed by Abolitionists: Benevolence in Washtenaw County

Benevolent activity in Washtenaw County commenced shortly after the initial settlement by whites, and it was more pervasive than in Tuscaloosa County, Alabama. The foremost reason for this greater magnitude was that there were many more Presbyterians and Congregationalists in Washtenaw County than in Tuscaloosa County—in the former, there were twelve different "Presbygational" bodies prior to 1860, while in the latter there were but five Old School Presbyterian congregations.[1] Presbyterians and Congregationalists were far more animated in their support for the ostensibly nonsectarian projects of the benevolent empire than were the Baptists, Methodists, or Episcopalians, who often devoted greater attention to their own denominational benevolent concerns. Further, agents of the American Bible Society, the American Sunday School Union, and the American Tract Society were more likely to labor in Michigan than in Alabama, probably because they, like most of Michigan's settlers, were from New York and New England and felt comfortable among their fellows. Consequently, the story of these operations is filled with more successes in Washtenaw County than in Tuscaloosa

---

1. Social schedule of the 1850 census, Washtenaw County, Michigan Historical Collections, Bentley Library; social schedule of the 1850 census, Tuscaloosa County, ADAH. Although the published census and the manuscript social census also list six Cumberland Presbyterian congregations in addition to the five Old School bodies in Tuscaloosa County, local newspapers referred only to the congregation in the town of Tuscaloosa. There were no Congregational churches in Alabama in 1850; J. D. B. De Bow, *Statistical View of the United States . . . Being a Compendium of the Seventh Census* (Washington, D.C., 1854), 136.

County. Nevertheless, aside from the fact that abolitionists in Washtenaw occasionally attacked the leaders of national and local benevolent societies as being too concessionary to slaveholders, and accordingly broke away to form their own benevolent societies, benevolence in both places was, on balance, similar with respect to objectives and ideology. In both places the success of benevolence had as much to do with the health of the economy as with the zeal of its participants.

Similar to their allies in Tuscaloosa County, Washtenaw evangelicals promoted revivals, denounced the wickedness of unbelievers, endeavored to provide their fellow citizens with otherworldly salvation, and asserted that the widespread endorsement of benevolent enterprises would aid in the spread of market capitalism and provide Americans with prosperity. But Washtenaw evangelicals—undoubtedly due to the greater presence of Catholics in their midst—were more likely than Tuscaloosa activists to raise the ante in their crusades and proclaim that the preservation of America was at stake. Uniting their exertions was the conviction that unless Americans embraced the moral and religious agenda of evangelical Protestantism, the resultant proliferation of vice would fragment American society and prevent the establishment of a stable social order.

One measure of the greater strength of the benevolent empire in Washtenaw than in Tuscaloosa County was the lack of strident opposition in Washtenaw, even during the first years of benevolent activity. In county newspapers, there were few stabs at the efforts of evangelicals—even though, among themselves, evangelicals frequently lamented that the wickedness of county residents was a hindrance to their work. Support for evangelical programs was widespread. One piece of evidence that suggests the tolerance or acceptance of evangelical activity among Washtenaw residents is the backing given to Samuel W. Dexter, the Antimasonic Party candidate for territorial representative to Congress in 1831, the chief organizer behind Washtenaw County's first temperance society, proprietor of the Antimasonic *Western Emigrant,* and later president of the Washtenaw County Bible Society. Although Dexter lost the election, he carried Washtenaw County with 410 of 648 votes (63.3 percent)—indicating that most residents did not find his well-known moralism so objectionable as to prevent them from voting for him.[2] Indeed, some portions of the

2. *Western Emigrant,* December 30, 1829, February 17, June 2, 1830; *Emigrant,* July 20, 1831; Charles G. Clarke to the American Home Missionary Society, February 16, 1830, in American Home Missionary Society Papers, Bentley Library [hereinafter cited as AMHS Papers]; *History*

county were receptive to reform from the beginnings of white settlement. The Reverend Charles G. Clarke of Dexter village wrote in January 1830 that intemperance "is a vice scarcely known here." One modern scholar has called most of the eastern three-fifths of the county part of a "piety belt or 'burned-over district,'" reminiscent of western New York's famed "psychic highway" where many spiritual and reformist enthusiasms flourished during the first half of the nineteenth century.[3]

The mere fact that Samuel Dexter did well in the election, however, does not mean that there were not significant antievangelical forces in the county. Later, during the lifetime of the second party system, nonevangelicals—and assuredly antievangelicals—became an important constituency of the Democratic Party, and it is likely that many Washtenaw voters registered their protest against evangelical Whigs at the ballot box. In a few townships, most notably Northfield, Freedom, and Dexter—the latter place to be distinguished from the village of the same name—Democrats were always victorious by large margins, and doubtless these places' residents, who were mostly Irish or German Catholics, resented evangelicals or felt threatened by them. It is possible, however, that as recent immigrants they were either reluctant or too marginal to express publicly the opposition that was described in Tuscaloosa in chapter 1.[4]

For reasons that are not clear, newspapers in Washtenaw County did not

---

of Washtenaw County, 250. Dexter, a Methodist, later served as president of the Michigan State Temperance Society in 1843 and 1851 and vice-president of the Washtenaw County Temperance Society in 1835. He was a Free Soil candidate for Congress in 1852 and was described in 1854 as a man of "piety and leisure" who preached at revivals and to people living remote from churches: ABS *Annual Report,* XXX (1846), 147, XXXI (1847), 144; *Signal of Liberty,* March 6, 1843; *Washtenaw Whig,* November 19, 1851, *Michigan Whig,* February 12, 1835; *Washtenaw Whig,* November 24, 1852; *History of Washtenaw County,* 267–69; Journal of Judson D. Collins, August 14, 1845, in Bentley Library; Andrew Ten Brook comment dated June 29, 1854, in Andrew Ten Brook Papers, Bentley Library.

3. Charles G. Clarke to AHMS, January 27, 1830, January 4, 1836, both in AHMS Papers; Formisano, *Birth of Mass Political Parties,* 143–46; Cross, *Burned-Over District,* 3. Although Washtenaw's temperance partisans complained often about drinking among their fellow citizens, intemperance was not universal throughout the county. Clarke's comments about Webster Township were echoed in August 1844 by the Reverend Justin Marsh of Augusta, who reported that intoxicants were seldom used in his vicinity and that he had not seen a drunkard for at least a year. Justin Marsh to AHMS, September 25, 1844, in AHMS Papers.

4. Formisano, *Birth of Mass Political Parties,* 104–10, 139–40, 160–64, 180, 183; *History of Washtenaw County,* 642–43, 648–49, 657–67, 718–19, 1292–94.

celebrate revivals to the extent that their Tuscaloosa counterparts did. In fact, fewer revivals were reported in Washtenaw papers than in Tuscaloosa papers. Nevertheless, contemporary sources reveal that revivals in the northern county were ubiquitous. A few individuals publicly expressed reservations about these events. In 1838 an essayist in the *Michigan Argus* decried the excessive enthusiasm of revivals—a "disgraceful means to procure proselytes"—which resulted in neglected business, misspent time, "perversions of holy writ," and "constitutions undermined by an attendance upon religious services at all seasons and times"; he compared the "discordant cries and imploring agonies of the maniac and the victim of religious excitement" to the "lunatic asylums of the east." Two decades later, the *Local News and Advertiser* editorialized that the "unprecedented" revivals of the previous few months were rooted in the panic of 1857, and concluded that "the history of all nations shows the proneness of men in times of public distress or calamity to throw themselves into the arms of the prevailing religion as a shield and protection," while others "will fly to the bottle and to the gaming table." Convinced that many editors had uncritically welcomed the revivals, the *Local News* denounced the abundant fanaticism that it detected in protracted meetings. A writer to the Ann Arbor *Journal* immediately charged the *Local News* with reductionism but found the *Local News* ready to defend its position and provide examples of local revivalistic excesses.

Additionally, an episode in neighboring Jackson County suggests that opposition to benevolence may have existed in Washtenaw but gone unrecorded for posterity. In 1839 the "friends of humanity and reform" in Jackson planned a Sabbath-school, temperance, and abolition celebration but were harassed by opponents who printed a mock program that ridiculed the planned festivities. Prior to the event, rowdies removed the seats from the site, burned them in the town square, and subsequently placed a disinterred corpse in an *"upright position"* in a church pulpit. Although the festivities continued as scheduled, at the close of the celebration the "liquor outlaws" fired a cannon into the throng and covered them with smoke.[5] To be sure, if adverse sentiments regarding benevolence were muted in Washtenaw County, such was not the case with respect to temperance and abolition (opposition to these endeavors is discussed in chapters 4 and 6, respectively).

5. *Michigan Argus*, February 8, 1838; *Local News and Advertiser*, March 16, 1858; Ann Arbor *Journal*, March 17, 1858; *Local News and Advertiser*, March 30, 1858; George W. Clarke to Moses Smith, March 28, 1877, undated newspaper clipping in George W. Clarke Papers, Bentley Library; Formisano, *Birth of Mass Political Parties*, 163.

Although reaction against evangelical benevolence was not as strong in Washtenaw County as in Tuscaloosa County during the late 1820s and early 1830s, evangelicals in Washtenaw, like their Tuscaloosa counterparts, lamented the wicked behavior of their nonbelieving fellow settlers. One early Presbyterian settler wrote from Ann Arbor in 1827 that the high incidence of people living outside matrimony was of consternation to believers. Ira M. Wead testified that when he arrived in Ypsilanti in 1830, "wickedness prevailed; in the village it triumphed. The original settlers were those who knew no Sabbath and practically at least knew no God. . . . The tide of opposition to the truth soon rose high and threats of personal violence were dealt out with an unsparing hand." Some evangelicals were convinced that vice kept people from their message. William Jones wrote to the American Home Missionary Society that during his stay in Ypsilanti for a few months in 1832, his thoughts were "directed towards the moral wastes of this Territory." He mourned that "intemperance was within the church. . . . I need not say that vice in its varied forms prevailed. Nothing I felt could be done until the demon was expelled. . . . A besotted community must be reduced to sobriety before they can be made to listen to the Gospel calls." Five years later, Albert L. Payson felt that Ypsilanti had not improved; he wrote the ASSU that the place was "exceedingly wicked. Much infidelity much intemperance."[6]

Like their Tuscaloosa counterparts, Washtenaw County churches took positions against gambling, Masonry, dances, circuses, and the theater, and disciplined their members who indulged in these activities. Rather than devote their energies exclusively to combating these vices, evangelicals encouraged the observance of the Sabbath and promoted Sunday schools, Bible and tract societies, and revivals. Although the precise extent of revivalism in Washtenaw County is, as with Tuscaloosa County, not possible to measure, extant primary sources suggest that its influence was far-reaching. As we noted in chapter 1,

---

6. Ira M. Wead to AHMS, July 20, 1836, in AHMS Papers; unsigned letter (possibly Ezra Maynard), January 25, 1827, in Lorenzo Davis Papers, Bentley Library (see also Lucy W. Stow Morgan to her siblings in Connecticut, July 31, 1831, in Robert M. Warner, ed., "A Document of Pioneer Michigan Life: A Letter from Ann Arbor," *Michigan History*, XL [June 1956], 215–24); William Jones to AHMS, January 15, 1833, in AHMS Papers; A. L. Payson to ASSU, May 1, 1837, in ASSU Papers. In 1835, Ira M. Wead reported to the AHMS: "I should be glad to cheer your heart with the intelligence that God has visited his work [in Ypsilanti]. But this I cannot do. The Devil still reigns in this village and to a great degree in the surrounding country." Ira M. Wead to AHMS, October 15, 1835, in AHMS Papers.

both revivalism and reform urged people to cast aside hedonistic behavior, embrace self-restraint, and engage in individual introspection that often produced a greater moral dimension in their lives. Further, the underlying premise of nineteenth-century revivalism—that people play an active role in bringing about their own salvation, rather than being subject to the predestined judgments of an omnipotent God—led many to participate in the various movements described in this study, which were governed by the like assumption that earnest-minded citizens could work together in pursuit of the social and moral betterment of their society. And as in Tuscaloosa, revivals in Washtenaw County were seen by some to have an importance beyond otherworldly salvation. Just as proponents of the benevolent empire insisted that Bibles, tracts, and Sunday schools were essential for the maintenance of American liberty, Henry Root, a Presbyterian minister in Sylvan, was convinced that "it is only through revivals that this delightful[,] this beautiful country is to be kept from falling under the dominion of the Man of Sin." Contemporaries also acclaimed the social good wrought by revivals; in 1851 the *Michigan Argus* praised a revival at the Ann Arbor Baptist Church that had caused several reformed thieves to return goods that they had confiscated. The Reverend Silas Woodbury of Manchester was pleased that the young people of his congregation were able "since our last revival to control the popular amusements of the day," while in 1850, Albert Payson, the American Tract Society's agent for Michigan, hoped that "the recent revivals of religion—will prepare the way for more efficient benevolent arrangements." Others reported that revivals were a consequence of virtuous living; both William Jones of Ypsilanti in 1830 and the Washtenaw Presbytery in 1842 remarked that revivals often commenced among those who had previously embraced temperance.[7]

Unlike Tuscaloosa County, Washtenaw had been the site of revivals from the beginning of white settlement. In fact, Methodists began holding camp meetings in adjacent Wayne County in 1822, prior to Washtenaw County's first influx of white pioneers in 1823. In 1828, William Page reported that nine members had been added to the Ann Arbor Presbyterian Church during a recent "refreshing season," and in 1830 the Reverend Charles G. Clarke of Dexter village and the Reverend William Jones of Ypsilanti both reported revivals in

7. Quist, "Social and Moral Reform," 298–99, 377–78; Henry Root to AHMS, December 23, 1835, in AHMS Papers; *Michigan Argus,* April 23, 1851; Silas Woodbury to AHMS, July 13, 1842, in AHMS Papers; ATS (New York) *Annual Report,* XXV (1850), 61; William Jones to AHMS, May 24, 1830, in AHMS Papers; *Michigan State Journal,* June 29, 1842.

their midst. Oren C. Thompson recalled that "protracted meetings were very common in the Territory in 1831 and 1832," and he compared these gatherings to the "great revival" in New York that was occurring simultaneously. Little is known of these early revivals and camp meetings. Contemporaries usually noted only their occurrence and the number of converts. Alexis de Tocqueville, however, left a description of a Methodist camp meeting related to him in 1831 by Amasa Bagley of Pontiac, Michigan:

> Almost every summer, it is true, some Methodist preachers come to make a tour of the new settlements. The noise of their arrival spreads with unbelievable rapidity from cabin to cabin: it's the great news of the day. At the date set, the emigrant, his wife and children set out by scarcely cleared forest trails toward the indicated meeting-place. They come from fifty miles around. It's not in a church that the faithful gather, but in the open air, under the forest foliage. A pulpit of badly squared logs, great trees felled for seats, such are the ornaments of this rustic temple. The pioneers and their families camp in the surrounding woods. It's there that, during three days and three nights, the crowd gives itself over to almost uninterrupted religious exercises. You must see with what ardour these men surrender themselves to prayer, with what attention they listen to the solemn voice of the preacher. It's in the wilderness that people show themselves almost starved for religion.[8]

Throughout the antebellum years, ministers supported by the American Home Missionary Society reported whether the season's revival had been successful and how many had been converted. In 1831, Ira Wead wrote that a heightened religious feeling in Ypsilanti had resulted in a four-day revival with forty to fifty converts. A year and a half later, John Beach noted that many of the sixty-three recent additions to the Ann Arbor church had ensued from a revival. The following year, Wead revealed that in Ypsilanti "there has been a deeper interest manifested on the subject of religion for the last four or five weeks than I have seen for the last two years. . . . Some have indulged the hope of having met with the great change which results in everlasting life . . . and we

8. Margaret Burnham Macmillan, *The Methodist Church in Michigan: The Nineteenth Century* (Grand Rapids, 1967), 54–55, 60; William Page to AHMS, July 9, 1828, Charles G. Clarke to AHMS, May 3, December 30, 1830, William Jones to AHMS, May 24, 1830, all in AHMS Papers; O. C. Thompson, "Observations and Experiences in Michigan Forty Years Ago," *Michigan Pioneer and Historical Collections*, I (1877), 401–402; George Wilson Pierson, ed., *Tocqueville in America* (abridged ed.; Gloucester, Mass., 1969), 163, 166.

are hoping for a general revival." He added that such meetings were becoming widespread: "One recently holden in Ann Arbor has resulted in good. Another is to commence in Saline this week, and others are to follow." In 1835, John G. Kanouse of Saline was absent from his congregation for a month attending revivals in Ann Arbor and Ypsilanti, and in 1836, membership at the Sylvan Presbyterian Church doubled because of revivals. Ira Wead disclosed in this latter year that the sixty-nine additions in Ypsilanti surpassed his wildest expectations. Charles G. Clarke, who conducted a revival in 1837 that brought twenty-eight new members into the Webster Presbyterian Church, reported in 1839 that "in no year, since the settlement of this state, have so many precious revivals been enjoyed. . . . I believe more than twenty such revivals might be enumerated." And on it went. A revival later that winter in Manchester converted one hundred, while in Lima, thirty-four were added to the Presbyterian church in 1844.[9]

Although most of the extant primary sources discuss the aspirations of Presbyterian revivalists, Methodists and Baptists were at least as active, if not more so, in promoting revivals in Washtenaw County. In 1835, Methodists held a large camp meeting three miles east of Ann Arbor. It assembled people from Wayne, Washtenaw, and Livingston Counties and converted from sixty to seventy. Baptists throughout the county participated in revivals, but perhaps the most poignant evidence of Baptist dedication to this institution was the moaning of the *Michigan Christian Herald* from 1847 to 1849 over the paucity of revivals in the state and nationwide.[10]

9. Ira Wead to AHMS, September 28, 1831, John Beach to AHMS, January 31, 1833, Ira Wead to AHMS, October 7, 1834, John G. Kanouse to AHMS, January 5, 1836, William Page to AHMS, June 6, 1836, Ira Wead to AHMS, July 20, 1836, Charles G. Clarke to AHMS, October 3, 1837 and May 7, 1839, all in AHMS Papers; A. L. Payson to ASSU, August 17, 1840, in ASSU Papers; G. L. Foster to AHMS, June 25, 1844, in AHMS Papers.

10. On Methodist revivals in 1835: Records of the Ann Arbor Circuit, March 14, 1835, located in the Records of the First United Methodist Church of Ann Arbor, Bentley Library; *Michigan Argus,* April 30, 1835, June 18, 1835; Macmillan, *Methodist Church in Michigan,* 104. On other Methodist revivals: Justin Marsh to AHMS, March 21, 1842, February 3, 1845, both in AHMS Papers; *Michigan State Journal,* June 11, July 30, 1845; Collins Journal, August 14, 1845; *Family Favorite,* May 24, 1849. On Baptist revivals: John Kanouse to AHMS, January 19, 1842, Justin Marsh to AHMS, February 3, 1845, both in AHMS Papers; *Michigan Christian Herald,* March 1, 1847, March 9, 1849; *Michigan Argus,* April 23, 1851. For Baptist lamentations over the dearth of revivals: *Michigan Christian Herald,* January 4–June 7, 1847, *passim,* August 30, 1847, November 8, 1847–February 18, 1848, *passim,* July 14, 1848, January 19, 26, 1849.

Many revivals in Washtenaw County, though, were interdenominational efforts. In 1835, Methodists, Baptists, and Presbyterians in Dexter, Lima, and Sylvan cooperated in revivals, and a revival conducted by Ann Arbor's Methodists and Presbyterians during the winter of 1837–1838 resulted in 118 conversions for the Methodists alone. Joint efforts by the Methodists and Presbyterians occurred in Lodi in 1837, Dexter in 1841, and Ann Arbor again in 1846. Of the latter event, the *Signal of Liberty* reported in March that for "several weeks" the "attendance has been full, and the meetings continue with unabated interest." The Congregationalists, Baptists, and Methodists also engaged in collaborative revivals in 1849.[11]

Despite the difficulties in making significant comparisons between revivalism in Washtenaw and Tuscaloosa Counties—other than to remark that protracted meetings were held in both places and devotees uniformly praised the conversions that followed from them—comparing the operations of the national benevolent societies in these two counties holds greater promise. The functional pattern of the American Bible Society and its auxiliaries in Washtenaw County was similar to the cycle that we observed in Tuscaloosa County—namely, enthusiasm for the cause was frequently ephemeral, and auxiliaries commonly atrophied and fell into disuse. Also, the effort in both places was often hampered by economic downturns, as any shortage of cash made the purchase and circulation of the Scriptures exceedingly difficult. Of course, the ideology of the cause was similar in both counties, in that its advocates believed that social disorder could be remedied if only more people read the Good Book. But judging from the successes of the Washtenaw County Bible Society, the biblical destitution there was not as great as it was in Tuscaloosa County, for on several occasions Washtenaw proponents of the Bible successfully supplied it to all of the destitute households in the county.

Although William Page provided his congregation with Bible classes at Ann Arbor's Presbyterian church from 1827 to 1830, little was done in either Washtenaw County or the Territory of Michigan to circulate Bibles to those

11. Henry Root to AHMS, December 23, 1835, in AHMS Papers; Macmillan, *Methodist Church in Michigan*, 130; John G. Kanouse to AHMS, March 16, 1837, and Charles G. Clarke to AHMS, July 1, 1841, both in AHMS Papers; *Signal of Liberty*, March 23, 1843; Records of the First Congregational Church of Ann Arbor, November 18, 1849, p. 42, in Bentley Library.

without them. In the summer of 1830, the Reverend Charles G. Clarke, the Presbyterian pastor of Dexter village, wrote to the American Home Missionary Society that he and his coreligionist, the Reverend Ira Wead of Ypsilanti, were attempting to form a county Bible society and a Sunday-school union. A month later, the *Western Emigrant* announced that the Washtenaw County Bible Society would be formed at the Presbyterian church in Ann Arbor, and that it would assemble on the same day as the Washtenaw County Temperance Society. This new society set the ambitious goal of providing all the destitute families in the county with a Bible in less than six months. The idea caught on; Bible societies were formed in many of the county's townships, where local enthusiasts canvassed their fellow citizens and circulated Bibles. In November, Luther Shaw expected that the destitute should be supplied in Superior Township in two or three weeks, and in January 1831, Ira Wead wrote that the work for the county was almost finished. Five months later Charles G. Clarke reported that "all the destitute families" in Dexter village "who were willing to receive [a Bible] have been supplied."[12]

After completing its task, the Washtenaw Bible Society quickly atrophied. Although its annual joint meeting with the Washtenaw County Sunday School Union in late September 1831 was a revitalizing session in which "40 expressed submission to God," the fact that the county had been supplied must have made further meetings seem less urgent.[13] Perhaps in an effort to keep an interest in the cause, the society resolved in 1833 to raise $400 for the foreign distribution of the Scriptures. No such sum, however, was ever donated to the national society, and only $10 was submitted from the Washtenaw auxiliary to the national society from 1833 to 1842. Elsewhere in the territory, though, enthusiasm for the endeavor grew and new auxiliaries continued to be formed until 1838. By this time, Michigan, like Alabama, was distressed by depression, and virtually no money was submitted to the parent society for the next four

12. William Page to AHMS, May 1, July 23, October 21, 1827, January 25, 1828, Charles G. Clarke to AHMS, July 1, August 2, November 30, 1830, Luther Shaw to AHMS, November 11, 1830, Ira Wead to AHMS, January 26, 1831, all in AHMS Papers; ABS *Annual Report*, XIII (1829), 41, XIV (1830), 43; *Western Emigrant*, September 1, 8, 1830; *Emigrant*, February 23, 1831.

13. *Emigrant*, September 14, 1831; Charles G. Clarke to AHMS, October 1, 1831, in AHMS Papers. In 1834, Luther Shaw reported to the AHMS that the Macomb County Bible Society had provided Bibles to all the scripturally destitute in that county; Shaw to AHMS, February 15, 1834, as cited in William Warren Sweet, ed., *The Congregationalists* (Chicago, 1939), 313, Vol. III of Sweet, ed., *Religion on the American Frontier, 1783–1850: A Collection of Source Materials*, 4 vols.

years. Nevertheless, the Bible cause did not collapse in Michigan as completely as it did in Alabama. In 1838, the Bible Society of Michigan was formed in Detroit, and Marcus Lane of Ypsilanti was selected as one of four vice-presidents. This organization was still functioning in February 1839, when its annual meeting was addressed by some of the state's leading ecclesiastics and a member of the state senate.[14]

The Michigan society fared better than the Alabama society in part because the depository in Detroit contained "a good stock of books," which were probably made available on credit to the county auxiliaries in the southeast corner of the state. But despite the continued activity of the state society during the depression—at a time when the society was virtually nonexistent in Alabama—its operations were much curtailed, as the "deranged condition of the currency . . . has been peculiarly unfavorable."[15] One agent, the Reverend William Bacon, reported that these conditions had

> greatly discouraged and paralyzed the friends of the cause. Whenever the agent comes, he is told, with lamentable uniformity, that he can do little in the way of raising funds for his object. In these circumstances the work of systematic supply must be the more slow and difficult. There is difficulty both in raising the funds and in distributing the Bibles. The work of distribution must be done by voluntary agents or distributers [*sic*]; for when money is so scarce it is inexpedient to raise funds to pay an agent for distributing, and when the work is committed to voluntary agents it is apt to be much delayed and very imperfectly performed.

Bacon continued his lament by asserting that *"the destitution* of Michigan must still be very great"; he was aware of some neighborhoods where one-fifth of the households were without Bibles. The reasons behind the scarcity were varied. Some immigrants to Michigan had inadvertently left their Bibles behind; others had worn out their books or lost them since arriving. On the other hand, some settlers had left their former residences for the purpose "of getting away from religious restraints" and were naturally hostile to Bible enthusiasts. Finally, aside from the scarcity of currency, people who desired Bibles were often frustrated "because they knew not where Bibles could be found." In some

---

14. Ira Wead to AHMS, January 7, 1834, in AHMS Papers; Quist, "Social and Moral Reform," 559–61; ABS *Annual Report*, XVIII (1834), 15, XIX (1835), 37, XX (1836), 49, XXII (1838), 40; *Michigan State Journal*, November 15, 1838; *Michigan Argus*, March 7, 1839.

15. ABS *Annual Report*, XXIII (1839), 36, XXIV (1840), 45, XXV (1841), 37–38.

counties—particularly those distant from Detroit—"it is not known that there is a single Bible for sale."[16]

The moribund Washtenaw County Bible Society was resuscitated in January 1841 and selected the Reverend Charles G. Clarke of Webster as its president. Again, its primary object was to "supply every destitute family in this county with the Bible." The executive committee was empowered to appoint one person in each township to supervise the carrying out of this resolution. After the depression ended, Bible societies in Washtenaw County and throughout the state continued active until the Civil War. There were, however, a few downswings. The Washtenaw auxiliary held its annual meetings in 1843 and 1844, but its gathering in 1845 almost failed to materialize, as the society was "nearly dead." Early that year, Henry Colclazer reported that the other auxiliaries in the state were in an "embarrassed condition" due to the failure of the wheat crop; concurrently, "the state society [had] gone out of existence." Colclazer and others again breathed fire into the cause. In April 1845 they held a quarterly meeting of the Washtenaw County Bible Society. They hoped to have the county resupplied shortly, and their zeal again lasted sufficiently long to accomplish this object: nine months later, an agent reported that the "Washtenaw Co. B. S. is totally vigorous. The work of supplying the county is nearly completed." Further evidence of the effort's success comes from William Ruckman, an agent for the American Tract Society, who reported in 1849 that of the 1,465 families he visited in the county, only 98 lacked a Bible. Two years later, the Reverend J. A. Baughman told the American Bible Society that in Washtenaw County there were six townships "in which there is not a single family without a Bible, and three others in which there is but one destitute family in each." Statewide, American Tract Society colporteurs found that less than 5 percent of the Michigan families that they visited between 1851 and 1857 lacked Bibles.[17]

16. *Ibid.*, XXVI (1842), 44–46.

17. *Michigan State Journal,* January 12, 26, 1841; *Democratic Herald,* January 27, 1841; Quist, "Social and Moral Reform," 559–62; *Michigan State Journal,* December 21, 1842, December 27, 1843; *Michigan Argus,* December 27, 1843; Henry Colclazer to ABS, February 1, April 24, 1845, James V. Watson to the ABS, February 15, October 1, 1846, both in Agent Papers, ABS Archives, New York (see also D. R. Dixon to AHMS, June 9, 1843, in AHMS Papers); ATS (New York) *Annual Report,* XXIV (1849), 63; ABS *Annual Report,* XXXIII (1850), 48, XXXIV (1851), 45; Quist, "Social and Moral Reform," 563 (*cf.* 551); Nord, "Religious Reading and Readers," 258.

As had happened previously, the county auxiliary largely fell into inactivity after its success. But as antebellum Americans were an extremely geographically mobile people, the work of providing Bibles to the destitute could never be considered permanently finished. The urgency was undoubtedly compounded during the early 1850s by the increased immigration to America of Irish and German Catholics, many of whom lacked a Bible and were hostile to native Protestants who offered them one. Northern evangelicals were horrified by the growing strength of Catholicism in America during the middle decades of the nineteenth century. In this particular, devotees of benevolence in Washtenaw County differed from their Tuscaloosa counterparts, as Catholicism in Tuscaloosa and throughout most of the South was too insignificant a force to raise evangelical fears. For the most part, evangelical Protestants disliked the Catholics' toleration of alcohol consumption and failure to observe the Sabbath rigidly, feared that allegiance to the pope would make Catholics incapable of assimilation, and viewed the Catholic priesthood as nothing more than a network of agents bent on delivering America to the Vatican. One of the principal objectives of the benevolent empire was to subdue this power, and evangelicals were convinced that providing Bibles to Catholics would make clear to them their doctrinal and behavioral errors. Thus, in February 1854, the Bible auxiliary met for the first time in over three years, on which occasion speeches were presented and officers selected. More urgent was a meeting held on a Sunday evening the following October—several of Ann Arbor's Protestant congregations suspended their evening services and encouraged their members to attend. The object of the gathering was the formation of the Ann Arbor branch of the Washtenaw County Bible Society, which included in its purview Northfield Township—a Catholic stronghold—and the city and township of Ann Arbor. At this meeting, "statistics were presented showing the necessity for actions in order that the destitute may be supplied and a great good accomplished." In a short time, the two towns were divided into twenty-two districts; eighteen women and ten men canvassed more than 800 families and supplied 105 destitute households—although 50 others refused "any portion of the scriptures." After this start, women continued to play an active role in the Ann Arbor auxiliary, and by 1859 a number of women served on its executive committee.[18]

18. *Michigan Argus,* October 13, November 10, 1854; ABS *Annual Report,* XL (1856), 73. See

Concurrent with the initial establishment of the Washtenaw County auxiliary of the American Bible Society, several village auxiliaries of the American Tract Society were formed. In fact, the creation of a tract society was frequently one of the first objectives of a newly formed church in the years following the initial white settlement of Washtenaw County; often, ministers would mark the formation of the Female Tract Society as one of the benchmarks of strength of their new congregations. During the late 1820s and early 1830s, the operations of several Washtenaw County auxiliaries of the American Tract Society were noted in the society's *Annual Report*. In Dexter village, a male-led tract society and a female one had submitted $16 and $26, respectively, to the national society in donations and remittances for tracts by 1834, after which time they apparently ceased functioning. A female society in Ann Arbor had sent nearly $50 to the American Tract Society by 1834 but afterward became moribund; it rebounded briefly after 1843, selecting new officers and over the next five years submitting another $43.[19]

This limited activity of such local groups as the Ann Arbor Female Tract Society did not constitute the bulk of the American Tract Society's work in Washtenaw County. As noted in chapter 1, many auxiliaries stagnated with the onset of the 1837 depression, and after 1842 the national society utilized colporteurs to circulate its publications. The names of seven colporteurs who labored in Washtenaw County during the 1840s and 1850s appear in the *Annual Re-*

also ABS *Annual Report,* XXXIX (1855), 74, and *Michigan Argus,* January 21, 1859. In Ann Arbor in 1846, nativists ran a ticket of candidates in township elections and began publishing the Ann Arbor *American,* whose editor, Edward L. Fuller, maintained that both parties ignored nativist concerns. Nevertheless Whigs—and later, Republicans—courted nativist votes. On the nativist party in Ann Arbor: *Michigan Argus,* October 28, 1845, April 15, 1846; *Michigan State Journal,* April 1, 1846; *Signal of Liberty,* November 7, 1846; Ann Arbor *American,* January 22, 1847. On Whig and Republican appeal to nativists: *Michigan Argus,* February 26, 1835, April 8, 1846, October 5, 1851, March 28, 1856; *Michigan Whig and Washtenaw Democrat,* April 16, 30, May 14, August 6, 1835; Ypsilanti *Sentinel,* May 13, 1846, June 2, 1847. On political nativism in Michigan, see Formisano, *Birth of Mass Political Parties,* 71, 82, 87, 89–92, 249–53, 256–65, 330–31. For the larger picture in the North, see Tyler Anbinder, *Nativism and Slavery: The Northern Know Nothings and the Politics of the 1850s* (New York, 1992).

19. William Page to AHMS, May 1, July 23, October 21, 1827, October 7, 1828, May 19, December 15, 1829, Charles G. Clarke to AHMS, January 27, May 3, 1830, July 1, 1831, May 8, 1832, Luther Shaw to AHMS, November 11, 1830, Ira Wead to AHMS, April 11, 1831, January 7, 1834, all in AHMS Papers; ATS (New York) *Annual Report,* VIII (1833), 96, IX (1834), 97, XIX (1844), 147, XXV (1850), 159.

ports. Most noteworthy was the Reverend David R. Dixon, a Presbyterian pastor who canvassed much of Washtenaw County and occasionally worked in Livingston and Jackson Counties as well: he often visited more than two thousand families per year between 1843 and 1857. Although he was not a full-time colporteur, Dixon's duties took more time than simply depositing reading material; he and other colporteurs asked questions about people's religious practices and beliefs, and whether they owned a Bible and other religious books. An agent would also endeavor to pray with a family, attempt to sell or give away religious tracts that he was carrying, and hold public meetings. Besides partially supporting these seven colporteurs, the American Tract Society sent at least 111,450 pages of tracts to eleven other Washtenaw residents during the 1840s and 1850s. This material was provided for "gratuitous distribution," and since many of those who received shipments of tracts from the national society were ministers, the tracts were probably circulated among church members, who were then encouraged to distribute them among their friends and neighbors. There were also four ministers and two minister's wives in Washtenaw who were life members of the American Tract Society—granted upon the donation of $20 to the society—and two life directors of the tract society, which required a contribution of at least $50.[20]

20. On colporteurs: ATS (New York) *Annual Report*, XIX (1844), 67, XXIV (1849), 63, XXV (1850), 79, XXVI (1851), 84, XXVII (1852), 73, XXVIII (1853), 63–64, XXIX (1854), 76, XXX (1855), 54, XXXI (1856), 55, XXXIII (1858), 53, 60, 130–131, XXXV (1860), 55. On gratuitous distribution: *Ibid.*, XVIII (1843), 112, XX (1845), 131, XXV (1850), 49, XXVI (1851), 29, XXVII (1852), 31, XXX (1855), 27, XXXII (1857), 25, XXXIII (1858), 25, XXXV (1860), 30. On life members and directors: *Ibid.*, XIII (1838), 180, 200, XVII (1842), 116–17. John P. Cleaveland of Ann Arbor in 1837 and Mrs. E. M. Sheldon of Ypsilanti in 1860 and 1861 received for gratuitous distribution 23,900 and 42,405 pages of tracts, respectively, from the ATS, Boston (of which Cleaveland was a life member); ATS (Boston) *Annual Report*, XXII (1836), 95, XXIII (1837), 11, XLVI (1860), 23, XLVII (1861), 39. The Boston-based body of the ATS was formed in Andover in 1814 as the New England Religious Tract Society, and in 1823 changed its name to the American Tract Society. In 1825, when the ATS in New York was formed, the Boston body subordinated itself to the New York group yet maintained its separate organization. In 1843 the Boston society claimed that "only the best harmony" existed between the two bodies; the one in Boston centered its efforts in New England and united its resources with the one in New York "for the benefit of our whole country and the world." Although differences over slavery caused these bodies to separate on the eve of the Civil War, they reunited in 1878 under the common name and habitat of the New York society. ATS (Boston) *Annual Report*, XXIX (1843), 20; XLVI (1860), 6, 145–89; ATS (New York) *Annual Report*, XCVI (1921), 25; John R. McKivigan, *The War Against Proslavery Religion: Abolitionism and the Northern Churches, 1830–1865* (Ithaca, 1984), 122–23.

~~

As noted, the Washtenaw County Sunday School Union was formed concurrently with the county Bible society in September 1830. And just as the Bible society pledged to supply the destitute with Scriptures, so the Sunday-school union resolved at its first meeting to "have a Sun. School organized in every neighborhood through the county during the ensuing year." Despite frontier conditions, a scattered population, and "a host who through ignorance or wickedness opposed every attempt to instruct the rising generation into a knowledge of the Bible," a year later the union had fifteen schools and three hundred students. But Sabbath schools had existed in the county before the organization of the union. Miss Harriett Parsons taught a Sunday school in Pittsfield Township in 1825, and a school connected with the Presbyterian church in Ann Arbor was operating by 1827. Not much is known of these early Sabbath schools, save that they were sometimes mentioned in ministerial correspondence and occasionally placed notices in Ann Arbor's newspapers. Unlike in Tuscaloosa, there are no extant minutes of any Washtenaw County Sabbath school. But as in Tuscaloosa County, the cause in Washtenaw County did not progress in a linear fashion. The Reverend Charles G. Clarke of Dexter village wrote to the American Home Missionary Society that the greatest impediment to the success of Sabbath schools was a shortage of teachers, and he pleaded for pious people to emigrate westward. Winters also took their toll, especially in the early years: rural schools in particular curtailed or closed their operations during the cold months. Some schools died completely, as occurred in the settlement of Panama in Superior Township, where a Sabbath school organized in 1832 had vanished by 1837. Nevertheless, there appears to have been more coordination of Sabbath-school efforts in Michigan than in Alabama. During the 1830s the Michigan Sunday School Union provided a forum for Sabbath-school advocates to discuss their concerns, and its officers coordinated the efforts of the ASSU with the needs of schools in the state. By the late 1840s, agents called by the national society recruited part-time missionaries who, instead of laboring as statewide itinerants, concentrated their efforts into a single county or two.[21]

21. *First Annual Report of the Michigan Sunday School Union Society* (Detroit, 1832), 15–16 and *passim; History of Washtenaw County,* 1255; William Page to AHMS, May 1, 1827, Charles G. Clarke to AHMS, January 27, May 3, August 2, November 30, 1830, April 1, 1831, March 8, 1832, January 5, 1835, January 4, 1836, William Page to AHMS, January 25, 1830, Ira Wead to AHMS,

Although there were far fewer Antimission Baptists in Michigan than in Alabama, opposition to the efforts of Sunday-school agents was nonetheless present.[22] Proponents of Sabbath schools were sometimes imprecise about whether their adversaries were sectarian or irreligious, but generally the ASSU agents in both Michigan and Alabama complained about Methodists, as members of that denomination were initially adverse to the union, its representatives, and its publications. This opposition often caught ASSU agents by surprise. Unlike the Hardshell Baptists, Methodists embraced the institution of the Sabbath school as beneficial—in 1850, the Michigan Annual Conference passed a resolution declaring it a "censurable delinquency for any preacher having charge of a circuit or station, not to take up an annual collection in behalf of the Sabbath School Union of the M. E. Church." But Methodists were leery of the Presbyterian-dominated ASSU. Even as late as the 1830s, the Arminian Methodists continued to express animosity toward the Calvinist Presbyterians despite their occasional cooperation in revivals. The differences between these denominations extended beyond theological disparities: Methodists often viewed Presbyterians and the national union as pillars of the religious establishment against which they were rebelling.[23]

In Washtenaw County, Methodists organized Sabbath schools in Scio, Dexter, and Ann Arbor, all under the jurisdiction of the denomination's Ann Arbor Circuit. These Methodists, though, were clearly suspicious of interdenominational Sabbath schools, as they reported in 1834 that the school in Dexter was "now extinct in consequence of its injudicious amalgamation with another on the principle of union."[24] Albert Payson reported to the ASSU in

April 11, 1835, all in AHMS Papers; I. M. Wead to ASSU, March 27, 1832, Oren C. Thompson to ASSU, October 30, 1832, January 24, 1833, July 25, 1832, A. L. Payson to ASSU, January 3, June 24, December 23, 1837, W. E. Boardman to ASSU, June 9, 22, July 10, 24, November 8, 1849, all in ASSU Papers; Detroit *Journal and Courier*, August 12, 1835, as cited in Arthur Raymond Kooker, "The Antislavery Movement in Michigan, 1796–1840: A Study of Humanitarianism on an American Frontier" (Ph.D. dissertation, University of Michigan, 1941), 88–89.

22. Rev. John Booth, an exploring agent for the American Baptist Home Missionary Society, reported the presence of Antimission Baptists in Fairfield, Lenawee County, and noted that this was "the only section of the State where they have much influence." ABHMS *Annual Report*, XXVII (1849), 58–59.

23. Hatch, *Democratization of American Christianity*, 170–72; Macmillan, *Methodist Church in Michigan*, 47; *Family Favorite and Temperance Journal*, I (October 1850), 235.

24. Church Records for the Ann Arbor Circuit, June 28, 1834, October 18, 31, June 28, 1838, in Records of the First United Methodist Church of Ann Arbor, Bentley Library. In 1827, Detroit

1837 that he had always endeavored to form schools that embraced all the families in a town, "setting aside all names and creeds." Despite his labors to convey this impression, he claimed that Methodists generally opposed the union and refused to send their children to a school that had been visited by an agent or had ASSU books in its library. One Methodist in Macomb County told Payson that he felt no ill will toward Payson, but that if Payson visited a joint Methodist/Presbyterian school there, the Methodists would "break it up & then we will have none." Because of such hostility, Payson felt that separate denominational schools were best, even though he preferred that a school align with the ASSU. In the fall of 1837, the Michigan Annual Conference of the Methodist Episcopal Church passed a resolution explicitly asking its members not to work with the ASSU or any of its agents. Although the Annual Conference had no objection to occasional visits by agents such as Payson, it preferred its own books to those of the national union and did "not want the ag't to have the general oversight, to receive reports, & c." But as was the case in Tuscaloosa, Methodists soon shed much of their antagonism toward Calvinists. By the mid-1840s, Independence Day in Ann Arbor, Ypsilanti, and other southeastern Michigan communities was celebrated by large gatherings of Sunday-school children, and Methodists were always a part of such festivities. Baptists also established their own Sunday schools, but these were often aligned with the ASSU.[25]

Contemporaries asserted and scholars have long recognized that these two benevolent efforts—to establish Sunday schools and to circulate Bibles and tracts—had not only similar agendas, but often the same supporters. Gilbert Hobbs Barnes proposed in his 1933 work *The Antislavery Impulse, 1830–1844* that the leadership of the national benevolent societies "was exercised through

Methodists separated from a preexisting union Sabbath school and formed their own denominational school. Macmillan, *Methodist Church in Michigan*, 75–76.

25. Macmillan, *Methodist Church in Michigan*, 128; *Michigan State Journal*, June 14, July 19, 1843; *Michigan Argus*, July 17, 1844, July 10, 1850, August 7, 1857; *First Annual Report of the Michigan Sunday School Union*, 14; Oren C. Thompson to ASSU, July 25, 1832, A. L. Payson to ASSU, March 15, July 25, December 26, 1837 (see also Payson to ASSU, October 10, 1837), all in ASSU Papers; Detroit *Journal and Courier*, August 12, 1835, as cited in Kooker, "Antislavery Movement in Michigan," 89.

a series of interlocking directorates composed of a relatively small number of prominent clergymen and philanthropists." Although Clifford S. Griffin has added a few corrections to Barnes's argument—chiefly that Barnes misunderstood the actual power of officers and life members of these societies—in Michigan the data suggest that these reform efforts shared both membership and agents. Oren C. Thompson, for instance, served the American Tract Society, the American Sunday School Union, and the American Bible Society as an agent, and David R. Dixon, a longtime colporteur for the American Tract Society, also circulated Bibles for the Washtenaw County Bible Society. Many others served as leaders of several state and local benevolent organizations. For example, John P. Cleaveland, who had been secretary of the Michigan Sunday School Union in 1837, addressed the Michigan Bible Society in 1839 and was also a life member of both the New York and Boston bodies of the American Tract Society. Charles G. Clarke, a director of the Washtenaw County Sunday School Union in 1832, was corresponding secretary and later president of the Washtenaw County Bible Society from 1834 to 1845 and a life member of the American Tract Society. Ira M. Wead was the secretary of both the Washtenaw County Bible Society and the Washtenaw County Sunday School Union and a director of the Michigan Sunday School Union. Ezra H. Platt was treasurer of the Washtenaw County Bible Society and a director of the Washtenaw County Sunday School Union. Donald R. McIntyre was a director of the Washtenaw County Bible Society in 1854, president of the Ann Arbor Bible Society in 1859, and president of an Ann Arbor organization called the "Friends of Sabbath Instruction and Moral and Religious Improvement" in 1857. William C. Voorhies was secretary of the latter association and treasurer of the Washtenaw County Bible Society for over fifteen years.[26] Ob-

26. Gilbert Hobbs Barnes, *The Antislavery Impulse, 1830–1844* (New York, 1933), 19; Griffin, *Their Brothers' Keepers*, 63–64, 274–76. On Thompson: Oren C. Thompson to ASSU, April 12, 1832, July 25, 1832, in ASSU Papers; ABS *Annual Report*, XXIII (1839), 37. On Dixon: ATS (New York) *Annual Report*, XIX (1844), 67; D. R. Dixon to AHMS, June 9, 1843, in AHMS Papers. On Cleaveland: *Michigan Argus*, March 7, 1839; ATS (New York) *Annual Report*, XIII (1838), 199; ATS (Boston) *Annual Report*, XXII (1836), 95; A. L. Payson to ASSU, December 23, 1837, in ASSU Papers. On Clarke: *Democratic Herald*, January 27, 1841; ABS *Annual Report*, XVIII (1834), 134, XXIX (1845), 145; ATS (New York) *Annual Report*, XIII (1838), 200; I. M. Wead to ASSU, March 27, 1832, in ASSU Papers. On Wead: *Emigrant*, September 21, October 12, 1831; I. M. Wead to ASSU, March 6, 1832, in ASSU Papers. On Platt: ABS *Annual Report*, XV (1831), 133; I. M. Wead to ASSU, March 27, 1832, in ASSU Papers. On McIntyre: *Washtenaw Whig*, February

viously, much of Washtenaw County's benevolent activity was orchestrated by a coterie of enthusiasts.

Multiple participation in reform is also evident among the benevolence rank and file. Altogether, 75 Washtenaw County residents—10 of them women—were identified from various sources as having either attended a meeting of, served as an agent or a local officer for, or contributed money to the American Tract Society, the American Bible Society, and/or one of their auxiliaries by 1861. Among these promoters of Bibles and tracts, 39 were linked with one or more other reform efforts. For example, 32 were active in the temperance crusade, 21 were abolitionists, Free Soilers, or had signed an antislavery petition prior to 1854, 15 participated in the antebellum Sabbath-school movement, 2 advanced a more restrictive public observance of the Protestant Sabbath, 2 were colonizationists, and 4 were proponents of the common school; further, 11 supported temperance, Sabbath schools, and the Bible/tract cause, and 7 endorsed these three reforms as well as abolition/Free Soil. Among Sabbath-school advocates, 92 names—chiefly of superintendents, teachers, speakers at public meetings sponsored by Sabbath schools, and officers of Sabbath school associations—were obtained primarily from Ann Arbor and Ypsilanti newspapers, church minutes, and the correspondence of the ASSU. Of these Sabbath school enthusiasts—all of whom were men—at least 53 were involved in other reform activities: 43 were linked to the temperance movement, 27 were abolitionists, Free Soilers, or signed an antislavery petition prior to the formation of the Republican Party, and 19 were active in all three endeavors—Sabbath schools, temperance, and abolition/Free Soil. Additionally, 3 advanced the common school, 2 actively favored a more restrictive public observance of the Protestant Sabbath, and 1 was a colonizationist.

Other aspects of the collective profile of these devotees are worth mentioning. As one might expect, most of the 49 proponents of Bibles and tracts with an identifiable church affiliation were Congregationalist and Presbyterian—9 and 21, respectively. There were 13 Methodists and 5 Episcopalians. Only 1 Baptist was identified, probably because Baptists were active promoting their own Bible and tract efforts. Almost all of the 33 individuals in this group with identifiable places of birth were from New England or New York—20

8, 1854; *Michigan Argus,* January 21, 1859; Ann Arbor *Journal,* May 6, 1857. On Voorhies: Ann Arbor *Journal,* May 6, 1857; ABS *Annual Report,* XXX (1846), 147. See also the activities of Francis M. Lansing, W. W. Wines, and Charles Mosely in n. 66 this chapter.

and 11, respectively—with 1 each from England and Ohio. The occupations of 58 men (including the husbands of 4 female advocates of Bibles and tracts) could be ascertained, and they were overwhelmingly professional—46 individuals (79.3 percent), 37 of whom were ministers—followed by 5 shopkeepers/ proprietors, 3 farmers, 2 clerks, and 2 artisans. The median real-estate holding of the 25 individuals found on the 1850 census was $1,000, and the mean was $1,633. Among Washtenaw County households at large, the mean real-estate holding in 1850 was $1,485; statewide, it was $1,048.[27]

Of the Sabbath-school proponents, the church affiliation of 57 could be determined: Baptist, 7; Catholic, 1; Episcopal, 3; Methodist, 10; Presbyterian, 27; Congregationalist, 7; Unitarian, 1; and Wesleyan Methodist, 1. Like Washtenaw's advocates of Bibles and tracts, these individuals were overwhelmingly from New York and New England—18 and 20, respectively—while the other 2 with traceable places of birth came from Pennsylvania and Canada. Again, the occupational profile heavily favored professionals, although not to the extent found among Bible and tract proponents:

Occupation	Number	Percent
Artisan	1	1.7
Clerk	1	1.7
Shopkeeper/proprietor	6	10.3
Farmer	15	25.9
Professional	33	56.9
Other	1	1.7
None listed on census	1	1.7
Totals	58	99.9

The lesser preponderance of professionals probably reflects both the larger participation of the laity in the Sunday-school movement and the fact that the Sabbath schools were established in rural neighborhoods. Nevertheless, the professionals were still overwhelmingly ministers—20 of 33; there were also 4

27. The mean real-estate holdings for the county and state were calculated from *Statistics of the State of Michigan, Compiled from the Census of 1850, taken by authority of the United States. Condensed for Publication by the Secretary of State of the State of Michigan* (Lansing, 1851), 158, 159, 170, 171.

physicians and 3 attorneys. The real-estate holdings of Sabbath-school devotees exceeded those of Bible and tract enthusiasts; for the 31 members of the former group located on the 1850 census, the median holding was $2,000 and the mean was $3,617. The somewhat lower percentage of ministers in the Sunday-school group probably accounts for much of this difference, as the median real-estate holding of both groups of ministers ($500 for Bible and tract, $1,200 for Sabbath schools) was much lower than for the others in their cohort. And as with Tuscaloosa's proponents of Bibles, tracts, and Sunday schools, the devotees of these causes in Washtenaw County who could be linked to the 1850 federal census were more likely to send their children to school than the population at large. Over eight-tenths of the children of Washtenaw's benevolence enthusiasts went to school, whereas only seven-tenths of Michigan's and Washtenaw County's children aged five to nineteen did so.[28]

Two national benevolent societies, the American Education Society and the American Home Missionary Society (AHMS), did not establish local auxiliaries in the same manner as the American Bible Society, the American Tract Society, and the ASSU, and thus their presence in Washtenaw County took a form different from that of the latter associations. The American Education Society, which partially subsidized the educational costs of economically disadvantaged youths aspiring to the ministry, received financial contributions from a few "Presbygational" congregations in Washtenaw County, and its agents addressed the Presbytery of Michigan in 1830 and the Sylvan Presbyterian Church in 1837. The Michigan Education Society, an auxiliary of this national body, was formed in 1830, and Ann Arbor resident John Allen served as its president in 1834 and its vice president in 1835. By early 1831, a Female Education Society, auxiliary to the state body, was functioning in Ypsilanti.[29] The AHMS, however, was much more influential in the religious affairs of

28. School attendance for these groups was as follows: 28 of the 35 (80.0 percent) children of Washtenaw Bible and tract devotees went to school, while 57 of the 65 (87.7 percent) children of Sunday-school activists attended school. School attendance figures for Michigan (69.9 percent) and Washtenaw County (70.0 percent) were calculated from De Bow, *Seventh Census*, 882, 901.

29. *Western Emigrant*, September 1, 1830; Henry Root to AHMS, June 20, 1837, in AHMS Papers; *Michigan Argus*, September 24, 1835; Detroit *Journal and Courier*, November 5, 1835, as cited in Kooker, "Antislavery Movement in Michigan," 88; Ira M. Wead to AHMS, January 26, 1831, in AHMS Papers. Washtenaw County Presbyterian and Congregational churches contributed frequently to the American Education Society, particularly before 1838. See the yearly reports of the AHMS agents in AHMS Papers, *passim*.

Washtenaw County.[30] Formed in 1826, it undertook to subsidize Congregational and Presbyterian congregations that were unable to pay a minister a full salary.

Contemporaries viewed the AHMS as a part of the evangelical united front, but it was also a logical outgrowth of the Congregational and Presbyterian Plan of Union of 1801. This agreement sanctioned the collaborative efforts of the two denominations in the joint establishment of churches in the new settlements of New York and, later, the Old Northwest where there were too few church members to sustain ministers of both faiths. The doctrines of these denominations were very similar, and their differences arose mainly in their respective forms of church government. Under the Plan of Union, congregations could select ministers of either denomination, choose a Congregational or Presbyterian polity, and send representatives to either Congregational consociations and associations or to Presbyterian presbyteries, synods, and the General Assembly. This working agreement, though, was often strained. Presbyterians were greatly divided on the Plan of Union and on the AHMS, as well as on other issues of theology and church polity. New School Presbyterians favored a broad subscription to the Westminster Confession, interdenominational cooperation for missions and ministerial training, and "new measure" revivalism. Old School Presbyterians opposed their coreligionists in these and other particulars. The eventual consequence of these differences was the denominational schism of 1837. New Schoolers were also more favorable to antislavery, and although most of the New School Presbyterians were in the North—virtually all Presbyterian congregations in Michigan were New School—and a majority of Old School Presbyterians were in the South, the schism was not entirely sectional. Prior to the break, Congregationalists were drawn more closely to the New School Presbyterians; Old Schoolers so de-

30. Except in Missouri, Kentucky, and Tennessee, the AHMS had few missionaries in the South, partly because of the low number of Presbyterians and Congregationalists in the region. Further, after the Presbyterian schism of 1837, the AHMS was considered anathema by most Old School Presbyterians—which faction was dominant among southern Presbyterians. Accordingly, there was very little contact between benevolent Tuscaloosans and the AHMS. Colin Brummitt Goodykoontz, *Home Missions on the American Frontier* (Caldwell, Idaho, 1939), 180–81; Kuykendall, *Southern Enterprize,* 64, 65, 67, 74–75, 80, 105–106, 110–11. Regarding Tuscaloosan contact with the AHMS, see J. F. Wallis to AHMS, November 18, 1834, and Emily H. Williams to AHMS, October 27, 1834, both in American Home Missionary Society Papers, Samford University, Birmingham, Alabama (microfilm).

spised the Plan of Union that they annulled it upon separating from their Presbyterian rivals. By the 1840s, however, New Schoolers and Congregationalists began to drift apart, with each claiming that the other denomination had benefited more from the Plan of Union. This alliance effectively ended in Michigan in 1846 and ceased operating nationally in 1852. It was abrogated in both instances by the Congregationalists. The AHMS continued to disburse funds to ministers of both denominations until the Presbyterians withdrew from the society in 1861. In the meantime, the antislavery-oriented American Missionary Association attracted the financial support and devotion of people—most of whom were Congregationalists—who felt that the AHMS was too willing to compromise with slavery.[31]

Whereas Methodists addressed the religious needs of isolated communities by employing circuit riders who traveled from settlement to settlement and preached along the way, the AHMS for the most part supported a settled, rather than an itinerant, ministry. Proponents of the AHMS policy believed that occasional visits by traveling preachers were less effective than having a permanent minister who devoted all of his time to pastoral duties.[32] Generally, the society subsidized one-fourth of the minister's salary and expected the congregation to cover the remainder (which, on the frontier, was often in kind). This support was ostensibly intended only for the first few years of a church's existence and was expected to end when the church became self-sustaining. This policy, however, was more likely to be applied to churches located in towns such as Ann Arbor and Ypsilanti; rural congregations, like the one in Webster Township, not infrequently received assistance from the national society for many years. The society also provided aid to churches in Dexter village, Lodi, Salem, Manchester, Augusta, Sylvan, and Lima. Although the ministers received their subsidies directly from the AHMS, the society required that requests for such aid be made by the churches and that applications be endorsed by a Committee of Correspondence in Detroit. Church lay leaders were expected to explain to the AHMS why they could not pay a full

31. Goodykoontz, *Home Missions*, 149–51; George M. Marsden, *The Evangelical Mind and the New School Presbyterian Experience: A Case Study of Thought and Theology in Nineteenth-Century America* (New Haven, 1970), 10–11, 59–103, 250–51; Necia Ann Musser, "Home Missionaries on the Michigan Frontier: A Calendar of the Michigan Letters of the American Home Missionary Society, 1825–1846" (Ph.D. dissertation, University of Michigan, 1967), 22–53; Frederick Irving Kuhns, "The Breakup of the Plan of Union in Michigan," *Michigan History*, XXXII (June 1948), 157–80; Griffin, *Their Brothers' Keepers*, 185–91.

32. Although most missionaries for the AHMS labored in a single congregation, not all did.

salary to their pastor. The Committee of Correspondence (and after 1838, when the committee ceased operating, any two ministers) generally rubber-stamped such requests but occasionally recommended against sending assistance if the minister devoted too much time to farming or subscribed to an unorthodox theology.[33]

Similar in its objectives was the American Baptist Home Missionary Society (ABHMS), which supported a number of Washtenaw County Baptist congregations. More itinerant than the preachers of the AHMS, the ABHMS-sponsored pastors in Washtenaw sometimes ministered to as many as seven congregations. Another difference between the two organizations was that while the AHMS usually employed ministers from the East who then migrated west, the ABHMS made greater use of local preachers.[34] The ABHMS was organized in New York in 1832, but home mission work among the Baptists in Michigan began in 1822 under the direction of the Baptist Missionary Convention of the State of New York. After the foundation of the ABHMS, Michigan was one of that organization's chief fields of labor, and by 1843 its *Annual Report* listed thirty-two missionaries in Michigan. Not all of these individuals, however, were aided by the ABHMS: between 1836 and 1847, as many as two-thirds of them were appointed and sustained by the Michigan Baptist State Convention. In the latter year, the State Convention turned over the work to the ABHMS. A few years later, the convention praised the national body for sustaining "no fewer, perhaps, than fifty Churches . . . in the time of their greatest need" and cited congregations in Ypsilanti, Manchester, Saline, and elsewhere, "all of which now sustain themselves, though in all probability they could never have risen to their present state of prosperity, but for the assistance they received from the Home Mission Society." Still, the support that the ABHMS provided to infant churches was significantly less than that provided

For example, in 1835 the society had 716 agents and missionaries, of whom 481 ministered to single congregations, 185 had two or three congregations, and 50 were employed in larger districts; Musser, "Home Missionaries," 102. It should also be noted that the National Methodist Missionary Society helped support a number of Methodist itinerants in Michigan during the years following initial white settlement. Macmillan, *Methodist Church in Michigan*, 46, 47, 73, 90.

33. Goodykoontz, *Home Missions*, 181–83, 185; Musser, "Home Missionaries," 1–2, 80–84, 102–108.

34. On the itinerancy of the American Baptist Home Missionary Society, see for example the cases of Lyman H. Moore of Ypsilanti and William G. Wisner of Manchester in ABHMS *Annual Report*, XVI (1848), 30–31, and M. E. D. Trowbridge, *History of Baptists in Michigan* (N.p. [published by the Michigan Baptist State Convention], 1909), 34–35; Goodykoontz, *Home Missions*, 205–206.

by the AHMS. In 1850 the State Convention was grateful that the Baptist society had sent as much as $500 annually to Michigan.[35] The AHMS, on the other hand, generally provided $100 per year to each of its pastors. This greater support was the consequence of the AHMS's insistence upon educated and settled ministers who often preached four sermons a week and devoted their time exclusively to their pastorate. Baptist ministers who served several congregations were unable to preach this often at each one, and most had to work in nonreligious pursuits in order to make ends meet.[36]

Although these home mission societies were active in Michigan and many of their concerns were identical to those of the other national benevolent societies, their organizational activity will not be discussed in further detail because they existed in Washtenaw County primarily as a result of out-of-state financial backing and not from the widespread activity of local voluntary societies like the other movements examined in this study. Nevertheless, letters to these national organizations—particularly to the AHMS—are frequently cited in this study, as they often provide trenchant insights into other reform efforts. Indeed, ministers supported by the AHMS were often the foremost proponents of Bible and tract societies, Sabbath schools, and temperance; a few— most notably Alexander B. Corning of Manchester, Gustavus L. Foster of Dexter village, Hiram S. Hamilton of Salem, and George P. King of Lima—actually endorsed abolition.[37]

Another prominent cause among Washtenaw's evangelicals was their effort to persuade people to observe the Sabbath. As they saw things, Sunday ought to be devoted to contemplation, prayer, and church attendance, rather than to the secular pursuits in which people engaged during the rest of the week. Evangelicals viewed the proper keeping of the Sabbath as both a necessary re-

35. ABHMS *Annual Report*, XI (1843), 50–51, XVIII (1850), 44–45; Trowbridge, *Baptists in Michigan*, 31, 132–34; Goodykoontz, *Home Missions*, 205.

36. In spite of the greater financial support that AHMS ministers received from their parent body, they complained often that their annual salary of $400 was insufficient in the West, where the cost of virtually everything, they insisted, was higher. Musser, "Home Missionaries," 69–77, 90–92; Goodykoontz, *Home Missions*, 33–34, 182, 185.

37. On Corning: Musser, "Home Missionaries," 140; Manchester Township Minutes, April 4, 1842, April 7, 1845, April 6, 1846, April 5, 1847, April 2, 1849, April 4, 1853, Manchester Town Hall, Manchester, Michigan. On Foster: Musser, "Home Missionaries," 148, 596; *Signal of Liberty*, February 17, 1845. On Hamilton: Musser, "Home Missionaries," 152; *Signal of Liberty*, August 11, September 1, 22, 1841, April 6, 1842; H. S. Hamilton to AHMS, April 5, 1841, in AHMS Papers. On King: Musser, "Home Missionaries," 162; *Signal of Liberty*, August 11, 1841.

newal and a way to maintain an orderly, God-fearing population. Although it is difficult to be precise as to whether evangelicals in Washtenaw or Tuscaloosa County were the more likely to mourn the neglect of the Sabbath, the volume of Washtenaw primary sources containing this lament suggests that the northern evangelicals held the Fourth Commandment nearer to their heart. Upon his arrival as a missionary for the AHMS in Ypsilanti and Dixboro in 1829, William Jones bemoaned that the people there were "truly . . . without a Sabbath. Open Sabbath profanation & its concomitant evils—intemperance, licentiousness & litigation extensively prevailed." Sentiments such as these caused a number of Michiganians to form associations that urged stricter observance of the Sabbath. In 1836 three of the territory's prominent ministers of the Baptist, Presbyterian, and Methodist Episcopal churches encouraged Michigan's Protestants to select delegates to a proposed Sabbath convention to be held in Buffalo, New York. There they would "discuss and adopt suitable measures for arresting the appalling profanation of that holy day, which now prevails in this Western country." Those who could not send representatives to Buffalo were admonished to "take up, in good earnest, the subject of an immediate and radical reformation in regard to the observance of the LORD's day."[38]

In the minds of evangelicals, desecration of the Sabbath seemed to multiply with the expansion of the means of transportation. Whereas the three ministers pointed to abundant violations of the Fourth Commandment in 1836 "on our inland waters and travelled routes," the expansion of the railroads during the late 1830s and 1840s caused Sabbatarians to wage their battle on this front. Because the Michigan Central Railroad was owned by the state until 1846, evangelicals spent much of the 1840s attempting to convince the state government to prohibit the operation of trains on Sunday. In February 1840, the Washtenaw Presbytery requested that the churches within its bounds petition the legislature on this issue, and in March, the Michigan House of Representatives, recently captured by the Whigs, passed a resolution forbidding the functioning of railroads on Sunday, except to transport government mail.[39]

---

38. William Jones to AHMS, February 15, 1830, in AHMS Papers; *Michigan State Journal,* May 19, 1836. See also Richard R. John, "Taking Sabbatarianism Seriously: The Postal System, the Sabbath, and the Transformation of American Political Culture," *Journal of the Early Republic,* X (Winter 1990), 517–67, esp. 530–31; Abzug, *Cosmos Crumbling,* 106, 111–16.

39. Minutes of the Washtenaw Presbytery, February 13, 1840, p. 94, in Bentley Library; Formisano, *Birth of Mass Political Parties,* 123–24. The attitude of the Synod of Michigan toward the Sabbath can be found in L. G. Vander Velde, "The Synod of Michigan and Movements for So-

State Representative Munnis Kinney, a Whig from Webster who later deserted to the Liberty Party, was appointed chair of a Michigan House of Representatives select committee created in response to the flood of petitions calling for the state's railroads to cease operating on Sunday. Kinney explained in
the committee's report that the "sanctification of the Sabbath . . . has been
found the best safeguard of public morals, and eminently conducive to social
and intellectual, as well as moral improvement. Industry, health, frugality,
temperance and order prevailed in those districts where it is observed, and just
in proportion as it is revered and honored; while idleness, dissipation, intemperance and vices, injurious to the public weal, have abounded, wherever, and
just as the first day of the week has been robbed of its sacredness and prostituted
to secular uses." The Sabbatarian legislation passed, but the Democrats softened it in 1842 shortly after they regained political power. This action angered
evangelical Whigs. The Ann Arbor *Michigan State Journal* reprinted the outraged response of the Detroit *Advertiser:* "Any exhibition of regard for [Sun-
day], would have been set down as heresy by the loco foco ultraists."[40]

The animosity of evangelicals toward the functioning of railroads on Sunday remained strong. In 1844 a protest authored by "Many Citizens" appeared
in the abolitionist *Signal of Liberty* and asked, "How long shall the feelings of
the religious part of the community be outraged by the running of the cars on
the Central Rail-Road on the Sabbath?" In 1846, *Signal* editor Theodore Foster—an elder in the Webster Presbyterian church who endorsed temperance
and a number of other benevolent projects—remarked, "The Sabbath will not
generally be observed in a community where Railways or canals are [in] operation on Sunday."[41] Clark Lockwood, the Congregational minister of Dexter
village, was convinced that the running of trains on Sunday, coupled with the
rapid migration of Catholics to his village, was causing widespread immorality

cial Reform, 1834–1869," *Church History*, V (March 1936), 63–66. Regarding the sale of Michigan's
railroads, see Formisano, *Birth of Mass Political Parties*, 37; Dunbar and May, *Michigan*, 314–15.

40. *Documents Accompanying the Journal of the House of Representatives of the State of Michigan,
at the Annual Session of 1840. Volume II* (Detroit, 1840), 467; *Michigan State Journal*, February 22,
1842.

41. *Signal of Liberty*, June 10, 1844, November 14, 1846; Records of the First United Church of
Christ, Webster Township, June 29, 1838, p. 15, in Bentley Library. For other examples of abolitionist support for Sabbatarianism, see *Signal of Liberty*, May 5, July 7, September 1, 1841, September 5, 1842, February 11, 1846, and Bertram Wyatt-Brown, "Prelude to Abolitionism: Sabbatarian
Politics and the Rise of the Second Party System," *Journal of American History*, LVIII (September
1971), 316–41.

and nullifying his churchly labors. Although Lockwood admitted that "there may be some professedly good men belonging to the company in Boston" that purchased the Central Railroad from the state, he wished "they could see what a tide of wickedness is created by the rolling of cars through our otherwise peaceful village on the Sabbath, attracting the gaze of the youth, & drawing vast companies of the idle to their depots, & even disturbing the congregations of worshippers in our sanctuaries, by their bells & whistles & thunder roarings, as they pass at all times of the day. We believe little good will all the money do them that is thus acquired at the expense of God's holy law, & the Salvation of the Souls of thousands."[42]

In 1848, Sabbatarians held a state convention in Jackson, and its delegates appointed Ann Arbor residents Solomon Mann, William Kingsley, Daniel B. Wheedon, John Holmes Agnew, and Andrew Ten Brook—the latter three of whom were University of Michigan professors—to be members of the state central committee. Although nothing is known of the affairs of this organization after its first convention, John Holmes Agnew explained why he felt committed to this cause. As with Munnis Kinney, Agnew regarded "the proper observance of the Lord's Day . . . as most intimately connected with the health, decorum, intelligence and morals" of Americans, and "essential to the life of this Republic." In 1849, the Michigan Annual Conference of the Methodist Episcopal Church declared that it was wrong for stagecoaches, steamboats, and railroads to operate on Sunday.[43]

Much of the support for the benevolent empire in Washtenaw County came from the contributions of individuals through their churches. In addition to the organizations that we have already discussed, the county's Presbyterian

42. Clark Lockwood to AHMS, December 3, 1847, reproduced in Maurice Cole, ed., *Voices from the Wilderness* (Ann Arbor, 1961), 155–56. A year earlier at the Congregationalist General Association of Michigan meeting in Dexter village, the annual Narrative of the State of Religion complained that the "observance of the Sabbath is diminishing among us" and reported with "deep sorrow" that the "principal Railroad of our state [was] recently renewing its trips upon the Sabbath. . . . We had fondly hoped when this public desecration was stopped a few years ago, it would never be resumed. But though we have been disappointed, it becomes us not to be discouraged in the use of all appropriate means until the dreadful evil is brought to a perpetual end." *Minutes of the General Association of Michigan, at Their Meeting in Dexter, Sept. 1846* (Detroit, 1846), 15.

43. *Michigan Christian Herald,* March 31, May 5, 12, 1848; J. Holmes Agnew to Dear Sir, April 12, 1848, in James Dubuar Papers, Bentley Library; Macmillan, *Methodist Church in Michigan,* 178.

and Congregational churches also submitted contributions to the American Board of Commissioners for Foreign Missions.[44] But as the Plan of Union between the Congregationalists and Presbyterians fell apart, the former denomination increasingly asserted its independence. By the 1850s, Ann Arbor's Congregationalists supported their own Doctrinal and Tract Society and the American Missionary Association—a home missionary cause that took a stronger stand against slavery than did the AHMS—but still contributed to the American Bible Society and the ASSU.[45] The operations of the Baptist and Methodist benevolent associations were less extensive than the others that we have discussed so far, and thus less is known of them. It is likely, as Whitney Cross suggested in his study of western New York, that the straightforward denominationalism of the Baptist and Methodist societies limited their appeal, and the ostensibly interdenominational associations did better because of their nonsectarian facade and assistance from wealthy contributors—principally Congregationalists and Presbyterians—in the East. According to their church minutes, Baptist congregations in Saline, Ann Arbor, and Manchester supported denominational benevolent causes such as the American and Foreign Bible Society, the Missionary Union, the ABHMS, the Free Mission Society, and the American Baptist Board of Foreign Missions. The Michigan Annual Conference of the Methodist Episcopal Church supported its own tract society and missionary society, and an auxiliary of the latter was formed in Ann Arbor.[46]

44. The yearly reports of the ministers to the AHMS contain the amounts that churches contributed to these organizations; seldom did a church contribute more than $50 a year to any of these causes. AHMS correspondence, *passim.*

45. Records of the First Congregational Church of Ann Arbor, February 1, 1852, July 7, 1853, February 29, 1856. On the American Missionary Association, see Griffin, *Their Brothers' Keepers,* 185–86, 188–91; Frederick Irving Kuhns, *The American Home Missionary Society in Relation to the Antislavery Controversy in the Old Northwest* (Billings, Mont., 1959), 10, 14; Goodykoontz, *Home Missions,* 292; Bertram Wyatt-Brown, *Lewis Tappan and the Evangelical War Against Slavery* (Cleveland, 1969), 292–300; McKivigan, *War Against Proslavery Religion,* 114–19.

46. Cross, *Burned-Over District,* 26; *Michigan Christian Herald,* November 18, 1844; Records of the First Baptist Church of Saline, September 25, 1851, May 1, 1852, December 1, 1854, March 17, 1855; Records of the First Baptist Church of Ann Arbor, January 8, 1849, May 16, 1851, January 26, 1852; Records of the First Baptist Church of Manchester, January 1853, all in Bentley Library; Macmillan, *Methodist Church in Michigan,* 72, 122; Church Records of the Ann Arbor Circuit, December 31, 1837, in Records of the First United Methodist Church of Ann Arbor, Bentley Library.

Washtenaw's benevolent causes evoked strong commitment from some of their supporters. Oren C. Thompson wrote to the ASSU in 1833 that he had surrendered a teaching position at an academy in Ann Arbor in order to serve as an agent for the society, and that although his salary would decline by one-half, "my heart is in the work of Sabbath Schools. And duty bids me go. . . . I would cheerfully sacrifice my earthly interests in this cause as any. All I want is to enable me to be useful in this cause, for here I would be willing to live and die." Similar in their beliefs to their Alabama counterparts, Thompson and other evangelicals in Michigan felt a deep passion toward Sabbath schools. They attributed to these institutions the power to provide moral ballast and self-control for their fellow citizens and to enable America to persist and prosper. An examination of the ideology of benevolence shows that devotees were filled with both hope and fear regarding the future of their country. They were optimistic about its economic development but uneasy regarding its moral condition. Although reformers were committed to American liberty, they feared that society might become atomistic and repudiate the law and moral authority. They frequently stressed the need for individuals to become masters of themselves, for if Americans surrendered to their base passions, society would disintegrate. The nation's destiny, to benevolence partisans, depended on whether their fellow citizens could subvert licentiousness and selfishness. They were convinced that liberty could not long exist unless Americans embraced the self-discipline inherent to Protestant Christianity. The benevolent causes discussed in this chapter endeavored to convert Americans not merely for the other-worldly salvation of souls, but also for the temporal salvation of the country.[47]

The importance of centering society on evangelical morality and respect for authority was attested by State Representative Grove Spencer, a Whig from Ypsilanti who strongly favored a state law forbidding railroad traffic on Sunday. Spencer, who was also a temperance stalwart, told the legislature that the "perpetuity of our republican institutions, [and] the safety of the republic itself

47. Oren C. Thompson to ASSU, April 3, 1833, in ASSU Papers; *History of Washtenaw County*, 929; O. C. Thompson, "Observations and Experiences in Michigan," 400; Ashworth, *"Agrarians" and "Aristocrats*," 196–98; Howe, *Political Culture of American Whigs*, 29, 33, 36–37, 300–301; Kohl, "Concept of Social Control," 21–34; Kohl, *Politics of Individualism*, 69–78, 148–57; Welter, *Mind of America*, 253–64.

is intimately connected with" the "reverence and respect for the Sabbath." The greatest threat to America, according to Spencer, was "licentiousness," which was

> the rock upon which we as a republic are destined to founder and break into pieces. . . . Do we not know that the desecration of the Sabbath will lead to the production of that polluted state of moral feeling and sentiment from which will germ and mature the noxious seeds of vice, infamy, and crime! . . . Demolish this day and you knock down the foundation upon which is based the moral principles which support the laws, good order, and correct deportment in society. Demolish the Sabbath, and you open the way for . . . the condition of France when she discarded religion and raised the national standard of infidelity.

Spencer's sentiments on the Sabbath were echoed by Munnis Kinney, who insisted that "no christian nation has guarded effectively against the prevalence of vice and immorality, who have not required the sanctification of the Sabbath, and prohibited by law, those things which are inconsistent with its sacred character and holy uses and designs."[48]

The fear that a society which ignored Protestant morality would disintegrate was also expressed by an unidentified writer in the *State Journal* in 1836. The maintenance of American liberty, the essayist claimed, required that Americans lead virtuous lives and lean upon God. They could not afford to be lascivious like the French, who had "an iron government there, to keep the passions of men within bounds. We have to govern ourselves." He proclaimed that "the gospel is the last and only hope of the friends of human freedom," since it "tam[ed] the ferocity of man's heart, and fitt[ed] him for virtuous society and domestic enjoyment." America could "only be preserved by God's spirit, sent down to give efficacy to God's means to prepare our country for enlightened self-government, making us willing to make laws and obey them. It must come to us through the medium of the Sabbath day. As soon as the sun of the Sabbath withdraws from us, darkness and cold chills come over us. It is the chord that binds us to heaven, as we see one strand after another part, we hang over the precipice, till the last fiber is out, and we thunder down to ruin." Fur-

---

48. *Michigan State Journal,* March 25, 1840; *Documents Accompanying the Journal of the House of Representatives of the State of Michigan at the Annual Session of 1840,* p. 467. On Grove Spencer, see *History of Washtenaw County,* 1142, 1161, 1177, 1231; *Emigrant,* February 23, 1831; "History of the Temperance Movement in Washtenaw County" (undated; *ca.* 1885), in Lorenzo Davis Papers, Bentley Library.

ther, if "christianity is to lend us her aid in preserving our liberties, she will do it only through her own institutions. . . . The bible must be read, God must be worshipped, the gospel must be preached, or all is lost. And for this we must have the Sabbath day observed and honored. If this flood of business shall be allowed to go over the Sabbath, no man can resist it or turn it back."[49]

George Corselius, editor of the *Michigan Emigrant,* similarly believed that liberty must be based upon the self-restraint taught by Protestant Christianity. In 1834 he insisted that students must be taught the Bible in schools because a "mere intellectual education" would only create a "highly intellectual community without moral principle and the habits of self-denial which religion imposes, [and] would only prove a sleeping volcano, ready to awaken every moment, ready to overthrow those institutions which it had fostered." In order that the young might "be trained in the ways of virtuous self-control, and piety and righteousness wrought in the understanding and in the whole habit of man," Corselius urged the necessity of a "Bible education" aimed at both the "acquisition of secular knowledge" and the "formation of the Christian Character."[50] Others agreed. In 1845, the Washtenaw Presbytery affirmed that "it is not right to send children to schools where the Bible is excluded," and less than two years later a state educational convention assembled in Ann Arbor and passed a resolution "in favor of . . . reading the Bible in schools."[51]

Proponents of benevolence viewed the educational process in general as something more than the mere instilling of intellectual knowledge or the bestowal of cognitive abilities, and Sabbath schools in particular as more than a means to provide children with scriptural literacy or to prepare them to meet their maker. They saw both as a way of providing children with skills that would enable them to achieve self-mastery, self-restraint, and accompanying virtues such as honesty, frugality, and industry. A "Bible education" would eliminate unbridled passions that prevented people from reaching their full human potential, liberate individuals from vice, and provide a progressive

49. *State Journal,* August 31, 1836.

50. *Michigan Emigrant,* August 14, 1834. Among those who encouraged Bible reading in common schools was Monroe resident Ira Mayhew, who served as Michigan superintendent of public instruction from 1845 to 1849 as a Democrat and again from 1855 to 1859 as a Republican. Ira Mayhew, *Popular Education for the Use of Parents and Teachers, and for Young Persons of Both Sexes* (New York, 1850), esp. 203–24.

51. Minutes of the Washtenaw Presbytery, September 1, 1845, p. 265, in Bentley Library; *Michigan Temperance Journal and Washingtonian,* July 15, 1847.

course for American society. And believing in the malleability of the human character, Sunday-school advocates saw childhood as the time to do all this. Oliver C. Comstock, a University of Michigan regent between 1841 and 1843 and the superintendent of public instruction for the state from 1843 to 1845, warned that "unless [the child's] mind be rightly impressed—his memory stored with the proper things—his action wisely directed, and his associations suitably guarded, he may embrace principles, imbibe a spirit and imitate manners, over which parental affections and Christian charity may weep in hopeless despair." Thus, when the "virtuous and benevolent man" considered the Sabbath school, and became "acquainted with its necessity, designs, and results—when he rightly reflects upon the capacities and susceptibilities of the tender mind—upon the strong and abiding influence of early habits, and upon the economy of God's moral government, he also becomes the fast and generous friend of the institution."[52] Albert Payson reflected similar views when he decried the shortcomings of the Presbyterian Sunday school in Ypsilanti. It was "distressing to see [churches] like this who might do so much good by way of Sab[bath] Sch[ool] instruction to lie dormant, & sleep while the characters of many youth rising into life are forming." J. H. Sanford, editor of the Universalist *Primitive Expounder,* concurred regarding the importance of fashioning youthful minds properly. Although many youths from poor backgrounds had become great through the help of Sabbath schools, ignorance and vice had befallen those who lacked this instruction. Sanford urged parents not to delay the religious training of their children, lest they acquire habits of "rambling about town on the Sabbath, and congregating for social converse, in places where religious subjects are not the theme of the company."[53]

The beneficial prospects of Sunday schools filled some commentators with

52. *Michigan Christian Herald,* February 13, 1843. Comstock, a former member of Congress from New York, was also an intermittent pastor of Ann Arbor's Baptists during the 1840s and 1850s; *Biographical Directory of the United States Congress, 1774–1989* (Washington, D.C., 1989), 814.

53. A. L. Payson to ASSU, May 1, 1837, in ASSU Papers (see also Payson to ASSU, August 6, 1840, as printed in the ASSU *Annual Report,* XVII [1841], 18); *Primitive Expounder,* November 1, 1849. Sanford also saw a pragmatic side of Sunday schools, as he was convinced that such a course would lead to denominational stability: "And when a person has received his religious education under the direction of any particular denomination, if he ever breaks off from his connexion with that denomination and embraces the sentiments of another, or advances to any new position, no one but those who have experienced it can tell the mental pains and labor attendant upon the change. How necessary it is then, that our children and youth should be correctly educated." *Ibid.*

optimism that the fears expressed by Spencer, Corselius, and others would not come to pass. Writing on behalf of the Michigan Presbytery in 1830, Charles G. Clarke hoped that Sabbath schools—"nurseries of knowledge and piety"— might be opened in every neighborhood in the territory, as they would have a positive bearing "upon the future well being of society." In 1832 the Michigan Sunday School Union claimed that against the instability that might result from a "spreading population in a new country," Sunday schools would produce "moral and enlightened children, trained up in the path of religion," who would prove to be "so many bulwarks of our nation, and so many pledges of the perpetuity and augmentation of our national prosperity." Accordingly, one could only conclude that "the cause of Sabbath Schools [is] emphatically the cause of freedom, of religion, and of God." Albert Payson explained to the ASSU that his principal motive in serving as their agent was "to do good to benefit the rising generations," and Oliver Comstock similarly intoned that because the Sabbath school was "divinely blessed, it is capable of completely improving the mind, extending the usefulness, and crowning the happiness of the rising and following generations." A Methodist writer explained in 1850 that "Sabbath Schools are the Edens of our children and youth, in which the teachers are as good angels to keep them from the seductive power of that serpent whose head is already bruised." An announcement for a Sabbath-school convention to be held in Detroit in 1857 asserted that the cause was "intimately connected with the happiness and prosperity of our whole population." The abolitionist *Signal of Liberty* proclaimed Sabbath schools to be "of great importance to the productive energies of a nation," since "whatever has a tendency to improve the morals of a people, tends also to augment their wealth."[54]

Washtenaw County writers did not regularly make such an explicit connection between benevolence and economic progress as did the *Signal of Liberty*. More often, it seems, they were preoccupied with vice—or with combating what they saw as the source of considerable vice, Roman Catholicism. Nevertheless, the references of writers to the "prosperity" and "the future well being of society" can be construed to have economic implications. Further, the causes for which evangelicals labored were compatible with the demands of market behavior. Distributors of Bibles and tracts stressed that these materials

54. *Emigrant,* September 8, 1830; *First Annual Report of the Michigan Sunday School Union,* 8; A. L. Payson to ASSU, July 25, 1837, in ASSU Papers; *Michigan Christian Herald,* February 13, 1843; *Family Favorite and Temperance Journal,* I (October 1850), 235; *Michigan Argus,* June 12, 1857; *Signal of Liberty,* April 10, 1843.

were to be circulated systematically and efficiently, and one effect of the installation of bells in Sunday schools was to make both students and teachers more time-conscious. Indeed, according to Anne M. Boylan, Sunday-school lessons "placed a heavy emphasis on punctuality, obedience, self-discipline, and order." The congruence of benevolence and the emerging industrial age was perhaps expressed most explicitly in 1854 by the Reverend Charles Peabody, the general agent for the American Tract Society and superintendent of colportage for Missouri, Illinois, Iowa, and Arkansas. Peabody praised the spreading of railroads for giving a "new life and impulse to every branch of enterprise. They will soon enable us to reach places and accomplish results in a few hours, which have heretofore required weary days to compass." The railroad also enabled colporteurs to obtain supplies that had previously taken months to obtain. Moreover,

these channels of trade and enterprise are having an important bearing upon the ready ability of the masses of the agricultural people to purchase books. Before railroads were built, the colporteur, in visiting many agricultural neighborhoods, would behold great abundance of the fruits of the earth, but find perhaps no ready money. People anxious to procure the rich treasures of Christian truth offered them, but no available means of doing it. Now the case is beginning to be different. Corn, wheat, oats, potatoes, are the same as money, whenever the iron horse stands ready to take them to market. These improvements, which have been enjoyed a longer time in some of the older states, are beginning to wake up the energies of the people here. They are coming to take a more correct and higher view of their position. They are beginning to see in what a glorious garden the providence of God has placed them; and now that railroads can be made over their fertile heritage in all directions so easily, they begin to contemplate the nature of these wide-spread, almost boundless prairies. We look for great results in our work, caused, or at least highly promoted, by this feeling of enterprise and hope among the people. We do not mean to stand idle, while commerce and enterprise are waking up in our field with such amazing energy and power. We intend to press on into the very midst of the whirl of progress, and bearing aloft the banner of our glorious cause, to make to work, with God's blessing, a prominent and effective means of evangelization in our field. The progress of the past year encourages us to go forward, and aim at still greater progress during the year to come.[55]

55. Boylan, *Sunday School,* 38, 46; ATS (New York) *Annual Report,* XXIX (1854), 53–54.

In 1851, the Michigan Baptist State Convention also identified benevolence with the course of American progress. Not only was benevolence necessary to defeat Catholics or to enable America to achieve greatness, but it also figured into America's sense of mission. The convention explained that America was "the arena which God has chosen for the genius and prowess of the Anglo-Saxon race to develop themselves." Accordingly, their country was "destined to inculcate its ideas, and plant its institutions in every region of the habitable globe." With such sublime promises awaiting their country, it was the current generation, "entrusted with responsibilities from God and posterity," that must seriously address the question, "What shall be the character of our religious institutions; and from ours, as the type, the religious institutions of mankind, for the indefinite future?" How Americans answered this question was significant, since "the elements out of which these institutions are to be formed are now *plastic,* but by an inevitable law, they will soon *consolidate;* and the mould or shape which they receive at our hands, they will not soon or easily lose." These considerations thus increased the importance of *"Domestic* or *Home Missions"* and made "our country . . . the most interesting and important missionary field in the world."[56]

As this and other contemporary statements suggest, underlining many benevolent efforts was a fear among evangelicals of social dislocation in the larger community—an anxiety that a moral, orderly, and God-fearing society would not be replicated in the West, and that in the end, the region and the country would be delivered to Roman Catholicism. This consternation that society was becoming increasingly disorderly was already evident during the first few years of settlement and was perhaps best summarized by John Allen, a founder of Ann Arbor, in a letter to the AHMS in 1828. Writing on behalf of the First Presbyterian Church in an appeal for aid to its pastor, William Page, Allen claimed: "We are on the frontier of the Kingdom of Christ in America, and exposed to the attacks of enemies on all sides, from the circumstance of our population, being made up of individuals from all parts of the world, and who are not under the influence of that restraint imposed on them by the presence of their acquaintances." In 1835, afraid that citizens would be influenced by sources that would not insist upon Sabbath adherence and self-restraint, the Monroe Presbytery—which at that time included Washtenaw County—expressed alarm over the "rapid increase of the Roman Catholic Church in this

56. ABHMS *Annual Report,* XIX (1851), 54–55.

country." Convinced of the "dangers which threaten our civil and religious institutions from this source," the Presbytery called "upon the whole community to awake to greatly increased efforts in the Sabbath school cause, and in every other species of benevolent effort, which may tend to counteract the plans of that sect."[57] The Democratic *Michigan Argus* was more optimistic. In praising the work of the ABHMS, the editor explained in 1835 that "not only every Christian, but every *republican* should bless the Baptists for the good they are doing. . . . At this moment they have schools established in the valley of the Mississippi to a great extent. . . . Give the West the light of education and the gospel, and we shall have no fears of Prince Metternich or the pope."[58]

Chauvinistic fears, however, were not easily discarded by Michigan's evangelicals, and persisted throughout the antebellum era. Echoing Allen, a Sabbath convention held in 1848 in Jackson reminded "the People of the State of Michigan" that it was important to keep the Sabbath so that the growing foreign-born population would adopt this practice and not be "tempted on the verge of the wilderness to throw off the restraints of law and order." Immigration and Catholicism in particular, as well as rapid urbanization, infidelity, and recent national territorial acquisitions were seen by the Michigan Baptist State Convention in 1851 and 1852 as problems that could be solved only by widespread missionary activity. Pointing specifically to the religious fate of the unsettled western territories, the convention proclaimed that it was the duty of the ABHMS and "their coädjutors of kindred societies . . . [to] secure the preöccupancy of a virgin soil; and in the name of 'God and Truth' take possession of a most interesting and important territory which Romanism and infidelity are rampant to enter and control." Although nativism was a significant political force in Michigan from the early 1830s, it blossomed during the mid-1850s with the emergence of the American (or Know-Nothing) and Republican Parties.[59]

Thus the Michigan Sunday School Union's concern, noted earlier, over "the

57. Allen to AHMS, November 11, 1828, in AHMS Papers; *Michigan Whig and Washtenaw Democrat*, May 14, 1835. Ira Wead of Ypsilanti requested that this specific resolution of the Monroe Presbytery be published as "it is belived [*sic*] you would gratify many of your readers and promote the cause of truth."

58. *Michigan Argus*, June 13, 1835.

59. *Michigan Christian Herald*, May 12, 1848; ABHMS *Annual Report*, XIX (1851), 54–55, XX (1852), 77; Formisano, *Birth of Mass Political Parties*, 71, 82, 87, 89–92, 249–53, 256–65, 330–31. See also Charles G. Clarke to AHMS, January 24, 1843, in AHMS Papers.

spreading population of a new country," expressed an ongoing anxiety that the West might turn to anarchy rather than into communities of steady habits. Other advocates of the benevolent empire in Washtenaw County repeated this refrain. The Reverend Charles G. Clarke, a pastor of the Presbyterian and Congregational churches in Dexter village and Webster from the late 1820s through the 1850s, an active proponent of temperance and Sabbath schools, and president of the Washtenaw County Bible Society, informed the AHMS in 1832 that the Bible class he was leading in Webster had been "neglected on account of the scattered state of the people." Oliver Hill in Augusta Township reported to the AHMS that "many families, and whole neighborhoods are so circumstanced that they have no benefit of a preached Gospel, except by occasional sermons, which do not promise to do them much good." If, as evangelicals believed, Protestant churches contributed to a community's moral restraint, the absence of such churches meant that vice and sin would proliferate. Hill used harsh language to describe neighboring communities that lacked churches: "The desecration of the holy sabbath & profane swearing are very prevalent. Many families of children are growing up in ignorance and vice." Henry Horatio Northrup of Lima Township and Silas Woodbury of Manchester described the numerous areas of the state that were destitute of preaching as "a moral waste." Presbyterian minister Justin Marsh wrote that a neighborhood just beyond the proximity of his Augusta Township congregation suffered from insufficient ministerial oversight, "much looseness, and considerable open infidelity." Accordingly, Marsh reminded the AHMS to urge "all christians in the East who have friends in the new settlements" to remember them and "affectionately write to them on the concerns of their souls. Let them press the duty of attatching [*sic*] themselves to some evangelical congregation & combining with the friends of temperance & the Sabbath to promote good order in the community around them."[60]

Like evangelicals in Alabama, Sabbath-school proponents in Michigan were convinced that the moral tone of a community improved noticeably upon the introduction of their program. Oren C. Thompson expressed his conviction in 1832 that communities with Sunday schools and other benevolent institutions enjoyed religion and good society, while poor morals ruled elsewhere.

60. Charles G. Clarke to AHMS, October 1, 1831, March 8, 1832, Oliver Hill to AHMS, October 31, 1838, H. H. Northrup to AHMS, March 1, 1841, Justin Marsh to AHMS, September 29, 1842, all in AHMS Papers; A. L. Payson to ASSU (quoting Woodbury), August 17, 1840, in ASSU Papers. See also ATS (New York) *Annual Report*, XXXIV (1859), 132.

In 1840, Albert Payson wrote that prior to the introduction of the Sabbath school in Clintonville, in Oakland County, the people "acted more like the heathen than a civilized people." But upon the organization of a Sabbath school, "the morals of this place are now greatly changed. Instead of noise & confusion on the Sab[bath] the chil[dren] collect in the Sab. Sch." The "wickedness" of the settlers of Lowell, in Superior Township, had, according to Payson, "long been a proverb and a bye word in the towns around." In particular, their crimes consisted of inappropriate activities on Sunday: "The Sab. became a continued scene of profanation. The [Huron] river on this day was covered with people, fishing & sporting—The Sab resounded from morn till night with the sounds of hunters guns & their dogs." After the establishment of a Sabbath school in Lowell, "tho many of the inhabitants continue their Sab breaking & other immoral habits—yet the children and a majority of the parents now attend to the observance of the Sab." Justin Marsh believed that his preaching, a Bible class, and the Sunday school connected with his church were transforming the Augusta Township vicinity, as "a stronger tide is evidently setting in this community against the open vices. We see less of Sabbath breaking & much less Intemperance, yet far too much of both." Among local youth, there was a "more decided disapprobation to things that are low and improper. Dancing is becoming less common."[61] Whether vice was in fact becoming less prevalent is, of course, impossible to verify. What is significant is that these evangelicals believed that their programs had positive social consequences and that this process of individual betterment led to the improvement of communities and would eventually prove to be the salvation of America.

As in Tuscaloosa County, women participated in a number of benevolent efforts in Washtenaw. Also similar to their Tuscaloosa counterparts, Washtenaw newspaper editors generally reported less about women's than men's organizations, and likewise only a few manuscript records of women's benevolent associations have persisted to the present. William Page and Charles G. Clarke, in correspondence to the AHMS during the late 1820s and early 1830s, reported the establishment of Female Tract Societies in their respective con-

61. Oren C. Thompson to ASSU, May 22, 1832, A. L. Payson to ASSU, undated [1840], A. L. Payson to ASSU, August 6, 1840, all in ASSU Papers; Justin Marsh to AHMS, June 28, 1843, in AHMS Papers.

gregations in Ann Arbor and Dexter village. Each society raised money for the American Tract Society in New York; in Ann Arbor, the seventy-five members were obliged to contribute dues of twenty-five cents. Women also served as Sunday-school teachers, and newspaper accounts of public Sabbath-school Independence Day celebrations noted that local women prepared refreshments. Religious women in Washtenaw County formed other associations. At Stoney Creek Presbyterian Church in Augusta Township, Oliver Hill reported, "the females hold prayer meetings, which are interesting." In Salem, Presbyterian and Congregational women formed a Female Home Missionary Society auxiliary to the AHMS, and in Ann Arbor, as mentioned previously, women constituted the bulk of the twenty-eight enthusiasts who canvassed for the Ann Arbor Bible Society—a few women even served on its executive committee. But the most widespread form of women's voluntary association in antebellum Washtenaw County was usually designated as the Female Benevolent Society. Again, little is known of these associations, other than that they were usually connected with a church. The contexts of the passing references to them suggest that many of these societies raised money either for the poor or to improve the facilities of their churches. The Female Benevolent Society in Lima and the Ladies' Aid Society in Webster raised money for the Presbyterian bodies in these locales, and the Ladies' Aid Society of the Ann Arbor Presbyterian Church reportedly met every two weeks to sew. In 1843 the women of the Ann Arbor Ladies' Aid Society raised money to assist in making their pastor a life member of the American Bible Society. Female benevolent societies are also known to have existed as auxiliaries of Baptist churches in Saline and Manchester, the Methodist church in Chelsea, and the Presbyterian church in Manchester. The Female Benevolent Society of Augusta Township's Stoney Creek Presbyterian Church was formed in 1835, and in 1837 its members renamed their society the Female Missionary Association and made it an auxiliary of the Michigan Home Missionary Society.[62]

62. William Page to AHMS, July 23, October 21, 1827, October 7, 1828, May 19, 1829, Charles G. Clarke to AHMS, July 1, 1831, Henry Northrup to AHMS, September 4, 1840, all in AHMS Papers; A. L. Payson to ASSU, March 15, 1837, in ASSU Papers; *Michigan State Journal,* July 6, 1841; *Michigan Argus,* July 10, 1850, January 21, 1859, *Local News and Advertiser,* August 4, 1857; Oliver Hill to AHMS, July 19, 1838, Chester Pratt, Salem, Michigan, to J. A. Murray, Geneva, New York, July 8, 1839, Henry Northrup to AHMS, September 4, 1840, Charles G. Clarke to AHMS, January 24, 1843, all in AHMS Papers; ABS *Annual Report,* XL (1856), 73; Francis L. D. Goodrich, *Historical Facts Concerning the First Presbyterian Church of Ann Arbor* (Ann Arbor, 1961), copy

The Congregational Ladies' Sewing Society of Ann Arbor was formed in April 1847—shortly after Ann Arbor's Congregationalists separated from the town's Presbyterian church. The group's first objective was to "raise funds to procure a Communion service: and other necessary furniture for the church: and likewise to aid any benevolent enterprise they shall think proper." A year later, one of the directors, Mary A. Irish, suggested that the society ought to make a more pronounced effort to "raise our feelings and expand our ideas," as she felt that the women of Ann Arbor had not lived up to their obligation of exerting their moral influence in their town. "Does it not appear," she queried, "that the Gentleman are A going a head of us in improving theire minds and trying to do good to there fellow beings[?]" Irish doubted that the successes male reformers had achieved in Ann Arbor had resulted from the encouragement of women, "since wee have all more or less been disposed to be rather prejudist against therie procedings." Women, in her view, ought to "have charity enough to think that some of them are right and sincere if not able."[63]

The concerns of this society eventually went beyond Washtenaw County, in a direction suggested by the dying wishes of Mrs. Jennab Kingsley in May 1848. Three weeks prior to her death at thirty-two, Kingsley met with several officers of the Congregational Ladies' Sewing Society and "expressed a deep anxiety that something should be done for the home of the Friendless. She prepared with her own hands some garments—expressly for that purpose, requesting that they should be made in our society." Over the next dozen years, members of the society gathered to sew clothing, some of which went to the local poor, but much of which was sent to the Home for the Friendless—a haven for indigent women in New York City. Many entries in the society's minutes mention the sewing of articles for this purpose. In 1852, Jane Louisa Hobart, the wife of pastor L. Smith Hobart, "gave us an interesting account of a visit she made to the 'Home' during her abscence." These meetings of the society were devoted

---

in Bentley Library; *Michigan State Journal*, February 1, 1843; *Michigan Christian Herald*, November 6, 1843, November 4, 1844; Ronald A. Brunger, "The Ladies Aid Societies in Michigan Methodism," *Methodist History*, V (January 1967), 31–33; Annetta English, "History of Manchester Township" (typescript, 1930), copy in Manchester Area Library; Minutes of the Female Benevolent Society, in Records of the First Presbyterian Church of Stoney Creek (Augusta), Bentley Library.

63. Records of the Congregational Ladies' Sewing Society, Vol. I, p. 1, in Records of the First Congregational Church of Ann Arbor, Bentley Library; Mary A. Irish to Dear Sisters, April 9, 1848, inserted in Vol. I of Records of the Congregational Ladies' Sewing Society.

to both charity work and religious fellowship, as the minutes note in March 1853: "Society met at Mrs Wheelers 11 Ladies were present, one hour was spent in prayer, the remainder of the time was occupied in work for the poor." Two years later, those present "worked on various garments for the little ones in the home. Reading a portion of Scripture and prayr by Mr. Baldwin."[64]

In chapter 1, we saw how the antebellum benevolent message resonated among slaveholders in Tuscaloosa County. Although abolitionists and slaveholders saw each other as the epitome of America's ills, many members of both groups embraced the agenda of benevolence. Abolition proved a far more fractious issue among benevolence devotees in the North than in the South. As we shall see more fully in chapter 5, Tuscaloosa Baptists advocated severing their ecclesiastical and benevolence ties to northern Baptists because of abolitionist attacks upon slavery. But otherwise there was little widespread effort to denounce national benevolence societies in Tuscaloosa after 1835, and few suggestions that any benevolence cause in Alabama was suspect because of its alleged association with abolitionists. Abolitionist enthusiasts of benevolence combated their antagonists differently. Viewing slavery as a sin, they insisted that it be considered the equal of any other violation of morality. Many believed that their association with any organization that tolerated slavery tainted them with slavery as well. Thus, even though some abolitionists endorsed the objectives of benevolence, they could not in conscience pursue those ends by collaborating with national societies that refused to denounce slavery sufficiently. As a result, they formed their own benevolent societies, which stayed clear of slaveholder influence and contamination.

For many abolitionists, benevolence and abolition were closely intertwined. During the early 1840s, the friends of abolition, Sabbath schools, and temperance assembled together in the village of Jackson to celebrate Independence Day. Delegates to the annual meeting of the Washtenaw Presbytery likewise considered abolition, temperance, and benevolence to be part of a common

64. Nancy Walker to the Congregational Ladies' Sewing Society, undated [April 1849], inserted in Vol. I of Records of the Congregational Ladies' Sewing Society, Bentley Library; Records of the Congregational Ladies' Sewing Society, October 13, 1852, March 23, 1853, May 9, 1855 (Vol. II, pp. 23, 31, 37). Regarding the Home for the Friendless, see Barbara J. Berg, *The Remembered Gate: Origins of American Feminism: The Woman and the City, 1800–1860* (New York, 1978), 231–33.

agenda, as they passed resolutions condemning slavery and supporting benevolent efforts at the same meeting.[65] A number of individuals were leaders in both abolitionist and benevolent organizations. Their multiple affiliations suggest that many Washtenaw residents viewed benevolence, abolition, and temperance as allied causes—even though such connections, particularly in nonabolitionist publications, were seldom made explicitly. Perhaps the most notable individual who was active in these three causes was John P. Cleaveland, a Congregationalist who served as a Presbyterian pastor in several Michigan communities, including Ann Arbor. Cleaveland spoke often at state gatherings of temperance, abolition, and benevolence groups, and served, in addition to his already-mentioned benevolence responsibilities, as a leader of Michigan's Sabbatarians in 1836, a member of the Detroit Committee of Correspondence for the AHMS from 1836 to 1838, president of the Michigan State Anti-Slavery Society in 1841, president of the state Liberty Convention in 1842, and president of the Michigan State Temperance Society in 1843. Others who engaged in both abolition and benevolence included Francis M. Lansing of Pittsfield Township, who served as an agent for the Washtenaw County Bible Society, a colporteur for the American Tract Society from 1849 to 1850, and a vice-president of the Washtenaw County Temperance Society in 1835, was a devoted abolitionist who was active in the Michigan State Anti-Slavery Society and was frequently a Liberty candidate for township office and the state legislature; and Munnis Kinney of Webster, who in addition to his previously cited Sabbatarian activity, was also a missionary for the ASSU in 1849, president of the Washtenaw County Temperance Society in 1831, a perennial Liberty candidate for town, county, and state offices, and the vice-president of the state convention in 1842 and 1843.[66]

65. *Michigan Freeman*, July 15, 1840; *Signal of Liberty*, June 23, 1841, June 5, 1843, April 29, 1844; Minutes of the Washtenaw Presbytery, February 13, 1840, pp. 94–96, in Bentley Library; *Signal of Liberty*, March 9, 1842. Resolutions favoring both abolition and benevolence were passed by the Michigan Synod in 1843 *(Signal of Liberty*, November 13, 1843). George Duffield, however, pastor of the Detroit First Presbyterian Church from 1838 to 1867, disliked abolitionists and, as the most powerful voice of the Michigan Synod during these years, prevailed upon his coreligionists to soft-pedal most antislavery resolutions. Vander Velde, "Synod of Michigan and Movements for Social Reform," 59, 67–68.

66. On Cleaveland: *Michigan State Journal*, May 19, 1836; Musser, "Home Missionaries," 104, 106; *Michigan Argus*, February 15, 1843; *Signal of Liberty*, April 28, 1841, October 24, 1842. On Lansing: *History of Washtenaw County*, 1252; ATS (New York) *Annual Report*, XXV (1850), 79, XXVI (1851), 84; *Michigan Whig*, February 12, 1835; *Signal of Liberty*, October 27, 1841, January 12, Sep-

Theodore Foster, editor of the *Signal of Liberty,* endorsed the objectives of benevolent organizations, and occasionally pointed to the congruence between benevolence and abolition. Foster felt that slavery impeded the spread of Bibles in the South. He noted that the North contributed five times more money to the American Bible Society than did the southern states, and he

tember 5, October 24, 1842, February 20, 1843, July 22, August 26, 1844, July 7, September 29, 1845, October 10, 1846, October 30, 1847, February 5, 1848; Pittsfield Township Records, April 5, 1841, in Bentley Library; Pittsfield Township Records, April 4, 1842, April 5, 1847, in Pittsfield Township Hall, Pittsfield, Michigan. On Kinney: W. E Boardman to ASSU, June 9, 22, July 10, 24, December 31, 1849, in ASSU Papers; *Emigrant,* April 27, 1831; *Signal of Liberty,* October 24, 1842, February 20, 1843. Others worthy of mention would have to include John Chandler of Ann Arbor, who chaired a Sabbath-school celebration held on the Fourth of July, 1844, served as the secretary of the Ann Arbor Temperance Society in 1841, and was active in the Liberty Party, of which he was also a frequent candidate and served as secretary of the state convention in 1843; Charles Mosely, president of the Washtenaw County Sunday School Union in 1832, treasurer of the Washtenaw County Bible Society from 1834 to 1845, a vice-president of the Washtenaw County Temperance Society in 1831, and chair of the Ann Arbor Total Abstinence Society in 1841, who was also a delegate to the Washtenaw County Liberty Convention in 1841 and protested the congressional gag rule in 1842; W. W. Wines, an executive committee member of the Ann Arbor City Bible Society in 1859 and treasurer in 1857 of the Ann Arbor-based Friends of Sabbath Instruction and Moral and Religious Improvement, who was also active in the Sons of Temperance, served as a delegate to the state temperance convention in Jackson in 1854 and the state Liberty convention in 1842, and was a Free Soil candidate for local office in 1852 and 1853; John S. Twiss, Ann Arbor's Baptist pastor from 1830 to 1837, who was also a Sabbath-school superintendent in 1833, a vice-president of the Washtenaw Temperance Society in 1835, and attended a Liberty Party meeting in Ann Arbor in 1845; Jacob Doremus of Scio, a vice-president of the Washtenaw County Sunday School Union in 1832, a subscriber to the *Home Missionary* (published by the AHMS), and president of the Scio Liberty Association, who also pushed for a resolution against slavery by the Webster Presbyterian Church in 1839; and J. A. Parks of Sylvan, a colporteur for the ATS in 1851 and 1852 and a Liberty Party candidate for township office in 1842 and 1843. On Chandler: *Michigan State Journal,* June 5, 1844, June 15, 1841; *Signal of Liberty,* February 20, 1843. On Mosely: I. M. Wead to ASSU, March 27, 1832, in ASSU Papers; ABS *Annual Report,* XVIII (1834), 134, XXIX (1845), 145; *Emigrant,* April 27, 1831; *Michigan State Journal,* June 1, 1841; *Signal of Liberty,* September 1, 1841, March 23, 1842 (see also August 11, 1841, and *Michigan State Journal,* August 4, 1840). On Wines: *Michigan Argus,* January 21, 1859; Ann Arbor *Journal,* May 6, 1857; *Michigan Argus,* January 19, 1848, June 15, 1854; *Signal of Liberty,* October 24, 1842; *Michigan Argus,* October 6, 1852; *Washtenaw Whig,* April 6, 1853. On Twiss: *History of Washtenaw County,* 920; Oren C. Thompson to ASSU, July 11, 1833, in ASSU Papers; *Michigan Whig,* February 12, 1835; *Signal of Liberty,* July 7, 1845. On Doremus: I. M. Wead to ASSU, March 27, 1832, in ASSU Papers; C. G. Clarke to AHMS, April 1, 1835, in AHMS Papers; *Signal of Liberty,* August 19, 1844; Records of the First United Church of Christ, Webster Township, October 25, 1839, in Bentley Library (in 1860 this church switched

blamed this discrepancy on the fact that the mostly illiterate slave population was barred by law from being taught to read anything, including the Bible. He later maintained that Gerrit Smith's abolition lectures on Sunday were not a violation of the Fourth Commandment, since they were part of an effort promoting "the ultimate extension of the Bible, Tract, Sunday School, Temperance and Common School enterprises among millions of our countrymen who are now chiefly excluded." In 1842, Foster and other abolitionists expressed outrage at the extent to which denominational missionary societies tolerated slavery and profited from slave labor: "We have a national custom of robbing a portion of our population called slaves, and employing the proceeds of the robbery for the distribution of the Bible and the preaching of the gospel in foreign countries."[67] Later that year, the *Signal of Liberty* endorsed a position promoted by the New York City *Emancipator* urging "the Benevolent Societies to adopt a position of actual antagonism to slavery"—and to place slaveholding in the same category of transgression as "stealing, intemperance, profanity, or any other sin." Consequently, benevolent societies would be obliged to refuse any contributions from people so tainted. The *Signal* also pointed out that the American Bible Society had "never been much disturbed in its deliberations by the consideration that slavery is the *greatest* obstacle to the accomplishment of its own work" and blasted the society for refusing to ratify a resolution requesting its auxiliaries in the South "as far as practicable to supply every person in their vicinities able to read whether *bond* or *free* with a copy of the Holy Scriptures."[68]

The *Signal* further rebuked the American Board of Commissioners for its tepid stance on slavery. Recalling the biblical story of the Good Samaritan, Foster compared the commissioners to the "Priests and Levites" who bypassed a "brother who has fallen among thieves." In 1853 at the Ann Arbor convention

---

from a Presbyterian to a Congregational body, and in the twentieth century merged with the United Church of Christ). On Parks: ATS (New York) *Annual Report*, XXVII (1852), 73, XXVIII (1853), 63; Sylvan Township Records, April 4, 1842, April 3, 1843, in Bentley Library; *Signal of Liberty*, August 11, 1841.

67. *Signal of Liberty*, June 2, 1841, September 25, 1843, June 6, 1842. See also the remarks of Guy Beckley at the Michigan State Anti-Slavery Society, *ibid.*, February 5, 1844, in which he argued that the "American churches were the bulwark of slavery," as slaveholders were received into "all the large denominations," where they were "promoted to the highest ecclesiastical honors," and "made officers of Bible, Tract, and Missionary societies," while "every attempt to censure or exclude them is steadfastly resisted by the ecclesiastical bodies."

68. *Signal of Liberty*, September 5, 1842, November 27, 1843.

of the Congregationalist General Association of Michigan, delegates devoted considerable time to discussing "whether any of our prominent benevolent Societies hold such a relation to slavery as tends to sustain that stupendous wrong." The following year, these Congregationalists called upon the American Tract Society to issue a tract clearly pronouncing slaveholding to be a sin and, among other things, to provide "god's teaching concerning the universal brotherhood of our race." Of course, the General Association was greatly disappointed when the ATS's Executive Committee decided to withhold from circulation *The Duties of Masters,* described in chapter 1 of this study. While hoping that the society would reverse its decision, in the interim the General Association called upon its churches to "turn their contributions into other channels so long as the Tract Society shall persist in this unrighteous policy." Ann Arbor's Congregationalists likewise were deeply concerned lest any of their benevolent contributions be too closely tied to the peculiar institution, and thus resolved that "[we] cannot approve the attitude of the American Tract Society of New York on the subject of Slavery." And although T. W. Hunt was pleased with his church's condemnation of slavery and its refusal to have fellowship with any "supporter of this evil," he withdrew from the Saline Baptist Church because it sent some of its foreign mission money to the American Baptist Missionary Union. Hunt felt that this organization had compromised too much with slavery; he sought to have all of its missionary donations—rather than a portion—sent to the abolitionist American Baptist Free Mission Society.[69]

Of course, these protestations were not accepted kindly by all proponents of benevolence in Michigan. The *Michigan Christian Herald,* whose editorial stance was mildly antislavery, denied in 1844 that the ABHMS and the American Baptist Board of Foreign Missions were "incurably pro-slavery," for if they

69. *Signal of Liberty,* October 6, 1845; *Michigan Argus,* June 8, 1853; *Minutes of the General Association of Michigan at their Meeting in Detroit, May 30th, 1854* (Ann Arbor, 1854), 20–39; *Minutes of the General Association of Michigan at their Meeting in Adrian, May 20, 1858* (Adrian, 1858), 11; Victor B. Howard, *Conscience and Slavery: The Evangelistic Calvinist Domestic Missions, 1837–1861* (Kent, Ohio, 1990), 117; "Clerk's Record of the Ann Arbor Congregational Church," December 1, 1859, p. 121, in Records of the First Congregational Church of Ann Arbor, Bentley Library; Records of the First Baptist Church of Saline, September 15, 1854, March 17, 1855, Bentley Library; *History of Washtenaw County,* 445; John R. McKivigan, "The Antislavery 'Comeouter' Sects: A Neglected Dimension of the Abolitionist Movement," *Civil War History,* XXVI (June 1980), 152–53; McKivigan, *War Against Proslavery Religion,* 88–89, 99–101.

were, "we should instantly dissolve our connexion with them, and so, we believe, would the 3,000 Baptists of Michigan." There was no reason, argued the *Herald,* to forsake these enterprises, which were "giving the world the Gospel of Christ," when *"slaveholders* denounce them."[70] Others, though, were less willing to acknowledge the virtue of abolitionists' positions with respect to benevolent societies. In 1843 the Jackson *Gazette* protested the Independence Day celebration joining the enthusiasts of Sabbath schools, temperance, and abolition because, as the *Signal of Liberty* reported the *Gazette*'s position, such a gathering would have "a tendency to clog the onward progress of Temperance and Sabbath Schools by the opposition that a portion of the community will manifest to the cause of Human Rights." According to the *Signal,* the attendance at the consolidated festivities in Jackson that year was lower because many citizens of Jackson held their own Sabbath school celebration "in a grove in another part of the village in a manner more congenial, to say the least, to a pro-slavery spirit."[71]

Not always able to reform benevolent associations that they believed were too closely aligned with slavery, Michigan's abolitionists either formed their own societies or sustained those operated by other abolitionists. The *Signal of Liberty* editorialized in 1842: "Those who cannot conscientiously put in their offerings with the price of blood, should not therefore cease to contribute for the spread of the Gospel through all the earth. Other channels are now open in various parts of the globe. The Mendi Mission, the West India Missions, and the condition of the refugees in Canada have claims on the sympathies of the Abolitionists. And may we shortly look for the time when the Southern Prison House shall begin to open, and the Bible shall there be presented 'to every creature.'" A few months earlier, a band of abolitionists assembled at the Ann Arbor Methodist Church to form the interdenominational Union Missionary Society. In the preamble to their constitution, the society's members explained that they felt an "imperious duty" to spread Christianity in a fashion that was "entirely disconnected with oppression and [would] in no way be made directly or indirectly to sanction sin"—in contrast to the "leading Missionary societies of our Nation [which] support and sanction American Slavery." Membership in the Union Missionary Society was open to "any person who is not a slave-

70. *Michigan Christian Herald,* November 18, 1844. On Baptist disputes over slavery, see the correspondence in *Signal of Liberty,* November 24, 1841.

71. *Signal of Liberty,* June 26, 1843, July 10, 1843.

holder," and with respect to the collection of funds and the selection of fields of labor, the society would "discountenance Slavery, and especially by refusing to receive the known fruits of unrequited labor."[72]

Although there is no evidence that the Union Missionary Society met more than once, the sentiments its members expressed at that meeting were not ephemeral. Abolitionists frequently made pleas for their fellow reformers to support missionary work among escaped slaves in Canada. W. M. Sullivan explained in 1841 that many fugitives in Canada were poor and were forced to resort to begging, and he suggested that abolitionists form a missionary society to labor among these refugees—particularly since the positions of Protestant denominational and interdenominational missionary societies were "too flagrant for abolitionists . . . to continue much longer the patrons and supporters of such professedly benevolent operations. I believe there might be an organization which would gratify abolitionists of every Christian order, and much to the honor of our holy religion." In the mid-1840s, Detroit abolitionists commissioned the Reverend Thomas Willas to "solicit funds for purchasing lands in Canada, on which to erect a schoolhouse and church: and to parcel out the residue in small lots to destitute colored people without sectarian distinction." Willas subsequently spent over six months journeying through Michigan and at least four other states as an agent for this objective. And in the 1850s the Reverend C. C. Foote advanced the Refugee Home Society—which body also sought to preach the gospel to former slaves in Canada—before the Congregationalist General Association of Michigan.[73]

Most studies of antebellum benevolence have examined only its northern manifestations. The last two chapters have attempted to describe how the be-

---

72. *Ibid.,* June 6, January 19, 1842. Evidently the Union Missionary Society received its impetus from the Michigan Wesleyan Anti-Slavery Society, which met the day before and denounced the Missionary Society of the Methodist Episcopal Church for "receiving slaveholders without reproof," accepting "the contributions of slaveholders into its Treasury without hesitancy," and "appointing slaveholders to its chief offices"; the body called for the creation of a "pure" missionary society "uncontaminated by the price of blood, and eternally hostile to slavery." *Ibid.,* January 19, 1842.

73. *Ibid.,* December 15, 1841, March 16, 1846 (see also May 26, 1845); Detroit *Daily Democrat,* June 19, 1854; *Minutes of the General Association of Michigan, at Their Meeting in Detroit, May 30th, 1854,* p. 9; *Minutes of the General Association of Michigan at Their Meeting in Adrian, May 20, 1858,* p. 9.

nevolent empire functioned in both a southern and a northern county. One is struck by the parallels between the places. The foremost similarity is that the drive for establishing Sunday schools and Bible and tract societies was typified by cycles of enthusiasm followed by moribundity. Also, in both counties, attempts to circulate religious publications were often hampered by economic downturns. And the ideology behind benevolence was similar in both places, in that its advocates linked their exertions to the spread of market capitalism and believed that their crusades would eliminate vice, spread the gospel, and provide Americans with a moral compass that would ensure social stability.

But there were also significant distinctions between benevolence in the two counties. Partisans in Michigan sometimes resorted to nativism in their rhetoric, arguing that benevolence was the best defense against the spread of Roman Catholicism. In contrast, immigrants and Catholics were relatively few in Alabama, and fear of them far less likely to be aroused. Additionally, it appears that the American Bible Society, the American Tract Society, and the American Sunday School Union were more active in Washtenaw County than in Tuscaloosa County and that Washtenaw Bible devotees may have been slightly more successful than Tuscaloosans in eliminating scriptural destitution in their county. This disparity stemmed not from southern suspicion of these organizations, but from the fact that Presbyterians and Congregationalists— often the principal supporters of these bodies—were more numerous in the North than in the South.[74]

It was actually in Washtenaw County—not Tuscaloosa County—that slavery proved to be a divisive issue for proponents of benevolence. In Washtenaw, many abolitionists viewed slavery as a sin and believed that their association with any organization that tolerated slavery would taint them with the sin as well. Even if they endorsed the objectives of benevolence, they could not in conscience pursue those ends by collaborating with national societies that refused to denounce slavery sufficiently. As a result, they formed their own benevolent societies which stayed clear of slaveholder influence and contamination—which, as we shall see in chapter 6, was similar to the logic used by aboli-

74. By the 1840s, however, Methodists throughout America were wholeheartedly endorsing the ABS and thus became its largest denominational supporter. Peter J. Wosh, "Bibles, Benevolence, and Emerging Bureaucracy: The Persistence of the American Bible Society, 1816–1890" (Ph.D. dissertation, New York University, 1988), 260–61. Regarding Presbyterianism's lack of success in Alabama, see Flynt, "Alabama," 10–11.

tionists to separate themselves from mainstream Protestant churches and national political parties.[75]

Notwithstanding the creation of separate benevolent societies by abolitionists, both abolitionists and slaveholders endorsed benevolence itself. Thus, support for Sunday schools, tracts, and Bibles extended across a gulf that seemed very wide to many Americans of these years. Nevertheless, the most important study of benevolence in the antebellum South, John W. Kuykendall's *Southern Enterprize,* concludes that the Bible and tract causes and the promotion of Sabbath schools were occasionally hindered in the South because of fears of possible abolitionist contamination.[76] To be sure, white Tuscaloosans were greatly fearful of abolitionists. But in spite of these anxieties, the national and regional benevolent societies in Tuscaloosa County were not stigmatized as abolitionist tools until protests were voiced against a publication of the American Tract Society in 1856. Even in this case, Basil Manly and other white southerners protested what they believed was a change in policy of the society; they did not attack the larger concept of evangelical benevolence. White Tuscaloosans who were inclined toward a suspicious view of benevolent efforts would surely have recognized that most of the Tuscaloosans active in evangelical benevolence—especially the leaders—were slaveholders, and that some of them were among the county's harshest critics of abolitionism.

It is also important to note that these particular slaveholders, despite the exceptional wealth of a few, were not members of a leisured planter class who resisted the era's economic and social changes.[77] The commercial and professional occupations of benevolence devotees in both counties, along with their willingness to send their children to school, suggest their commitment to ma-

75. Quist, "Social and Moral Reform," 294–351, 551, 563; Wosh, *Spreading the Word,* 186; McKivigan, *War Against Proslavery Religion,* 111–27.

76. Kuykendall, *Southern Enterprize,* 76–79, 107–109.

77. Among the most important expressions of the view that the antebellum South was governed by a plantation aristocracy that resisted the era's social and economic changes is Genovese, *Political Economy of Slavery,* 3–36. Although Genovese's complex argument has evolved in the years since it was first stated—see, for example, his *Slaveholder's Dilemma: Freedom and Progress in Southern Conservative Thought, 1820–1860* (Columbia, S. C., 1992)—the point of view expressed in *Political Economy of Slavery* has continued to have a wide following. Faust, "The Peculiar South Revisited," 78–119. In contrast, examples of other southern reformers who worked to orient their fellow citizens toward the market economy may be found in Robert Eno Hunt, "Organizing a New South: Education Reformers in Antebellum Alabama, 1840–1860" (Ph.D. dissertation, University of Missouri, 1988).

terial as well as moral progress. The concerns and objectives of their benevolent associations were similar to those of the American Whigs in that they saw both spiritual and physical deficiencies in America's remote regions and they welcomed technological advances as omens of a better age. Further, advocates of benevolent enterprises argued that their efforts assisted Americans in controlling their passions and provided citizens with a moral compass that directed them toward voluntary compliance with civil law and thus bonded American society into a cohesive whole.

3

Toward the Sober Slaveholder: Temperance in Tuscaloosa County

Evangelicals were not content merely to preach the gospel, circulate religious literature, or establish Sunday schools. During the pre–Civil War years, they waged extensive attacks on behaviors that they concluded distanced a person from God. Tuscaloosa's evangelicals assailed the theater, Masonry, and gambling and were to a considerable extent successful in suppressing these activities and organizations in their community.[1] But temperance was by far the most extensive and successful of these crusades.

Similar to the other Tuscaloosa County reform movements examined in this study, temperance went through cycles of enthusiasm and inactivity. Of all these endeavors, though, temperance had by far the greatest public visibility, and unlike the other enterprises, it developed an explicitly political dimension. Its agenda also met with greater success than any other reform effort in Tuscaloosa. Although temperance originally met with considerable opposition, during the 1830s white Tuscaloosans decreased their alcohol consumption and made abstinence from hard liquor into a virtue, particularly among those who identified themselves as enterprising and respectable. Later, prohibitionists captured political power in Tuscaloosa and strove to shut down liquor retailers by raising license fees to extraordinary levels. As we examine Tuscaloosa temperance activity in the decades before the Civil War, we will note how this cause's strategies oscillated between moral suasion and legal prohibition. Also, the membership of Tuscaloosa's temperance movement, originally dominated by the local elite, opened up during the 1840s and 1850s to include whites from the middle and lower ranks of society. Further, the activities described in this

1. Quist, "Social and Moral Reform," 47–69.

chapter will demonstrate that temperance, which has sometimes been discounted by historians as an insignificant movement in the South during the
antebellum years, actually thrived in Tuscaloosa, and that white slaveholders
constituted the bulk of the temperance rank and file.[2]

Tuscaloosa's earliest settlers provided little evidence of enthusiasm for temperance. During the 1820s, political candidates treated the local electorate to liquor, and county elites celebrated American liberty and the virtues of republicanism with toasts at political dinners and Independence Day celebrations.
Occasionally, toasters would drink to alcohol itself, as did R. C. McAlpin in
1824, when he honored "Old Madeira—may it ever remain tax free, to drink to
death ill advised measures." Writing of Tuscaloosa in 1821, William H. Ely lamented that the "highest & lowest Classes in Society . . . are much adicted [*sic*]
to excessive drinking." But Ely's complaints were private murmurings, written
to his wife in Connecticut. During these years, the drinking habits of Tuscaloosans were rarely questioned publicly, as the newly emergent temperance
movement gained its foothold in the Deep South only in July 1827, when a temperance society was formed in Eaton, Georgia. Shortly afterward, though,
Tuscaloosans heard initial rumblings of an issue that would persist for the next
century. In the summer of 1828, one writer in the *Tuscaloosa Chronicle* complained that politicians campaigning for electoral office "hunt up . . . worthless
vagabonds, drench them with some whiskey with a supper of Oysters to obtain
their votes." A few months later, "Capt. Grose" wrote the paper to express concern about the behavior of local residents. Having encountered a saloon while

2. Based on the weak support for the American Temperance Society in the South in 1831,
John A. Krout and others have concluded that enthusiasm for temperance was minimal throughout the region during the antebellum years. Even if Krout's figures are correct—and it is possible
that many proponents of temperance in the slave states belonged to state and local associations
that were not affiliated with the American Temperance Society—they say nothing for the support that temperance received in subsequent decades. John A. Krout, *The Origins of Prohibition*
(New York, 1925), 129–31. See also the citation upon which Krout bases his assertion, *Journal of
Humanity, and Herald of the American Temperance Society* (Andover, Mass.), II (March 10, 1831),
165. Although this source lists only ten temperance societies in Alabama, it acknowledges that its
figures for Alabama and South Carolina were over a year and a half old. Nor does the *Journal*
mention the Tuscaloosa Temperance Society, which by this time had been active for almost two
years. Seven months later the *Journal* remained unaware of the Alabama State Temperance Society. *Ibid.*, III (October 20, 1831), 86; *Alabama State Intelligencer*, August 6, 1831.

strolling through the city, he was disgusted with its "effluvia of certain death." He lamented that there were several of these "hovels of destruction" in town and that they were frequented by "men of families, and claiming the name of respectability." Grose announced that intemperance and other vices were "so prevalent throughout the Southern States, & no where more so than in this town." Local turpitude, he repined, was "not confined to the professed faro dealler, or the lounging votary of the back room of a grogshop." It was "predominant in almost evry class of society, christians *perhaps* excepted."[3]

Captain Grose believed that vices such as liquor consumption begat idleness and destroyed individual initiative. When he first visited Tuscaloosa, Grose entered the "business part of the town" and found "several little groups of men, sitting and standing at the shop doors, *whitling* sticks." He characterized Tuscaloosa's liquor stores as being surrounded by "sloth and depravity." Instead of hearing a "busy hum" one morning in the town's business district, he discovered that "silence reigned as predominant as at midnight: or perhaps more so." With the exception of saloons, "not a shop has yet unloosed a window, nor a door yet open." The problem with intemperance, according to Grose, was that it directed people away from disciplined and structured living; alcohol was a subtle beast that enslaved its victims to their most vile passions and craftily led them to gambling and then to "inevitable ruin."[4]

By 1840, the editors of Tuscaloosa's newspapers would similarly condemn intemperance, gambling, and other vices. During the late 1820s and early 1830s, however, some Tuscaloosans did not permit such moralistic condemnations to go unchallenged. Critics complained of Grose, for example, that his description of their town was mistaken and that the fault-finding moralism of his beratings was nauseating. Nevertheless, the intensity of the critics' remarks suggests that they were not simply boosters highly conscious of their town's image, but that they feared the growing power of evangelicals and their secular allies who were obsessed with respectability. "Truth" was outraged, labeling

3. *American Mirror,* July 10, 31, 1824; Tuscaloosa *Chronicle,* July 6, 1829; *Alabama Sentinel,* July 11, 1829; Tuscaloosa *Inquirer,* February 23, May 4, July 21, 1831; *Alabama State Intelligencer,* July 17, 1831; *Flag of the Union,* March 28, 1838; William H. Ely to Clarissa May Davis, June 2, 1821, in Hoole, ed., "Elyton, Alabama," 67; Tuscaloosa *Chronicle,* July 19, October 30, November 10, 1828; Douglas Wiley Carlson, "Temperance Reform in the Cotton Kingdom" (Ph.D. dissertation, University of Illinois, 1982), 13. See also Amos Warner to Peter Wainright, June 18, 1820, in James Austin Anderson Papers, Hoole Special Collections (typescript).

4. Tuscaloosa *Chronicle,* October 18, 30, November 10, 1828.

Grose as the epitome of "the insidious spy, the mean contemptible inter-
meddler—the base calumniator and malignant LYAR!!" and advising him to
mind his own affairs, find honest employment, and beware of tar and feathers
if he continued to "amuse himself and the public at the expense of innocent individuals." Less threatening but still indignant was "Tom Diggery," who
warned Grose that if he continued to make his "meditation rambles," he would
be brought before the law and punished as "an idle straggler." Tom informed
Grose that "if he really intends to bring about a reformation in [Tuscaloosa], he
will certainly miss his end, because he is mistaken in their manners." Tuscaloosans were not prone to vice, but more important, local citizens "stay at home
and mind their own business, and let our neighbors do the same."[5]

Five months after the *Chronicle* published Grose's jeremiads, Tuscaloosans
assembled to form their town's first voluntary association to suppress the excessive use of liquor. The "Anti-Electioneering Association" protested the practice of political aspirants who "ride all over the country" seeking votes. More
specifically, it objected to candidates who treated the electorate to whiskey (the
term *electioneer* referred to this custom). Members of the body pledged not to
vote for any such candidate and announced that they would "use all laudible
means to prevent the election of any person . . . guilty . . . of such immoral
practices." The *Alabama State Intelligencer* agreed that electioneering was a serious problem, as many "intelligent and patriotic persons" avoided running for
office because they had neither the time nor the money to waste "the spring and
summer in posting through the county, from house to house, spending their
substance at grog shops." Under the current custom, "only the more wealthy or
vicious" could run for office. The *Intelligencer* further concurred that the electioneering system created "swarms of degraded wretches" who "lounge and loi-
ter about the haunts of vice . . . in the hope of drinking the candidate's treat."
But the *Intelligencer*'s editors saw a greater threat in "leagued associations
formed for the purpose of affecting an election," which endangered the vitality
of a republic based upon "freedom of election." The paper therefore opposed
the Anti-Electioneering Association.[6]

5. *Ibid.*, November 10, 17, 1828. "Truth" and "Tom Diggery" may have been encouraged by
Tuscaloosa *Chronicle* editor Dugald McFarlane, who, as one contemporary later recalled, was
"sorely beset with the sin of intemperance." William Russell Smith, *Reminiscences of a Long Life:
Historical, Political, Personal and Literary* (Washington, D.C., 1889), 24.

6. *Alabama State Intelligencer*, April 17, 1829; on electioneering in Madison County, see Dupre, "Barbecues and Pledges," 479–512. Before Tuscaloosa's temperance controversy erupted, the

In spite of the *Intelligencer*'s protests, opponents of electioneering formed the Tuscaloosa Society for the Promotion of Temperance in April 1829. Although the core of the members' pledge—"not to drink ardent spirits, nor to give it to others, unless as a medicine, and then in cases only of imperious necessity"—should come as no surprise, their avowal not "to support for any office any man who is in the habit of the intemperate use of ardent spirits, or who shall be known to treat, directly or indirectly, for the purpose of securing his election" suggests that the objectives of the Anti-Electioneering Association were subsumed by the cause of temperance. The executive committee of the Tuscaloosa Society for the Promotion of Temperance explained their agenda more explicitly in a statement published in the *Intelligencer.* Intemperance was "destructive of individual advantage—domestic prosperity—social pleasure and political improvement." If treating the electorate continued, it would result in the loss of political virtue and the rise of "total corruption," thus making Americans incapable of self-government and leading to the country's downfall. The temperance society sought to "destroy . . . the embryo contagion before it incorporates itself with our institutions." But the problem went beyond electioneering: it was the "deliberate opinion of the temperance society that there is no evil, with which society is cursed, so huge and unmanageable as that which originates from the *use* of ardent spirits—(we will not say the abuse.)"[7]

Like the assertions of Captain Grose, the declarations of the new temperance society met with hostility from some of the town's residents. One objector, writing under the pseudonym "Thumbscrew," alluded to the close ties between temperance activists and evangelical ministers—"those travelling gentlemen, yclept Circuit Riders." Their efforts were evidence that "the spirit of fanaticism is stalking abroad throughout the land," for it was "well known by believers that these supposed inroads on our personal liberties are for the good of our souls." Another critic, "A Friend to Mental and Personal Liberty," objected to the society's prohibition of ardent spirits. He doubted whether "a

---

editors of the *Intelligencer* expressed the following perspective in the inaugural issue (April 10, 1829) of their paper: "Extreme religious fanaticism is not more pernicious in its tendencies, or unfavorable to truth, than great political excitement. By it communities are distracted and torn asunder, strife and animosity are kept up between individuals, slander and falsehood are countenanced; the real object of all good government, left out of view, is never pursued." The editors' response to temperance was thus another manifestation of their dislike of partisan animosity.

7. *Ibid.,* May 17, 8, 1829.

little spirit taken merely to alleviate fatigue, or to exhilarate the mind over-stretched by long and strenuous application to study, can really be prejudicial to morals." Particularly objectionable to this writer was the society's constitution restricting its members from supporting intemperate candidates or those who treated the electorate. "Friend" agreed with Thumbscrew that the Methodist clergy were behind all of this temperance commotion. He regarded these oaths as contrary to the United States Constitution because they "bound up" citizens "in the trammels of individual authority." Additionally, he considered that the temperance society threatened to violate privacy, and he asked Tuscaloosans if they would

> suffer a set of meddlers to enter the privacy of your dwellings and persuade you to deny the rights of hospitality, the dearest right of a Southerner, to a friend, or even a stranger, who does not think as they do on the subject of ardent spirits? Will you deny to your old friend . . . his accustomed drink of spirits and water, because some brutal, weak, fools cannot taste without making themselves drunk? If we must have follies, let them be of our own growth; let us not ape the yankee puritans who bow in all submission to whatever their minister dictates.[8]

The temperance society was thus seen by its enemies as a group of imperious zealots who espoused ideals that ran counter to accepted local customs.

The partisans of temperance did not permit these assaults on their cause to go unanswered. "Whiskey Punch" charged "Friend" with anticlericalism and mockingly denied that to listen "to the voice of Methodist preachers is to sacrifice personal liberty. . . . The friends of temperance had not interfered with his liberty . . . they had not, with rash hand, attempted to dash the delicious toddy from his lips." On the contrary, it was "Friend" who was guilty of being intolerant; if people had the right to drink what they pleased, how could it be intrusive if people endeavored "to abstain from drinking what . . . they may deem pernicious"? In response to this counterattack, "Friend" protested that the meaning of his previous essay had been distorted. Reiterating his opposition to the "narrow, illiberal spirit which confounds the *use* with the *abuse* of spirits," he contended that the logical extension of the temperance society's rhetoric would be to abolish love lest it lead to libertinism. He insisted that anticlerical accusations against him were unfounded, adding that a minister who "recommend[s] any particular measure to his fellow citizens" was as accountable "to the tribunal of public opinion" as anyone else. "Friend" was pleased, however,

8. *Ibid.*, May 8, April 24, 1829.

that in spite of the agitation promoted by the temperance workers, only a few of his fellow Tuscaloosans had enlisted in their ranks.[9]

The emerging controversy caught the attention of the editor of the *Augusta Courier,* who reported that a society had formed in Tuscaloosa "for the suppression of Intemperance and Electioneering." The editor's opinion was that "the society has undertaken a difficult task, and will find that last nearly as difficult as the former." In one instance, the editors of the *Intelligencer* (W. W. McGuire, W. E. Henry, and H. M. McGuire) attempted to inject humor into the temperance struggle when they reported that Daniel Craigham, boating in the Black Warrior River while intoxicated, fell overboard and drowned: "We understand there is a warm dispute between the Temperance and Anti-Temperance folks whether his death was produced by 'ardent spirits' or 'cold water.'" Although irritated by the temperance activists, the *Intelligencer* maintained an ambivalent position on temperance, possibly attempting to offend as few readers as possible. On the one hand, the editors concluded that "all the low abuse, vulgar epithets, invidious personal allusions, the actions of the angry passions with which the papers have teemed, for the last few weeks" were due to the antielectioneering plank of the society's constitution, which the *Intelligencer* had opposed from the beginning. They further agreed with "Friend" that it was wrong for even ministers "to interfere with us in the exercise of our elective franchise," and they objected to anyone's prescribing different qualifications for public office from those outlined in the state constitution. But the editors also conceded that some of the charges made by antitemperance writers had demeaned the clergy, and they agreed with the temperance forces that intoxication produced considerable human misery and needed eradication. In this spirit, the *Intelligencer* praised a temperance sermon by Tuscaloosa's Methodist minister, the Reverend Robert L. Kennon, who "Friend" had suggested was the inspiration behind the most objectionable features of the temperance society. The editors believed that if everyone could hear such a sermon, "great comparative sobriety would ensue."[10]

9. *Ibid.,* May 1, 8, 1829. From the extant sources it is impossible to determine the numerical strength of the Tuscaloosa Society for the Promotion of Temperance—later known simply as the Tuscaloosa Temperance Society. Support for temperance in 1829, however, was not confined to the town of Tuscaloosa, as another temperance society was formed that year in the county's rural village of Carthage. *Journal of Humanity, and Herald of the American Temperance Society,* II (March 10, 1831), 165.

10. *Augusta Courier* quoted in *Alabama State Intelligencer,* June 5, 1829; *Alabama State Intelligencer,* June 12, May 8, 1829.

The *Intelligencer*'s effort to mediate the conflict by plowing a middle ground did not set partisans at ease. One unidentified writer blamed the temperance forces for upsetting the peace of the town and insisted that they were seeking to impose their religious values on everyone else. Tuscaloosa's temperance movement, this writer announced, mostly consisted of local elites who were angered that some of their fellow residents had become "so brutified by drink as to be incapable of discriminating between" the "superior virtues" of this gentry "and the squalid wretch who wields a mallet, or toils at the plough handles!" Naturally, this unsigned attack triggered a reply. "Zeta" asserted that liquor "produced a thousand fold more evil than good to the community," and those "persons capable of sober reflection," who recognized this fact, would seek its ban entirely, even if their efforts were despised and ridiculed with the "sharp weapons of *wit* and *satire.*" Zeta alleged that his adversaries held that the evils of intemperance "are very limited in their extent, only here and there a contemptible drunkard who deserves no pity . . . and whose death will be an advantage to society."[11] Temperance proponents such as Zeta believed that they held the high ground regarding human life. It was obvious, they claimed, that the anti-temperance people had no regard for the victims of alcohol abuse and simply blamed the individual drunkard for his or her difficulties. Temperance activists saw things differently: if society's members did not endeavor to banish ardent spirits, then they were accomplices in the evils of intemperance.

There seems to be one point, however, on which both adversaries and proponents of temperance agreed: the significance of individual independence. The differences between the two groups stemmed from the divergent ways in which they understood this concept. Opponents of temperance believed that independence meant autonomy and consisted of the right of individuals to make choices in the absence of external constraint. Thus, they complained that temperance proponents' efforts were intrusive and diminished the agency of individuals to decide for themselves whether or how much they would drink. Temperance forces, on the other hand, were convinced that independence consisted of freedom from vices that inhibited the individual from attaining his or

11. *Alabama State Intelligencer,* May 29, June 5, 1829. The controversy over temperance upset the tranquillity of Huntsville at the same time, while in Mobile a temperance society, an ATS auxiliary, and the Female Benevolent Society were organized in 1829. Fladeland, *Birney,* 33–34; Daniel Dupre, "Liberty and Order on the Cotton Frontier: Madison County, Alabama, 1800–1840" (Ph.D. dissertation, Brandeis University, 1991), 326–33; Harriet E. Amos, *Cotton City: Urban Development in Antebellum Mobile* (University, Ala., 1985), 17.

her true potential. The inactivity that Captain Grose found in Tuscaloosa's business district was deplorable to him and to others who believed that the diminished use of liquor would result in greater industry and prosperity for their town. Further, in the minds of temperance devotees, a person who was dependent upon alcohol was not free. The drunkard could not make a responsible decision when voting, nor could the inebriate approach God and be converted to Protestant Christianity, and neither could that person have the internal drive that would lead to self-improvement.[12]

Although opposition to the temperance society was often ferocious in 1829, it quickly subsided, at least in the town's newspapers. It is not clear why the opponents and skeptics ceased their written protestations. Perhaps they recognized that popular opinion no longer favored them and thus felt bludgeoned into silence, or possibly a new generation of temperance-minded editors refused to publish anything denunciatory of temperance. Maybe the one-time adversaries of temperance were converted to the principles of cold water. Probably, though, the most significant cause behind this shift is that the commencement of temperance activism in Tuscaloosa coincided with the demise of Jeffersonian rationalism and the emergence of revivalism. As evangelical Protestantism gained the intellectual ascendancy in Tuscaloosa—as it already had elsewhere in the early-nineteenth-century South—public opposition to virtuous living declined. Nevertheless, looking at Tuscaloosa beyond the editorial pages of its newspapers, one clearly sees that many Tuscaloosans refused to give up the bottle. Liquor continued to be sold with few, if any, restrictions—merchants and grocers listed in the town's newspapers the "wines and liquors" available at their stores.[13]

An examination of the county's tavern licenses from 1820 to 1832 further illustrates that new drinking patterns were not present among the entire population. The largest number of tavern and liquor licenses was issued in 1826 (see Table 6) and probably reflects hopes of profiting from Tuscaloosa's new status as a state capital. It is true that ten licenses to sell liquor were issued in 1829 and

12. For a similar dichotomy between the ideology of Alabama's Whigs and Democrats, see Thornton, *Politics and Power,* 54–58, and J. Mills Thornton III, "The Ethic of Subsistence and the Origins of Southern Secession," *Tennessee Historical Quarterly,* XLVIII (Summer 1989), 72–73.

13. The transition from rationalism to evangelicalism is traced in May, *Enlightenment in America,* 324–36. Regarding the sale of liquor in Tuscaloosa, see *State Rights Expositor and Spirit of the Age,* December 15, 1832; *Flag of the Union,* June 6, 1838; *Alabama State Intelligencer,* June 12, 1829, January 8, 1831; *Spirit of the Age,* May 2, 1832; and *Independent Monitor,* April 30, 1845.

only six in 1830, but it is not clear whether this decrease was due to greater temperance activity, business failures, or a consolidation of Tuscaloosa's drinking establishments. The record also shows that John Meek was the only tavern operator in Tuscaloosa who purchased a less expensive license that precluded him from selling spirits. At his establishment, Meek, a proponent of Sabbath schools who was also employed as a slave trader, pledged that he would try to please "every sober, genteel person & as he keeps no BAR, he will refuse to entertain any who may be intoxicated. He therefore hopes that none of that description will trouble him with a call." Although Meek's establishment may have appealed to some Tuscaloosans, apparently there was only enough demand to keep one temperance tavern operating.[14]

In spite of the persistence of drinking in Tuscaloosa, the executive committee of the temperance society claimed in 1829 that public sentiment was shifting in their direction. For example, without being solicited by temperance devotees, Tuscaloosa's candidates for the state legislature pledged that year not to treat the electorate in the upcoming election. Temperance activists believed that a reformation in electoral habits was occurring throughout the state, and they reported that electioneering was now a rarity. In place of the former customs, "sober citizens" were now performing "their patriotic duty, or rationally canvassing the *true merits* of the persons offering to represent them." The temperance enthusiasts denied charges that they "intended to establish a proscriptive censorship, and impose aristocratic restrictions on the freedom of elections." On the contrary, they sought to keep the franchise "in the vigor of untarnished purity" and to "preserve the *morals* of the sovereign people from the demoralizing influence of unblushing bribery." A republican government, they believed, required an independent and moral electorate. The committee also claimed that the "moral influence of temperance" was being felt increasingly as more talented individuals rallied around its banners. Indeed, they an-

---

14. William H. Williams to the ASSU, January 31, 1832, in ASSU Papers; *State Rights Expositor and Spirit of the Age,* December 15, 1832; *Alabama Sentinel,* June 20, 1829. In 1831, Meek purchased a $10 license that permitted him to operate a tavern without selling liquor; in 1832, he purchased a $20 tavern license, which presumably permitted him to sell spirits. Tuscaloosa County Tavern License Docket, 1818–1832, Tuscaloosa County Courthouse. Whether he ever sold liquor under this license is not known; in 1829, however, he advertised that his tavern, the Rising Sun, had no bar, and in 1834 he described his "City Hotel" as a "Temperance House." *Alabama Sentinel,* June 20, 1829; *State Rights Expositor and Spirit of the Age,* December 7, 1833; *State Rights Expositor,* March 8, 1834; *Alabama Intelligencer and State Rights Expositor,* October 3, 1835.

nounced that the "spirit of radical reform, in this particular, has been aroused." Despite "the denunciations of prejudice, the lash of wit, and the impositions of nameless essayists" brought against Tuscaloosa's temperance community, its members were convinced that a transformation in public attitudes toward drink was occurring as a result of their efforts and the labors of temperance activists throughout the state. Believing that triumph was within reach, the temperance society congratulated itself and passed a resolution proclaiming that the members "deserve[d] the thanks of all good men."[15]

Although total victory for the temperance forces continually proved to be illusive, public objections to the movement appeared to be receding, and the cause shortly became a widely embraced institution of respectable Tuscaloosans. Two examples from 1830 demonstrate that this transition was already well under way. In June of that year, members of the temperance society were notable in the planning of the town's Fourth of July festivities, and they assumed a distinctive position in the Independence Day procession. A few months later, the comments of "Jeremiah Sneak" suggest that women were among the first converts to temperance and that their proddings encouraged their husbands to embrace a temperate lifestyle. A resident of rural Tuscaloosa County, Sneak complained that "the women our way seem determined to deprive us of all of our privileges; if I offer to take a drink of whiskey as I used to do, my wife tells me of the *Temperation Society*, and says its mean, and low, and sinful."[16]

With the decline of vocal opposition, Tuscaloosa's temperance society grew rapidly. In early 1833 the society requested that the pastors of each church in Tuscaloosa preach a temperance sermon before the society's annual meeting in April, and that each temperance society member persuade at least one additional person to enlist in the cause. This effort was an overwhelming success: seventy-three new members—thirty-six men and thirty-seven women—joined the ranks. Two months later, twenty-seven more enlisted in the cause. Such activism caused one rural Tuscaloosan to remark wryly that the "Temperance Societies have done away (pretty much) with strong drink."[17] It is

15. *Alabama State Intelligencer,* July 24, 1829. The sentiments of all Tuscaloosans had not progressed as far as the temperance society would have liked, as on this occasion the *Intelligencer* forsook its middle position and ridiculed the society's self-congratulatory resolution.

16. *Ibid.,* June 4, July 2, August 6, 1830.

17. *State Rights Expositor and Spirit of the Age,* March 2, April 6, June 8, 1833; *Alabama Intelligencer and State Rights Expositor,* November 7, 1835.

likely, however, that the temperance society in Tuscaloosa merely organized the atomized enemies of alcohol into groups of activists and made the consumption of strong drink disreputable among society's respectable elements. There are no indications suggesting that temperance societies reformed many inebriates at this stage of the movement, especially among the lower classes.[18]

But the growing strength of temperance sentiment, coupled with Tuscaloosans' boosterism, may have caused officials to place greater restrictions upon unregulated tippling. In early 1831 Tuscaloosa's civil authorities passed an ordinance that sought to regulate the large number of vendors selling liquor from their wagons, who were found throughout the town's streets but were concentrated in its commons. This new law penalized such vendors five dollars "for each and every offence, one half to the informer, and the other half to this corporation." Evidence that the unregulated sale and consumption of alcohol was perceived as a threat to the community was manifested most strongly in "An Ordinance to Regulate Slaves in the Town of Tuscaloosa," which will be discussed in chapter 5. Additional restrictions were enacted in 1835, when a local ordinance prohibited the sale of liquor after 10 P.M.[19]

Improved regulation of alcohol sales, however, did not quell demand among those unmoved by the temperance cause, and in no case is this better illustrated than with electioneering. Despite the claims made in 1829 regarding the disappearance of this practice, the campaign for governor and state legislature in 1831 witnessed a resurgence of candidates' treating the electorate, illustrating further that whatever changes may have occurred in the public's drinking habits, devotion to temperance principles was far from universal. The *Intelligencer* lamented that "all well wishers of good order and sobriety must deeply deplore the prevalence of [this] disgraceful evil," and the *Inquirer*'s Erasmus Walker believed that the practice was more widespread than ever and praised the halcyon election of only two years before, when opposition to treating "took such a deep hold."[20] "Cornfield Observer" was incensed that a candidate for gover-

18. Nationally, temperance was an affair of the middle and upper classes until the 1840s, when the Washingtonians and the Sons of Temperance emerged. The Tuscaloosa manifestations of these organizations are discussed later in this chapter.

19. *Alabama State Intelligencer,* March 30, 1831; *Alabama Intelligencer and State Rights Expositor,* October 17, 1835. This ordinance was passed shortly after Tuscaloosa's gamblers were driven from town, and may have been part of the city's effort to curtail gambling.

20. *Alabama State Intelligencer,* June 4, 1831; Tuscaloosa *Inquirer,* July 21, 1831. Although Walker expressed disapproval of electioneering, he also questioned the numerical strength of the

nor, and another for Congress, treated Tuscaloosa's electorate without even announcing their political views. Instead of stumping or submitting their arguments to the press, these candidates spent all of their time in Tuscaloosa's liquor establishments or mingling with "some multitudes of *rowdies* in the streets." Such candidates recognized all too well that they could not win "in competition with the man of qualification. They have to resort to the grogshop." Cornfield concluded that they were unworthy "to fill the offices which they seek at the hands of a free people."[21]

Opponents of electioneering worried that the best-qualified candidates would be denied office and that the community's lowest moral denominator would reign supreme. The result would be the continued growth of liquor consumption, and voters would fall prey to scheming politicians eager to promote their own selfish agenda rather than the good of society. Denunciations of electioneering in 1835 by Samuel Mills Meek, by the Tuscaloosa Temperance Society in 1839, and by the Tuscaloosa Baptist Association in 1846—whose delegates lamented that they had seen this practice continued "for years"—demonstrate that many citizens still responded more affirmatively to the candidates' treat than to the pleas of temperance societies. Nevertheless, Meek's protest of electioneering by other candidates reveals the extent to which Tuscaloosa's public discourse had changed since 1829, when opponents

Anti-electioneering Association. Benjamin Fontaine provided the *Inquirer* with a copy of the association's principles, and 100 signatures affirming solidarity. Walker challenged Fontaine, claiming that the notice supplied to the *Inquirer* was merely a copy of a manifesto circulated two years earlier and questioning whether 100 people actually subscribed to the principles of the association. Tuscaloosa *Inquirer,* June 30, 1831.

21. *Alabama State Intelligencer,* June 4, 1831. Both the *Intelligencer* and one of its correspondents later accused John Gayle of being the gubernatorial candidate guilty of treating the voters. Gayle partisans were outraged. "Cato" insisted that such charges were full of "slander and falsehood" and were a desperate attempt to revive the sagging candidacy of Nicholas Davis. He acknowledged that Gayle traveled about the state, mingling with voters and explaining issues to them, and countercharged that Gayle's behavior was better than Davis', whose failure to campaign revealed that he was blue-blooded. *Inquirer* editor Erasmus Walker's response was less direct; he avoided the charge of Gayle's guilt in treating the voters but suggested that Davis stayed indoors in 1831 because he had demonstrated, while treating the voters in 1829, that he "could not restrain himself occasionally from actual *intoxication*." Tuscaloosa *Inquirer,* July 21, 1831. Interestingly, although Gayle was a supporter of temperance in 1829, a contemporary later wrote that "the social nature of Gov. Gayle, and the common usages of his day, betrayed him into habits of intemperance." *Alabama State Intelligencer,* July 24, 1829; Garrett, *Reminiscences of Public Men in Alabama,* 459.

of temperance pilloried their adversaries as moral extremists. Meek, who had been president of the Tuscaloosa Temperance Society since 1831 and refused to treat the voters in his 1835 campaign for the Alabama legislature, could have been similarly excoriated by his political opponents had they thought that such a tactic would be politically useful. Instead, they labeled Meek as a nullifier, which he claimed was a distortion concocted by his adversaries "striving to deprive me of my good name and fair standing in the community with those who have been under their Bacchanalian influence."[22]

Despite the persistence of drinking among much of the population, it is nonetheless clear that in just a few years many Alabamians embraced the temperate lifestyle—a change that reflected both the successes of the temperance movement and the greatly decreased per capita consumption of alcohol nationwide. As one Alabama merchant reported to the New York *American*, in 1824 he had required "100 barrels of whiskey, with a large quantity of American and English rum, and American and French brandies" to satisfy the demands of his customers for that year. Subsequently, though, local demand for liquor decreased, so that by 1831 he needed only five barrels of whiskey and one pipe of brandy to meet the annual needs of his increasingly temperate neighbors. After praising the temperance effort in Tuscaloosa, the Mobile *Chronicle* marveled in 1839 at how "the habits of society have been so far improved within a few years, that it would now be almost as difficult to meet a party of gentlemen in a state of beastly inebriety, as it would formerly have been to find a sober man in an assemblage convened for hilarity and mirth." Of course, intemperance had not yet been permanently defeated, and the *Chronicle*'s writer was saddened that social censure had made drunkenness into a "solitary" vice. His remarks, though, comport with the findings of modern scholars, who have concluded that alcohol consumption in the United States declined by over 50 percent during the 1830s.[23]

22. *Flag of the Union*, August 22, 1835; *Alabama State Intelligencer and State Rights Expositor*, August 22, 1835; *Flag of the Union*, October 2, 1839; *Independent Monitor*, August 29, 1846.

23. New York *American* quoted in American Temperance Society, *Annual Report*, VI (1833), 105–106; Mobile *Chronicle* quoted in *Flag of the Union*, September 11, 1839. Per capita consumption of alcohol in the United States decreased from nearly four gallons in 1830 to about two gallons in 1840. W. J. Rorabaugh, *The Alcoholic Republic: An American Tradition* (New York, 1979), 232; Jack S. Blocker, *American Temperance Movements: Cycles of Reform* (Boston, 1988), 28–29, 34; Mark Edward Lender and James Kirby Martin, *Drinking in America: A History* (Rev. ed.; New York, 1987), 46, 71, 205–206.

At this point, it is imperative to ask why some Tuscaloosans became so vigilant regarding temperance and benevolence during these years. Unfortunately, the reformers did not always explain to posterity why they strove to promote their agenda; to them the correctness of their positions was self-evident. Nevertheless, the alcohol consumption of which they complained was not merely imagined, but was greater in 1830 than at any time before or since in the history of the United States. Also important to temperance devotees was the segment of the population most likely to imbibe heavily: highly mobile, single, adult males. Not only were these individuals, when inebriated, frequently obnoxious and boisterous to morally estimable citizens, but their rootlessness made it difficult to restrain them through family pressure and other traditional means of social control. Temperance, then, set a new standard of respectability to which enthusiasts hoped all worthy members of society would aspire, while concurrently elevating self-control into a greater social virtue. Temperance also proved to be extraordinarily compatible with the expansion of market capitalism, a point to which reformers often alluded. Temperate workers and proprietors were more efficient in their labors, it was claimed, and money saved from people no longer purchasing liquor could be invested more profitably.[24]

The expansion of revivalism was unquestionably a factor in this cultural and behavioral transformation, for evangelicals believed that an inebriate lacked the mental wherewithal to plead for God's grace. The evangelical churches disciplined their members for drunkenness, although in the years before the Civil War only Tuscaloosa's Presbyterians insisted upon total abstinence from all intoxicants. Baptists and Methodists often embraced the cause by permitting temperance meetings to be held in their churches, through editorials in religious newspapers, or by direct clerical endorsement.[25] The intense moral

24. Rorabaugh, *Alcoholic Republic*, 11–12, 140–46; Peter Way, "Evil Humors and Ardent Spirits: The Rough Culture of Canal Construction Workers," *Journal of American History*, LXXIX (March 1993), 1412–14. See also Jed Dannenbaum, *Drink and Disorder: Temperance Reform in Cincinnati from the Washingtonian Revival to the WCTU* (Urbana, Ill., 1984), 1–12.

25. Session Book No. 1 of the Tuscaloosa Presbyterian Church, September 1, 1834, in possession of the First Presbyterian Church of Tuscaloosa; W. D. Blanks, "Corrective Church Discipline in the Presbyterian Churches of the Nineteenth Century South," *Journal of Presbyterian History*, XLIV (June 1966), 99, 102. On Baptists: *Minutes of the Eleventh Annual Session of the Tuscaloosa Baptist Association; Minutes of the Eighteenth Annual Session of the Tuscaloosa Baptist Association, Held at the Friendship Meeting-House, Tuscaloosa County, Alabama* (Tuscaloosa, 1850); *Alabama Baptist* (Marion), February 4, November 4, 1843, March 16, June 15, 1844; *Alabama Baptist Advocate*, April 20, October 31, 1849; *South Western Baptist*, October 9, December 4, 1850, October

vision that revivals stamped upon many evangelicals doubtless caused them to look upon temperance favorably. If drunkenness was part of the fallen and sinful world that Christians were to shun, many evangelicals undoubtedly felt that taking the additional step of abstaining from hard liquor—or even from all intoxicants—was fulfilling the spirit of their religious obligations.

Despite their successes in the 1830s, many temperance devotees in Tuscaloosa were disappointed that their victory was not complete. Realizing that a significant portion of the population refused to relinquish spirits, many reformers grew impatient with moral suasion and, by 1838, sought to enact limitations on the retail sale of alcohol. From the beginning of temperance activity in Tuscaloosa, there had been division in the movement regarding the means by which their objectives could best be achieved, with one camp favoring persuasion and another endorsing coercion. This division was never resolved in antebellum Tuscaloosa. Indeed, as we shall see, many temperance organizers worked for legal restrictions on the sale of liquor in the late 1830s and 1850s, but during the 1840s, they chiefly embraced moral suasion.[26] In 1829 "Temperance and Freedom" wrote in the *Chronicle* that "the formation of temperate societies, I say is right, and I am glad the opinion is general." Nonetheless, he was outraged at the Tuscaloosa Society for the Promotion of Temperance, as that body had allegedly presented memorials to the Alabama legislature "for legal power to force obedience to certain rules of the Society" (which rules, unfortunately, he failed to specify). Like flatly antitemperance writers, Freedom saw Tuscaloosa's temperance forces as part of a clerical drive to obliterate individual liberty and freedom of conscience, which he insisted was the "grand hallmark and safeguard of religion pure and undefiled." This attempt violated the spirit of Christianity, as it sought to compel the public "to observe measures, which all the eloquence of the scribes and pharisees throughout the land cannot enact." Christ did not command his apostles to present "memorials to the existing

8, 1851, October 28, 1852, April 1, 8, 29, August 12, 1853, June 5, 1854, March 13, 1856. On Methodists: *Alabama State Intelligencer,* April 24, May 1, 1829; *Spirit of the Age,* March 14, 21, April 4, June 3, 1832; *State Rights Expositor and Spirit of the Age,* April 6, 1833; *Independent Monitor,* January 4, 18, February 1, 1843, January 1, 1845; James Sellers, *First Methodist Church,* 159–60.

    26. One scholar of American temperance has concluded that its proponents have remained divided on the question of persuasion versus coercion, and that the history of this reform "reveals no simple progression toward coercion." Blocker, *American Temperance Movements,* xv and *passim.*

powers" when they preached the gospel, for "they were strong in themselves, the power of God was with them." Freedom contended that all the laws in the world "cannot make a christian," and legislative efforts to impose temperate behavior would fail and were subversive of American liberty.[27]

It is not known which measures, if any, the temperance society tried to enact at this time. Tuscaloosa's earliest recorded proponent of prohibition explained his views under the pseudonym "Zerotes" in 1831. He argued that as a consequence of living in a community, people surrender the right to behave in ways that injure others. Thus, the sale of ardent spirits should be prohibited through legislative action because of the incalculable harm that liquor inflicted upon the community. Those who sold liquor were a greater scourge to humanity than murderers. Whereas murderers took the lives of a few individuals, vendors of spirits were responsible for the sacrifice of "hundreds" on the "bacchanalian altar." Unlike Freedom, who defined liberty as the preservation of individual autonomy and the absence of external constraint, Zerotes emphasized that freedom existed only following the removal of impediments that precluded individuals from attaining their highest potential. The alcohol seller not only prevented drinkers from striving toward perfection, but also inhibited their dependents from earnest improvement. Zerotes concluded that "every resident, occasioned by the formation of a law which is productive of the general good, is an actual accession to individual liberty." The legislature's refusal to abolish the retail of ardent spirits could only signify that legislators had breached their charge to promote the general welfare of society, and they could thus be esteemed as "unworthy the confidence of a free people."[28]

A coordinated effort to carry this logic into law commenced in 1838, when the corresponding committee of the Tuscaloosa Temperance Society declared in a circular to the "friends of Temperance throughout the State of Alabama" that it was actively petitioning the legislature to end the retail of liquor "in small quantities." Because the committee acknowledged that people had a right to use their money for their own ruin, its members focused their wrath not on the users of spirits, but on those who sold it. And although they denied that the legislature had "the power to regulate morals in all their bearings," they nevertheless asserted that the lawmakers were empowered to "prevent the seller from selling that which produces the distress and beggary of the pur-

27. Tuscaloosa *Chronicle*, July 20, 1829.
28. *Alabama State Intelligencer*, January 26, 1831.

chasers family; especially if the practice has become so general as to affect a large portion of the community." Retailers were like professional gamblers, as "the winner takes his neighbors money without consideration, producing probable ruin at least to the looser's family." Laws against gambling demonstrated that the legislature was not powerless to halt the retail sale of liquor, as its effects, like those of gambling, were "against the moral sense of the community." The corresponding committee regarded the retailing of liquor as an "inequitable and immoral traffic" and a "fruitful source of idleness, poverty, and bloodshed," producing "by far the larger amount of our paupers and prisoners, for the maintenance of whom every citizen is *taxed.*" The circular urged "every friend of good order and morals" to join the committee in the effort to prohibit the "retailing of ardent spirits in small quantities, and to abolish every grog shop in the land."[29]

In order to convince lawmakers that support for their cause was widespread, Alabama's temperance societies circulated petitions statewide that pleaded for the end of retail trade in ardent spirits. In doing so, they found plenty of verbal support from the state's leading politicians, a number of whom had enlisted in the cause. Governor Arthur Bagby declared his abhorrence of intemperance in a September 1838 address before the Tuscaloosa Temperance Society.[30] Speaking later before the legislature, Bagby remarked that "of all the evils that beset and waylay the path of civilized society, I am satisfied, that intemperance is the greatest; and that it tends more than any other . . . to retard the advancement of the American people to that high state of moral and intellectual eminence, which, I hope awaits them." The legislative committee that received the petitions was also effusive. It praised "the strength which public . . . sentiment is gathering in its efforts to crush this great evil." The committee members were pleased that ten thousand signatures had been gathered and were certain that "thousands more might have been obtained by more active exertions. It is believed too that public sentiment now powerfully aroused, and thus diverted against this alarming Vice, will in time succeed in subduing it."

Despite such sentiments, the lawmakers remained unconvinced that the answer lay with suppression of the retail trade. In their rejection of prohibition, elected officials expressed their reservations carefully and gently, suggesting

29. *Flag of the Union,* August 29, 1838.

30. *Journal of the American Temperance Union,* II (November 1838), 169, 173. See also *Independent Monitor,* June 21, 1843.

that they recognized the widespread public support for temperance principles. Governor Bagby himself refused to endorse prohibition, possibly because of his Jacksonian views that glorified the autonomy of the individual. He explained to the solons that "if the Legislature possessed the legitimate power to suppress this evil, without the infraction of private rights, I should rejoice to see it exercised." The legislative committee also cautiously rejected prohibitionism. After examining the petitions, the committee voiced concern that any action of the legislature to suppress the liquor trade "at this time might injure the cause which it was designed to aid." Nevertheless, the committee encouraged "the friends of the Temperance cause, to persevering and unceasing exertions, and hoped to see it achieve at no distant day, a conquest which while it honors them will bless mankind."[31]

These platitudes may have ingratiated the politicians with some of the electorate, but members of the temperance vanguard refused to be co-opted. One writer to the *Flag of the Union* could scarcely contain his outrage: "our property, our character, our sacred honor, the welfare of our dear wives and children—the welfare of the community—yea our lives, and our *souls*, are all involved in this all important subject." He felt that the legislature's decision was utterly inconsistent. It could "pass a law granting license to those men who keep retailing shops; which proves destructive of the life-blood of the community: but cannot pass a law to suppress the evil!!! . . . To raise a revenue by licensing a traffic that is thus injurious, is to commit murder for hire." He promised eternal vengeance on a recalcitrant legislature; if they could not "hear the cry of 10,000 of their constituents, during this session, we hope that they *will* hear the united voice of 100,000 at their next election. We beseech the people of Alabama, to pour their incessant cries into the ears of the Lord of hosts, and reiterate them through the legislative halls, and continue to sound them aloud to the boundaries of the State in every direction; elect none to the high and responsible office of legislators but sober men, and the monster will soon be subdued."[32]

A committee of the Tuscaloosa Temperance Society was less acerbic toward the legislature's report, conceding that it was "perhaps as much as could have been expected at the time." Moreover, the report was "corroborative of the

31. *Flag of the Union*, January 2, October 2, 1839.

32. *Ibid.*, January 2, 1839. This call to arms was endorsed in neighboring Jefferson County, where temperance activists pledged that they would not vote for any candidate who failed to support prohibition. *Ibid.*, May 15, 1839.

views and designs of the petitions" and even invited renewed action by temperance workers, "for it speaks of the inexpediency of legislating upon the subject *'at this time,'* as much as to say that the time *may* come when it will be otherwise." Needless to say, though, the leaders of the temperance crusade in Tuscaloosa were far from satisfied and, like many other contemporary devotees, directed their wrath toward the proprietors of the "doggeries." It was there, they lamented, that "hundreds contract habits of indolence," resulting in "poverty and disgrace" for their families and the "moral putrefaction" of society. The local temperance leadership concluded that the only solution to these problems was to abolish the system of licensing liquor retailers. Since the law forbade drunkenness, they asked, "why should it license the means to create it?" Ought it not to be the duty of the legislature "to break up the sources of pauperism? Why should the citizen be taxed to support vice[?]" Realizing that they simply could not wait for the legislature to change its ways, the Tuscaloosa Temperance Society issued a call to arms and asked "all philanthropists, and all good citizens" in Alabama to put forth "redoubled exertions, to save the wretched from further wretchedness" and "to lose no time" in circulating prohibition petitions.[33]

The temperance campaign was hindered by division on the issue of legislation. Daniel P. Bestor, a Baptist minister and a former member of the legislature from Greene County, recognized the futility of the petition drive as it was getting under way. Speaking before a temperance convention in Tuscaloosa, he asked, "What is to be expected upon the subject of temperance from a body of men, a majority of whom were wafted to their seats upon the tide of ardent spirits?" Other temperance stalwarts believed that legal measures would be counterproductive. One "warm friend of the temperance cause" objected to legally imposed prohibition as contrary to the spirit of the movement, as he believed "that it would be ineffectual—that it was not by such means the reformation was to be accomplished—that it was by the lamp of love, fed by the oil of charity, and borne by the hand of benevolence, the wanderers were to be conducted back into the paths of virtue, peace, and safety." Similar sentiments were expressed by Samuel A. Hale, the editor of the *Flag of the Union.* Although an unwavering supporter of temperance—he held membership in three different temperance associations during his years in Tuscaloosa—he feared that suppression of the traffic by legislation would only result in univer-

33. *Ibid.,* October 2, 1839.

sal disregard for the law. Writing in the *Flag* in August 1838, he asked the members of the Tuscaloosa Temperance Society's committee to examine present statutes "and see how many of the laws enacted for the suppression of similar evil practices remain there a 'dead letter,' while the vices at which they are aimed, stalk abroad through our streets in open day, laughing to scorn the enactments of the legislature, and the officers appointed to carry them into effect." This Democratic editor insisted that vice be "eradicated in some other way than by force."[34]

A. J. Holcombe of the corresponding committee, however, was unpersuaded by Hale's reasoning. If the laws were not enforced, the problem lay not with the law, but with the officers appointed to execute the law. A "large proportion" of law enforcement officers were either timorous or "men of corrupt minds, who have been promoted through the influence of drinkers and grog dealers, and are dependant on the corrupt portion of society for continuance in office." To solve this problem, Holcombe saw only one solution: "Remove the grog-shops, and let the voters be sober when they come to the ballot box. Then, we can elect to office men of firmness, sobriety, and integrity; then, and not until then will we have our laws executed with promptitude . . . and energy." Nevertheless, the *Flag* remained firm in its position. Over a year later, it reiterated its solid support for temperance through moral suasion, while objecting to "that mode of conversion, which holds a written creed in one hand and a drawn sword in the other."[35]

The *Flag*'s aversion to prohibition on the grounds that it was coercive and denied individuals their autonomy was consistent with the political ideology of the Democratic Party. Democrats often distinguished themselves from their rivals by emphasizing that they were forever laboring to defend the freedom of Americans against the enslaving devices of the Whiggery. In 1837, Hale expressed the fears of many Alabama Democrats when he charged that the true

34. Garrett, *Reminiscences of Public Men in Alabama,* 60–61; *Flag of the Union,* August 29, 1838.

35. *Ibid.,* September 26, 1838, December 25, 1839. In his study of the antebellum temperance movement in South Carolina, Georgia, Alabama, and Mississippi, Douglas Carlson explains that temperance activists in all of these states, and throughout the Union, submitted petitions and memorials to their state legislators in 1838–1839 calling for the repeal of state laws that provided for the licensing of liquor retailers. Although organized opposition to changes in Alabama's licensing laws was not as strong as in other states of the Deep South, the petition campaign in Alabama during these years was more significant than Carlson suggests. Carlson, "Temperance Reform," 162–219, esp. 170–71.

intent of the "money princes" of the Whig Party was to obtain all power for themselves, and that unless they were stopped, "they will not only tell you whether you shall 'HAVE RAIL ROADS OR NOT'—'CANALS OR NOT,' but they shall also tell you, whether your CHILDREN SHALL BE EDUCATED OR NOT, YOUR FAMILIES FED AND CLOTHED, AND YOUR-SELVES REMAIN FREE MEN." Characteristically, the *Flag* in 1841 criticized a requirement imposed by the Whigs in Washington, D.C., that obliged their clerks to take a pledge of total abstinence, never gamble, maintain respectable company, and observe Sunday as the Sabbath. Noting the moral lapses of Henry Clay and Daniel Webster, and the "hard cider and log cabin" presidential campaign the previous year, the *Flag* denounced these requirements as "disgustingly hypocritical" and a "positive violation of the rights of conscience secured to every citizen by the . . . constitution. No Jew or Sabbatarian could take office under such regulations."[36]

Democrats adapted temperance to their particular political culture in other ways. For example, in a lengthy serial article on the credit system, a frequent object of Democratic wrath, the *Flag* commenced one essay as follows: "Vivid and elaborate descriptions have been given of the evils of intemperance; a striking parallel may be seen between these and such as are attendant upon the credit system." Like so many tales from the temperance literature, this particular story recounts the sad fate of a young man with flattering prospects for success. But instead of falling victim to drink, he becomes the prey of credit, which, like liquor, was understood to be "demoralizing" in its effect upon society, since the "proper and natural stimulus to industry is taken away." In addition, the Democrats could use temperance to refute Whig charges that their party consisted of mere *lumpen*. Hale relayed the report of a local citizen who had witnessed a praiseworthy crowd of 7,500 at a Democratic Party rally. He could scarcely contain his joy at seeing such an assemblage "conducting themselves with so much propriety, and good order, exhibiting not a solitary instance of drunkenness" or fighting, as "every day" he read of his party "abused and slandered as agrarians, infidels, and disorganizers." He felt that such a gathering should be "gratifying in the extreme both to the friends of temperance and democracy." Witnessing such a scene "argued so strongly to his mind the intelligence and love of order in the people, that he could never again doubt it[,] let federal editors deny it and abuse them as they may."[37]

36. Thornton, *Politics and Power*, 54–57; *Flag of the Union*, July 26, 1837, June 9, 1841.
37. *Flag of the Union*, December 18, 1839 (see also December 4, 1839), October 2, 1839.

In Tuscaloosa, 69 of the 123 (56.1 percent) temperance enthusiasts whose political affiliation could be identified during the antebellum years were Whigs. This majority is not surprising, since the temperance agenda had much in common with Whig ideology. Of course, people rallied under the temperance banner for many reasons. But a central theme of the Whig Party was the need for collective efforts to remove the impediments that kept people ignorant and dependent and subjugated their potential—barriers that, Whigs believed, hindered economic progress. For these reasons, among others, Whigs supported internal improvements, public schools, and easy credit through a national banking system, and argued that such efforts would provide opportunity—or freedom—to Americans whose lives were unnecessarily constricted. Similarly, temperance, throughout its various antebellum manifestations, endeavored to deliver people from the enslavement of alcohol; it further appealed to the Whig mind-set because it promised efficiency in the workplace and self-discipline in one's personal life.

The role of Democrats, however, was not insignificant in Tuscaloosa's temperance movements. Besides providing nearly one-half of the membership over the span of three decades, many Democrats served as officers of temperance societies. In some phases of Tuscaloosa's temperance reform, Democrats were more numerous than the Whigs. Of the 24 members of the Tuscaloosa Temperance Society (1829–1840) who had an ascertainable political party membership, 16 were Democrats, while only 8 were or would later become Whigs. Of those affiliated with the Alabama Total Abstinence Society in 1843, 24 were Democrats and 24 were Whigs. Whigs were more dominant in the Young Men's Total Abstinence Society of 1839–1840, accounting for 19 of the 29 members with a traceable political identification. Similarly, in the Sons of Temperance between 1846 and 1859, 25 of 37 such members were Whigs. It should be noted, though, that in the absence of poll lists, the only individuals whose party identification was traceable were political activists, and that the political predilections of the majority of the 324 male temperance enthusiasts identified in Tuscaloosa between 1829 and 1859 remain unknown.

As with a number of the Democrats who endorsed benevolence, some members of this party who embraced temperance also showed a considerable proclivity for the political and cultural styles of the Whiggery. Since Alabama was a strong Democratic state throughout the antebellum years, it is not inconceivable that some ambitious politicians attached themselves to the Democrats when they might otherwise have joined the Whigs. Most noteworthy was Henry W. Collier, who was president of the Alabama State Temperance Society during the early 1830s and of the Alabama Total Abstinence Society in 1843. According to one scholar of antebellum Alabama politics, Collier's "views on the bank question were, without qualification, Whig." He was also a promoter of expanded public education in Alabama, endeavored through the Alabama State Agricultural Society (of which he was president) to increase agricultural production by improving the skills of farmers, and zealously advocated the development of manufacturing in the South.[38]

Another Whiggish Democrat who supported temperance was Alexander B. Meek. President of the Young Men's Total Abstinence Society in 1839–1840, vice-president of the Alabama State Temperance Society in 1840, and an officer in the Alabama Total Abstinence Society, Meek was also a Democratic newspaper editor, assistant secretary of the United States Treasury during the Polk administration, Democratic speaker of the Alabama House of Representatives, and the father of Alabama's public school system. Edward F. Comegys, secretary of the Tuscaloosa Society for the Promotion of Temperance in 1829, and James H. Dearing, an officer of the Tuscaloosa Temperance Society in 1833, were both organizers of Tuscaloosa's Democratic Party. Both also later endorsed a three-year property tax of 3 percent in order to fund a railroad through Tuscaloosa, and Dearing, who served as president of the Tuscaloosa Female Academy and later as a school commissioner of Tuscaloosa Township, was the marshal of ceremonies at the inauguration of the Northeast and Southwest Alabama Railroad. Dearing eventually aligned himself with the Know-Nothings, Whiggery's remnant, during the late 1850s. Pleasant H. May, another officer in the Tuscaloosa Temperance Society, served in the Alabama House of Representatives, where he advocated public schools during the 1830s. Longtime Democrat George D. Shortridge, who had been active in the Tuscaloosa Temperance Society during his student days at the University of Alabama, left his party and ran as the Know-Nothing candidate for governor in 1855. Democrat Warfield Creath Richardson, who headed the Warrior Division of the Sons of Temperance upon its organization in 1848 and later edited the temperance-oriented *Orion* in Montgomery, was also the headmaster at

38. *Independent Monitor,* December 31, 1845; *State Journal and Flag of the Union,* January 9, 1846; *Spirit of the Age,* January 18, 1832; *State Rights Expositor and Spirit of the Age,* December 7, 1833; *Independent Monitor,* January 18, 1843; Thornton, *Politics and Power,* 182, 300; *Independent Monitor,* December 28, 1842. Indeed, rumors spread during Collier's campaign for Alabama's governorship in 1849 that he had voted Whig in 1840—which Collier's Democratic allies denied. Huntsville *Democrat,* June 20, 1849. Regarding Alabama's "Collier-Democrats," see chap. 1, n. 72, and the text associated with that note.

Tuscaloosa's Classical and Scientific School and advocated Alabama's public schools during the 1850s.[39]

With these and other prominent Democrats actively participating in the temperance movement, the cause easily transcended local party differences and was seldom, if ever, used by one party to distinguish itself from the other. Both parties contained a spectrum of opinion on the issue (for example, Tuscaloosa merchant Henry Adams Snow, a Whig, sold liquor in his store), which made moral suasion attractive to both Whig and Democratic newspaper editors, since that approach was generally tolerable to people of all temperance persuasions in both parties. As we shall see, though, by the mid-1840s the editor of Tuscaloosa's Whig *Independent Monitor*, Stephen F. Miller, was partial to prohibitory license laws.

All of the known political exchanges regarding temperance involved Democrats attacking Whigs. The Whigs whom the Democrats ridiculed, however, were not locals. *Flag* editor Samuel Hale became incensed when Henry A. Wise, a Whig member of Congress from Virginia, charged that some officials in Martin Van Buren's administration "are and have been *notorious drunkards.*" Hale responded that "in the abundance of their spleen, the whigs have ever been ready to excite opposition to the administration, by any means, however base," and asserted that Wise, having libeled "men infinitely superior to him in moral worth," deserved expulsion from the House. The presidential election of 1840 in particular saw the Democrats ridicule the Whig style of campaigning, although again, Tuscaloosa Democrats failed to point to any local examples. The *Flag* lamented that "the cause of temperance will be greatly retarded, if not put back fifty years, by the log cabin drinking scenes which the federalists are enacting in different parts of the country." The editor estimated that each log cabin would create fifty drunkards during the election and thus would have an influence more "deleterious on public morals, than a regular grog-shop."[40]

39. On Meek: *Flag of the Union*, August 28, 1839, January 22, April 8, 1840, September 13, 1843; Owen, *History of Alabama*, IV, 1183–84. On Comegys: *Alabama State Intelligencer*, May 8, 1829; *State Rights Expositor and Spirit of the Age*, April 6, 1833; *Flag of the Union*, October 31, 1835; *Independent Monitor*, July 15, 1853; *State Rights Expositor and Spirit of the Age*, February 9, 1833; *Independent Monitor*, December 29, 1846, December 14, 1854, June 25, 1857. On May: *State Rights Expositor and Spirit of the Age*, April 6, 1833; *Flag of the Union*, June 28, November 15, 1837. On Shortridge: *State Rights Expositor and Spirit of the Age*, June 8, 1833; Thornton, *Politics and Power*, 325. On Richardson: Owen, *History of Alabama*, IV, 1437; *Independent Monitor*, September 28, December 28, 1848; *Dallas Gazette* (Cahaba, Ala.), April 25, 1856.

40. *Flag of the Union*, August 9, 1837, May 27, 1840 (see also June 24, 1840), September 16, 1840; *Independent Monitor*, August 7, 1840.

Clearly, the response of the legislature and of the newspapers of both political parties to this resurgent temperance activism was different from the reaction that temperance workers received in the late 1820s. Then, temperance devotees who called for moral suasion were denounced as overbearing extremists. But in the late 1830s there were few, if any, arguments expressed publicly against moral suasion. The focus of dispute among both temperance proponents and opponents had shifted to the question of whether temperance objectives ought to be pursued through persuasion or through legislation. While the *Intelligencer* tepidly endorsed moral suasion over legal compulsion during the late 1820s, it also, on occasion, ridiculed the temperance forces for their self-righteous attitude. The *Flag* in 1839 also preferred moral suasion to legislation, but Hale did not emphasize his objections to the petition drive nearly as much as he stressed the beneficial qualities of temperate living. Shortly afterward, the *Flag* endorsed total abstinence from all intoxicants, including wine—a stand more stringent than the one Tuscaloosa's temperance forces had taken only a decade before.[41]

Although temperance and alcohol moderation gained unprecedented approbation during the 1830s, some people of course continued to imbibe and to oppose temperance activism. In late 1838 one temperance enthusiast was threatened at gunpoint by a drunken man for having advocated the suppression of the retail trade. The following year, a temperance meeting in Tuscaloosa was interrupted by an intoxicated man who repeated incessantly the biblical injunction to "take a little wine for thy stomach's sake."[42] Yet these instances point to the changed nature of temperance in Tuscaloosa: by the late 1830s, the principal recorded opposition to temperance came from inebriates. Many of the public disputes regarding temperance, however, were far more subdued than these altercations and were generally between those favoring prohibition and those for moral suasion.

The failure of temperance proponents to achieve their objectives during the petition campaign of 1838 did not deter them from advancing their agenda. In August of 1839, Tuscaloosans saw the emergence of a new temperance association in their town, the Young Men's Total Abstinence Society. When the Tus-

41. *Flag of the Union*, September 11, 1839. Unfortunately, there are few extant Tuscaloosa Whig newspapers from the late 1830s. For one endorsement of temperance, however, see *Alabama State Intelligencer*, November 9, 1838.

42. *Flag of the Union*, January 2, 1839; September 11, 1839. The biblical reference was to 1 Timothy 5:23.

caloosa Temperance Society was formed in 1829, it condemned spirits but tolerated the use of wine. Early opponents of temperance saw this policy as an inconsistency: "Thumbscrew" thought it ludicrous that people would censure any "anti-fogmatic or phlegm-cutter" yet permit wine-drinking; "A Friend to Mental and Personal Liberty" reminded the temperance forces that the first miracle of Christ was to turn water into wine and that their willingness to drink wine but abjure hard liquor was a "shallow, weak distinction," since the consumption of wine, even "among gentlemen, occasionally make[s] them very drunk." The issue of total abstinence was first raised in connection with the 1838 petition campaign. While explaining his position on legal suasion, Hale confessed in the *Flag*, "We are a warm friend of the cause of temperance, though not a professor of total abstinence—we believe in the virtues of cold water, though we do not abjure wine." In less than a year, though, Hale was avidly supporting total abstinence. Suggesting that "intemperance in the use of wine" was possibly "the very worst form in which this vice can exhibit itself," he applauded the formation of the Young Men's Total Abstinence Society—of which he was corresponding secretary—and asserted that "there is no argument employed against the use of ardent liquors, that is not just as applicable against vinous and fermented ones."[43]

Hale's views on total abstinence clearly shifted during the excitement surrounding the emergence of the Young Men's Total Abstinence Society. Tuscaloosa was now graced with two temperance societies simultaneously. Doubtless there were members of the Tuscaloosa Temperance Society who embraced total abstinence, but the fifty-two "young men" who formed the new association made teetotalism fundamental to their pledge: "We do hereby pledge ourselves to abstain entirely from the use of ardent and vinous liquors of any kind whatever." The persistence of both associations is evidence that not all of Tuscaloosa's temperance supporters were prepared for complete abstinence. Despite his continued reservations about prohibition, Hale accepted total abstinence; concurrently, there must have been members of the Tuscaloosa Temperance Society who favored the elimination of retail licenses yet saw no need to pledge not to drink wine. The question of total abstinence quickly be-

43. *Alabama State Intelligencer,* May 8, April 24, 1829; *Flag of the Union,* August 29, 1838, August 21, August 28, 1839. When the Temperance Society of the University of Alabama adopted a constitution in 1831 "on the principles of entire abstinence," the members were probably rejecting the moderate use of hard liquor. *Spirit of the Age,* December 28, 1831. See also *State Rights Expositor and Spirit of the Age,* February 16, 1833, for a later meeting of this society.

came the central concern of temperance disciples. When it issued a call for the formation of a state temperance society in Tuscaloosa on December 10, 1839, the Tuscaloosa Temperance Society revealed that a consensus had yet to be reached on teetotalism, as its members asked the delegates to consider beforehand "the propriety or impropriety of adopting the wine pledge, that the convention may act more advisedly upon the subject."[44]

Thirty-four delegates were present at the formation of the Alabama State Temperance Society. Despite the implications of the society's name, twenty of the delegates hailed from Tuscaloosa County and at least two others would shortly reside there. The organizations represented at this meeting provide some idea of the disparate nature of the movement in late 1839. Present were delegates from the Alabama Baptist Convention; the Young Men's Total Abstinence Society of Clinton, Greene County; the Fayette County Temperance Society; the Yorkville (Pickens County) Temperance Society; the Marion (Perry County) Temperance Society; the Tuscaloosa Temperance Society; the Young Men's Total Abstinence Society, Tuscaloosa City; the North Tuscaloosa Temperance Society; the Grant's Creek (Tuscaloosa County) Temperance Society; the Talladega Temperance Society; the Benton County Temperance Society; and the Livingston (Sumter County) Temperance Society.[45]

The delegates called for the establishment of a *"State Temperance Journal,* to be devoted to the enlightenment of public opinion, and the interests of the temperance reform exclusively." They also condemned treating of the electorate with alcohol, denounced the "retail traffic of ardent spirits" as "productive of incalculable injury to the most vital interests of the community," and requested that local societies continue to circulate petitions calling for the legislature to cease issuing retail licenses. Although they agreed that the society would follow "the principle of total abstinence from all intoxicating liquor," the delegates were still not of one mind regarding strategy: the minutes reveal that notwithstanding the majority's affirmation of the constitutionality of abolishing the retailing of ardent spirits, several delegates refused to sustain this resolution.[46]

44. *Flag of the Union,* August 28, October 2, 1839.

45. All of the non–Tuscaloosa County delegates came from central to north-central Alabama—mostly counties that bordered Tuscaloosa. This small representation should not be understood to mean that these were the only counties in the state with temperance societies. It is more likely a commentary on the difficulty of travel in the state.

46. *Flag of the Union,* January 22, 1840. See also Tuscaloosa *Whig,* January 21, 1840.

The enthusiasm expressed at the formation of the state temperance society quickly subsided during the 1840 presidential campaign, which dominated the attention of Tuscaloosans and their newspapers for the entire year. After an announcement of a meeting of the Young Men's Total Abstinence Society in April 1840, no temperance meetings were advertised in the city's newspapers for almost two years. When temperance meetings were held again, nothing further was heard of the Young Men's Total Abstinence Society or of the Tuscaloosa Temperance Society, which latter group had persisted, if intermittently, since 1829. As we noted previously, accusations of intemperance were sometimes heard from the Democrats during the hard-cider campaign of 1840. But aside from the Alabama Baptist Convention's demand that the legislature suppress the licensing of liquor establishments, temperance was temporarily moribund.[47]

Temperance activity reemerged into Tuscaloosa's public view in 1842 with the commencement of the Tuscaloosa Total Abstinence Society, a body committed to moral suasion. After the failure of the 1838 petition campaign, many temperance partisans may have felt that legal measures were for the moment ineffectual, and until the early 1850s most temperance enthusiasts in Tuscaloosa County embraced persuasion instead. In a speech before the newly formed society, A. S. Gore noted that there were two kinds of societies devoted to suppressing intemperance: *"Temperance Societies,* which prohibit the use of ardent spirits, but . . . tolerate the substitution of wine, malt liquors, &c.," and *"Total Abstinence Societies,* which . . . denounce every species of intoxicating liquor." Gore suggested that there were significant class differences between these two groups, as the principal purpose of temperance societies was to "reclaim and benefit the poor," whereas total abstinence societies sought to eradicate the use of all intoxicants, including "the vinous indulgences of the rich." Gore revealed that he had long been troubled by the hypocrisies of temperance societies and had never joined one. He was especially bothered by temperance members "who would not take a glass of grog for the world, but who had no objections to lend their very efficient aid in discussing the merits of a bottle or two of wine" and then became inebriated. This inconsistent policy was "why the *'temperance cause,'* so called, has experienced so many fluctuations": temperance society members had fought valiantly against ardent spirits but had not suc-

---

47. *Flag of the Union,* April 8, 1840; *Independent Monitor,* February 23, 1842; *Flag of the Union,* November 25, 1840. See also *Independent Monitor,* June 30, 1841.

ceeded in "banishing intemperance altogether . . . from among their own members." Total abstinence societies, claimed Gore, were a "higher order" of the temperance cause.

Gore's ultimate ambition was not merely to eliminate intemperance among the professed friends of the cause. He aimed to end the consumption of alcohol altogether. This goal was imminently attainable, he explained, because his contemporaries were "living in an age of reform" in which the human mind was constantly seeking ways to "enlighten the understanding and ameliorate the condition of the human species." He esteemed temperance and total abstinence societies "to be one of the greatest blessings, next to the promulgation of the gospel, ever bestowed upon the human race." He was certain that this cause would continue to "multiply and to spread 'till [it] cover[s] the habitable parts of the earth as the waters cover the great deep; working out an entire revolution in the habits and manners of every individual in every class of society."[48]

This belief in the power of their cause to transform human behavior was foremost among the tenets of temperance partisans in Tuscaloosa. Writing the following month in the *Flag,* one correspondent praised the "Temperance revival" as virtually "sufficient to characterize our present age." Especially praiseworthy were those "brutalized victims of intemperance" who were "shaking themselves free from the rags of poverty, from the foulness and filth of vice" and, after putting aside "all the cravings of an appetite, which is tyrannical in the same proportion that it is unnatural," reappearing "as freemen, capable of forming high resolves, and with sufficient firmness to execute them."[49] Adherence to the principles of temperance, in the minds of activists, not only ended domestic violence and made people more inclined to accept the gospel, but it also created responsible citizens capable of self-government and instilled the character traits essential to proper behavior in an expanding market.

Despite Gore's zeal and optimism, this phase of the temperance movement ignited only ephemeral passion, and no sooner than it appeared was it in decline. A few weeks after Gore's invigorating speech, Stephen Miller of the *Independent Monitor* wondered why the designated meetinghouse of the Total Abstinence Society was dark and empty during the time of a scheduled meeting. A writer to the *Flag* further queried why none of the eleven officers of the

48. *Independent Monitor,* February 23, 1842. Later that year, Stephen Miller, editor of the *Independent Monitor,* similarly declared temperance to be "the best of causes, next to Christianity." *Independent Monitor,* October 26, 1842.

49. *Flag of the Union,* March 16, 1842.

"Temperance Society recently formed in this city" was present at two recent meetings, and hoped that the cause in Tuscaloosa "will not prove a mere flare up, resulting in failure and disgrace." Perhaps these reprimands spurred the movement's temporary resurgence, as the city's newspapers advertised and reported temperance meetings for the following month and a half. Nevertheless, enthusiasm again faded quickly. In May 1842, J. Harris, the new editor of the *Flag of the Union*, observed that national sentiment had changed dramatically over the past month or two: "What has become of the numerous temperance societies throughout the country, the proceedings of which occupied nearly one fourth of every paper we received?" Harris' conclusion was that temperance, "like every other undue excitement, either on the subject of morals, politics, or religion," could be perpetuated only "by a continuation of the means which first produces it—numerous assemblies, and exciting and inflammatory lectures and addresses. Whenever these causes cease to exist, their effects must and will necessarily subside."[50]

The following months saw no revival of temperance in Tuscaloosa. While promoting Tuscaloosa's lyceum, Harris added his hope that the interest his townspeople had manifested in the lyceum "will not, like the cold water excitement, cool off as suddenly as it was exhibited." This rapid demise caused some people in the movement to blame others. Teetotalers of a radical hue, such as A. S. Gore, who had only a few months previously blamed the movement's lack of complete success on the inconsistencies of nonteetotalers, were now seen by some to have damaged the cause by being too uncompromising. Suggestive is an article published without comment in the *Flag* from the New York *Courier and Enquirer*. The writer asserted that the cause began to falter when fanatics took it over and tried to exclude communion wine. A few months later a correspondent requested that the *Flag* publish an extract from the proceedings of the General Assembly of the Presbyterian Church in the United States of America, which had refused to deny communion to manufacturers or retailers of spirits. While praising the successes of the "temperance reformation," the assembly expressed its concerns about the "disastrous effects produced by fanatical advocates of temperance," especially the quasi-religious and revivalistic measures used by temperance devotees.[51]

---

50. *Ibid.*, March 9, 1842; *Independent Monitor,* March 9, 1842; *Flag of the Union,* May 18, 1842.

51. *Flag of the Union,* July 20, May 18, August 24, 1842. On the disagreements in the temperance movement, even among teetotalers, regarding the use of communion wine, see Ian R. Tyr-

This hiatus, though, was brief. The temperance cause in Tuscaloosa was revitalized in December 1842 with a public display of temperance enthusiasm that was followed by a sequence of regular meetings. Initially, the adherents of the new temperance society identified themselves as "Washingtonians." The Washingtonian phase of temperance commenced in Baltimore in May 1840, when six drunkards committed themselves to total abstinence after attending a temperance lecture. The Washingtonians were more secular and less likely to seek ties with churches than earlier temperance reformers had been. Further, they did not attempt to advance temperance from above through self-appointed executives who considered themselves to be the moral vanguard of society. Rather, they were, in most locales, explicitly a working-class movement that sought to convert inebriates to the ways of sobriety. Like the Sons of Temperance—who later adopted a number of Washingtonian techniques— the Washingtonians undertook to re-create the conviviality of the barroom. In the course of this new approach, however, some Washingtonians eschewed any connection with religion, a rejection that alienated some longtime temperance activists.[52]

Tuscaloosans were first visited by Washingtonians in April 1842. J. J. Johnson and a Mr. Cady gave several speeches during a two-week stopover on a southern tour that took them to more than twenty cities in Louisiana, Alabama, Georgia, and South Carolina. The *Independent Monitor* reported that their remarks in Tuscaloosa were well received, and later assigned Johnson "a foremost rank among the active philanthropists of the day." Nevertheless, there is no evidence to suggest that the Tuscaloosa Total Abstinence Society adopted the Washingtonian label at this time. Nor does it appear that the temperance effort in Tuscaloosa, when it did embrace Washingtonianism, was marked by a shift toward greater working-class participation, which characterized the movement in many places throughout the United States.[53]

---

rell, *Sobering Up: From Temperance to Prohibition in Antebellum America, 1800–1860* (Westport, Conn., 1979), 145–49.

52. Dannenbaum, *Drink and Disorder*, 32–42; Tyrrell, *Sobering Up*, 159–209; Blocker, *American Temperance Movements*, 39–47.

53. *Flag of the Union*, April 13, 1842; *Independent Monitor*, April 27, October 26, 1842. Although Washingtonianism generally involved increased participation in the temperance movement from the lower classes and among reformed drunkards, this was not always the case; occasionally, existing organizations merely added "Washingtonian" to their name. Blocker, *American Temperance Movements*, 42–43.

On December 28, 1842, "a very large meeting of the Tuskaloosa Temperance Society" assembled at the Methodist Episcopal Church and, undaunted by their previous institutional failures, resolved to form another state temperance society, later designated the Washingtonian Total Abstinence Society of the State of Alabama. Although the *Monitor* reported that "some 75 or 80 persons signed the Washingtonian pledge," this group was not an insurgency from below, as were Washingtonian meetings elsewhere in the United States. Like previous phases of temperance reform in Tuscaloosa, this gathering of Washingtonians was dominated by the state's leading political officials. Writing three decades later, William Garrett recalled that "nearly all the members of the legislature were present . . . besides a vast concourse of citizens." Speeches were given by General Felix Grundy McConnell of the state senate and militia; Nathaniel Terry, president of the state senate; and former legislators Samuel F. Rice and James E. Belser. Henry Collier was elected president of the society. Collier, of course, was no plebeian: at the time, he was chief justice of Alabama's supreme court, and he would serve from 1849 to 1853 as the state's Democratic governor. McConnell and Belser were shortly afterward elected to the United States House of Representatives, Rice later served as chief justice of the Alabama Supreme Court, and Terry was the Democratic nominee in a losing bid for governor in 1845.

Despite the elite character of the Washingtonian leadership in Alabama, during this gathering drunkards were apparently called upon to change their ways, and at least one habitual inebriate was touched by the proceedings:

> After the lecture had ended, Gen. McConnell rose in the audience and moved that a temperance society be at once formed, which he would be the first to join. . . . A number of beautiful speeches were made on the occasion, but none had the pathos and overwhelming effect of Gen McConnell's. He confessed and mourned how he had trifled away his past life; how he had abused his faculties by the too free indulgence in the use of ardent spirits; but his eyes were now opened, and he was clothed in his right mind, resolved by the assistance of Heaven to be a new man in future. His friends heard the resolution with delight, and hoped that he might have the self-control to make it good by a permanent reform.[54]

54. *Independent Monitor*, January 4, 1843, January 18, 1843; Owen, *History of Alabama and Dictionary of Alabama Biography*, III, 131–32, 380; IV, 1095, 1435; Garrett, *Reminiscences of Public Men in Alabama*, 163.

The following week, an even larger assemblage was present to adopt the society's constitution. Newspaper reports of the meeting present further evidence that this group of Washingtonians was top-heavy: of the ninety-four who accepted the Washingtonian pledge and the society's constitution, sixteen were members of the Alabama legislature. Notwithstanding McConnell's public confession of his erroneous past and his expressed determination to reform his habits—utterances characteristic of Washingtonian temperance elsewhere in the United States—the reformation of drunkards on their own terms did not merit mention in the society's constitution or in any of the newspaper accounts of the progress of local Washingtonians. Rather, Stephen Miller opined in the *Monitor* that total abstinence in Tuscaloosa would "receive a strong impulse" from the new movement, "supported as it is by many of the representatives of the people, and other gentlemen of intelligence from different parts of the state." Perhaps the disparity between local temperance efforts, which were dominated by social elites, and the connotation that *Washingtonian* generally carried of working-class temperance efforts was obvious to this new society. In any case, after the first meetings, the organization was seldom called "Washingtonian," but was usually referred to as the Alabama Total Abstinence Society. Members pledged to abjure the use of all intoxicants, except for "medicinal or sacramental purposes," and approved a report proclaiming "that cold water, is the proper drink for man" because it is highly "consistent with physical strength, mental cultivation, intellectual greatness, family concord, and domestic peace."[55]

Like the Alabama State Temperance Society that was formed in 1839, the Alabama Total Abstinence Society was in many respects a Tuscaloosa-based, rather than a statewide, association. A large number of the signatories to its constitution were local Tuscaloosans. Although the constitution mandated an annual meeting to be held on the last Wednesday in December, meetings of the society were held in Tuscaloosa regularly throughout the rest of the year. But as with previous efforts, leaders found it difficult to sustain the initial enthusiasm. When announcing the April 1843 meeting, James M. Norment, the society's secretary, hoped that "there will be no flagging and holding back on the part of

---

55. *Independent Monitor,* January 18, 1843; *Flag of the Union,* August 30, 1843. James M. Norment described his prospective newspaper, the *Alabama Temperance Recorder and State Journal of Agriculture,* as being aligned with the Washingtonians. Although the proposed Tuscaloosa newspaper was endorsed by the state temperance society, it apparently never commenced publication. See also *Flag of the Union,* February 1, 1843.

those who . . . belong to this division of the *Great Cold Water Army."* His plea fell upon deaf ears. Although Colonel R. S. Inge gave a speech that was "well received by the whole assembly" at the April 1843 meeting, other speakers "who had promised to address this meeting, from some cause unknown to the secretary, did not attend." Nevertheless, after an extemporaneous address by a pastor of one of the town's churches, twenty-nine people signed a total abstinence pledge, which according to Norment was a "very considerable accession in these hard times." In July the city's only public celebration of American independence was held at the Methodist church and was sponsored by the Alabama Total Abstinence Society. Norment proposed that the festivities be a "grand Cold Water Celebration" and told Tuscaloosans that the Fourth would be "a most appropriate day to throw off all allegiance to King Alcohol, and declare our independence of him and all his lesser lights." The ceremonies were marked by temperance songs and poetry, and State Representative Benjamin F. Porter delivered an address "commemorative of the Jubilee of Freedom, and the triumph of Temperance."[56]

In October the Alabama Total Abstinence Society issued a call for a state temperance convention in Tuscaloosa on December 27. The objectives of this convention differed significantly from the goals of temperance workers only a few years earlier. There were no proposals urging activists to petition the legislature to end the traffic in liquor. Instead, the agenda was oriented exclusively toward moral suasion. The foremost objective was to devise new ways "to arrest drunkenness, and to promote temperance, and thereby expel from the state a vast amount of crime and misery." The delegates also wanted to "meet together, face to face, from all parts of the state, and compare notes in this grand enterprise" and to "adopt some means for the advancement of temperance, through the influence of the press, thereby sending 'glad tidings' to remote and obscure places of degradation and vice, where the voice of the temperance orator is never heard." Here is a clear admission that temperance activists, like the proponents of benevolence discussed in chapter 1, viewed the rural population of Alabama as the segment of society that stood to gain the most from their activity.[57]

The spread of temperance to Alabama's hinterlands, as well as temperance

56. *Flag of the Union,* March 29, 1843; *Independent Monitor,* April 5, 1843; *Flag of the Union,* May 24, June 28, July 5, 1843.

57. *Flag of the Union,* September 13, November 1, 1843.

activity in Tuscaloosa, took a back seat as voters prepared for the election of 1844. That year, a committee at the Alabama Baptist State Convention lamented that the temperance cause "is rapidly retrograding. Its professed friends have in good degree deserted it." Although the *Monitor* announced that another state temperance society meeting was to be held in Tuscaloosa in January 1845, the fact that the minutes were never published in the paper suggests that the gathering was poorly attended and no significant measures were proposed. Despite this fluctuation in activism, many Tuscaloosans remained abstinent; numerous witnesses continued to testify that alcohol consumption in Alabama had diminished considerably during these years. This shift paralleled a national drop in adult per capita alcohol consumption from 7.1 gallons in 1830 to 1.8 gallons in 1845. Changes in the drinking habits of Alabamians were evident from the fact that twenty-eight of the thirty steamboats that operated on the state's rivers were reported to be willing to "banish the use of liquor on their boats, provided the custom will be generally adopted." This news delighted Miller at the *Monitor*: "It is indeed gratifying to the friends of moral order, to see the holy cause take that wide direction, where inebriety was supposed to have its deepest foundations." Another Tuscaloosan later praised the well-ordered operation of the steamer *Dallas*. There was but little card playing on the ship, and there were no decanters at the dinner tables, "as was the case some few years since. . . . We think the boats, generally of our waters, have quit the practice of putting spirits on the table." The 1842 meeting of the Alabama Baptist State Convention reported that the influence of temperance societies was "felt through all classes of the community" and that sobriety reigned where drunkenness had formerly ruled. In particular, delegates rejoiced that Independence Day celebrations, which had only recently been festivals of bibulousness, were "now observed on temperance principles."[58]

Political meetings, too, were more temperate than in former days. At a dinner given by Tuscaloosa Whigs on behalf of Arthur Hopkins, the chair of the 1844 Whig nominating convention in Baltimore, no ardent spirits were served. The *Monitor* expressed its hope that "the time has come when the practice of using intoxicating drinks, on such occasions, will be discontinued altogether." When English geologist Sir Charles Lyell visited Alabama in 1846, he reported

58. *Journal of the Proceedings of the Baptist State Convention in Alabama at its Twentieth Anniversary*, 9; *Independent Monitor*, January 1, 1845; Rorabaugh, *Alcoholic Republic*, 232; *Independent Monitor*, May 11, 1842; *Alabama Baptist* (Marion), January 25, 1845; *Minutes of the Nineteenth Anniversary of the Baptist State Convention of Alabama*, 7.

that "everyone here speaks of the great reform which the temperance movement has made, it being no longer an offense to decline taking a dram with
your host." Yet he complained that drunkenness prevailed throughout the state
to such an extent that he feared for slaves at the hands of inebriated slaveholders.[59]

And certainly, not all Tuscaloosans embraced the widespread reformation
of alcohol consumption. Beneath the masthead of the *Independent Monitor,*
Stephen Miller reported that John A. Mears had recently been "found dead,
and standing up in one of the state rooms" of the steamer *Tuskaloosa.* Miller's
laconic analysis: "Probable cause, *intemperance.*"[60] In 1843, the *Flag* lamented
the persistent "general prevalence" of intemperance in Alabama but, like Lyell,
reported that temperance principles were gradually gaining ground: "There is
not so much gluttony or drunkeness now as there have been in former times."
But the *Flag* was less willing than Lyell to credit temperance societies with the
change in public habits: "The gradual extension of, and improvement in, the
moral education of the lower classes of society, backed by good examples of
those who give tone to public opinion, has effected a more salutary change
than all penal enactments, all the denunciations of legislatures [or] all the
anathemas of the pulpit could ever have done." And with a touch of self-
adulation, the editor praised the work of newspapers in promoting temperance, and announced himself convinced that newspapers had done more for
the advancement of alcoholic abstinence "than all the sanctimonious admoni-
tions have ever done, and is at this day a more effective advocate of it than all
the ranting pseudo saints in christendom or all the temperance societies put
together."[61]

Concerned about the recurrent cycles of declining enthusiasm for temperance
and about the numerous Washingtonians who relapsed into inebriety, sixteen
Washingtonians gathered in New York City in September 1842 and formed the

59. *Independent Monitor,* as quoted in *Alabama Baptist* (Marion), June 15, 1844, which praised
the *Monitor* as "one of the most influential Whig papers in the South"; Charles Lyell, *A Second
Visit to the United States of North America* (2 vols.; New York, 1849), II, 60.

60. *Independent Monitor,* February 12, 1845. Miller had previously reported that convicted
murderer Ervin E. Brookshire had confessed "*intoxication from spirituous liquors,* as the CAUSE!"
of his crime in Huntsville. *Independent Monitor,* March 5, 1841.

61. *Flag of the Union,* June 14, 1843.

Sons of Temperance. A fraternal organization, the Sons of Temperance was highly structured, with a hierarchy of officers and societies (called divisions) on the local, state, and national levels. The brotherhood, aside from its pledges of total abstinence, resembled the Masons and Odd Fellows in some respects, incorporating secret handshakes, sickness and death benefits, rituals, ceremonies, and ornate regalia. Local divisions met often, and their meetings were explicitly aimed to replace the camaraderie of the tavern. Members were encouraged to convert drunkards to total abstinence. The Sons of Temperance grew rapidly. By 1845, divisions were found in most of the northern states, and by 1847, they had spread throughout the Deep South. The national body peaked in 1850 with 238,000 contributing members, but it remained in existence through the Civil War. The Sons found fertile soil in the slave states, which despite containing only 32.1 percent of the nation's white population in 1850, were the home of 44.2 percent of the American members of the Sons of Temperance.[62]

In Tuscaloosa the initial effort to create a Sons of Temperance chapter appears to have failed. In 1846 a notice in both of the city's newspapers announced that George W. Rives was to present an address before the Alabama Division of the Sons of Temperance at the Methodist church. Although Tuscaloosa could possibly boast of having the first Sons of Temperance division in the Gulf South, nothing more was heard of this division or this organization in Tuscaloosa until September 1848. In the meantime, divisions appeared throughout the state. A temperance newspaper, the *Orion*, edited by former Tuscaloosan James M. Norment, commenced publication in Montgomery in December 1847.[63]

The organization of the Warrior Division of the Sons of Temperance on September 26, 1848, marked the start of the strongest and longest-running

62. Carlson, "Temperance Reform," 27–31; De Bow, *Statistical View*, 45; W. J. Rorabaugh, "The Sons of Temperance in Antebellum Jasper County," *Georgia Historical Quarterly*, LXIV (Fall 1980), 263–79; Dannenbaum, *Drink and Disorder*, 42–62; Tyrrell, *Sobering Up*, 203–204, 211–18; Blocker, *American Temperance Movements*, 48–51; "Lecture on the Obligation of the Order," n.d., in Matthew P. Blue Papers, ADAH.

63. *Independent Monitor*, July 21, 1846; *State Journal and Flag of the Union*, July 24, 1846. James Benson Sellers, *The Prohibition Movement in Alabama, from 1702 to 1943* (Chapel Hill, 1943), 23–25; M. P. Blue *et al.*, *City Directory and History of Montgomery, with a Summary of Events in That History, Calendarically Arranged* (Montgomery, 1878), 41, 43, 72, 87. Carlson, "Temperance Reform," 30, notes that by the end of 1846 the Sons had established divisions in the upper South and Georgia, but that they appeared in the Gulf South only in 1847.

manifestation of the antebellum temperance crusade in Tuscaloosa. Warfield Creath Richardson gave a temperance oration that stirred twenty-five people to be initiated with "the greatest enthusiasm and zeal" into the order the following day. Richardson outlined the horrors of alcohol and the history of temperance agitation and promoted the Sons as an organization that would supersede all previous temperance associations: "It is sufficient to say, that in every previous attempt at organized resistance to the monster evil, there was wanting an element necessary to secure complete and permanent success. There was wanting . . . something to secure co-operation, extension, and perpetuity— some social organization and influence, as well as some systematic provision for mutual assistance and relief. . . . These essentials are furnished by the organization of the Sons of Temperance, and these things . . . give it an efficiency, which no other association for similar objects is believed to have hitherto attained." The Masonic forms, ceremonies, badges, and processions were designed, according to Richardson, to give "permanence and stability to the order," to "keep alive the zeal of the members, to promote social feeling and brotherly love among them, and to render the association a reality and not a mere idea."[64]

Richardson's thoughts on temperance echoed the arguments advanced by his predecessors in this crusade. Like them, Richardson pointed out that his contemporaries lived in "an age of revolution and reform. . . . The mind of man has burst its chains asunder, kings reign no more by divine right; superstition holds no more the nations in awe; ignorance no longer wraps the world in darkness." Improvements in communication, linking peoples previously separated, "have multiplied with almost miraculous rapidity," while the "thoughts of men are no longer tied down to the little spot in which they were born, but they take in with easy grasp, whole empires and continents." And like the proponents of Bibles, tracts, and Sabbath schools, Richardson warned that if these great advances were "unaccompanied by a corresponding *moral* counterpoise," the consequence would be the acceleration of the "growth of noxious principles, and . . . the prevalence of corrupting habits."[65]

The *Monitor* reported that the inauguration of the Sons division in Tuscaloosa generated a "lively and general interest." Although promoters of temperance undoubtedly exaggerated any positive reception that they received from

64. *Independent Monitor,* September 28, October 19, 1848.
65. *Ibid.,* October 19, 1848.

the public, in this instance there seems to have been real enthusiasm. In the month following Richardson's speech, divisions were organized across the Black Warrior River in Northport and at McMath's and Foster's Settlement in rural Tuscaloosa County. In November a division was formed among University of Alabama students, and in December the Alphadelphia section of the juvenile Cadets of Temperance was formed in Tuscaloosa. For over four months, the *Monitor* consistently filled its pages with temperance songs, excerpts from other newspapers on temperance, and reports on the doings of the Sons of Temperance in Tuscaloosa. The *Monitor* conveyed to its readers that the Sons had ignited a revolution throughout the nation: "We hardly take up a paper which does not tell us of the glorious progress which this able and philanthropic Order is making." The editor added that in Tuscaloosa, "its strength and numbers are rapidly increasing, and the salutary effect of its presence is palpably obvious."[66]

Tuscaloosans may have embraced the Sons of Temperance with such fervor because they found the 1848 presidential campaign boring in comparison with the two previous contests. Many Alabama Democrats were unenthusiastic about Lewis Cass and either stayed home on election day or reluctantly voted for Zachary Taylor. Whigs, on the other hand, had lost so many times in Alabama that they had all but conceded the state to Cass. The *Monitor* devoted less space to preelection hoopla than Tuscaloosa newspapers had in previous elections, and unlike in the 1844 contest, no weekly campaign sheet was published consistently prior to the election.[67] For people accustomed to electoral vitality, the lack of it may have created a vacuum that assisted in the rapid growth of the Sons of Temperance. In addition, the fraternal aspects of the Sons probably appealed to the affection that some of Tuscaloosa's males had for the Masons and Odd Fellows. As we noted in chapter 1, the Antimasonry of the early 1830s— though less vibrant than its manifestation in many northern states—had suppressed a once strong Masonic presence in Alabama. Antimasonry, however, had waned by the early 1840s, and the number of lodges in the state then began to increase. By the 1850s, Masons were again found throughout Alabama. In this society of joiners, Alabamians were pleased to have another place to meet.

66. *Ibid.*, October 19, October 26, November 13, November 23, December 14, 1848.

67. Thornton, *Politics and Power,* 177–80. The Tuscaloosa *Democratic Mentor* was published during the 1844 campaign, and the campaign sheet *Old Zach* appeared briefly in the spring of 1848 but was then discontinued. Rhoda Coleman Ellison, *History and Bibliography of Alabama Newspapers in the Nineteenth Century* (University, Ala., 1954), 182, 185.

But more important for this study, the weaker residual effects of Antimasonry in the South undoubtedly contributed to the stronger reception of the Sons of Temperance there.[68]

The Sons quickly assumed a prominent place in the affairs of the community. In November 1848, plans were made for a public celebration on Christmas Day, and the anticipation of this festive occasion doubtless maintained temperance sentiment and talk at a high pitch for a few additional weeks. Of the festival itself, the *Monitor* reported that the size of the gathering and the "deep interest, common feeling, the good order, [and] the quiet, all-pervading satisfaction" were unprecedented. The Sons gathered at 11:30 A.M. at the city hall and commenced a procession that took them to the Methodist church by noon. A receptive audience filled "every nook of the house," and even the aisles were packed with people sitting on the floor. The church was the largest in Tuscaloosa, but the crowd was so great that some celebrants had to be turned away.

After an invocation, A. W. Richardson summarized the history of the temperance cause, noting that it was "sweeping away drunkenness from the entire surface of our land" and that "the movement is particularly a christian movement." Several "Temperance odes" were sung, the words of which were published in the *Monitor* prior to the celebration. A banner bearing the words "LOVE, PURITY, and FIDELITY" was presented to the Warrior Division from the women of Tuscaloosa, with accompanying remarks by Miss Harriette Wallace and Captain John G. Barr, a reformed inebriate. After these exercises, a procession repaired to the statehouse, where a large feast was held. The following day, the remaining food was "distributed gratuitously among families whom it might benefit," suggesting that not all of the city's classes participated in the festivities and that those present possessed at least a modicum of wealth.[69]

The presentation of the banner during this festival furnishes some insights into the place of women in the order, and provides an opportunity to discuss the role of Tuscaloosa women in the temperance crusade. As was the case with the benevolent empire that we addressed in chapter 1, little information is

68. Quist, "Social and Moral Reform," 53–56.

69. *Independent Monitor,* December 28, 1848. On Barr's earlier drunkenness, see Basil Manly Diary No. 3, July 11, 1845, in Manly Family Papers. Regarding his contributions as a "Southwestern Humorist," see G. Ward Hubbs, ed., *Rowdy Tales from Early Alabama: The Humor of John Gorman Barr* (University, Ala., 1981).

available regarding the participation of women in Tuscaloosa's several antebellum temperance associations or how women's position in society changed over these years. Although women held no offices in any of Tuscaloosa's pre–Civil War temperance societies and seldom spoke at temperance gatherings, it is clear that women played a significant role in the temperance movement in Tuscaloosa. They were encouraged to attend meetings as early as 1832, when the Tuscaloosa Temperance Society announced that the "members and friends of the Temperance cause . . . male and female" were requested to attend one of its gatherings. A year later, thirty-seven women and thirty-six men united with the society at its annual meeting. The constitution of the Alabama Total Abstinence Society in 1843 permitted women to be members, although no female names ever appeared in the society's published minutes. Their place in that organization and in Tuscaloosa's other temperance societies, though, was principally to encourage men to be temperate (and of course, women who feared that their husbands might fritter away the family's income on drink or commit acts of violence while intoxicated had an immediate interest in the cause). A few months after the commencement of the Total Abstinence Society, James Norment reported that at a recent gathering, "we observed more ladies than has been our good fortune to see at any previous meeting. This is a sure guarantee that the Temperance cause will prosper in this city." Norment echoed the sentiments of another writer, who had remarked a few years earlier that women were responsible for controlling men's appetite for alcohol, as "within her own home, to her own circle, woman is called upon vigilantly to observe this encroaching vice."[70]

These and other contemporaries understood how women could influence men toward paths of temperance and morality. Yet Tuscaloosa's temperance rhetoric carried two conflicting messages. One was that women were the movement's most valuable asset. The other was that because women were mentioned so infrequently and were absent from the leadership hierarchy, they bordered on irrelevance.

Over a month before the Sons of Temperance–sponsored Christmas festivities in 1848, the *Monitor* suggested that the celebration would be "a suitable occasion for the presentation of the banner" and that this would be a fine activity

---

70. *Spirit of the Age*, April 4, 1832; *State Rights Expositor and Spirit of the Age*, April 6, 1833; *Independent Monitor*, January 18, April 5, 1843; *Flag of the Union*, September 11, 1839. See also *Flag of the Union*, May 31, 1843.

for the town's women: "Such gifts come most appropriately from the hands of the fair; and the fair, every where, have been most prompt and most cheerful in encouraging by their smiles, an effort which has done and is doing so much to banish misery from the hearth-stone. Will the ladies of Tuscaloosa think of this?" These remarks, coupled with the eventual delivery of the banner, suggest that some sort of female temperance network was operative in Tuscaloosa during this phase of the temperance crusade—although it was evidently dormant at this time, as the *Monitor* noted: "Since making the suggestion to the ladies, last week, in regard to a temperance banner, we have been inclined to think that our fair friends must be afraid of speaking all at once." As we saw in chapter 1, Harriette Wallace spoke at the festival in approving tones of the different roles that men and women had played in the temperance effort. The position of males was preeminent, and she compared their struggle with that of the European crusaders of the Middle Ages: "Theirs the glory of winning the Holy Sepulchre from the infidels, be yours the noble aim of delivering the immortal souls of men from the degrading thraldom of intemperance." Women were to provide moral support to men engaged in this worthy cause, and the presentation of the temperance banner by the "ladies of Tuscaloosa" was their way of expressing to the Sons "our heart-felt approbation of your high enterprise" in seeking to "exterminate that moral scourge" from the land. "Man will thank you for encouraging and fortifying him in his resolution to resist the tempter; woman will bless you for placing such a safe-guard around her domestic peace and happiness."[71] This latter remark further underlines the fact that some women supported temperance because they feared the disruption of their households at the hands of intemperate husbands.

Accepting the banner for the Sons, John G. Barr praised the pageantry of the festival and the generosity of Tuscaloosa's women, then rhapsodized on woman in general: "At no period in the worlds history has her position been so well-defined and so truly elevated, or her position more universally felt, or more widely acknowledged than at the present time." Denying the belief that as "man progresses in cultivation and refinement . . . woman sink[s] into unimportance and obscurity," Barr argued that the role of women had been also transformed into a "more elevated and glorious position. No longer adorned as divinity, she becomes what God intended her, the 'helpmeet' of man; not flattered as a child, she becomes man's councellor and advisor; not his inferior, but

71. *Independent Monitor,* November 23, 30, 1838, January 4, 1849.

his equal." A woman was to be a comfort when a man's heart became heavy. Moreover, "shielded by society and unexposed to the rude shocks and rough buffetings of the world, she has a freer field for the culture and a wider scope for the display of those higher virtues of our nature." When a woman combines all of her qualities, she assists the "great chariot of humanity. . . . This done, she is fulfilling her high destiny" of using her influence to transform the moral condition of the world.[72]

The increased participation of Alabama's white women in the temperance agitation of the 1850s forced men to acknowledge—in unprecedented ways—the significance of women in the crusade. Further, this increased conspicuousness of Alabama women coincided with the even greater power that women were achieving in the temperance movement in the urban North. At a ceremony similar to the Christmas celebrations of 1848, Miss Mary Vaughn addressed Tuscaloosa's Warrior Division in June 1851 and presented it a temperance banner. The *Crystal Fount* reported similar ceremonies in Jonesboro and Fayetteville. Women in Selma formed their own temperance society, and in 1853 the Alabama State Temperance Convention "earnestly requested" that "all the Ladies of Alabama . . . circulate petitions and obtain signatures, praying the passage of a suitable law on the subject of Temperance."[73]

And more than ever, men in the temperance movement placed responsibility upon women as the backbone of the cause. After receiving the banner from Mary Vaughn in 1851, Harvey H. Cribbs told the women present: "You are the arbiters of fashionable entertainments. Your influence is omnipotent in the social circle. The wine cup being banished from these, and your frowns of displeasure resting on all who taste or handle any intoxicating liquid, we feel indeed that 'OMEN OF A BETTER AGE' is here." *Crystal Fount* editor John Warren agreed. Upon the formation of the women's temperance society in Selma, Warren proclaimed that "it is well known that the female portion of the community exert a very great influence upon the destinies of men, and now they have arrayed themselves against the indulgence in intoxicating drinks—we

72. *Ibid.*, January 4, 1849.

73. Ian R. Tyrrell, "Women and Temperance in Antebellum America," *Civil War History*, XXVIII (June 1982), 128–52; Dannenbaum, *Drink and Disorder*, 181–94; Ruth M. Alexander, " 'We Are Engaged as a Band of Sisters': Class and Domesticity in the Washingtonian Temperance Movement, 1840–1850," *Journal of American History*, LXXV (December 1988), 763–85; *Crystal Fount*, July 4, August 2, 1851, August 3, 1849, June 20, 1851, January 30, 1852, May 27, 1853. See also *South Western Baptist*, August 10, 1853.

hail it as the harbinger of a better day in Alabama."[74] Some of Tuscaloosa's women followed through on this advice, and reportedly dropped "hints to their husbands that they had better quit their liquor," and then bragged among themselves "when their husbands join the 'Sons.' "[75] The activities of Tuscaloosa's white women in the temperance movement were mostly restricted to such persuasive means. Aside from their gathering of petitions, there is no evidence that women in Alabama engaged in any forms of direct action—especially the assault upon liquor retailers—that were more common in the North. Nor does it appear that the activity of Tuscaloosa's women in temperance during the antebellum years led them to demand suffrage.[76]

One quarter in which Tuscaloosa's temperance forces were continually challenged was among the students of the University of Alabama. Although some students and faculty embraced temperate living, university president Basil Manly was continually aggrieved at the degree of alcohol consumption among the university community. Most noteworthy was Manly's long-term feud with Frederick Augustus Porter Barnard, the university's most distinguished faculty member. Manly, a Baptist foe of intemperance and an ardent proponent of southern rights, clashed often with Barnard, a Yankee by birth, a Unionist

74. *Crystal Fount*, August 2, 1851, January 30, 1852. Although John Warren admitted that some men were opposed to women's forming their own temperance societies, he claimed that the "propriety" of such female associations "is now no longer doubted. . . . We cannot, for the life of us, conceive why, good citizens should object to any *honorable* means, in the hands of *any class* of people, of arresting the destroying and soul-damning influence of spirituous and malt liquors"; *ibid.*, April 30, 1852. It cannot be ascertained how widespread Warren's sentiments were among Alabamians. Although no correspondence was published in the *Crystal Fount* that repudiated Warren's views, the Selma female temperance society was the only such women's association that was reported in that paper.

75. *Crystal Fount*, March 12, 1852. In neighboring Greene County, one young man wrote to a friend: "My gal asked me the other day if I drank liquor in town . . . I was obliged to admit that I sometimes take a 'drop' . . . she considered it very unbecoming in a young man to drink *in public* . . . I promised her that I would not drink any more in town if she would not care should I drink at home. So we struck a bargain." Letter dated April 18, 1848, cited in Minnie Clare Boyd, *Alabama in the Fifties: A Social Study* (New York, 1931), 176.

76. That women's rights grew out of temperance and other reform causes in which women participated is contended by Dannenbaum, *Drink and Disorder*, 184–200, *passim*, and Tyrrell, "Women and Temperance," 144–52. In the conclusion of this study, I will address the question of why reformers in the South rarely embraced such "ultraist" measures.

Whig in politics, an Episcopalian, and a frequent tippler. By the late 1840s, Barnard (who later became president of the University of Mississippi and Columbia University) embraced the Sons of Temperance, but prior to this conversion Manly often noted in his diary Barnard's inebriate ways. In one entry, he wrote: "Barnard, with Barr, Blevins, & Walker, spent the Governor's fast Day, in a drunken frolic in Barnard's house. They got so drunk by dinner time that they could not eat; they slept till sundown. I have heard of Barnard being Drunk at several parties in the course of the past spring."[77]

Alcohol consumption by students was an even greater concern for Manly. He kept track of their drunken behavior and other moral infractions—such as playing cards or billiards, hooting at women, swearing, and singing religious hymns or quoting from the Bible in a mocking tone—in a series of notebooks. A number of pranks suggest that some students resented the dominance of evangelical religion at the university and in the larger society. In 1842 Manly reported finding that the university's Bible in the school rotunda "had been destroyed before morning prayers" and that "some scurrilous words also were written on the Rostrum in relation to Prof. Brumby and myself." A few years later, on a day "set apart by public authority as a Day of fasting & c.," some students, rather than offering their devotions, vandalized the university's rotunda and hung up "numerous placards—all foolish & sacriligious [*sic*]." Manly also reported in 1848 that students held a "mockery of a religious meeting" that was "loud and disorderly."[78]

Manly's efforts to curb students' drinking—in particular, their drunken behavior in downtown Tuscaloosa—must have seemed futile. By 1847 he had begun confronting students who had been found drunk and extracting from them a signed pledge to "abstain entirely from all that may intoxicate, during their stay in college." Finding this method to be ineffective, a January 1848 faculty meeting adopted as a "principle of our action that if a student is known to have been drunk, or to keep liquors in his room he shall, without fail, be required to leave the University." Possibly in response to this growing adminis-

---

77. John Fulton, *Memoirs of Frederick A. P. Barnard* (New York, 1896), 105–108; Basil Manly Diary No. 3, July 11, 1845. Further information regarding Manly's displeasure at Barnard's drinking may be found in William J. Chute, *Damn Yankee! The First Career of Frederick A. P. Barnard* (Port Washington, N.Y., 1978), 96–98, 121–22, and James Sellers, *History of the University of Alabama*, 71–73.

78. Basil Manly Diary "Blue Book," February 22, 1842, in Manly Family Papers; Basil Manly Diary No. 3, December 4, 1846, June 25, 1848.

trative heavy-handedness, student misbehavior increased. After less than a week of the faculty's new policy, "the bible was removed from the rotundo. The Rostrum was decorated with liquor bottles, surrounded by playing cards. . . . A placard of the lowest description in all respects, was struck up." After replacing the stolen Bible, Manly and the faculty were outraged to have the new volume removed only a few days later.[79]

In light of this riotous behavior, university officials must have been ecstatic with the enthusiasm that the Sons of Temperance generated the following autumn. Perhaps the students who had proved the most troublesome to Manly and the faculty were expelled or chose not to return to the university. Other students, who may have been irritated by their hedonistic classmates, possibly embraced the Sons of Temperance as a way to distinguish themselves as virtuous. In any case, Manly recorded fewer infractions in his notebooks during the 1848–1849 academic year, suggesting that the student body had mellowed. The university's Sons of Temperance division remained active for at least three years, the university providing facilities for the meetings. In 1849 the school authorized some repartitioning in Franklin Hall so that the Sons could have a permanent place to gather. After the division had been on campus for nearly two years, Manly wrote in his diary that "the degree of order prevailing among the students of the University during this college year has been commendable; no violation of rule, worthy of notice here, having occurred. . . . A division of the order of the Sons of Temperance has been established among them, consisting [of] nearly half their number."[80]

Manly's notebooks, however, also indicate that by 1849, those students who did not join the Sons of Temperance became increasingly hostile to the organization and more inclined toward drunken behavior. In December 1849, hecklers attended a temperance meeting and caused "much disorder." Almost two years later, Manly noted that "an old white horse was put into the Rotundo; with the badges of the Sons of temperance hung on him." This gradual loosening of the Sons' grip upon the student body, plus some possible recidivism on the part of those who had pledged themselves to the order, lessened the faculty's enthusiasm for this manifestation of temperance. Although Manly had earlier defended the right of individual Baptists to join the Sons, he feared that

79. Basil Manly Diary No. 3, March 11, 1847, January 18, 24, 26, 31, 1848.
80. Basil Manly Diary No. 4, October 15, December 1, 1849, January 18, 1850, October 31, 1851, Basil Manly Diary No. 5, July 10, 1851, both in Manly Family Papers.

a report from the University of Virginia in May 1850 might foretell the University of Alabama's fate. At Virginia, 100 of the 238 students had joined the Sons; but of that number, 50 had withdrawn, and now drinking problems at the school were worse than ever. Ten days earlier, Manly was irritated by the remarks of a Sons promoter at the University of Alabama, and afterward gave the speaker only a lukewarm endorsement. Although Manly called intemperance "the greatest curse that afflicts mankind" and cited the "duty of all to bind themselves to this mighty movement, by adopting habits of total abstinence," he also told the students, "I am not certain that it is my duty to join the 'Sons of Temperance'; but if any man thinks that his joining will make him a soberer, steadier, more useful or a happier man, I advise him to join." A year later, Manly declined to speak before the Warrior Division, citing pressing duties. He added, however, that at "a future day, if the advocacy of that 'temperance' which the Bible teaches, and which induces far more than abstinence from intoxicating drink be desired from me,—as a Xtn & minister of the Gospel, I will cheerfully give my earliest leisure to the matter."[81]

After the failure of the petition drive of 1838–1840, A. J. Holcombe proposed a new strategy to enact prohibition in 1841—namely, that local magistrates be required to call for an election within twenty days from the time that an individual applied for a liquor license. Voters in each electoral beat would then decide whether they would license the sale of liquor in their community or prohibit it by refusing to issue licenses. Holcombe was convinced that the enactment of such a law—designated as "no license" by contemporaries, while the adversarial position of permitting liquor sales was labeled "license"—would cause the sale of liquor to cease. Unfortunately for Holcombe, his appeal fell upon deaf ears in the legislature. Nevertheless, his goal of seeking local option proved to be the next phase of legal suasion. In 1844 the voters of Marion elected a village council that was determined to "abate groggeries and all other public nuisances." The council's strategy was to do an end run around the question of no license by merely raising the license fee to a prohibitive level, thus making the affordable operation of a grog shop virtually impossible. Marion's $1,000 li-

---

81. Basil Manly Diary No. 4, November 30, December 3, 1849, October 31, 1851; George Little, *Memoirs of George Little* (Tuscaloosa, 1924), 16–17; *Alabama Baptist Advocate*, August 29, October 31, 1849; Basil Manly Diary No. 4, May 10, 20, 1850; Basil Manly Diary No. 5, November 17, 1851. For more information on the conflicts between students and faculty at the University of Alabama during these years, see James Sellers, *History of the University of Alabama*, 197–257.

cense law on retailers of liquor was challenged and was eventually argued before the Alabama Supreme Court. The court, in an opinion authored by Chief Justice Henry Collier, ruled in favor of the law. The justices held that the ordinance was consistent with the village's act of incorporation granted by the legislature in 1835, which authorized Marion officials "to restrain and prohibit every species of gambling, drunkenness, & c.; to grant licences to the retailers of spirits and liquors; to regulate and restrain them when deemed a nuisance." The court explained that this statute gave the corporation power to see "that good morals may be preserved; and if this should become impracticable, and it is supposed that retailers incommode or annoy, or are offensive or noxious to the people of the town, then to withhold, and thus suppress the business." This ruling came as no surprise to the law's opponents, who protested that Collier, because of his well-known temperance sympathies, could not rule on the case impartially.[82]

In 1845, though, Marion officials reduced their village's license fee from \$1,000 to \$200, which action outraged Stephen Miller of the *Monitor*. Tuscaloosa did not have such a law at this time, nor is there any indication that its temperance societies pressed for one during the 1840s. Nevertheless, Miller had hoped that Marion's example would prove contagious: "From the superior tone of society and morals, as evidenced by the flourishing schools and general order which existed in Marion, the friends of Temperance throughout the state regarded the prohibition, by the Town Council, of the retail of ardent spirits, as an example which other communities would in due time follow." In Marion, "not a drop of liquid fire was to be found," and the town "was considered the modern Athens, and her stern morality, as well as elevated position in learning, made her the pride of Alabama." The \$200 license fee, claimed Miller, was inequitable, as it afforded the operation of "a genteel doggery, patronized by the select," while excluding the "small retailers, with their jugs and half pints." Calling the measure an "odious distinction," Miller proclaimed: "Let there be general competition in the sale or use, or let there be none at all."[83]

82. *Independent Monitor*, June 30, 1841; *Alabama Baptist* (Marion), March 16, 1844; *The Intendant and Council of the Town of Marion* v. *Chandler*, 6 Alabama Reports 899–904 (1844); S. A. Townes, *The History of Marion, Sketches of Life, & c. in Perry County, Alabama* (Marion, Ala., 1844), 32–33.

83. *Independent Monitor*, April 9, 1845. After moving to Georgia, Miller was among the 6 percent of voters who supported Basil H. Overby, the prohibitionist candidate for governor in 1855. Stephen F. Miller, *The Bench and Bar in Georgia: Memoirs and Sketches* (2 vols., Philadelphia, 1858), II, 440–41.

The decision of the Alabama Supreme Court, however, seems to have given other polities in the state the impetus to regulate their liquor traffic similarly. Although the temperance movement had succeeded in lessening the consumption of liquor, it was obvious that some people remained unmoved by pleas for abstinence. Disillusioned with moral suasion, the resurgent temperance campaign of the late 1840s and early 1850s embraced prohibitively high liquor-license fees as a way to combat the sale of spirits in each community. But many temperance devotees, finding this method unsatisfactory, eventually called for a legislative ban on the granting of liquor licenses.

As we saw earlier in this chapter, Tuscaloosa had always regulated the sale of liquor by the issuing of liquor licenses. Up through 1835, tavern licenses cost $20 and liquor licenses sold for $15 (see Table 6). By 1839, a tavern license had risen to $30 and a license to sell spirits to $50. The extent to which license fees rose, if at all, in the following twelve years is not known. In February 1851, however, the voters of Tuscaloosa elected a mayor and aldermen who opposed the sale of spirits. These officials subsequently passed a $1,000 liquor license law. The fee was, according to Basil Manly, "designed to be prohibitory"—especially since current Alabama law mandated that liquor licenses in towns of one thousand or more inhabitants be no less than $75. The new measure was sustained "by a direct vote of the people" a few months later. It was further endorsed the following October when *Crystal Fount* editor John Warren, who also served as a city alderman, resigned his post because his "dry" views were reputed to be out of touch with those of his constituents, and another "dry" won the seat in a special election.[84]

In June 1851, Northport officeholders passed a $1,000 license ordinance. Warren praised the measure, which he believed was tantamount to prohibition—although a "positive prohibitory statement would have pleased us better." Warren anticipated that "complaints . . . will be uttered by the thirsty

---

84. *Flag of the Union*, April 24, 1839; *Crystal Fount*, November 7, 1851, February 20, 1852; Basil Manly Diary No. 5, July 12, 1851; *American Temperance Magazine and Sons of Temperance Offering*, II (January 1852), 63; John J. Ormond, Arthur P. Bagby, and George Goldthwaite, comps., *The Code of Alabama* (Montgomery, 1852), 134. Although the aldermen construed the results of this 1851 special election as an endorsement of their high-license law, apathy to the election—and perhaps to the issue as well—may have been a better interpretation of the voters' mood, as J. W. Turner, the victorious dry candidate, defeated Mr. Cooper, the wet candidate, 21 to 16. In contrast, during the 1848 presidential election, 598 ballots were cast in the city of Tuscaloosa. Assuming that this ward's electorate constituted one-sixth of the total in Tuscaloosa, there should have been at least 99 eligible voters for this special election. *Independent Monitor*, October 9, 1851, November 10, 1848.

ones" but recommended that they "learn . . . to slake their thirst with nature's own pure beverage, and it will save them many a headache and many a dime." These Tuscaloosa and Northport ordinances also pleased University of Alabama officials. In his annual report to the trustees, Basil Manly admitted that some students continued to imbibe and a few had wandered into the town of Tuscaloosa and been disruptive. But he added that despite these problems, Tuscaloosa's new liquor law "has diminished exposure & thus has had a salutary bearing on the University." Since the law's passage, Manly claimed, there had been "more general & more vigorous applications than usual to study. At no period, within our knowledge, has there been so small a proportion of idlers in our classes." Both John Warren and the Tuscaloosa Board of Aldermen agreed that "the large accessions of students to the University" in the fall of 1851 occurred because "the fact has gone abroad that we have closed all our 'licensed retail establishments.' "[85]

Of course, not everyone was satisfied with this ordinance. Appealing to their sense of moderation, Mathew Duffee petitioned the board of aldermen in the fall of 1851 for a $400 license. He may have argued that his proposed establishment would cater to the well-to-do and price its spirits beyond the reach of the poor, or even that as the only liquor retailer in town, he could better regulate alcohol consumption, but "from a profound conviction of duty," the board refused his request. Citing the three electoral manifestations of the voters' will mentioned previously, the aldermen were "of opinion, that the citizens of Tuscaloosa are disposed to give this experiment a *fair test,* and to satisfy themselves fully, before they yield the point, whether the *'no license law'* works *well,* or *ill;* especially at this time, when Tuscaloosa is daily becoming more and more prominent throughout the State as an educational point." In light of the removal of the state capital from Tuscaloosa only five years earlier and the town's subsequent decline in population, this latter topic was stressed by Warren when he endorsed the aldermen's decision in the *Crystal Fount:* "We believe that Tuscaloosa is coming up; that real estate is going to advance; that business will ere long increase; that people from various quarters will move here to educate their children."[86]

85. *Crystal Fount,* June 6, 1851; Basil Manly Diary No. 5, July 12, 1851; *Crystal Fount,* October 10, November 7, 1851. In 1851, 126 students enrolled at the University of Alabama, up from 91 the year previous, and the highest since 158 students enrolled in 1836. After the $1,000 license fee was reduced to $400, enrollment dipped to only 117, and never went below 112 during the following five years. James Sellers, *History of the University of Alabama,* 581.

86. *Crystal Fount,* November 7, 1851.

In the subsequent three months, however, the board must have sensed that public opinion was shifting, as they called an election for February 11, 1852, when the voters would be presented with the option of reducing the license fee. Predictably, John Warren opposed a decrease, arguing that "the true policy of the people is, in sustaining the law as it exists." To change the law would, in his view, sacrifice the interests of the community for the selfish designs of one person. As things stood, Tuscaloosa was recognized as a "sober, industrious and thrifty community," one "approbated" nationally for having "no licensed Bar-room." "Should we not, therefore, for our own credit's sake, sustain the present license law? . . . Shall it be said that [Tuscaloosa] is retrograding?" Reminding his readers that enrollment at the University of Alabama had increased after the passage of the $1,000 license law, Warren suggested that reopening the bar-rooms could cause the university to relocate. He admitted that he could not determine the correctness of the growing opinion that "there is more drinking in the city now than there was before the Bar-room was closed" but asserted that regardless of whether this notion was true, the law was a positive good. Since the passage of the high license fee, drinking had become "an individual affair. Each man must be personally responsible for the improprieties committed. If we authorize a Bar-room, we transfer all the responsibility and odium of the traffic to the shoulders of the people. For ourself, we do most sternly object to bearing any part of any such responsibility."[87]

The Tuscaloosa division of the Sons of Temperance took no official position on the license-fee issue. Before the election, however, they published an open letter to "the Merchants and Traders, who sell intoxicating Liquors in the City of Tuscaloosa, Ala.," in which they reminded the public of the debilitating consequences of the liquor trade. Implicitly recognizing that the sale of liquor continued in spite of the high-license law, the Sons appealed to the city's merchants to stop selling liquor "on account of the misery you are inflicting on the innocent mothers and helpless children of those whose vitiated appetites prompts them to buy this pernicious fluid from your stores," and also "on grounds of self-interest to banish it from your stores. By doing so you would at once change every drunkard who trades to Tuscaloosa into a sober man; and where he now earns and spends one dollar with you, he would spend ten dollars, and for articles which would pay a much better profit than that miserable stuff called whiskey."[88]

87. *Ibid.*, February 6, 1852.

88. *Ibid.* This plea followed a series of resolutions passed by the local Sons of Temperance the preceding December, in which they blamed retailers of spirits for the misery arising from drunk-

In spite of these pleas, Tuscaloosans voted to reduce the license fee from $1,000 to $400. John Warren expressed his disappointment in a sardonic essay, commenting that "a majority of the good citizens of our town . . . discovered that the best plan to diminish the consumption of intoxicating liquors, was to legalize the retail sale thereof." He also pointed out that the new law favored the rich, as now the only people who would retail liquor were those who could afford the license fee. With further sarcasm, he suggested that the fee be reduced to the cost of paying a clerk to perform the necessary paper work. This low fee would open the opportunity of selling spirits to everyone, which would create much "improvement in the quiet and good order of the city." Warren's bitterness was shared by others in the temperance forces. In subsequent weeks, a correspondent of the *Crystal Fount* charged that liquor retailers who had been driven out of business by the $1,000 license law had provided free bottles of liquor to everyone who promised to get drunk and make a lot of noise. "In a short time, not a few of the better sort of folks began to talk about the street, that they did believe there was more drinking going on now, than there was before the $1,000 ordinance was passed."[89]

As much as Warren fought to preserve Tuscaloosa's $1,000 license ordinance, he nonetheless considered it a "half loaf." His goal was total prohibition. Throughout his tenure as editor of the *Crystal Fount*, he continually argued in favor of prohibitionist laws that would end the licensing of liquor sales altogether. Of course, by taking this position, he and others demonstrated that they had given up any hope of using persuasion to complete a moral revolution. And in surrendering persuasion for coercion, they placed less stress upon the highly moral society that they believed would inevitably develop when everyone embraced the temperate lifestyle. Instead, prohibitionists explained that respectable people were endangered by the retail sale of alcohol, and they vigorously contended that moral suasion was insufficient to protect society from the consequences of liquor consumption. Warren conceded that "to coerce any man by legal law to conform to any code of morals, the non-conformance to which would not result in public injury, is clearly a violation of the principles

---

enness and called upon "all respectable citizens" to place "the vendor of intoxicating liquors on a level with the degraded victim of their vile traffic." *Ibid.*, December 5, 1851.

89. *Ibid.*, February 27, March 12, 1852. Basil Manly also became disillusioned with the high-license law as a means to keep university students from drinking; he reported to the university's trustees in 1852 that the "evils" of alcohol "are in no degree diminished by any municipal restrictions thrown upon the sale of liquor;—there are always means at hand by which students inclined to it may be intemperate." Basil Manly Diary No. 5, July 10, 1852.

of free government." But vices that "endanger public security" required a legal remedy. Moral suasion "may go a great way with moral men," but it was insufficient to "change the liquor dealer's insatiate thirst for gain."[90]

As they brought the social impact of alcohol consumption to the public's attention, temperance devotees further directed their attacks on liquor retailers. Retailers "take no delight in the improvement of society, and glory only in that which tends to its shame." The fact that a liquor proprietor "was guided by honest intentions" and "rigidly adhered to the letter of the law" was irrelevant: the goodness of the seller could never "deprive the fatal beverage of its bane, nor yet prevent the formation of the alcoholic appetite." Nor was there ever "a bar-room opened, that did not engulph some in perdition. . . . The *respectability* of the establishment, no more than the lowest places of debauchery, strips it of its fearful power." And as long as the state continued to license liquor retailers, it kept "the dealer in countenance, and the business respectable." Because the sale of liquor exposed the public to "acts of violence and deeds of darkest hue," no legislative body "on earth has the right to legalize the traffic in intoxicating liquors; . . . such legislation is an outrage committed on the rights of the people." Indignant, Warren appealed to the temperance faithful to "send a petition to the Legislature to repeal the license feature, and to pass a law forbidding the traffic."[91]

Numerous petitions from throughout the state were sent to the legislature during the 1851–1852 session. In January 1852, the Alabama house's Committee on Ways and Means "reported adversely on the bill to regulate the granting of licenses to retailers of spirituous liquors." After the full house approved the committee's report, Warren concluded that the people were ahead of the legislature on this issue: "We will venture the assertion, that if the sense of the people, in this section, were taken on the subject, they would render a different verdict." But Warren was not deterred by this setback. Two weeks later he was singing the praises of Maine's recently enacted law prohibiting unauthorized persons from selling or manufacturing intoxicants throughout the state. Warren glowed over reports that the liquor traffic in Maine had "almost entirely ceased—giving place to thrift and a high standard of morals." He continued: "Some of its features are very stringent, yet, nevertheless, it has many warm friends, who think—and very properly too—that severe cases require severe treatment. It is viewed by them as the only sure and effectual method of re-

90. *Crystal Fount,* June 6, 1851, March 25, May 21, 28, 1852.
91. *Ibid.,* June 20, December 12, September 12, June 6, 1851.

straining altogether the abominable liquor traffic, which has so long afflicted mankind." A few months later, Warren reported with "unspeakable pleasure" that a similar law had been approved by the Massachusetts Senate. Listing the other states that were expected to adopt statewide prohibitory laws, Warren queried, "When shall we have it in our power to class Alabama among the galaxy of Temperance States?" Hoping that the day was not too distant, Warren prodded his fellow temperance devotees: "to accomplish such a proud preeminence we must be active—zealous—fully alive to the great work." And although Warren's ideal was the Maine law, he was also pleased that a local-option bill had been passed by the Mississippi legislature. Although it was "not so stringent as the Maine law," it was "equally as efficacious. . . . Would that we had a similar law in Alabama—we would ask for no better. Such a law is greatly desired in our state."[92] Believing that majority opinion was on his side—even after Tuscaloosa voters elected to reduce liquor license fees—Warren was certain that widespread prohibition would be enacted only if the people were permitted to vote on it.

Tuscaloosa's temperance forces thrived for several years before the cause again atrophied, and during this time temperance activity throughout the state became more extensive than ever before. Several Baptist churches in Tuscaloosa County became increasingly concerned about alcohol consumption by their members. The Big Creek Baptist Church so aligned itself with the Sons of Temperance that the two groups discussed the joint construction of a new meetinghouse. In the early 1850s this church and the Bethany and the Dunn's Creek Baptist churches all amended their articles of decorum to prohibit their members from retailing spirits. These changes were highly significant in that they were the only such modifications in the behavioral requirements of these churches during the antebellum years. The Baptist church in Tuscaloosa town enacted no such restrictions upon its members, but its pastor and many in its congregation were aligned firmly with the temperance camp. The Reverend Azor Van Hoose gave a prayer at a major temperance celebration in 1851, and a year earlier he discoursed on the text "No drunkard shall inherit the kingdom of heaven."[93]

92. *Ibid.*, January 9, 23, March 25, May 28, 1852.

93. Big Creek Baptist Church Minutes, October 13, November 10, 1849, January 10, September 12, 1852; Bethany Baptist Church Minutes, September 27, 1851; Dunn's Creek Baptist Church Minutes, November 1850, p. 164, February 1851, p. 166, May 1851, p. 170, April 1853, p. 191 [photocopies of all these records are in Hoole Special Collections]; *Crystal Fount*, July 4, 1851, May 10, 1850.

By mid-1851, however, the growth of the Sons of Temperance had peaked in Alabama. John Warren lamented almost weekly that enthusiasm for the cause had waned—he complained that subscription expirations outnumbered new subscribers to the *Fount.* The Sons were also in decline institutionally, as many members were behind in their dues and numerous divisions had ceased operating. Warren pleaded with his readers to contribute money so that the statewide Sons could hire a lecturer to visit the divisions that were languishing. In 1852 one newspaper editor in Talladega was saddened that "the subject of temperance" had "lost much of its interest" in his town. Even though the community was "evidently improving in everything else, and although our citizens are, most of them, sober and discreet men, perhaps as much so as can be found in any town in the state, yet that interest necessary to advance the cause of total abstinence, is, in some small degree, wanting." In Tuscaloosa as well, Warren noted that the regular meetings of the divisions "are not so crowded as they used to be on the introduction of the Order into this place." Yet he praised a committed cadre who "have enlisted for life, and intend to pursue the path of duty through evil and through good report."[94]

This temperance vanguard was still a significant force in local affairs. In July 1853, members of the Warrior Division participated with Tuscaloosa's other fraternal associations and civil leaders in the cornerstone-laying ceremonies of the Alabama Asylum for the Insane. The *Monitor* attested to the division's continued existence ten months later when it printed resolutions mourning the death of an activist. But in December 1854, when Tuscaloosa's Masons, Odd Fellows, municipal authorities, and University of Alabama officials were present at the groundbreaking ceremonies of the Northeast and Southwest Alabama Railroad, the Sons of Temperance were absent, suggesting that their local division had ceased operating. A few other Tuscaloosa County divisions persisted, however, and in August 1858, the Grant's Creek Division celebrated its tenth anniversary as "the first Division ever established in this country during the Temperance Reformation ten years ago." Although the presence of three to four hundred people at these festivities may have suggested to some that the movement still had widespread support, one correspondent knew otherwise, noting that the Grant's Creek and the Buck Creek Divisions were the only two functioning auxiliaries "of the now almost extinct order of the Sons

94. *Crystal Fount,* June 20, September 5, October 17, June 27, September 19, November 7, 1851; January 2, 1852; *Democratic Watchtower* (Talladega, Ala.), May 12, 1852; *Crystal Fount,* March 25, 1852. In 1850, the *Fount* had 1,400 subscribers. Social schedule of the 1850 census, ADAH.

of Temperance, of which we have any knowledge. All others within the circle of our acquaintance, have yielded to the power of the enemy, and their banners, 'all tattered and torn,' are ingloriously trailing in the dust."[95] Meanwhile, the *Crystal Fount* had ceased publication sometime during the spring of 1854.[96]

Much temperance activity occurred in Alabama during the 1850s prior to this collapse. In fact, a protracted effort to enact prohibition marks this period as the pinnacle of Alabama's temperance agitation during the antebellum years. Temperance proponents, encouraged by the lower levels of alcohol consumption in the state, believed that total victory was within reach. In 1850 John Warren was "much gratified" to report that an election had transpired in Tuscaloosa "without the exhibition of drunkenness and disorder, which have so frequently heretofore attended popular elections," and he ascribed this welcome change to the diligence of the Sons of Temperance. Temperance had brought about "the general improvement of morals and condition of society," as society was "less frequently disgraced by the drunken revel and the midnight orgie"; it had resulted in "the almost general paralysis . . . to public drinking." In neighboring Jefferson County, Elyton, a place formerly renowned for its "idleness and dissipation," and whose "respectable" citizens were "daily saluted with the bitter and vulgar oaths of the inebriate," had undergone radical changes: "The Village Groceries are closed—Their keepers have become respectable members of society and all engaged in honorable callings—The inebriate has become a sober man and the dissolute character has amended his ways."[97] The power of the temperance crusade may be further attested by Newton L. Whitfield. The Tuscaloosa city attorney from 1852 to 1858 and afterward a member of the Alabama House of Representatives and the president of the

95. *Independent Monitor,* July 15, 1853; Basil Manly Diary No. 5, July 14, 1853; *Independent Monitor,* May 25, 1854, December 14, 1854, August 12, 1858. The Grant's Creek Division was still operating a year later when it passed resolutions mourning the death of one of its members; *Independent Monitor,* August 6, 1859.

96. *Independent Monitor,* August 12, 1858. The *Fount* was cited in the Penfield (Ga.) *Temperance Banner,* April 15, 1854, but when the editor of the *South Western Baptist* announced two months later the inauguration of the Montgomery *Temperance Times,* he implied that the *Times* would be the only temperance paper in Alabama. *South Western Baptist,* June 22, 1854.

97. *Crystal Fount,* May 10, 1850, August 8, 1851, May 21, 1852; *Jones Valley Times* (Elyton, Ala.), November 3, 1854. In Eutaw, in neighboring Greene County, one young medical student affirmed that an aversion to alcohol had taken hold upon the young men of his community: "I drink whenever I feel like it, but the young men here are not so much inclined that way. It is very seldom you see a young man go into a grocery . . . to drink." Letter dated April 18, 1848, as cited in Boyd, *Alabama in the Fifties,* 176.

Northeast and Southwest Alabama Railroad, Whitfield would have surely been an officer in any of Tuscaloosa's temperance societies had he joined them. Although there is no record of his ever uniting with the temperance movement during his lengthy residence in Tuscaloosa, Whitfield was greatly disturbed that Thomas J. Burke had "disgraced himself by a violation of his Sons of Temperance pledge, and returned to excessive drink. After years of degradation he had resumed decent habits. . . . Now to return to his beastly habits, places him beyond all hope of reformation, while it justly subjects him to the lasting execration of all his friends. . . . Surely the greatest, incomparably the greatest curse ever inflicted on frail humanity is ardent spirits. I have a mind to pledge myself never to taste a drop of it again."[98]

The push toward legislatively sanctioned prohibition commenced in September 1852 when Alabama's Grand Division of the Sons of Temperance called for a convention to meet in Selma in November "for the purpose of considering . . . the best means of promoting the Temperance reformation." The time had arrived, announced the leaders of the Grand Division, when advocates of the cause "should act in concert and have a perfect and distinct understanding to the object to be accomplished, and the mode and manner of accomplishing it." J. B. Stiteler, corresponding editor of the *South Western Baptist,* assumed that delegates would discuss the feasibility of pursuing a Maine-style liquor law for Alabama. As for himself, Stiteler was sold on prohibition and discounted arguments that a Maine-type law was subversive of individual freedom. He drew an analogy to southern statutes that punished those who circulated antislavery tracts: "Should an abolition fanatic propose to distribute incendiary publications in our midst, and ask on the ground that he was a free citizen that his work might be legalized, who would think that the general good would be sacrificed to, or even endangered by his cupidity? And yet it may be questioned if this is not the policy on which our laws are at present framed." The convention was well attended, drawing 237 delegates from thirty-two of Alabama's fifty-two counties. After a spirited debate, only a minority of delegates endorsed pressing the legislature immediately for a law "similar in its spirit to the Maine

98. Newton L. Whitfield Journal, December 11, 1849, in James Austin Anderson Papers (typescript); Tuscaloosa Scrapbook No. 5, "On the History of Tuscaloosa," 3, in Hoole Special Collections. Prior to his activity in the Sons of Temperance, Thomas J. Burke had also served in the leadership of Tuscaloosa's Young Men's Total Abstinence Society from 1839 to 1840, and was also an attorney, town alderman, and editor of the Whig *Independent Monitor. Flag of the Union,* February 20, August 28, October 30, 1839; Tuscaloosa *Whig,* January 21, 1840; *Independent Monitor,* April 21, July 15, 1853.

Liquor Law." The majority report, which was unanimously approved after the defeat of the minority report, favored only a local-option law. Yet this was the first time a state temperance society had endorsed prohibitory measures since the Alabama State Temperance Society had done so in 1839, and undoubtedly many delegates who might otherwise have approved the pursuit of statewide prohibition were convinced that public opinion was not yet ready for such legislation.[99]

The majority of the delegates at the Selma convention approved what eventually came to be known as the "Alabama Law." This proposed bill, entitled "An Act to enable the inhabitants of every county, city, town, village and election precinct within the State of Alabama to protect themselves from the evils arising from the sale of intoxicating liquors," permitted the citizens of each polity to "increase to any amount" the cost of a liquor license or to "suppress entirely the sale, either by wholesale or retail" of intoxicants. Although a number of Alabama towns and villages had already enacted proscriptive license fees, the state supreme court had upheld the ordinances of only those polities whose legislative acts of incorporation, in the opinion of the court, permitted such prohibitory efforts. The promoters of the Alabama Law sought to provide all polities with at least the right currently reserved to those relatively few locales. Many temperance partisans, like John Warren, hoped for more: that citizens would use the proposed law to abolish the license system in their communities completely. The process of enacting local prohibition would commence when fifty qualified voters of a county, or ten voters of a smaller polity, petitioned the judge of probate to call a special election, which was to be held between thirty and sixty days after the judge gave notice to the electorate. If the voters rejected the proposition, no new election could be held for six months; if they approved the measure, then it would take effect thirty days after the results were posted. Violators of the new law would be liable to a fine of not less than one hundred dollars for each offense and imprisonment for up to three months.[100]

After endorsing this proposed act, the delegates at the Selma convention voted to reconvene six months later to discuss the progress of their crusade and consider further political activity. Three hundred enthusiasts of legal suasion assembled in Selma in May 1853. Although they declared that they did

99. *South Western Baptist*, October 20, 28, 1852; Carlson, "Temperance Reform," 236–37. Regarding temperance in Alabama during the 1850s, see also James Sellers, *Prohibition Movement in Alabama*, 32–38, and Carlson, "Temperance Reform," 236–48.

100. *Crystal Fount*, May 27, 1853; *Intendant and Town of Marion v. Chandler*, 6 Alabama Reports 899–904 (1844); *The Mayor, &c. of Mobile v. Rouse*, 8 Alabama Reports 515–517 (1845).

not "propose to intermix" their prohibitionist agenda with partisan politics, the delegates nevertheless concluded that additional political measures were necessary, as temperance was "a question of paramount importance." Realizing that the success of their cause depended upon the "complexion of the legislature," they resolved that no friend of temperance should vote for any legislative candidate who refused to endorse the Alabama Law, and they encouraged local temperance devotees to nominate their own candidates if no others proved favorable. In addition, gubernatorial candidates would henceforth be scrutinized with respect to their views on prohibition. Statewide, local activists were "earnestly requested to take immediate steps to insure the full discussion of the temperance reform question" by holding mass meetings and by circulating petitions favoring the Alabama Law that would be presented before the legislature. Throughout their proceedings, the delegates took pains to deny that they were imperious zealots. They insisted that the proposed law was simply a manifestation of majority rule. The present license system was "seriously objectionable and anti-republican," since a local licensing board of six men "can locate retail drinking houses in every community, although every voter may oppose their establishment." In the *Fount*, John Warren concurred with this assessment, insisting that the convention's resolutions were "moderate," as there was nothing in the proposed law that "conflicts with the rights of anyone. As we understand it, all that is asked is, that the state cease to legislate upon the subject of the liquor traffic, leaving it to the *people*, who are the best judges of their own wants to say whether or not they will continue or discontinue it."[101]

It is not known how many legislative candidates were endorsed by temperance enthusiasts. In the 1853 gubernatorial race, the Whigs' inability to decide upon a successor to the party's regular nominee, Richard W. Walker, who resigned from the race due to illness, resulted in a crowded field. Both John A. Winston, the Democratic nominee, and A. Q. Nicks, a Union Democrat supported by some Whigs, refused to take a definite position on the proposed local-option law but replied to temperance questionnaires that they would approve any laws passed by the legislature on this subject. Whig William S. Earnest flatly favored local option, which brought him an endorsement from the state's temperance forces. This approval, though, failed to help Earnest significantly. Alabama's Democrats united behind Winston,

---

101. Carlson, "Temperance Reform," 238; *Crystal Fount*, May 27, June 14, 1853.

and he was overwhelmingly victorious with 30,116 votes. His divided opposition floundered, and Earnest and Nicks received only 10,127 and 3,763 votes, respectively.[102]

This failure of prohibition to resonate in the gubernatorial race appears to have been matched in the legislative contests as well. Despite the appeals of 100,000 Alabamians—almost one-fourth of the state's white population—to the legislature, calling for the enactment of the Alabama Law, the committees on temperance in both the state senate and house recommended that their bodies reject local option, and the house defeated a proposal to submit the issue for a statewide referendum. Furious but still undaunted, disciples of temperance called for another state convention to be held in Montgomery in late May, 1854. The response was less enthusiastic than at the previous state convention, as only 150 delegates appeared. They nevertheless reaffirmed previous strategies and beliefs—denouncing the license system for its harmful effects upon society and its antirepublican qualities, urging local activists to maintain their vigilance, and reiterating the pledge not to vote for any candidate for the governorship or the legislature who refused to endorse the Alabama Law. Suspecting, though, that no gubernatorial hopeful would embrace their platform, the conventioneers issued a call to meet again the following January to consider nominating their own candidate.[103]

At this convention in January 1855, R. C. Holifield reported that he had recently organized eighty-four temperance leagues in Alabama and believed that a "great and salutary change in public opinion" in the state "was fast maturing into prohibitory enthusiasm." In spite of Holifield's optimism, the small number of delegates at this gathering—the minutes do not reveal how many were present—indicated that the cause was again beset with apathy. Accordingly, the delegates deemed it "inexpedient to nominate a candidate for Governor at this time" but gave the Central Executive Committee the authority to call a later convention either to nominate a candidate or to endorse one who supported the Alabama Law. A few weeks later, proponents of state aid to railroads solicited Dallas County planter Robert A. Baker to run against incumbent governor John A. Winston. C. E. Haynes, editor of the Cahaba *Dallas*

102. Dorman, *Party Politics in Alabama*, 86–87; Thornton, *Politics and Power*, 325, 352; James Sellers, *Prohibition Movement in Alabama*, 34.

103. *South Western Baptist*, June 22, 1854; James Sellers, *Prohibition Movement in Alabama*, 35; Carlson, "Temperance Reform," 242; Huntsville *Democrat*, May 11, 1854; *South Western Baptist*, August 10, 1854.

Gazette, commented that Baker's views on temperance "prove him to be as big-oted on that question as any man in the country," making him the candidate most likely to gain the movement's endorsement. George D. Shortridge, how-ever, was nominated by the emergent Know-Nothing Party in June 1855, and his support of local option earned him the backing of Alabama's temperance leadership. Shortridge was no recent convert to temperance, as he had actively participated in the Tuscaloosa Temperance Society while a student at the Uni-versity of Alabama more than two decades earlier. Again, it is difficult to de-termine the extent to which Shortridge's position on prohibition assisted or hindered; in any case, he was soundly defeated by Winston, 42,238 to 30,639. State aid to railroads and the character of the Know-Nothing Party, rather than local option, were the dominant issues in the campaign.[104]

After Shortridge's defeat, the temperance cause in general, and the promo-tion of prohibition in particular, continued their downward spiral. By 1855, op-ponents of the Alabama Law reacted with hostility to prohibitionist efforts. The *Dallas Gazette*'s editor, although admitting that the "temperance party of this State" may not have favored a law as stringent as the Maine Law, was con-vinced that they would seek a stronger law upon the passage of a local-option bill and then "continue the march of bigotry and fanaticism, until the country is filled with a swarm of informers, and no man's dwelling safe from the inva-sion of a search warrant!" But the *Gazette* recognized that temperance was al-ready on the wane: the paper had reported a month and a half earlier that the Sons of Temperance division had ceased to exist in Cahaba and in many other places. Further evidence of this decline came when the *South Western Baptist,* which had enthusiastically endorsed prohibition—and presumably continued to do so—nonetheless removed the caption "Devoted to Religion, Temper-ance, Education, Morality, & c." from its masthead with the May 27, 1856, is-sue. Although secular newspapers usually said nothing on the disappearance of the temperance struggle, Baptists lamented it. On the one hand, in 1857 the Temperance Committee of the Alabama Baptist State Convention praised the changes wrought by the temperance movement over the past three de-cades—in particular the great decrease in the use of alcohol as a "common bev-erage" among "enlightened society," the virtual abandonment of liquor among the "laboring classes" when performing "fatigueing labor," and a "gratifying

104. *South Western Baptist,* February 1, 1855; Dorman, *Party Politics in Alabama,* 104–105; *Dal-las Gazette* (Cahaba, Ala.), February 2, 1855 (see also February 16, March 9, March 16, 1855); James Sellers, *Prohibition Movement in Alabama,* 36; Thornton, *Politics and Power,* 325, 327, 352–60; *State Rights Expositor and Spirit of the Age,* June 8, 1833.

change in the public conscience" in which "multitudes of the people" were no longer "enraged almost to madness" toward temperance activists. But the committee also mourned that the "friends of Temperance have become weary in well doing—have ceased to discuss and agitate on the subject." Members of the Liberty Baptist Association of Randolph County and the Ten Islands Baptist Association expressed similar regret over declining temperance activity in their vicinities. Nevertheless, in the remaining years of the decade a few communities in Alabama—often areas located near churches or schools—successfully petitioned the legislature for permission to prohibit the sale of intoxicants within their borders (one such locale was the village of New Lexington in Tuscaloosa County). These actions demonstrated that even during the late 1850s, the yearning for prohibition was not completely dead.[105]

In the town of Tuscaloosa, however, prohibitionist support was diminishing by this time. After Tuscaloosans lowered their license fee to $400 in 1852, prohibitionists recaptured public power and raised the cost of a liquor license to $5,000. Yet by late 1857, W. H. Fowler, editor of the *Independent Monitor*, was complaining that prohibition in Tuscaloosa had been counterproductive. Although he asserted that he had been a strong opponent of the license system prior to the introduction of the most recent high-license ordinance, Fowler contended—as had opponents of the $1,000 license law six years previously—that private drinking was "fifty times" greater than it would have been "if the city had a licensed Bar under the control of a genteel proprietor." The current law forced people to purchase their liquor in larger quantities and to consume it behind closed doors: "the result of this is, that a quart is often used where a single drink only would be taken if we had a genteel licensed Bar." Fowler also charged that the current law was hazardous to University of Alabama students, and that a "well regulated license system would protect the College ten-fold better."[106]

---

105. *Dallas Gazette* (Cahaba, Ala.), February 2, 1855, December 15, 1854; *Minutes of the Thirty-fourth Anniversary of the Alabama Baptist State Convention,* 10–11; *South Western Baptist,* October 23, 1856, October 22, November 12, 1857; James Sellers, *Prohibition Movement in Alabama,* 37–39; *Acts of the Seventh Biennial Session of the General Assembly of Alabama* (Montgomery, 1860), 588–89.

106. *Independent Monitor,* December 24, 1857. Alabama statute permitted any white citizen "to sell ardent spirits to any other citizen of industrious or temperate habits, in quantities not less than one quart," provided that the intoxicants were not consumed on the premises of purchase. C. C. Clay, comp., *Digest of the Laws of the State of Alabama* (Tuscaloosa, 1843), 557; Ormond, Bagby, and Goldthwaite, comps., *Code of Alabama,* 244–45; *Harris* v. *The Intendant and Council of Livingston,* 28 Alabama Reports 579 (1856).

Two months later, in a letter purportedly from a student to his mother, "Harry" explained why he favored the licensing of a bar. Echoing the sentiments of Fowler, Harry stated that the present law "caused many persons who drank scarcely any before, to buy and keep bottles and other large quantities of liquors in their private rooms, and to which the young men of the town have private but free access; and it is very certain that there is now more drinking done in Tuscaloosa, and more temptations of that sort thrown before the young men here, than there was before the retail law was abolished." In spite of the high-license law, many merchants maintained barrels of spirits "in their cellars or back rooms" for their customers. These merchants, however, complained that this practice had become a burden—one swore that he would rather pay a $300 license than give away an equivalent amount of liquor—while another explained to Harry that because of the difficulties most people had in obtaining liquor, merchants could be employed, if they were willing, from morning to evening doing nothing but "'sponging' friends."[107]

Of course, not everyone favored repealing Tuscaloosa's license law. One anonymous correspondent reiterated some oft-heard temperance rhetoric of the past three decades—for example, that it "requires more nerve than most young men possess to refuse the very polite invitation to drink, and when he has drank, it is quite easy to persuade him to amuse himself at cards, then step by step he is lead until he is lost." Thus, if the city council were to license a bar, "many a mother will bitterly regret the decision of the *so-called* Council, and many a youth will curse the day that he was born." The worst fears of this latter correspondent were realized in June 1858 when the council voted to reduce the license fee from $5,000 to $200. Interestingly, though, the *Monitor* did not attribute this change to a shift in local opinion. Rather, it pithily reported that the council was "compelled because the [Alabama] Supreme Court decisions upon the subject declare exorbitant fees to be utterly void." These judicial rulings did not settle the matter, nor did prohibitionist sentiment wither completely, as within two years the license fee was increased to $500.[108]

107. *Independent Monitor,* February 18, 1858, December 24, 1857; see also February 25, 1858.

108. *Independent Monitor,* February 18, June 10, 1858, April 7, 1860. The *Monitor* was probably referring to *Ex Parte James T. Burnett,* 30 Alabama Reports 461–470 (1858), in which the court held that only municipalities that had been given explicit authority from the legislature to grant prohibitory license fees might do so. Previously, in *Intendant and Town of Marion* v. *Chandler,* the court had implied that municipalities that had been granted the right to issue liquor licenses could set the fee at whatever level they desired. Although Chief Justice Samuel F. Rice had been a proponent of Washingtonian temperance in 1843, he, as well as his two fellow justices, were less

Despite Fowler's pronouncement that he at one time supported no license, his aversion to alcoholic beverages did not run as deep as it had among previous editors of the *Monitor,* for at one point he published a recipe for tomato wine. Such a step was possibly indicative of deeper changes in the feelings of Tuscaloosans toward alcohol, because no editor had so endorsed an intoxicant for over a quarter century. Moreover, when new editors took charge at the *Monitor,* they brought an even greater tolerance of alcohol: A. Robertson and J. S. Garvin printed a letter in 1860 that celebrated the scuppernong wine that some merchants had provided to them. Perhaps even greater evidence of the shift in Tuscaloosans' attitudes may be seen in the example of John Warren, former editor of the *Crystal Fount.* After his paper folded, Warren eventually became editor of the Democratic *Tuscaloosa Observer.* Although very few issues of this paper have survived, which precludes us from examining Warren's views in detail, in March 1861 he also praised a bottle of scuppernong wine, a gift to him from William H. and N. P. Lawrence: "We can bear testimony to its superior quality, having sampled a bottle politely presented to us by these clever advertisers, and pronounce it the pure juice of the grape—a No. 1 article—good for bodily ailments generally. Be it understood, we are under no spirit-inspiration while inditing this paragraph." This declaration is truly remarkable, given that it was written by a man who less than nine years previously had fervently announced, "It is the great principle of Total Abstinence of all that can intoxicate, for which we are battling."[109] Evidently Warren became disillusioned with temperance and embraced the ways of his former opposition. Although a cynic may charge that Warren never altered his beliefs but only exchanged one set of readers for another, his sentiments expressed in the *Observer*—as well as the remarks published in the *Monitor*—clearly run contrary to the views that had become widely accepted during the previous decades in Tuscaloosa, and suggest the depths to which temperance had sunk by the eve of the Civil War.

---

willing than the Henry Collier–led court to affirm local prohibitory license fees. *Independent Monitor,* January 4, 18, 1843; see also *Harris* v. *Intendant and Council of Livingston,* 28 Alabama Reports 577–80 (1856).

109. *Independent Monitor,* August 12, 1858, August 27, 1859, July 21, 1860; *Observer,* March 13, 1861; *Crystal Fount,* April 2, 1852. Ellen Eslinger, "Antebellum Liquor Reform in Lexington, Virginia: The Story of a Small Southern Town," *Virginia Magazine of History and Biography,* XCIX (April 1991), 164, contends that "In the South, the main population targeted for prohibition was black." Although prohibitionists and enthusiasts of temperance occasionally directed their rhetoric toward alcohol consumption by slaves and free blacks—a point further developed in chap. 5— such a concern was not a dominant theme among Tuscaloosa's activists.

Writing a generation ago, Joseph R. Gusfield concluded that "the identification with antislavery was strong enough to stifle completely the organization
of the Temperance movement in the South. Although Temperance agitation
had developed in southern states during the 1820s, by the late 1830s Temperance was unable to gain any strength in the South." Since Gusfield wrote, however, other studies have demonstrated that temperance was a vital force in the
South through the 1850s.[110] In Tuscaloosa, temperance was never denigrated in
print for being too closely aligned with abolitionism. As we shall see in chapter
5, a number of temperance proponents were fervent defenders of slavery and of
the South. But which elements of white southern society were most likely to
support temperance? Ian Tyrrell, in an examination of Alleghany County, Virginia, and Rowan County, North Carolina, found Sons of Temperance advocates to be overwhelmingly urban-oriented in their occupations—dominated
by artisans, with much smaller percentages of professionals and merchants and
a disproportionately low number of farmers. Tyrrell also claimed that although
"slaveholding and temperance support were not incompatible," few of the temperance devotees he examined were substantial slaveholders. W. J. Rorabaugh
similarly found that Sons of Temperance members in Jasper County, Georgia,
were far less likely to be farmers and more likely to be artisans or skilled laborers than the rest of the county's population of adult white males; however, a
slightly larger percentage of these temperance devotees (57 percent) were slaveholders than was the case among adult white males countywide (47 percent).[111]

    How do Tyrrell's and Rorabaugh's conclusions as to these southern commu-

110. Gusfield, *Symbolic Crusade*, 54; Carlson, "Temperance Reform"; R. Lyn Rainard, "An
Analysis of Membership in Temperance Organizations in Antebellum Virginia" (Paper presented at the Eighty-fourth Annual Meeting of the Organization of American Historians, April
13, 1991, Louisville, Ky.); Rorabaugh, "The Sons of Temperance in Antebellum Jasper County,"
263–79; Anne C. Loveland, *Southern Evangelicals and the Social Order, 1800–1860* (Baton Rouge,
1980), 130–58; Stanley K. Schultz, "Temperance Reform in the Antebellum South: Social Control and Urban Order," *South Atlantic Quarterly*, LXXXIII (Summer 1984), 323–39. Both Tyrrell,
"Drink and Temperance," 485–510, and Eslinger, "Antebellum Liquor Reform," 163–86, however,
conclude that the temperance movement in the antebellum South was significantly weaker than
in the North.

111. Tyrrell, "Drink and Temperance," 493–94; Rorabaugh, "Sons of Temperance," 266–68.
The numbers of subjects for Alleghany County, Rowan County, and Jasper County were 42, 81,
and 51, respectively.

nities compare with the temperance experience in Tuscaloosa? Before proceeding to this question, we should note that one of the advantages of looking at this community over time is that one can more readily observe how the temperance constituency in Tuscaloosa County during the early 1850s differed from that of the early 1830s. The members of the Tuscaloosa Temperance Society, which persisted from 1829 to 1840, held the highest status of any temperance advocates. Of the 45 identifiable activists who participated in this phase of temperance, the occupations of 38 could be ascertained from various sources; of this number, 36 were professionals, 1 was a shopkeeper/proprietor, and 1 was a farmer. Predominant in the professional group were 16 attorneys and 14 clergy. Thus, almost one-third of the known members of the Tuscaloosa Temperance Society were ministers—confirming the allegations of early temperance opponents who lambasted the strong clerical voice of this association. Slaveholding data were available for twenty-three of these subjects, of whom twenty-one (91.3 percent) owned slaves; among these slaveholders, the median holding from the 1830, 1840, and 1850 censuses, respectively, was 10 (mean 13.4), 7.5 (mean 18.2), and 20 (mean 37.5).[112] The elite characteristics of the members of this society, and their acceptance of wine consumption, give credence to the conclusions of "A Friend to Personal and Mental Liberty," A. S. Gore, and others who charged that early temperance proponents in Tuscaloosa and elsewhere were upper-class males who endeavored to proscribe the consumption of spirits—particularly among the lower classes—while reserving the option of enjoying wine themselves.[113]

The society's members were also born earlier than those who followed them in the temperance effort:

112. Of these individuals, 17, 12, and 6 were slaveholders according to the 1830, 1840, and 1850 censuses, respectively. Establishing the slaveholding status of individuals on the 1830 and 1840 manuscript census is simple, since the enumerator listed the number of slaves owned by a head of household on the same line that his or her name appeared. Unfortunately, the names of non-heads of household are not recorded in these censuses, but the family relationships of non-heads of household to heads of household can often be determined through the corroborative use of *Pioneers of Tuscaloosa County, Alabama, Prior to 1830* (Tuscaloosa, 1981). Regarding the determination of an individual's slaveholding status from the 1850 census, see my comment in chap. 1, n. 82. A more complete 1850 slave schedule would probably yield even more slaveholders than are listed in nn. 114, 115, and 117, this chapter.

113. *Alabama State Intelligencer,* August 24, 1829; *Independent Monitor,* February 23, 1842; Blocker, *American Temperance Movements,* 22; Tyrrell, *Sobering Up,* 139–40.

Year of birth	Age in 1840	Number	Percent
1811–1820	20–29	6	20.0
1801–1810	30–39	4	13.3
1791–1800	40–49	12	40.0
1781–1790	50–59	7	23.3
1771–1780	60–69	0	
1761–1770	70–79	0	
1751–1760	80–89	1	3.3
Totals		30	99.9

The median age at which the names of these individuals first appeared in temperance proceedings was thirty-four, and their median year of birth was 1796. In contrast, those who joined Tuscaloosa's Young Men's Total Abstinence Society in 1839 were—as the name would imply—considerably younger, although 6 of 54 identifiable YMTAS members belonged to both this organization and the Tuscaloosa Temperance Society:

Year of birth	Age in 1840	Number	Percent
1821–1823	17–19	1	4.0
1811–1820	20–29	16	64.0
1801–1810	30–39	7	28.0
1791–1800	40–49	0	
1781–1790	50–59	1	4.0
Totals		25	100.0

The median age at which its members joined was twenty-five, and their median year of birth was 1814. But because of their younger age, fewer subjects appeared on the 1840 census, which listed the name only of the head of household. YMTAS members held fewer slaves than did the members of the Tuscaloosa Temperance Society. Slaveholding data were available for 22 subjects, of whom 17 (77.3 percent) owned slaves. The median slaveholding from the 1830, 1840, and 1850 censuses, respectively, was 4 (mean 9.7), 5 (mean 12.8), and 4 (mean 4.6).[114] The group also held fewer high-status occupations, as there were 9 professionals (all attorneys), 8 shopkeepers/proprietors, 5 artisans, and 1 farmer. The smaller slaveholdings, less prestigious occupations, and relative youth of the YMTAS members suggest that participation in the temperance cause during the late 1830s was expanding beyond the elite constituency of the Tuscaloosa Temperance Society.

Members of the 1843 Alabama Total Abstinence Society—the group that initially espoused the Washingtonian label—were similar in their social profile to the Tuscaloosa Temperance Society in that they were generally older and held higher status than did the members of the YMTAS. Of the 104 individuals whose names were identified with this organization, most were newcomers to the temperance fold. Only 7 had participated in both the Alabama Total Abstinence Society and the YMTAS, 6 had previously been members of the Tuscaloosa Temperance Society, and 3 had belonged to all three organizations. The occupations of 51 members of the Alabama Total Abstinence Society were ascertained, the greatest portion of whom were professionals (24, including 16 attorneys), followed by farmers and shopkeepers/proprietors (8 each), 6 artisans, 2 laborers, 1 clerk, and 2 who had no occupation listed in the 1850 census. Slaveholding data were available for 38 subjects, of whom 36 (94.7 percent) owned slaves; the median slaveholding from the 1830, 1840, and 1850 censuses was 10 (mean 13.0), 4 (mean 20.4), and 9 (mean 17.7) slaves, respectively.[115] Members were slightly older (median birth year 1807) at their time of joining than was the case with the members of Tuscaloosa's first temperance society:

Year of birth	Age in 1843	Number	Percent
1821–1828	15–22	4	7.3
1811–1820	23–32	13	23.6
1801–1810	33–42	22	40.0
1791–1800	43–52	10	18.2
1781–1790	53–62	3	5.5
1771–1780	63–72	3	5.5
Totals		55	100.1

114. Of these individuals, 7, 9, and 7 were slaveholders according to the 1830, 1840, and 1850 censuses, respectively.

115. These individuals included 17, 23, and 20 slaveholders according to the 1830, 1840, and

The number of legislators and other notables who aligned with this organization may have encouraged the activity of older individuals of wealth who would not have otherwise participated.

Spanning the years from 1846 to at least 1859, the Sons of Temperance was not only the longest-lasting temperance organization in Tuscaloosa County during the antebellum years, but the largest as well, even though only 136 of its members—most of whom were officers—could be identified from temperance proceedings. Like the other new temperance societies, the Sons opened the doors of temperance activity to individuals who had not previously participated, as only 8 of the identified members had belonged to the Alabama Total Abstinence Society, 4 had been members of the YMTAS, and only 1 had joined the Tuscaloosa Temperance Society. The Sons appealed to a younger and less affluent constituency than did the Alabama Total Abstinence Society. The median age of these activists when their name first appeared in a source linking them to the organization was twenty-nine (median birth year 1820). And as is evident from the following table, several joined the Sons of Temperance while in their early teens:

Year of birth	Age in 1850	Number	Percent
1831–1838	12–19	14	13.3
1821–1830	20–29	37	35.2
1811–1820	30–39	29	27.6
1801–1810	40–49	17	16.2
1791–1800	50–59	4	3.8
1781–1790	60–69	4	3.8
Totals		105	99.9

Comparing the birth-year breakdown for these different groups, we find that although most people who joined the movement did so by their mid-thirties, support for temperance was not restricted to a single age cohort. The Tuscaloosa Temperance Society drew its members largely from among people born

1850 censuses, respectively. Among the 25 members of the Alabama Total Abstinence Society who appeared on the population schedule of the 1850 census, the median real-estate holding was $1,000, and the mean was $3,216.

between 1781 and 1800, the YMTAS and the Alabama Total Abstinence Society from people born between 1801 and 1820, and the Sons of Temperance from people born between 1810 and 1830. Although it can be said that temperance galvanized most of its adherents during their young adulthood, the message resonated at different times among different people who were separated in their year of birth by as many as five decades. Part of the success of the temperance movement must be seen as its ability to appeal across generations.

Of all the temperance groups that we have examined, the Sons of Temperance was the most likely to appeal to individuals from households headed by farmers and artisans. Nevertheless, professionals again were the largest occupational category in this group:

Occupation	Number	Percent
Artisan	19	18.4
Clerk	9	8.7
Shopkeeper/proprietor	9	8.7
Farmer	27	26.2
Laborer	1	1.0
Professional	34	33.0
Illegible	1	1.0
Other	1	1.0
None listed on census	2	1.9
Totals	103	99.9

This occupational profile differs significantly from that of the general population of both Tuscaloosa County and Tuscaloosa town. Countywide, almost three-fourths of the free male heads of household were farmers, while the city of Tuscaloosa had a larger proportion of artisans (29.2 percent) and a slightly lower percentage of professionals (26.6 percent; see the occupational breakdown for Tuscaloosa County and city heads of household in chapter 1). The percentage of Sons who were professionals, though, was lower than in previous temperance endeavors. Additionally, the Sons had a smaller proportion of attorneys (8, or 7.8 percent of this cohort who were linked to an occupation) than any other group. The lawyers were joined by 6 physicians, 7 clergy, 5 teachers, 3 newspaper editors, 3 minors whose fathers were professionals, and 2 other professionals.[116]

The real-estate holdings of Sons of Temperance members from the 1850 census demonstrates that although a few of its adherents were from wealthy households, most owned little or no real estate:

Household real property ($), Sons of Temperance members, 1850	Number	Percent
0	38	41.3
1–999	12	13.0
1,000–2,499	18	19.6
2,500–4,999	15	16.3
5,000–9,999	6	6.5
10,000 and over	3	3.3
Totals	92	100.0

Among this group, the median real estate holding was $175, and the mean was $2,542. The median was similar to the countywide figure for male heads of household (median $200, mean $909), while the mean was closer to the mark for the town of Tuscaloosa (median $0, mean $1,882):

Real property ($), Tuscaloosa Co. male heads of household, 1850	Number	Percent
0	640	37.1
1–999	714	41.4
1,000–2,499	216	12.5
2,500–4,999	75	4.4
5,000–9,999	50	2.9
10,000 and over	28	1.6
Totals	1,723	99.9

116. Of the 103 Sons of Temperance members whose occupations were traceable, 6 individuals were minors, and the occupations of their fathers were listed in the table instead.

Real property ($), Tuscaloosa town male heads of household, 1850	Number	Percent
0	97	50.5
1–999	28	14.6
1,000–2,499	22	11.5
2,500–4,999	16	8.3
5,000–9,999	17	8.9
10,000 and over	12	6.3
Totals	192	100.1

And although the majority of the identified Sons of Temperance members owned slaves, a smaller percentage (61 of the 91 for whom slaveholding data are available, or 67.0 percent) were slaveholders than in any other group of temperance activists. The relative youth of this cohort may have prevented them from accumulating the wealth of the members of other temperance groups. Nevertheless, the size of slaveholdings among those who owned slaves was approximately the same as the slaveholdings of other temperance cohorts, as the median slaveholdings from the 1830, 1840, and 1850 censuses were 13 (mean 16.7), 3.5 (mean 14.2), and 5.5 (mean 10.6).[117]

A number of scholars have contended that the temperance drive was hindered in the slaveholding states by the powerful influence of a class of planters who valued leisure and conspicuous consumption, disavowed the work ethic, and followed a code of hospitality that required generous offers of wine and whiskey to guests.[118] Although such a class may have been present in antebellum Tuscaloosa County, the data provided in this chapter show that such sentiments were not universally felt among the county's slaveholders. Not only were strong majorities of each temperance cohort overwhelmingly slaveholding, but overall, of the 328 identifiable temperance activists in Tuscaloosa between 1829 and 1859, the slaveholding status of 164 is known, and 125 (76.2 percent) were

117. Including 11, 22, and 56 slaveholders according to the 1830, 1840, and 1850 censuses, respectively.

118. See esp. Tyrrell, "Drink and Temperance," 503–504. For a contrary position, see Douglas Carlson, "The Ideology of Southern Temperance" (Paper presented at the Eleventh Annual Meeting of the Society for Historians of the Early American Republic, July 1989, Charlottesville, Va.).

slaveholders. In contrast, only 35.4 percent of Tuscaloosa County's free households in 1850 held slaves. Moreover, an even greater proportion of Tuscaloosa's
temperance proponents were native-born southerners. Although 93.4 percent
of the 1,723 male heads of household in Tuscaloosa County listed in the 1850
federal census were born in the slaveholding states, only 72.9 percent of the
male heads of household in the town of Tuscaloosa—whence most of the temperance society members came—were southern-born. But of the 182 temperance activists with traceable places of birth, 154 (84.6 percent) were born in the
South, as against 21 (11.5 percent) born in the North and 7 (3.8 percent) outside
of the United States. These statistics were surely not unnoticed by Tuscaloosans and would have made it implausible for opponents of temperance to label
the temperance effort as Yankee subversion. The conclusion of Joseph Gusfield, cited earlier, is simply inaccurate with respect to Tuscaloosa County.

The conclusions of Ian Tyrrell and W. J. Rorabaugh should be qualified. In
addition to the larger extent of slaveholding found among temperance enthusiasts in Tuscaloosa County than in either of their studies, the data presented
here demonstrate that the occupational profile of temperance reformers was
not consistent over time, as members of both the Tuscaloosa Temperance Society and the Alabama Total Abstinence Society were more likely to hold prestigious occupations than members of the Young Men's Total Abstinence Society
or the Sons of Temperance. Tuscaloosa obtained a smaller percentage of its
temperance support from artisans than was the case in either of these other
studies of temperance in the South, which points again to the elite character of
temperance support in Tuscaloosa.

But the congruities between temperance in Tuscaloosa County and the locales studied by Tyrrell and Rorabaugh (Alleghany County, Virginia; Rowan
County, North Carolina; and Jasper County, Georgia) are important as well.
The majority of temperance proponents in Tuscaloosa County held urban-
oriented occupations, sustaining the conclusions of Tyrrell and Rorabaugh
that the temperance movement found its supporters among individuals who
embraced the emerging market economy and welcomed the ethic of self-
control that was so central to the temperance message. Also supportive of their
positions is the fact that Tuscaloosa's temperance activists—similar to the supporters of the benevolent empire—were eager to send their children to school.
As we saw in chapter 1, parents who sent their children to school were themselves generally more receptive to the market skills that were taught there—
arithmetic, literacy, punctuality and abstemiousness—than were people who

did not send their children to school. Of the 279 children between the ages of five and nineteen identified from the 1850 census for Tuscaloosa County as living in the households of temperance activists—and as sharing the surname of the activist—202 (72.4 percent) attended school. Although this percentage is considerably higher than the statewide and the countywide school attendance figures of 35.9 percent and 37.9 percent, respectively, it is roughly the same as the school attendance mark of 69.2 percent for the city of Tuscaloosa—which is also where most (151) of these children resided. School attendance of this cohort who did not reside in the city of Tuscaloosa, however, was also much higher than the county figure (91 of 128, or 71.1 percent). This high incidence of temperance advocates sending their children to school is further indicative of their receptivity to the expansion of the market. Very likely, many temperance enthusiasts looked forward to meetings where they could gather with others who not only sought to eradicate intemperance, but who were ambitious as well.

Of course, a social-economic interpretation of temperance can go too far. Few people, if any, would have asserted that they joined the temperance movement in order to help spread market capitalism. Most saw alcohol consumption as a debilitating vice that led many to personal ruin, and viewed their enterprise as a humanitarian effort. In fact, it was not uncommon for a temperance proponent to criticize, as did the *Fount*'s John Warren, the liquor retailer's "insatiate thirst for gain." Nevertheless, many relished the self-control that the cause endorsed, and believed that such a virtue was a prerequisite to approaching God sincerely. But self-control also had its place in the growth of an urban-oriented economy, where one who exercised this trait in conjunction with delayed gratification could excel. Temperance devotees undoubtedly viewed those who continued to enjoy alcohol as less likely to succeed in the world, and certainly suspected that imbibers were more inclined to be slothful. Although not often an explicit theme in Tuscaloosa's temperance literature, these connections were clearly expressed in a newspaper in neighboring Jefferson County. In the *Jones Valley Times*, edited by James Norment, a former temperance leader in Tuscaloosa, a writer in 1854 identified temperance with "Young America," the spirit of which also favored waking at daybreak, getting to business early, preparing one's crop as soon as the previous one was harvested, raising a surplus of agricultural produce, paying one's creditors promptly, building good roads and railroads, and promoting the spread of education. "Young America" embraced the Sons of Temperance, whose dues were "a mere trifle to the industrious, or to the man who is not *hide bound.*" In contrast, "Old Foger" enjoyed "my dram when I want to" and insisted that the Sons were "seeking to take our Liberty away from us." Those who endorsed Foger's agenda maintained that there was "no use in hurrying through life," awoke late into the day, asserted that "there is no use in working so much on roads, for we get nothing for it," saw no need for a county newspaper, and believed that "we are doing very well without a railroad." Similarly, a rural Alabama merchant reported in 1833 that as his neighbors curtailed their consumption of liquor, they commenced educating their children, saving their money, improving their homes, and increasing their agricultural production.[119]

The role of religion in the temperance movement is more difficult to assess. In the early 1830s, some of Alabama's Protestants were not yet persuaded that temperance societies were necessary. One Jefferson County writer complained that he encountered too many of the cause's opponents "among the expressed friends of God." To be sure, the major evangelical faiths—the Baptists, Methodists, and Presbyterians—all eventually supported temperance, probably for reasons similar to those expressed by the temperance committee at the Alabama Baptist State Convention in 1857, which explained that it did not desire to "magnify the cause of temperance above an humble instrumentality to lead men to sobriety and to God." Few churches insisted that their members be totally abstinent—although they may have held to it as an ideal—but the Alabama Baptist State Convention did endorse prohibition. Further, while the state convention admitted that "we cannot infringe on the liberty of the churches so far as to make temperance a test of membership," it nonetheless recommended that all Baptists join a temperance society, reported annually on the progress of the temperance movement in the state, urged its ministers to preach temperance sermons, endorsed the Sons of Temperance, and reminded congregations to discipline drunkenness rigidly. The Tuscaloosa Baptist Association adhered to this counsel in 1849, when its leadership discountenanced the treating of the electorate and encouraged its members to abstain from intoxicants. And as we have seen, some Baptist churches went beyond this advice and disciplined their members for selling spirits.[120]

119. *Crystal Fount,* May 28, 1852; *Jones Valley Times* (Elyton, Ala.), May 27, 1854; New York *American* quoted in American Temperance Society *Annual Report,* VI (1833), 105–106.

120. *Journal of Humanity, and Herald of the American Temperance Society,* July 21, 1831; *Minutes of the Thirty-fourth Anniversary of the Alabama Baptist State Convention,* 11; *Minutes of the Alabama Baptist State Convention, 1842,* 7; *Journal of the Proceedings of the Baptist State Convention in Ala-*

These actions notwithstanding, the extent to which temperance society members viewed their participation in the movement as an extension of their spiritual obligations is not clear. And although the religious affiliation of 136 of Tuscaloosa's temperance proponents can be ascertained from church records, the religious ties of the remaining 194 must remain a mystery. Were they church members whose names were absent from Tuscaloosa's often incomplete church records? Were they religious people who had not yet formally joined a church, and left the county before so doing?[121] Or did they find organized religion to be irrelevant? Newton L. Whitfield fell into this latter category. Although he cannot be linked to any of Tuscaloosa's antebellum temperance organizations, he professed abstinence in his diary, the following sentiments from which may speak for some temperance society members whose names were absent from church records—and possibly for some church members as well: "Have not been to church today, nor for several weeks past. 'Tis strange I used to feel out of place on Sunday if I did not go to Church, and the habit of attending Church every Sunday would have continued with me if I had never associated with George P. Blevins [a skeptic] . . . . I am no sceptic however, though I do not believe I could tell what I do believe in reference to religion."[122] Clearly the skepticism that was present in Tuscaloosa during the 1820s was not completely eliminated by the subsequent wave of revivals, nor was a deep religious commitment a prerequisite to temperate behavior in antebellum Tuscaloosa.

The religious affiliations of temperance enthusiasts were spread more evenly across the evangelical spectrum than was the case among the proponents of the benevolent empire (Table 7). Although the Catholic and Episcopal church records are the most incomplete, listing only the names of parents who presented

---

bama at Its Twentieth Anniversary, 9; *Minutes of the Alabama Baptist State Convention, 1847* (N.p., 1847[?]), 9; *Minutes of the Alabama Baptist State Convention, 1848* (N.p., 1848[?]), 29–30; *Minutes of the Alabama Baptist State Convention, 1849* (N.p., 1849[?]), 19; *Alabama Baptist Advocate,* October 31, 1849.

121. In the antebellum churches, members were often outnumbered by noncommunicants during Sunday services. For instance, although not a member of any of the city's churches, Alexander Meek often visited the different Protestant congregations. The minister of Tuscaloosa's Presbyterian church estimated in 1842 that one thousand people attended his services "with more or less regularity"—possibly seven to ten times the number of Presbyterians who were members of that church. A. B. Meek Diary, January 5, 12, 1840, in ADAH; Clifford Merrill Drury, *William Anderson Scott: "No Ordinary Man"* (Glendale, Calif., 1967), 76.

122. Whitfield Journal, December 11, 22, 1849.

children for baptism and—the Episcopal only—the names of financial donors, it should come as no surprise that far fewer members of these denominations belonged to the temperance societies than did members of the evangelical faiths. For one reason, communicants of these liturgical churches were few in Tuscaloosa. For another, whereas the evangelical churches frequently disciplined members for moral infractions, the Catholic and Episcopal faiths maintained less restrictive codes of conduct. Nevertheless, ministers of both these churches preached public temperance sermons, and members of their congregations may have embraced total abstinence without joining a temperance society. (And of course, many Episcopalians, and especially Catholics, were undoubtedly uninterested in temperance meetings dominated by evangelicals.)[123]

The strength of the Presbyterians during the early years of the temperance movement may reflect their greater experience with and confidence in extradenominational voluntary associations than their Methodist and Baptist contemporaries. The dramatic increase in the Baptist participation in temperance during the Sons of Temperance years may seem out of place, given the secret, Masonic-like character of the order and the fervent opposition that some Baptists expressed to Masonry.[124] And it appears that some Baptists objected to the Sons of Temperance on these grounds, judging from two widely circulated letters written by Basil Manly. Manly defended the right of the Sons to hold their meetings in private and to use secret passwords, and he insisted that the order "is an alliance not contrary to, nor inconsistent with church obligations." He denied that the Sons, the Masons, or the Odd Fellows "propose to take away our liberties," and although not a member of any of these bodies, he encour-

123. *Flag of the Union*, February 9, 1842 (sermon by Rev. Patrick Hackett, Tuscaloosa's Catholic priest); *Independent Monitor*, August 28, 1851 (sermon by Episcopal bishop Nicholas Hamner Cobb). Although not a dominant theme in Tuscaloosa's antebellum newspapers, anti-Catholic rhetoric occasionally reared its head even before the formation of the Know-Nothing Party in 1854. See *American Mirror*, May 15, 1824; Tuscaloosa *Chronicle*, October 30, 1828, July 20, 1829; *Alabama Baptist* (Marion), June 8, October 12, 1844; *Independent Monitor*, August 17, September 7, 28, October 5, 1842, April 16, 1845, June 11, 1857, May 6, 1858, July 15, 1858. Regarding Tuscaloosa church affiliations, see chap. 1, n. 47.

124. *Alabama State Intelligencer*, June 1, 1831; *Minutes of the Twelfth Annual Session of the Tuscaloosa Baptist Association, Held at Spring Hill Meeting House, Tuscaloosa County from the 14th to the 17th of September 1844* (Tuscaloosa, 1844), 3.

aged Baptists to join the Sons if it would help them lead temperate lives.[125] His approval, coupled with the endorsement of the Alabama Baptist State Convention, must have removed many misgivings of individual Baptists about the Sons.

The temperance crusade in antebellum Tuscaloosa was not monolithic. Its strategies varied over time, and activity repeatedly went through cycles of peaks and troughs. Finding persuasion to be ineffectual in converting everyone to temperance principles, proponents attempted to end the sale of intoxicants during the late 1830s and early 1850s. Their failure to achieve legislative victories should not be interpreted to mean that the movement was weak or powerless; the legislature's refusal to submit a prohibition statute to popular referendum during the early 1850s indicates that politicians knew temperance and prohibition were explosive issues in Alabama. Further, the numerous reports of decreased alcohol consumption—even if restricted to that portion of society that considered itself "respectable"—is additional evidence of the great impact that the temperance movement had upon the behavior of white Alabamians. The temperance movement encouraged numerous Alabamians to reform their inebriate ways. But the movement was not omnipotent, and after the enthusiasm for a new temperance episode had dimmed, a number of stalwart proponents of temperance proved incapable of permanently maintaining their temperate lifestyles, suggesting that recidivism was not uncommon.[126]

125. *Alabama Baptist Advocate,* August 29, October 31, 1849. Primitive Baptists—who were deeply hostile to temperance—and their Regular Baptist sympathizers were most likely the source of Baptist antagonism to this cause. *South Western Baptist,* October 8, 1851; Dorman, *Party Politics in Alabama,* 110.

126. A public acknowledgment that many members of the Alabama Total Abstinence Society had returned to the bottle was made in a March 13, 1843, resolution, which affirmed that if a member of the society should "violate his pledge of total abstinence," and were to remain "delinquent . . . after having been affectionately remonstrated with, . . . and still persist in the abuse of his pledge, then the President of this Society, shall have said delinquent's name stricken from the roll of said Society, and publicly read out from the Secretary's desk, at the next regular monthly meeting." *Flag of the Union,* March 15, 1843. Aside from Thomas Burke—mentioned in connection with n. 98 this chap.—recidivists included Felix G. McConnell, William B. Martin, Backus W. Huntington, John Gayle (Garrett, *Reminiscences of Public Men in Alabama,* 162–64, 302–303, 364–65, 458–59), Alexander B. Meek (Basil Manly to Basil Manly Jr., January 21, 1846, in Manly Family Papers), Henry McGown (*Flag of the Union,* August 29, 1839; Basil Manly to Basil Manly Jr., January 21, 1846, in Manly Family Papers), and Milford F. Woodruff (Basil Manly to Thomas Herndon, September 6, 1850, in Manly Family Papers; *Crystal Fount,* January 2, 1852; *Independent*

Not surprisingly, the temperance movement in Tuscaloosa received strong endorsements from all the town's churches. Additionally, temperance in Tuscaloosa was noteworthy for the degree to which it drew activists from among the prosperous—although the Sons of Temperance did successfully appeal to classes previously excluded from the movement. Also significant is the extent to which Tuscaloosa's temperance proponents were the owners of slaves, indicating that they saw no contradiction between their cause and the peculiar institution. We have observed variations with respect to age, wealth, occupation, and religion among the activists enlisted in Tuscaloosa's four principal temperance manifestations. Nonetheless, in all these cohorts, the local cause mirrored the movement elsewhere in America in that it was dominated by a class of individuals closely linked to the nation's material development.[127] Although temperance had reached a low point prior to the firing upon Fort Sumter, it would rise again, phoenixlike, in the years following the Civil War, and eventually prove victorious—if only for a season—in establishing legal prohibition in Alabama.[128]

Monitor, August 12, 1858; Session Book No. 3 of the Tuscaloosa Presbyterian Church, February 27, October 29, November 9, 1857, February 14, 1858).

127. Dannenbaum, *Drink and Disorder,* 46–47, 65–66, cites studies showing this same trend in Georgia, North Carolina, Mississippi, Massachusetts, New York, Vermont, Virginia, Ontario, Ireland, and England. Of these works, see esp. W. J. Rorabaugh, "Prohibition as Progress: New York State's License Elections, 1846," *Journal of Social History,* XIV (Spring 1981), 425–43.

128. James Sellers, *Prohibition Movement in Alabama, passim.*

4

Prohibition Attempted and Refuted: The Temperance Movement in Washtenaw County

Temperance in Washtenaw County, as in Tuscaloosa County, was a cyclical phenomenon. The pattern was much the same in both places. In both, an elite-dominated movement that tolerated the use of wine but fervently condemned the use of hard liquor moved gradually—but not without dissension and loss of adherents—toward total abstinence and prohibition during the mid-1830s. In both, the cause suffered setbacks when legislators patronizingly received petitions and then refused to ban the sale of liquor. During the early 1840s, temperance activists in both counties retreated to moral suasion, but later in the decade pursued local option. Agitation peaked in both places during the 1850s as enthusiasts strove for prohibitory legislation patterned after the so-called Maine Law. Partisans failed to implement such a statute in Alabama, and although general prohibition laws were enacted in Michigan in 1853, 1855, and 1857, none proved successful. In other parallels, temperance partisans in Tuscaloosa and Washtenaw Counties held urban-oriented occupations and demonstrated an affinity for the growing market economy. But whereas temperance in Tuscaloosa was dominated by slaveholders, abolitionists were represented in Washtenaw's temperance ranks in numbers disproportionately large in comparison to the general population.

As with Washtenaw's benevolent activity, temperance societies in the county formed shortly after white settlement began. Although there does not appear to have been the same degree of opposition to temperance in Washtenaw County as there was in Tuscaloosa County, some contemporaries insisted that early settlers in Washtenaw were also heavy drinkers. L. D. Norris recalled in 1874 that Ypsilanti's inhabitants fifty years earlier had deemed whiskey to be a "necessity" that "cured rattlesnake bites, and alleviated 'fever and fatigue.'" Cooperation with one's fellows was essential on the frontier, and Norris explained that it was only "the 'churl' who, in those days, did not 'put the bottle to his neighbor's lips.'" The construction of log cabins and barns was communal work, and those who aided their neighbors expected to be reciprocated with whiskey. The inaugural issue of Ann Arbor's first newspaper, the *Western Emigrant*, announced on November 18, 1829, that Hawley, Nash, and Company had erected a distillery that would shortly produce "a superior quality of rectified whiskey," which product could be "exchanged for grain, on liberal terms."

In July 1828, William Page, Ann Arbor's Presbyterian pastor, told the American Home Missionary Society that he and some others, with the aid of the Presbytery of Detroit, were "forming a temperance society, with pleasing prospects for its usefulness." His optimism may have resulted from the fact that the newly built Presbyterian "meeting house was raised without ardent spirits." Page was probably also enthused by the conversion of Simeon Mills to temperance principles. After returning from a visit to Detroit that had infected him with energy for the temperance cause, Page happened upon Mills, "who had always supposed that whiskey was an essential element of a person's diet." Mills was nevertheless convinced by Page's earnestness, swore off whiskey at that moment, and convinced three of his brothers to unite with him and Page in the newly formed temperance movement. Unfortunately for this vanguard, only seven other residents of the village of Ann Arbor joined them. According to a local historian recalling the circumstances several decades later, "This society met with great opposition at first, as it was customary at house and barn 'raisings' to always have a jug of the 'ardent' on hand, and no body thought of assisting at such an occasion unless their spirits were kept up by pouring 'spirits' down. These persons, and there were very few who did not coincide with them, considered it utterly impossible to dispense with whiskey on such occasions, and therefore for several years the society had only a very feeble support from the general community." Benjamin Packard likewise recorded that during the late 1820s, several Ann Arbor residents died of delirium tremens.[1]

---

1. *History of Washtenaw County*, 338–40, 524, 679, 692, 955–56; Andrew Ten Brook, "Sketches of the Early History of Ann Arbor," 36, in Andrew Ten Brook Papers, Bentley Library; *Western Emigrant*, November 18, 1829; William Page to AHMS, July 9, 1828, July 7, 1829, in AHMS Papers; Notes by Benjamin Packard, as cited by Marwil, *Ann Arbor*, 11.

In late 1829 and early 1830, however, temperance societies in Washtenaw County experienced phenomenal growth. Much of the activity focused around Samuel W. Dexter and John Allen. These men purchased the *Western Emigrant* a few weeks after it began publication and turned it into an organ that devoted its primary attention to Antimasonry. Temperance, however, was a closely monitored secondary preoccupation. In the fifth issue of the *Emigrant,* Dexter announced that on January 1, 1830, a public meeting of the citizens of Dexter village would be held in his home "to take into consideration, the best method of arresting the use of ardent spirits." This assembly concluded that the "best method" of promoting abstemiousness was to organize a temperance society, which was done on January 6, 1830. Samuel Dexter was selected as president, and a constitution was framed by the village's Presbyterian minister, Charles G. Clarke, who noted that although the society was small, "some of the leading men in town have become members." Three weeks later, Ann Arbor's temperance adherents reorganized their forces and formed the Ann Arbor Society for the Promotion of Temperance, said to comprise members of "different religions, as well as political principles."[2] The occasion filled the devotees with sufficient optimism that they called for the formation of a county society in April, which would thereafter meet annually on Independence Day.

The Ann Arbor Society for the Promotion of Temperance met again in February at the Presbyterian church, and following an address by John Allen, twenty-three new members joined, demonstrating that temperance had reached a threshold of vitality. William Jones reported to the AHMS that wickedness in Ypsilanti had been dealt a blow by the formation of a temperance society there, which had grown to more than seventy members by February 1830. Jones added that "one of the strong opposers to the Temperance Society confessed before three weeks had passed after the first effort that '*much good had been done.*' " A half century later, a local historian recalled that "a grand wave of temperance swept over the whole land" at this time: "In every city, village and hamlet the enthusiasm was caught." Charles G. Clarke reported in May that although benevolent efforts were lethargic, "the Temperance cause flourishes among us & throughout the county." The temperance addresses presented at the monthly meetings in Dexter village proved to be popular, and attendance increased with each passing month: "We began the year with twelve members;

---

2. *Western Emigrant,* December 30, 1829, January 27, 1830; Charles G. Clarke to AHMS, January 27, 1830, in AHMS Papers; *History of Washtenaw County,* 338–40.

we now have about seventy." In Ypsilanti temperance likewise continued its ascendancy. In May 1830, William Jones was pleased to recount that "the cause of
temperance is in rapid progress in this county. The Presbyterian Church at Ypsilanti have resolved to form themselves into a temperance Society on the principle of total abstinence." Jones added that revivals had recently commenced
"in the very neighborhood & with the same persons" who were the first to embrace temperance "in this section of the county."[3]

On the occasion of the first annual meeting of the Washtenaw County
Temperance Society, July 4, 1831, Dexter village's Mill Creek Temperance Society had 53 members—less than the number reported by Charles Clarke a year
before. It was dwarfed, however, by the county's other societies, as Panama
(later Dixboro) reported 75 members, Ann Arbor 140, and Ypsilanti 150. Other
signs of progress included merchants who had purportedly "discontinued the
sale of ardent spirits," the closing of all the county's distilleries (even though
some of them shut down "from want of grain"), and the newly opened temperance taverns in Ann Arbor and Ypsilanti, where travelers could "rest free from
the annoyance of a grog shop."[4]

Recognizing that temperance appealed to some people who had no interest
in Antimasonry, and fearing that temperance could be discredited in the eyes
of people who loathed the Antimasonic cause, the *Western Emigrant* insisted in
March 1830 that temperance "be kept perfectly distinct from Masonry, Antimasonry, and Politics generally"—particularly since rumor had it that temperance "was about to be mingled with our elections." Upon announcing the passing of editorial duties to George Corselius two months later, Dexter and Allen
assured their readers that the *Emigrant* would not forget the cause of temperance, and that they viewed temperance as "perfectly distinct from Antimasonry, and as embraced by all parties without distinction; we shall watch
over this cause with jealous eyes, and if ever we find it associated with politics,
we shall sound the alarm." In a subsequent issue of the paper, though, Corselius
acknowledged that while many Antimasons embraced the temperance cause,

3. *Western Emigrant*, March 3, 1830; Minutes of the Ann Arbor Temperance Society, February 17, 1830, Bentley Library; William Jones to AHMS, February 15, 1830, in AHMS Papers; *History of Washtenaw County*, 954, 1113–14; Charles G. Clarke to AHMS, May 3, 1830, William Jones
to AHMS, May 24, 1830, in AHMS Papers. See also *Journal of Humanity, and Herald of the American Temperance Society* (Andover, Massachusetts) II (March 24, 1831), 175, III (June 30, 1831), 22.

4. *Emigrant*, July 20, April 6, 20, 1831. See also *Journal of Humanity, and Herald of the American
Temperance Society*, II (March 24, 1831), 175, III (April 12, 1832), 186.

some held back from joining temperance societies because they did not "believe that antimasons can go hand in hand with masons" in temperance societies and were convinced that Masonry was "so essentially bad that nothing good can mingle with it with impunity." As for himself, Corselius hoped that temperance would triumph. He promised "occasionally [to] lend the temperance cause a helping hand" and wished it "success from the bottom of our hearts; but the first great cause with us is antimasonry, now and forever." Nevertheless, he again urged that temperance societies be kept separate from politics. Otherwise, "powerful parties will be organized against them, and the reult [*sic*] might be the prostration of their usefulness."[5]

The Ann Arbor Society for the Promotion of Temperance was similar to the earliest temperance society in Tuscaloosa, in that its gatherings assumed a strongly religious tone. Meetings generally assembled at the Presbyterian church, where they were always opened by prayer and often followed by addresses from the clergy; occasionally passages from the Bible were read aloud. The society was also dominated by the socially prominent who were especially bothered by working-class intemperance. In January 1832, Israel Branch explained that intemperance was at its worst during the winter, when "a large portion of the population in the neighborhood of navigable waters are thrown out of business & hang as idlers around town & grogshops." He was convinced that the lower classes emulated the upper classes: "The rich man calls for his bottle of brandy & the poor man apes him as far as possible by robbing his family of their support to enable him to have a jug of whiskey." Branch explained that "the sure way" to eliminate working-class intemperance was to "effect a change in the morals fashions & manners of the most influential part of the community. We must use some means to effect a change in those who give tone to fashions[.] Let those who lead the fashions propose one in relation no matter how absurd & multitudes are surely to follow their tracks as far as their abilities will permit . . . regardless the consequences as to themselves & families."[6]

As in Tuscaloosa, by the mid-1830s the temperance movement in Washtenaw County became divided over the issues of no license and teetotalism, although these relatively radical doctrines surfaced in Washtenaw County several years earlier than in Tuscaloosa. In New England, the temperance vanguard were ahead of their Washtenaw counterparts and were pressing for pro-

5. *Western Emigrant,* March 31, May 19, July 14, 1830.
6. Minutes of the Ann Arbor Temperance Society, March 9, 1832, and *passim.*

hibition by the early 1830s. Nevertheless, it is evident from a speech of George Corselius given at the Mill Creek Temperance Society in early 1833 that the issue had already been broached in Washtenaw County. Corselius explained that legal sanctions could not effectively guard against all evils; with some infractions, the "sole security against them is in the enlightened moral sense of community, that public opinion which for many purposes, is more potent than the civil law." Curtailing the consumption of "ardent spirits," Corselius continued, was "a case peculiarly appropriate" for public opinion rather than the force of law because the "machinery of the law is too coarse and too clumsy to be applied in this case." He called for a "moral force" to govern human behavior and was certain that the "more our actions are controlled by this power, and the less by human laws, the better." Although Corselius' belief in the effectiveness of moral suasion would change within a few years, at this time he was convinced that only the proper cultivation of public opinion could cure America of intemperance.[7]

Recognizing, however, that moral suasion would not convince everyone to lead abstemious lives, other temperance activists called for legal remedies. Public authorities used liquor licenses to raise revenue, and presumably to regulate the sale of alcohol, well prior to the commencement of widespread temperance activity in Washtenaw County: at the first session of the Washtenaw County Court, in January 1827, Erastus Priest was indicted for selling liquor in quantities of less than one quart without a license (he was later acquitted). But with the advent of the temperance movement, some advocated using the license system to control the sale of liquor further. Perhaps because of the rapid rise of the temperance movement in Ypsilanti—in January 1834, there were 450 persons in the Ypsilanti vicinity pledged to abstinence—prohibitory license laws first took root there. Ira M. Wead reported that the grocers of Ypsilanti were "in a great wrath" because a law that took effect on January 1 prohibited them from selling liquor in quantities of less than a quart.[8] In February 1834,

7. Tyrrell, *Sobering Up*, 226–27; *Michigan Emigrant*, March 6, 1833.

8. *History of Washtenaw County*, 220–24; Ira M. Wead to AHMS, January 7, 1834, in AHMS Papers. A similar ordinance was enacted in Detroit in 1834, but later proved ineffectual following a judicial challenge and the subsequent decision of the Detroit city council to abandon this law. Peter Donald Slavcheff, "The Temperate Republic: Liquor Control in Michigan, 1800–1860" (Ph.D. dissertation, Wayne State University, 1987), 91–92. The fate of the Ypsilanti statute is unknown, but the lack of any subsequent mention of it suggests that it too was soon abandoned. Significantly, Wead noted a year later that liquor retailers were still present in Ypsilanti. Ira M. Wead to AHMS, January 6, 1835, in AHMS Papers.

the *Michigan Emigrant* followed this lead by proposing that temperance devotees open a petition campaign "to increase the tax on taverns retailing ardent spirits, and to except those entirely that do not sell the poison."[9]

But later that year, a few writers were denouncing the licensing system altogether and calling for an end to what they believed was government sponsorship of vice. In July, the *Michigan Emigrant* declared the traffic in liquor to be an "immorality" and that "the system of granting licenses to sell ardent spirits, is productive of no public benefit, but is unequal and unjust, legalizing wrong and furnishing an apology for an employment which can find no justification in morality, patriotism or humanity." "Wilberforce" denounced the license system in a December 1834 essay; how, he asked, "can our laws countenance a practice so destructive of the highest ends of society?" Two months later, at its annual meeting, the Washtenaw County Temperance Society resolved that the "laws licensing the sale of ardent spirits are morally wrong, and ought to be abandoned," since "they form the greatest existing obstacle to the complete success of the temperance cause." Nevertheless, this declaration was tempered with sentiments favorable to moral suasion: the convention also resolved that "a purified public sentiment is the only means of safely legislating on the subject of Temperance"—suggesting that the delegates were divided over the best course to achieving a temperate society. In the midst of this rising protest over the license system, the Ann Arbor Village Council in October 1834 passed an ordinance that prohibited individuals from selling "any wine or spirituous liquors in any quantity" and permitting it to be consumed on the premises where it was sold, unless the seller held a tavern license. Violators were to be fined ten dollars for each offense. Apparently the law proved ineffectual, as nine months later "Common Sense" protested the operation of three "grog shops kept under the color of groceries," which were presumably functioning in violation of this ordinance. Common Sense suggested using moral suasion before resorting to a legal remedy: "The persons who keep them should be kindly asked to quit the sale of spirits. . . . And they should be apprised that the laws *shall*, at all events, be respected. The friends of good order *can* suppress the evil; and it is not acting justly to permit it any longer."[10]

The Washtenaw temperance body, though, proved to be ahead of the

9. *Michigan Emigrant*, cited in Detroit *Journal and Courier*, December 15, 1834, as quoted by Slavcheff, "Temperate Republic," 82.

10. *Michigan Emigrant*, July 24, 1834, December 25, 1834; *Michigan Whig*, February 12, 1835; Ann Arbor Village Minutes, October 29, 1834 (p. 11), Bentley Library; *Michigan Whig and Washtenaw Democrat*, August 13, 1835.

Michigan State Temperance Society, which continued to hold that persuasion was the best means by which to effect a temperance revolution. In October 1834, for example, the executive committee of the state organization issued a circular that condemned the retail sale of liquor. Rather than attacking the license system, however, the committee appealed to the moral sentiments of retailers and requested that liquor sellers ask themselves, "Can it be right for me to derive my living" from the sale of alcohol, which the committee asserted debased the minds and ruined the souls of its users and caused "nine-tenths of all the crimes that are perpetuated against society," a like fraction of pauperism, and the destruction of the "domestic circle." The state executive committee affirmed this position three months later when it announced that the annual meeting of the society was to assemble shortly and asked the local societies to forward answers to a number of questions, including "How many have renounced the traffick in ardent spirits?" None of the questions endorsed or suggested legal suasion.[11]

Measured by the number of essays and comments appearing in Ann Arbor's newspapers, sentiment there favoring the abolition of the license system was clearly on the upswing. In January 1835, "A. B." wrote: "The time has come which calls upon the people of this territory to investigate the practice of granting lisence for the sale of ardent spirits. The influence of our lisences system is obvious and extensive." That same month, the *Michigan Whig* published an essay from the *Temperance Recorder* urging that liquor sellers be made liable for the damage occurring as a result of liquor consumption. Several months later, the *Whig* endorsed a bill rejected by the Massachusetts legislature that would have permitted local voters to have ultimate veto over the issuance of liquor licenses. In April, the Democratic *Michigan Argus* praised the women of Batavia, Ohio, who had petitioned their legislature to suppress "ardent spirits." The *Argus* hoped that their example would be "followed by all the females in the U. S." The following month, the "Ann Arbor Young People" announced that they would shortly hold a county convention at which they would discuss "the propriety of petitioning" the territorial legislature "to abolish the Law granting Licenses for the sale of Ardent Spirits."[12]

At the convention, delegates unanimously adopted several resolutions decrying retailers, the licensing system, the money collected from liquor licenses,

11. *Michigan Emigrant,* October 23, 1834; *Michigan Whig,* January 15, 1835.

12. *Michigan Whig,* January 1, 22, April 23, 1835; *Michigan Whig and Washtenaw Democrat,* May 7, 1835.

and the scarcity of grain occasioned by its conversion into whiskey; they also favored a law that would enable local communities to make the final determination on the questions of granting liquor licenses. Significantly, these resolutions were coauthored by George Corselius, who only two years earlier had defended moral suasion as the only method capable of accomplishing temperance objectives. His conversion to legal measures is indicative of the great changes that occurred in temperance strategy and suggests that he—and others—were frustrated when their intemperate neighbors were unresponsive to their glaring disapproval. Following this convention, moral suasionists were seldom heard from during the subsequent half dozen years. In July, the *Michigan Whig and Washtenaw Democrat*—also edited by Corselius—announced that the petition drive mandated at the recent convention would commence soon, and posed a question that may have been directed toward the diminishing number of moral suasionists: "What has become of the petitions to be presented to the dealers in this town to desist from dealing out alcohol to the poor men who are dying under the effects of the poison?"[13]

Concurrent with the growth of no-license sentiment was a shift in temperance doctrine, with abstinence only from hard liquor giving way to teetotalism. Early devotees of temperance principally attacked the sale and consumption of whiskey, but during the early 1830s even their leaders, such as Corselius, consumed beer and hard cider. Indeed, even after Corselius had abandoned moral suasion, he permitted an advertisement to be run in the *Michigan Whig and Washtenaw Democrat* in August 1835 for the Ann Arbor Brewery. Ironically, in this same issue of the *Whig*, "Wilberforce" regretted that temperance societies did not generally "embrace the principle of abstinence from *all* intoxicating drinks," as he felt it was virtually impossible for one to recover from the use of hard liquor by continuing to use "wine or strong beer," which were "sufficient stimulants to keep in full life the seeds of his distemper. They keep alive the morbid appetite for stimulants." Sometime during the early 1830s, Lorenzo Davis recalled, he "took the ground that no one could be a thorough temperance advocate in theory or practice who drank wine. . . . And I called a few of my associates together and formed a total abstinece [*sic*] Society[,] the pledge including wine and all alcoholic drinks." Davis, who was elected the society's president, believed at the time that it was the first such temperance organization in the territory.[14]

13. *Michigan Whig and Washtenaw Democrat*, June 11, July 16, 1835.

14. Marwil, *Ann Arbor*, 11; *Michigan Whig and Washtenaw Democrat*, August 13, 1835; "History of the Temperance Movement in Washtenaw County," undated [c. 1885], Lorenzo Davis Papers,

Others soon followed. Many citizens took a total-abstinence pledge that was administered in Ypsilanti in December 1834, although not until February 1836 was a temperance society formed there based on this principle. Some Ypsilanti activists, however, refused to endorse teetotalism. Ira Wead wrote in April that "our old Temperance Soc. during the year has been rather inefficient and still remains so, except in its opposition to TeeTotalism." On the other hand, the new society "embraces most of the efficient members that belonged to the old society," although both organizations were said to number about 120 adherents. In July, Wead wrote to the AHMS that the "old society" in Ypsilanti had "become defunct," temperance throughout the state was receiving a new impulse, and "Teetotalism is the doctrine that prevails." The Reverend Charles G. Clarke similarly reported the following March that the old temperance society in Webster was "dead" and had been replaced by a "Teetotal" body. Henry Root wrote that his Presbyterian/Congregational church in Sylvan was converted to teetotalism, and Edward B. Emerson and John G. Kanouse revealed that total abstinence societies had been formed in Pittsfield, York, and Lodi.[15] The spread of teetotalism to the county's large settlements, as well as its rural townships, demonstrates the rapid rise and immense power of this idea during the mid-1830s.

At the statewide Young Men's Temperance Association meeting in Ann Arbor in January 1836, however, delegates from other corners of Michigan were not as enthusiastic about total abstinence as were the members from Washtenaw. After prolonged debate, teetotalers and moderates reached a compromise under which both groups would continue to affiliate. Permanent cooperation, though, was ruined in March when state teetotalers reassembled in Ann Arbor to form the Michigan Total Abstinence Temperance Society and condemned all who would not accept complete abstinence. According to the *State Journal*, one speaker insisted that old temperance hands who refused to adopt a pledge of total abstinence were "nothing but a dead weight to the cause of

---

Bentley Library, 9–10. In Detroit, Isaac Stetson gave a total abstinence address as early as 1831. Detroit *Journal and Courier*, February 16, 1831, as cited in Slavcheff, "Temperate Republic," 328.

15. Detroit *Courier*, December 24, 1834, as cited in Slavcheff, "Temperate Republic," 97; I. M. Wead to AHMS, April 11, 1836, July 20, 1836, Edward B. Emerson to AHMS, December 23, 1836, April 4, June 28, 1837, John G. Kanouse to AHMS, March 16, 1837, in AHMS Papers. Lorenzo Davis recalled that "there was a severe contest" among temperance partisans over total abstinence, which "in some instances broke up societies." "History of the Temperance Movement in Washtenaw County," 17–18.

Temperance" and "had only joined at all because it was popular to do so." He added that "all such friends could be profitably spared—that they were more injurious to the cause than open enemies." When another speaker tried to raise objections to total abstinence, teetotalers responded, according to the *Journal*, "not by open fair, manly argument, but by low scurrility, black guardism and ridicule." The editor, himself a temperance partisan but not a teetotaler, was convinced that teetotalism in particular and temperance in general suffered a major setback as a result of this meeting.[16]

Opposition to total abstinence resurfaced in December 1837, when "S."—who described himself as "a temperance man, upon the first pledge of the Temperance Society, i.e., that he would abstain from the use of ardent spirits, by which was meant, in those days, brandy, rum, gin, & c. wine, cider, and malt liquor not being included"—charged in the *Michigan Argus* that "an opinion is prevailing in one class of society, that a wine cup is an immorality." S. complained that such a position was not sustained by the Bible, which he claimed denounced only drunkenness; the moderate use of wine was in effect endorsed by Jesus when he converted water into wine at Cana. A few weeks later, "W.," a self-professed "total abstinence man," disputed this interpretation of Scripture, arguing that teetotalism was indeed sustained by divine writ. In response, S. asserted that he was "as violently opposed to intemperance as 'W.,' " and after another scriptural exegesis, lamented that teetotalers were unintentionally injuring the cause of temperance "by the high and exclusive position that they have taken." In addition to rejecting total abstinence, S. denounced the trend in temperance circles toward favoring legal measures. He defended moral suasion as the only feasible means of eliminating vice and irreligion, and he was skeptical that legislation "on keeping the sabbath—on moral reform, temperance, and abolition" would ever result in much good.[17]

Although people in sympathy with S. did not prevail in Washtenaw County, the friction between teetotalers and moderates may have slowed the cause throughout most of 1837 and 1838, when there were scarcely any temperance notices published in Ann Arbor's newspapers. An announcement in August 1838 proclaimed that in a few weeks a "County Temperance Society will be organized," indicating that the movement had previously waned. In the fol-

16. *The Proceedings of the Young Men's State Temperance Convention, Held at Ann Arbor, January 20, 1836* (Detroit, 1836); *State Journal*, March 17, 1836. See also *Journal of the American Temperance Union*, I (March, 1837), 45.

17. *Michigan Argus*, December 7, 28, 1837, January 4, 1838.

lowing months, the focus on the November gubernatorial election drowned all temperance activity. But in early November, Washtenaw temperance devotees opened a petition drive directed toward the state legislature and demanding an end to the sale of intoxicants. "The most active Temperance men in each town" were called upon to collect the signatures of sympathetic men and women. The county temperance society also urged that all "ministers of the Gospel . . . preach a sermon on the immorality of the traffic in intoxicating drinks." The executive committee of the Michigan State Temperance Society praised this effort and recommended "the holding of county temperance meetings throughout the state, immediately, to take speedy measures to follow the noble example of Washtenaw County."[18] The editor of the *State Journal* was convinced that such a measure would "serve to promote the welfare of all classes," but he doubted that the people of Michigan were "prepared for such a law. We are less enlightened, and less moral than the people of Massachusetts" (whose legislature had recently passed a prohibitory liquor law). Nevertheless, the editor favored a measure that would allow a majority of local citizens to determine "in town meeting whether they will allow any spirituous liquors to be retailed within their town."[19]

This petition campaign occurred at about the same time as a similar one in Alabama. Whereas the Alabama drive gathered 10,000 signatures, Michigan temperance activists secured only 1,450.[20] The response of legislators in Michigan was similar to that of the lawmakers in Alabama: they praised the objectives of the temperance movement but disagreed that prohibition would bring about a temperate society. Instead, the house Temperance Committee, chaired by Justus Goodwin, a Democrat, and the senate committee, chaired by Whig William Woodbridge, encouraged temperance workers to continue their la-

18. *State Journal,* August 16, November 11, 1838; *Journal of the American Temperance Union,* II (December 1838), 188. The "County Temperance Society" organized in August 1838 was probably the Washtenaw County Total Abstinence Society, which met again the following June. *Michigan Argus,* June 6, 1839.

19. *State Journal,* December 6, 1838. As county and state activists were mounting their petition drive, George W. Clarke began publishing the *Michigan Temperance Herald* in November 1838. Published briefly in Ann Arbor, it subsequently relocated to Jackson where it was printed at least through November 1839. George W. Clarke to Moses Smith, March 28, 1877, undated clipping, George W. Clarke Papers, Bentley Library; *Michigan State Journal,* August 16, November 1, 22, 1838; *Michigan Argus,* January 24, 1839. The staff at the Burton Historical Collection, Detroit Public Library, has been unable to locate its copy of the *Michigan Temperance Herald* (November 1839).

20. Slavcheff, "Temperate Republic," 332.

bors through moral suasion. Not surprisingly, temperance advocates were outraged, and like their Alabama counterparts, some threatened to vote only for political candidates who supported no license. Nevertheless, the issue played little part in the state electoral campaigns of 1839, and although the Whigs captured the governorship and both houses of the legislature, they proved unwilling to act on the wishes of their prohibitionist constituents.

In 1840 temperance activists handed the legislature new petitions, which were referred to a select committee chaired by Munnis Kinney, a Whig (and later a Libertyite) from Webster. Although Kinney's report denounced in thundering tones the evils of alcohol, he was forced to admit that public opinion did not yet support prohibitory legislation. He hoped, though, that "the time will soon come when the public voice will be so loud and united, that our beautiful state will be saved from the scourge they are now called on to deplore. But in a free government, all enactments which are not sustained by a correct public opinion are a mere nullity, if not worse." And whatever temperance flame remained in 1840 was quickly doused by the Whig hard-cider presidential campaign of that year. The Democratic *Michigan Times* accused Ann Arbor's Presbyterians of violating the spirit of their total-abstinence pledges by ringing their church bell to announce the "log cabin and hard cider carousals" and even openly joining in the "bacchanalian" festivities. The *Times* further charged that because of their willingness to compromise their moral principles for the possibility of electoral victory, Presbyterians throughout the country "have let their Temperance Societies go down by default."[21]

Following the failed petition drives, activity in Ann Arbor was at a nadir until the spring of 1841, when the abolitionist *Signal of Liberty* announced that "an effort is being made to revive and *advance* the good cause in our village."[22] By late May, 175 names had been subscribed to the "Total abstinence Pledge," and the Ann Arbor Total Abstinence Society was reorganized. A communication to the *Michigan State Journal* assured "our friends abroad that we are *beginning* to wake up. . . . we will not suffer our beautiful and beloved village to fall behind Detroit, or Marshall, or Monroe, or any other place"; later, the *Journal* editorialized its pleasure at the reinvigoration of the cause in Ann Arbor.[23]

Although the reborn society was firm in its position of total abstinence,

21. *Documents Accompanying the Journal of the State of Michigan, at the Annual Session of 1840. Volume II* (Detroit, 1840), 554; *Michigan Times,* June 16, 1840; Slavcheff, "Temperate Republic," 108–20.

22. *Signal of Liberty,* April 28, 1841.

23. *Michigan State Journal,* June 1, 8, 1841.

some of its early resolutions suggest that members believed that the radicalism of the late 1830s had hindered the temperance cause. Despite affirming that "the *common good* requires that the manufacture of all intoxicating drinks should be discontinued," the society did not propose prohibitionist measures. Instead, it embraced moral suasion and proclaimed that the manufacture of intoxicants would be accomplished only "when the demand for their use ceases; and . . . the demand will only cease when the whole community, acting upon total abstinence principles, shall cease to drink." The members may also have felt that earlier radicalism had offended others in the community and caused such doubters to believe that the temperance effort was a haven for imperious zealots. The Ann Arbor Total Abstinence Society made a deliberate effort to counteract this perception. While reiterating their stout certainty of the rightness of their efforts, the members assured one and all that their convictions did not mandate "that we should arrogate to ourselves the prerogative of judging motive and denounce as unchristian and void of patriotism those who do not at once unite with us in effort or feeling." They further deprecated "all undue influences to force the pledge upon any one" and maintained that "the solemn determination never to use one of the *favorite luxuries* of the day, should not be hastily and unadvisedly formed."

Although the tenure of the Ann Arbor Total Abstinence Society probably did not extend beyond August 1841, two large assemblies in which its membership participated nevertheless demonstrate the extensive—yet ephemeral—interest in temperance. The first was the Sunday-school celebration in Ann Arbor on July 4, at which many temperance enthusiasts were present and the "cold water song" was sung. More noteworthy was a widely advertised temperance gathering held under the auspices of the state temperance society in Ypsilanti a month later. People assembled mostly from Wayne and Washtenaw Counties—a chartered train picked up six hundred passengers from Scio, Dexter village, and Ann Arbor—and those present estimated that between 2,000 and 4,000 clustered along the banks of the Huron River. There, they heard temperance speakers, participated in processions, listened to music, and feasted.[24]

Not all of Washtenaw County's temperance advocates were willing to re-

24. *Michigan State Journal,* June 22, 1841, July 6, 20, August 10, 1841; *Democratic Herald,* July 28, 1841; *Signal of Liberty,* August 11, 1841; Lucy Mary Henderson to William Woodbridge, August 8, 1841, in William Woodbridge Papers, Burton Historical Collection, Detroit Public Library.

treat from prohibitory goals. Theodore Foster, editor of the Liberty Party paper, the *Signal of Liberty*, did not speak ill of the Ann Arbor Total Abstinence Society and had only lavish praise for the temperance gathering in Ypsilanti, but he thought that the temperance cause was fighting a losing battle. Claiming that "indifference and inaction have extensively prevailed" in the movement, that the number of distilleries and the consumption of intoxicating drink was increasing, and that most temperance activity had "but little influence with the great mass of those who shall drink or sell intoxicating liquors," Foster asserted that "so long as the law licences the sale of intoxicating drink as a beverage, as it now does, *moral suasion cannot remove the evil, and* DRUNKENNESS WILL SURELY CONTINUE." But he also recognized that petitioning the legislature for legal sanctions would come to nothing. Since the majority of legislators "use intoxicating drinks, and are opposed to the suppression of the traffic," it was unreasonable to expect them to act contrary to their interests.

Not surprisingly, Foster thought that both the Whigs and the Democrats were unreliable with respect to this issue. The "great majority of the Democratic Party" in Michigan were "most decidedly opposed" to the suppression of liquor sales, and the Whigs had forfeited any claims to carrying the temperance banner as a result of their hard-cider campaign in 1840. Foster urged voters to consider the temperance credentials of the Liberty Party: "The Abolitionists in this State are strenuous temperance men, with but few, if any exceptions." In August, at a county convention to select Libertyite candidates for the state senate, the delegates resolved not to vote for anyone "who is not known as an uncompromising temperance man, as well as an inflexible abolitionist." Foster commented that he was unaware of an abolitionist in the state "who is not in favor of carrying the principle of temperance to the ballot box." In the campaigning prior to the November 1841 election, and afterward as well, Foster and other abolitionists in Washtenaw County generally insisted upon enacting legal prohibitions against the sale of alcohol, maintaining that "drunkenness will never cease among us, until the license system is abolished; and that will never be abolished until the people declare BY THEIR VOTES that it shall be done."[25]

For the time being, though, nonabolitionists generally ignored Foster's pleas for prohibition. Despite the Ann Arbor Total Abstinence Society's disappearance roughly simultaneous with the commencement of the Michigan

25. *Signal of Liberty*, August 4, 1841, September 1, 29, October 6, 20, 1841.

gubernatorial campaign in September 1841, temperance activity in Ann Arbor reemerged the following winter—again under the banner of moral suasion—with the onset of the Washingtonian movement. On January 25, 1842, three members of the Detroit Washingtonian Tee Total Society, which had been organized only two months previously, formed a Washingtonian body in Ann Arbor, and 214 persons signed a pledge of total abstinence. Of this group, "large numbers" were "accustomed to moderate drinking and not a few . . . were confirmed inebriates." The community seemed so receptive that another meeting was held the following evening, in which 110 more citizens pledged total abstinence, and during the following week, two additional meetings were held in which 32 and 80, respectively, forswore all intoxicants.[26] As mentioned in chapter 3, Washingtonians differed from previous temperance groups in that they made a greater effort to reclaim drinkers and were more secular in their orientation. But unlike in Tuscaloosa, where the name "Washingtonian" was rarely invoked, a Washingtonian organization persisted in Ann Arbor for more than three years, until its tactics of moral suasion were undermined by another widespread appeal to prohibition.

The secular dimension of Washingtonianism can be easily overdrawn. Although the Methodists refused the Washingtonians the use of their building, Washingtonian meetings in Ann Arbor were generally held in either the Presbyterian, Baptist, or Universalist church, and in July 1842, Ann Arbor's Sabbath-school proponents joined with local Washingtonians in a joint Independence Day celebration. Nevertheless, some evangelicals questioned whether the Washingtonians were worthy of the praise sometimes showered upon them. In mid-1842 the Reverend Justin Marsh of Augusta reported that some local Washingtonians had violated their pledge and returned to alcohol "like a dog to his own vomit." In Leoni, in Jackson County, the Reverend George Barnum, who also pastored part-time in Sylvan, in Washtenaw County, noted in late 1844 that Washingtonians were one by one "induced to drink a little beer" from a temperance landlord, and subsequently drinking became "the order of the day."[27] Samuel Chipman told the executive committee

26. *Michigan State Journal,* November 30, December 7, 1841, January 25, February 8, 1842; *Signal of Liberty,* February 2, 1842.

27. *Signal of Liberty,* February 2, 1842; *Michigan State Journal,* February 1, 8, June 15, July 11, 1842; Justin Marsh to AHMS, June 29, 1842, George Barnum to AHMS, December 2, 1844, both in AHMS Papers. See also the remarks of Sylvester Cochrane of Howell in neighboring Livingston County in his letter to the AHMS, September 8, 1843, in AHMS Papers.

of the Michigan State Temperance Society that although the Washingtonian movement had "worked wonders in reclaiming the drunkard," he believed that it had succeeded in doing so only where it and the older temperance organizations had cooperated. In those places where "in their zeal to avoid sectarianism, they have discarded all religion" and prohibited the opening of their meetings with prayer, Washingtonians had "very extensively returned to their 'wallowing in the mire.' "[28]

Some evangelicals were even less charitable toward the Washingtonians. Although it originally praised the movement, by 1843 the *Signal of Liberty* commented on the secular dimension of Washingtonianism as its greatest failure: "The attempt to reform the world of its vice independently of religion has never been successful." Oliver C. Comstock differed with the Washingtonian prescription of drunkenness as "a mere unavoidable misfortune." Temperance workers, he explained, were obliged to "call things by their right names. Drunkenness is a very disgraceful sin. It is a prolific source of multifarious and aggravated evils." He also denied the contention of some Washingtonian lecturers that temperance had heretofore been too closely affiliated with churches. No one, Comstock asserted, was ever obliged to join a church after signing a temperance pledge, although he admitted that many church members joined temperance societies and that "when individuals were about to connect with some churches, they were invited to sign the temperance pledge."[29] But perhaps the harshest criticism of the Washingtonians was recorded by Lorenzo Davis, an occasional Methodist preacher and long a temperance partisan, who later insisted that the Washingtonians "no doubt retarded the cause of temperance and set it back practically for quite 10 years."[30]

Although calls for prohibition during the heyday of Washingtonianism came mostly from abolitionists, others occasionally denounced the license system. "With indignation," Samuel Chipman "spoke of our foolish system of li-

28. *Signal of Liberty*, August 7, 1843; *Michigan State Journal*, June 14, 1843. Without specifically mentioning the Washingtonians, Thaddeus Osgood of Ann Arbor complained that some "very zealous advocates for the temperance reform have said nothing respecting religion, or our dependence on God." *Michigan Argus*, July 29, 1846.

29. *Signal of Liberty*, August 7, 1843, March 4, 1844. Almost two years earlier, however, Comstock addressed an Independence Day celebration sponsored by the Washingtonians. *Michigan State Journal*, July 6, 1842.

30. "History of the Temperance Movement in Washtenaw County," Lorenzo Davis Papers, Bentley Library.

censing drunkeries" during a speech in December 1842. In a few of the county's townships, according to L. W. Osgood in July 1843, "no licenses have been granted to tipling shops during the past year under the delusive hope that they would disappear." Osgood was outraged that authorities in Ypsilanti failed to enforce that village's license laws and permitted "four or five grog shops" to operate. He was further appalled when Governor John S. Barry, to whom he complained after being dismissed by Ypsilanti's peace officers, ignored him too. In January 1844, the executive committee of the Michigan State Temperance Society praised the good accomplished by moral suasion but pointed out that some people were never sober long enough to hear a reasoned argument. This small group of people, claimed the committee, constituted the majority of inmates at poorhouses and caused extraordinary suffering to women and children: "Must three-fourths of the men be annoyed by day and disturbed by night, and taxed annually . . . and the rising generation inherit nothing but rags and disgrace, in order that a heartless few may live by [liquor] manufacture and sales[?]" The executive committee proposed a local-option law providing communities with the right to vote directly on "the question of License or no License," believing that such a law would generally accomplish "what moral suasion cannot." The annual convention of the Michigan State Temperance Society endorsed this proposal, and of the "fifteen or twenty" speakers at the convention, only two opposed this shift in strategy. Those who questioned the usefulness of a local-option law argued that "Washingtonians had done well, and all we needed was to keep on in the same track, only with more diligence." Guy Beckley, the financial backer and coeditor of the *Signal of Liberty*, countered that moral suasion alone "could not expel drunkenness from the community.—The Washingtonian movement had been found insufficient, and hence he was for legislative action." Indeed, some Washingtonians had already concluded prior to the state society's meeting that moral suasion alone was inadequate, as the Washingtonian Temperance Society of Medina instructed its delegates to favor a local-option law.[31]

Despite the failure to enact statewide prohibition during the late 1830s, this local-option proposal met with a favorable reception from many in the move-

31. *Democratic Herald*, December 14, 1842; *Michigan State Journal*, July 26, 1843; *Michigan Argus*, February 14, 1844; *Signal of Liberty*, March 25, 1844; *Michigan Argus*, February 28, 1844. By 1846 Dexter village's Washingtonians were serving as a vigilance committee to ensure that liquor retailers complied with local license laws. (Jackson) *Michigan Temperance Journal and Washingtonian*, I (July 15, 1846), 53.

ment. In Washtenaw County, the growing hostility to liquor sellers may have arisen because of the persistent evidences of alcohol abuse, and out of frustration over the continued sale of spirits by unlicensed retailers. In April 1844, the Washtenaw County District Court issued twenty-seven indictments of people accused of selling liquor without a license "in the central and eastern parts of the county," and the district's grand jury complained that township supervisors had failed to exercise their duty to prosecute people who sold unlicensed liquor.[32] Prior to the Ann Arbor Village election on July 1, 1844, "Temperance" urged readers of the Democratic *Michigan Argus* to vote only for temperance proponents "who will not, for a few paltry shillings" license "dram shops," and suggested that Ann Arbor's temperance societies nominate a slate of candidates to accomplish this end. Rejoicing to see this letter in the *Argus*, the *Signal of Liberty* proclaimed its delight "that many of our most influential citizens, disgusted by the almost daily scenes of drunkenness that disgrace our Village, the inevitable consequence of *legalized dramshops*, are considering what is the most effective remedy for this enormous evil." Perhaps fearing that temperance activists would run their own candidates for village officers, the town council, "by request of the citizens," permitted the electorate to determine whether the council ought to cease licensing liquor retailers. Unfortunately for the prohibitionists, they were unable to rally those numerous supporters who had signed the Washingtonian pledge only two years earlier, and the measure was narrowly defeated, 106 to 114.[33] But sensing citizen disgust with the ubiquity of barrooms, the council asked the village marshal to compile a list of people selling liquor without a license and directed the corporation's attorney to prosecute all such cases in the future. The following October, twenty-nine additional indictments were presented to the Washtenaw County District Court.

32. Washtenaw County District Court Journal, April 5, 1844 (pp. 44–45), April 8, 1844 (pp. 49–51), April 9, 1844 (pp. 52–55), April 10, 1844 (pp. 56–59, 67, 68), Washtenaw County Courthouse. *Signal of Liberty*, April 15, 1844, contains a report of the grand jury, of which abolitionist and temperance adherent Munnis Kinney of Webster served as foreman.

33. *Michigan Argus*, June 19, 1844; *Signal of Liberty*, June 24, 1844; Record Book of the Ann Arbor Village Council, July 1, 1844 (pp. 92–93), Bentley Library. Three months earlier, the council rejected a motion by Norton R. Ramsdell to enact a prohibitionist no-license statute. Ramsdell was a reform-minded Democrat who also favored abolition; while a member of the Michigan House of Representatives he worked to provide suffrage for African American males and labored to secure a legislative act of incorporation for Ann Arbor's Fourierist Alphadelphia Association. *Ibid.*, April 2, 1844 (p. 82); *Signal of Liberty*, November 6, 1843, March 11, 1844; *Michigan State Journal*, April 10, 1844.

But these measures were largely unsuccessful. Since violations of license laws were prosecuted as civil and not criminal cases, liquor retailers, if caught, merely paid the fine and then proceeded with their business. This failure to stop the traffic in alcohol led only to discouragement and inactivity among temperance stalwarts. In January 1845, the *Argus* complained that no temperance society or citizens' group protested the twenty well-patronized liquor retailers in Ann Arbor.[34]

In the meantime, temperance activists throughout the state urged the legislature to pass the local-option law proposed by the Michigan State Temperance Society, and in March 1845, the legislators did so. The new law was praised by the Ypsilanti *Sentinel,* and editor Charles Woodruff charged temperance adherents to "revive old societies and establish new ones," and then place the question of license or no license "directly before the people"—which actions, he believed, would eventually halt the sale of ardent spirits. In Ann Arbor, a public discussion on the merits of this law was scheduled at the courthouse "from evening to evening as long as the discussion may seem to be necessary and profitable." On election day, Ann Arbor's voters overwhelmingly chose no license; the measure was also successful in Bridgewater, Manchester, Northfield, Pittsfield, Sharon, Salem, Webster, and Ypsilanti, but lost in Sylvan and Scio. Nevertheless, one-third of the voters in Ann Arbor who voted for township supervisor did not cast a ballot on this measure, suggesting either apathy or confusion. Sylvan and Ypsilanti showed a rate of participation on the license question that was roughly equal to the number of votes residents in those townships cast for supervisor, but participation on the license issue was only 71 percent in Webster and 50 percent in Manchester (Table 8). Another reason for the lower votes on license may be the fact that voters throughout the state were required to cast a distinct ballot on the license question and to place it in a separate box.[35]

Of course, passage of these laws entailed the expectation that they would eliminate the sale of spirits. And some opponents of prohibition feared that li-

34. Record Book of the Ann Arbor Village Council, July 16, 1844 (p. 97), August 2, 1844 (p. 99), August 8, 1844 (p. 101); Washtenaw County District Court Journal, October 3, 1844 (pp. 77, 94); Oliver C. Comstock to Seymour B. Treadwell, December 13, 1844, Treadwell Papers, Bentley Library; *Michigan Argus,* January 15, 1845.

35. Oliver C. Comstock to Seymour B. Treadwell, December 13, 1844, Treadwell Papers; Ypsilanti *Sentinel,* March 12, 1845; *Michigan Argus,* March 19, 1845; Slavcheff, "Temperate Republic," 342–43.

quor would indeed be greatly suppressed. In Ann Arbor, the prosecution of Charles Brewill for selling liquor without a license in June, along with another no-license victory at the village elections in July, caused some of the town's wets to retaliate. The *Signal of Liberty* reported that following these two elections and the subsequent commencement of "several" prosecutions against those who had continued to sell liquor "in defiance to the Law," pro-liquor vigilantes attempted to "strike terror into all who would oppose these violations of the Law." Things came to a head in August 1845, when the awning attached to the store of David and Erastus Lesuer was "cut and damaged" and the "door and window shutters bedaubed and inscribed, 'No License, Judge Lynch is after you.'" The editors of the *Signal of Liberty,* Foster and Beckley, were particularly outraged when the mob visited a store that they jointly operated. At least three of the other six objects of the vigilantes' wrath—the barns of Dr. Martin H. Cowles and David T. McCollum, and the well of McCollum and Robert Davidson—belonged to prohibitionists who were also members of the Liberty Party. The barns were left with inscriptions, blue paint, or tar, and a well was defiled with tar, turpentine, and oil, which "rendered [it] . . . useless." The front door of Theodore Foster's dwelling "was changed in color from white to blue, and we were complimented by a card from his honor, painted on our fence—'Look out, old chap! Judge Lynch.'" Two men were arrested and charged with committing these acts. Such vandalism was not restricted to Ann Arbor. The following year, Foster attributed a fire in nearby Plymouth, Wayne County, to an incendiary, "as much excitement has prevailed in that vicinity on the license question, and threats of injury have been made."[36]

The expectation that no license would eliminate liquor sales was frustrated. Again, violators were tried as civil offenders, and since legal authorities were powerless to impose any penalty beyond fines, liquor retailers usually regarded such intrusions as another cost of doing business. But many citizens believed that the authorities were shirking their duty. In September 1845, a writer complained in the *Michigan Argus* that the village authorities, who had pledged prior to the last election to "bring about a new order of things," were unresponsive to Ann Arbor's disheveled appearance, which was caused largely "by rowdies made drunk with liquor sold without license, amid yells and shrieks worthy of Milton's Pandemonium." In December, the *Signal of Liberty* lamented that the no-license laws were being ignored—which sentiments were echoed

36. *Signal of Liberty,* August 11, 18, 1845, May 4, 1846.

by Halmer H. Emmons of Detroit in February 1846, when he stated that the law was being "enforced in very few instances" statewide—and charged that legal challenges to liquor retailers had proved futile because lawyers as a group favored the "rumsellers." While the *Signal* praised the no-license law, as it removed the legal sanction from liquor, editor Foster expected that alcohol would continue to be sold "until the temperance people in each town shall UNITEDLY arise and put away the abomination, by a general, systematic and persevering prosecution of the law." Although there was some dissent at the state temperance convention in Marshall in February 1846—a Mr. Bates of Jackson, a member of the state society's executive committee, remained ardently committed to moral suasion and opposed to any legal action—the society continued to embrace the local-option law.[37]

Abiding support for no license persisted in Ann Arbor, as prohibition won 390 to 38 in the April 1846 township election. The measure also proved victorious in Scio, Pittsfield, and Webster, winning in the latter two places 96 to 10 and 71 to 7. The shift in sentiment in Scio Township from rejecting no license in 1845 to embracing it in 1846 was certainly an outcome of the temperance agitation in Dexter village—most of which was in Scio Township—during the intervening winter. According to Mrs. N. A. Bronson, secretary of the Ladies' Total Abstinence Benevolent Society in Dexter village, the three hundred pledges to total abstinence that temperance partisans had obtained, plus the visit of a temperance lecturer in May, resulted in "a great moral change." Nevertheless, not everyone who embraced no license in 1845 continued to do so in 1846, as it was defeated in both Ypsilanti and Manchester, where it had won previously. And although the percentage of people who voted on both the license question and for township supervisor rose in Manchester, it decreased in Webster, Ann Arbor, and Ypsilanti (Table 8). Participation percentages on the ballot proposal ebbed and flowed in the local elections of most townships—possibly because in some elections the location of the ballot box for the license/no-license referendum may not have been convenient to the ballot box for township officers. And in the face of continued liquor sales in most townships, voters doubtless became cynical about ending the traffic by casting their ballot for no license. Consequently, either most polities eventually failed to comply

37. *Michigan Argus*, September 9, 1845; *Signal of Liberty*, December 1, 1845, February 9, 16, 1846.

with the state law that mandated these referendums, or voters no longer bothered to cast their ballots on this question, or both.[38]

Township votes on the license question continued until 1851, although the only township in the county known to have put the issue before its electorate that year was Pittsfield (where no license won all 36 votes cast). Voters of some townships favored issuing licenses one year but opposed them the next. The residents of Ann Arbor village and Ann Arbor Township were especially capricious on this question. After the voters there had overwhelmingly favored no license in April 1846, the stirring temperance lectures of Alonzo Hyde the following month further roused them. According to George Corselius in the *Michigan State Journal,* they became "pretty well waked up; and we believe, determined to have the traffic in intoxicating drinks discontinued." At one public meeting, citizens appointed a committee to visit every liquor establishment in Ann Arbor "for the purpose of remonstrating with the vendors, and inducing them to abandon the illegal traffic." The reception of this committee was mixed. Although one retailer agreed to convert his establishment into a "Temperance House," others were less compliant: "Some dealers would give up the business if others would: some were willing to give up the sale of all but beer and cider: some would not converse on the subject at all: some planted themselves on their constitutional right to sell liquor: and one dealer seized an axhelve and drove the committee out of his shop." In light of such animosity, the *Michigan State Journal* urged that prosecutions continue against liquor sellers who proved recalcitrant.[39]

By April 1847, however, support for no license in Ann Arbor Township diminished considerably, winning only 347 to 314. That the public had become disillusioned with this remedy was even more apparent from the village referendum the following month, when prolicense forces defeated no-license partisans, 215 to 198. Evidently some opponents of no license used the argument that their Tuscaloosa counterparts would advance during the 1850s: that alcohol consumption would diminish with the reemergence of licensed liquor establishments. The editor of the *True Democrat,* disappointed with the referendum

38. (Jackson) *Michigan Temperance Journal and Washingtonian,* I (July 1846), 53; *Acts of the Legislature of Michigan Passed at the Annual Session of 1845* (Detroit, 1845), 56; *Acts of the Legislature of the State of Michigan Passed at the Annual Session of 1849* (Lansing, 1849), 295–96; *The Revised Statutes of the State of Michigan, Passed and Approved May 18, 1846* (Detroit, 1846), 187–88.

39. *Michigan State Journal,* May 20, 1846; *Signal of Liberty,* May 23, 1846.

results, was skeptical of this logic but hoped to be proved wrong. Perhaps recognizing the uncertainty of public opinion on the question, the Ann Arbor Village Council passed an ordinance in June 1847 that prohibited liquor retailers from selling intoxicants to individuals identified by the council as "common drunkards," and affixed the penalty as the loss of the liquor license. But in April 1848, the township overwhelmingly chose no license again, and subsequently, the village narrowly favored the granting of liquor licenses, thus rescinding the vote of the previous month in the village but not in the larger township. Clearly, voters of the rural portion of Ann Arbor Township were more favorable to prohibition than were their village counterparts.[40]

An identical pattern occurred in April and May 1849 (Table 8). Despite complaints by S. S. Shoff, editor of the *Washtenaw Whig*, that the streets of Ann Arbor had lately become "the scene of brawling drunkenness," the voters in Ann Arbor village shortly afterward narrowly rejected no license. A correspondent to the *Whig* who considered this electoral outcome a mistake was nevertheless convinced that even Ann Arborites who had voted for licenses did not want the unlimited sale of liquor. He urged the town council to issue licenses only to responsible people of high moral character, requested the council to "direct the Marshal to execute the law against all who sell without license," and—analogous to Tuscaloosa's prohibitionists—warned that parents would refuse to send their children to the University of Michigan if Ann Arbor developed a reputation as a haven for liquor sellers.[41] Although no license won the following year in both the village and the township elections, the fact that

40. Ann Arbor Township Records April 5, 1847, April 3, 1848, Ann Arbor Township Hall; Record Book of the Ann Arbor Village Council, May 3, 1847 (p. 1), June 14, 1847 (p. 26), July 16, 1847 (p. 29), Bentley Library; *True Democrat*, May 4, 1847; *Michigan Argus*, May 3, 1848. Ann Arbor township was one of twenty townships in Washtenaw County, each of which had an area of thirty-six square miles. Like most townships in Michigan during the mid-nineteenth-century, it was largely rural and dotted by farms. Contained within Ann Arbor township was the village of Ann Arbor, which was unincorporated until 1851. Prior to incorporation, though, the village participated in township elections in April each year, and then selected village officers between one and three months later. From 1845 to 1850, voters of Ann Arbor village and town also cast their ballots on the license/no license referendum, both of which were legally binding on the village until the following license/no license vote.

Despite the stronger support for prohibition in the rural portion of Ann Arbor township, temperance activists, as we shall see later in this chapter, were more likely to reside in the village. Opponents of prohibition were, presumably, also more likely to live in the village.

41. *Washtenaw Whig*, April 25, May 9, 1849; see also *ibid.*, December 5, 1849; *B'Hoy's Eagle*,

less than 12 percent of the voters for township supervisor cast their ballots on the local-option referendum shows the extent to which an electorate sympathetic to prohibition had become cynical about the existing local-option law. Unfortunately, extant primary sources fail to provide any clues regarding the changing temperament of voters on no license. The constant shifting of votes and the failure of many citizens to vote on this question at all suggest that many people in Washtenaw County were internally divided as to the best method to halt widespread alcoholism and its attendant social problems. They found that neither license, no license, licensing only responsible citizens to sell liquor, nor prohibiting the sale of liquor to chronic inebriates solved the problem. Nevertheless, these failures did not keep people from seeking remedies for these problems, nor did the public cease demanding that their politicians do something. This willingness to experiment eventually culminated, as we shall see shortly, in residents of Washtenaw County considering the application of the Maine Law to their state.

Not long after the implementation of Michigan's local-option law, most temperance stalwarts conceded that it had failed to extinguish liquor sales. Like Theodore Foster, however, they remained committed to the law and believed that continued vigilance would enable them eventually to attain their objective of effective prohibition. In February 1847, the Michigan State Temperance Society renewed its support of the local-option law, disapproved of efforts to repeal it, and urged temperance adherents to attend the conventions of their respective parties and nominate candidates who, if elected, would endeavor to carry out the existing no-license mandates. The Jackson-based *Michigan Temperance Journal and Washingtonian* praised the local-option law, as it had "taken away the sanction of law to the unholy traffic, and shown . . . the hostility of a great majority of the people to the sale of intoxicating drinks in their midst." Although the morals of some communities had purportedly improved since the passage of the law, the *Journal and Washingtonian* admitted that the ordinance had generally had "very little effect in preventing the traffic in liquors, not because of any real defect in the law, but on account of the lack of interest and action on the part of the friends of temperance." The executive committee of the Michigan State Temperance Society concurred with this as-

October 11, 1849. As of April 2, 1849, all local option elections in Michigan were reversed, and liquor sales in the state were prohibited except in those communities where pro-liquor license supporters placed the local option question on the ballot. Slavcheff, "Temperate Republic," 183–84.

sessment and attributed the failure of no license's enforcement "to the apathy of temperance men, and the difficulty in procuring evidence."[42]

Several obstacles prevented temperance devotees from improving the execution of local-option laws. Foremost was the reluctance of either Whigs or Democrats to commit fervently to prohibition. Although Ann Arbor's Whig and Democratic newspapers endorsed the local-option law and supported no license with a few occasional sentences of encouragement, neither party devoted itself to prohibition. Party leaders undoubtedly feared offending voters who still enjoyed alcohol. In this important respect, the Washtenaw County newspapers of the major parties differed little from their counterparts in Tuscaloosa County. Nevertheless, Whigs were more likely to favor prohibition than Democrats, and within some Michigan townships Whigs and Liberty-ites occasionally united behind a single ticket in order to elect a prohibitionist supervisor or town council. The *Signal of Liberty* discouraged such actions, claiming that they were aimed at destroying the Liberty Party and that voting for a proslavery township supervisor was merely the first step toward voting for a proslavery president. Notwithstanding the importance of the cause of temperance to most abolitionist voters, many viewed it as secondary to combating slavery.[43] And despite the significance of temperance to voters belonging to other parties, there were doubtless few among them who viewed it as paramount over all other issues.

Concurrent with the fight over the local licensing of liquor retailers, the Sons of Temperance emerged. First appearing in Michigan in 1847, the organization met with a considerably cooler reception there than in Alabama—probably because of the stronger residual Antimasonic sentiment in the northern state. Although Antimasonry was present in Alabama during the late 1820s and early 1830s and caused the closure of many Masonic divisions there, its influence in Michigan was much stronger, with Antimasons forming their own political party. The epicenter of Antimasonry in Michigan was in Washtenaw County, where the *Western Emigrant*, the territory's Antimasonic paper, was published and where Samuel Dexter, one of the four vice-presidents of the 1830 national Antimasonic Party convention, resided. Even though Antimasonry as a political force had disappeared by the mid-1830s, sentiment adverse to se-

42. *Michigan Temperance Journal and Washingtonian*, II (February 1847), 12, 14–15, II (March 1847), 21.

43. *Signal of Liberty*, March 13, 1847.

cret societies persisted. This attitude is perhaps best illustrated by a heated controversy that arose in 1849, when many Ann Arbor residents and the University of Michigan clashed over whether students should be permitted to belong to fraternities.[44]

Of course, such views did not disappear in Alabama either. Basil Manly's insistence to Alabama Baptists in 1849 that the Sons of Temperance was an organization to which Baptists could in good conscience belong suggests that many Alabamians continued to hold secret societies in suspicion. In Washtenaw County, however, no figure of Manly's stature came to the Sons' defense. In fact, only three months after the formation of the Sons of Temperance in Ann Arbor, the village's Baptist church inserted a clause into its covenant whereby the members pledged "neither to unite or receive into the Church any who are connected with any secret association"; those who continued their connection with secret societies after being entreated to leave would be expelled from the church. In November 1847, the church withdrew fellowship from four members "for refusing to withdraw from Societies with which they are connected, one of whose conditions of membership is a pledge of secrecy." Among those excluded was Earl P. Gardiner, who served several terms as editor of the *Michigan Argus* from 1835 to 1854, was later a justice of the peace, and held the rank of "Worshipful Patriarch" in Ann Arbor Division No. 10, Sons of Temperance.[45]

R. Powell of Clinton, a Baptist whose congregation denounced the Sons of Temperance, admitted that the Sons had done much good in reclaiming inebriates but saw no reason why "the same good, or even more good, might not

44. William Preston Vaughn, *The Antimasonic Party in the United States, 1826–1843* (Lexington, Ky., 1983), 54; *Washtenaw Whig,* January 2, 9, 16, March 6, 1850; Walter A. Donnelly, ed., *The University of Michigan: An Encyclopedic Survey* (Ann Arbor, 1958), volume 4, 1799–1801.

45. Records of the First Baptist Church of Ann Arbor, July 29, November 4, 1847; Louis W. Doll, *A History of the Newspapers of Ann Arbor, 1829–1920* (Detroit, 1959), 22, 30, 44, 45, 47, 48; *Michigan Argus,* September 25, 1857. On August 4, 1847, Gardiner published the church resolution in the *Michigan Argus.* Because this issue of the *Argus* is not extant, it cannot be known whether Gardiner appended any editorial comments, or the full context under which it appeared. The announcement of this policy in the *Signal of Liberty,* however, which was based on the *Argus* account, mentioned only "associations whose conditions of membership require a pledge of secrecy," and said nothing explicitly regarding the Sons of Temperance. *Signal of Liberty,* August 7, 1847. Further, those in Ann Arbor who were inclined to view the Sons of Temperance with suspicion may have had their fears confirmed when the Ann Arbor Division was organized at the village Odd Fellow's hall in April 1847. *Michigan Argus,* April 14, 1847.

have been done by the same men with equal exertions, under an organization without secrets and passwords." Michigan's Free Will Baptists were likewise antagonistic to the Sons and to all other secret societies. Not all churches in Michigan, though, were hostile to the Sons of Temperance. The Washtenaw Presbytery was ambivalent. In May 1848, the Presbytery discussed whether it was "expedient" for members and ministers to unite with the Sons, but arrived at no conclusion until September 1849, when it resolved to leave the question of association "to the intelligence and conscience of its members." Congregationalists in Washtenaw County were more receptive. The Ladies' Sewing Society of the Ann Arbor Congregational Church constructed the regalia for the local members of the Sons of Temperance, who held meetings in the church. The Reverend Clark Lockwood of Dexter village's Congregational church was active in Dexter's Phoenix Division. Sons of Temperance meetings were held in the Dexter village Methodist Episcopal Church as well.[46]

In Washtenaw County, the Sons of Temperance was first organized in April 1847, when the Ann Arbor Division was formed at the town's Odd Fellows hall. As it did in Tuscaloosa, the organization spread quickly to the surrounding villages. A few weeks after the formation of the Ann Arbor Division, another was created in Ypsilanti, followed by divisions in Saline, Dexter village, and Manchester; eventually, Ann Arbor hosted three divisions. But there were others, besides the churches, who withheld their enthusiasm. Charles Woodruff, editor of the Ypsilanti *Sentinel,* praised the Sons for providing the greatest revitalization of the temperance movement seen in several years, but he acknowledged that some "old and efficient friends" of temperance had stood aloof from the new society because of its secrecy. Woodruff defended the Sons by noting that some churches held their meetings in private and that the Sons made no pretensions to exclusive knowledge, nor did they have any obnoxious oaths or penalties. Earl Gardiner explained that a ceremony in which "the Ladies of

46. *Michigan Christian Herald,* February 18, 25, 1848; Michigan Association of Free Will Baptists, Records, June 9, 1848, Bentley Library; Minutes of the Washtenaw Presbytery, May 9, 1848 (volume 1, p. 315), September 25, 1849 (volume 2, pp. 23–24); Records of the Congregational Ladies' Sewing Society, early 1848 (volume 1, pp. 11–15), located in the Records of the First Congregational Church of Ann Arbor, Bentley Library; Records of the Phoenix Division No. 79, Sons of Temperance, *passim,* Bentley Library; *Washtenaw Whig,* May 1, 1850; *Michigan Argus,* February 27, 1850. Some Presbyterians, however, were more hostile to the Sons of Temperance; the Ripley (Ohio) Presbytery regarded the Sons of Temperance as a secret society and excluded members who belonged to the order. *Signal of Liberty,* January 15, 1848.

this village" presented a Bible to the Ann Arbor Division was calculated to strengthen members of the order and "do away with much of the unfounded opposition which exists against the Sons of Temperance." Later that year, "M. J. T." wrote from Ann Arbor to the *Michigan Temperance Journal & School Advocate* to promote the Cadets of Temperance, an auxiliary of the Sons designed for males aged twelve to eighteen. Despite the numerous temperance societies that had sprung up in America over the past few decades, all had been ephemeral, for as soon as "their novelty wears away, the members lose all interest in the cause." Though secret, the Cadets of Temperance strove to "possess sufficient attractions of its own to keep the members constantly interested." M. J. T. feared that if the meetings were thrown open to the public, the Cadets would then "share the fate of its many predecessors." And like Woodruff, M. J. T. explained that the order's rites were "simple and to the point" and that the group eschewed the pomp of the Odd Fellows and did not boast of their antiquity, as did the Masons.[47]

These arguments failed to persuade all nay-sayers. Among those who stood aloof from the Sons of Temperance were abolitionists, most notably the editors of the *Signal of Liberty*. Despite its fervent advocacy of temperance, this paper was editorially silent regarding the Sons and only reprinted one piece from the *Michigan Argus* that noted the formation of a division in Dexter village. Perhaps more indicative of the paper's view of the Sons is a letter of former co-editor Guy Beckley, who in October 1847 denounced "Masonry, Odd Fellows, Rechabitism, and the Sons of Temperance. . . . Not a Journal, political or religious, to my knowledge, has commenced the discussion of the question of *secret societies* . . . but what has been compelled to give up the discussion. The friends of these societies will not tolerate the investigation, and their enemies stand in awe of them, and so the matter rests. For one I maintain uncompromising hostility to them all."[48]

Greater lingering hostility to Masonry may explain why the Sons of Temperance received a cooler reception in Washtenaw County than in Tuscaloosa County, but the opposition to the organization can also be overstated. The

47. *Michigan Argus*, April 14, May 5, 26, June 23, 1847, January 19, 1848; Ypsilanti *Sentinel*, June 9, 1847; *Michigan Argus*, September 15, 1847; *Michigan Temperance Journal & School Advocate*, II (December 1847), 94–95.

48. *Signal of Liberty*, July 10, 1847, November 13, 1847. Antebellum conspiracy theorists were doubtless further convinced of Beckley's charges when Beckley died only six weeks after these words were published.

Sons of Temperance in Washtenaw County appealed to a constituency that was less affluent and also far less likely to be connected to a church or a political party than the county's other temperance cohorts. Additionally, the existence of at least seven divisions in Washtenaw County alone attests that the group's message resonated well with some segments of the population. And after the initial outbursts of hostility that I have mentioned, the antagonism toward the Sons seems to have faded. Although Ann Arbor's First Baptist Church continued to have a low regard for secret societies, in February 1849 the church rescinded the penalty of expulsion for members who continued to associate with such organizations. Quite possibly the decision of the Washtenaw Presbytery to be ambivalent regarding the affiliation of its members with the Sons was also the result of the Sons' improving image. Antagonism to the Sons had apparently diminished in April 1850, when Samuel F. Cary, the head of the National Division, spoke in Ann Arbor. Although all three of the Ann Arbor divisions had disappeared by this time, the town's newspapers reported that Cary's two addresses were presented to "crowded audiences at the Congregational Church," in which "many were forced to listen, standing."[49]

The minute book of Dexter's Phoenix Division provides some insights into the operation of the Sons of Temperance. This division met weekly from its creation on July 10, 1848, until its demise on February 27, 1851—much longer and more consistently than any other known temperance body in antebellum Washtenaw County—and was one of two divisions in the village of Dexter. At its peak, it had about twenty-two members. Each Sons of Temperance division had ten officers, and since new officers were chosen quarterly, virtually every member in the Phoenix Division held, at one time or another, a position of responsibility. Also, each officer played a distinct role in the order's ritual that was enacted during each weekly meeting. After the ritual, members planned activities such as special lectures, picnics, and public celebrations; listened to temperance speeches; formed auxiliary organizations such as a glee club and committees to visit inactive members; read communications from other divisions; proposed strategies to combat intemperance locally; discussed disciplinary measures for members who had violated their pledge of total ab-

49. Records of the First Baptist Church of Ann Arbor, February 8, 1849, Bentley Library; *Michigan Argus,* May 1, 1850; *Washtenaw Whig,* December 5, 1849, May 1, 1850; Records of the Phoenix Division of the Sons of Temperance, August 20, 1849, Bentley Library.

stinence; and levied fines—usually only twenty-five cents—on members who violated protocol, such as speaking without rising.

The members also grappled with what it meant to be temperate. On September 11, 1848, the division debated whether it was a violation of the pledge to "drink the unfermented juice of the apple," and the following week, division members voted to count apple juice among their banned beverages. Previously the division had debated whether members of the order ought to be censured for speaking with "profane language" or using tobacco in the division's meeting hall.[50] A majority of members eventually condemned the use of tobacco during meetings. They later concluded, however, that this prohibition was "disastrous to the good order of brothers" and rescinded it, although agreeing to fine members twenty-five cents for the "spitting of tobacco juice upon the floor of the Division room." The division members also endorsed a prohibitionist Maine Law and resolved in the meantime to "watch the liquor sellers if possible to obtain evidence for prosecution" against those who violated local license laws. One member was appointed to present complaints about violators to the township supervisor. Thus the Phoenix Division was in some respects a standing vigilance committee for temperance and prohibition. Nevertheless, not all members favored a resolution presented in March 1850 requiring all Sons of Temperance to use their energy to secure a no-license vote in the upcoming township election; the resolution passed by only 11 to 5.

Eventually, the novelty of the Sons of Temperance diminished in Dexter village and elsewhere, and attendance at meetings dwindled. The Phoenix Division, however, outlasted many other divisions of the order. Prior to its collapse, the Phoenix received notice of members from other divisions who failed to pay their dues and were no longer to be welcomed as fraternal brothers. In August 1849, for example, the Ann Arbor Division reported that thirty-nine of its members had been suspended for the nonpayment of dues, thus ending the division's existence. Although the cause persisted in Dexter village longer than it did in Ann Arbor, by November 1850, the Dexter Division and the Phoenix Division were discussing a merger of their lodges. In January 1851, the uninsured meeting hall of the Dexter Division was destroyed by a fire. Although the Phoenix met at the Odd Fellows hall, the cause was afterward so dispirited

50. Records of the Phoenix Division of the Sons of Temperance, September 4, 11, 18, 1848, Bentley Library.

that at the end of February, the division's remaining members voted to dispose of its regalia and other property "to the best advantage." A month later, when the Ypsilanti Division's hall was destroyed by fire, too, the Sons of Temperance in Washtenaw County effectively ended, almost four years after it began.[51]

The inadequacies of the local-option law neither caused the proponents of legal measures to retreat nor encouraged the friends of moral suasion to take control of the movement, as had happened in the late 1830s and early 1840s. The Detroit *Michigan Christian Herald* in 1848 denied claims that the local-option law was unpopular and that suppressing the sale of alcohol only increased consumption. It was the duty of temperance forces to take a firm stand against the repeal of local option and to sustain it until they obtained a law that would abolish the power to grant liquor licenses altogether. In January 1849 the Michigan State Temperance Society resolved to draw up petitions "praying the Legislature . . . to pass a law prohibiting the sale of intoxicating drinks as a beverage." On a number of occasions in the subsequent two years, the Phoenix Division circulated petitions and passed resolutions calling for a prohibitory liquor law. But the issue of statewide prohibition failed to capture the zeal of temperance partisans and the attention of the general public until the passage of Maine's prohibitory law in 1851.

At the time, the Michigan State Temperance Society was at a nadir of activity. The delegates to its October 1851 meeting in Ann Arbor represented only six of the state's counties, and a committee was appointed to revise the society's constitution, as the previous one "could not be found." Public concern over alcohol control, however, continued to assert itself independently of the state temperance organization. The preceding June, the Michigan legislature had enacted a "Wisconsin Law." This legislation abolished the license system but permitted liquor retailers to continue selling spirits in quantities under twenty-eight gallons so long as they posted two sureties and paid a bond of between $500 and $1,000 biennially—or annually, at the option of local officials. Anyone who suffered damages as a result of the sale of liquor could then file a lawsuit against the bond's principal and sureties.[52]

51. Records of the Phoenix Division, September 4, 11, 18, 1848, January 29, February 12, May 14, 1849, February 27, 1851; *Washtenaw Whig*, January 29, 1851; *Michigan Argus*, April 2, 1851.

52. *Michigan Christian Herald*, January 28, 1848, March 16, 1849; Records of the Phoenix Division of the Sons of Temperance, January 8, 29, December 17, 1849, January 27, 1851; *Washtenaw*

Delegates to the Michigan State Temperance Society in October 1851 endorsed the "Temperance law of the State of Maine," but they did not push for its passage in Michigan. Instead, they praised Michigan's "present law in relation to the traffic in intoxicating drinks, as a valuable advance on any previous legislation upon this subject" and requested that Michigan's temperance devotees actively support the existing statute. In February 1852, the state's few remaining Sons of Temperance embraced the Maine Law and urged the enactment of similar legislation in Michigan. But it was not until the following June that temperance forces began widespread agitation for complete prohibition in Michigan.[53]

Shortly after the Michigan State Temperance Society called for a meeting to be held in Detroit in July to discuss the possibility of embracing "more stringent" legal measures, thirty residents of Manchester affixed their names to an announcement for a "mass meeting" in that village to "discuss the propriety and practicability of adopting the MAINE LAW." Following an address by James W. Hill, those present endorsed a resolution that deemed the passage of the Maine Law in Michigan to be of "paramount interest to all other questions of State policy now pending" and pledged to "support no person as a Member of the Legislature whose sentiments are not known to be in favor of such a law." Eight days later, Hill advocated the Maine Law in Ann Arbor, and prohibitionists there adopted a resolution favoring it. A second "mass temperance meeting" was later scheduled for August, when speakers were to explain why the Maine Law was necessary for Michigan, after which planners expected to "adopt such measures as will secure the passage of a similar law in our own state."

Support for the passage of the Maine Law in Michigan continued to swell, not only among temperance proponents, but among politicians as well. Many leading and rank-and-file members of both the Whigs and Democrats in Michigan were active in temperance and endorsed prohibition, but neither party had been willing to take a position on temperance, fearing the loss of

Whig, November 19, 1851; Slavcheff, "Temperate Republic," 205; Clark F. Norton, "Early Michigan Supreme Court Decisions on the Liquor Question," *Michigan History,* XXVIII (January–March 1944), 44. Regarding the implementation and enforcement of the Wisconsin Law in the city of Ann Arbor, see Records of the City of Ann Arbor, October 16, 1851 (p. 34), October 17, 1844 (p. 35), October 20, 1851 (p. 36), Bentley Library.

53. *Washtenaw Whig,* November 19, 1851; *Michigan Argus,* February 25, 1852; Slavcheff, "Temperate Republic," 210.

drinkers' votes. Further, the disastrous consequences of injecting the issue into politics during the late 1830s had left partisans reluctant to do so again. In 1852, however, widespread enthusiasm for the Maine Law brought the question into that year's gubernatorial campaign. Democrat Robert M. McClelland and Whig Zachariah Chandler both answered the entreaties of the Michigan State Temperance Society and acknowledged that they would sign a Maine Law bill if it passed the legislature, while Free Democrat Isaac P. Christiancy pledged not only to sign such a bill, but also to pressure the solons to enact one.[54]

Following the November election, Maine Law enthusiasm continued to grow. The *Michigan Free Democrat* reported in late December that throughout the state, "our correspondents express an earnest purpose and strong confidence on the part of the people" to secure a similar law from the next legislature, and claimed that the public was eagerly signing prohibitionist petitions. The *Michigan Argus* reported in January that 40,000 names had already been submitted to the legislature. By the end of the legislative session, the signatures of more than 100,000 men, women, and children—or one-fifth of the state's population—had been gathered by prohibitionists. The prohibitionist law was signed by Governor McClelland on February 12, 1853. It was virtually identical to the law enacted in Maine in 1851—although voters were to determine its final approval in a referendum in June.[55] If approved, the law would take effect in December 1853; if rejected by the voters, it would nevertheless become binding in 1870.

Partisans of prohibition continued their well-organized campaign in preparation for the June referendum. In late April, proponents of the Maine Law planned to meet at the courthouse in Ann Arbor to establish the political machinery to make certain that temperance voters made it to the polls. Throughout the state, the upcoming election was a constant subject of discussion in

---

54. *Washtenaw Whig,* June 2, 16, August 11, October 20, 1852; *Michigan Argus,* October 27, 1852; *Michigan Free Democrat,* September 7, 1852; Slavcheff, "Temperate Republic," 212–16. The most significant opposition to the enactment of the Maine Law came from the Detroit *Free Press.* Formisano, *Birth of Mass Political Parties,* 230–31.

55. *Michigan Free Democrat,* December 29, 1852; *Michigan Argus,* January 26, 1853; Slavcheff, "Temperate Republic," 218, 223. See also "Narrative of the State of Religion in the Church of Webster—to the Presbytery of Washtenaw," in James Dubuar Papers, Bentley Library, dated February 1, 1853: "The church, & with few exceptions, the community around us, have asked of our legislature the passage of a law prohibiting the sale of intoxicating drinks."

newspaper columns. Most papers, both Whig and Democrat, favored passage of the law. The Democratic Detroit *Free Press* was the principal dissenter from this emerging consensus. The Ypsilanti *Sentinel* accused the *Free Press* of endeavoring to give prohibition "a party character, hoping thereby to rally the democratic majority against it" and vilified the Detroit paper for being "so destitute of philanthropy as to oppose, violently, the adoption of this benevolent enactment." Although prior to the election the *Free Press* continually carried editorials and letters opposed to the passage of the referendum, it denied the *Sentinel*'s charges and called prohibition a "moral question" that would "retard rather than advance the cause of temperance." In contrast, the Democratic *Michigan Argus* displayed an ambivalence on prohibition, as the paper was silent on the referendum until June 8, when it called attention to the upcoming election and merely asked its readers to give the issue thorough consideration. The following week, though, it published a letter from "H." urging readers to vote for prohibition, reminding them of the social consequences of intemperance, and disabusing them of the rumor that the Maine Law would prohibit the manufacture of nonfermented cider. The Maine Law was overwhelmingly approved by Michigan voters, 40,449 to 23,054 (63.7 percent), and obtained an even larger proportion of the vote in Washtenaw County, where it won by 3,162 to 1,444 (68.6 percent), losing only in the lightly populated townships of Bridgewater, Dexter, Freedom, and Lyndon. Although turnout was lower than in the November 1852 United States presidential contest, it was higher than in the township elections the preceding April. Statewide, the measure did best in large towns and in highly developed agricultural areas.[56]

Determined not to have another prohibitory law become ineffective, and undoubtedly recalling the unwillingness of municipal governments to prosecute the violators of such laws, temperance activists throughout the state—in advance of the implementation of the new law on December 1, 1853—formed the Carson League. In each local Carson League, members contributed to a common fund that would be used to defray the expense of prosecuting people who manufactured or sold alcoholic beverages. One Carson League covered

56. *Washtenaw Whig*, April 6, 1853; Ypsilanti *Sentinel*, quoted in Detroit *Free Press*, June 15, 1853; see also Detroit *Free Press*, June 16, 17, 18, 1853; Slavcheff, "Temperate Republic," 223–25; Formisano, *Birth of Mass Political Parties*, 230–31; *Michigan Argus*, June 8, 15, 1853; Quist, "Social and Moral Reform," 567–68. The position of the *Washtenaw Whig* on the Maine Law election is unknown, as there are no extant copies of this paper for the two months prior to the June 20, 1853, election.

the city and township of Ann Arbor and the townships of Northfield, Superior, and Salem. Its members were morally earnest individuals who proclaimed that the creation of this body arose "from our obligation as men, and duties as parents and citizens, and our responsibilities as Christians." By February 1854, prosecutions of violators were proceeding in Ann Arbor and Ypsilanti. These actions, however, were frustrated early that month when the Michigan Supreme Court split 4–4 on the Maine Law's constitutionality. This decision, as well as two others by the court, left the status of the law murky and effectively gutted the measure. As a result of this first ruling, the *Washtenaw Whig* recognized that the "anomalous state of affairs" would cause prohibitionists "much difficulty in attempting to enforce" the Maine Law and expected that the present law would "most likely be suffered to remain in quiescence until the meeting of the next Legislature." The *Whig*'s prescience was confirmed the following week when it reported that prosecutions in Ann Arbor were effectively halted after countersuits were instituted against the constables who arrested the violators and seized their alcohol. In one instance, after the justice of the peace presiding over the case proclaimed the Maine Law to be unconstitutional, the jury ruled in favor of the liquor seller. In Ypsilanti, confusion on the issue led liquor sellers and prosecutors to reach a compromise: those trafficking in liquor were to cease selling it, and each side would incur its own legal costs.[57]

The changed sentiment toward prohibition was revealed by the outcome of township elections in early April. According to the *Argus,* the Maine Law was the principal issue in the elections, and "in a large majority" of places, "the opponents of the law have triumphed." For the *Argus,* the most striking election was in Kalamazoo, where Maine Law opponents, who had lost the referendum the previous June, won by a hundred votes. A few weeks later, the *Argus,* which claimed that Whigs and Free Soilers had been endeavoring to politicize the Maine Law, asserted that these parties' newspapers—in particular the Whigs'—were retreating in light of the law's perceived repudiation.

---

57. *Washtenaw Whig,* November 16, 1853, February 8, 15, March 22, 1854; Tyrrell, *Sobering Up,* 293–96; Clark Norton, "Early Michigan Supreme Court Decisions," 48–60; *John J. Ortman, plaintiff in error,* v. *William B. Greenman et al., defendants in error,* 4 Michigan Reports 291–294 (1856). In 1856, the Michigan Supreme Court censured the Ann Arbor judge for declaring the Maine Law unconstitutional. John J. Ortman, the liquor seller who successfully prevailed in the Ann Arbor court in 1854 and the Michigan Supreme Court in 1856, was represented by Olney Hawkins. In 1860, Hawkins publicly protested the lax enforcement in Ann Arbor of municipal and state liquor laws. *Ibid.;* Ann Arbor *Journal,* February 22, 1860.

The Michigan State Temperance Society recognized by late April that the new law had been gutted beyond repair, and urged the friends of prohibition to interrogate each political candidate on this issue and to vote for no one who would not "publicly pledge himself to support by his vote and influence, the passage and enforcement of such a law."[58]

The most significant political development in Michigan in 1854, though, was not the evisceration of the Maine Law but the demise of the Whig and Free Soil Parties and the creation of a fusion movement that became the Republican Party. Riding upon opposition to the Kansas-Nebraska Act, hostility to the South, nativism, and widespread dissatisfaction with the Democrats— who had held the governorship and both legislative branches since the 1841 elections—Republicans swept into office in November. Although they did not explicitly incorporate the passage of another Maine Law into their platform— reckoning, undoubtedly, that the results of that year's township elections proved prohibition to be a fickle issue among the voters—the large number of temperance partisans in the Republican Party nonetheless created a general perception that fusionists were the "Maine Law Party" and that the Democrats were the "Whiskey Party."[59] Consequently, expectations were high that a new law would be enacted.

Of course, both the Republican and Democratic Parties were broad-based coalitions, and each contained wets and drys. In Ann Arbor, Elihu Pond, the Democratic editor of the *Michigan Argus,* was a prohibitionist who urged the friends of temperance to petition the legislature for a new Maine Law, as "legislative bodies are not in the habit of conferring favors unsolicited. We believe there is no trouble in passing a constitutional effective liquor law, one that will restrain the traffic in Alcoholic preparations as a beverage and yet not prevent their free sale for medicinal and mechanical purposes." The *Washtenaw Whig,* edited by Stephen B. McCracken, was more ambivalent. Following the November 1854 Republican victory, McCracken—a former officer of the Ann Arbor Division of the Sons of Temperance and an early supporter of the 1853

58. *Michigan Argus,* April 13, 27, May 4, 1854. Prohibition was not an issue in the Ann Arbor city election in April 1854; in this election, Whigs and Free Democrats ran a fusion ticket that presaged the formation of the Michigan Republican party in July. Fusionists won in Ann Arbor City and in nine of Washtenaw County's twenty townships. *Ibid.,* March 30, April 6, 1854; *Washtenaw Whig,* March 29, April 5, 1854.

59. Formisano, *Birth of Mass Political Parties,* 239–53; Slavcheff, "Temperate Republic," 254–58.

Maine Law—explained that in light of the state's other pressing needs, the "precious time of the Legislature will be wasted in useless debate" if prohibition were to occupy the solons' attention. "In our opinion, the least said about the 'Maine Liquor Law,' the better," particularly since McCracken expected that any law passed by the legislature would have "some useless provision engrafted upon it which will render it valueless."[60] Even after recognizing that it was "inevitable that the vexed question" of prohibition would "engross" the legislature, McCracken remained steadfast in his opposition. He doubted that "any law for that purpose can be made even measurably effective," preferred a return to the license system, and with respect to "cider, beer, ale, and porter," could see "no good reason for restricting their use by law." In February 1855 the legislature passed a new prohibitory act outlawing the sale of distilled liquor. Manufacture of alcohol for industrial use was permitted, though, and bonded druggists were allowed to sell it for medicinal purposes. The production and sale of wine and cider in quantities over one gallon and ten gallons, respectively, were exempted.[61]

Expecting this law to be enforced effectively, A. DeForest announced in an advertisement headlined MAINE LAW in late April that he was cutting his prices on wines and liquors in order to eliminate his stock prior to the May 14, 1855, implementation. With a new editorial team that included longtime temperance devotee Lorenzo Davis, the *Washtenaw Whig* joined the *Argus* in welcoming the law. Both papers reported that the law was generally obeyed during its first month, although the *Whig* warned one violator to change his ways, "for we are inclined to think that the Maine Law is on your track, and by your peculiar scent, will smell you out. So look out old chap." The *Argus* also defended the law against charges that drinking only increased with the onset of prohibition. Simple observation revealed that there had been an improvement, as "exclusive drinking shops" had "all been closed," liquor sales were "no longer the leading business in *groceries*," and drunken assemblages had disappeared. In endorsing the Maine Law, however, the *Whig* touched upon an element that even some proponents of the law found potentially troubling. While the *Whig*

60. *Michigan Argus,* December 22, 1854; *Washtenaw Whig,* November 29, 1854. McCracken was a Whig who was never comfortable with the Republican party, and later edited newspapers in Ann Arbor and Ypsilanti for the American and Democratic parties, respectively. *Ibid.,* July 18, 1856, June 22, 1860.

61. *Washtenaw Whig,* December 13, 20, 1854, February 14, 1855; Slavcheff, "Temperate Republic," 258.

urged prohibitionists to "stand up in defence of our law and see that its provisions are carried out," it also counseled them to "be careful and not encourage insubordination to the law, by harsh and overbearing measures, when, by mild and persistent efforts, we may secure the end we desire." In particular, the *Whig* feared a repetition of the recent Chicago riots, where violence stemming from antiprohibition protests left one dead and several wounded.[62]

The *Whig* proved to be prescient. In early June, Americans were shocked by the violence in Portland, Maine, where Mayor Neal Dow, father of the Maine Law, ordered the city's militia to fire upon a mob angered by his illicit purchase of liquor intended for medicinal and industrial purposes. Seven of the antiprohibitionists were wounded and one was killed.[63] Antiprohibitionists in Michigan flaunted the Portland riot as evidence that a police state was the consequence of the Maine Law. In many places, this allegation alone resulted in diminished support for prohibition in Michigan. Particularly opprobrious were the Maine Law's search and seizure provisions, which gave public officials considerable powers of enforcement.[64]

Not unexpectedly, committed prohibitionists remained steadfast. Elihu Pond defended Neal Dow's actions, charging that the "mob was raised, not upon the spur of the moment, but by a pre-concerted arrangement," and that it then took the law into its own hands in an effort "to prevent the new law from going into operation." Pond felt that public debate ought not to focus on the legitimacy of the Maine Law or whether Dow had acted properly in purchasing liquor for the city of Portland, but on the "infuriated mob." Even if Dow had

62. *Michigan Argus*, April 27, May 11, 18, June 15, 1855; *Washtenaw Whig*, May 2, 13, 1855; Tyrrell, *Sobering Up*, 296.

63. Under prohibition in Maine, municipalities were empowered to appoint bonded agents who were in turn permitted to sell liquor only for medicinal and industrial uses. Dow purchased $1,600 of liquor before the Portland City Council had appointed a city agent, and his political and anti-prohibitionist enemies charged that Dow had speculated in this liquor for his own profit. After knowledge of this liquor purchase became general, a mob formed outside of city hall, where the liquor was stored, and demanded its immediate destruction, which, according to state law, was the required consequence of all confiscated alcohol purchased illegally. Following prolonged stone-throwing by the mob upon the militia, and after several rioters had broken into the place where the liquor was stored, Dow instructed his forces to shoot. The irony of Neal Dow's using armed force to defend improperly—if not illegally—purchased liquor was not lost upon antiprohibitionists. Tyrrell, *Sobering Up*, 295–96; Blocker, *American Temperance Movements*, 30–34.

64. Slavcheff, "Temperate Republic," 261–63.

erred in purchasing the alcohol, Pond reminded his readers that "there was a remedy, but not in a mob." In July, Pond further demonstrated his commitment to prohibition when he protested the attacks by the Detroit *Free Press* upon newspapers that differed with its antiprohibitionist position. Pond denied that the position of the *Free Press* represented the view of the members of the state's Democratic Party: "The mass of democrats of the State, not as democrats, *but as individuals,* are in favor of a law prohibiting the traffic in alcoholic liquors as a beverage." And while acknowledging that the law was "not fully enforced," Pond asserted that it was "accomplishing much good," as "the open traffic is done away with, and liquor rows and public drunkenness are numbered among the things that were." The renamed Ann Arbor *Journal and Washtenaw Whig* also took exception to the antiprohibitionist position of the *Free Press* and the Pontiac *Jacksonian* and praised the effect of prohibition upon "public health [and] public morale."[65]

Despite such staunch defense of the Maine Law, the number of violations increased throughout the state in the months following the Portland riot, and by the end of 1855, the law was widely ignored. In September, the *Journal and Washtenaw Whig* published an editorial, "A Lecture to Loafers," that blasted the town's young men who loitered "about the grocery and liquor stores" and harangued paying customers for a "treat." The following month, the Washtenaw County Board of Supervisors refused to pay the costs of "prosecuting violators of the liquor law," as the board maintained that the law was not constitutional. This decision was rebuked by the *Journal,* which insisted that the board was motivated by politics, as two unreconstructed Whigs and "two of the strongest kind of Democrats" had voted not to pay for liquor-law prosecution. It was the board's responsibility to sustain the law "and not seek to nulify [*sic*] the acts of our legislators by this extra-judicial mode of operation." The *Journal* felt certain that the law would in the end be approved by the Michigan Supreme Court.[66]

In March 1856, in *The People* v. *Thomas Gallagher,* the Michigan Supreme Court sustained the authority of the legislature to prohibit the manufacture and sale of liquor, but in another decision eviscerated the law by striking down its search and seizure provisions. Moreover, a growing number of Michigan-

---

65. *Michigan Argus,* June 22, July 27, 1855; Ann Arbor *Journal and Washtenaw Whig,* August 22, 1855. See also *Washtenaw Whig,* August 8, 1855.

66. Slavcheff, "Temperate Republic," 266; Ann Arbor *Journal and Washtenaw Whig,* September 12, 1855; Ann Arbor *Journal,* October 31, 1855.

ders wanted the court to overturn all prohibitionist legislation completely. Democrats in the township of Dexter in late March 1856 denounced the court's decision in *People* v. *Gallagher* as a "full endorsement of the fusion Legislature Liquor Law" and an affirmation that the solons "may exercise any power, however despotic, tyrannical, oppressive, and unjust, which the Constitution does not in express terms prohibit to them." Also in late March, Ann Arbor City Democrats passed a resolution that "entirely" disapproved of the Maine Law and called for its repeal and for replacing it with a "well-regulated license system, under such restrictions as will effectively subserve the cause of temperance." The *Argus,* still edited by Maine Law devotee Elihu Pond, did not print this resolution. Its existence was thus stressed by Lorenzo Davis of the Ann Arbor *Journal,* who doubted whether "rank and file" Democrats would "swallow and support" the resolution and gloated over the inconsistency between party regulars and their newspaper editor on this important issue.[67]

If the Maine Law was a compelling issue among the city of Ann Arbor's electorate, then they gave their votes to the party that favored its repeal, as the Republicans lost all but one of the city's fourteen electoral races in April 1856. *Argus* editor Pond also had the last word with respect to Republican allegations that the Democratic constituency held prohibitionist views at variance with those of their party leaders. Prior to the election, Pond asked how either of the *Journal'*s editors could "consistently be a Maine Law man and yet vote the Republican City ticket?" He insinuated that there were more temperance partisans and fewer sellers of liquor among Democrats than among Republicans. Pond's commitment to the Maine Law did not wane. Later, when the Detroit *Tribune* charged him as a hypocrite who mouthed pieties about the Maine Law and proceeded to vote for politicians who promoted its repeal, Pond countered that the *Tribune'*s editor was among those *"model* temperance men . . . who advocate prohibition for political purposes, and take a glass of grog at every saloon they come to. These are the kind of temperance men which have ruined the cause of prohibition. Their interested harping has done a hundred fold more to make prohibition unpopular than the opposition of all the open enemies in the State."[68]

Democrats in Dexter Township and Ann Arbor City were not the only

67. Slavcheff, "Temperate Republic," 266, 364 n. 109; *Michigan Argus,* April 4, 1856; Ann Arbor *Journal,* March 26, April 2, 1856; *The People,* v. *Thomas Gallagher,* 4 Michigan Reports 244–285 (1856).

68. *Michigan Argus,* April 4, 11, May 2, 1856.

members of their party demanding the repeal of the Maine Law; other local caucuses throughout the state called for repeal in April 1856. At its statewide convention in August, the divided party endeavored to take a middling position on the Maine Law so that Democrats could campaign on either side of the issue. Significantly, this was the first occasion in which a major political party in the state had addressed temperance in its platform. The Republicans, however, who made no mention of liquor control in their party's resolutions, captured over 57 percent of the vote and handed Michigan's Democrats their worst antebellum political defeat. The following year, the Republican-led legislature, recognizing the diminished public support for the Maine Law, further enfeebled it by repealing the search and seizure provisions of the 1855 law—thus affirming the Michigan Supreme Court's decision of the previous year—and also permitted the unlimited sale and production of wine, cider, and beer. Although spirits remained prohibited, the new measure represented a major setback for legal suasionists. Among those who mourned its passage was the Reverend J. S. Smart, a Methodist minister in Ypsilanti, whose sentiments were recorded in his pamphlet *Funeral Sermon of the Maine Law and Its Off-spring in Michigan.*[69]

Other temperance regulars continued ardently committed to the Maine Law. In a debate before Ann Arbor's Young Men's Association in May 1858, Donald McIntyre, who later served as president of the Michigan State Temperance Society, set forth "in an elaborate speech . . . the superior advantages of the law of 1855 over that of 1857 to suppress drunkenness." The Ann Arbor *Journal* was in complete agreement with McIntyre, maintaining that the supremacy of the Maine Law "was entirely unanswerable." The *Journal* argued that the provisions of the 1857 law allowing for the sale of wine, cider, and beer were counterproductive: "The fact is there is no middle ground upon this subject. Total abstinence is the true ground, and whatever effort may be made by friends of the law . . . must be made upon this principle or it will fail of success." A year later the Michigan State Temperance Society proclaimed that although it favored a "thorough enforcement of the present law," it continued to stand behind the 1855 Maine Law and, of course, demanded "restoring that clause in relation to wine, beer and cider, which was stricken out by the Legislature of 1857."[70]

69. Slavcheff, "Temperate Republic," 267–68, 364 n. 110; *Michigan Argus,* September 18, 1857, May 14, 1858.

70. Ann Arbor *Journal,* May 26, 1858; *Michigan Argus,* May 14, 1858, July 1, 1859.

The demise of the Maine Law did not mean that prohibitionists surrendered or that municipal efforts to control liquor retreated entirely. Shortly after the 1857 liquor law took effect, the city of Ann Arbor passed an ordinance that prohibited the sale or distribution of intoxicants to minors without the written consent of a parent or guardian, or to anyone "already drunk," and affixed heavy fines and jail sentences to multiple offenders. City officials took this ordinance seriously enough to prosecute offenders during the subsequent months. In December 1857, though, the University of Michigan faculty complained that too many students were still purchasing liquor. Consequently, the city council pledged to do "all in our power to remedy the evils complained of" and to direct the mayor to prosecute "whenever such proof is offered him, as will in his opinion ensure a conviction of the offender." The collection of evidence remained a major stumbling block to the enforcement of this and other liquor laws.[71]

Aside from such municipal efforts at liquor control, temperance activity in Washtenaw County was nonexistent following the passage of the 1857 law. In fact, the existence of temperance societies was not mentioned in Washtenaw's newspapers for almost four years after the enactment of the 1855 Maine Law. It is easy to imagine that many rank-and-file temperance enthusiasts considered their work completed once the Maine Law was implemented, reasoned that enforcement was the responsibility of municipal authorities, and then became dispirited following the Portland riots, the successful legal challenges to the 1855 law, and the passage of the watered-down 1857 law. These defeats, piled on top of one another, resulted in the most serious downturn of the county's antebellum temperance activism. Because temperance enthusiasm waned throughout the country during the late 1850s, some scholars have attributed this decline to the increased preoccupation with sectionalism. But across the nation, prohibitionists were either defeated when they tried to implement their measures, or found them unenforceable once passed into law. Like temperance promoters in Washtenaw and Tuscaloosa Counties, enthusiasts elsewhere were probably smitten with discouragement following the failure of their most vigilant effort to date.[72]

71. Ann Arbor City Council Minutes, May 11, 1857 (p. 209), December 11, 1857 (p. 226), December 29, 1857 (p. 227), May 17, 1858 (p. 241), May 24, 1858 (p. 244), in Bentley Library; *Michigan Argus*, September 25, 1857; Peckham, *Making of the University of Michigan*, 42.

72. Both Dannenbaum, *Drink and Disorder*, 173, and Lender and Martin, *Drinking in America*, 85, attribute the movement's decline in the late 1850s to increasing sectionalism, whereas Nor-

In late 1858, however, temperance in Ypsilanti finally received a boost with the formation of the Ypsilanti Total Abstinence Society, which announced that the "present alarming increase of intemperance, and its accompanying evils" was "scarcely less alarming" than the widespread apathy among "temperance men, and women." The cause, however, was not vibrant elsewhere in the county, as the Ypsilanti society's "desideratum" of forming a "County Society with its various Town and District auxiliaries" failed to materialize. Statewide, temperance took a beating as well: the state society itself had at that time become inoperative. It was resurrected the following June when a circular endorsed by forty-six of the state's temperance enthusiasts called for a meeting in Jackson to discuss the "general interests of the cause" and "re organizing (if deemed desireable,) the State Temperance Society." Those present at the Jackson meeting urged that the county and town auxiliaries be formed. A year later the reinvigorated state body broke with its past by framing a new constitution and renaming itself the Michigan State Temperance Alliance.[73]

Concurrent with the rebirth of the state temperance body, the Ann Arbor *Journal* complained about the vandalism and other "drunken frolics" of youths, which were greatly offensive to the "sober minded thinking and intelligent portion of the community." Shortly afterward, the Ann Arbor City Temperance Society was formed and commenced meeting on Sunday afternoons in the city's Protestant churches. The principal objective of the temperance movement in Ann Arbor, however, shortly became advocating the enforcement of the existing laws. On July 5, 1859, "a number of citizens" concerned about the "present state of the morals of this place and of the University particularly, in regard to intemperance" assembled. They later issued a report that, like many proclamations by similar bodies during the previous three decades, identified their cause with the city's prosperity, described the "habitual use of ardent spirits" as "the greatest curse of our land," and claimed that it was their obligation to "do all in our power to abolish it." But rather than resolve to carry their message to the intemperate or to call upon lawmakers to frame a new law, the group announced that present "laws and city ordinances, if properly en-

---

man H. Clark, *Deliver Us from Evil: An Interpretation of American Prohibition* (New York, 1976), 48–49, believes that prohibition waned because the movement lacked a political sponsor after the collapse of the Whig Party. Tyrrell, *Sobering Up*, 307, favors a position similar to the one presented here.

73. Ann Arbor *Journal*, December 8, 1858; *Michigan Argus*, June 10, July 1, 1859, February 10, 1860.

forced, are sufficient to entirely eradicate the evil"; urged city officers "to prosecute all glaring breaches of the law"—particularly those liquor sellers "who habitually sell to or harbor drunkards," who sold liquor on the Sabbath, and who permitted gambling on their premises; and pledged never again to vote for city council candidates who continued to cast their lot "with the opposers of morality."[74]

At a February 1860 meeting, concerned citizens again praised the existing law, but complained that there was no "efficient mode . . . for enforcing it," particularly since, as they maintained, public officers were "elected by sellers and consumers of ardent spirits." Especially disappointing to this group was the continued unauthorized sale of liquor to minors. The attendance at the meeting of University of Michigan president Henry P. Tappan—who was himself a drinker of wine and had opposed the Maine Law in 1854—suggests that drinking by university students and Ann Arbor's statewide image were what most concerned these citizens. Those present insisted that city officials enforce the local ordinance forbidding the sale of liquor to minors, and they urged liquor traffickers to abide by this restriction (some retailers reportedly agreed, provided that other retailers in the city would do the same).[75]

In subsequent weeks, several meetings were held in Ann Arbor to protest illegal liquor sales and again call upon municipal authorities to enforce the laws. This constant flow of activity caused the city's mayor, attorney, and marshal, along with the county prosecuting attorney, to declare "themselves ready to enforce the laws of our state and ordinance of our city relative to [the] sale of intoxicating drinks." But again, because of difficulties in procuring evidence without the search and seizure provisions of the 1855 Maine Law, even the cooperation of the legal authorities was insufficient to eradicate the sale of intoxicants. Thus following a "meeting of the citizens of Ann Arbor," a three-member committee selected "one hundred persons, good men and true, to act as a vigilance committee, to report to the proper officers all violations" of state

74. Ann Arbor *Journal*, June 1, 1859; *Michigan Argus*, June 10, 24, July 1, 22, 1859. A speaker before one of the society's meetings complained that there were thirty-nine places in Ann Arbor "where intoxicating drinks are sold," and lamented that the eighty-two employees of these establishments outnumbered the city's shoemakers, clothiers, and merchants. *Young Men's Temperance Journal and Advocate of Temperance* (Detroit), September 10, 1859.

75. Ann Arbor *Journal*, February 22, 1860; Andrew Ten Brook to *New York Baptist Register*, June 30, 1854, in Andrew Ten Brook Papers, Bentley Library (typescript); Peckham, *Making of the University of Michigan*, 40; Marwil, *Ann Arbor*, 39, 46.

and local liquor laws. This method proved, for a while at least, to be effective, as by the end of April 1860 the *Argus* reported that "quite a number of suits are pending in court." The editor was pleased to add that "the evidence is positive, and conviction morally certain." Perhaps the best measure of the success of this rejuvenated temperance drive was the announcement of a meeting to be held in May, where "the friends of sobriety, peace, good order, and a due observance of law" were to discuss "whether the rumsellers shall escape their just desserts" after threatening the assistant city marshal with placards "ordering him to select his gravestone, and threatening to send him to 'h——ll' if he should continue faithful to the discharge of his official duty."[76]

The power of this movement, however, was limited. In June former Michigan governor Alpheus Felch submitted a petition signed by him and 1,583 others to the Ann Arbor City Council, requesting that Ann Arbor's "Drinking and Gaming Saloons" be closed on Sunday—which measure the council eventually laid upon the table. Later that year, county citizens petitioned the Washtenaw County Board of Supervisors, asking that the board and the supervisors in their respective townships be more diligent in enforcing the liquor laws. Notwithstanding this agitation, the extent of its success and of the protracted efforts of Ann Arborites to control the sale of liquor is perhaps best attested to by a comment in the *Michigan Argus* in February 1861: "It is said that the stringent City ordinance prohibiting the sale of liquors to minors is being daily violated. Parents should call upon City authorities for its enforcement."[77] By this date, Washtenaw County's temperance movement—particularly Ann Arbor's—had undergone considerable evolution. Beginning as a moral suasion effort, then mutating into a prohibitionist crusade, it had by the late 1850s and early 1860s finally altered into an informal endeavor to secure the enforcement of existing liquor laws.

As in the temperance crusade in Tuscaloosa County, the activity of women in the movement in Washtenaw is difficult to measure due to the paucity of pri-

---

76. *Michigan Argus,* March 9, 1860 (see also February 24, March 2, 1860); Ann Arbor *Journal,* February 29, March 7, 14, 21, 1860; *Michigan Argus,* April 27, May 18, 1860.

77. Ann Arbor City Council Minutes, June 4, 11, July 2, 1860, in Bentley Library; Ann Arbor *Journal,* November 21, 1860; *Michigan Argus,* November 30, 1860, February 15, 1861. See also Ann Arbor *Journal,* February 22, 1860. Regarding the contest over prohibition in another Michigan community, see Bruce Tap, " 'The Evils of Intemperance Are Universally Conceded': The Temperance Debate in Early Grand Rapids," *Michigan Historical Review,* XIX (Spring 1993), 17–45.

mary sources that describe their role and efforts. Fragmentary evidence shows that Washtenaw women, like their Tuscaloosa counterparts, were not excluded from the earliest temperance meetings: notices in the *Western Emigrant* in 1830 announced that both "ladies and gentlemen" were invited to attend. In 1835 the *Michigan Whig* listed the names of all 118 members of the Mill Creek Temperance Society, 59 of whom were women. Concurrently, the leading resolution of the Washtenaw County Temperance Society acknowledged that the cause "has been greatly promoted by the influence of women" and speculated that if the effects of women in the movement were extended, the triumph of temperance "would be certain, and its benefits extended to all future generations." But for the most part, the men who wrote reports of temperance societies for local newspapers scarcely mentioned the activities of women. And often when women were mentioned, it was only in terms of their importance in encouraging men to be sober. Their supporting role took several forms. At an Independence Day celebration in 1841, several of Ann Arbor's leading moral men spoke, while "the Ladies of the village . . . provided a bountiful supply of refreshments." In Augusta the following year, Justin Marsh reported that "most of our young men" were initially opposed to temperance, "but in part by the influence of the young ladies, but more especially by the Spirit of God, they have relinquished their opposition and joined the Society." A visitor to Ann Arbor's Mechanics' Temperance Society in 1845 praised the number of women in attendance. Because women as a group felt the brunt of intemperance most severely, their interest "augurs well for the cause and for themselves. . . . Let their presence ever uphold the arms of laborers in their behalf." Although the Sons of Temperance did not initiate women into the order, women were often called upon to make regalia and to repair "the carpet and the fixtures" of the meeting hall at the Phoenix Division in Dexter village, and this division occasionally planned social activities that included the women of the village. In a public ceremony in Ann Arbor, "the Ladies of [the] village" presented one division there with "an elegant Bible."[78]

In contrast to Tuscaloosa County, though, in Washtenaw County women

78. *Western Emigrant,* February 17, May 19, 1830; *Michigan Whig,* February 12, 1835; *Michigan State Journal,* July 6, 1841; Justin Marsh to AHMS, March 21, 1842, in AHMS Papers; *Signal of Liberty,* March 24, 1845; Records of the Ann Arbor Congregational Ladies' Sewing Society, Vol. I, 11–14, in Records of the First Congregational Church of Ann Arbor, Bentley Library; Records of the Phoenix Division No. 79, August 14, September 4, December 4, 1848, April 23, 30, 1849, June 24, 1850; *Michigan Argus,* September 15, 1847. Women were also explicitly invited to a Maine Law meeting in 1852. *Washtenaw Whig,* August 11, 1852.

were far more likely to form their own temperance associations and to engage in female-sponsored direct action against liquor retailers. Such activity occurred on several levels. According to the *Washtenaw Whig*, some women in Saline became distraught over their husbands' late hours and heavy drinking, which occurred whenever the men assembled to play euchre. After they "put their heads together," these women "gently administered" a rebuke to their husbands and persuaded them to desist. But women in Washtenaw County engaged in public activity as well, although it was not until the spring of 1846 that women's temperance associations commenced activity. In May, Alonzo Hyde, a Washingtonian and the agent of the State Temperance Society, spent a week in Ann Arbor holding temperance meetings; he also organized a Martha Washington Temperance Society—later officially designated as the Ladies' Total Abstinence Benevolent Society of Ann Arbor—which soon had four hundred female members. This society complained that the intemperance of men too often "beggarded" their wives and "converted into an earthly hell the once lovely home with all its endearments." Because of these afflictions, "woman . . . should feel herself called upon to go forth in the spirit of kindness, to reclaim the inebriate, to clothe, educate, and comfort all who by fault or otherwise are feeling in their own person the withering curse of dissipation, and to do all in her power to restore the unfortunate, to all the comforts and joy, the dignity which their nature asks, and the word of God promises." The society's constitution stated that other objectives were to "prevent the manufacture, sale, and use, of intoxicating drinks . . . and in every honorable way to discountenance their use throughout the community." Ann Arbor women were among those who in May 1846 pleaded with the village's liquor retailers to comply with the local no-license ordinance and cease the sale of alcohol.[79]

Hyde also organized a women's temperance society in Dexter village; it numbered ninety-six members within two months. These women confronted the village's liquor sellers, asking them to cease the sale of all intoxicants. Some dealers initially promised only to cease selling liquor if others did the same, but a few purportedly complied with the entreaties of the women. N. A. Bronson, secretary of Dexter's Ladies' Temperance Society, reported with glee that as a

79. *Washtenaw Whig*, October 13, 1854; *Michigan Argus*, April 23, 1835; *Michigan Temperance Journal and Washingtonian*, I (April 15, 1846), 27; *Michigan Argus*, May 20, 1846; *True Democrat*, June 4, 1846; *Michigan State Journal*, June 3, 17, 1846; *Signal of Liberty*, May 23, 1846. See also New York *Pearl*, June 27, 1846, as cited by Tyrrell, "Women and Temperance," 142. Unfortunately, only 19 officers of these 400 women could be identified by name, and these officers proved difficult to link with other sources.

result of the increased interest in temperance in Dexter, liquor had lost all respectability and retailers now sold spirits clandestinely so as to "avoid the disapprobation of the multitude, or to elude the prosecuting committee of the Washingtonian society." Theodore Foster of the *Signal of Liberty* lauded the emergence of female temperance societies but suggested that not everyone shared his enthusiasm: "Success to the ladies, we say. We are glad to see them at work for the substantial benefit of society.—Let no aristocratic old bachelor sneer at them as being out of their place."[80]

Primary evidence of other actions conducted by women is scarce. Fernando Jones, editor of the Jackson-based *Michigan Temperance Journal and Washingtonian*, however, placed a number of essays in his monthly publication that were directed toward women, and occasionally collected such writings under the heading "Ladies' Department." Jones praised the commitment of women to temperance and contrasted them to men, whose zeal was often ephemeral and whose effectiveness was frequently diminished as a result of debates over means. Jones also endorsed a bill introduced into the Mississippi legislature that would have permitted all women over fourteen to vote on liquor-license questions, reasoning that if "the ladies" were granted this privilege, then "authorized tippling shops" would "be scarce as hen teeth." And although Jones in 1847 lamented the disbanding of many Washingtonian societies, he was nevertheless gratified that many "noble *women*" continued "adhering to the counsels of peace, charity, and a steady performance in the line of duty." In October 1854, at the Ann Arbor Congregational church, a Mrs. Shepard spoke "from the heart" in favor of a prohibitory law. Like earlier activists, she argued that many women suffered by their husbands' drunkenness. Following her remarks, "a Ladies Temperance Society was organized, officers elected, and committees appointed." The *Michigan Argus* wished the women Godspeed and hoped that they would "never cease to labor until every husband, son, and brother are reclaimed."[81] Nothing more, though, was recorded of the body.

Undoubtedly other temperance associations of women existed in Washtenaw County whose activities were not recorded for posterity by male newspaper editors. But in contrast, the complete absence of any record of female temperance organizations in Tuscaloosa County and the lack of evidence that they ever participated in any form of direct action, as the women of Ann Arbor

80. *Michigan Temperance Journal and Washingtonian*, I (July 15, 1846), 53; *Signal of Liberty*, May 23, 1846.

81. *Michigan Temperance Journal and Washingtonian*, II (February 1847), 13, I (April 15, 1846), 31; *Michigan Argus*, October 13, 1854.

and Dexter village did when they requested liquor retailers to cease their sales, suggests that women in Washtenaw County were socially less constrained than were their southern sisters.

As with temperance in Tuscaloosa County, different manifestations of the movement attracted different elements of the population in Washtenaw County. The people of the county were not homogeneous. In the countryside, of course, most people were farmers, but the villages of Ann Arbor, Ypsilanti, and Dexter—where most of the county's temperance activity occurred—were understandably dominated by professionals, artisans, and shopkeepers/proprietors. As Israel Branch suggested in his previously cited speech before the Ann Arbor Society for the Promotion of Temperance in 1832, members of the early temperance movement in Washtenaw County were enlisted from the ranks of the social elite. Of the 39 temperance devotees from 1829–1834, the occupations of 28 could be ascertained, of whom 18 (64.3 percent) were professionals (including 5 attorneys and 7 clergy), followed by 5 farmers (17.9 percent), 4 shopkeepers/proprietors (14.3 percent), and 1 artisan (3.6 percent). This group was also the wealthiest of all temperance reformers, with an average real-estate holding in 1850 of $9,992 (median, $3,000). The real-estate holdings of only 13 individuals could be found in the 1850 census, however; their wealth and persistence in Washtenaw County after two decades were probably related to each other.

Only 11 of the 205 traced to the legal suasion campaigns of 1835–40 were also linked to the earlier cohort. Although 59 of these activists were women, no further information is available on virtually all of them; men were easier to associate with other sources. In contrast to the earlier temperance activists, a larger proportion of this group were farmers. Of the 146 males who could be tied to temperance activity between 1835 and 1840, there were 65 with identifiable occupations; the largest segment was farmers (27, or 44.6 percent), followed by professionals (23, or 35.4 percent, including 8 attorneys, 3 editors, and 8 clergy), shopkeepers/proprietors (7, or 10.8 percent), artisans (4, or 6.2 percent), clerks, and other (each with 1, or 1.5 percent, respectively). A contemporaneous cohort of temperance personnel was the 263 male Washtenaw County subscribers to the Ann Arbor–based *Michigan Temperance Herald*, published during 1838 and 1839, to which only one county subscriber was a woman. These subscribers were likewise dominated by farmers. Of the 126 with ascertainable occupations, 52 (41.3 percent) were farmers, followed by 35 (27.8 percent) professionals (including 15 clergy, 13 physicians, 3 judges, and 3 attorneys), 19 artisans (15.1 percent), 13 shopkeepers/proprietors (10.3 percent), 1 laborer (0.8 percent), 2 other (1.6 percent), and 4 (3.2 percent) who had no occupation listed in the 1850 census. Of course, it is not possible to know the extent to which newspaper subscribers were also subscribers to temperance principles. Only 41 of the county's 264 subscribers could be linked to other temperance activity (8 were traced to the 1829–1834 cohort, 18 to the 1835–1840 group, 12 to those active from 1841–1846, 4 to the Sons of Temperance, and 8 to the 1851–1860 prohibitionists)—a much smaller proportion than of abolitionists traced to the *Signal of Liberty*, discussed in chapter 6. Undoubtedly some received the *Michigan Temperance Herald* simply because it was locally published. The geographic distribution of individuals on this subscription list, however, suggests that the temperance cause had many supporters among people whose rural residences precluded them from frequently attending organized temperance activities, which were usually held in villages such as Ann Arbor, Ypsilanti, or Dexter.

The next distinct body of temperance activists was the moral suasionists of 1841 to 1846; only 5 and 9 were linked to the 1829–1834 and 1835–1840 cohorts, respectively. Virtually all of these identified individuals were residents of Ann Arbor, and thus their more urban occupational profile should not be surprising. Of the 85 males and 21 females in this cohort, the occupations of 55 males and the husbands of only 3 females were identified, of whom 28 (48.3 percent) were professionals (including 10 clergy, 5 newspaper editors, and 4 attorneys), followed by artisans and shopkeepers/proprietors (10 each, or 17.2 percent), farmers (8, or 13.8 percent), and clerks and other (1 each, or 1.7 percent). This group of temperance partisans included the Washingtonians. Despite their active presence in Washtenaw County—Ann Arbor in particular—the names of only 32 Washingtonians were culled from various sources.[82] The occupations of only 18 Washingtonians could be traced—7 professionals, 5 farmers, 4 artisans, and 2 shopkeepers/proprietors—which, albeit suggestive that this was not necessarily a working-class temperance organization, is inconclusive because of the lack of data. These data do suggest, though, that Washtenaw's Washingtonians did not draw from the same elite constituency as did their Tuscaloosa counterparts.

Data for the Sons of Temperance, Washtenaw County's subsequent temperance manifestation, are more complete. Although Ann Arbor and Ypsilanti

82. Included in this figure are 15 members of the Mechanics' Temperance Society, a Washingtonian-like group that met in Ann Arbor from 1844 to 1845, and 1 agent for the Jackson-based *Michigan Temperance Journal and Washingtonian*.

newspapers did not celebrate the Sons as much as did the Tuscaloosa *Independent Monitor,* the names of the organization's officers—which positions were
many and spread throughout the membership—were often published in local
papers. Even more useful are the records of Dexter village's Phoenix Division
No. 79 and the "Black Book" of Sons of Temperance—mostly from the Phoenix, Dexter, Ann Arbor, and Huron (Ann Arbor) divisions—whose membership in the order had lapsed because of nonpayment of dues or, sometimes, violation of the teetotal pledge. Both sets of records often list both the ages and
occupations of those connected with this fraternity, and in conjunction with
the 1850 federal census and other sources they enable us to ascertain the occupations of 206 of the 269 identified members of the order:

Occupation	Number	Percent
Artisan	105	51.0
Clerk	8	3.9
Shopkeeper/proprietor	19	9.2
Farmer	30	14.6
Laborer	13	6.3
Professional	21	10.2
Other	6	2.9
Illegible	2	1.0
None listed on census	2	1.0
Totals	206	100.1

The larger extent to which artisans participated in the Sons of Temperance
in comparison to Washtenaw County's other temperance cohorts—and the
smaller percentage of professionals—demonstrates that this order opened
temperance activity to people who had not heretofore participated in the
movement. This point is further underscored in that no Sons of Temperance
members were linked to Washtenaw County's earliest temperance cohort, and
only 6 and 5 were traced to the 1835–1840 and 1841–1846 cohorts, respectively.
The breakdown of professionals in the Sons of Temperance—which included
5 attorneys, 5 newspaper editors, 4 physicians, and 4 clergy—shows that this
society had fewer from the ranks of the clergy than any other Washtenaw
temperance cohort, and was certainly a result of the hostility it sometimes engendered from churches. Members of this group also generally owned less real
estate than those who participated in other temperance organizations:

Temperance cohort	Total	Found on 1850 census	Mean RE	Median RE
1829–34	39	13	$9,992	$3,000
1835–40	205	48	$3,773	$2,250
1838 subscribers	264	94	$3,189	$2,000
1841–46	106	43	$4,274	$1,500
Sons of Temp.	269	106	$1,390	$425
1851–60	124	63	$3,812	$1,000

Devotees of the Sons of Temperance were also far more likely to be listed in the 1850 federal census without any real-estate holdings:

Temperance cohort	# without RE	% of cohort without RE on 1850 census
1829–34	2	15.4
1835–40	7	14.6
1838 subscribers	18	19.1
1841–46	5	11.6
Sons of Temp.	43	40.6
1851–60	15	23.8

The lesser wealth holdings among the Sons of Temperance results, in part, from the fact that they, like their Tuscaloosa counterparts, were generally younger than the members of other temperance cohorts in 1850. Thus, they had had less time to accumulate property:

Temperance cohort	# with known age	Median yr. of birth	Median age first appeared in movement
1829–34	17	1796	33
1835–40	53	1804	32
1838 subscribers	101	1804	34
1841–46	48	1805	36
Sons of Temp.	136	1815	33
1851–60	72	1812	42

Although their median years of birth ranged over two decades, most of Washtenaw County's temperance enthusiasts became active in the movement by the time they reached their early to mid-thirties. Notwithstanding the differences in Washtenaw and Tuscaloosa Counties' temperance movements, it is worth noting that the earliest cohort in each place was, on the whole, born earlier than its successors. Also, the ability of the temperance movement—in both counties—to recruit new devotees into its ranks with each succeeding cohort is different from colonization in Tuscaloosa and abolitionism in Washtenaw (to be discussed in chapters 5 and 6, respectively). Although abolitionists and temperance devotees who were active between the mid-1830s and the mid-1840s have median ages that are fairly close, the Sons of Temperance opened the temperance movement to a younger generation from whom Washtenaw County abolitionists had failed to recruit in large numbers. Whereas most colonization and antislavery supporters were born near the year 1800, temperance appealed to people in both counties of a broader generational and class base.

As with Washtenaw County's other temperance cohorts, a few of the enthusiasts from the 1850s could be linked to previous temperance activism (only 3, 6, 8, and 7 were traced to the 1829–34, 1835–40, 1841–46, and Sons of Temperance cohorts, respectively; none of the 1850s enthusiasts were found in all these groups, while only 3 of the 1850s devotees could be found in 3 of these other cohorts). In addition to their greater wealth, Washtenaw County's temperance activists of the 1850s were similar to those antedating the Sons of Temperance in that artisans constituted a smaller portion of their membership. Of the 123 male activists from this period, the occupations of 85 could be determined, of whom a near majority (42, or 49.4 percent) were professionals (including 17 clergy, 9 professors, 7 attorneys, and 6 physicians), followed by artisans (15, or 17.7 percent), shopkeepers/proprietors (13, or 15.3 percent), farmers (11, or 12.9 percent), clerks (3, or 3.5 percent), and nothing listed on the census (1, or 1.2 percent).[83]

The occupational breakdown of temperance partisans differed from that of

83. Most temperance personnel were identified from newspaper reports of temperance meetings; see also Records of the Phoenix Division No. 79 and *History of Washtenaw County*, 652. In addition to these latter two sources, most occupational and age data were extracted from the 1850 federal manuscript census, as were all the values of real-estate holdings. The records of the Phoenix Division are described in David M. Fahey, "Who Joined the Sons of Temperance? Livelihood and Age in the Black Book and Minutes, Phoenix Division, Dexter, Michigan, 1848–1851," *Old Northwest*, XI (Fall–Winter 1985–86), 221–26.

the 1850 population of the state of Michigan in general, which was far more dominated by farmers:

Occupation	Number	Percent
Artisan	17,860	16.4
Clerk	1,406	1.3
Shopkeeper/proprietor	2,957	2.7
Farmer	65,731	60.3
Laborer	16,679	15.3
Professional	3,148	4.2
Other	1,189	1.1
Totals	108,970	100.0

In comparison with the occupational profile of Michigan, activists from all temperance cohorts were more urban-oriented. In all groups there were lower percentages of farmers and laborers, and higher percentages of professionals, commercial occupations, and with the exception of the 1829–1834 cohort, artisans.[84]

In contrast, the occupational profile for males fifteen and older in the village of Ann Arbor, Washtenaw County's largest "urban" locale in 1850, is worth considering:

Occupation	Number	Percent
Artisan	478	47.0
Shopkeeper/proprietor	65	6.4
Farmer	53	5.2
Laborer	82	8.1
Professional	126	12.4
Other	68	6.7
Illegible	4	0.4
None listed on census	140	13.8
Totals	1,016	100.0

84. Compiled from De Bow, *Seventh Census*, 902–903. Only the occupations of males fifteen and older were enumerated on the 1850 federal census. Occupational classifications for the state of

Although these figures approximate those for the Sons of Temperance, they underline the extent to which people of professional and commercial occupations were overrepresented in Washtenaw County's other temperance cohorts. Aside from the Sons of Temperance, each temperance cohort had over two times, and as much as five times, the percentage of professionals and twice the percentage of shopkeepers/proprietors found in Ann Arbor village in 1850. Further, temperance activists as a group had greater real-estate holdings than did the population at large. In Washtenaw County, the mean household real-estate holding in 1850 was $1,485; statewide it was $1,048. True, the mean real-estate holding of Sons of Temperance members was slightly below the county mean. This at-large county figure, however, was strongly influenced by farmers, who generally held more real estate than nonfarmers and were comparatively few among the Sons of Temperance. The mean value of farms in Washtenaw County and statewide in 1850—$1,956 and $1,489, respectively—raised the mean value of household real estate in both the county and the state. The mean value of real estate held by nonfarmers—a better figure with which to compare the real-estate holdings of Sons of Temperance members—was only $894 in Washtenaw County and $628 statewide; in Ann Arbor, where many of the Sons described in this chapter lived, the mean real-estate holding was $963, the median was $0, and 63.1 percent of this group held no property. It can be safely claimed, then, that temperance members of all cohorts held more real estate than their nontemperance peers, and as was true in Tuscaloosa County, Washtenaw's temperance partisans were concentrated in occupations highly amenable to the growing market economy.[85]

As in Tuscaloosa County, the church affiliation of an individual suggests only part of the story of a person's commitment to temperance. Furthermore, the names of most temperance participants could not be found in any of Wash-

---

Michigan and for the subjects in this study were derived from a pattern used by John Barkley Jentz, "Artisans, Evangelicals, and the City: A Social History of Abolition and Labor Reform in Jacksonian New York" (Ph.D. dissertation, City University of New York, 1977), 318–21.

85. The 1850 federal manuscript census does not explicitly distinguish Ann Arbor village from its more rural township of the same name. There were few agricultural occupations listed in the first 677 households of the census for Ann Arbor, however, and agricultural occupations prevail beginning with household number 678. The occupation and real estate figures were calculated from the first 677 households in Ann Arbor. These households contained 3,660 residents; in the *Michigan Argus*, August 21, 1850, a contemporary estimated that 4,025 of the 4,868 residents of Ann Arbor Township who were enumerated in the 1850 federal census lived in Ann Arbor village. The figures for real estate and value of farms for the state and county were derived from *Statistics of the State of Michigan, Compiled from the Census of 1850*, 170–71.

tenaw County's extant church records; of the 988 names that I extracted from newspapers, temperance records, and county histories, only 291 were linked to the membership of a church (the larger number of temperance activists in Washtenaw County, compared to Tuscaloosa County, is not a reflection of stronger temperance enthusiasm in the North, but a consequence of a greater base population and more extant temperance-related manuscripts).[86] Analogous with Tuscaloosa County, the church affiliation of temperance activists and the proportion who were connected to a church varied according to the cohort. A key difference, however, was the greater religious diversity exhibited by Washtenaw County (see Table 9). And similar to the temperance cause in Tuscaloosa, disproportionately large numbers of Presbyterians were present in all of these organizations. This dominance is even more apparent if we consider Congregationalists and Presbyterians as belonging to a single religious unit. Under the Plan of Union described in chapter 2, members of these denominations almost always formed churches together in Michigan and other western states during the first few decades of white settlement, and both shared a similar theology. In fact, of the thirty-one Congregationalists, eighteen were at one time connected with a Presbyterian body. Baptists were proportionately fewer in Michigan than in Alabama during the mid-nineteenth century, and members of that denomination were not as prevalent in Michigan's temperance circles as they were in Alabama's. Episcopalians were best represented in the Sons of Temperance; as nonevangelicals, they were less likely to be offended by the Masonic parallels of that order. And although there were at least five Catholic churches in Washtenaw County, only four Catholics were ever identified as belonging to any of these temperance societies. One scholar has argued that the devotion of Michigan's antebellum Catholics to temperance was obscured by their hesitancy to join organizations dominated by Protestants, and that they formed their own temperance societies. Although there is no record of any Catholic temperance society in Washtenaw County during the pre–Civil War years, the fact that the Sons of Temperance attracted the only Catholics linked to the county's antebellum temperance movement underlines the lesser influence of evangelicals within the Sons.[87]

86. Although accounted for in the composite figures of Table 9, the series of cohorts in that table do not include the 66 student members of the University of Michigan's College Temperance Society in 1844, 8 of whom—5 Baptists, 2 Methodists, and 1 Presbyterian—belonged to Ann Arbor churches. See Records of the College Temperance Society, in Bentley Library.

87. Slavcheff, "Temperate Republic," 133–38. Since Catholic records contain only birth, marriage, and death records, and not a registry of all the members within a parish, it is likely that

While it is not always a simple task to link temperance-society members to churches, Washtenaw County churches were often in the thick of the temperance crusade. The connection was obvious to contemporaries, as temperance meetings were often held in Presbyterian, Congregational, Methodist, or Baptist churches. As noted in chapter 3, it should not be surprising that members of the evangelical faiths showed the greatest attraction to temperance: consciously accepting Christ required a commitment, as well as mental concentration, that evangelicals believed was beyond the grasp of drunkards enslaved by alcohol. This point was emphasized by Grove Spencer, a Methodist, in a speech before the Temperance Society of Ypsilanti in January 1831:

> Indeed, who will not acknowledge, that, were it not for the successful operation of the temperance cause, the efforts of other benevolent institutions would not only be retarded, but in numerous cases, frustrated and destroyed. What benevolent design can reach the man who is under the spell of the inebriating cup? Of what importance will it be to a man to have been made acquainted with the sublime truths and maxims of the Bible, if he is to become a victim of intemperance? Or what will a man's intelligence avail him, when debased by ardent spirits?

Aside from its social costs, alcohol thus stood between an individual and salvation—or as expressed by George W. Clarke, editor of the Ann Arbor *Michigan Temperance Herald,* the costs of the liquor traffic were "of health, of sobriety, of virtue and domestic happiness; yes of blood and immortal souls."[88] The best way to prevent the drunken condition, concluded many temperance devotees, was to abstain totally from all intoxicants; the temperance literature was abundant with examples of poor souls led to a drunkard's grave as a consequence of taking the first drink.

Presbyterians and Congregationalists generally made adherence to temperance principles a test of fellowship. The Ypsilanti Presbyterian Church "resolved themselves into a temperance Society" in 1830 and later refused to admit as members people who would not assent to the church's article on temperance, and disciplined members who violated it. Members of the Stoney Creek Pres-

there were many Catholics who could not be identified from the records of St. Thomas the Apostle Church in Ann Arbor, St. John the Baptist Church in Ypsilanti, and St. Patrick's Church in Northfield. The number of Catholic churches is taken from the 1850 social census; see Table 4.

88. *Emigrant,* February 23, 1831; *Michigan Temperance Herald,* undated clipping *ca.* 1838–39, in George W. Clarke Papers, Bentley Library.

byterian Church in Augusta were expected to "abstain from the use, traffic, and manufacture of ardent spirits except for medicinal & mechanical purposes," as were those connected with the Presbyterian church in Webster. The Washtenaw Presbytery regarded the use of intoxicants as a beverage to be a sin, and enjoined its churches "to labor with such members as are guilty of this sin."[89] Similar strictures were adopted by Washtenaw's Congregational churches. The Congregationalist General Association of Michigan endorsed the adoption of the Maine Law in 1853, while the church in Ann Arbor in 1849 adopted nonfermented "juice obtained from Raisins" for its communion instead of "common alcohic [*sic*] wines."[90]

Although the Michigan Baptists as a body endorsed the Maine Law, and notwithstanding the fact that their paper, the *Michigan Christian Herald,* was a strong and consistent supporter of temperance and prohibition, neither the Ann Arbor nor the Ypsilanti Baptist congregations are known to have adopted any resolutions prohibiting the use of intoxicants among their members before 1860. In contrast, the First Baptist Church of Saline forbade its members to make, vend, or use "distilled Spirits." The Michigan Association of Free Will Baptists called for vigilance on the temperance issue and supported the Maine Law. Methodists of the Ann Arbor Circuit resolved in 1834 that "no persons can be considered as members in good standing in our societies" who used "ardent spirits." They also disapproved of their members' trafficking in spirits, and strongly recommended Methodists to join temperance societies. In 1850 the Michigan Annual Conference formally endorsed temperance, and in 1856

89. William Jones to AHMS, May 24, 1830, in AHMS Papers; Records of the First Presbyterian Church of Ypsilanti, January 12, 1833, March 20, 24, April 3, 1835 (pp. 19–20, 45–50), in Bentley Library; Records of the First Presbyterian Church of Stoney Creek (Augusta), October 25, 1833, in Bentley Library; Records of the First United Church of Christ, Webster Township, May 8, 1836 (pp. 8–9), in Bentley Library; Minutes of the Washtenaw Presbytery, February 13, 1840 (pp. 94–95), April 10, 1860 (p. 265), in Bentley Library. See also John G. Kanouse to AHMS, July 12, 1835, William Page to AHMS, June 6, 1836, and Alexander B. Corning to AHMS, March 20, 1840, all in AHMS Papers, regarding the temperate character of the Saline, Sylvan, and Bridgewater Presbyterian churches.

90. *Michigan Argus,* June 8, 1853; Records of the First Congregational Church of Ann Arbor, November 16, 1849, in Bentley Library. See also the Records of the First Congregational Church of Lima, August 28, 1846, February 18, 1848, Records of the First Congregational Church of Chelsea (Sylvan), February 1, 1849, Records of the First Congregational Church Salem, October 1, 1851, and Records of the First Congregational Church of Ann Arbor, November 25, 1852, all in Bentley Library.

the conference charged every minister to preach a temperance sermon at least once a year. Although few temperance meetings occurred at Washtenaw County's Episcopal churches and members of this denomination generally kept aloof from the movement, the Rev. D. F. Lumsden of Ann Arbor's St. Andrew's Church preached a sermon in 1859 that heralded temperance as one of the most important issues of the age and urged members of the clergy to be impeccable examples of sobriety and "abstain totally" from the use of wine.[91]

As in Tuscaloosa County, there were more Whigs than Democrats among Washtenaw's temperance partisans. The political constituency of the temperance movement in Washtenaw County, however, was complicated by the more complex evolution of political parties there. Prior to the emergence of the rivalry between the Whigs and Democrats, the Antimasons fielded candidates during the early 1830s; from 1840 to 1848, the abolitionist Liberty Party ran candidates for national, state, and local offices, receiving as much as 8.4 percent of the county vote and an even larger percentage in a few townships. As mentioned in chapter 2, most of the Liberty Party's support came from former Whigs. The Liberty Party was largely succeeded by the Free Soil or Free Democrat Party, which generally received a larger percentage of the vote than did the Liberty Party. Again, the Free Soil Party was mostly composed of former Whigs and Libertyites, although the 1848 presidential campaign of Martin Van Buren inspired some Democrats to vote Free Soil in that election only. The Free Soilers persisted until 1854, when both they and the Whigs were superseded by the Republican Party. The Republicans, however, were not merely a conglomeration of Whigs and Free Soilers; in the process of this voter realignment, some former Whigs joined the Democrats, and a number of Democrats joined the Republicans.

91. Records of the First Baptist Church of Saline, July 1, 1837, in Bentley Library; Records of the Michigan Association of Free Will Baptists, June 8, 1855, in Bentley Library; Records of the First Baptist Church of Ann Arbor, *passim*, in Bentley Library; Records of the First Baptist Church of Ypsilanti, 1854–71, *passim*, located at the First Baptist Church in Ypsilanti; George H. Waid, *Centennial History of the Michigan Baptist Convention* (Lansing, 1936), 34; "Church Records of the Ann Arbor Circuit," April 5, 1834, in Records of the First United Methodist Church, Ann Arbor, Bentley Library; *Family Favorite and Temperance Journal*, I (February 1850), 41, I (October 1850), 235; Macmillan, *Methodist Church in Michigan*, 198–99; Ann Arbor *Journal*, October 5, 1859. Although there were few Universalists in Washtenaw County, the Ann Arbor (and later Jackson, Kalamazoo, and Lansing) *Primitive Expounder*, an organ of that denomination, embraced temperance. See esp. *Primitive Expounder*, II (July 10, 1845), 265–66, III (April 23, 1846), 172, IV (June 18, 1847), 214, V (April 20, 1848), 164, V (August 10, 1848), 288.

A consequence of these political convulsions is that the party identification of some individuals is often imprecise. Not only did people move from the Democrats or Whigs into the Liberty or Free Soil Parties, but occasionally they returned to their original party after flirting with the politics of anti-slavery. Additionally, many voters and some political activists would some-times abandon the Whigs for Democrats or the Democrats for the Whigs. Thus the following data on the political affiliations of Washtenaw temperance supporters cannot be conclusive. When an individual has been traced to both the Whig and Democratic Parties, I have placed that person in the party that was closest in time to his temperance activity. In order to underline the correla-tion between antislavery proclivity and temperance activity, I have designated all individuals who ever participated in the Liberty Party as affiliated with that body, reasoning that even a brief flirtation with the politics of antislavery sug-gests that a person was moved by its message. I have used a similar logic to identify individuals as Free Soilers, but individuals who were active in both the Liberty and Free Soil Parties are listed as Libertyites. The only people that I have classified as Republican, though, were those persons for whom no pre-1854 party affiliation could be found:

Temperance cohort	Males in cohort	Whig	Dem.	Lib.	FS	Rep.
1829–1834	39	12	5	3	2	0
1835–1840	147	47	11	18	3	0
1838 subscribers	263	59	24	52	7	0
1841–1846	85	16	10	20	7	0
Sons of Temp.	269	18	22	12	5	0
1851–1860	123	24	12	12	8	4

Overall, the political affiliation of only 337 of the 815 male temperance activists could be found, of whom 144 (42.7 percent) were Whigs, 74 (22.0 percent) were Democrats, 93 (27.6 percent) were Libertyites, 22 (6.5 percent) were Free Soil-ers, and 4 (1.2 percent) were Republicans.[92]

92. The political predilections of most individuals were gathered from lists of people at-tending county and township party meetings, as printed in various Washtenaw County news-papers, and from the following township poll lists at the Bentley Library: Dexter, Manchester,

In light of the fact that temperance and abolition were rarely, if ever, linked as consanguineous causes in Tuscaloosa County, it is important to underline the strong representation of affiliates from the antislavery parties among temperance proponents in Washtenaw. As mentioned previously, some members of the Liberty Party stressed that the rank and file of their party was also ardently committed to temperance. Although J. Carpenter of Adrian warned in 1841 that the Liberty Party risked losing the support of the opponents of temperance if it continued to link temperance and abolition, he was generally ignored. Nathan Power of Farmington responded to Carpenter by urging the Liberty Party to increase its support of temperance. According to Power, it was impossible to separate the two movements: "Without the temperance cause, the righteous one of abolition cannot move one inch. We make no dependence here on a man professing abolition unless he is a temperance man. . . . The temperance road is the great highway in which the holy cause of emancipation must travel . . . ; in the same proportion that we progress in temperance, the cause of the slave will move on. . . . Slavery will never be abolished until drunkenness shall cease among the slaveholders." The belief among activists that temperance and abolition were mutually dependent is evident from the fact that the delegates to the Michigan State Anti-Slavery Society in 1842 were "with very little exception" the "same persons" who had been present at the annual meeting of the Michigan State Temperance Society the day previous. Further, in that same year the outgoing president of the abolitionist body, John P. Cleaveland, was made president of the state temperance society, and the former chief of the temperance organization, Charles H. Stewart, became the new presiding officer of the Michigan State Anti-Slavery Society. Indeed, until the Michigan State Anti-Slavery Society ceased functioning in 1849, the annual meetings of the state temperance and abolition societies were always held on consecutive days in the same locale.[93]

Northfield, Saline, Sylvan, Webster (all 1840), and York (1852). An 1840 poll list for Ann Arbor is located at the Ann Arbor Township Hall. These figures do not include the 67 members of the University of Michigan's College Temperance Society of 1844, none of whom could be identified with a political party; nor do they encompass an individual from the 1829–1834 cohort who could be linked only to the Antimasonic Party, and another from the 1835–1840 cohort who could only be traced to a small nativist party that contested Ann Arbor's 1846 township election. On the prior political associations of Libertyites and Free Soilers, see Formisano, *Birth of Mass Political Parties,* 27–30.

93. *Signal of Liberty,* November 24, December 15, 1841, January 26, March 16, 1842, January 23, November 6, December 18, 1843, December 16, 1844, February 17, 1845, February 6, 1847, January

Abolitionist partisans were least likely to be found in the early years of the temperance movement and during the 1850s after the antislavery parties had ceased functioning. But among subscribers to the *Michigan Temperance Herald*, and temperance activists from 1841 to 1846, 42 and 51 percent, respectively, of those individuals with a traceable political affiliation were linked to the Liberty and/or Free Soil Parties. Additionally, ninety-three other temperance advocates (from all temperance cohorts) who could not be linked to the Liberty or Free Soil Parties demonstrated abolitionist sentiments through such means as subscribing to the *Signal of Liberty*, signing an antislavery petition, protesting the United States congressional gag rule in 1842, publicly opposing the nominations of the Liberty Party in 1840 while professing to hold abolitionist views, belonging to the Michigan State Anti-Slavery Society, donating money to an antislavery lecturer, embracing Garrisonian abolitionism, or participating in the underground railroad.[94]

Although it has long been recognized that temperance was strongly endorsed by abolitionists, these findings indicate that the converse was also true: abolition was widely embraced among northern temperance partisans. Both causes, after all, focused upon freedom—from either the lash of an overseer or the inveterate addiction to alcohol. Nevertheless, as we saw in the preceding chapter, the temperance movement was by no means dependent upon abolitionists for its support, as it enjoyed a separate life of its own in a land where antislavery was not tolerated, and found recruits among generational cohorts that proved less successful for abolitionists. Nevertheless, in light of both the large numbers of abolitionists found in the temperance ranks and the fervent

---

8, 1848; *Michigan Argus*, February 15, 1843. See also *Signal of Liberty*, April 6, October 17, 1842, January 2, 1843, and *Michigan Argus*, June 5, 1844, where the state temperance body requests that its proceedings be published in the *Signal of Liberty*. A few other temperance partisans, however, joined Carpenter in being displeased with the close association between temperance and abolition; Slavcheff, "Temperate Republic," 146.

94. *Signal of Liberty* subscription list, in Theodore Foster Papers, Bentley Library; *Michigan Argus*, March 2, 1837 (petition); *Signal of Liberty*, March 23, 1842 (protest of gag rule); *Michigan State Journal*, August 4, 1840 (oppose Liberty Party). Other references to the antislavery activity of individuals were obtained from *Monroe Times*, September 22, 1836; *Report of the Proceedings of the Anti-Slavery State Convention held at Ann Arbor, Michigan, the Tenth and Eleventh of November, 1836* (Detroit, 1836), 4; *Signal of Liberty*, June 2, 1841, February 20, 1843, March 20, 1847, February 5, 1848; *Primitive Expounder*, May 7, 1845; *Ann Arbor Journal*, October 5, 1859; and the antislavery petitions sent from Washtenaw County to Congress that I located in the National Archives. These antislavery organizations and activities will be more fully discussed in chap. 6.

efforts taken by whites in Tuscaloosa and elsewhere in the South to prevent the circulation of antislavery ideas among both whites and blacks—which we shall detail in chapter 5—it may seem extraordinary that Tuscaloosa's opponents of temperance did not endeavor to paint their antagonists as the tools of their section's common enemy. The fact that opponents of temperance and prohibition did not do so suggests that they recognized what we discovered in the last chapter—that these causes were too widely endorsed by too many slaveholders to give credence to such a proposition.

The scarcity of Democrats in most manifestations of antebellum temperance in Washtenaw County is also a stark contrast to Tuscaloosa County, where Democrats made up 45 percent of all temperance partisans with an identifiable party affiliation, and constituted a majority in some cohorts. Although one Washtenaw Democrat charged in 1835 that the Whigs were striving to unite church and state and to make "the temperance cause a stepping stone in that awful catastrophe," such partisan intrusions into the temperance movement were rare.[95] Additionally, the lack of representation of Democrats in Washtenaw County cannot be attributable to the hostility of local party newspapers to the cause, for as we have noted, two longtime editors of the *Michigan Argus*, Earl P. Gardiner and Elihu Pond, were often in the forefront of temperance activity. Among only the Sons of Temperance, however, were there more identifiable Democrats than Libertyites or Whigs, but even there they were outnumbered by the combined Liberty, Whig, and Free Soil total.

But perhaps the most significant feature with respect to the political affiliation of all temperance cohorts was how few individuals could be linked to any political party, either through attendance at a township party meeting, candidacy for township or state office, or through the few surviving poll lists. This feature was most pronounced among the Sons of Temperance; of the 269 members of this organization, only 57 had any traceable political ties. Their lack of political activity, less valuable real-estate holdings, fewer high-status occupations, and apparent disinclination toward church membership again bears out the fact that the Sons of Temperance brought into the temperance fold a sector of the population that had previously remained aloof—and possibly alienated—from Washtenaw's political parties and other voluntary associations.

Given that most of the support for the Liberty and Free Soil Parties came

95. *Michigan Whig*, February 26, 1835. See also the denial by Whigs in Superior Township of similar charges, *ibid.*, May 5, 1835.

from former Whigs, it becomes clear again that despite the failure of Michigan's Whigs to endorse temperance formally, temperance drew many of its supporters from people who belonged, at least at one time or another, to the Whig Party. Furthermore, temperance activists in Washtenaw County—like their Tuscaloosa counterparts, and similar to benevolence supporters in both counties—also shared the trait of being more likely to have their children attend school than the rest of the population:

Temperance cohort	Children 5–19 of parents in cohort	Children in school	Percent
1829–34	26	26	100.0
1835–40	103	88	85.4
1838 subscribers	188	164	87.2
1841–46	75	63	84.0
Sons of Temp.	129	109	84.5
1851–60	72	59	81.9
All temp. activists	507	431	85.0

Only 70.0 percent of the county population on the 1850 census between five and nineteen attended school in 1850; statewide, the figure was 69.9 percent.

One area in which the temperance constituency of Washtenaw County differed greatly from its Tuscaloosa counterpart was with respect to adherents' places of birth. Just as Tuscaloosa's temperance members were more likely to be southern-born than were the county's heads of household who were enumerated in the 1850 census, so Washtenaw's temperance community was disproportionately northern-born:

Place of birth	Number
New England (Conn. 32, Vt. 33, Mass. 31, N.H. 11, R.I. 5, Maine, 1)	113
New York	184
Other Middle States (Pa. 9, N.J. 7)	16
Old Northwest (Mich. 5, Ind. 1)	6
South (Va. 2)	2
Foreign (Canada 5, England 8, Germany 1, Ireland 3)	17
Total	338

Scholars have long recognized that Michigan was overwhelmingly settled by New Englanders and New Yorkers, and that many of those from New York were recent New England transplants. Unfortunately, the published census did not compile places of birth by county or statewide for adult males. This problem can be somewhat remedied, however, by comparing these figures with another control group compiled for a different study. In his examination of early-to-mid-nineteenth-century officeholders in south-central Michigan, Gregory Rose found that 651 of 849 of these leaders, or 76.7 percent, were born in New England or New York. Of course, one would expect this figure to be higher than the population of adult white males at large, since foreign-born males would be less likely to be elected to office. Among Washtenaw County's temperance activists, though, 87.9 percent were Yankee-born. On the one hand, the Yankee origins of these reformers may appear to have much significance for Washtenaw County's temperance movement. Indeed, some scholars have argued that the prevalence of antislavery and other reform activity in antebellum Michigan resulted from the heavy domination of transplanted New Englanders and New Yorkers who brought with them an intense moral earnestness inherited from the Puritans. Nevertheless, the importance of Yankee birth as a determinative factor in temperance activity can easily be overstated, especially when we remember the dominance of native-born southerners in Tuscaloosa's temperance crusade. It is possible that Washtenaw residents from other areas of the country and from abroad may have subscribed to temperance principles but were not often appointed to leadership positions, or they may not have felt welcome in associations dominated by Yankees.[96]

On balance, then, one of the greatest differences between temperance in Washtenaw and Tuscaloosa Counties was the heavy involvement of abolition-

---

96. Gregory Rose, "South Central Michigan Yankees," *Michigan History*, LXX (March-April 1986), 32–39; Morris C. Taber, "New England Influence in South Central Michigan," *Michigan History*, XLV (December 1961), 305–36; Dunbar and May, *Michigan*, 200–201. See also Jeremy Atack and Fred Bateman, "Yankee Farming and Settlement in the Old Northwest: A Comparative Analysis," in David C. Klingaman and Richard K. Vedder, eds., *Essays on the Economy of the Old Northwest* (Athens, Ohio, 1987); Fred Bateman and James D. Foust, "A Sample of Rural Households Selected from the 1860 Manuscript Censuses," *Agricultural History*, XLVIII (January 1974), 75–93. Don Harrison Doyle, *The Social Order of a Frontier Community: Jacksonville, Illinois, 1825–1870* (Urbana, Ill., 1978), 120–22, shows that Yankees and southerners clashed during the early years of the settlement in a community with fewer northerners and considerably more southerners than Washtenaw County. The 1850 school attendance figures for Washtenaw County and the state of Michigan were derived from De Bow, *Seventh Census*, 882, 901.

ists in temperance activity in the northern county. If the editorial opinion of the *Signal of Liberty* can be trusted as a guide to abolitionist sentiments on temperance, then abolitionists were often the force behind radical temperance measures. This fact notwithstanding, the issue of slavery seldom interfered with temperance. Tuscaloosans made few, if any, connections between aboli- tion and temperance, and slaveholders probably constituted the bulk of the county's temperance rank and file. Nor is there any evidence to suggest that Washtenaw's prohibitionists abandoned their cause in the mid-1850s to focus on the slave question. The decline of their crusade, as with the concurrent dis- appearance of temperance and prohibition in Tuscaloosa County, owed more to failure and discouragement.

Although temperance advocates in both counties showed a preference for the Whigs, Democrats appear to have constituted a larger proportion of the temperance faithful in Tuscaloosa County than in Washtenaw County. Ow- ing to a smaller residual mistrust of Antimasonry, Tuscaloosans—and white southerners in general—also displayed more enthusiasm for the Sons of Tem- perance than did their northern counterparts. Nevertheless, temperance parti- sans in Michigan achieved political victories that were denied to enthusiasts in Alabama. The most notable of these included the Michigan legislature's pas- sage of a local-option law in 1845, the "Wisconsin Law" in 1851, and the state- wide implementation of various prohibitory statutes in 1853 (by referendum), 1855, and 1857—each of which endeavored to compensate for the shortcomings of the former act. Despite a considerable outpouring of prohibitionist activism in Alabama during the 1850s, the legislature there refused to consider a local- option law similar to the 1845 Michigan statute. Finally, although women in both counties were generally relegated to a supporting role, women in Wash- tenaw were far more likely to form and operate their own societies.

But because some scholars have exaggerated the distinctions between the southern and northern temperance movements, it is important to underscore the similarities of this cause in Washtenaw and Tuscaloosa Counties. In both Alabama and Michigan, strong temperance movements resulted in diminish- ing alcohol consumption after 1830. In 1848 the *Primitive Expounder* pointed to the progress achieved, noting that the extensive public drinking so common thirty years earlier had retreated, and drinkers were now on the defensive be- cause of the widespread successes of the temperance movement.[97] In fact, after

97. See esp. Tyrrell, "Drink and Temperance," 485–510, and Eslinger, "Antebellum Liquor

the mid-1830s, opponents of legal suasion rarely pursued the argument that drinking was a personal decision. Instead, the opponents of statewide and local prohibition insisted that such legal measures were the wrong strategy and that a temperate society would be achieved only through persuasion. Undoubtedly these arguments were sometimes uttered disingenuously. Nevertheless, their use demonstrates the widespread acceptance of temperance principles.

In both counties, temperance personnel generally held occupations linked to towns, owned a larger than average amount of real estate, and were more likely to send their children to school—all suggesting that they found the emerging market economy compatible with their way of thinking. Temperance enthusiasts also invoked similar strategies in both places, resorting to legal measures in the late 1830s after persuasion proved unsuccessful earlier in the decade. In both states prohibitionists were frustrated—particularly in Alabama, where they enlisted broader support in the late 1830s—by legislatures that ignored their demands. Discouraged by their failures, temperance advocates returned to moral suasion in the early 1840s. Beginning in 1845, reformers in Michigan gave legal suasion another chance, to which position Alabama activists had returned by 1851. But in neither Alabama nor Michigan could statewide prohibition, no license, or high license achieve the ultimate objectives of temperance devotees—a permanent ban on the sale of liquor and the complete elimination of its consumption.

Reform in Lexington, Virginia," 163–86; *Primitive Expounder,* V (August 10, 1848), 288. Washtenaw County liquor-consumption estimates by local temperance societies in the 1830s must be considered unreliable as they demonstrate an unreasonable degree of fluctuation. Taken together, they point to a per capita consumption of 10.7 gallons of liquor in 1831 (more than twice the national average of 5.2 gallons) that decreased to 3.0 gallons in 1835 (lower than the national figure of 4.2 gallons), rose again to 8.5 gallons in 1838 (nearly three times the national mark of 3.1 gallons in 1840), and diminished to 3.3 gallons in 1841. Nevertheless, even these figures suggest a trend of decreased drinking. Minutes of the Ann Arbor Temperance Society, January 1, 1831; *Michigan Whig,* February 12, 1835; *Journal of the American Temperance Union,* II (December 1838), 188; *History of Washtenaw County,* 339; Rorabaugh, *Alcoholic Republic,* 232; Slavcheff, "Temperate Republic," 71–73, 108, 339–40.

5

Colonization, Plantation Missions, and the Limits of Southern Reform

In chapters 1 and 3, we observed that the antebellum reform impulse was not generally understood by white Tuscaloosans to be incompatible with chattel slavery. In fact, slaveholding was more widespread among Tuscaloosans who were active in temperance and benevolent enterprises than among the white population at large, and although the activists came mostly from households with fewer than ten slaves, the participation of individuals from plantation households was not uncommon. Even a few slave traders—a class that some slaveholders themselves were said to despise—such as John Meek and James M. Norment, were active in some of these causes. We also observed that temperance and benevolence were not widely perceived by Tuscaloosans as Yankee imports or threats to slavery, for born southerners constituted the vast majority of the members of these societies in Tuscaloosa.

In this chapter we shall see that southern reformers were not lax in the defense of slavery: a number of proponents of reform vigilantly defended the peculiar institution, such as during the abolitionist mail scare of the 1830s. Slavery also added a few dimensions to reform that were not encountered in the North. For example, the fear of slave rebellion contributed to a far more hostile reaction to abolition in the South than in Washtenaw County, while colonization—at least in Tuscaloosa—was more likely to be received with muted hostility or cold indifference. Yet slaves were occasionally the objects of benevolent zeal, as a number of whites were concerned about the drinking habits of, and the large numbers of unconverted among, these African Americans. This latter effort, often designated as the "mission to the slaves" or "plantation mission," is the most explicit example of reform as a measure of social control, as its advocates openly proclaimed that they hoped to use evangelical Protestantism to restrain what they saw as a potentially dangerous population. But as we shall discover, the plantation mission was more than a cynical effort to modulate slave behavior, as it also aimed to fulfill the religious needs of both whites and blacks.

As we noted in the introduction, the geography of Tuscaloosa County precluded it from having the extensive slave population of Alabama counties in the black belt and the Tennessee Valley, in many of which slaves outnumbered whites. Slaveholding in Tuscaloosa County was concentrated in the rich alluvial soils south of the town of Tuscaloosa, and most white households in the county did not possess slaves. Although the town and its immediate environs were home to many of the county's wealthiest planters, many whites there—such as artisans, attorneys, and laborers—owned few if any slaves. The slave population of Tuscaloosa County, however, grew faster than the white population during the antebellum period, and by 1860 slaves constituted slightly less than one-half of the county's population. The slaveholding size among the households owning slaves also increased over these years (see Tables 1 and 2).

Just as they did regarding religion and drink—as discussed in chapters 1 and 3—white Tuscaloosans tolerated a greater diversity of opinion regarding slavery and abolition during the 1820s than afterward. For example, in 1824 the Tuscaloosa *American Mirror* printed an advertisement promoting Benjamin Lundy's Baltimore periodical, the *Genius of Universal Emancipation*. In this ad, Lundy expressed his desire to expose "to public view the naked deformity and odious peculiarities of that soul-debasing system of individual oppression which is yet tolerated in the United States" and to promote means "whereby that system may be completely annihilated." Thomas Davenport, the editor of the *Mirror*, tacitly endorsed Lundy's appeal by noting that subscriptions for the *Genius* would be received at his office. (Davenport, however, was not an avowed emancipationist; on the same page, he also printed a runaway-slave notice.)[1]

The fact that Davenport ran Lundy's ad for five weeks suggests that during the 1820s, not all white Tuscaloosans felt threatened by criticism of slavery. A similar spirit was expressed by the editor of the *Alabama Sentinel*, who two years later scoffed at United States Senator John Randolph. The senator had

1. *American Mirror*, August 7, 1824. Davenport apparently wanted all emancipated slaves to leave America but recognized the immensity of this task when he noted that it cost $50 to send each person to Africa and that the "whole number of blacks, both bond and free, is estimated at 1,900,000, and the annual increase 58,000." *Ibid.*, January 3, 1824.

warned that if the United States entered into an alliance with Simón Bolívar, American slaves would revolt, "cut the throats of their masters," and drench the country in blood. "For our part," responded the *Sentinel,* "we do not apprehend the dangers which the imagination of Mr. R. has conjured up to terrify and affright us." Rather, good relations with the revolutionary powers in Latin America would "result in lasting benefits to our country, that will strengthen the ties of friendship between us and the rising republic of the South, and secure to us commercial advantages which a cold refusal of the invitation would have forever lost on us."[2]

The *Sentinel*'s response to Randolph may not have been the dominant view in Tuscaloosa, but it is unlikely that such a perspective would have gone unchallenged a decade later. The reaction of some white Tuscaloosans to several local violent conflicts between whites and slaves during the late 1820s, however, suggests that white anxiety—which would flower abundantly in the 1830s—had already begun to set in. In late 1827 two slaves were sentenced to be executed, one for "Rape on the body of a white female" and the other for arson. A year later the *Chronicle* was pleased to announce the breakup of "the gang of runaway negroes who have been committing depredations, and keeping the adjacent country in continued alarm for the last eight or nine months." While two men and two women were captured after a fight with white authorities, "the chief of this predatory band, has, as yet, eluded the vigilance of his pursuers, although wounded." Several others were reported to be still at large with him.[3]

Incidents such as these undoubtedly led white Tuscaloosans to insist that increased order be imposed upon the local slave population. At a meeting of the town council in 1827, whites protested that they were "annoyed" by slaves who were hiring their own time beyond the immediate supervision of their masters. Thereafter the town authorities were required to pay closer attention to all slaves within the corporation, and all citizens were obliged to notify the town's intendant if they noticed a slave "thus going at large or hiring his or her own time." Some white Alabamians, however, wanted to do more than merely place additional controls on slaves. Fearing that there were already too many African Americans in the state, the legislature passed a bill in early 1827 that made it illegal to bring slaves into Alabama for the purpose of selling them.

2. *Alabama Sentinel,* April 7, 1826.
3. Tuscaloosa *Chronicle,* October 20, December 1, 1827, October 30, 1828.

Offenders were to be subject to a $1,000 fine and three months' imprisonment, with a further fine of $500 for each additional slave thus imported. Citizens could bring slaves into the state for their own use but were prohibited from hiring or reselling them for two years. This law proved difficult to enforce, was unpopular in some quarters, and was repealed in 1829.[4]

Heightened concern about the slave population, coupled with the concurrent rise of the temperance movement, possibly provided the impetus for the enactment by the town of Tuscaloosa in early 1831 of new statutes that increased restrictions on the sale of intoxicants to slaves. Whoever sold liquor to a slave without the written permission of the slave's master would be fined as much as twenty dollars, and free blacks who violated this law would receive the additional penalty of "not less than fifteen stripes on the bare back." Slaves were prohibited from being "intoxicated in the street, or in anywise disorderly or indecent on the Sabbath day"; such behavior would merit "not more than fifteen stripes." A year later, the town stiffened the punishment for slaves found intoxicated on the streets: they would now receive twenty lashes and be "confined to the guard house" until the following morning. Also, liquor retailers who sold ardent spirits to a slave without the written consent of the slave's master would lose their liquor license and pay a fine of ten dollars. Although this penalty was less than the one imposed by the ordinance of the previous year, the new law gave citizens an incentive to reveal the names of violators, as the fine was payable to the informer. And increased fears that free blacks would incite slaves to question the system of slavery resulted in "An Ordinance to Prevent Free Persons of Color from Trading with Slaves," by which unenslaved African Americans who violated its provisions were to receive, upon conviction, "thirty-nine lashes well laid on."[5]

The rise of immediatism among northern abolitionists and, in particular,

---

4. Tuscaloosa *Chronicle*, November 10, 1827; *Acts Passed at the Eighth Annual Session of the General Assembly of the State of Alabama* (Tuscaloosa, 1827), 44–45; *Acts Passed at the Tenth Annual Session of the General Assembly of the State of Alabama* (Tuscaloosa, 1829), 63. See also William Birney, *James G. Birney and His Times* (New York, 1890), 56–57, and Fladeland, *Birney*, 40–41, 49. In January 1832, the Alabama legislature again restricted the importation of slaves into the state, possibly in reaction to the Nat Turner insurrection. These laws were repealed, however, at the following session of the legislature. *Acts Passed at the Thirteenth Annual Session of the General Assembly of the State of Alabama* (Tuscaloosa, 1832), 12–15; *Acts Passed at the Extra and Annual Sessions of the General Assembly of the State of Alabama* (Tuscaloosa, 1832), 5.

5. *Alabama State Intelligencer*, March 30, 1831; *Spirit of the Age*, May 2, June 13, 1832.

their efforts to use the United States mails to disseminate tracts and newspapers in the South produced a siege mentality among white southerners regarding any criticism of slavery. Their anxieties were exacerbated by Nat Turner's bloody slave revolt in Southampton County, Virginia, in August 1831. The efforts of whites to control slaves, however, were not mere paranoia that flared up after Turner's rebellion and then quietly dissipated after the mid-1830s. After Turner had provided a tangible dimension to their greatest fears, whites fretted about slave uprisings until emancipation. This consternation—in particular, whites feared those slaves whom they did not know—resulted in the frequent revision of slave codes. Although a Tuscaloosa ordinance prohibiting slaves from merchandising was amended to permit slaves to carry "cakes or apples through the city from place to place for sale," restrictions on slaves residing apart from their masters, hiring out their time, or vending alcoholic beverages were retained. In 1839 a town ordinance prescribed that all capable white males in the town have their names placed on a patrol list; each week, six men were to be selected for patrol duty. They were expected to report anyone who engaged in "unlawful traffic" with slaves—such as selling liquor to them—and to "visit all negro quarters, all places suspected of entertaining unlawful assemblies of slaves or other disorderly persons." A loud bell was rung nightly at 9 P.M.; all slaves were to be on their master's premises by this hour. The slave patrol was to confront any slave "going at large through the streets after the ringing of the bell." A slave who was caught "without a pass from his or her owner" was to receive "any number of lashes not exceeding ten" and incarceration for up to twelve hours. Apparently this penalty was an insufficient deterrent, for by 1844, slaves were to suffer as many as twenty lashes when found by the town patrol and could receive up to thirty more after a hearing before the mayor's court. The extent to which these ordinances were carried out is unknown; in 1845, however, Mayor R. Blair printed a notice that the town's slave ordinances "will in future be strictly enforced."[6]

Some in the community, though, felt that the laws were inadequate. In February 1861, a vigilance committee of forty-two Tuscaloosans met to consider the fate of L. W. O'Neil and Louis McCullough, the latter a "free negro." These partners in crime were accused of trading with local slaves and providing them with intoxicants, resulting in "the great injury of the community and

6. Eaton, *Freedom-of-Thought Struggle*, 89–117, 196–205; *Flag of the Union*, April 2, 1836, August 28, 1839; *Democratic Gazette*, May 9, 1844; *Independent Monitor*, February 5, 1845.

the demoralization of the slaves." The committee believed that "a sufficient remedy for this grievance does not exist by law," and thus ordered O'Neil and McCullough to leave the county immediately or "abide by the consequences."[7]

Concurrent with the spread of laws that tightened the manacles of slavery was the advent of sectionalism as a major political issue and the growth of immediate abolition in the North. Threatened by these developments, Richard T. Brumby, the nullificationist editor of the *State Rights Expositor and Spirit of the Age*, warned in 1833 that southerners were living perilously in permitting themselves to be the minority party in the Union. Brumby told his readers that the "spirit of opposition to slavery is spreading, with fearful rapidity, in all the states north of the Potomac," and that northern newspapers were already encouraging slaves to rise against their masters; eventually, Brumby was convinced, northerners would attempt to liberate southern slaves physically. Pleasant H. May, editor of the Jacksonian *Flag of the Union*, protested that such fears were overblown; abolitionists amounted to only a "few visionary enthusiasts" who were scorned by the "thinking portion of the community in which they reside." May asserted confidently that "our undisturbed right to our slaves is a position which does not admit of controversy."[8]

In spite of May's reassurances, on August 25, 1835, at least fifty-four Tuscaloosans formed a vigilance committee in response to abolitionist use of the U.S. Mail to distribute their publications. Southern whites were sure that such literature would eventually fall into the hands of slaves and inspire them to revolt, causing what *Flag of the Union* editor Alexander B. Meek predicted would be "one of the severest scourges with which a nation was ever afflicted —a scourge in comparison with which the Inquisitorial rack, or the Revolutionary guillotine would be instruments of mercy."[9] Headed by Tuscaloosa mayor John Owen and the town's aldermen, the committee complained that "a number of organized bodies of reckless and infatuated persons were organizing in the

---

7. *Independent Monitor*, February 15, 1861. In March 1861, Tuscaloosa Baptists excluded O'Neil from fellowship "for unchristian conduct in unlawfully trading with Negroes, receiving from them various articles, and giving in exchange, whiskey or other intoxicating drinks," and ordered that "he be informed of the action if he could be found." Fourteen years earlier, the Baptists excluded O'Neil for fraudulently selling a free "Negro boy" whom he claimed was a slave. In the intervening years, though, O'Neil had been reinstated. Records of the First Baptist Church, Tuscaloosa, 1842–1867, *passim*; Porch, *History of the First Baptist Church*, 39–41.

8. *State Rights Expositor and Spirit of the Age*, April 20, 1833; *Flag of the Union*, July 11, 1833.

9. *Flag of the Union*, September 19, 1835.

North" and circulating antislavery pamphlets in the South that would "excite insurrections destructive of the good order of our society, involving consequences shocking to contemplate, in the destruction of property and life, with the accompanying brutalities which have heretofore marked such outrages." The committee resolved that any persons who assisted the abolitionists in circulating this literature should be considered "as enemies of God and Man, deserving severe punishment," and declared that the committee had the right "to use all means to feret [*sic*] out, confine and bring to punishment" anyone who distributed "inflammatory papers ... calculated to excite insurrectionary movements."[10] The committee further requested all postmasters in Tuscaloosa County to "withhold from distribution, and to deliver to some member" of the committee "all papers ... of an insurrectionary character." This controversy animated Tuscaloosa newspaper editors for a month and a half, until another vigilance committee—this one to suppress gambling—arose in the town. In the meantime, white Tuscaloosans expressed unequivocal support for the anti-abolitionists. "Never before were the feelings of our citizens so much excited," wrote Meek.[11]

White Tuscaloosans also attacked abolitionism through legal channels. On September 25, 1835, the grand jury of Tuscaloosa County, "after a calm and deliberate investigation of the subject," indicted Ransom G. Williams, an agent of the New York City *Emancipator*, "for circulating within our State, pamphlets and papers of a seditious and incendiary character, and tending, by gross misrepresentation, and illicit appeals to the passions, to excite to insurrection and murder, our slave population."[12] Although efforts to extradite Williams to

10. In January 1832, the Alabama legislature passed a law that made the circulation of seditious or incendiary literature a capital offense. The law further prohibited the teaching of reading or writing to any African American, slave or free, limited the assembly of slaves away from their place of residence, and forbade free blacks from associating with slaves without the consent of the latters' masters. *Acts Passed at the Thirteenth Annual Session*, 16–17.

11. *Flag of the Union*, August 29, 1835; *Alabama Intelligencer and State Rights Expositor*, August 29, 1835. Resolutions condemning the abolitionists were also adopted by the Tuscaloosa Presbytery and by the Alabama and Elyton Presbyteries, the latter two of which were Cumberland Presbyterian bodies that included churches in Tuscaloosa County. *Flag of the Union*, October 24, 1835; *Alabama Intelligencer and State Rights Expositor*, November 7, 1835.

12. *Flag of the Union*, October 3, 1835. The *Flag* incorrectly identified *Emancipator* agent Ransom G. Williams as that paper's editor and erroneously referred to him as Robert G. Williams. On this episode, see Dwight Lowell Dumond, *Antislavery: The Crusade for Freedom in America* (Ann Arbor, 1961), 209; Walter M. Merrill, ed., *The Letters of William Lloyd Garrison* (6 vols.;

Alabama were futile, the case demonstrates how greatly white Tuscaloosans feared abolitionist literature. It also marks a turning point in their attitude toward slavery itself. After 1835 there was a solid consensus that slavery was not to be questioned. The *Alabama Intelligencer and State Rights Expositor* objected to a public discussion of the pros and cons of slavery because it would "divide the South on a question on which it is important that they should present an undivided front to the meddlers of the North." Such a discussion would further cause the wrong people to ask the wrong questions: "How shall the unenlightened Southern people know whether the arguments of the abolitionists are refuted, unless they know what these arguments are? The discussion, if entered upon, cannot be confined to the prudent, and the reflecting. No, it seems to be intended for the unenlightened, and to the unenlightened, the ignorant and the imprudent, nay even to the slaves themselves it would be likely to extend."[13]

The defense of slavery never disappeared from Tuscaloosa's newspapers for the remainder of the antebellum period, but it would be incorrect to focus solely upon the mail controversy of 1835 and conclude that the defense of chattel slavery was white Tuscaloosans' foremost public preoccupation. On the contrary, the lack of activism in defending slavery after 1835 suggests that whites believed that their vigilance had rooted out the menace of abolition. Henry Adams Snow, a Tuscaloosa merchant and Massachusetts native, reflected this view in an 1841 letter to his brother in New England: "Abolition movements give us no disturbance, the subject is only agitated for political effect." Nevertheless, the frequent revision of slave codes and the presence of slave patrols demonstrates that not all white fears had evaporated. Widespread discussion of slavery and southern rights emerged again in connection with the election of 1844. In the meantime—and after 1844 when sectional issues were not being agitated—the defense of slavery and the ferreting out of abolitionists were matters upon which white Tuscaloosans almost universally agreed. So strong was the consensus on these issues that during presidential elections, each party tried to outdo its adversary by proclaiming that the other candidate

Cambridge, Mass., 1971), I, 335–36 [where Garrison refers to Williams as a "colored preacher"]; Louis Ruchames, ed., *The Letters of William Lloyd Garrison* (6 vols.; Cambridge, Mass., 1971), II, 12 n. 18; Louis Filler, *The Crusade Against Slavery, 1830–1860* (New York, 1960), 75–76; Leonard L. Richards, *"Gentlemen of Property and Standing": Anti-Abolition Mobs in Jacksonian America* (New York, 1970), 47–49.

13. *Alabama Intelligencer and State Rights Expositor,* October 3, 1835. Although this newspaper's title was similar to the *State Rights Expositor and Spirit of the Age,* the *Intelligencer* was not nullificationist.

was a threat to the South and slavery, and that the opposition party in the North was the stronghold of abolitionists. But when Alabamians competed against one another for state offices, they contended over issues that characterized the second party system, and did not debate issues associated with slavery.[14]

Although abolitionists operated under the "sacred garbs of benevolence and christianity," their philanthropy was, in the mind of Democrat Alexander B. Meek, that of "deluded and unholy fanatics." According to the Whig *Independent Monitor*, abolitionists and other northern reformers were a "band of restless visionaries" who were "always in motion, to draw off the masses from their true interests, and to embitter them against the established order of things." The Alabama planter turned abolitionist, James G. Birney, though, was worse than a "visionary." In the words of Meek, Birney "followed the *ignis fatuus* of his imagination, until it . . . bewildered him amidst all the errors of Immediate Emancipation." Birney was rumored "to labor under a mental hallucination in regard to slavery; a species of monomania, that would effect its paramount desire at the sacrifice of every obstacle, however pure or beneficial." Thus, despite the abolitionists' altruistic pretensions, reformers in Tuscaloosa were convinced that abolition was dangerously extremist, a reform gone wild. Instead of protesting the sufferings of southern slaves, Tuscaloosa reformers such as Meek—who was later elected vice-president of the Alabama State Temperance Society and in the 1850s was the state's leading advocate of the common school—insisted that abolitionists "look to their own degraded and starving poor. Let them feed their beggars—clothe their paupers, and instruct their own ignorant and miserable peasantry."[15] John G. Davenport, editor of the Whig *Alabama Intelligencer and State Rights Expositor*, who had served as an

14. Henry Snow to Peter Snow, April 6, 1841, in James Austin Anderson Papers, University of Alabama (typescript); Thornton, *Politics and Power*, 165–68, and the following examples: *Alabama Intelligencer and State Rights Expositor*, September 26, 1835; *Flag of the Union*, March 11, 1840; *Independent Monitor*, August 14, October 23, 1840, March 5, 1845, March 18, 1858; *Democratic Mentor*, April 3, May 8, 1844; *State Journal and Flag of the Union*, October 16, November 6, 1846. The most detailed public defense of slavery in Tuscaloosa was presented in 1860 by University of Alabama president Landon C. Garland, who gave four lectures on behalf of Tuscaloosa's Female Benevolent Society, which was collecting funds to help 200 people who suffered economic displacement after a town factory ceased operating. *Independent Monitor*, January 7, March 3, 10, 17, 31, April 21, 1860. Garland's first three lectures are conveniently summarized in James Benson Sellers, *Slavery in Alabama* (University, Ala., 1950), 352–54.

15. *Flag of the Union*, August 29, 1835; *Independent Monitor*, February 18, 1846; *Flag of the Union*, September 19, 1835; Tuskaloosa *Whig*, January 21, 1840; Hunt, "Organizing a New South."

officer in several local temperance societies and was active in the antigambling movement, argued that the abolitionist agitation would only "tighten the chains of slavery wherever it exists," as in the past few years laws had been passed throughout the South that prohibited the teaching of slaves to read and write and restricted their assemblage "except under the guardianship of their masters. . . . These are consequences at which the heart of the *true philanthropist* must bleed."[16]

The hostility of white southerners to abolition was often expressed as animosity toward anything northern. On the eve of the Civil War, Tuscaloosa merchant Charles J. Fiquet informed his customers that all of his merchandise was manufactured in the South, and that "neither Senator [Henry] Wilson, Wm. H. Seward, Dr. [George] Cheaver [*sic*], Wendell Phillips, Henry Ward Beecher, nor any of their abolition constituents, had any part, whatever, in getting up his splendid stock of Spring and Summer Goods." Nearly two decades earlier, Basil Manly had judged Yankees generally inadequate as tutors at the University of Alabama. He was irritated, though, that more people in the South did not see things his way: "The southern people have practiced long enough the silly presumption that Northern men are better for Southern institutions than Southerners themselves." Not surprisingly, Manly also argued that southern women made better wives than northern women.[17]

Despite such displays of sectionalism and overt hostility to abolitionists, antagonism toward any reform effort as a northern importation was, as chapters 1 and 3 have shown, seldom expressed in Tuscaloosa after the early 1830s. This attitude may have prevailed because some of Tuscaloosa's most prominent reformers actively condemned the abolitionists. Manly, a supporter of foreign

16. *State Rights Expositor and Spirit of the Age*, February 16, June 15, 1833; William H. Williams to ASSU, June 1, 1834, in ASSU Papers; Minutes of the Teachers Association of the Tuscaloosa Union Sunday School, October 24, 1832, in possession of the Tuscaloosa First Presbyterian Church; *Alabama Intelligencer and State Rights Expositor*, August 22, 1835. Contemporary observers and modern scholarship have generally concluded that while slave access to freedom and citizenship declined during the antebellum period, the material conditions of slave life improved, and that this improvement was in part the consequence of slaveholders' reexamining the peculiar institution in light of the mounting abolitionist critique. Eugene D. Genovese, *Roll, Jordan, Roll: The World the Slaves Made* (New York, 1974), 54–57. See also Michael Hindus, "Black Justice Under White Law: Criminal Prosecutions of Blacks in Antebellum South Carolina," *Journal of American History*, LXIII (December 1976), 575–99, who demonstrates that the punishment of recalcitrant slaves became harsher during the 1850s.

17. *Independent Monitor*, March 3, 1860; Basil Manly to E. B. Teague, September 2, 1841, Manly to James L. Reynolds, September 12, 1841, both in Manly Family Papers.

missions, temperance, and colonization, never hid his antiabolitionist and anti-Yankee sentiments, and when secession finally occurred, he could hardly contain his exuberance.[18] Fiquet was the treasurer of the Tuscaloosa Bible Society from 1854 until 1861 and was long active in the Tuscaloosa Union Sunday School. Marmaduke J. Slade embraced temperance, actively promoted the circulation of Bibles, and occasionally printed antiabolition material in his Whig newspaper, the *Independent Monitor.* Meanwhile, Alabama Supreme Court justice and future governor Henry Collier and attorney and legislator Benjamin F. Porter, both active reformers, were the principal speakers at a meeting in 1847 to denounce the proposed Wilmot Proviso; both men excoriated abolitionists and defended slavery.[19]

Perhaps even more significant was the presence of consequential local reformers on the vigilance committee that in 1835 protested the mailing of abolitionist literature. At least fourteen of the fifty-four members were participants in temperance or benevolence activities. Twelve of these fourteen individuals were identified on the 1830 federal census, and all twelve were slaveholders. Their holdings ranged from the one slave owned by Aaron Ready to the thirty-four possessed by Alfred Battle. The median holding was 11, and the mean was 14.1. Seven were temperance activists during the antebellum years, and they included Aaron Ready and Dennis Dent, both members of the Executive Committee of the Tuscaloosa Society for the Promotion of Temperance in 1829 (Ready was also secretary of the Society of the State of Alabama for the Promotion of Temperance in 1830); Thomas Owen, president of the Tuscaloosa Society for the Promotion of Temperance in 1829; and Samuel Mills Meek, vice-president of the Tuscaloosa Society for the Promotion of Temperance in 1829, treasurer of the Alabama State Temperance Society in 1831, and president of the Tuscaloosa Temperance Society from 1831 to at least 1835.[20]

18. Manly was present in Montgomery during the passage of Alabama's secession ordinance; a few weeks later, he gave the invocation at the inauguration of Jefferson Davis. Basil Manly to Sarah Manly, January 11, 1861, Basil Manly to Basil Manly Jr., February 5, 1861, both in Manly Family Papers.

19. ABS *Annual Report,* XXXVIII (1854), 152, XLV (1861), 18; *Independent Monitor,* October 15, 1859; Minutes of the Teachers' Association of the Tuskaloosa Union Sunday School, in possession of First Presbyterian Church of Tuscaloosa, *passim; Independent Monitor,* February 19, 1845, February 18, June 17, 1846, October 10, 26, 1847; Theodore H. Jack, *Sectionalism and Party Politics in Alabama, 1819–1842* (Menasha, Wisc., 1919), 33.

20. *Alabama State Intelligencer,* May 8, 1829, August 6, 1830; *Spirit of the Age,* November 17, 1831, January 18, June 13, 1832; *State Rights Expositor and Spirit of the Age,* March 23, 1833; *Alabama Intelligencer and State Rights Expositor,* August 15, 1835.

Activists of the benevolent empire were also well represented on the vigilance committee. In addition to Meek, who served as the Alabama Bible Society's Tuscaloosa agent and had presided at a state Bible society meeting in 1830,
there was Alfred Battle, a planter and vice-president of the Alabama State Bible Society in 1837 and treasurer of that organization from 1837 to 1845. Three
superintendents (Benjamin Whitfield, David Buck, J. Holbert) and one corresponding secretary (Robert S. Foster) of the American Sunday School Union–
affiliated schools were also on the vigilance committee. Although some southerners protested that temperance and benevolent enterprises were tinged with
abolitionism, such arguments lacked credibility in Tuscaloosa, given the vigilant antiabolitionism and widespread slaveholding among front-line reformers.[21]

The attitudes of Tuscaloosans toward colonization were more complex. Of
all the major reforms preached in Tuscaloosa, colonization was the most likely
to be questioned as a threat to slavery.[22] Formed in December 1816 in Washing-

21. *Alabama State Intelligencer,* January 8, 1831; *Flag of the Union,* February 24, July 26, 1837;
ABS *Annual Report,* XXIX (1845), 145; William H. Williams to Frederick W. Porter, January 31,
1832, Thomas M. Cox to Frederick W. Porter, December 31, 1834, both in ASSU Papers; Tyrrell,
"Drink and Temperance," 485–510; Kuykendall, *Southern Enterprize,* 78–79, 105–106, 108–109,
133–45. See also the discussion in chap. 1 herein regarding the increased hostility of white southerners to national benevolent societies during the 1850s.

22. The major works about colonization include Charles I. Foster, "The Colonization of Free
Negroes, in Liberia, 1816–1835," *Journal of Negro History,* XXXVIII (January 1953), 41–66; Frederic
Bancroft, "The Early Antislavery Movement and African Colonization," in Jacob Cook, ed.,
Frederic Bancroft, Historian (Norman, Okla., 1957), 147–91; Staudenraus, *African Colonization
Movement;* Donald G. Mathews, *Slavery and Methodism: A Chapter in American Morality, 1780–
1845* (Princeton, 1965), 88–110; Eric Foner, *Free Soil, Free Labor, Free Men: The Ideology of the Re-
publican Party Before the Civil War* (New York, 1970), 267–80; George M. Fredrickson, *The Black
Image in the White Mind: The Debate on Afro-American Character and Destiny, 1817–1914* (New
York, 1971), 6–21; Floyd J. Miller, *The Search for a Black Nationality: Black Emigration and Coloni-
zation, 1787–1863* (Urbana, Ill., 1975); Lawrence J. Friedman, "Purifying the White Man's Coun-
try: The American Colonization Society Reconsidered," *Societas,* VI (Winter 1976), 1–24; David
M. Streifford, "The American Colonization Society: An Application of Republican Ideology to
Early Antebellum Reform," *Journal of Southern History,* XLV (May 1979), 201–20; Andrew E.
Murray, "Bright Delusion: Presbyterians and African Colonization," *Journal of Presbyterian History,* LVIII (Fall 1980), 224–37; Thomas D. Matijasic, "Whig Support for African Colonization:
Ohio as a Test Case," *Mid-America,* LXVI (May–July 1984), 79–92, and "The African Coloniza-
tion Movement and Ohio's Protestant Community," *Phylon,* XLVI (Spring 1985), 16–24; Douglas
R. Egerton, " 'Its Origin Is Not a Little Curious': A New Look at the American Colonization Society," *Journal of the Early Republic,* V (Winter 1985), 463–80; and Marie Tyler McGraw, "Rich-

ton, D.C., the American Colonization Society had as its principal goal the removal of African Americans to the society's settlement in Liberia. The American Colonization Society exercised colonial control over this west African territory before finally recognizing its independence in 1847. Supporters of the society disagreed over whether its goal should be the expatriation of all blacks, slave and free, or of free blacks only. The genius behind the colonization movement was its ability to represent different things to different people. Many northerners, and a few southerners, saw in it the means to eradicate slavery, gradually and peacefully, from the United States. Although a number of northern colonizationists departed the cause and embraced immediate emancipation in the 1830s, particularly after the publication of William Lloyd Garrison's *Thoughts on African Colonization,* antislavery colonizationists generally eschewed radical reform. While uncomfortable with slavery, they greatly respected the social order and were repulsed by anything suggesting controversy or ultraism. Many of these individuals, however, supported colonization not only because they wanted to emancipate America's slaves, but also because they believed that American institutions could attain perfection only in a racially homogeneous nation. One anonymous Tuscaloosan expressed such views in a letter to the *Alabama State Intelligencer* when he praised the colonizationists as "men of virtue, piety, and reflection" who were performing God's will as they commenced the "gradual separation of the black from the white population, by providing for the former some situation where they may enjoy the advantages to which they are entitled by nature and their creator's will." A considerable number of southern colonizationists, moreover, saw colonization as a way to strengthen slavery by ridding their section of free blacks, whose presence served constantly to remind slaves that their condition was not universal or immutable. Nevertheless, this observation should not be taken to mean that colonization enjoyed strong support from white southerners. From the movement's beginning, many white southerners mistrusted it, suspecting that colonization was merely a front for the complete elimination of slavery. Even before the organization of a colonization society in the state, an anonymous Alabamian

mond Free Blacks and African Colonization, 1816–1832," *Journal of American Studies,* XXI (August 1987), 207–24. Useful comparisons of colonization in Mississippi may be gleaned from Charles Sydnor, *Slavery in Mississippi* (New York, 1933), 203–30, and Norwood Allen Kerr, "The Mississippi Colonization Society (1831–1860)," *Journal of Mississippi History,* XLIII (February 1981), 1–30. The Mississippi Colonization Society was one of the strongest in the United States during the 1830s but became moribund by 1840.

wrote to the American Colonization Society that "the impression which mostly obtains in this section of country" was that a number of the society's leaders "would plunge us into all the miseries that would result from an indiscriminate emancipation of slaves, to gratify their mistaken ideas of humanity."[23]

Despite colonization's ambiguous agenda, its adherents shared a number of assumptions. Regardless of their position on slavery, few colonizationists believed that free blacks could be absorbed into white American society. Most were so committed to white supremacy that they never seriously considered African Americans as potential fellow citizens. A smaller group believed that only white prejudice stood in the way of black progress but that this prejudice was unchangeable; therefore, like their more bigoted counterparts, they concluded that blacks were unassimilable into white society. Colonizationists also believed that a harmonious, culturally uniform society was essential to the permanency of the republic, and saw their effort as part of the benevolent network. Like the enthusiasts of other reform endeavors, they believed that they were promoting social perfection by seeking to eliminate elements that threatened the stability of the nation—in this case, free blacks, slaves, or both. As with other enterprises within the benevolent empire, colonizationists used agents to circulate their message and to collect money. Because of these similarities, many whites viewed colonization as another manifestation of the missionary ideal, and they were convinced that as African Americans took knowledge of American institutions with them to Africa, colonization would facilitate the spread of Christianity and American civilization. Those colonizationists who believed that free blacks were incapable of attaining their human potential in America expected that expatriation would result in their uplift. They further maintained that colonization would rescue America from amalgamation and eventual race war, thus making their cause contribute to the progress and glory of America. Like advocates of Bibles, tracts, and Sunday schools, colonizationists saw religious and material progress as intertwined propositions; most of the major Protestant sects in America—Methodists, Baptists, Presbyterians, Episcopalians, and Quakers—embraced colonization as a means to ameliorate America's racial divisions.[24]

23. Staudenraus, *African Colonization Movement,* 173, 193–206; Mathews, *Slavery and Methodism,* 105; *Alabama State Intelligencer,* January 22, 1830; *African Repository,* III (June 1827), 116.

24. Matijasic, "Whig Support for African Colonization," 80, 81; Mathews, *Slavery and Methodism,* 91–92.

A few of Alabama's colonizationists believed that slavery was wrong and ought to be abolished eventually. One such individual was a University of Alabama professor, Henry Tutwiler, a resident of Tuscaloosa from 1831 to 1837. As he explained in a private letter, Tutwiler was certain that "almost all of the moral and political evil in our Country may be traced to this fruitful source— it exhausts our soil, corrupts our morals, and is the chief cause of that diversity of interest which is fast tending to rend asunder our political fabric." Although he hoped for a providential interposition that would rid America of slavery, Tutwiler believed that everyone was obliged to "exert himself to the utmost" to eradicate "this dreadful evil and reproach." Convinced that colonization was the best means of stimulating widespread manumission, which he hoped would gradually end slavery, Tutwiler was perhaps more strongly committed to colonization than anyone else in Alabama. He was a devoted contributor to the cause; through the years he sent hundreds of dollars to the society's headquarters in Washington, D.C., his last remittance of one hundred dollars being acknowledged in the *African Repository* in December 1860. Nevertheless, colonizationists of Tutwiler's stripe were reluctant to voice their antislavery sentiments publicly for fear of retaliation. Further, they supported only a very gradual effort that would cause minimal social and economic dislocation among whites. Tutwiler personally loathed northern abolitionists, who he believed had turned southerners away from colonization.[25]

Another adversary of the peculiar institution was James G. Birney, a resident of Huntsville, Alabama, where he had been a planter, mayor, and state representative. Although Birney served as the American Colonization Society's agent for Alabama, Tennessee, Mississippi, Louisiana, and Arkansas in 1832 and 1833, his views later progressed beyond colonization. Birney eventually became one of America's best-known abolitionists; he was the Liberty Party's nominee for president in 1840 and 1844 and for governor of Michigan in 1843 and 1845. As an abolitionist, Birney became a hiss and a byword among Tusca-

25. Henry Tutwiler to James Birney, August 20, 1832, in Dumond, ed., *Birney Letters,* I, 17, 19; *African Repository,* XXI (March 1845), 94, XXIII (October 1847), 312–13. Tutwiler's remittances to the American Colonization Society amounted to $775. See *ibid.,* XXI (March 1845), 95; XXIII (July 1847), 226; XXIV (July 1848), 224; XXV (May 1849), 159; XXV (September 1849), 287; XXVI (March 1850), 96; XXVIII (February 1852), 96; XXX (July 1854), 222; XXXI (June 1855), 190; XXXII (October 1856), 319; XXXIII (September 1857), 288; XXXV (June 1859), 191; XXXVI (December 1860), 383. See also Paul M. Pruitt Jr., "The Education of Julia Tutwiler: Background to a Life of Reform," *Alabama Review,* XLVI (July 1993), 199–226.

loosans. In 1835, A. B. Meek wrote that this former University of Alabama trustee was "the most deluded of the abolitionist fanatics." Shortly afterward, Birney was expelled from the university's Philomathic Society, of which he was an honorary member, because of his abolitionist views. In 1833, however, Birney's beliefs were compatible with his agency for the American Colonization Society, and Henry Tutwiler could still say that his and Birney's thoughts on slavery went "hand in hand." At this stage, Birney was apparently motivated in part by Negrophobia, as he lamented that if slaveholders in the Southwest refused to expatriate their slaves, Alabama, Mississippi, and Louisiana "in 20 years must be overrun by the blacks."[26] Also in 1833, at least one of Birney's essays on colonization was published in the Tuscaloosa *Alabama State Intelligencer.* In it, Birney explained that colonization's great objective was to send "the free people of color" in the United States to Africa, which effort, he believed, was motivated by humane concerns. The "intellectual and moral progress" of free African Americans had been stymied, as "barriers deemed insuperable" had been placed before them. "A noble benevolence" motivated the colonizationists, who in Birney's view were "impelled . . . to place this portion of their fellowmen in a situation where no unusual obstacle would debar them from the enjoyment of life, liberty, and the pursuit of happiness—in the land of their fathers."[27]

Another agent of the American Colonization Society, Josiah F. Polk, reported in 1830 that potential support among Alabamians for colonization was widespread but sprang from a dislike of African Americans rather than from wellsprings of goodness. White Alabamians, he claimed, considered "the colored population" to be "an immense evil to the country—but the free part of it . . . the greatest of all evils." He added that slave labor was "already becoming unprofitable," which had prompted several wealthy families to relocate from Alabama's Tennessee Valley to Texas, while the "labouring white population"

---

26. Fladeland, *Birney,* 1–74; Robert Paul Lamb, "James G. Birney and the Road to Abolitionism," *Alabama Review,* XLVII (April 1994), 83–134; *Flag of the Union,* September 19, 1835, October 25, 1837; University of Alabama Philomathic Society to James Birney, November 12, 1832, in Birney Papers; Henry Tutwiler to Birney, January 26, 1833, Birney to Ralph R. Gurley, September 24, 1833, in Dumond, ed., *Birney Letters,* I, 38n, 90, respectively.

27. *Alabama State Intelligencer,* June 1, 1833. Birney published fifteen essays on colonization in the spring and summer of 1833. For a discussion of these works, see Fladeland, *Birney,* 65–69. The files of the *Intelligencer* are incomplete for 1833, and it is not known how many of Birney's essays were published in Tuscaloosa.

was said to be "emigrating to states where the best of land is abundant, and where to labor is no degradation. They feel severely the effects of the deleterious influence which the free negroes exert upon the slaves—and they look moreover into futurity, and there they behold an appalling scene—in less than 100 years . . . 16,000,000 of blacks." Polk was convinced that Alabamians "see that the time is not far distant when an outlet *must* be sought for them [African Americans] beyond the limits of the United States."[28]

Neither racially motivated antislavery sentiments nor philanthropic voices praising colonization as a way to eliminate slavery gradually and peacefully were often heard in Alabama after the mid-1830s. The reaction of white southerners to the Nat Turner rebellion and the abolitionist mail controversy caused a complete stifling of public debate on either universal or partial emancipation, and in any case, the economic profitability of slavery virtually precluded slaveholders from emancipating their chattels without a fight. In this atmosphere James Birney's apostasy from colonization to immediate emancipation must have confirmed the suspicions of many Alabamians that colonization was crypto-abolitionism.[29] Henceforth, colonizationists in Alabama explained that they sought the deportation only of free African Americans—an action that would in turn, they reasoned, buttress slavery. Writers sometimes pointed out the "benefits" that colonization would provide for free blacks, but they more often followed Polk's lead and placed greater emphasis on how colonization would make southern whites feel more secure.

For example, in the *African Repository,* a writer from Mobile lamented the "radical error in legislation in many of the slave-holding States, in permitting individuals to manumit slaves, without adding a condition, that they be removed from the country." This style of manumission—which he termed "a mistaken philanthropy"—was contributing to the "evils" of an ever-increasing number of free blacks. In light of the Haitian insurrection, the plot of Denmark Vesey, and the Turner rebellion, unenslaved blacks were particularly worrisome: "That such a population is a positive and dangerous nuisance in a

28. *African Repository,* VI (May 1830), 77.

29. Less than three years after Birney's visit to Tuscaloosa as a colonization agent, and after his views had moved away from colonization toward antislavery, Alexander Meek suspected that Birney's embrace of colonization had led him to become "by a kind of retrograde progression, . . . a violent and flaming abolitionist." Meek also recalled that the ideas Birney had expressed as a colonizationist struck him then as "wild, visionary, and dangerous." *Flag of the Union,* September 19, 1835.

slave-holding community scarce needs argument to prove." In Baldwin County, Alabama, members of an auxiliary of the American Colonization Society echoed these fears when they alarmingly reported that the lack of constraints upon free African Americans made them too accessible to "designing fanatics [abolitionists]. . . . We cannot, therefore, but look upon the rapid increase of the free blacks as dangerous, and affording probable grounds for the partial realization of these expectations, unless the process of removal be soon commenced and steadily prosecuted." The Baldwin County colonizationists also saw in their enterprise a benevolent dimension, although it was not their principal emphasis: the emigration of free blacks to Liberia would assist in the spread of some of the "cherished . . . principles of our own institutions; and so far as the race is susceptible of improvement, the field is a favorable one for their success." Indeed, deporting blacks to Africa could result in "the creation of a rich and varied commerce . . . and the ultimate suppression of the slave trade."[30] But Baldwin County colonizationists had no intention of using colonization to emancipate their slaves.

This apprehensive attitude manifested toward African Americans was more representative of Alabama colonizationists than the emancipation-by-inchmeal views of Birney and Tutwiler. But regardless of their perspective, colonizationists of all stripes were convinced that black people were inferior to white people, and many were certain that slaves would be unable to care for themselves adequately if they were emancipated. For example, Basil Manly, an ardent antiabolitionist who "aided and encouraged" colonization, did not believe that slavery would continue in perpetuity. Emancipation, when it came, "will certainly be decided as a question of expediency; not of right or morals." Although Manly often pondered the problems surrounding emancipation, he arrived at no answers. For the moment, he was convinced that "slavery is better for the slaves as a mass," for when manumission occurred, the circumstances of the emancipated would be painful: "But what then? They cannot be left in the country. Where will they go? Who will bear their expenses? and who will support them for the first year, till they can make a living?" Manly claimed that only three of his slaves could support themselves; the rest would suffer, and as a race, freed blacks, "would disappear much faster than the Indians."[31]

30. *African Repository*, XIV (Aug 1838), 235, XV (March 1839), 90–91.

31. Basil Manly to Basil Manly Jr., May 18, 1849, January 21, 1846, January 24, 1845, all in Manly Family Papers; John B. Pinney to American Colonization Society, February 24, 1846, in American Colonization Society Papers [hereinafter cited as ACS Papers], Library of Congress.

Arthur Hopkins, a resident of Tuscaloosa during the mid-1840s, was present at the formation of the Alabama Colonization Society in 1830; he was also James Birney's law partner in Huntsville, a leader of the state's Whig Party, president of the Alabama State Sabbath Convention, a temperance activist, and an officer in the Alabama Bible Society. Hopkins confessed to Birney that if he "could better the condition of my slaves by emancipating them, I do not think that I would hesitate to let them go free." Yet, like Manly, Hopkins considered his slaves incapable of living as free citizens: "With no other restraints upon their vicious propensities than those created by the laws of which they know scarcely anything, & their disposition to be idle, the slaves would, I believe, if immediately set free, become miserable vagabonds & hopeless paupers."[32]

The remarks of Manly and Hopkins probably represent the sentiments of southern colonizationists who viewed the cause as something other than a means to eliminate free blacks from their midst and thus strengthen slavery. Unconvinced that slavery was an ideal institution, they were nevertheless certain that emancipation would pose even greater problems for blacks and their former masters. Such individuals stressed the benevolent side of colonization and saw it as the best that could be done in circumstances impossible to surmount. Yet colonization hardly provided these large slaveholders with a means of resolving their dilemmas. Despite their support for colonization, there is no

---

Manly favored colonization as early as 1821, and at this time felt private misgivings regarding the institution of slavery; by the mid-1830s, however, many of his doubts about the morality of slavery of evaporated. Loveland, *Southern Evangelicals*, 214 n. 39; David T. Bailey, *Shadow on the Church: Southwestern Evangelical Religion and the Issue of Slavery, 1783–1860* (Ithaca, 1985), 215, 226. According to the 1850 slave schedule of the federal census for Tuscaloosa County, Manly owned 30 slaves in two holdings of 18 and 12.

32. Arthur Francis Hopkins to James Gillespie Birney, August 25, 1834, in Birney Papers. Hopkins was a charter member of the Alabama State Colonization Society (T. Nixon Van Dyke to James Birney, November 25, 1832, in Dumond, ed., *Birney Letters*, I, 42), and visited Tuscaloosa often on business, as attested by his numerous letters written from that place that are present in the Birney Papers. Hopkins and his wife were accepted as members of the Tuscaloosa Presbyterian Church on August 3, 1844, and dismissed in January 1846; Tuscaloosa Presbyterian Church communion roll, Session Book No. 2, in possession of Tuscaloosa Presbyterian Church. For Hopkins' activities with the Alabama Bible Society, see *Alabama State Intelligencer*, January 1, 1830, January 8, 1831; his role in the Alabama State Sabbath Convention is reported in the *Independent Monitor*, June 5, 1846. On temperance, see James Sellers, *Prohibition Movement in Alabama*, 21.

evidence that Basil Manly or Arthur Hopkins ever emancipated his slaves and sent them to Liberia. Manly may have relieved his uncertainties by embracing the plantation mission, which will be discussed shortly. Hopkins' language in the passage just quoted may represent nothing more than self-serving justification. Or perhaps he found his internal conflicts to be unresolvable, resulting ultimately in his doing nothing. Henry Collier similarly believed that blacks were incapable of living outside the confines of slavery, and he foresaw dreadful calamities for both blacks and whites if slaves were freed. Collier—the governor of Alabama from 1849 to 1853, one of the many vice-presidents of the American Colonization Society, and an important figure in state temperance, Bible, and Sunday-school societies—believed that emancipation would result in racial violence and, eventually, the extinction of African Americans: "If the connection of master and slave were dissolved, without the removal of one or the other, riots, murders, and the most heinous offenses would become matters of every day occurrence, until at length the white race being the superior . . . would extirpate the colored." Not surprisingly, Collier's support for colonization emphasized the removal of Alabama's free blacks, not the state's slaves. Indeed, as governor, Collier called for the state to pay for the deportation of free blacks to Liberia.[33]

The formation of the Alabama Colonization Society in January 1830 marked the beginning of colonizationist activity in Tuscaloosa. The thirty-six men—there were also two women—who attended the organizational meeting, held at the state capitol, were described as "not only gentlemen from Tuskaloosa, but gentlemen from a distance of the most distinguished character in the State." Indeed, five judges of the state's supreme court were among those present. Josiah Polk, the American Colonization Society agent who organized the Alabama society, was "politely allowed the use of the Representative chamber" of the capitol.[34] Tuscaloosans were well represented in the society's leadership; Methodist Episcopal minister and temperance activist Robert L. Ken-

---

33. *Independent Monitor,* October 10, 1847; *African Repository,* XXVIII (March 1852), 90; Sydnor, *Slavery in Mississippi,* 217; *Alabama State Sentinel* (Selma), December 31, 1853. See also Collier to American Colonization Society, May 18, 1854, ACS Papers.

34. *Alabama State Intelligencer,* January 22, 1830; T. Nixon Van Dyke to James Birney, November 25, 1832, in Dumond, ed., *Birney Letters,* I, 42–43; *African Repository,* V (February 1830), 379, VI (May 1830), 76; Josiah F. Polk to American Colonization Society, January 12, 1830, ACS Papers.

non and attorney Elisha Wolsey Peck were both vice-presidents.[35] T. Nixon Van Dyke, who was at this time the secretary of Tuscaloosa's Protestant Episcopal Sunday School, was selected as secretary of the colonization society, and David Johnston, an officer with the Baptist Missionary Society of Tuscaloosa County, the Alabama Bible Society, the Tuscaloosa Society for the Promotion of Temperance, and the Tuscaloosa Union Sunday School, was chosen as treasurer. Samuel M. Meek, who was as active in reform enterprises as David Johnston, was a manager, as were his fellow Tuscaloosans B. G. Sims and William Marr. Indeed, during the early 1830s, the constituencies of temperance, benevolence, and colonization were considered to be interchangeable. As we saw in chapter 1, the annual meetings of the Alabama Colonization Society during these years were held simultaneously with the state Bible and temperance societies, and at one of these meetings, William H. Williams hoped to promote the Sunday-school cause by meeting with "clergymen and others from different parts of the state."[36]

Of these 38 charter members of the Alabama Colonization Society, at least 19 were residents of Tuscaloosa County, while the residence of 6 could not be ascertained. Although this is too small a group from which to make sweeping generalizations, it is worth noting that 9 of the 19 Tuscaloosans participated in activities connected with the benevolent empire such as a Sunday school or a Bible, tract, or missionary society, and that 7 of these 19 were temperance activists. We are able to make broader judgments regarding the social constituency of Alabama colonization of the 1830s, however, if we include the names of 69 additional colonizationists gleaned from the minutes of meetings from Baldwin, Franklin, Lauderdale, Lawrence, and Madison Counties because they provide us with 109 Alabama colonizationists, including the non-

35. Peck lived in Elyton in 1830 but moved to Tuscaloosa in 1838 and lived there for the remaining fifty years of his life. After the Civil War, he became a Republican and served as president of the Reconstruction constitutional convention in 1867 and as chief justice of the Alabama Supreme Court from 1868 to 1874. However, he "was one of the few men of that [the Republican] party opposed to granting suffrage to the negro." Owen, *History of Alabama*, IV, 1334.

36. For Van Dyke, see *Alabama State Intelligencer,* October 5, 1830, and Dumond, ed., *Birney Letters,* I, 42n. For Johnston, see *American Mirror,* July 10, 1824; *Alabama State Intelligencer,* May 8, 1829, July 1, 1830, January 8, 1831; Tuscaloosa *Chronicle,* December 15, 1827; William H. Williams to ASSU, December 23, 1830, January 31, 1832, both in ASSU Papers; and *African Repository,* V (February 1830), 379.

Tuscaloosans present at the organizational meeting of the Alabama Colonization Society.[37]

Of this larger group, additional information was obtained on 74 from the 1830 United States Census or from state histories.[38] Most evident is the "distinguished character" alluded to previously, as many of the colonizationists were members of the political and social elite. The Tuscaloosa contingent included Alabama Supreme Court justice Sion L. Perry; planter William M. Marr (who with 101 slaves, was Tuscaloosa County's largest slaveholder in the 1830 census); Benjamin B. Fontaine, a state legislator; T. Nixon Van Dyke, clerk of the Alabama House of Representatives in 1829; Samuel M. Meek, an alderman from Tuscaloosa's second ward in 1832; Congressman Robert E. B. Baylor, who later served on the Texas Supreme Court, and for whom Baylor University was named; Robert Lewis Kennon, the town's Methodist minister, who in 1837 gave the prayer at the inauguration of Governor Arthur Bagby; and University of Alabama professor Henry Tutwiler. Similar support for colonization came from the rest of the state. In addition to the other members of the state supreme court—Reuben Saffold, Dallas County; Abner Lipscomb, Mobile County; John White, Lawrence County; and John M. Taylor, Madison County[39]—14 colonizationists held a prestigious political office: state attorney general, governor of Alabama, judge, member of the state legislature, or U.S. presidential appointee. Of the 60 who were identified in the 1830 census, 52 were slaveholders. Their size of slaveholdings ranged from 1 slave to the 101 owned by Marr; other significant holdings included those of Albert J. Vaughan (Madison County, 45), Reuben Saffold (Dallas County, 47), Arthur F. Hopkins (Madison County, 53), John M. Taylor (Madison County, 55), and David Moore (Madison County, 100). The median slaveholding was 6.5, and the mean was 14.8. This predominance of large slaveholders suggests that they may have sup-

---

37. *African Repository,* V (February 1830), 379–80, VI (August 1830), 179, XV (March 1839), 92. The names of five other Tuscaloosa colonizationists are taken from Josiah F. Polk to American Colonization Society, January 12, 1830, ACS Papers; T. Nixon Van Dyke to James Birney, November 25, 1832, and Henry Tutwiler to Birney, January 26, 1833, in Dumond, ed., *Birney Letters,* I, 44, 38 n. 3.

38. Especially useful were Vols. III and IV of Owen, *History of Alabama,* and Garrett, *Reminiscences of Public Men in Alabama.*

39. At this time, the Alabama Supreme Court was simply the state's circuit judges meeting as a group; a separate Supreme Court was created in January 1832. *Acts Passed at the Thirteenth Annual Session,* 19.

ported colonization because they saw it as a means to strengthen slavery by ridding the state of free blacks. Arthur Hopkins' comments cited earlier, though, may be indicative of the sentiments of a large slaveholder who would have endorsed the forced removal of slaves if all slaves—not just his—were deported.

Although the preponderance of slaveholders among these Alabama colonizationists of the 1830s may imply a strong agricultural orientation of this group, occupational data suggest otherwise, as only 2 of the 38 colonizationists with identifiable occupations were farmers. Of the remainder, 34 held professional occupations such as attorney (17), minister (6), physician (5), university or academy professor (3), and surveyor general of Alabama (1); one was a merchant and one became a wealthy industrialist by 1850. Although the extensive slaveholding among many of these individuals is evidence that agricultural pursuits occupied much of their energies, their overwhelmingly professional background further suggests that colonization drew its support from people who were town-oriented.

Of the 69 colonizationists of the 1830s for whom information regarding age is available, their ages in 1830 were as follows:

Year of birth	Age in 1830	Number (%)
1801–1810	20–29	18 (26.1)
1791–1800	30–39	27 (39.1)
1781–1790	40–49	17 (24.6)
1771–1780	50–59	6 (8.7)
1761–1770	60–69	0
1751–1760	70–79	1 (1.4)
Total		69 (99.9)

Thus, 90 percent of identifiable colonizationists were, in 1830, between the ages of twenty and fifty. The median year of birth was 1795, and the median age at which they first participated was 35.[40]

40. The ages of many of these colonizationists—especially those who did not live in Tuscaloosa—were determined from the 1830 and 1840 censuses, which only placed the age of a person within a decade. When determining the median year of birth and the median year of participation of subjects whose age was known only from the 1830 or 1840 census, I have assigned those subjects the middling age of that decade. In the case of a person whom the 1830 census identified as 30–39, I assigned that person the age of 35 and 1795 as the year of birth.

Of the 34 colonizationists with ascertainable places of birth, five were born in northern states (Connecticut, Vermont, and New York) and two were born abroad (Ireland and Scotland). The remaining 27 (79.4 percent) were native-born southerners (Virginia, 11; South Carolina, 5; Kentucky, 4; Georgia, 2; North Carolina, 2; Tennessee, 1). Like the other Tuscaloosa reforms discussed in previous chapters, colonization in Alabama was dominated by southerners, although not to the extent that temperance was.

The religious affiliations of only 26 colonizationists could be determined, 11 of whom were Tuscaloosans; of the 26, there were 4 Baptists, 3 Episcopalians, 13 Methodists, and 6 Presbyterians. The preponderance of Methodists may be significant, as there were virtually as many Baptists in Alabama as Methodists.[41] As we shall see, Methodists in the South had long been antipathetic toward slavery; some Methodist supporters of colonization may have seen this cause as a middle way. Also noteworthy is the comparatively large number of Presbyterian colonizationists, as that denomination had far fewer adherents in Alabama than either the Baptists or Methodists. The American Colonization Society's claim as a national benevolent society on the order of the American Bible Society, the American Tract Society, and the American Sunday School Union—all of which were dominated by Reformed Calvinists—undoubtedly attracted Presbyterians to its banner.[42]

The dynamics of the colonization movement in Tuscaloosa were similar to the vicissitudes of its kindred reforms of temperance and evangelical benevolence. Like those two efforts, colonization commenced with great enthusiasm but was unable to sustain itself permanently. In July 1830, members of the colonization society marched in Tuscaloosa's Independence Day procession, and the following January, the Alabama State Colonization Society met again in Tuscaloosa. After this January 1831 meeting, however, the energy behind the cause waned. In November 1832, T. Nixon Van Dyke, the society's secretary, wrote that there had been no meeting of the society in almost two years and that "the President [Alabama Supreme Court chief justice Abner S. Lipscomb] has sent in his resignation—nor have we been able to get a meeting of the Managers although many efforts have been made by some of them to do so." Nevertheless, legislators had not forgotten colonization. Fears aroused by the Turner rebellion, rather than the altruistic optimism expressed by the Ala-

41. Flynt, "Alabama," 9–11, 17; Posey, *Frontier Mission*, 418. On the religious composition of Tuscaloosa County and the state as a whole, see n. 15 in the introduction herein and Table 3.

42. Fred J. Hood, *Reformed America: The Middle and Southern States, 1783–1837* (University, Ala., 1980), 124, 129.

bama Colonization Society, were probably the impetus behind the formation, by the Alabama House of Representatives in late 1831, of a special committee "to inquire into the propriety and best practicable mode of removing from among us, free persons of color." The editor of the *Intelligencer* added that "every friend of this unfortunate class of beings, and lover of domestic security, must desire that their deliberations may conduct to a happy result."[43] But unlike some legislatures in the North and upper South that expended money for the expatriation of free blacks, Alabama's lawmakers took no such action.

In some quarters, a renewed interest in colonization was manifest in late November 1832, when James Birney visited Alabama's principal settlements as an agent of the American Colonization Society. On November 25 he was well received by Tuscaloosans, who contributed forty-five dollars after his address—the second-largest collection that he received in Alabama (in addition, the Tuscaloosa firm of Caruthers, Hawn, & Co. offered Birney free travel on their stage line connecting Tuscaloosa, Montgomery, and Huntsville).[44] Despite this mild success in Tuscaloosa, Birney found much of Alabama unreceptive to his reveille. In Mobile, small audiences precluded his either taking a collection or organizing an auxiliary. He found the "deadness to the subject of African Colonization in this portion of Alabama" to be "altogether discouraging" and wondered whether it was worthwhile for the American Colonization Society to maintain an agent in the Deep South or to make, "for the present, any additional effort." Even the enthusiasm engendered by Birney's reception in Tuscaloosa was incomplete and short-lived. In the fall of 1832, Henry Tutwiler conferred with "several gentlemen" regarding local sentiments toward colonization; they concluded that it would be unwise "to attempt a reorganization of the Society" prior to Birney's visit to Tuscaloosa, as "an opposition might be aroused, which would afterwards be kept up merely because it had been begun." This feared reaction did not occur during Birney's visit, but two months later Tutwiler complained that "the office-hunters of Tuscaloosa" would never promote colonization effectively, and he inquired whether he could become a member of the Huntsville society.[45]

43. *Alabama State Intelligencer,* July 2, 1830, December 10, 1831; T. Nixon Van Dyke to James Birney, November 25, 1832, in Dumond, ed., *Birney Letters,* I, 44.

44. James Birney Account Book, November 25, 1832, Henry Tutwiler to Birney, November 7, 1832, in Dumond, ed., *Birney Letters,* I, 32, 37–38, respectively; Caruthers, Hawn, & Co. to Birney, November 28, 1832, in Birney Papers; *African Repository,* VIII (January 1833), 344.

45. James Birney to Ralph R. Gurley, December 27, 1832, Henry Tutwiler to Birney, November 7, 1832, January 26, 1833, in Dumond, ed., *Birney Letters,* I, 49, 37–38, 38, respectively. Perhaps

After traveling as an agent throughout the Deep South, Birney despaired for the prospects of colonization and decided that he could advance his cause more effectively by moving to Kentucky. During his travels he constantly addressed objections that "the Am. Col. So. is a Northern Institution, set on foot by fanatics etc. etc., and that the subject ought not to be discussed in the Slave States, and that it has a tendency to produce a restless and agitated feeling amongst the Slaves." The belief that colonization was an abolitionist plot proved to be the principal impediment that prevented the public from responding positively to the society's appeals. "The proceedings of the abolitionists of the North have a very injurious effect here," wrote Birney; "they seem to furnish a kind of justification of slavery itself to the southern slaveholders."[46] As a result of this attitude, colonization advocates in Alabama—including Birney—steadfastly denounced abolitionism and insisted that abolitionists were the most vehement opponents of colonization, which in fact they were.[47] But Birney also blamed the failure of colonization in Alabama on the "insensitivity of the *religious* community on the subject of slavery. . . . They will give their dollar or their 25 and talk in favor of colonization but when you ask them to rise up and give the world an example of Christian magnanimity by sending their slaves to Liberia, you drive them to espouse slavery itself and they plead that they cannot live in the South without slaves."[48]

After Birney's departure to Kentucky, colonization in Alabama lacked an agent and the cause further declined.[49] And, as with other benevolent enterprises, the influx of cash into colonization coffers dropped significantly follow-

---

the most noteworthy event at a December 1832 colonization meeting in Tuscaloosa was that it was disturbed by at least one drunkard. Session Book No. 1, First Presbyterian Church, Tuscaloosa, 1820–1836, March 28, 1833, in possession of First Presbyterian Church of Tuscaloosa.

46. James Birney to Ralph R. Gurley, December 27, 1832, September 24, 1833, in Dumond, ed., *Birney Letters*, I, 48–49, 90, respectively.

47. See, for example, James Birney to Ralph R. Gurley December 27, 1832, *ibid.*, I, 50; *African Repository*, XIV (August 1838), 234–37; XV (March 1839), 89–92.

48. James Birney to Ralph R. Gurley, September 24, 1833, in Dumond, ed., *Birney Letters*, I, 89.

49. David Bailey notes that colonization sentiments persisted in the Old Southwest after 1830, but he restricts his examination to the colonization strongholds of Kentucky and Tennessee and neglects to distinguish the extent to which colonization activity in those states differed from that in the deep Southwest, where the cause met a more hostile reception. Bailey, *Shadow on the Church*, 221–22. See also Sydnor, *Slavery in Mississippi*, 216–17, and Kerr, "Mississippi Colonization," 19–20.

ing the economic depression that commenced in 1837.[50] In 1846, the national society lamented that Alabama, Georgia, North Carolina, and South Carolina were devoid of state colonization societies. None of these states had been visited by an agent "for many years past," and the *African Repository* bemoaned the fact that church pastors in the Deep South "have neglected to bring the subject before their people." The *Repository* was optimistic, though, and reported that in many places in these states, "considerable interest is manifested in the operations of the society." Henry Tutwiler, who had since removed from Tuscaloosa to become a professor at LaGrange College, in Franklin County, hoped that the spirit of colonization would return to "those better feelings which prevailed on this subject before the Abolitionists commenced their officious intermeddling." Tutwiler was sure that if the objectives of colonization were better understood, "a host of zealous friends would rise up in its support, particularly in the South," as southerners were a "benevolent and magnanimous people."[51]

Such magnanimity could still be aroused in Tuscaloosa if the right approach was made. Shortly after the *Repository* analyzed the colonization situation in the Deep South, the Reverend John B. Pinney, an agent of the American Colonization Society and former governor of the society's colony in Liberia, visited Tuscaloosa. Pinney had hoped to advance colonization among state officials, but was frustrated by the legislature's imminent adjournment. Nonetheless, he delivered three lectures at the town's principal Protestant churches, collected $108.50 from thirty-six Tuscaloosans, and was "cordially received & hospitably entertained."[52] These contributors were overwhelmingly (32) male. No data could be found on 11 of these individuals, but informa-

---

50. *African Repository,* XIV (October 1838), 314. Other problems of the American Colonization Society, such as some northern benefactors' turning from colonization to abolition, and financial mismanagement, added to the national society's pecuniary woes. Staudenraus, *African Colonization Movement,* 224–39. In December 1838, some citizens of Baldwin County formed a colonization society, called for meetings to be held elsewhere in Alabama, and proclaimed that the "state society formed, several years ago, at Tuscaloosa, ought to be revived, or a new one organized"; *African Repository,* XV (March 1839), 92. However, there is no evidence to suggest that such a movement ever gained support.

51. *African Repository,* XXII (February 1846), 39–40, XXI (March 1845), 94.

52. John B. Pinney to American Colonization Society, February 12, 1846, ACS Papers; *African Repository,* XXII (April 1846), 136. Staudenraus, *African Colonization,* 167. Although the mean donation of three dollars may seem minor considering the wealth of the contributors, single collections of this size in Tuscaloosa by proponents of national benevolent associations—both in terms of money and the number of donors—were not common.

tion on the remaining 25 is further suggestive of the sources of colonization support. The religious profile of these donors is similar to that of the colonizationists of the 1830s. Although there were equal numbers of Methodists and Presbyterians (eight; there were also three Episcopalians and two Baptists), the numerical superiority of the Methodists and Baptists in antebellum Alabama suggests that Presbyterians here, as in the other reforms that we have examined, were represented disproportionately to their numbers, and that colonization was more highly favored by Methodists than by Baptists.[53]

The colonizationists of 1846 were, on the whole, born slightly later than their counterparts from the 1830s, although they were noticeably older at the moment of participation in colonization:

Year of birth	Age in 1846	Number (%)
1811–1820	26–35	5 (22.7)
1801–1810	36–45	6 (27.3)
1791–1800	46–55	9 (40.1)
1781–1790	56–65	1 (4.5)
1771–1780	66–75	1 (4.5)
Totals		22 (99.1)

The youngest colonizationist was twenty-seven, the oldest was seventy; their median birth year was 1800. Though the data are limited, they nonetheless suggest, when considered in conjunction with the birth years of the colonizationists from the 1830s, that the appeal of colonization was strongest among an older generation of white southerners who had come to maturity before the rise of immediate abolitionism in the North. As such, they were less likely to regard colonization as a threat to slavery. The attraction of colonization to people born before 1800 contrasts significantly with temperance, whose adherents came from a broader generational and class base.

Like their counterparts of the previous decade, these colonizationists were generally southern-born. Of the 22 colonizationists whose place of birth could be determined, 14 were from the South (Georgia 1, Maryland 1, North Carolina 3, South Carolina 2, Tennessee 2, Virginia 5), 6 were northern-born (Con-

53. Despite this low support for colonization among Baptists, the ACS was endorsed by the denomination's state newspaper. *Alabama Baptist Advocate*, May 8, 1850.

necticut 1, Massachusetts 2, New York 2, Pennsylvania 1), and 2 were born abroad (England and Scotland). That only 64 percent of these colonizationists—and 76 percent of colonizationists from the 1830s—were southern-born is noteworthy when we recall that 85 percent of the temperance activists in antebellum Tuscaloosa were natives of the slaveholding states. It may be that the smaller figure for colonizationists is the consequence of our having data about fewer people. It is possible, however, that these nonsoutherners were attracted to colonization because of unsettled feelings regarding slavery. If so, their opinion of the peculiar institution did not keep them from owning slaves or associating with the planters active in this enterprise.

Although Tuscaloosa County voters—particularly those living in the town of Tuscaloosa—regularly favored the Whig Party, contributors to colonization whose party affiliation could be identified favored Whigs by a greater margin than that party received on election days (14 Whigs, 5 Democrats). The 5 Democratic contributors included Alabama's sitting governor, Joshua L. Martin, Alabama Supreme Court justice and future governor Henry Collier, and three former or future members of the Alabama House of Representatives—including William Garrett, chosen Speaker of the Alabama House in 1853, and Lincoln Clark, later elected a member of the United States House from Iowa. Clearly, these Democrats were not socially or economically representative of Alabama's yeomanry. Other socially high-ranking contributors to colonization included the pastors from Tuscaloosa's Episcopal, Baptist, Methodist, and Presbyterian churches; University of Alabama president Basil Manly; Alabama Supreme Court justice John J. Ormond; Chancery Judge Elisha W. Peck; editor of the Whig *Independent Monitor* Stephen F. Miller; and two of the town's longstanding merchants, Henry Adams Snow and David Woodruff, the latter of whom was elected Tuscaloosa's mayor in 1855.

Every one of the seventeen colonizationists who could be identified on the population schedule of the 1850 census for Tuscaloosa County was a slaveholder. Holdings ranged from a single slave to large holdings: John J. Ormond held 10 slaves; Joshua Martin, 13; Elisha Wolsey Peck, 14; Henry Adams Snow, 16; Basil Manly, 30; Henry Collier 88; and Alfred Battle, 134; the median holding was 7. The median value of real estate owned by these colonizationists was $2,500 (mean $5,259)—considerably greater than the median among male heads of household in both Tuscaloosa County as a whole ($200, mean $909), and the town of Tuscaloosa ($0, mean $1,882).

All seventeen colonizationists found on the census lived in the town of Tuscaloosa or, as in the case of Basil Manly, just outside the town. But whereas Tuscaloosa's temperance advocates included many artisans and small farmers, only one artisan provided money to colonization. (One might have expected white artisans' fears of economic displacement by free blacks to have generated support for colonization, but Tuscaloosa's white artisans were clearly uninterested in this cause.) The other twenty-two contributors' identifiable occupations suggest that these colonizationists, like those of the 1830s whom we discussed earlier, were more urban-oriented than the rest of the population. The only colonizationist listed as a farmer on the 1850 census was Alfred Battle, who possessed the third largest slaveholding in Tuscaloosa County. The others included eight shopkeepers/proprietors and thirteen professionals—such as attorneys, clergy, government officials, and physicians—although the large slaveholdings of some colonizationists suggest that agriculture frequently remained an important avocation. Additionally, at least ten of these thirty-six contributors to colonization participated in the temperance crusade, and thirteen were active in local Bible, tract, missionary, or Sunday-school societies. Eight colonizationists embraced both temperance and at least one benevolent cause.

In sum, when compared with the other Tuscaloosa voluntary societies that we examined in chapters 1 and 3, Alabama colonizationists of the 1830s and 1840s found less support among Baptists, artisans, and small farmers; were more likely to own slaves, to work as professionals, and to be of nonsouthern birth; and were slightly older than contemporary temperance devotees. With respect to real estate, colonizationists in the 1840s were far wealthier than other Tuscaloosa town and county residents, and more urban in their occupations. Although Alabama experienced considerable urban growth during the decade and a half prior to secession, residents of the state were still overwhelmingly farmers.[54] More than any other reform that we have examined in antebellum Tuscaloosa, colonizationists came from the ranks of the elite.

Nationally, interest in colonization was revived in the early 1850s. In the North, the growing desire to keep slavery—as well as free blacks—out of the territories encouraged this revival, as did the frustration among some abolitionists that America was incapable of overcoming racism. In the North and

---

54. Thornton, *Politics and Power*, 268–321. In the 1850 census (the first year for which such data are available) 61 percent of Alabama's adult males identified themselves as farmers; De Bow, *Seventh Census*, 903.

South alike, colonization—as with other benevolent enterprises—benefitted from the period's economic expansion, as money, the scarcity of which had caused the benevolent empire to curtail its operations by the late 1830s, was once again making its way into the society's coffers. The growing controversy surrounding slavery, moreover, inspired some white southerners to attempt to extricate their region from the threat of unenslaved African Americans. The Reverend A. E. Thom, an agent of the American Colonization Society, visited the new state capital, Montgomery, in the spring of 1850. In a series of lectures there, Thom was more explicit than Alabama's previous colonizationists. He announced flatly that the objective of colonization was to rid the country of free blacks, whom he labeled "a useless, and in many cases, a burdensome class of people," adding that "as a body, they are a clog in our political and social machinery."[55]

In December 1851, a group of Alabamians formed a new Alabama State Colonization Society. Among the founders were Tuscaloosans Robert Jemison— an industrialist and planter, the owner of 114 slaves in 1850, a state senator, and eventually a member of the Confederate Senate—and John J. Ormond, a former justice of the Alabama Supreme Court, who was selected as the society's president. Agent Thom's reassurances about the goals of the national society were, however, insufficient to mollify concerned Alabamians. The organizers of the new state body admitted that the prevailing view in Alabama was that the American Colonization Society was controlled by people who used it "as a means of indirectly assailing the institution of slavery in the Southern States." Thus, despite offers of financial assistance from the national group, the state society refused association with "the Society at Washington," and its constitution only permitted it to "have connection with other similar Societies in the Southwest."[56]

Nevertheless, white Alabamians did not completely end their relationship

55. Fredrickson, *Black Image*, 115–17, 147–49; Kuykendall, *Southern Enterprize*, 123–24; *Daily Montgomery Journal*, March 30, April 2, 1850. One writer in Tuscaloosa pointed to the incendiary potential posed by free blacks and called for either their removal from Alabama or their enslavement; *Independent Monitor*, August 6, 1857. A modern scholar, however, argues that such a position was not passionately felt by most Alabama whites, as free blacks in the Cotton State were too few to cause serious alarm; Gary B. Mills, "Miscegenation and the Free Negro in Antebellum 'Anglo' Alabama: A Reexamination of Southern Race Relations," *Journal of American History*, LXVIII (June 1981), 16–34.

56. *African Repository*, XXVIII (May 1852), 141–44.

with the American Colonization Society. Whereas virtually no money from Alabama had gone to the national society from the mid-1830s to the mid-1840s, the 1850s witnessed a large-scale revitalization of the movement in Alabama in terms of the money collected, the number of contributors, and the quantity of subscribers to the *African Repository*.[57] The ACS honored the Alabama society's president, Ormond, and the state's governor, Collier, by making each of these Tuscaloosans one of the national society's multitudinous vice-presidents—Collier was vice-president number sixty-eight, and Ormond was vice-president number ninety. There is no evidence, however, to suggest that the principal goal of the Alabama State Colonization Society, as expressed explicitly in the second article of its constitution, was compromised: "The object of the Society is to promote the emigration of free colored persons from the State of Alabama to Africa." In an accompanying "Address to the People of the State of Alabama," the state society reiterated the dangers stemming from free African Americans living among slaves. But as had the other colonization societies organized in Alabama during the 1830s, the Alabama State Colonization Society again played upon the note of altruism. The leadership explained that "there is a higher elevation from which it [colonization] may be viewed, and one which comes home to the bosom and conscience of every Christian and Philanthropist, who acknowledges the obligation of doing all the good in his power," because, as these colonizationists believed, their efforts constituted a way to introduce civilization and Christianity to the "benighted region" of Africa.[58]

When given the choice, most African Americans rejected colonization as an unattractive deportation scheme; in some northern towns and cities where the black community was large and well informed, tales of hardship, mistreat-

---

57. Quist, "Social and Moral Reform," 557–58. Unfortunately for the purposes of this study, none of these contributors from the 1850s came from Tuscaloosa. Most of this money was collected by ACS agents, generally in Montgomery and Mobile. Apparently no agents ventured into Tuscaloosa after John B. Pinney's visit in 1846.

58. *African Repository*, XXVIII (May 1852), 141–44; *Crystal Fount*, December 12, 1851; *Independent Monitor*, December 23, 1851; *African Repository*, XXVIII (March 1852), 90, XXX (February 1854), 45. Similar emphases on the colonization agenda were explained by John Morris Pease in the Mobile *Daily Advertiser*, reprinted in the *African Repository*, XXVII (September 1851), 273–75. In this context, see the position of Henry Collier discussed in the text in connection with n. 33 this chap.

ment and disease among expatriates in Liberia created rampant anticolonization sentiment.[59] Where blacks were dependent upon whites for their information, colonization was sometimes an attractive option, especially when a
master presented a slave only two alternatives: continued bondage or expulsion
to Liberia. Some slaves chose the first option, which was a source of frustration
to white colonizationists. In the mid-1840s, the American Colonization Society received 25 slaves from the will of the Reverend Witherspoon, an Alabamian, on the condition that they be deported to Liberia. Agent John Pinney was
incredulous when he reported that those slaves "will not accept the offer of liberty preferring slavery!" Certain that the desire of these black Alabamians to
remain in the land of their birth was based on "ignorance," Pinney felt convinced that his persuasive powers and first-hand experiences in Liberia as its
former governor would change their minds. Unwilling to rely on persuasion
alone, Pinney consulted with Tuscaloosa attorneys and colonizationists Elisha
W. Peck and Lincoln Clark, and reported to the national society their opinion
"that the will could be sustained in the courts."[60]

In a similar case, former governor Collier informed the American Colonization Society in 1854 that it had been named as a beneficiary in the will of Celia Burgess, "a free woman of color." By "her industry and good management,"
Burgess "acquired the money to purchase her children and grandchildren."
Alabama law, however, did not permit a slaveholder to liberate his or her slaves
without a specific "legislative act authorizing it," and thus Burgess was a slaveholder of her own family members. Obviously acquainted with Alabama's laws
relating to slavery, Burgess bequeathed her descendants to the American Colonization Society "in the confidence" that this body would "cause them to be
sent to Africa." Celia's posterity, though, did not like the predicament that this
will and Alabama law imposed on them. There is no evidence suggesting that
they preferred slavery under a new master, but they did make clear to Collier
their desire to continue living a "wretched existence" in Alabama rather than
face the uncertainties of emigration and life in a strange land. The fates of nei-

59. Staudenraus, *African Colonization Movement*, 188–93. Black hostility to colonization was
well founded; a twentieth-century demographer has concluded that immigrants to Liberia "experienced the highest mortality rates in recorded human history." Antonio McDaniel, "Extreme
Mortality in Nineteenth-Century Africa: The Case of Liberian Immigrants," *Demography*,
XXIX (November 1992), 581–94.

60. John B. Pinney to American Colonization Society, February 12, 1846, ACS Papers.

ther Celia's family nor the Witherspoon slaves are known, and their names do not appear on any of the Liberian passenger lists published by the American Colonization Society in the *African Repository*.[61]

Occasionally, though, some free blacks were convinced by colonization propaganda and found the prospect of Liberia appealing. The author of an anonymous "letter from a colored man in Alabama" was convinced that those who had emigrated were "emphatically sitting under their own vine and fig tree, and enjoying the blessings of social and political freedom in the Republic of Liberia." He also believed that if a fleet of steamers could be procured to assist in this emigration, the fears of many free blacks could be eliminated, and that within ten years "there will not be a free man of color left in the southern or slave-holding states." S. W. Jones, a free black living in Tuscaloosa, planned to leave for Liberia in early 1852. He asserted that "those of us who want to go to Liberia are men who have been striving to do something for ourselves," and he hoped that other free African Americans would "let national pride be kindled up in their hearts, and go to and make us a great nation of our own, [and] . . . in a word, cease to be 'hewers of wood and drawers of water,' and be men." In 1846, John Pinney reported that Tuscaloosan Henry Dent, "an interesting freeman of colour," had "expressed an earnest desire" to go to Liberia. Edenborough and Nancy Carroll of Tuscaloosa County purchased their freedom, obtained letters of dismission from Tuscaloosa's First Baptist Church, and left for Liberia in December 1856. Lincoln Clark, who while a resident of Tuscaloosa was active in temperance, the Alabama Bible Society, and the Tuscaloosa Union Sunday School, left his slaves in Tuscaloosa after he moved to Iowa in 1847. Nevertheless he manumitted Frederick and Charlotte Clark by 1856, and they too, emigrated to Liberia with letters of dismission from Tuscaloosa's First Baptist Church—though their emancipation was probably contingent upon their emigration. Between April 1830 and May 1857, 105 Alabamians departed for Liberia, constituting about 1 percent of the American Colonization Society's 9,709 total emigrants as of the latter date. One of these expatriates from Alabama, Harrison W. Ellis, became a high school teacher and wrote favorably of his new home abroad. It is not known how other immigrants fared in Liberia, but given the high mortality rates from disease, it is not likely that many prospered.[62]

61. Henry W. Collier to American Colonization Society, May 18, 1854, ACS Papers.

62. *African Repository*, XXVI (September 1850), 276–77, XXVIII (May 1852), 148–49, XXXII (August 1856), 253, XXXIII (January 1857), 25; John B. Pinney to ACS, February 12, 1846, in ACS

Colonization perhaps best demonstrates the limits under which African Americans could participate in the white world of reform, especially in the Deep South. When Sunday school, temperance, or evangelical religion was presented before the white population, it was done in part with the hope of assisting Americans to internalize behavior patterns that were formerly enforced through external community pressure. A potentially dangerous white population would not only then be harmless in a frightening and atomized world, but would also be transformed into a virtuous citizenry that would meet the demands both of republican government and of the expanding market economy. They would be worthy free agents and fully capable of making the correct decisions that would add to the glory of America and the progress of humanity. Reform among enslaved African Americans was done with a few of the same goals in mind: whites believed that slaves who internalized the values of the reformers would be more efficient workers and less inclined to rebel against the social order, and most evangelicals also believed that slaves were worthy of salvation, and thus attempted to preach the gospel to them. But a conversion of any sort made little, if any, difference in an African American's political or social status. As far as most whites were concerned, blacks were unassimilable, a detriment to cultural homogeneity, and thus not worthy to participate as citizens in the American republic. Their only utility was to serve as cheap labor in America or to spread American values in Africa.

The consumption of alcohol among slaves was an object of concern to white Tuscaloosans. As we have seen, state and local laws prohibited the sale of alcohol to slaves. Notwithstanding these efforts, ending the use of alcohol among slaves was never a central theme of temperance rhetoric in Tuscaloosa. Local temperance writers seldom expressed such a goal. Even so, the occasionally stated fear of alcohol falling into the hands of slaves constitutes a key difference between northern and southern temperance rhetoric. In their efforts to inspire temperance activists to petition the legislature for a prohibition law, the executive committee of the Tuscaloosa Temperance Society reminded Alabamians that it was "at the doggery" where "the slave population was corrupted and

Papers; Records of the First Baptist Church of Tuscaloosa, 1842–1867, May 10, December 15, 1856; *African Repository*, XLIII (April 1867), 109–17, XXVII (January 1851), 2–4; Staudenraus, *African Colonization Movement, passim;* McDaniel, "Extreme Mortality," 581–94.

made dishonest."[63] John Warren, editor of Tuscaloosa's temperance weekly, the *Crystal Fount*, lamented in 1851 the widespread intemperance among slaves. He felt that it diminished their value and was a direct consequence of the legal sale of alcohol, "which will continue to injure the slaveholder directly, and indirectly the interests of the whole South." Although Warren insisted that the only way to make liquor less accessible to slaves was through statewide prohibition, he also encouraged the development of Tuscaloosa's Colored Total Abstinence Society. Little is known of this organization, as Tuscaloosa's newspapers rarely reported on slave activities. Formed in 1839, it had a membership in 1851 of nearly four hundred. Warren believed that their purported temperance had made an enormous difference in the lives of these slaves, and that the "good which has resulted from this organization is incalculable. The benefit has been to both the master and the slave; enhancing the value of the latter, and rendering him physically and morally happier." Intemperance, on the other hand, was the bane of slavery, as slaveholders "all know that the habitual use of liquor makes a servant lazy and indifferent to the interests of his master, and renders him physically and morally miserable and worthless."

The 1851 anniversary meeting of the Colored Total Abstinence Society assembled at the Methodist Church, where the large crowd heard "an address from one of their members, who entertained them with a brief but spirited expose of the history, progress and plan of the association." After the speech, the assemblage formed a procession that extended a quarter mile in length to the rotunda of the old Capitol. Approaching the Capitol, the streets were illuminated by "blazing piles of pine." Warren was moved by the occasion, and he described this "imposing spectacle" as "truly brilliant, and the effect picturesque in the extreme." Nor were those present content with the clothing of bondservants, as they were "all gaily attired in holiday costume, and full of smiles and good humor." Awaiting them at the Capitol was a table "some fifty yards in length" covered with "sumptious [*sic*] viands barbecued," the "rich results of many days' labor."[64] John Warren's description of the celebration casts doubt on

63. *Flag of the Union*, October 2, 1839. See the similar sentiments in *Crystal Fount*, December 5, 1851. At a state temperance meeting in Selma in 1853, delegates voted to appeal to the legislature for a law that would prohibit the establishment of "doggeries" at the edge of a plantation; *Crystal Fount*, June 14, 1853.

64. *Crystal Fount*, September 26, 1851; *Independent Monitor*, September 25, 1851. Masters desirous of temperate slaves certainly used heavier-handed tactics to achieve their objective. Basil

his contention that all of the participants at this anniversary meeting were genuine teetotalers. It does not strain credulity to believe that virtually anyone would espouse temperance principles for an evening if he or she could enjoy such a festive diversion from the daily rigors and monotonies of slave labor.

White Tuscaloosans made a more sustained effort to promote the plantation mission, evangelical Protestantism's drive to promulgate the gospel among slaves.[65] Although African Americans were often among the founders of churches in Tuscaloosa (as in the rest of the Old Southwest), by the 1840s a significant number of slaves had not received the evangelical message. At about this time, some white evangelicals expressed an increased interest in converting African Americans. Promoters of the plantation mission, however, faced opposition from a number of white southerners who suspected that it undermined slavery. Some slaveholders feared that abolitionists were using the cause clandestinely to foment incendiarism. Others wanted slaves to be kept away from Christianity altogether; the knowledge that Nat Turner and Denmark Vesey were highly religious only made these whites more convinced that the Christian faith was subversive when preached among slaves. Opponents of the plantation mission undoubtedly felt uneasy regarding the concept that both blacks and whites had immortal souls and would someday be equally accountable before God, and when African American preachers encouraged members of both races to rally to Christ. Regardless, the lives of blacks and whites in the antebellum South intersected at many points, and even prior to the widespread promotion of the mission to the slaves, members of both races shared their reli-

---

Manly, for example, threatened his slave Moses that he would sell him unless he quit his intemperate ways. Basil Manly Diary No. 4, January 13, 1851.

65. On the plantation mission, see: Mathews, *Slavery and Methodism*, 62–87, and Donald G. Mathews, "Charles Colcock Jones and the Southern Evangelical Crusade to Form a Biracial Community," *Journal of Southern History*, XLI (August 1975), 299–320; Albert J. Raboteau, *Slave Religion: The "Invisible Institution" in the Antebellum South* (New York, 1978), 152–80; Loveland, *Southern Evangelicals*, 219–56; John B. Boles, "Introduction," and Blake Touchstone, "Planters and Slave Religion in the Deep South," in *Masters and Slaves in the House of the Lord: Race and Religion in the American South, 1740–1870*, ed. John B. Boles (Lexington, Ky., 1988), 1–18, 99–126; Hatch, *Democratization of American Christianity*, 102–107, 110–13; Cornelius, *"When I Can Read My Title Clear";* Ruth Alden Doan, "Race and Revivalism in *The Southern Christian Advocate*" (Paper presented at the Thirteenth Annual Meeting of the Society for Historians of the Early American Republic, July 1991); and Mitchell Snay, *Gospel of Disunion: Religion and Separatism in the Antebellum South* (Cambridge, Eng., 1993).

gious faiths with each other. A pious slave was the catalyst in Basil Manly's conversion during the latter's youth in South Carolina, and Henry Tutwiler remarked that several conversations with his slave Frances had dispelled some of Tutwiler's skepticism: "What a humiliating lesson!"[66]

Some whites feared that such interaction between master and slave would diminish the social distance between the races and cause widespread questioning of the essential inferiority of blacks and superiority of whites. Neither thing came to pass. Although possibly subversive of slavery, the plantation mission was not destructive of it, as the peculiar institution was too wrapped up in the economic life of the Old South to be discarded easily. Nevertheless, plantation missionaries labored hard to reassure their critics that their gospel posed no threat and that slaves under their care would be obedient and profitable servants rather than rebels. In order to attain this proslavery objective, it was necessary for plantation missionaries to instruct slaves in religion orally to make certain that they remained illiterate and ignorant of portions of the Bible that could undermine their position as chattels. Slaves heard Ephesians 6:5–6 preached to them incessantly ("Servants, be odedient to them that are your masters according to the flesh, with fear and trembling, in singleness of your heart, as unto Christ; Not with eyeservice, as menpleasers; but as servants of Christ, doing the will of God from the heart"). Most slaves, however, rejected such a submissive faith; among themselves, they sang spirituals praising the mortal deliverances of Daniel, David, Joshua, Jonah, Moses, and Noah.[67]

For many whites, "doing the will of God from the heart" meant that religious slaves would internalize the values of their masters and be more efficient and obedient workers. Of course, white southerners who embraced evangelical religion and who recognized the humanity of the slave felt deep concern over anyone who was not converted. But evangelicals also knew that the person who was converted to the gospel and had experienced an internal change of heart would no longer need external compulsion to obey God's will, as such behavior was a manifestation of genuine conversion. Like the promoters of Bible, tract,

    66. Bailey, *Shadow on the Church*, 180–96; Porch, *History of the First Baptist Church*, 7, 24; Henry B. Foster, *History of the Tuscaloosa County Baptist Association* (Tuscaloosa, 1934), 24, 241; Harold Wilson, "Basil Manly, Apologist for Slavocracy," *Alabama Review*, XXXVIII (January 1962), 39; Henry Tutwiler to James Birney, May 8, 1833, in Birney Papers. On the interaction between whites and blacks in the course of religious conversion, see Doan, "Race and Revivalism."

    67. Lawrence W. Levine, *Black Culture and Black Consciousness: Afro-American Folk Thought from Slavery to Freedom* (New York, 1977), 50–51; Genovese, *Roll, Jordan, Roll*, 208, 244, 252–55.

and Sunday-school societies—and to a lesser extent, temperance, which was ostensibly more secular in its orientation than the benevolence crusades— these reformers desired to have a population that was both converted and would voluntarily control its passions and reorient itself toward greater productivity. In the end, most white southerners came to view a converted slave as a safe slave, provided that whites could control the words that were preached to the enslaved. Such a view eventually was supported by Alabama's highest court, which ruled in 1857 that "though [slaves] are property, they are intelligent beings, and under moral accountability. The master . . . is morally bound to furnish to his dependent and subject class such moral and religious instruction as is adapted to its political status. Such instruction, properly directed, not only benefits the slave in his moral relations, but enhances his value as an honest, faithful servant and laborer."[68]

There were a number of plantation mission advocates in Tuscaloosa, particularly among the Baptists. Members of this sect became increasingly vocal during the 1840s, when disputes between northern and southern Baptists over slavery led to the breakup of the American Baptist Foreign Mission Society and American Baptist Home Missionary Society. Preceding this disintegration of Baptist benevolence, many northern Baptists wanted to know if the money they contributed to foreign and domestic missions was supporting missionaries who held slaves, while many southerners took umbrage at such inquiries and wondered whether they should support enterprises that excluded slaveholders. Led by Basil Manly, members of the Tuscaloosa Baptist Church were especially troubled by the controversy. Manly was set on edge by northern cries about "the offensiveness of union with slaveholders." He felt that slavery was strictly the concern of southerners, and northerners had no right to interfere: "We have examined that matter, & come to the deliberate conclusion that it is not wrong to hold property in our slaves. . . . Now it is for them to say, whether, with this understanding, they are willing to work with us on equal terms—acknowledging us as brethren—*Let us alone.*" Manly's congregation asked their delegates to the 1844 Alabama Baptist Convention to submit the following question for the convention's consideration: "Is it proper for us at the South to send any more money to our brethren at the North, for missionary

---

68. *Pickens Adm'r.* v. *Pickens' Distributees,* 35 Alabama Reports 452. See also James D. Hardy Jr. and Robert B. Robinson, "A Peculiarity of the Peculiar Institution: An Alabama Case," *Alabama Review,* XLV (January 1992), 18–25.

and other benevolent purposes before the subject of *Slavery* be rightly understood by both parties?"[69] After responding in the negative, the convention then
passed several resolutions that asked the Boston-based board of managers of
the American Baptist Home Missionary Society whether a slaveholder could
be appointed as a missionary. The board's negative answer exacerbated a growing sectional split among American Baptists that led to the formation of the
Southern Baptist Convention in 1845.[70]

Although Basil Manly was a thoroughgoing sectionalist, he was not gleeful
when he realized that a denominational split was inevitable; he believed that
the "consequences of separation" would be "deplorable in various respects."
The cause of foreign missions had been a favorite of Manly's, and he was convinced that it would "be an injury, a vast injury, to the cause of benevolence, for
the South to be divorced from it." Baptist foreign missions would not wither
away completely—beachheads had been established in many lands, and
Manly was sure that "the northern people will still send, the work will go on, &
spread." He felt, though, that the time was ripe for a shift in the strategy of
southern benevolence. White southern evangelicals, he argued, had work to do
among slaves, among American Indians, and in advancing "evangelization at
the west." The obnoxious interference of northerners, Manly believed,

> may be the occasion, under God, of directing the Southern churches to these
> Heathen at home. My mind is running strong in that channel: I find many in
> just the same situation; and excited by discovering the unexpected coincidence
> of views and feelings. If the Northern people will not have our counsels and con-
> tributions, we have a cause at home that demands them. I believe that this is now
> the appropriate miss[ionar]y field of the Southern Churches. None but the
> Southern Churches can do it. And it must be done. It is an immediate absorbing
> enterprize. If one more word is said, by the northern people, about the offen-

69. Basil Manly to Basil Manly Jr., September 23, November 22, 1844, in Manly Family Papers; Records of the First Baptist Church of Tuscaloosa, 1842–1867, November 11, 1844.

70. Baker, *Relations Between Northern and Southern Baptists*, 72–87; William Barnes, *Southern
Baptist Convention*, 12–42; Putnam, *Baptists and Slavery*; Porch, *History of the First Baptist Church*,
21–23; Posey, *Frontier Mission*, 363–71. See also *Minutes of the Seventeenth Anniversary of the Bap-
tist State Convention of Alabama*, 4–6; *Journal of the Proceedings of the Baptist State Convention in
Alabama at its Twentieth Anniversary*, 2; *Minutes of the Twenty-first Anniversary of the Alabama
Baptist State Convention*, 23; *Minutes of the Twenty-second Anniversary of the Alabama Baptist State
Convention*, 21; and *Alabama Baptist*, November 20, 1846.

siveness of union with slaveholders; I shall be in favor of making a disunified adieu: and attending to our own business, in our own way.[71]

Manly took the lead in promoting the mission to the slaves among southern Baptists. A month and a half prior to the Alabama Baptist Convention in Marion in November 1844, he planned to plead with his coreligionists "to begin missionary work for the colored people." After the convention, he was pleased with the favorable notices that his remarks elicited in the Tuscaloosa *Democratic Gazette* and the Marion *Herald.* He confided to his son, "I made as forcible an effort as I could; & the thing took wonderfully." Like Manly, Alabama's other Baptists present at the convention probably viewed the plantation mission as the best way to advance the evangelical agenda in light of the impending schism with northern Baptists. Moreover, evangelicals who were troubled by abolitionist charges and harbored secret misgivings regarding the inhumanity of slavery found the plantation mission to be a way to salve their troubled consciences. Although he despised abolitionists and was an ardent sectionalist, Basil Manly may have been among this group, as he felt private apprehensions about both slavery and emancipation. Such individuals must have reasoned that a population of pious slaves and pious slaveholders was the most humane solution for the present.[72]

Of course, advocates of the plantation mission only hoped to strengthen the peculiar institution; they often claimed that the circulation of the gospel among the slaves would be the best protection against insurrection. Manly had expressed this view earlier that year when he addressed a congregation of Baptists, Methodists, and Presbyterians. Appealing for a united evangelical effort to take the gospel to the slaves, Manly told his listeners that "the dissemination of moral truth . . . will always be found at once the cheapest & most effective support of law & order, the most certain check of incendiarism & turbulence." He also pointed out that many slaves did not pose an insurrectionary threat. The labor of these devoted servants —and the labor of those not devoted to their masters, for that matter—procured for slaveholders "the luxuries & comforts of life; they constitute a great part of our wealth." Thus masters were in-

71. Basil Manly to Basil Manly Jr., November 22, 1844, March 31, 1845, September 23, 1844, all in Manly Family Papers.

72. Basil Manly to Basil Manly Jr., September 23, November 22, December 3, 1844, *ibid.* Regarding Manly's views of slavery, see n. 31 this chap. and the discussion in the text associated with that note.

debted to their slaves: "They kindly nurse us in infancy, they relieve the fatigue of our journeys, they contribute to the care & hospitality of our festive houses, they watch & support us in sickness, they risk their lives for us in danger, and when we die, the faithful old servant follows us to our grave, & vents his undissembled grief." Despite what Manly believed were ample material rewards for slaves' services, he suggested that "it will be more useful to them and acceptable to God, to pay also in spiritual things." Further, Manly maintained that slaves constituted one of the most promising missionary fields available, as they were easily accessible and more likely to convert than other peoples across the globe. Their lack of formal education would only encourage their conversion, as "they have not been educated under any prevailing systems of false doctrine or worship. . . . Their weak and dependent condition in the world disposes them for the peculiar doctrines of the gospel. . . . From our acknowledged superior relation, what we say or do attracts their confidence at once and exerts great power over them."[73]

Possibly the earliest Baptist congregation in Tuscaloosa County to express an interest in the mission to the slaves was the Grant's Creek Baptist Church in Foster's Settlement. After several months of discussion, this body resolved in early 1837 to "procure the services of some suitable persons whose duty it shall be to visit plantations and all others in this vicinity where their services may be accept[ed] once a month and spend as much time as he may think in preaching and instructing the Negroes in the fundamental doctrine of the Scriptures." But it was the white members of Tuscaloosa's Baptist church, where Manly was a prominent member and often preached, who endeavored to make the spiritual welfare of slaves a paramount issue among Baptists. Delegates from the Tuscaloosa church to the November 1844 Alabama Baptist State Convention were instructed to seek "the commencement of a fund for employing suitable persons as missionaries to labor among our own colored people after having obtained consent of their owners," as the "most recent action of the Baptist Home Missionary Board seems to us, in the Providence of God, to point out *this* as the appropriate sphere, at the present time, for our Home Missionary operations." The delegates also reported on the progress that had been made in Tuscaloosa: "During the past year, we have commenced a system of *oral religious* instruction of our colored people upon a plan that has

73. Basil Manly, "National Stability" (Manuscript dated June 21, 1844, as cited in Loveland, *Southern Evangelicals*, 223–26).

been in approved operation in many parts of G[eorgi]a and S. Carolina. . . . We have found it attended with highly satisfactory results & can cordially recommend it to Southern Churches generally." Basil Manly similarly reported that "our colored Sunday School numbers over 100 of various ages—and is working very well. Every one, who has examined it, seems well pleased. The people seem docile—and have given no trouble in the managemt. of their discipline."[74]

Reuben Dodson, a Baptist minister who preached at several rural churches in Tuscaloosa County, responded enthusiastically to this new emphasis on the evangelical agenda by "preaching to the negroes in his congregations with encouraging prospects." Benjamin Whitfield, a Sunday-school superintendent who in 1850 held thirty-two slaves in Tuscaloosa County, hired Dodson to preach once a month at his plantation. After emancipation, former Tuscaloosa resident James H. DeVotie recalled that for thirty-five years about one-third of his preaching was among the "colored people," and that he had baptized "about 800 of these Ethiopian believers."[75] But despite such fervor in some quarters, Baptists in Tuscaloosa and throughout the South made no formal, institutional efforts to spread the gospel among African Americans. Although some Baptists spoke enthusiastically regarding the importance of the plantation mission, such efforts were individual pursuits, rather than coordinated operations on the scale of their denomination-sponsored and white-oriented Bible, tract, and Sunday-school societies.

The enlarged emphasis upon the spiritual welfare of slaves, ironically, resulted in increased segregation in southern white churches. During the settlement of the Old Southwest, blacks and whites either worshiped side by side or met concurrently but sat in separate sections. This pattern began to change during the 1840s. When the Tuscaloosa Baptist Association encouraged its churches to pay special attention to the "conversion and religious instruction of the colored people," it also suggested that the spoken word needed to be administered differently to slaves than to whites. Writing on behalf of the association's Committee on the Religious Instruction of the Colored People, Tusca-

74. Records of the Grant's Creek Baptist Church, Fosters, Alabama, in Samford University Library, Birmingham, Alabama (microfilm typescript); Records of the First Baptist Church of Tuscaloosa, 1842–1867, November 11, 1844; Basil Manly to Basil Manly Jr., October 25, 1844, in Manly Family Papers.

75. Basil Manly to Basil Manly Jr., December 3, 1844, in Manly Family Papers; J. H. DeVotie to S. S. Cutting, July 15, 1877, as cited in William Barnes, *Southern Baptist Convention*, 60.

loosa pastor Thomas F. Curtis recommended in 1848 that ministers "preach to the white congregation in the morning . . . [and] to the blacks in the evening," since "special services intended for and addressed to [the blacks], are alone equal to the difficulty of reaching their capacities." Curtis' suggestions had already been implemented by the Grant's Creek and Tuscaloosa Baptist Churches. African American Baptists in both congregations also experienced increased supervision from the white body; in accordance with state law, blacks were not permitted to assemble without the presence of a white superintendent. At the Grant's Creek church, the statute was carried out more fully, as Anthony, an African American preacher of that body, was prohibited from preaching unless "5 respectable slaveholders" were present and was required to consult with a committee of eight white members before making any preaching appointments.[76]

The success of the Baptist plantation mission varied widely. Some congregations, planters, and pastors embraced the cause with great enthusiasm. Nevertheless, the Baptist belief in congregational autonomy made it difficult for Baptist churches to act collectively in this or other enterprises. Added to this obstacle was the long-time paucity of Baptist missionaries in the South. Because the American Baptist Home Missionary Society had been unable to send many missionaries to the region, southern churches and associations often had to improvise in order to maintain a missionary in their midst. Institutionally, it often appeared that little was being done. After the Baptist schism, the Domestic Mission Board of the Southern Baptist Convention was not able to do much better. Recognizing that its limited resources were unable to penetrate deeply a field covering fourteen states, nearly 900,000 square miles, and a population of about eight million, the board suggested that state conventions and local associations take up the slack. Exhortation and encouragement was thus provided by the Baptist leadership, but ultimate responsibility lay with local churches and individuals.[77] Resolutions approved by mem-

---

76. Bailey, *Shadow on the Church*, 178–96; *Minutes of the Sixteenth Annual Session of the Tuscaloosa Baptist Association, held at Concord Meeting-House, Fayette County, Alabama* (Tuscaloosa, 1848), 7; Porch, *History of the First Baptist Church*, 24–36; Records of the Grant's Creek Baptist Church, January 4, February 2, 29, May 2, July 4, 1840, October 1, 1842, July 1, 1843, February 3, 1844. See also Records of the Big Creek Baptist Church, May 9, August 9, 1857, in Hoole Special Collections (photocopy).

77. William Barnes, *Southern Baptist Convention*, 39–40. In 1849, the Alabama Baptist State Convention placed the responsibility of a slave's religious education upon the slave's owner. It was

bers of the Gilgal Baptist Church in rural Tuscaloosa County in 1853 suggest that institutional patronage had not succeeded in making many white Baptists feel an urgency in this matter. Although the church members explained that they felt a high responsibility "imposed on us by our ownership of slaves" and recognized a "duty to provide them with the means of religious instruction," they had as yet done little preaching among their chattels. They intended, however, to improve matters and they resolved to raise enough money "to preach to the colored people of the vicinity," requesting other churches in the association "to adopt a similar plan, and thus co-operate with us in this good work."[78]

Gilgal's resolutions may have changed this inertia, since in the long run, Baptist efforts to evangelize African Americans resulted in a significant increase in the percentage of black church members. In 1846, the first year for which such figures are available, 13.6 percent (258 of 1,893) of the Baptists in the Tuscaloosa Association were African American; this statistic rose over a third to 18.7 percent (471 of 2,531) by 1857. The Tuscaloosa church expressed the most enthusiasm for sending the gospel to the slaves. As it was the home church of Basil Manly and had Thomas F. Curtis as its pastor, this attitude should not be surprising. Further, as many of the county's planters lived in or near the town of Tuscaloosa, their slaves were often easily accessible to receive the word. The church was also the only one in the association with a majority of African American members; over the same period, the percentage of African Americans increased from 50.7 percent (71 of 140) to 58.5 percent (148 of 253).[79] Countywide, however, blacks were disproportionately absent from the Baptist church. Unfortunately, extant sources do not reveal the extent to which this lack of African American Baptist church members was a consequence of reluctance on the part of whites to extend the hand of gospel fellowship to slaves, or

---

no longer necessary, declared the convention, to debate the propriety of providing slaves with religion; the pious master should provide his or her slaves with the gospel. *Minutes of the Alabama Baptist State Convention*, as cited in James Sellers, *Slavery in Alabama*, 315.

78. *Minutes of the Twenty-first Annual Session of the Tuscaloosa Baptist Association, Held at the Hepzibah Meeting House, Tuscaloosa Co., Ala., from the 17th to 20th Sept., 1853* (Tuscaloosa, 1853), 7.

79. *Minutes of the Fourteenth Annual Session of the Tuscaloosa Baptist Association* (Tuscaloosa, 1846), 9; *Minutes of the Twenty-fifth Annual Session of the Tuscaloosa Baptist Association, Held at Mount Moriah Meeting House* (Tuscaloosa, 1857), 11; Henry Foster, *Tuscaloosa County Baptist Association*, 73. While there was some fluctuation in these figures, both absolute numbers and percentages increased gradually between 1846 and 1857. In contrast, the racial mixture of Tuscaloosa's Methodist church (see n. 81 this chap.) showed a far greater yearly variation.

whether slaves found the message unappealing. Of course, participation in any religious activity could occur only with the consent of a slave's master. A master who was irreligious or believed that religion subverted slavery would have been unlikely to permit his or her slaves to worship. Conversely, though many African Americans obtained solace worshiping at biracial congregations where their spiritual equality was occasionally acknowledged and they were sometimes addressed as "brother" or "sister," many a slave undoubtedly "converted" only after being pressured by his or her master. Also, many blacks were probably convinced that the gospel preached at Baptist and other churches was essentially a message of docility, and thus rejected it as a "white man's religion."[80]

Although they lacked advocates of slave evangelism such as Basil Manly and Thomas Curtis, Methodists in Tuscaloosa were more successful than their Baptist counterparts in providing African Americans with the gospel, in that a larger number and a higher percentage of Tuscaloosa town's Methodists were African Americans than was the case in the Baptist, Presbyterian, Episcopalian, or Catholic churches.[81] Most authorities conclude, however, that statewide and throughout the South, more blacks affiliated with the Baptists than with the Methodists.[82] Slaves may have leaned toward the Baptists because congregations in that denomination were self-governing and permitted blacks to have some voice in the church, whereas authority in Methodism proceeded downward from white bishops. At Tuscaloosa's First Baptist Church, for ex-

80. Raboteau, *Slave Religion*, 176–77. See also *Flag of the Union*, October 31, 1838, in which a writer complains of the "assemblages of noisy negro men and boys"—presumably unconverted— who regularly disturbed Tuscaloosa's churchgoers.

81. Regarding missionary efforts among slaves by Tuscaloosa Catholics and Episcopalians, see James Sellers, *Slavery in Alabama*, 298–99, 323–25.

Between 1825 and 1860, blacks outnumbered whites at the Tuscaloosa Methodist church, except for 1836–1839. Church membership statistics varied considerably, and numbers are available for only thirty of these years. However, during thirteen of these years, African Americans constituted at least 60 percent of church members. Black membership reached 415 in 1857 and peaked at 541 in 1864. Upon emancipation, African Americans left the Tuscaloosa Methodist church en masse to form the African Methodist Episcopal Zion Church of Tuscaloosa. James Sellers, *First Methodist Church*, 51, 66, 102, 124–25. See also Katherine L. Dvorak, *An African-American Exodus: The Segregation of the Southern Churches* (Brooklyn, 1991).

82. Raboteau, *Slave Religion*, 175–76; Mathews, *Slavery and Methodism*, 66–67, 83. According to James Benson Sellers, "of the three denominations competing for the allegiance of the slave, the Presbyterian stood third. The Baptist came first, with the Methodist a close second." The Catholic church, and other Protestant denominations, trailed far behind the three major evangelical faiths. James Sellers, *Slavery in Alabama*, 318.

ample, African American members, despite their close supervision by whites, enjoyed limited autonomy in some matters of church government.[83]

Although many slaveholders were Methodists, some masters may have felt hesitant to have their slaves hear Methodist preaching in light of the mildly antislavery legacy of the Methodist Episcopal Church. Methodism's founder, John Wesley, had denounced slavery, and in the late eighteenth and early nineteenth centuries numerous Methodist conferences in the South had prohibited their ministers from owning slaves. One significant illustration is the case of Dudley Hargrove. In 1819, Hargrove, a resident of Big Sandy Creek in rural Tuscaloosa County, was recommended by the Quarterly Conference of the Tuscaloosa Circuit as a candidate worthy of ordination as a deacon. Nevertheless, after an extensive debate at the October 1819 meeting of the Tennessee Annual Conference in Nashville, Hargrove was rejected as unworthy to hold this office because he was a slaveholder. In another case involving a church leader, Joshua Boucher resigned his Tuscaloosa town pastorate in 1827 because of his repulsion toward slavery, and relocated to Ohio. During the ensuing decades, however, the antislavery dimension of Southern Methodism declined. In 1844, American Methodists split into Northern and Southern denominations because of their disagreements over slavery. The particular issue around which the schism centered was whether James O. Andrew, who became a slaveholder upon marriage to a woman owning slaves, could continue to function as a bishop. Northern Methodists insisted that he either resign or divest himself of his new properties; southern Methodists stood firm in maintaining that he continue in his position. In neighboring Greene County, Methodists proclaimed that more was at stake than mere sectional honor. Had Andrew resigned his position, "he would have closed the door (now open) for preaching the gospel in the South." After the church divided, the Southern Methodist clergy obviously felt compelled to live up to the ideals for which they seceded.[84]

83. Porch, *History of the First Baptist Church*, 24–36. See also James Sellers, *Slavery in Alabama*, 319; Genovese, *Roll, Jordan, Roll*, 232–33. Sellers notes that Alabama Baptists accepted the testimony of slaves in church trials as being on par with the words of any other church member (*Slavery in Alabama*, 321). Considering the secular power granted to whites, however, it is not likely that slaves often brought the sins of their masters to the attention of the church.

84. West, *Methodism in Alabama*, 155–56, 642; James Sellers, *First Methodist Church*, 41. West, 599, 604, notes that "many slave owners" in Alabama resisted Methodist preaching to their slaves because they believed that it would "foster insubordination, encourage abolition sentiments, complicate civil affairs, and hasten emancipation"; see also Raboteau, *Slave Religion*, 160. Regarding the reaction of Tuscaloosa's Methodists to the schism of 1844, see *Independent Monitor,*

Methodists were not as daunted by collective action as the Baptists were, and their denomination promoted the plantation mission with greater vigor than the Baptists—although throughout the South these Methodist missionaries were obviously not as successful as the less-organized Baptists. As was the case with the other churches in Alabama, Methodism numbered African Americans among the faithful from the time that Methodists commenced preaching in the state. In 1831 two missionaries were appointed "to the people of color" in northern Alabama. Although Methodists occasionally discontinued plantation mission appointments during the early 1830s, after 1838 the Alabama Conference at its annual meetings regularly designated individuals to labor among the slaves. The Methodists' mission to the slaves peaked in 1856, when the Alabama Conference established thirty-seven missions to provide preaching for the state's African Americans. Two of these missions, the Greensboro Mission and the Prairie Creek Mission, were located in the Tuscaloosa District. The latter mission served twelve plantations in 1856 and had 694 members.[85]

Tuscaloosa's Presbyterians similarly sought to carry the gospel to African Americans, and also to Africans. African Americans were listed among the communicants at the Tuscaloosa Presbyterian Church from the early 1820s. In the ensuing decades Presbyterians devoted increased attention to presenting the gospel to slaves. "We hope it may not be long till all the colored families in these United States shall enjoy the rich and inestimable blessings of a preached gospel," declared the Synod of Alabama in 1838. By 1848, the Tuscaloosa Presbytery disclosed that nearly all the churches within its bounds held special services for slaves. Over a decade later, the presbytery boasted that it had succeeded in "plainly and faithfully" declaring Presbyterian doctrines to the slaves' "unsophisticated . . . minds." The presbytery also felt that Presbyterians had made "our simple forms of worship . . . attractive to this people" in spite of claims by some whites that blacks only enjoyed preaching accompanied "by loud and boisterous demonstrations."[86]

September 17, 1845; West, *Methodism in Alabama,* 643, 648–51; and James Sellers, *First Methodist Church,* 67–72.

85. West, *Methodism in Alabama,* 598–99, 603–604, 710; James Sellers, *First Methodist Church,* 81.

86. James Sellers, *Slavery in Alabama,* 296, 298, 317. However, a church in the Presbytery also complained that nearly all of its African American members "have preferences for other

In April 1843, the Tuscaloosa session leadership announced to the congregation that the Synod of Alabama was attempting "to raise money to purchase the freedom of a certain Negro slave and his family with the view of sending them as Missionaries to Liberia."[87] With a special Sunday school for slaves, Tuscaloosa's Presbyterians may have had the most complete program for the religious education of African Americans of any of the town's churches. During his visit to Alabama in 1846, Sir Charles Lyell found that an "excellent Sabbath school had been established by the Presbyterians of Tuscaloosa, for the children of Negroes." He expected that such an institution would improve the literacy of free African American artisans, most of whom were uneducated. But some of Tuscaloosa's white Presbyterians hesitated before instructing their slaves and free blacks. In 1853, Charles J. Fiquet asked the session "to permit the teachers in the Sabbath School for colored people to teach them to read." The session agreed to allow the teachers to do so, "provided it did not infringe [upon] the Law of the State." If session members adhered rigidly to state laws, they probably did not teach free and enslaved African Americans in the Sunday school to read, as laws in effect since 1832 prohibited this practice. Fiquet and the session must have been aware of these laws; his inquiry suggests that some slaves and free blacks were taught to read, regardless of the letter of the statute.

Of course, some white Alabamians reacted with hostility to the instruction of African Americans in Sunday schools, as a literate slave could read not only the Bible, but abolitionist tracts as well. In 1831, Thomas Manning reported that ASSU-affiliated schools in Dallas County had "met with some serious opposition on account of the blacks being admitted and taught in them. There

---

churches"; *ibid.*, 317. Hatch, *Democratization of American Christianity*, 102–106, suggests why slaves preferred the Baptist and Methodist denominations.

87. Session Book No. 3 of the Tuscaloosa Presbyterian Church, 1842–1871, April 1, 1843, in possession of First Presbyterian Church of Tuscaloosa. This individual was undoubtedly Harrison W. Ellis of Greene County, whose name Charles Lyell heard mentioned frequently while visiting Alabama in 1846. He was a "blacksmith, who had taught himself Greek and Latin. He is acquiring Hebrew, and I was sorry to hear that the Presbyterians contemplate sending him as a missionary to Liberia. If it were an object in the South to elevate the blacks, he might be far more instrumental in forwarding the cause of civilization and Christianity by remaining at home, for the negroes like a preacher of their own race." Lyell, *Second Visit to the United States*, II, 71–72; *African Repository*, XXIII (February 1847), 46–48, XXVII (January 1851), 2–4; James Sellers, *Slavery in Alabama*, 307–308.

is a law exists in this state against instructing the Blacks. The people prepose, now, proceeding upon a different plan, that of instructing white children only." But despite the animosity reported by Manning and the reluctance expressed by the session to Fiquet, some of Alabama's slaves learned to read. Undoubtedly some did so clandestinely. Others lived with masters who taught their slaves to read, in defiance of state laws. The Reverend Jonathan Lyons, the American Bible Society's agent for Alabama, rejoiced that the instruction of "servants in the great truths of the Bible is receiving more and more attention from all the Christian Churches in the state." After inquiring throughout Alabama, Lyons estimated that one-tenth of the adult slave population was literate and supplied with a Bible. Those slaves with Bibles usually received a copy from their masters. It was reportedly "not an uncommon thing for masters to hold out inducements for their servants to learn to read the Bible," and Lyons claimed that he had never heard of a case where a master had refused to supply a literate slave with a copy of the Scriptures.[88] The Reformation credo "every man his own priest" continued to be powerful in this Bibliocentric culture.

In this chapter, we have examined the intersection of slavery and antebellum reform in Tuscaloosa County. Increased white fear after the Nat Turner rebellion and the abolitionist mail controversy exacerbated hostility toward abolition. Although white Tuscaloosans linked neither temperance nor mainstream benevolent enterprises to antislavery, their fear of abolition augmented indifference and suspicion toward colonization and resulted in greater white control over the lives of slaves. Some whites were initially suspicious of white Protestant efforts to evangelize southern slaves, but most were won over when they concluded that a converted slave was a safe slave. Encompassing more than merely the increasingly restrictive state laws and the ordinances passed in Tuscaloosa, the mission to the slaves aimed in part to extend the authority of white evangelical culture over the lives of slaves. In an evangelical culture, whites knew that external controls were insufficient; the ubiquitous emphasis upon conversion made whites stress the importance of internal commitment to

88. Lyell, *Second Visit to the United States,* II, 71; Session Book No. 3 of the Tuscaloosa Presbyterian Church, April 11, 1853; James Sellers, *Slavery in Alabama,* 117; Thomas Manning to F. W. Porter, March 17, 1831, in ASSU Papers; ABS *Annual Report,* XL (1856), 90. Cornelius, *"When I Can Read My Title Clear,"* 8–9, corroborates Lyons' estimates.

the laws that regulate and govern society. In addition, such regulations were especially important in a fluid society where the authority of neighbors, family, church, and the old elite was not as powerful as it once was. This erosion of authority was true for blacks as well as for whites. It was becoming increasingly difficult for the ruling race to keep track of all its slaves, and to know them all personally.

This increased concern about the control of slaves caused some white southerners to take a second look at the enslaved. Scholars have noted that the antebellum period was remarkable for the increase in the restrictions placed upon America's slaves, while at the same time their physical living conditions improved. This dual outcome resulted in part from white anxiety stemming from the rise of northern abolitionism and the fear that Nat Turner's insurrection could be replicated. These factors were countered by the growing prosperity of white planters, the increased economic stability brought about by the demise of the frontier, advancing slave prices, and, ironically, from the reaction of slaveholders to abolitionist charges regarding the inhumane treatment of slaves. The president of Tuscaloosa's Athenaeum academy, Columbus Franklin Sturgis, insisted that poor treatment of slaves made it "impossible to gag the abolitionists."[89] But material improvements in the lives of slaves may have also resulted in part from the humanitarian sentiment of the age, expressed in the multitude of reform movements. The evangelical spirit that inspired Tuscaloosans to advance revivals and eliminate irreligion, skepticism, gambling, strong drink, and unenslaved African Americans from their midst may have also contributed to the amelioration—although by no means the elimination—of some of the harshest features of chattel slavery. But whether or not white reform improved some aspects of slave life, it is clear that the impulse of antebellum reform was insufficient to bring about an end to slavery in the nineteenth-century United States. Whites found slavery to be too profitable, and were unwilling to relinquish it without a fight.

89. Genovese, *Roll, Jordan, Roll*, 49–70. Sturgis is quoted *ibid.*, 56; additional information on him may be found in Porch, *History of the First Baptist Church*, 39; *Independent Monitor*, June 19, 1851; and Owen, *History of Alabama*, IV, 1637. A useful cross-time analysis of slavery in colonial America versus the nineteenth-century institution can be made by comparing Peter H. Wood, *Black Majority: Negroes in Colonial South Carolina from 1670 Through the Stono Rebellion* (New York, 1974), with Charles Joyner, *Down by the Riverside: A South Carolina Slave Community* (Urbana, Ill., 1984).

6

The Personification of Principle: The Crusade Against Slavery in Washtenaw County

Unlike temperance and benevolence, abolitionism was not present in Tuscaloosa County, where whites in the southern county violently resisted the presence even of abolitionist publications. Yet as chapters 2 and 4 have shown, abolitionists composed a significant segment of the constituencies of both temperance and benevolence in Washtenaw County.

The antislavery movement was institutionally more complex than any other reform effort examined in this study. Antislavery in Washtenaw County, as elsewhere in the North, began as a movement committed to moral suasion, and then shifted its strategy to political action. When they initially moved into the political arena, abolitionists merely questioned aspirants for office and voted for the candidate who best approximated their position. Finding this method unsatisfactory, abolitionists formed their own political organization in 1840, which they later christened the Liberty Party. During most of the party's eight-year existence, Ann Arbor served as an unofficial headquarters of the antislavery movement in Michigan, as it was where the party's organ, the *Signal of Liberty*, was published. In 1848, the Liberty Party was absorbed by the Free Soil Party, composed of ex-Libertyites and of Whigs and Democrats opposed to the expansion of slavery into the federal territories. Although the Free Soil platform expressed less outrage over the peculiar institution than had the Liberty Party's, the new party remained the political home of most voting abolitionists until it in turn was absorbed by the Republican Party in 1854.

Antislavery activity, however, was not restricted to political expressions. In the first place, abolitionists did not limit their agenda to the emancipation of slaves: many white abolitionists also eagerly promoted equal rights for African Americans, including suffrage for black males and the right to jury trials. Perhaps because of their greater willingness to press for the civil rights of black Americans, few abolitionists were found in the county's small colonization movement; if they believed that blacks could and should enjoy equal rights in America, they would have felt no urgency about encouraging them to emigrate to Liberia. Additionally, disciples of the abolitionist William Lloyd Garrison, many of whom rejected antislavery political parties and embraced nonresistance, were active in Washtenaw County, especially during the 1850s. More so than in any other reform endeavor in Michigan, male abolitionists encouraged women to form their own antislavery societies, which they did; a few abolitionists, both male and female, also endorsed women's rights. But the most important form of nonpolitical antislavery activity in Washtenaw County occurred among the evangelical churches. Many members of these churches agitated to have their congregations and denominations condemn slavery as a sin and to withhold fellowship and their pulpits from slaveholders and apologists of slavery. A few withdrew from churches that they concluded were hopelessly proslavery, and formed their own denominations.

Although the movement to abolish slavery mobilized fewer activists than did the temperance cause and was not as widespread geographically as support for temperance or evangelical benevolence, the activities of abolitionists always attracted the attention of contemporaries. Despite the apparent lack of any abolition society in Washtenaw County prior to 1836, Ann Arbor's newspaper editors wrote often on the question of slavery and on the actions of abolitionists elsewhere in the country. In 1829, in the third issue of Washtenaw County's first newspaper, the *Western Emigrant,* editor Thomas Simpson revealed his preoccupation with slavery when he devoted three-fifths of a page to a speech by James Monroe, in which the former president set forth the difficulties that he believed would follow emancipation and proposed that this objective could never be accomplished without federal assistance. Simpson argued that Monroe's comments, coming from a man raised in a slaveholding state, would "do more to influence the slaveholders of the South, than the volumes of declamation from the wholesale philanthropists of the North."[1]

Simpson's successor, George Corselius, regarded abolitionists as well intentioned but extremist, and eagerly embraced colonization as a moderate and

---

1. *Western Emigrant,* December 9, 1829.

reasonable solution to slavery. Colonization, Corselius wrote in 1830, "may be the means not only of relieving the African population of this country from the degradation to which they are subjected, of carrying the blessings of civilization into Africa, but also of relieving our own Country ultimately from the curse of slavery." He viewed colonization as the best prevention against future slave revolts and hoped that the insurrections in the West Indies in 1831 would cause all slaveholders to recognize the expedience of getting "rid of that species of property." With the Nat Turner rebellion in Virginia later that year, Corselius also hoped that white southerners would finally recognize "the appalling evils of Negro Slavery." Though he lamented the "apathy with which Americans look upon two millions of their fellow men wearing the chains of slavery," he was more concerned that the rapid increase in the numbers of slaves and free blacks, coupled with their continual oppression, would eventually result in a "general insurrection of the Slaves in the Southern States." Thus he urged that government revenues be devoted toward colonization, rather than toward internal improvements or armaments: "Our safety would be less hazarded by postponing the construction of fortifications and ships of war, than by the continuance of slavery. The removal of slaves is a measure of national safety of more pressing importance than any other."[2]

Colonization, according to Corselius' thinking during the 1830s, seemed to be a reasonable middle ground between the "fanatics" of both North and South. After a mob in Vicksburg, Mississippi, lynched two whites in 1835 for complicity in planning a slave revolt, Corselius commented that southerners had "surrendered themselves entirely to their passions." He also had unkind words, however, for abolitionists, "the most warmly, but, through the blindness of feeling, the most mischievously, benevolent people that ever lived." He doubted that the abolitionists were "truly solicitous for the slave population," as he believed their agitations had only created fear and mistrust between master and slave. Further, Corselius was convinced that slaves were not prepared for freedom, and he maintained that if abolitionists actually wished to bring about emancipation, they ought to devote "their efforts and their money" to "imparting to [slaves] that instruction which will fit them to be free; and the spirit and discipline of that religion which will fit them for any state of circumstances." But Corselius occasionally defended abolitionists when he felt that they had been treated unfairly. Following the antiabolition riots in New York

2. *Ibid.*, May 5, 1830; *Emigrant*, June 29, 1831, September 28, 1831 (see also August 29, 1832).

City in 1834, he asserted that although the abolitionists "deserved reprehen-
sion" and had "said and done some things offensive to property," in this case
they were "more sinned against than sinning" and were the victims of *"fanatical
intolerance"* bred by the city's "three thousand grog shops."[3]

Antiabolition riots in the North, and the hard line that white southerners
took against the circulation of antislavery literature in their midst—such as
when Tuscaloosans formed an antiabolition vigilance committee in 1835—
caused moderates such as Corselius to defend the rights of abolitionists more
often than they denounced antislaveryites for extremism. He condemned a
North Carolina grand jury in 1831 for returning an indictment against William
Lloyd Garrison, editor of the Boston *Liberator*, for circulating his paper in that
state. Corselius called the indictment "a miserable expedient, and a powerful
demonstration of the woes of slavery. If negro slavery is to be sustained by such
means, we shall soon have a nation of white slaves. . . . Are the people of the
South willing to sacrifice the first rights of human nature in order to keep negroes to do their work?" Five years later, the Whig *State Journal* published a letter from "Justitia" protesting the creation of a vigilance society in Kentucky
that assumed the power to arrest, prosecute, and inflict summary punishment
upon any person suspected of circulating antislavery publications. Though Justitia was "not one of those who favor the wild schemes of the immediate abolitionists," he was convinced that this vigilance committee was "far more subversive of the principles of justice and social order." Such actions, "unless
overwhelmed by public indignation, will speedily subvert our form of government" and undermine security for "life, liberty, or property."[4]

In February 1837, George W. Wood, editor of the *State Journal*, denounced
the violent disruption of an abolitionist meeting in Pontiac. Three weeks later,
Wood published a letter from "No Abolitionist," who reproved the Democratic
Michigan Argus for publishing the names of 141 male Washtenaw County residents who had signed a petition to Congress praying for the abolition of slavery
in the District of Columbia. The *Argus*, which proclaimed that the purpose of
the petition was to "assist in keeping up an excitement between the North and
the South," was accused by No Abolitionist of only seeking to "cast odium, disgrace, and public censure" upon many "honest and respectable citizens" for ex-

3. *Michigan Whig and Washtenaw Democrat*, August 13, August 27, 1835; *Michigan Emigrant*,
July 24, 1834 (see also October 9, 1834).

4. *Emigrant*, December 28, 1831; *State Journal*, August 11, 1836.

ercising "their undeniable rights." Later, *State Journal* editor Edwin Lawrence argued that actions that denied abolitionists their civil rights—such as Congress' refusal to accept their petitions, or the murder of Elijah Lovejoy—only made more converts to their cause.[5] Such deeds not only impelled more than a few individuals to demand the immediate end of slavery, but many more northerners developed a hostility toward southern culture and a suspicion of planters—whom northerners came to see as a threat to their own civil rights.[6]

In contrast to the *State Journal,* its adversary the *Argus* never defended the civil liberties of abolitionists during the 1830s. Instead, the *Argus* ridiculed churches in Massachusetts and Ohio that made "concurrence with the movements of the *abolitionists* a test of Christian character," and generally mentioned abolitionists only to reprove them. In 1838 the *Argus* rejoiced at the news of a sparsely attended abolition meeting in Massachusetts, concurred with the decision of the Congress to table all antislavery resolutions it received, and unapologetically reprinted articles that antislavery partisans claimed misrepresented the abolitionists. Early in 1839 the *Argus* acknowledged that it refused to publish a notice of the Washtenaw County Anti-Slavery Society, reasoning that abolition threatened the peace of the Union and should not "receive any favor at our hands." Although Washtenaw County's Whig papers published notices of antislavery meetings, they usually did so with little, if any, comment. Whereas the formation of a state benevolence or temperance society—especially if it occurred in Ann Arbor—would elicit considerable coverage and commentary in the village papers, the *State Journal,* for example, simply noted in 1836: "The friends of emancipation convened in this village on the 10th inst. and organized a State Anti-Slavery Society. The meeting was addressed by several respectable individuals, who explained the causes which impelled them to associate in the defence of suffering servitude."[7] Judging from these sources, local newspaper editors did not perceive antislavery to be a popular cause in Washtenaw County during the mid-1830s.

---

5. *State Journal,* February 23, March 16, 1837; *Michigan Argus,* March 2, 1837; *State Journal,* November 30, 1837, January 4, 1838. Indeed, while antiabolitionist mobs were widespread in the North and South, antislavery societies in the nation grew from 200 in May 1835 to 527 a year later; Merton L. Dillon, *The Abolitionists: The Growth of a Dissenting Minority* (DeKalb, Ill., 1974), 91.

6. James Brewer Stewart, *Holy Warriors: The Abolitionists and American Slavery* (Rev. ed., New York, 1996), 77–78, 87–88.

7. *Michigan Argus,* July 30, 1835, March 31, 1836, November 8, December 27, June 21, 1838, January 17, 1839; *State Journal,* November 17, 1836.

Antislavery activity in Michigan commenced among Lenawee County Hicksite Quakers, led by Elizabeth Chandler, in 1832. In 1834 the Farmington Anti-Slavery Society was created in Oakland County; it and the Lenawee County body were the first two auxiliaries of the American Anti-Slavery Society in Michigan. The members of the Farmington society, who specifically requested that the Ann Arbor *Michigan Emigrant* publish their preamble and constitution, explained that after waiting fifteen years for the colonization effort to emancipate "the people of color," they were "now left without any well-grounded hope or expectation of this scheme ever releasing the slave." Having no expectation, either, that the "slaveholding states" would "take the lead in abolishing slavery," the Farmington society aimed to persuade slaveholders of the injustice of their position: "We will therefore use all honorable and peaceful means . . . to arouse the people of the free states to a just conception of their responsibility and duty upon the subject of slavery, and to unite with them in making a solemn remonstrance with their Southern brethren on the guilt, inutility, and danger of their present system, in pointing out to them the safety of emancipation, and in earnestly appealing to their hearts and consciences to blot out the foul stain from their own and the character of the American people."[8]

Such were possibly also the sentiments of Washtenaw County's first known abolitionist body, the Webster/Scio Anti-Slavery Society. Though never mentioned in any extant county newspaper, this organization was listed in the third *Annual Report* of the American Anti-Slavery Society as being formed in March 1836 with twenty members, and Theodore Foster as its secretary. Increasing interest soon persuaded Michigan's abolitionists to recognize the need for a statewide body.[9] Antislaveryites initially intended to assemble in Ann Arbor in August 1836 but postponed this gathering twice before finally meeting in November. One advertisement for the meeting demonstrated the extent to which interest in abolition had spread throughout the state, as 254 individuals from nine counties attached their names to a circular addressed to "those who are anxious to see our nation redeemed from the guilt and injustice of de-

---

8. Merton L. Dillon, "Elizabeth Chandler and the Spread of Antislavery Sentiment to Michigan," *Michigan History*, XXXIX (December 1955), 481–94; *Michigan Emigrant*, September 25, 1834. The Farmington and Lenawee County societies were the only Michigan auxiliaries that the American Anti-Slavery Society listed in its *Annual Report*, II (1835), 84, 85.

9. American Anti-Slavery Society *Annual Report*, III (1836), 99.

priving one sixth part of its population of all rights which are inherent to man."[10]

Seventy-five delegates from Michigan—thirty-two of whom were Washtenaw County residents—and four visitors from Ohio assembled in Ann Arbor's Presbyterian church on November 10 and 11, 1836, and formed the Michigan State Anti-Slavery Society (MSASS). The delegates agreed to fourteen resolutions, which, in brief, denounced slavery as "a stain on our national character that ought to be effaced"; argued that recent events in the British West Indies demonstrated the "safety and practicability" of emancipation; condemned the domestic slave trade; proclaimed that slavery diminished the "moral influence of our otherwise free institutions on foreign nations"; repudiated emancipation by violence, as the delegates expected emancipation to occur primarily from "argument and moral suasion" and secondarily from "salutary and enlightened legislation"; maintained that Congress was entitled to abolish slavery in the District of Columbia and the federal territories; and condemned the congressional gag rule. The religious predilections of the delegates were demonstrated by resolutions denouncing attempts to justify slavery from the Bible, laws that effectively withheld the Bible from slaves, and Christians who admitted slaveholders to communion. Delegates also called for the "general observance" of a "Monthly concert of Prayer, for the immediate abolition of slavery throughout the world," and they endorsed petitioning the Michigan legislature to overturn laws that prohibited black males from voting. Finally, they urged abolitionists to labor in "educating the colored people" and "earnestly invite[d] the action and co-operation of females . . . to act in concert with us in the great work of emancipation."[11]

Although Ann Arbor's newspapers said little about this meeting, residents of the village commenced debating slavery and abolition among themselves. Less than two weeks after the convention, the *State Journal* reported that "animated discussion upon the subject of emancipating the slaves of the South has been and is still proceeding before the Young Men's Society in this village." The discussion continued at least an additional week. Then, in late January,

10. *State Journal,* August 4, 31, October 6, 1836; Monroe *Times,* September 22, 1836; Kooker, "Antislavery Movement in Michigan," 137–43. By county, these 254 signatories were as follows: Lenawee 106, Oakland 55, Monroe 36, Washtenaw 34, Wayne 8, Kalamazoo 6, Cass 4, Allegan 3, and Branch 2; a photostatic reproduction is provided in Kooker, "Antislavery Movement in Michigan," 139.

11. *Report of the Proceedings of the Anti-Slavery State Convention, Held at Ann Arbor,* 3–13.

John S. Cowles, a traveling agent of the American Anti-Slavery Society, debated the merits of abolitionism for three nights with Samuel Denton, an Ann Arborite who in the 1840s would represent Washtenaw County as a Democrat in the state senate, where—despite his opposition to abolitionism in 1837—he supported black suffrage. With this debate, reportedly attended by a "numerous audience," the editor of the *Michigan Argus*, Earl P. Gardiner, finally expressed his disappointment with the growing abolitionist presence: "We had hoped that while other parts of our country were excited and divided by the discussion of this question, our peaceful community would remain exempt from its vexations." Gardiner was convinced that abolitionists were willing to dissolve the Union in pursuit of their objectives—Cowles admitted as much—and urged his readers to "meet and put down this wicked attempt . . . at the ballot box" in order to prevent "these black-coated political partisans" from destroying the Union and reducing "our fabrick of Government to chaos." In the midst of these debates, auxiliaries of the American Anti-Slavery Society were formed in Ann Arbor and Dexter village, although neither body merited mention in either of Ann Arbor's papers.[12]

Because the Whig *State Journal* attempted to distance itself from abolitionism and the Democratic *Michigan Argus* displayed outright hostility to the cause, information regarding Washtenaw County abolition activities during these early years is scarce.[13] Unlike temperance or benevolent causes, which occasionally had the minutes of their meetings or favorable essays published in both newspapers, the abolitionists received little coverage. It is clear, though, that abolition activity continued. February 1837 brought the aforementioned petition of 141 Washtenaw County residents calling upon Congress to abolish slavery in the District of Columbia. At about this same time, the Manchester Lyceum debated the question "Ought American Slavery to Be Immediately Abolished?" Statewide, the growth of abolitionism was evident from the formation of thirteen new auxiliaries that were listed in the May 1837 *Annual Report* of the American Anti-Slavery Society. Later that year, Nathan Thomas in Kalamazoo County reported that within the past eight months, local subscribers to abolition newspapers had grown from two to fifty. Moreover, anti-

12. *State Journal*, November 24, December 1, 1836, January 26, 1837; *Michigan Argus*, December 1, 1836, February 2, 1837; *Michigan State Journal*, May 14, 1845; American Anti-Slavery Society, *Annual Report*, IV (1837), 140.

13. In 1837, the Whig Detroit *Daily Advertiser* closed its columns to abolitionists; Kooker, "Antislavery," 216.

abolition sentiment had subsided. Two years previously, according to Thomas, an antislavery lecturer in Kalamazoo had been prevented from speaking by a mob. "Since that time," however, "the publick feeling has undergone such a change upon the subject that I doubt whether a mob could now be raised for such a purpose." Five members of the Ann Arbor Anti-Slavery Society were present at the annual MSASS meeting held in Detroit in June. Delegates passed resolutions similar to the ones that the organization had embraced seven months earlier, including a renewed call for civil rights and social uplift for African Americans in Michigan.[14]

The following year brought more petitions to Congress from Washtenaw County abolitionists. Because southern members of Congress and their northern allies were outraged by antislavery petitions, they implemented the so-called "gag rule" in May 1836. The gag rule, which remained in effect until 1844, required that all antislavery petitions to Congress be delivered to a committee where they were automatically tabled. These actions only encouraged the further submission to Congress of antislavery petitions. Many members of Congress, however, discarded these petitions and never publicly acknowledged receipt of them. Consequently, many abolitionists forwarded their petitions to those few members who championed their cause, such as Whigs John Quincy Adams of Massachusetts and William Slade of Vermont.[15]

Although Washtenaw County abolitionists submitted at least three petitions to their representative, Democrat Isaac Crary, in January 1838, the surviving eight county petitions from the Twenty-fifth and Twenty-sixth Congresses (1837–1841)—which listed 202 signatures from 108 different petitioners—indicate that local abolitionists trusted Adams and Slade more than they did Crary. The complaints of these early petitions echoed the resolutions of the Michigan State Anti-Slavery Society. One petition, originally sent to the Michigan legislature from Dexter village but afterward forwarded to the U.S. House of Representatives, also included a call for the repeal of Michigan

---

14. *Michigan Argus*, March 2, 1837; *State Journal*, March 16, 1837; "Manchester Lyceum," in Jane Palmer, comp., "A History of Manchester Township" (typescript, 1964), Bentley Library; American Anti-Slavery Society, *Annual Report*, IV (1837), 140; Nathan Thomas to Jesse Thomas, December 29, 1837, in Nathan Macy Thomas Papers, Bentley Library; *Report of the Meeting of the Michigan State Anti-Slavery Society, June 28th, 1837, Being the First Annual Meeting* (Detroit, 1837). An announcement for this meeting was published in the *State Journal*, June 22, 1837.

15. Stewart, *Holy Warriors*, 83–84; Barnes, *Antislavery Impulse*, 109–45.

laws "which graduate the rights of the citizens of this state by the color of their skin."[16]

Concurrent with the proliferation of petitions was the formation of the Washtenaw County Anti-Slavery Society. In July 1838, this body's executive committee declared its intention to "disseminate, as speedily as possible, the principles of Abolition through all parts of the county." It urged "abolitionists in all the towns where no societies exist, to organize without delay, however small may be their numbers or influence. The cause cannot be systematically advanced in any other way. Its whole power and efficiency consists in the concentration of feelings and energies of many individuals with reference to a single subject." The committee also announced that it had "competent individuals" eager to deliver antislavery speeches anywhere in the county, and encouraged Washtenaw abolitionists to circulate as widely as possible copies of the *Emancipator* or *Human Rights,* both of which were available at bulk rates. But again the cause met resistance. When the nationally renowned abolitionist Alvan Stewart spoke in Ann Arbor, he was arrested and fined one dollar for circulating abolition petitions "at a meeting on a Sabbath evening where he had promised to deliver a temperance address." The *Argus* concurred in this treatment of Stewart and opined that the "conduct of Mr. Stewart was highly dishonorable in thus trifling with and insulting the feelings of his audience,

16. *Congressional Globe,* Twenty-fifth Congress, Second Session, 101; 7 inhabitants of Washtenaw County [Dexter Township] urge the rejection of Texas annexation (tabled February 14, 1838, HR25A-H1.1); 19 citizens of Washtenaw County [Dexter village] request diplomatic recognition of Haiti (undated, probably tabled February 1839), and 27 inhabitants of Bridgewater urge the rejection of Texas annexation (undated, both HR26A-H1.5); 52 inhabitants of Washtenaw County [Saline Township] pray for an end to the gag rule (tabled between January 7 and February 18, 1839, HR25A-H1.7); 44 citizens of Washtenaw County [Saline Township] call for the end of slavery in the District of Columbia and the federal territories; 16 citizens of Washtenaw County [Dexter village] to the Michigan legislature (and forwarded to the United States House of Representatives) urge the repeal of racially discriminatory laws and call upon the state legislature to instruct Congress on several slavery-related issues; 20 citizens of Washtenaw County [Dexter village] urge rejecting Texas' annexation and the admission of additional slave states into the Union, and 17 citizens of Washtenaw County [Dexter village] pray to end interstate slave trade and slavery in the District of Columbia and the territory of Florida (all tabled between February 4 and February 18, 1839, HR25A-H1.8). All of these petitions are located in the Petitions and Memorials Referred to Committees, Records of the U.S. House of Representatives, Record Group 233, National Archives, Washington, D.C. [hereinafter cited as RG 233].

and we do not wonder that the friends of good order and enemies of agitation should take a legal method of testifying their resentment."[17]

The *Argus* often appealed to racist sentiments when denouncing the abolitionists. The paper announced in June 1839 that "Abraham Sykes, the negro," who had been convicted of murder, had escaped from the state prison in Jackson. Immediately below this notice, the *Argus* printed the following: "It was stated at an abolition meeting held in our village sometime since, by one of the speakers from Detroit, that the negroes in that city were quiet, orderly, inoffensive inhabitants—guiltless of crime & c. We learn that some four or five of these lamb-like gentry passed this village, bound to state prison, the other day. What a comment on the abolition gentleman's veracity." A year earlier, the *Argus* reported that a white woman and a black man had planned to get married locally. Editor Gardiner surmised that "the many lectures and debates on abolition and the propriety of amalgamation, previously held in this vicinity . . . had induced them to commit this unhallowed act." These abolitionist speeches, however, failed to convince many local whites to forsake their repulsion to interracial marriage, as the *Argus* continued: "This shock to human nature and common sense was prevented by a large body of men, and the last the *black gentleman* was seen of, he was running towards the South with the speed of a quarter-horse."[18]

The sentiments behind such actions may have been why abolitionists in Ann Arbor found it difficult to procure a place to meet. That same month, the Ann Arbor Presbyterian Church—which only a year and a half before had been the meeting place of the MSASS and was where many local abolitionists worshiped—denied the state abolitionist body the use of its building, citing fears of antiabolition disturbances. The following year, a request of the Washtenaw County Anti-Slavery Society to assemble at the Presbyterian church was again denied, as was permission to use the Methodist church and the county courthouse. Finally, Ann Arbor's Baptists offered their meetinghouse to the abolitionists.[19]

Not infrequently, the *Argus* tried to use abolitionism for political gain by as-

17. *Michigan State Journal,* July 12, 1838; *Michigan Argus,* August 16, 1838.

18. *Michigan Argus,* June 6, 1839, June 28, 1838. In October 1837, an African American male was banished from Scio Township for his inability to post a $500 bond as required by an 1827 Michigan law; Kooker, "Antislavery," 263.

19. *Michigan Observer* as cited in *American Freeman,* May 21, 1839; *Michigan Argus,* June 6, 1839.

serting that the Whigs and abolitionists were closely aligned. In its last issue before the November 1838 election, the *Argus* alerted its readers that the "Anti-Slavery societies have come boldly into the political field as champions of federalism . . . and no man is to receive their suffrages unless he is willing to put himself upon a par with the negro." The *Argus* again raised the specter of miscegenation as a means to put down the abolitionists—and by inference, the Whigs—as it expressed what it saw as the implications of the purported abolitionist litmus tests: "If fathers are not willing that blacks shall marry their daughters, and farmers and mechanics are unwilling to have a swarm of locusts let loose upon them to eat their bread and compete with them in their business, they are unworthy of [abolitionist] confidence." After correcting Whig allegations that Alvan Stewart had been "arrested by the 'locofocos,' and brought before a 'locofoco' justice . . . for delivering a temperance lecture on the sabbath," the *Argus* countercharged that "as a champion of abolitionists," Stewart "will of course have the sympathies of the Journal, and its partisans," and that his abolitionist proposals would "be hailed by them as acts of the most exalted patriotism." The *Argus* also reprinted numerous pieces from other newspapers that pointed to an abolitionist/Whig connection, and in January 1839, published a series of essays entitled "Abolitionism and Whigism," in which the writer claimed that abolitionism represented, among other things, an unnecessary intrusion of religion into secular life: "The union of Church and State—Religion and Politics—Whigism and Abolitionism—meets with an approval at religious assemblies, is endorsed by resolutions adopted at Abolition Conventions, and even the sacred desk is polluted in this crusade against the rights of property and the interests of men." In response to such allegations, the *Michigan State Journal* did not proudly boast that members of its party were devoted antislavery activists. Rather, it countered that it was the Democrats and not the Whigs who were the true friends of abolitionists, and on at least two occasions pointed to examples in Ohio and New York where the abolitionist vote provided Democrats with their margin of victory.[20] Clearly, abolitionism in Washtenaw County during the 1830s was viewed by both parties as a political liability and was a label that each endeavored to attach to the other.

20. *Michigan Argus,* November 1, June 28, 1838, January 24, 31, 1839; *Michigan State Journal,* January 24, February 21, 1839. Though hostile to abolitionists, the *Argus'* editor did not regard himself as an apologist for slavery: "We are enemies of slavery in any and every shape, and we are also the enemies of those who would destroy our national peace, and neither the one, nor the

Their failure in Michigan and elsewhere to gain influence with either political party led many abolitionists eventually to espouse the creation of a separate political party. Nevertheless, this position was reached only after much debate and experimentation with other strategies. At the time of its formation in 1836, MSASS members announced that they expected "the extinction of slavery" to occur "primarily" by "moral suasion . . . addressed to the understanding and the heart of the slaveholder; and *secondarily,* [through] salutary and enlightened legislation, as the necessary fruit of correct public sentiment." Michigan abolitionists, however, soon began moving away from this strategy of appealing to white southerners. Like temperance partisans—and as we saw in chapter 4, many abolitionists were active in this cause as well—some abolitionists eventually recognized that their meetings and resolutions were accomplishing little, and thus they gradually increased their efforts in the political arena. Their initial step in the political realm—the increased petitioning of state and national legislatures—had long been used by abolitionists in the eastern states, and was a widely agreed-upon tactic among them. Abolitionists in Michigan and elsewhere, though, were frustrated that both national and state assemblies had generally ignored their entreaties. Therefore, in 1838, abolitionists in most northern states commenced questioning political candidates regarding their views on slavery. In some cases, abolitionists were asked to vote only for candidates who embraced immediate emancipation, while in other instances they supported the candidate whose responses best approximated their point of view. If no candidate was satisfactory, then antislavery partisans were either to withhold their votes or to scatter them among write-in candidates. The intent of this strategy was to encourage politicians to pursue the antislavery vote actively: given the nearly equal numbers of Whigs and Democrats in many voting districts, abolitionists hoped to hold the balance of power.[21]

Michigan abolitionists, however, were more reluctant to move beyond the questioning of candidates. In 1838, the MSASS directed its executive committee to ask the candidates for the state's single seat in the United States House of

<hr />

other, shall receive any favor at our hands"; *Michigan Argus,* January 17, 1839. See the similar sentiments of a Whig editor in *Michigan State Journal,* February 28, 1839.

21. *Proceedings of the Anti-Slavery State Convention, Held at Ann Arbor,* 9; Richard H. Sewell, *Ballots for Freedom: Antislavery Politics in the United States, 1837–1860* (New York, 1976), 10–15; Dumond, *Antislavery,* 245–48.

Representatives for their positions on abolishing slavery in the District of Columbia, the annexation of Texas, the interstate slave trade, and the nation's diplomatic and commercial relations with Haiti. The following year, abolitionists in Michigan questioned the gubernatorial candidates and a number of aspirants to the state legislature regarding their views on black male suffrage and jury trials for people of all races. Because no candidate answered these questions satisfactorily, the MSASS executive committee did not endorse anyone in either election. Nevertheless, the leadership did not encourage abolitionists to scatter their votes. An earnest appeal to increase the political activity beyond the mere questioning of candidates was presented at the 1838 MSASS meeting in Ann Arbor by Luther Humphrey, who urged abolitionists to vote only for candidates who met their approval. Humphrey's resolution, however, was tabled. This hesitancy of Michigan abolitionists to increase their political visibility was expressed again the following January at a meeting of the Washtenaw County Anti-Slavery Society, where the majority of those present were reportedly against "making a political question" of abolition.[22]

At the MSASS anniversary gathering in June 1839, Humphrey repeated his plea of the previous year, arguing that it was "the duty of *all freemen* to withhold their votes at the ballot box from those who are known in any way to patronize slavery," and predicting that the antislavery effort would eventually prove victorious if abolitionists utilized their votes properly. Again Humphrey was rebuffed, and his proposal was indefinitely postponed. The state body would do no more than submit questions to political candidates, after which abolitionists were simply to exercise their "unfettered suffrage." Political activity was not the answer. Rather, "moral influence, exercised in a spirit of kindness and Christian forbearance towards all concerned, remains, as it ever has been, the only appropriate means of accomplishing the Anti-Slavery enterprize."[23] As with the temperance cause in their state, Michigan abolitionists were not of one mind regarding the proper roles of political action and of moral suasion. Though Michigan abolitionists no longer expressed hope that they would directly persuade white southerners to emancipate their slaves, those favoring a

22. *Michigan Argus*, October 11, 1838; Kooker, "Antislavery," 287–301; *American Freeman*, July 2, 1839; *Michigan Argus*, February 7, 1839. The *Argus* correspondent was convinced, though, that the Washtenaw abolitionists "will shortly adopt" political action, "and the sooner the better. *They will soon find where their* WEAKNESS *(not strength) lies."* See also *Michigan State Journal*, January 17, 1839.

23. *American Freeman*, July 2, 1839.

heavier dose of moral suasion evidently anticipated that their exertions would at least result in a moral revolution in the northern states. Abolitionists hoped that public opinion would then prompt Congress to eradicate and control slavery where it had the power to do so, and would also provoke state legislatures to grant equal suffrage to black males and jury trials to everyone regardless of race.

The system of questioning the candidates, though, proved frustrating to abolitionists throughout the nation, as many antislaveryites were convinced that politicians forgot their promises made in the heat of an election. In many electoral districts abolitionists did not hold the balance of power and were ignored or ridiculed by candidates. Of course, for many abolitionists, other political issues influenced them to vote for their traditional party of preference, thus disregarding the implorings of antislavery societies. For all these reasons, some abolitionists argued that the best way for their voices to be heard in the political arena would be if they united their actions under a single, independent, political party. Such a conclusion, though, was not reached hastily. Indeed, many abolitionists remained firmly committed to moral suasion, and some, concentrated in New England and influenced by the teachings of William Lloyd Garrison, embraced nonresistance and eschewed voting altogether. In 1839 the annual meeting of the American Anti-Slavery Society debated whether abolitionists were obliged to express their convictions at the ballot box, which proposal won only narrowly. The ensuing year, further differences brought schism to the national society. Following the May 1839 convention of the American Anti-Slavery Society, proponents of political action, led by Alvan Stewart and Myron Holley, debated the merits of an independent political party at a series of conferences in Albany, Rochester, Cleveland, and again in Albany. At the second Albany gathering, in April 1840, delegates nominated James G. Birney and Thomas Earle for president and vice-president.[24]

In the nine months following the MSASS's rejection of Luther Humphrey's proposal to increase the political visibility of abolitionists, the state's antislavery leadership gradually embraced not only Humphrey's plea, but also independent political nominations. Undoubtedly the debates from the East during the summer of 1839 regarding the feasibility and necessity of forming a

24. Sewell, *Ballots for Freedom*, 14–23, 37–42, 47–75; Vernon L. Volpe, *Forlorn Hope of Freedom: The Liberty Party in the Old Northwest, 1838–1848* (Kent, Ohio, 1990), 30; Filler, *Crusade Against Slavery*, 126–36.

political party committed to abolitionist principles had reached Michigan by the fall of 1839. In his editorial debut with the Jackson *Michigan Freeman,* Seymour B. Treadwell may have evinced this growing debate when he announced in September that abolitionists were prepared to form their own party. Treadwell, however, hoped a separate party would never be necessary, and urged abolitionists to remain active within the Whig and Democratic Parties, provided that these parties presented candidates with solid antislavery credentials to the electorate. A pronounced shift in sentiment favorable to political action was evident at the MSASS anniversary meeting in October: eight of the meeting's nineteen resolutions either pointed to the necessity of political action among abolitionists or bemoaned the ways in which national affairs were "controlled by a rigidly disciplined political combination of slaveholders"; moral suasion was not mentioned at all. Most noteworthy was a measure proclaiming it to be the "duty of all Abolitionists in Michigan to carry their principles to the Ballot Box at the coming election, and to vote for and support" abolitionist objectives.[25]

Few abolitionists, however, were prepared to endorse a separate party. When, that same month, some abolitionists in Jackson nominated a ticket to compete in the November 1839 election, the MSASS executive committee denied that the group had their sanction. In accord with the resolutions passed at the MSASS meeting, the committee urged abolitionists to vote for the best antislavery candidate, and if they found no candidate acceptable, to scatter their votes. In December 1839, renewed sentiment for the formation of an independent third party surfaced at meetings of the Jackson County Anti-Slavery Society—which, after extended debate, rejected this strategy. Seymour Treadwell argued against the formation of an abolitionist party at the Jackson County convention and in a long essay in the *Freeman* that again called for abolitionists to work within the existing parties.[26] But while some abolitionists supported the Whig nominee William Henry Harrison, as being a lesser evil than Democrat Martin Van Buren, others were distraught by Harrison's onetime ownership of slaves and by what they believed was his proslavery record as governor of the Indiana Territory, and thus would not back either candidate. And Harrison's nomination may have been why the MSASS, at its February 1840 meeting, approved a resolution declaring that "the time

25. *Michigan Freeman,* September 25, October 23, 1839.
26. *Ibid.,* October 23, 1839, January 15, 29, 1840.

has now arrived . . . for Abolitionists throughout the country, to form themselves into a systematic and distinct political party." Even Treadwell shed his public antipathy toward an independent party only seven weeks after opposing one: in March he was convinced that the members of the Jackson County Anti-Slavery Society would now endorse the resolution favoring a separate political organization, which they had tabled less than three months earlier. This revolution in sentiment among the top ranks of Michigan abolitionists is remarkable, particularly since it occurred before the second Albany Convention, where Birney and Earle were nominated.[27]

Henceforth, Treadwell and Michigan's other abolitionist leaders ardently promoted the new, as-yet-unnamed political party. The executive committee now called for "moral suasion, effectively consummated through the ballot box," and Treadwell criticized the Reverend George Duffield, pastor of Detroit's First Presbyterian Church, who "takes very well with the politicians of that place—*talk, preach,* and *wish* against slavery, the greatest moral evil, as well as the most dangerous *political* power in the nation—but by no means VOTE against it." Political abolitionists received outside encouragement from Alvan Stewart and Gerrit Smith, who both wrote to the *Freeman* from New York urging Michigan abolitionists to pursue the political path and arguing that moral suasion had run its course. And as the enthusiasm for political abolitionism grew, the abolitionists' description of the Whigs and Democrats changed. No longer were these parties depicted as simply unresponsive to the implorings of abolitionists; they were part of slavery's stranglehold upon America, and to vote for either was to vote for slavery. When the *Freeman* announced that a meeting to select electors for Birney and Earle would be held in Jackson in August, Treadwell added that respect would be shown anyone, "should any such there be, who, while professing to be devoted abolitionists, still vote for slaveholders." Those who attended the convention, though, spoke with greater zeal. The delegates resolved that it was inconsistent for an abolitionist to vote for a political candidate who, once elected, would not use his power to promote the repeal of laws that tended to uphold slavery. Anyone who advocated moral suasion alone as the way to ameliorate slavery was either hopelessly blinded by love of party or an antiabolitionist. Treadwell balked at some abolitionists who maintained that the Whigs were a lesser evil and thus

27. *Ibid.,* January 15, March 4, 18, 1840; Dumond, *Antislavery,* 99, 122.

worthy of their suffrage; Whig stalwarts such as Harrison and Daniel Webster had continually demonstrated their "dangerous servility to the Slave Power in this country." Treadwell concluded that with respect to the Whigs and Democrats, "of two such evils I will have nothing to do with either." Of course he held no illusions about the outcome of the election, as he was convinced that Whigs and Democrats would not find the abolitionist candidates to be appealing. Only the purest abolitionists—"men in whom their principles are personified"—would vote for this ticket.[28]

Although a few abolitionists from throughout Michigan lent their support to the new party, the overwhelming majority of them did not immediately flock to it. In April, A. L. Porter informed Treadwell that the abolitionist leaders in Detroit were "all really 3^d party men and of course inclined to carry out our principles at the polls at the ensuing election." As for himself, Porter thought that the time to commence third party activity had arrived: "If we never make a beginning I see not how we can look for an ending of the great contest between liberty & despotism—personally *my* mind is made up.—I can never vote for Harrison." Porter was disappointed that more abolitionists did not see things his way. In Detroit, he believed, "not more than one in ten" antislaveryites would accept the independent party. Nearly all of them were Whigs, he added, among whom "Harrison rages like a pestilence." Guy Beckley of Ann Arbor, one of the foremost abolitionist and temperance lecturers in Michigan during the late 1830s and early 1840s, admitted that he initially doubted the wisdom of independent nominations, and announced shortly after the nomination of Birney and Earle his reluctant endorsement of the ticket. By August 1840, though, Beckley could see no course aside from casting his ballot for an abolitionist ticket, as he was now convinced that there was no substantial difference between the Whigs and the Democrats.[29]

Many abolitionists disagreed with Treadwell, Porter, Beckley, and the MSASS executive committee. Both Porter and Treadwell reported that "numerous Whig abolitionists . . . say only wait till after *this* election, and we will go with you *en masse*." By July, Whigs were declaring that abolitionist nominations were only a Democratic plot designed to divide the Whig vote and thus

28. *Michigan Freeman*, March 25, April 8, July 15, September 16, June 17, July 29, August 12, 1840.

29. A. L. Porter to S. B. Treadwell, April 23, 1840, in Seymour B. Treadwell Papers, Bentley Library; *Michigan Freeman*, April 22, July 29, August 12, 1840.

reelect Van Buren.[30] But Whigs did more than simply denounce the creation of a new party that they felt certain would hinder their chances of electoral victory. William R. Deland, a Whig abolitionist and a member of the MSASS executive committee, met in August with two other members of this eight-member council and passed resolutions proclaiming that the course pursued at the abolitionist ticket nominating convention "was 'unwise and inexpedient,' and originated in a desire to *favor* one of the existing political parties," and that the *Michigan Freeman* was no longer the organ of the MSASS because its editor supported the independent nominations. These measures were then heralded in an extra edition of the *Michigan State Gazette,* a Whig paper published in Jackson. Immediately, the remaining members of the executive committee assembled and rescinded these resolutions, and partisans of the new abolitionist party trumpeted out the clandestine way in which the measures had been passed. Whig abolitionists still tried to remove Treadwell from the editorial post of the *Freeman* but failed. The upshot of these proceedings was an abolitionist schism inversely analogous to the split in the American Anti-Slavery Society: the MSASS embraced the emerging abolitionist political party, while Whig antislaveryites left the state association.[31]

The emergence of the abolitionist party split Ann Arbor abolitionists as well. In early August, one assembly of abolitionists endorsed the nominations of Birney and Earle, declared that the "friends of Civil Liberty and Equal rights" should vote only for candidates committed to the "cause of human rights," and selected a delegate to attend the abolitionist nominating convention to be held in Jackson. Another abolitionist group, however, retorted that the nominations of Birney and Earle "were in opposition to the wishes of a large majority of the abolitionists in this state," and labeled such political actions counterproductive, as they would make "foes of those who are now favorably disposed towards us" and cause unnecessary divisions in the movement. This faction resolved to "stand aloof" from the nominating convention in

30. Porter to Treadwell, April 23, 1840, in Treadwell Papers; *Michigan Freeman,* May 5, July 15, 1840.

31. *Michigan Freeman,* August 12, September 23, 1840. A few subscribers may have reacted as did Amos Mead of Farmington, who, disgusted with the *Freeman's* endorsement of the abolitionist party, canceled his subscription, arguing that such actions only aided the "Van Buren party"; *ibid.,* September 23, 1840. However, the members of the MSASS executive committee maintained the following February that they found "no evidence" that support for the *Freeman* declined after it advocated "independent A. S. nominations"; *Signal of Liberty,* April 28, 1841.

Jackson and to "act in political matters as shall best accord with our private views." It also charged that the organizers of the Jackson convention were "gagging down and driving from the house a large number of those veterans in the cause who have stood forth at all times as its most able champions."

Even though these minutes were published by the Whig *Michigan State Journal*, this was not simply another Whig scheme to discredit the new abolitionist party. Some present at this meeting, such as Thomas M. Ladd and William A. Abel, were committed to both abolitionism and Whiggery. Ladd had been a delegate to the MSASS anniversary meeting in 1837 and served as editor of the *Michigan State Journal* during the early 1840s; Abel, a member of the Washtenaw County Anti-Slavery Society Executive Committee in 1838, remained with the Whigs through at least 1841. But others who opposed the nominations of Birney and Earle—including Martin H. Cowles, Belah Brown, Charles Mosely, and Roswell Parsons—shortly became some of the Liberty Party's most active enthusiasts in Ann Arbor. Calvin Townson, though, may have chosen the middle way. Townson was an executive committee member of the Washtenaw County Anti-Slavery Society in 1838 and was also among those who rejected the national abolitionist ticket. He quickly changed his opinion on this question, as he was an abolitionist candidate in the Ann Arbor Township elections of April 1841. Six months later, however, he was a delegate at a Whig county convention. Although Townson remained in Ann Arbor for a few more years—he was the corresponding secretary of the Washtenaw County Bible Society until 1845—there is no record of his involvement in party politics after 1841. These facts suggest that Townson, like some of Michigan's other antislavery Whigs, was torn by conflicting loyalties and chose to resolve his inner turmoil by becoming politically inactive.[32]

32. *Michigan Freeman*, August 12, 1840; *Michigan State Journal*, August 4, 11, 1840. On Ladd: *Report of the Meeting of the Michigan State Anti-Slavery Society, June 28th, 1837*, 3; Louis W. Doll, *A History of the Newspapers of Ann Arbor, 1829–1920* (Detroit, 1959), 27, 28; *Washtenaw Whig*, August 16, 1848. On Abel: *Michigan State Journal*, July 12, 1838, September 7, 1841. On Mosely: *Report of the Meeting of the Michigan State Anti-Slavery Society, June 28th, 1837*, 3; *Signal of Liberty*, August 11, September 1, 1841. On Brown: *Signal of Liberty*, August 11, September 1, 1841. On Parsons: *Proceedings of the Anti-Slavery State Convention, Held at Ann Arbor*, 4; *Michigan Freeman*, September 23, 1840 [Parsons embraced independent nominations a month and a half after he had publicly opposed them]; *Michigan State Journal*, April 6, 1841; *Signal of Liberty*, September 1, 1841, October 24, 1842, March 27, 1843, September 29, 1845. On Cowles: *Proceedings of the Anti-Slavery State Convention, Held at Ann Arbor*, 4; *Signal of Liberty*, August 11, 1841, March 23, 1842, March 27, 1843, March 18, 1844, September 29, 1845, April 6, June 27, October 10, 1846, October 16, 1847, February

The new party failed to create any major disturbances with respect to the election's outcome; it polled only 321 votes out of 44,350 that were cast in Michigan, and Whigs enjoyed their last statewide electoral victory. Nevertheless, the abolitionists' 0.7 percent of the vote in Michigan was higher than in any other state except Massachusetts, and Washtenaw County—Ann Arbor, Pittsfield, and Salem in particular—was ahead of the state proportion (Table 10). In the following months, the *Freeman* encouraged abolitionists to field candidates for county and township offices as well. At the MSASS anniversary meeting in February, the executive committee and the delegates further urged abolitionists "to unite their suffrages upon well-tried men of their own selection, who have absolved all connection with pro-slavery parties."[33] Although only a few locales ran abolitionist tickets in the April 1841 township elections, the total number of abolitionist votes in the Washtenaw County townships of Ann Arbor, Salem, and Scio surpassed the countywide figure for Birney of only five months earlier (Table 23).

The growth of abolitionist sentiment in Washtenaw County—and of the new abolitionist party, which was christened the Liberty Party in the spring of 1841—was greatly encouraged by the establishment of the *Signal of Liberty* in Ann Arbor in April 1841. The *Michigan Freeman*, which had ceased publishing in February, had been printed irregularly and, according to the state abolition body, had "greatly embarrassed the progress of our cause." In mid-February the executive committee was soliciting financial pledges from wealthy MSASS members, explaining that they expected the new paper to lose money for at least a year, but that a regularly published paper would better advance abolitionism.[34] Although the *Signal of Liberty* was initially under the editorship of the MSASS executive committee, most of the editorial work was performed by Theodore Foster, while Guy Beckley carried much of the paper's financial bur-

5, 1848; Ann Arbor Township Minutes, April 5, 1847, in Ann Arbor Township Hall. On Townson: *Michigan State Journal*, July 12, 1838, April 6, September 7, 1841; *Democratic Herald*, January 27, 1841; ABS *Annual Report* XXIX (1845), 145; Formisano, *Birth of Mass Political Parties*, 28, 59.

33. *Michigan Freeman*, December 9, 1840, February 5, 1841; *Signal of Liberty*, April 28, 1841; Svend Petersen, *A Statistical History of the American Presidential Elections* (Westport, Conn., 1981), 25; Volpe, *Forlorn Hope*, 47.

34. *Signal of Liberty*, April 28, 1841; Guy Beckley to Nathan Macy Thomas, February 16, 1841, in Nathan Macy Thomas Papers. One correspondent to the *Michigan State Journal* complained that the articles in the *Freeman* were "rendered almost intolerable by their almost interminable length" and that the answers to questions posed by abolitionists to political candidates appeared six weeks after the election; *Michigan State Journal*, December 18, 1839.

den. Beginning with the *Signal*'s second volume, both of their names appeared on the masthead as editors, but for all practical purposes Foster carried the weight of editorship until the paper's demise in February 1848.[35]

With the MSASS and its newspaper endorsing political nominations, abolitionists in Michigan who opposed such nominations lacked a forum, and they failed to unite under a new organization. Although it appears that most male abolitionists in Michigan eventually joined the Liberty Party, there is some evidence that a significant minority did not. In August the *Signal* claimed that as soon as abolition became associated with politics, some ministers ceased preaching against slavery lest they contribute to a political party and thus violate the sacred barrier separating church and state. One minister who had been known for years as an abolitionist reportedly warned his congregation against political abolitionism; he was convinced that the Libertyites would be unsuccessful because "political abolitionists had ceased to pray and depend upon the Lord, and were now relying on an arm of flesh." To such contentions, the *Signal* was conciliatory: the paper recommended that ministers continue to preach against slavery without making reference to a political party, urged churches to exclude slaveholders from their fellowship, and encouraged those who were sincerely attached to the exclusive use of moral suasion to continue in that direction.[36]

The following week the *Signal* commented on the "very considerable body of abolitionists who have not supported separate nominations." Rather than labeling these individuals as weak of heart, the *Signal* acknowledged that they included some of the movement's most stalwart members. Yet, maintained editor Theodore Foster, they were at present doing little to "hasten the day of universal liberty." In addition to pointing out that they had no newspaper or societies of their own through which to express themselves, Foster asserted that their continued participation with the major political parties had caused them to be no longer "known publicly as abolitionists," as they were now "recognized among pro-slavery partizans." He asked these individuals how they could "consistently ask God to deliver the oppressed . . . and then *vote* for a slaveholder, or a defender or supporter of the right of property in man?" Foster was optimistic, though, that many of these "true-hearted abolitionists will yet

35. John Edgar Kephart, "A Voice for Freedom: The *Signal of Liberty*, 1841–1848" (Ph.D. dissertation, University of Michigan, 1960), 9, 12. Foster became the *Signal*'s sole editor in 1846. *Ibid.*, 19.

36. *Signal of Liberty*, August 18, 1841.

come into the measure of anti-slavery nomination," as they would eventually recognize the need to *"vote,* as well as to pray, and talk, and write in favor of universal liberty." Abolitionists in Pittsfield Township agreed with the *Signal* and the state abolition organization; they resolved "that as moral suasion alone, is insufficient to accomplish our object in establishing liberty and equal rights, where people are bound by civil laws, therefore a resort to political action is our only remedy." And as noted in chapter 4, from its commencement the *Signal of Liberty* endorsed legal measures in the temperance crusade, and announced in September 1841 "that the Temperance cause, as well as abolition, in this State, will henceforth go on the *two* legs of moral suasion and political action." Inasmuch as temperance agents had been unsuccessful in using moral suasion alone to "prevent the making of drunkards" while "grog sellers, under the sanction of law, have carried on a work of opposite nature," so political abolitionists no longer regarded moral suasion as their principal weapon to combat slavery.[37]

In the three years following the 1840 election, there was virtually no dissent at the annual MSASS meetings regarding that body's endorsement of the Michigan Liberty Party. True, the two organizations were technically separate, but their meetings were often held in the same village on consecutive days, as happened in Ann Arbor in February 1843. At this MSASS gathering, though, the Reverend Nathaniel West of Monroe explained that "he could not consistently take a part in political anti-slavery conventions" due to a "strong prejudice against ministers entering the political caucuses" and an understanding that some people would reject his gospel if he was thus involved. The report of the meeting recorded that "he did not defend this feeling. He did not say it was right. He only said that such would be *the effect* of a given course."[38]

At the MSASS meeting the following year, however, at least eight speakers questioned the body's endorsement of the Liberty Party. This dissent struck Seymour Treadwell and Theodore Foster as extraordinary: both confessed that it was "the first time in three years that [they] had heard political action against slavery repudiated by one who called himself an Abolitionist." Only one speaker expressed Garrisonian views; many of the others charged that they had been read out of the movement by political abolitionists, insisted that moral suasion alone was sufficient to attain abolitionist objectives, and com-

---

37. *Ibid.,* August 25, 1841, January 12, 1842, September 1, 1841.
38. *Ibid.,* February 20, 1843.

plained that the Liberty Party had been too willing to denounce antislavery Whigs such as John Quincy Adams and Joshua Giddings. Guy Beckley countered that political abolitionists still adhered to moral suasion, but that this force alone "would never create or abolish a Bank or a Tariff, neither will it extinguish slavery, which exists only by force of law." Charles H. Stewart, president of the society, replied that Giddings had publicly opposed the Liberty Party and was "trying to put the slaveholders in power. At the top of his principles are the Bank and Tariff and [Henry] Clay, while his abolition is made subordinate. We go for Anti-Slavery at the top, and make financial questions subordinate."[39]

Stewart's response was common among Liberty Party members in Michigan. Antislavery Whigs insisted that their candidates, if elected, would do more to promote abolition than Liberty candidates ever could, as none of them had ever been elected to any office beyond the township level. For many Libertyites, such questions were moot. They viewed the two major political parties as hopelessly in the power of southern interests—the "Slave Power," as they called it—and were convinced that any show of support for these parties was tacit acceptance of slavery. In this important regard, many Liberty Party devotees were similar to members of "come-outer" religious sects, which we shall subsequently examine, who left mainstream churches that they believed were corrupted by slavery.[40]

As a political organization, the Liberty Party experienced many failures and few successes. None of its candidates in Michigan was ever elected to state, county, or federal office, and in none of the five hundred counties in the northern states did the party ever achieve majority status.[41] But while Liberty Party members would have certainly enjoyed winning elections, short-term electoral victory was not their sole objective; they saw their party as a means to bear witness against American slavery. And as a Liberty convention in Ann Arbor resolved in 1841, Libertyites believed their votes were "never thrown away," because a solid turnout at the polls would provide them with respect in the halls of power. Although they never received the regard they felt they deserved, the party's vote totals in Michigan rose significantly during its first few years, and by 1844 it was organized in every white-settled county in the lower peninsula.

---

39. *Ibid.*, February 5, 1844. See also the letter of Ann Arbor Universalist minister S. Miles, a committed moral suasionist, *ibid.*, December 1, 1845.

40. This point is well argued in Volpe, *Forlorn Hope, passim*.

41. *Signal of Liberty*, March 9, 1846; Sewell, *Ballots for Freedom*, 113, 164.

During these first few years, the election reports published in the *Signal* were often heady and full of optimism. Foster and the *Signal*'s correspondents often noted how the Liberty Party held the balance of power in many townships and counties, and delegates to a Liberty convention in Ann Arbor expected that the continual growth of the party would cause the present political system to disintegrate and a new antislavery party or parties to rise from the ashes. Election reports applauded the rapid increase in Liberty votes. One correspondent's response to the November 1842 election returns in Jackson County was exuberant. The 300 Liberty votes there accounted for 14.3 percent of the total and was "more than double what it was last year, and more than five times what it was the year before." In celebrating the increase of the aggregate Liberty vote in the free states from only 7,000 in 1840 to 57,000 in 1843, the MSASS executive committee again endorsed the party and proclaimed that "an increase in the same proportion for a very few years, will give the Liberty Party a decided ascendency in the councils of the nation." In the 1845 gubernatorial election, the party received its highest proportion of the state's vote, 7.6 percent. Nevertheless, the party polled 600 fewer votes than in its previous electoral outing, and the optimistic blustering of a few years previous was now seldom repeated. Thereafter, the party received both fewer votes and a smaller percentage of the total vote, until it was essentially absorbed by the Free Soil Party in 1848 (Tables 10 through 17).[42]

The *Signal of Liberty* also encouraged abolitionists to support the Liberty cause in township elections. Although township officers lacked the power of state and federal legislators to enact laws touching upon slavery or the status of free blacks, the Liberty Party fielded tickets in many townships and occasionally even won. As with general election returns during the early 1840s, the *Sig-*

42. *Signal of Liberty*, October 27, November 17, 1841, November 14, 1842, January 22, 1844, November 24, 1845. This drop-off in the number of Liberty votes was expected by Foster and others before the 1845 gubernatorial election; Theodore Foster to James G. Birney, July 7, 1845, in Dumond, ed., *Birney Letters*, II 952. Statewide, Michigan Liberty returns were as follows: 1840, U.S. president, 321 votes (0.7 percent); 1841, governor, 1,223 (3.2 percent); 1842, state senate, 1,949 (5.4 percent); 1843, governor, 2,776 (7.1 percent); 1844, U.S. president, 3,639 (6.5 percent); 1845, governor, 3,023 (7.6 percent); 1846, Congress, 2,885 (6.0 percent); 1847, governor, 2,585 (5.6 percent). County figures are provided in John W. Quist, "'The Great Majority of Our Subscribers Are Farmers': The Michigan Abolitionist Constituency of the 1840s," *Journal of the Early Republic*, XIV (Fall 1994), 332. A more complete accounting of county votes—and the basis for the figures in the 1842 state senate race—are available in the County Canvassers' Statements of Votes for County, State, and Federal Offices, in the State Archives of Michigan, Lansing.

nal celebrated increases in the Liberty township vote as evidence that its cause was in the ascendant. Some Washtenaw County townships—most notably Ann Arbor and Salem—consistently ran a Liberty slate from 1841 to 1848, but in many townships the interest in running candidates diminished by the middle of the decade (Tables 23 through 30). Nevertheless, even as late as March 1847, the *Signal of Liberty* reminded its readers of the importance of voting in the upcoming township elections. If Liberty voters "could be induced to vote for a proslavery man for Supervisor, why should they not support the *same* man for Senator or Representative?" It was better not to vote than to cast ballots for Whigs or Democrats—even if they were sound temperance candidates pledged to prohibition.[43]

In a few townships, the Liberty Party was actually competitive. Salem was clearly Washtenaw County's banner township, and after 1840 the Liberty ticket there never finished with less than 20 percent of the vote. Salem's Libertyites were victorious in the 1846 and 1847 township elections (Tables 28 and 29), outpolled the Whigs and Democrats in the 1846 election for the United States Congress (Table 16), and closely contested the 1845 and 1847 gubernatorial elections (Tables 15 and 17). The Ann Arbor Liberty Party received a smaller percentage of the vote than the party did in several other townships in the county; it nevertheless had one of Washtenaw's strongest Liberty organizations, which fielded a ticket in every township election from 1841 to 1848.

Contemporaries disagreed as to whether the Liberty Party hurt or helped the cause of abolition. Although the party—like all of the era's political organizations—generally excluded from participation those who were prohibited by law from voting, it provided white males of voting age the opportunity to participate in the antislavery cause in a new way that went beyond attending lectures, passing resolutions, and circulating publications and petitions. Such measures were always fundamental to temperance, abolition, and to a lesser extent, benevolent activities but, alone, were insufficient to maintain long-term enthusiasm in any of these causes. Electoral politics provided the abolitionists with activities that were interspersed throughout the year, most certainly helping to keep more people active in antislavery endeavors. Aside from elections every April and November, in which devoted party members un-

43. Quist, "Great Majority," 330 n. 7; *Signal of Liberty*, April 28, 1841, April 6, 13, 25, May 2, 1842, March 13, 1847. The *Signal*'s interest in township elections was best demonstrated during the 1843 township campaigns, when it printed the Liberty tickets of five local townships; *ibid.*, March 27, April 3, 1843.

doubtedly sought out like-minded antislaveryites and urged them to vote the Liberty ticket, there were also nominating conventions for these campaigns. These assemblies entailed not only the attendance of committed abolitionists, but at least the compliance of some other engaged antislaveryites who allowed their names to be used as candidates for county and township offices. The failure of some townships to run Liberty tickets most likely reflected the difficulty of finding thirteen to eighteen individuals to serve as abolitionist candidates. In some of the less-populated townships—Webster, Scio, Manchester, and Pittsfield in particular—the party generally ran a ticket for township office yet usually received only as many votes as candidates, which suggests that the party members in these locales were especially committed to maintaining a separate party status and were loath to participate in any manner with the "pro-slavery" parties.

The level of abolitionist activity in Washtenaw County was lower and less consistent during the years prior to the formation of an abolitionist political party than during the 1840s. Few delegates from eastern Michigan attended the 1839 MSASS meeting. *American Freeman* editor William M. Sullivan commented that this was not because of their lack of conviction. Despite their meager numbers, Sullivan noted the strength of the commitment of devotees in Ypsilanti, Scio, Webster, and Saline and praised the years that they had spent in the movement: "They espoused the cause . . . early in the days of Garrison's and Tappan's unpopularity." Six months later, however, Sullivan reported that Joshua Leavitt, editor of the New York City *Emancipator*, had commissioned Guy Beckley to "abolitionize" Washtenaw County "this winter" and that it would be "a task of no little magnitude." Sullivan continued: "Withal in passing through the wealthy and enterprising county of Washtenaw, my heart involuntarily ached, and my eyes filled with tears, when I reflected that but a little while ago, when a call was made for a meeting of the county society, there was hardly as many made their appearance as the 'souls' that floated in Noah's ark above a wretched world. Brethren of Washtenaw, will you be longer than your oars?" In contrast, at a Liberty county convention less than two years later, at least fifty-nine delegates were present, and of course many others expressed their solidarity with abolition by either running for township office or voting for the party.[44]

44. *American Freeman*, July 2, 1839; *Michigan Freeman*, December 25, 1839; *Signal of Liberty*, September 1, 1841.

During the life of the Liberty Party, Washtenaw County abolitionists also continued with traditional antislavery measures. Religious-minded opponents of slavery formed the Monthly Concert for the Enslaved, and a number of Washtenaw County abolitionists participated in the most romanticized form of antislavery activism, the so-called underground railroad. On a number of occasions, the *Signal of Liberty* reported the passing of fugitives through Ann Arbor on their way to Canada, and according to local tradition, Guy Beckley's home in Ann Arbor and Theodore Foster's residence in Scio served as "stations" on the "railroad." Stations were also reportedly located in Dexter village, Scio, Ypsilanti, Saline, Sharon, and Manchester. Contemporary evidence is lacking, however, with respect to the extent to which other Washtenaw abolitionists were engaged in this enterprise.[45]

Another tool used to maintain and build antislavery interest was the lecture. James G. Birney—who, as we noted in chapter 5, had addressed Tuscaloosans on colonization during the early 1830s—spoke at least twice in Ann Arbor, in 1841 and 1845. In 1846, Henry Bibb, a well-known expatriate from slavery who lectured throughout the North, spoke before audiences in Ann Arbor, Ypsilanti, Webster, Northfield, and Salem. Of Bibb's Ann Arbor visit, the *Signal of Liberty* reported that "every seat in the Court House was filled and a large number remained standing for more than two hours." In February and March of 1847, Samuel T. Creighton, a Virginian who had emancipated his 150 slaves, lectured in Ypsilanti, Ann Arbor, Saline, and Dexter village. At the latter site, Creighton reportedly kept his audience "spellbound" for three succes-

---

45. On the Monthly Concert for the Enslaved: *Signal of Liberty,* December 30, 1844. On the underground railroad: *ibid.,* May 12, 19, September 1, December 1, 15, 1841, June 27, December 26, 1842, March 4, June 24, 1844, July 28, 1845, January 5, 1846; *Local News and Advertiser,* December 1, 1857; Detroit *Daily Democrat,* January 14, 1854; inscription on photograph of Theodore Foster's residence in Pattengill Family Papers, Bentley Library; "School District No. 2" in Palmer, comp., "A History of Manchester Township"; Kooker, "Antislavery," 261–62 n. 13; "Brief History of the Residence and Property Owned by Mr. and Mrs. Ralph W. Hammett," undated typescript in Arthur Raymond Kooker Papers, Bentley Library; Dunbar and May, *Michigan,* 356–57; Larry Massie and Keith A. Owens, "Michigan's Railroad to Freedom" and Keith A. Owens, "Tracking Down Local Stations," both in Ann Arbor *News,* July 12, 1987; Colburn, *Ypsilanti,* 147–49; Albert P. Marshall, *Unconquered Souls: The History of the African-American in Ypsilanti* (Ypsilanti, 1993), 17–30; Larry Gara, *The Liberty Line: The Legend of the Underground Railroad* (Lexington, Ky., 1961), 110 and *passim*. Michigan's most renowned activist in the underground railroad was Laura Haviland, a resident of Lenawee County. See Laura S. Haviland, *A Woman's Life-Work: Labors and Experiences of Laura S. Haviland* (Cincinnati, 1882).

sive evenings. In May of that year, Lewis Washington, a "fugitive slave," spoke before audiences in Ann Arbor and Dexter village.[46] But most of the antislavery lectures in Washtenaw County at this time were provided by Michiganders active in the Liberty Party. Guy Beckley preached the abolitionist gospel before audiences in Superior, Sharon, and Northfield prior to the November 1841 election; Seymour Treadwell toured several of the county's western townships in 1844 and in 1846 accompanied Henry Bibb; and Chester Gurney, the Liberty candidate for governor in 1847, campaigned in Ann Arbor, Dexter village, Ypsilanti, and Manchester.[47]

In addition to planning strategy or voice protests, Liberty Party members gathered occasionally to hold meetings independent of explicitly political ends. In 1845, Washtenaw County Libertyites held their own Independence Day celebration. The following year, the "Friends of Liberty" in Saline organized a society that was to meet the last Saturday of every month, and its members recommended "abstinence from the products of slave labor, as far as practicable, as one means of antislavery efficiency."[48] Some protests of slavery and of the influence of slaveholders in national affairs occurred independent of the Liberty Party. In March 1842, sixty Washtenaw citizens called for a meeting to publicize their views on "the Right of Petition, the Creole case, and the series of aggressions continually [made] by Southern slaveholders upon the rights and interests of the Northern people." Not everyone who called for this meeting belonged to the Liberty Party, and none of the meeting's measures condemned slavery in the harsh moral tones common to Liberty Party resolutions; nor was there any remonstrance against the denial of rights to free blacks. Instead, the resolutions passed by this assembly condemned the South for its disproportionate power in national councils and its willful abuse of that power— at the expense of northern rights—to defend slavery. One resolution praised the actions of Whig congressman John Quincy Adams, suggesting that the organizers were attempting to find common ground among antislaveryites in different political parties. Later, a petition to the Michigan Senate from Ann

46. *Signal of Liberty*, September 22, 29, 1841; *Michigan Argus*, February 5, 1845; *Signal of Liberty*, May 4, 18, 1846; Ypsilanti *Sentinel*, May 6, 1846, February 24, 1847; *Signal of Liberty*, March 20, May 22, 1847 (see also August 7, 1843). Bibb was also scheduled to speak in Ann Arbor in July 1850. *Michigan Argus*, June 19, 1850.

47. *Signal of Liberty*, September 29, October 20, 1841, September 9, 1844, May 6, 1846, August 28, 1847.

48. *Ibid.*, November 6, 1843, December 30, 1844, June 23, 1845, May 23, 1846.

Arbor condemned the proposed admission of Texas into the Union and suggested the appropriation of Canada if Texas were to be annexed.[49]

Generally, though, Michigan abolitionists relied less on petitions during the 1840s than they had during the latter years of the previous decade. While the MSASS executive committee still hoped in February 1842 that a flood of petitions to the U.S. Congress would overturn the gag rule, by the following year, the executive committee reported that Michigan abolitionists had sent few petitions to Washington. In 1844 antislavery leaders explained that abolitionists had grown tired of their petitions being used as an excuse to "insult" them and their cause, and concluded that political action better promoted their message. Nevertheless, Washtenaw abolitionists collected at least 293 signatures from 134 sympathizers in late 1841 and early 1842, and submitted them to Michigan's Whig Representative, Jacob Howard. Though Howard voted against the gag rule, abolitionists were disappointed when he failed to be vigilant in opposing this restriction. Abolitionists, however, continued to urge the submission of petitions to the state legislature, as they were hopeful that Michigan's solons would act favorably on such issues as black male suffrage and prohibiting the use of state resources in the capture of fugitive slaves.[50]

The *Signal of Liberty*, the Liberty Party, and the MSASS not only repudiated in harsh moral tones the injustices suffered by American slaves, but they also condemned the impact of slavery upon both the national economy and the civil rights of nonslaveholders. In short, they endeavored to convince people who were not moved by the plight of the slave to acknowledge that slavery in-

49. *Ibid.*, March 23, April 6, 1842; *Michigan State Journal*, March 5, 1845.

50. *Signal of Liberty*, October 13, 1841, February 16, 1842, February 13, 1843, January 22, 1844; 54 legal voters of Washtenaw County [Ann Arbor] remonstrate against the gag rule, 49 legal voters of Washtenaw County [Ann Arbor] urge the repeal of all laws by which the federal government and people of the free states are implicated with slavery, and 50 legal voters of Washtenaw County [Ann Arbor] call for the repeal of all laws which sanction slavery on U.S. ships (all tabled December 15, 1841 and filed under HR27A-H1.6); 52 legal voters of Washtenaw County [Manchester and Sharon] urge the repeal of all laws by which the federal government and people of the free states are implicated with slavery, 61 legal voters of Washtenaw County [Manchester and Sharon] remonstrate against the gag rule, 14 legal voters of Saline call for the repeal of all laws sanctioning slavery on U.S. ships, 13 legal voters of Saline urge the repeal of all laws by which the federal government and people of the free states are implicated with slavery (all tabled between February 7 and February 28, 1842, and filed under HR27A-H1.7). All of these petitions are found in RG 233. Regarding use of petitions by Michigan abolitionists during the 1840s, see also *Signal of Liberty*, October 13, 1841, January 30, 1843.

fluenced many dimensions of their lives. Seymour Treadwell recognized the strength of this "Slave Power" argument in 1841, when in a letter to an anti-slavery confidant he praised the *Signal of Liberty* for its coverage of the *"moral part of our enterprise"* but confessed that its editors were thus far deficient in pointing to the "political and financial power of slavery" and the necessity of "independent political action to over throw these crushing powers." Treadwell continued:

> Very few men who have long been wedded to their old proslavery parties by a thousand (to them) *endearing* and almost indissoluble ties, will ever be induced to break away from these parties by *mere moral* considerations. They must be made to see clearly and forcibly that Slavery in all its bearings is not only *immoral* and *outraging* all the rights of human nature but that it is the OVERWHELMING political and financial power in the nation which has in *truth already subverted* AMERICAN LIBERTIES. To *tell* the people this merely is not enough. They must be made to feel the facts in the case, the *historical* whys and wherefores.[51]

Much to Treadwell's undoubted delight, the *Signal of Liberty* shortly there-after commenced pursuing this line of reasoning in its editorials. In an essay entitled "The Debt of Slaveholders," Foster argued that many of the financial woes in the northern states occurred because "the capital of the North is made to flow into the great southern gulph out of which it never emerges." In a sepa-rate piece, "The Necessity of a Liberty Party," Foster catalogued the injustices that northerners were forced to suffer on account of slavery: "unequal represen-tation of the slave States in the National Legislature," which resulted in one slaveholder's possessing "as much political power as two, three, and four north-ern voters"; the disproportionate share of revenues from the national treasury that went to the southern states; the stranglehold of southerners upon the presidency, the speakership of the House of Representatives, and federal office appointments; and the congressional gag rule, which deprived northerners "of the right of petition." A correspondent to the *Signal* further detailed the inten-tions of this sinister force: "By their unity, perseverance, and effrontery, the 250,000 slaveholders have obtained and continue to hold the ascendancy of po-litical power, in the whole nation." Additionally, "They deprive their slaves of

51. Seymour B. Treadwell to Nathan M. Thomas, August 21, 1841, in Nathan Macy Thomas Papers. See also Larry Gara, "Slavery and the Slave Power: A Crucial Distinction," *Civil War History,* XV (March 1969), 5–18.

the possession of every right, and they have sought to make the encroachments upon the rights of free laborers all over the Union." These "encroachments" were only the first step toward a much larger goal, the enslavement of northern laborers as well. The writer then quoted South Carolina governor George McDuffie, who "said that the North would be driven to the adoption of the slave system in less than twenty-five years. Slaveholders avow it as a desirable object to reduce society into two classes—the capitalist and the laborer—in other words, the master and the slave and thus bring about a uniform system of labor through the union."[52] Before long, the state Liberty Party made frequent references to the Slave Power. At a meeting of the state party in Ann Arbor in February 1843, the convention resolved "that the Liberty party was organized not for the purpose of testing a doubtful experiment, and to be abandoned on any reverse of fortune, but for the noble purpose of rescuing our government from the control of the slave power."[53]

These sentiments were expressed not only by high-ranking Liberty Party officials, but by people on the grass-roots level as well. A Liberty gathering in Jackson blasted the preoccupation of legislatures with corporations and internal improvements while a "relentless and despotic oligarchy of 250,000 slaveholders" trampled upon American liberties. It was not possible, concluded a Liberty convention in Grand Rapids, for a slaveholding community to support itself except through "depredations upon other communities, with which it holds intercourse. . . . Northern funds, to a vast amount, have been engulphed and lost forever in the Pontine marshes of Southern Banks and Southern State Stocks." Similarly, an assemblage in Shiawassee County proclaimed that slavery was "a greater evil in pecuniary point of view than the existence or nonexistence of a Tariff, U. S. Bank or Sub-Treasury, and in a *moral* sense, *infinitely* greater." These positions were personalized in some remarks of George W. Jewett, who prior to his association with the Liberty Party had been president of the Ann Arbor town council and a justice of the peace, and because of his position in the militia, was often addressed as "Colonel." He had always been a Democrat, and his politics, he claimed, remained unchanged. But, according to the minutes of a Liberty gathering,

52. *Signal of Liberty,* September 29, 1841, February 2, 1842. See also the essay from "F.," "Oppression of Slavery upon the Non-Slaveholding Portion of the Community in the Slave States," *ibid.,* September 1, 1841.

53. *Ibid.,* February 20, 1843; see also the address of the State Central Corresponding Committee of the Liberty Party, *ibid.,* October 10, 1842.

of late years he had received new light on the subject of slavery. He had ever abhorred it; but he ascertained that the people of the North were in one sense slaves to the slaveholders. They were not, indeed subject to the lash, but their purses were heavily drained, the honors and emoluments of office were largely monopolized by these few slaveholders, and our national policy controlled by them. Every thinking person could easily satisfy himself by a little reflection, that a slaveholding community, where only half the people are laborers, cannot support itself. But slaveholders live, and live in greatest splendor too, and it comes out of Northern laborers. They trade largely with the North, and every few years, by a bankrupt act or otherwise, wipe out their indebtedness of two or three hundred millions.

Indeed, the Slave Power even succeeded in winning over one of Ann Arbor's former residents, Franklin Sawyer, who had edited the Whig *Michigan State Journal* and had also served as the Michigan superintendent of public instruction. Upon his being named editor of the New Orleans *Tropic,* the *Signal* sarcastically noted that *"his* antislavery principles, it seems, are no bar to the confidence of the most rabid slaveholders." Five months later, the *Signal* reported that Sawyer was running slave advertisements in his paper, and Theodore Foster saw this development as a further example of how the Slave Power was able to subvert the principles of the "ablest men of New England and of the North, for pecuniary or political emolument."[54]

Such attacks on the Slave Power reflected the fears and mistrust that abolitionists had of slaveholders, but they also proved to be a powerful rhetorical weapon. While the Free Soil and Republican Parties did not protest the inhumanity of slavery or the denial of civil rights to northern blacks to the extent that the Liberty Party did, condemnations of the Slave Power served as a cornerstone of their rhetoric. The Ann Arbor Whigs eventually employed the concept in their political language, particularly after they sustained continued political losses due in part to the tergiversations of Whigs to the Liberty banner. Although the Liberty Party drew from both Whigs and Democrats, contemporaries in Washtenaw County frequently affirmed that the vast majority

54. *Ibid.,* November 17, December 1, 1841, July 22, 1844, November 6, 1843, October 6, 1845, March 9, 1846. In 1837, Sawyer wrote at length of several meetings of the Massachusetts Anti-Slavery Society that he attended and by which he was favorably impressed. Detroit *Daily Advertiser,* February 20, 1837.

of Libertyites were former Whigs.[55] Nevertheless, Washtenaw County Whigs initially gave scant attention to the abolitionist party. The only notice that the *Michigan State Journal* provided of the new party during the 1840 election was the publication of the heretofore mentioned protest meeting of abolitionists who opposed separate antislavery nominations—which proceedings appeared without any editorial comment. Indeed, the *Journal* made no effort to appeal to abolitionist votes in 1840. Never in the course of this long campaign did the *Journal* argue—as did some Whigs—that a Harrison administration would show consideration to abolitionist concerns. In fact, its editors ignored a question posed to it by its Democratic rival: "Why does not the Michigan State Journal publish . . . the remarks . . . proving [Harrison] an abolitionist?"[56] Evidently the *Michigan State Journal* felt that antislavery was not a driving issue among Washtenaw County voters likely to vote Whig in 1840.

Aside from responding to an article in the *Signal of Liberty* that charged Daniel Webster with "Bowing Down to Slavery," the *Michigan State Journal* also ignored the abolitionist paper during its first five months of publication. After the Liberty Party announced its nominations for the November 1841 state election, however, the *Journal* declared to its party stalwarts that the "avowed object of the Abolition Party" was the defeat of the Whigs, and pointed to the Washtenaw Liberty nominations to the legislature—of which seven of eight were former Whigs—as proof of this objective. "Knowing that the greatest majority of Abolitionists are Whigs they take the surest course to draw all they can from the support of the whig ticket, *and thus elect the Locofoco ticket.*" In its electoral postmortem, however, the *Journal* did not blame its party's defeat upon Liberty defections; rather, it insisted that Whigs were not dili-

---

55. The *Michigan State Journal,* October 19, 1841, asserted that three-fourths of the Liberty Party came from the Whigs. In 1843, the Marshall *Western Statesman* claimed that nine-tenths of the Liberty rank and file were drawn from the Whigs, to which the *Signal of Liberty,* May 29, 1843, responded, "Our acquaintance is 'pretty extensive,' and we are satisfied that scarcely three fourths are from the Whigs." See also *Michigan State Journal,* April 6, September 7, 21, 1842, June 7, November 15, 1843, and *Signal of Liberty,* September 9, 1844. Enthusiasm among Whig abolitionists for William Henry Harrison in 1840 may have been why Nathan Thomas reported that two-thirds of those who voted for Birney in 1840 had formerly been Democrats; Thomas to S. B. Treadwell, November 28, 1840, as cited in Kooker, "Antislavery," 301 n. 16 (see also 296, 300–301); Sewell, *Ballots for Freedom,* 77.

56. *Michigan State Journal,* August 11, 1840; *Michigan Times,* August 11, 1840; Sewell, *Ballots for Freedom,* 76–77.

gent and stayed away from the polls.[57] Between the November and April township elections, the *Journal*'s only mention of the Liberty Party was a piece, reprinted from the *Emancipator* and authored by Lewis Tappan, that argued against independent abolitionist nominations. But after the April township election, the *Journal* asserted that of the seventy-two Liberty votes, fifty came from former Whigs. Although victorious in this instance, the Whigs henceforth treated the Liberty Party as a foe with which they had to reckon (Tables 11 and 24).[58]

As the 1842 November election approached, the *Michigan State Journal* tried several approaches to discredit the Liberty Party. One was a continuation of its previous strategy of accusing the Liberty leaders of being "locos at heart" whose "foolish opposition to a tariff. . . proves conclusively to us, that their object is not confined to the emancipation of the slave."[59] The *Journal* also argued that supporting the Liberty Party was myopic and unpatriotic, since "that organization neglects and disregards all the important questions of the day, save abolition alone." Such singlemindedness, continued the *Journal*, "does not discharge most certainly the whole duty of a good citizen." The *Journal* pleaded with Liberty voters to view the Whigs as the lesser evil to the Democrats, who as a party had long been unsympathetic to any elements of the antislavery agenda. Prior to the election, the paper reminded voters that one of the inconsistencies of the "locofocos" was to "preach up democracy, and vote with southern slavery." Finally, the *Journal* argued that the Liberty Party was "daily losing

57. *Michigan State Journal,* June 8, October 5, November 16, 1841 (see also October 19, 1841).

58. *Ibid.,* January 4, April 6, 1842.

59. *Ibid.,* July 13, 1842, as quoted in *Signal of Liberty,* July 18, 1842; see also *Michigan State Journal,* September 7, 1842, June 7, November 1, December 6, 1843, October 30, 1844, and *Signal of Liberty,* January 1, September 9, 1844. Some Whigs were convinced that the Liberty Party was a Democratic plot to divide the Whigs; Liberty leaders, they claimed, were not sincere abolitionists, but Democratic conspirators whose aim was ultimately to stifle antislavery objectives. Thus, during the 1844 presidential campaign, the *Michigan State Journal* published an affidavit that charged *Signal of Liberty* coeditor Guy Beckley with favoring Texas annexation—which accusation Beckley vehemently denied. Later the *Journal* published the "Garland forgery"—a falsified letter of James G. Birney that purported to show that Birney was in league with the Democrats. And so strong was this belief in a Democrat/Liberty conspiracy that it was still repeated over six years after the demise of the Michigan Liberty Party. *Michigan State Journal,* August 14, 21, October 9, 16, 23, 30, November 20, 1844; Ypsilanti *Sentinel* quoted in *Washtenaw Whig,* September 6, 1854.

ground" in Michigan, as "the majority of this party are too honest not to regard other interests as well as those of the slave and [would] not willingly sacrifice those other objects, to the ambition and cupidity of abolitionist leaders." Although the number of Liberty voters in Ann Arbor declined from the township election in April, from the countywide perspective the *Journal*'s campaign analysis was flawed, as the Washtenaw Liberty vote surpassed the previous year's total and at 8.3 percent was the largest proportion that the party ever received in the county (Table 12). The following year the *Journal* again tried ignoring the Liberty Party but, following the Whigs' third straight loss in a state election—and their third consecutive defeat by the Democrats among Washtenaw County voters—admitted that defections to the Liberty Party, as well as widespread apathy among Whigs, had cost the Whigs the election.[60]

One consequence of the Libertyite appeals to antislavery voters to break from the two older parties was that the Whig and Democratic Parties changed their strategies toward the abolitionists. In 1844, the *Michigan State Journal* sought to win back Liberty voters—and to prevent additional defections—by taking a stronger stand against slavery. Initially, the *Journal* argued that slavery adversely affected the northern economy; later, George Corselius, the paper's new editor as of February 28, 1844, called upon Congress to abolish slavery in the District of Columbia and to put a halt to the coastal slave trade. The *Journal*'s position regarding slavery became more pronounced with the emergence of Texas annexation as a political issue in the spring of 1844, for the *Journal* strongly opposed annexation. But even prior to the national debate over Texas, the *Journal*'s increasing attention to slavery was immediately noticed by the *Michigan Argus*. The Democratic paper announced that the *Journal*'s posture "was obviously designed to conciliate the Abolitionists." Unlike during the 1830s, when it tried to link the Whigs to the abolitionists, the *Argus* now maintained that the Whigs were unworthy of any antislavery credentials. On this particular occasion, the *Argus* reminded its readers that the Whigs held power in Washington for two years and did nothing to rectify these problems, nor did the *Journal* urge its party leaders to action during these years. Therefore, the *Argus* thought that the Whigs would make "but little political capital by de-

<hr/>

60. *Michigan State Journal*, September 14, 21, October 19, September 28, 1842, November 15, 1843.

nouncing them now" and further pointed out that "their candidate for the Presidency being a slaveholder, does not speak well for their sincerity . . . to make friends with the abolitionists."[61]

Recognizing the bind in which the local Whig Party found itself—of trying to appeal for antislavery votes while endorsing a slaveholder for president—for three months the *Argus* printed under its masthead "MR. CLAY AND SLAVERY," to which it appended the following quotation from Henry Clay: *"I am the son of Virginia, a slaveholder in Kentucky.* AND I WOULD SUFFER THE TORTURES OF THE INQUISITION, BEFORE I WOULD SIGN A BILL HAVING FOR ITS OBJECT THE ABOLITION OF SLAVERY IN THE DISTRICT [of Columbia], OR IN ANY MANNER GIVE COUNTENANCE TO THE PROJECT." Although the *Argus* removed the quotation shortly before the Democrats nominated James K. Polk, a slaveholder from Tennessee, the paper continued to trumpet the Whigs' dilemma.[62] In July the *Argus* reprinted a list of quotations from Henry Clay in which he affirmed his commitment to slavery and defended his opposition to the reception of antislavery petitions by Congress. In the fall the *Argus* made additional efforts to discourage marginal Whigs from voting for Harry of the West by charging that Clay was a onetime slave trader and by printing his rebukes of abolitionists—including his cousin, Cassius Clay—for threatening the Union and exaggerating the crimes of slavery. So successful were the Democratic barbs at Henry Clay that they diverted attention from Polk's slaveholdings. A Democrat in Lima Township purportedly maintained that "Polk is not a slaveholder, and consequently all who are opposed to slavery ought to vote for him."[63]

To be sure, Henry Clay's opposition to the annexation of Texas satisfied some abolitionists that he was indeed a lesser evil than Polk, who favored it. And although Birney's position on abolition was unimpeachable for most abolitionists, they recognized that he stood no chance of winning the presidency. Thus the *Journal* constantly repeated Clay's position on annexation and main-

61. *Ibid.*, April 12, 1843, April 3, 1844; *Michigan Argus,* January 31, 1844, referring to *Michigan State Journal,* January 24, 1844.

62. *Michigan Argus,* February 7, May 8, 1844. Later the *Argus* denied the *Signal of Liberty's* contention that the quotation was removed because of the nomination of Polk; editor E. P. Gardiner maintained that the quotation was removed three weeks before the Democratic convention. *Michigan Argus,* June 12, 1844.

63. *Michigan Argus,* July 31, September 18, October 2, 1844; *Michigan State Journal,* August 7, 1844.

tained that under the present circumstances, a vote for Clay was the best way to combat slavery. The Whig Party, contended the *Journal*, was *"anti-*slavery in so far as a national party can legitimately take any action on the subject of slavery." The Liberty Party's objectives were commendable, but unattainable in the short term. A Whig victory guaranteed concrete action. In June, Corselius exclaimed: "Remember! We have no constitutional power to interfere with slavery in Sovereign states; but we do have the constitutional power to protect against the increase of slavery." If Texas annexation was defeated—which could only occur through a Whig victory—then slavery would be dealt a "death blow"; otherwise, "the evil" would "continue growing upon us." And on election eve, the *Journal* reminded its readers that "the restriction of slavery to its constitutional limits, and leaving the way open for its not distant extinction, is to be voted on."[64]

This line of reasoning was powerful enough to cause some Liberty Party members to announce prior to the election their intention of crossing party lines to vote for Clay. Although one of these twenty-nine defectors continued to insist that the Whigs were a "pro-slavery party," the signers of these two manifestoes that were prominently displayed in the *Journal* maintained that their vote for Clay was a necessary obligation of their abolitionist beliefs. They conceded that the "immediate overthrow of Slavery in the District of Columbia, in the Territories of the United States, or in the Slave States of this Union, by the direct action or influence of the liberty party, is idle to expect." Nevertheless, they believed that Libertyites could prevent the annexation of Texas "and the sanction of their government from being extended to Texan Slavery. To do this however, we must make the sacrifice of voting for a Presidential candidate who is himself a Slaveholder."[65]

Despite the Whigs' loss of this election in Michigan—as they had every election since their victory in 1840—Whigs in Washtenaw and throughout the state recognized that they had kept the Democrats under 50 percent of the vote. A few Whig leaders hoped that they could win over additional Liberty votes if they presented themselves as a genuinely antislavery party. Additionally, the dynamics of the 1844 election—namely the reaching out to Liberty voters, the championing of Clay's opposition to the annexation of Texas, and the conse-

64. *Michigan State Journal,* September 25, June 26, September 18, October 30, 1844.
65. *Ibid.,* September 4, 18, 1844; *Signal of Liberty,* August 26, September 16, 1844. The *Signal* responded to these manifestoes in its October 14, 1844, issue.

quent furor over the annexation during the winter and spring of 1845—may have caused some Whigs to detest slavery further. Indeed, although the *Argus* favored the annexation of Texas, it qualified its support by adding that if the South claimed "annexation as a measure which shall be the means of perpetuating the institution of slavery, we say let it be defeated at once." Following the election, the *Journal* not only continued to proclaim that the Whig Party was a pragmatic alternative to the Liberty Party, but also adopted some key elements of the Liberty platform as its own. Most notable were the *Journal*'s objections to slavery not merely as a blight on American ideals and an obstacle to economic progress, but also as an immoral institution whose greatest victims were the slaves themselves. Referring to the acquisition of Texas, the *Journal* blasted the "unscrupulous and shameless manner in which the annexation of this new market of human beings, is urged by Southern locofocos." Northern Democrats were complicit in this crime as well. Their support of Texas annexation served only to "strengthen and perpetuate our slave system . . . by opening a new and wide market where human beings, innocent men women and children, torn from all earthly ties, are sold like cattle!"[66]

Corselius also pointed to the inherent conflict between the Declaration of Independence and the "principle of despotism which regards MAN as PROPERTY," and he ridiculed the contention of the Charleston *Mercury* that slaveholders would never voluntarily surrender chattels because of their great financial value. Regardless of the slaves' worth "to their *masters*—they are worth infinitely more to *themselves!*" The *Journal* also reprinted articles under the headline "Horrors of Slavery!"; described the freed slaves of the British West Indies as the "most orderly, moral, industrious, benevolent, and kindly disposed people under the sun"; and condemned southern laws that made it "a penal offense to teach dark-skinned children to read."[67] Such comments were, of course, quite a change for the newspaper, which had previously attempted to paint the Democrats as the party of abolition, and for Corselius, who a decade earlier was much cooler toward antislavery objectives. Now he charged the Liberty Party with the responsibility for the "annexation of Texas, and the extension of slavery," labeled it as the "mere tool and cat's paw . . . of the fanatical and mischievous slavocracy," and proclaimed that the "Whig party is the only

66. *Michigan Argus*, January 1, 1845; *Michigan State Journal*, February 5, April 16, 1845.
67. *Michigan State Journal*, March 12, June 11, July 16, 1845, April 1, 1846.

true anti-slavery party. The liberty party appears to have lost sight of its ostensible end and become a mere faction."[68]

Not surprisingly, the *Signal of Liberty* noticed this shift in the *Journal*'s position. Foster labeled as absurd the *Journal*'s assertion that the Whigs were the true antislavery party: "No other paper has the news! Will the Journal name a single anti-slavery act which 'the whole Whig party' has ever performed, or a single anti-slavery principle which it has expressed through its conventions? If the party has not taken the first step, why talk of its becoming more anti-slavery?" Privately, though, Foster was more complimentary of the rival Whig sheet: "The Journal of our place is a thorough reform paper, Whig in little else but name." He was convinced that the Seward wing of the Whig Party was "calculating to take our antislavery grounds and *thus* swallow us up," and he was certain that Whigs in Jackson, Pontiac, and Ann Arbor desired to "bring over the Whig party in Michigan to anti-slavery ground." The present, he confided to James Birney, was "a most auspicious time to lay broad and deep the foundations of a great national party" whose "creed will be neither Whig or Democrat, but will be such a one that the Whigs cannot go it *without losing their own identity*." The results of the 1845 state elections further persuaded Foster that a crucial moment in party politics was at hand. Whereas he had earlier believed that northern Whigs would separate from "their Southern brethren" only with great reluctance, the heavy losses that Whigs had sustained in recent southern elections made it clear that "the slaveholders themselves are deserting the Northern Whigs." Without the encumbrance of their southern wing, the northern Whigs would become a strong advocate of antislavery, which then left a crucial question to be answered: "Shall we go to the Whigs, or shall they come to us?" Naturally, Foster wanted the Liberty Party to set the terms for any future "union of all true antislavery men at the North," and he urged Birney to join him in calling for an expanded Liberty platform that went beyond the "one idea" of emancipation.[69]

68. *Ibid.*, April 2, 30, May 14, 1845 (see also November 20, 1844, April 23, May 21, 1845). None of Ann Arbor's subsequent Whig—or Republican—sheets approached the antislavery tone that Corselius provided the *Journal,* particularly after the 1844 election. The sincerity of Corselius' views is evident in his defection from the Whigs to the Free Soilers in 1848. *True Democrat,* September 21, 1848.

69. *Signal of Liberty* quoted in *Michigan State Journal,* May 14, 1845; Theodore Foster to James G. Birney, September 29, October 16, 1845, in Dumond, ed., *Birney Letters,* II, 972–73, 979–80, re-

Foster requested Birney to submit his views on the expansion of the Liberty platform to the February 1846 MSASS meeting in Marshall. In a letter to the president of that body, Birney proposed that the party endorse not only emancipation and "legal and constitutional equality for all men," but also free trade, the gradual elimination of the army and navy, the reduction of travel perquisites to members of Congress, and the diminution of presidential power, patronage, and salary. Although Birney could not attend the meeting of the state body, Foster argued fervently that unless the party broadened its agenda, stagnation, already commenced, would continue: "The only inducement for recruits, was to show them some chance of success—otherwise the party would be dissolved and some other one would come up to accomplish the object."[70]

Others present at the meeting, however, were not easily persuaded by Birney, Foster, and Guy Beckley. Their objections did not stem from a disapproval of the issues favored by Birney and Foster but from a reluctance to surrender their allegiance to the "one idea" of emancipation. Foster and Beckley reported to Birney that the views in Birney's letter "were *new* to most of them," as they were "thoroughly wedded to the '*one idea*,' and were determined to know nothing else." Even the "most sensible" devotees "were still dreaming that they could gather one half the nation under their one idea *alone*. Hence they felt unpleasantly at having this delusion dispelled." Despite the cold reception to Birney's proposals, after the convention a number of delegates who originally opposed the expansion of the platform reconsidered Birney's letter, changed their

---

spectively. Although Foster proposed the expansion of the Liberty platform in a letter to Birney earlier in 1845, as early as 1843 he had called upon the National Liberty Convention to "define the position" of the party regarding a national bank, a protective tariff, the distribution of public lands, and the "other great interests" of the day. Interestingly, in 1842 Foster had opposed having the national convention address these issues. See Foster to Birney, July 7, 1845, in Dumond, ed., *Birney Letters*, II, 950–53, and *Signal of Liberty*, April 24, 1843, May 16, 1842. Despite Foster's fears that the "Seward Whigs" were aiming to destroy the Liberty Party, a decade later he expressed admiration for William H. Seward as one who had worked with a major political party yet successfully maintained his antislavery principles. Theodore Foster, "The Liberty Party," 72, in Theodore Foster Papers, Bentley Library.

70. Foster to Birney, December 7, 1845, Birney to President of the Michigan State Anti-Slavery Society, January 1, 1846, in Dumond, ed., *Birney Letters*, II, 982–84, 990–96, respectively; Jackson *State Gazette*, February 16, 1846, clipping in Treadwell Papers. Foster's agenda was similar to Birney's. Although he did not propose that the party adopt free trade, Foster also called for the election of national and state officers presently subject to appointment, judicial reform, complete liability for corporate stockholders, and a single district system of electing legislators. *Ibid.*, 983.

minds, and promised to advance this position at the Northwestern Liberty Convention, scheduled for Chicago in July. Although abolitionists in Ann Arbor and Salem approved the expansion of the platform, Birney's proposal was ignored or repudiated by Liberty Party presses outside Michigan. Three months prior to the Chicago convention, Foster was already pessimistic about the prospects of the party's seeing things his way: "The truth is, that most of our leaders and political speakers have been and are *ministers*—not statesmen or politicians. Hence their blindness to anything but the one idea. I have my doubts whether they will not destroy the party by their narrow-mindedness."[71]

Following the convention, where his proposals were defeated, Foster was resigned to political failure. As he wrote to Birney: "The Liberty party, as I think you must see, by this time, are determined to be no party at all. They are intent upon political suicide." Having surrendered any hope of a new political party led by Libertyites, he was convinced that eventually most political abolitionists who favored a broader platform would end up in the Whig Party "because they see that the Liberty party will not take the only stand on which it can live and go ahead." Likewise, Foster expected that the "one idea portion" of the party would also join the Whigs, since "they are fast becoming tired of a separate organization, which is heavily laborious, and which yet scarcely progresses at all." But even though Foster favored an antislavery union with an agenda set by the Liberty Party, he was opposed to making deals with the Whigs. In response to a proposal by the Cleveland *American* that the Liberty Party enter into a coalition with antislavery Whigs, Foster wrote that the Liberty Party would be destroyed if it made "compromises with parties that are now decidedly proslavery. When they manifest BY THEIR WORKS that they have become truly ANTI-slavery, it will be time enough to propose a formal union."[72]

After the failure of Foster, Beckley, and Birney's effort to create a national antislavery party subservient to Liberty principles, Beckley announced in March 1847 that he would in the future vote for any candidate who agreed with his agenda: equal rights for all citizens, passage of laws that prohibited granting assistance to the arrest of fugitive slaves, the repeal of all federal laws sanc-

71. *Signal of Liberty*, February 23, March 9, 30, April 6, May 23, 1846; Charles H. Stewart to Birney, February 19, 1846, Foster and Beckley to Birney, February 9, 1846, Foster to Birney, February 13, March 30, May 5, 11, 1846, in Dumond, ed., *Birney Letters*, II, 999–1000, 1002–1006, 1007–1009, 1014–17, respectively.

72. Foster to Birney, August 1, 1846, in Dumond, ed., *Birney Letters*, II, 1024–26; *Signal of Liberty*, July 4, August 8, 1846; Sewell, *Ballots for Freedom*, 113–17.

tioning slavery in the territories and the District of Columbia, the repeal of the
fugitive slave law of 1793, no more slaveholding states to be admitted into the
Union, and the appointment of no slaveholders to public office. Beckley believed that these points covered "the entire ground of antislavery action" and
that any candidate who honestly subscribed to them "would, for all practical
purposes, be a Liberty man." Of course, if no candidate from the major parties
merited his support, Beckley would continue to vote Liberty. He hoped, however, that since Libertyites "hold the balance of power in this State," they
would use it to "great advantage for the cause of freedom." Beckley soon found
that he had company in this view. Although Foster initially rejected coalitions
with other parties, several other correspondents—including Foster's brother,
Samuel W. Foster—embraced Beckley's plan, and by August 1847, Foster himself was in agreement. In the fall, despite a Washtenaw County Liberty convention's decision that none of the Whig or Democratic candidates for office
were worthy of their support, the delegates declared that they were "ready to
take up the gauntlet which the slaveholders have cast at the North—and would
be glad to join hands with every honest freeman in the County, in a grand assault on the Slave Power."[73]

Foster's glum appraisal of the Liberty Party's prospects are evident in the
subsequent issues of the *Signal of Liberty*, which he continued to edit for a year
and a half following the Chicago meeting. Lost was much of the paper's former
vitality; Foster inserted fewer of his own essays and relied more upon material
from other antislavery sheets. This shift was evident to James Birney by March
1847, when he wrote Foster that during recent months the *Signal* had "not been
so *decided* as I wished, as I expected—it would be." That summer, Foster asked
Michigan's abolitionist leaders to look for another editor, and at the conclusion
of the five-year tenure for which he had contracted with the MSASS, he formally resigned, citing the death of the paper's financial backer—Beckley—

---

73. *Signal of Liberty*, March 13, 20, April 3, 10, May 15, August 21, October 16, 1847. James Birney condemned Beckley's announcement, as he trusted the politicians of neither party to deliver
on their promises. Birney to Beckley, April 6, 1847, in Dumond, ed., *Birney Letters*, II, 1057–61.
The enthusiastic response of some Liberty Party members to Beckley's proposal may have also
been a consequence of abolitionists' sense of helplessness to prevent the Mexican War from being
waged; many antislaveryites were convinced that this war was a shameless effort to acquire more
territory for slavery. On opposition to the Mexican War in Michigan, see Jeffrey G. Charnley,
"'Swords into Plowshares,' A Hope Unfulfilled: Michigan Opposition to the Mexican War,
1846–1848," *Old Northwest*, VIII (Fall 1982), 199–222.

and "other causes." Although he had "devoted almost seven of the best years of my life" to the paper, he departed "without regret," as the question of slavery was now "being discussed in every political newspaper" in the country and would eventually "break up and scatter existing political organizations."[74]

and "other causes." Although he had "devoted almost seven of the best years of my life" to the paper, he departed "without regret," as the question of slavery was now "being discussed in every political newspaper" in the country and would eventually "break up and scatter existing political organizations."[74]

Two months after the *Signal of Liberty* ceased publication, the MSASS and the state Liberty Party began publishing the *Michigan Liberty Press* in Battle Creek, with Erastus Hussey as its editor. Despite the paper's designation as the "organ for the Liberty Party in this State," events soon made the party itself obsolete. Throughout the North—but in the northeast in particular—some Whigs and Democrats grew impatient with their parties' unwillingness to sustain the Wilmot Proviso. "Conscience" Whigs were furious at the prospect of Zachary Taylor, a Louisiana slaveholder, as the Whig nominee for president, while antiproviso Democrats in New York—known as "Barnburners"—mutinied after losing to the more conservative "Hunker" faction at a state party convention in 1847. After Democrats voted to recognize both Hunker and Barnburner delegations at their May 1848 national convention in Baltimore, thus splitting the state's convention votes, neither delegation participated in the nomination proceedings. Following the nomination of Senator Lewis Cass of Michigan, however, the Barnburners walked out of the convention and called for a state convention to be held in June. There they nominated Martin Van Buren for the presidency. At an August gathering in Buffalo, New York, that had been billed as a meeting of "all Friends of Freedom, Free Territory, and Free Labor," Van Buren was nominated to head the emergent Free Soil Party.[75]

Some Liberty Party members resisted the Free Soil movement, believing that their abolitionist principles would be compromised by an alliance with former Whigs and Democrats who wanted to keep slavery out of the territories, but cared little about the plight of the slaves themselves, or who failed to

74. Birney to Foster, March 27, 1847, in Dumond, ed., *Birney Letters*, II, 1041; Nathan M. Thomas to W. P. F. Denison July 20, 1847, Thomas to Chester Gurney, August 15, 1847, both in Thomas Papers; *Signal of Liberty*, February 5, 1848.

75. *Michigan Liberty Press*, April 13, 1848; Sewell, *Ballots for Freedom*, 138–64; Joseph G. Rayback, *Free Soil: The Election of 1848* (Lexington, Ky., 1970), 61–98, 186–91, 201–30; Frederick J. Blue, *The Free Soilers: Third Party Politics, 1848–1854* (Urbana, Ill., 1973), 29–80; John Mayfield, *Rehearsal for Republicanism: Free Soil and the Politics of Antislavery* (Port Washington, N.Y.), 101–19.

recognize sufficiently the moral sinfulness of the peculiar institution. Further, despite Van Buren's opposition to the expansion of slavery into the territories, his past positions on other slavery-related issues were abhorrent to abolitionists. Most Libertyites were won over, though, by the platform approved at the Buffalo convention, which gave concessions to the abolitionists by declaring that it should be the policy of the federal government to "limit, localize, and discourage, Slavery," to "RELIEVE ITSELF FROM ALL RESPONSIBILITY FOR THE EXISTENCE OR CONTINUANCE OF SLAVERY" wherever Congress possessed authority to legislate on that matter, and to use federal power to prevent "the extension of Slavery into territory now free."[76]

The emergence of the Free Soil Party in Michigan met with less opposition from members of the Liberty Party than elsewhere, possibly because abolitionists in the Wolverine State had been discussing broadening the platform for over two years. Additionally, the positive responses by other Michigan abolitionists to Guy Beckley's declaration of cooperation with antislavery politicians probably paved the way toward the abolitionists' generally positive reception of the Free Soil movement—even though the Free Soil platform fell short of Beckley's manifesto.[77] Prior to the convention, the *Michigan Liberty Press* had endorsed Senator John P. Hale of New Hampshire, who had been nominated by the Liberty Party for the presidency in October 1847. Hale was now a leading candidate for the Free Soil nomination, and the *Press* encouraged Liberty Party members to promote his candidacy by turning out in large numbers for a convention in Jackson, where delegates to the Buffalo Free Soil convention were to be selected. "It is necessary that the Liberty party, who have been the pioneers of reform, should be well represented," wrote Hussey, and he urged abolitionists to caucus actively but "never relinquish principle." Enthusiasm for the new movement ran high in Michigan. Although few actually at-

76. Volpe, *Forlorn Hope*, 125–46; Sewell, *Ballots for Freedom*, 152–54, 157–62, 170; Rayback, *Free Soil*, 225–26, 229 n. 17; Kirk H. Porter and Donald Bruce Johnson, comps., *National Party Platforms, 1840–1960* (Urbana, Ill., 1961), 13. Similar to most members of the Liberty Party, Free Soilers denied that Congress had power to legislate concerning slavery in the states; Porter and Johnson, comps., *National Party Platforms*, 13.

77. Although he recognized the distinctions between abolitionists, Barnburners, and Conscience Whigs, Scio resident Samuel W. Foster praised this emerging coalition of Free Soilers as evidence of the progress of antislavery principles over the past thirteen years. Previously, Foster had endorsed Beckley's cooperationist manifesto but had urged his fellow Liberty Party members to keep their organization intact. *Michigan Liberty Press*, June 2, 1848; *Signal of Liberty*, April 10, 1847.

tended the Jackson convention, at least 132 Free Soilers from Michigan traveled to the national convention in Buffalo.[78] Despite his disappointment that Hale did not receive the nomination, Hussey was pleased with the results of the Buffalo convention and announced "to the Liberty Men of Michigan" that the Free Soil platform was "essentially the same as has ever been advocated by the Liberty Party. . . . In the adoption of this we lose nothing—we still hold to our principles." A state convention of the Michigan Liberty Party in Jackson went even further than mere praise. Six days following the adjourned Buffalo gathering, Michigan's Libertyites hailed "the day as having now arrived, at which event we have all repeatedly declared for the last eight years, that we should greatly rejoice when the people would take up our principles with a full determination to carry them out to a speedy and glorious triumph." The Liberty Party then voted to disband and embrace the Free Soil banner, believing that "by so doing our principles will be more speedily and certainly advanced."[79]

The Free Soil movement in Washtenaw County gained impetus when one of Ann Arbor's two Democratic newspapers, the Barnburner-inclined *True Democrat,* endorsed Van Buren in mid-July 1848 and then, following the Buffalo convention, embraced the new party. Although many Free Soilers were former members of the Liberty and Whig Parties, the fact that editor Orrin Arnold was a onetime Democrat may have been why this paper was especially caustic toward Lewis Cass and his party. One *True Democrat* writer blasted the *Michigan Argus* and the Detroit *Free Press*—both of which allegedly "excommunicated all democrats, who dared openly or secretly" to favor the Wilmot Proviso—and rebuked the disciples of Cass, who he claimed were cowering before southern interests. Following the November election, Arnold concluded that "there is one circumstance at which every friend of Freedom should rejoice—LEWIS CASS, the most slavish of Northern men, the most unmitigated of Northern sycophants of the slave power, the eyesore of Freemen . . . has met the retribution he has so richly deserved."[80] Of course, the *True Democrat* also vented its spleen toward the Whigs, especially in response to local Whig

78. *Michigan Liberty Press,* August 25, 1848. Twenty-two of these delegates were from Washtenaw County. The minutes contended, though, that this list was compiled before all of the delegates had arrived and was incomplete.

79. *Ibid.,* August 25, 18, 1848.

80. *Washtenaw Whig,* July 19, 1848; *True Democrat,* August 17, November 16, 1848 (see also September 21, 28, October 5, 12, 1848).

claims that the election of Zachary Taylor represented the best hope for Free Soil principles. Retorting to one such proclamation in the Detroit *Advertiser,* the *True Democrat* labeled Taylor as a "dealer in human flesh and blood" and asked the *Advertiser* why "all the genuine Anti-Slavery portion of your party" refused to support the nominee. Later, Arnold reminded his readers of the general's enthusiastic following in the South, and observed that Taylor's constituency there was as certain that he was opposed to the Wilmot Proviso as his northern adherents were convinced that he favored it.[81]

But in other races in Michigan, Free Soilers and Whigs occasionally found common ground and formed coalition tickets. Although they failed to agree upon a common congressional candidate, Washtenaw's Whigs and Free Soilers united behind two candidates for the state senate, who were easily elected to office. In the county's other electoral contests, the results were mixed, with both Whigs and Democrats electing some of their candidates.[82] Building such coalitions was a wise move for Michigan's Whigs, since Free Soilers drew from that party more than they did from the Democrats. In most northern states, however, the opposite was true. Many Democrats—especially in New York— flocked to the Free Soil ticket headed by Van Buren, a former Democratic president. Initially, Michigan's Whigs expected that their party would benefit from Democratic defections. But after "multitudes" of their party rallied to the Free Soil banner, Whigs returned to their argument against Liberty voters in previous elections: that a vote for the Free Soil Party only ensured the defeat of their entire party platform. Undoubtedly the candidacy of favorite son Cass hindered Democratic defections in the Wolverine State.[83]

81. *Washtenaw Whig,* November 1, 1848; *True Democrat,* September 21, 28, 1848, October 5, 12, 1848.

82. *Michigan Argus,* September 27, 1848; *True Democrat,* October 12, November 23, 1848; *Washtenaw Whig,* September 13, November 1, 1848. In Michigan's Second Congressional District the Free Soil nominee, D. C. Lawrence, resigned after the Whig candidate, William Sprague, endorsed Free Soil principles; Sprague won in November. Kinsley S. Bingham, the Democratic nominee in the Third Congressional District, also embraced the Free Soil platform and, despite opposition from the *True Democrat,* was elected. Theodore Clarke Smith, *The Liberty and Free Soil Parties in the Northwest* (New York, 1897), 158–59; Ronald E. Seavoy, "The Organization of the Republican Party in Michigan, 1846–1854," *Old Northwest,* VI (Winter 1980–81), 349; *True Democrat,* October 5, 12, 1848; William McDaid, "Kinsley S. Bingham and the Republican Ideology of Antislavery, 1847–1855," *Michigan Historical Review,* XVI (Fall 1990), 43–73.

83. Formisano, *Birth of Mass Political Parties,* 30; Rayback, *Free Soil,* 284, 286, 300. In the 1848 presidential election in Michigan, the Whigs retained a lower percentage of their 1844 vote (84.3 percent) than in any other state except New Hampshire, while the Democratic vote retention

Despite the fact that former Liberty Party members made up the largest portion of the Free Soil Party in Michigan, and notwithstanding the references to Taylor as a "dealer in human flesh and blood," the Free Soil Party in Michigan did not exhibit the same concern for slaves as had the Liberty Party. Gone too were the calls for black male suffrage. Although one of the resolutions passed by the state Free Soil convention in Ann Arbor paraphrased the proclamation of the Apostle Paul that "God . . . 'has made of one flesh all the nations of mankind,'" the delegates also made clear that their central preoccupation was "mastery over the cruel and unjust pretensions of the Slave Power." This latter force had resulted in "northern bondage to southern interests." Accordingly, Free Soilers proclaimed their insistence upon *"no more slave states, and no slave territories."* Regarding the existence of slavery in the states, Free Soilers differed from Libertyites—who, particularly during the early years, often asserted that northerners who supported the main political parties were complicit in the evils of slaveholding. Michigan's Free Soilers, while asserting that they were not "indifferent to the suffering of any portion of the human family," also maintained that it was not their purpose to "reproach the understanding or humanity of the north by an argument upon the right or wrong of slavery," since they deemed themselves "not responsible for the existence of slavery in the Southern States." Nor did the Ann Arbor meeting pass any resolutions that called for an end to the domestic slave trade, abolition in the District of Columbia, or jury trials for accused fugitive slaves. The reaction of abolitionists to these shifts in emphasis is difficult to determine, but there is no evidence that they opposed the changes. On the contrary, *Michigan Liberty Press* editor Erastus Hussey was on the five-member committee that drafted resolutions at the meeting, and Nathan Power, a leader in the Liberty Party from Oakland County, viewed recruits to third-party politics as recruits to abolitionism: "I hope that many of those who have recently united with the Free Soil Party who have not previously acted with [the MSASS] will be . . . prepared to participate in its proceedings."[84]

(94.4 percent) was among the highest in both the North and South. In Washtenaw County, retention more closely reflected the pattern found elsewhere in the North, as Whigs there retained 90.8 percent of their 1844 vote; the figure for Democrats was 85.8 percent. One scholar has estimated that of the 1848 Free Soil vote in Michigan, 33 percent came from former Whigs, 28 percent from former Democrats, and 39 percent from former Libertyites; Rayback, *Free Soil*, 286, 300. See also Mayfield, *Rehearsal for Republicanism*, 195–97.

84. *True Democrat*, September 28, 1848; *Signal of Liberty*, November 14, 1842; Nathan M. Thomas to the *Michigan Liberty Press*, January 3, 1849, in Thomas Papers.

In Washtenaw County and throughout Michigan, the Free Soilers brought many new voters into the third-party ranks. The 16 percent of the state's voters who cast ballots for Van Buren in 1848 more than doubled the percentage that voted for Birney in his 1845 gubernatorial campaign. Free Soil fared even better in Washtenaw County. It was the victorious party in Salem Township, where it captured over 40 percent of the vote. The ticket placed second in Pittsfield, while Ann Arbor, Augusta, and Lodi delivered at least a fourth of their votes to Van Buren (Table 18).

At first glance, the 1849 township elections in Ann Arbor showed even greater Free Soil strength. These elections, however, both marked the pinnacle of local antislavery politics and signaled its unraveling. For the first time, an antislavery party in Ann Arbor had succeeded in electing its candidates to office, as voters chose Sumner Hicks to be a justice of the peace and Samuel R. Doty to be the commissioner of highways. Nevertheless these victories did not signify the growing support of antislavery principles so much as they represented the consequence of unprecedented ticket splitting and the willingness of Free Soilers to form coalitions as they had done the previous November. As the *Washtenaw Whig* reported with some surprise, the four tickets run in the election were "split up in every conceivable manner." Free Soilers united behind the Whig nominee for supervisor, and thus provided Israel Mowry with an overwhelming victory. Hicks's election was secured by the support of almost all the township's Democrats. Doty secured his office by merely one vote, and obviously won by broadening his appeal to Whigs and Democrats. In the eleven other contested races, though, Free Soilers nominated their own candidates; the number of votes received by the party's candidates ranged from 192 to 277, and their proportion of the vote varied between 25.0 percent and 36.4 percent, with a composite of 29.1 percent. Free Soilers seemed to benefit from ticket-splitting, even though such returns indicated that for some Free Soil voters, township elections were becoming increasingly centered upon the virtues of individual candidates, rather than upon the principles of antislavery. This trend significantly weakened the party's moral energy.[85]

Elsewhere, many Free Soilers did not follow through on their electoral successes from the previous November. Free Soilers posted tickets in Manchester and Scio for township elections but they failed to organize in Pittsfield, Sylvan, Webster, and Ypsilanti, where committed Libertyites had consistently fielded

85. *Washtenaw Whig,* April 4, 1849; Ann Arbor Township minutes, April 2, 1849.

tickets in previous years. In fact, third-party activity in most township elections virtually ceased until 1853 (Tables 31 and 32).[86]

It was at this time, too, that the MSASS disappeared. In early January 1849, Nathan Thomas was concerned that no notice had been given in the *Michigan Liberty Press* regarding the abolitionists' yearly convention. He asked Erastus Hussey "whether we shall have a gathering of all the old friends of freedom this winter in accordance with our annual custom or abandon the anniversary meeting as being no longer required to promote the interests of the Great Cause for which it was instituted." Hussey replied that Seymour Treadwell had asked him the same question, to which he pleaded ignorance, as he did not have the minutes of the previous anniversary meeting to consult. Hussey proposed that they gather on the second Thursday in February, but if they met on such short notice, no record has survived of this or any subsequent MSASS meeting.[87]

Notwithstanding their failure to field tickets in many of the county's township elections, Free Soilers in Michigan entertained the hope that at least some of the candidates would win statewide office by forming a coalition with either the Democrats or the Whigs. Some Free Soilers hoped that their gubernatorial nomination in July of Flavius J. Littlejohn—a former Democrat—would attract Democrats to their party or assist in forming a coalition with members of that party favoring the Wilmot Proviso. There was considerable sympathy in the Democratic Party for free-soil principles. In fact, one contender for the Democratic nomination, Robert McClelland, hinted that he would be willing to forge a coalition with Free Soilers. Lewis Cass, though, opposed such a union, and he and his faction not only labored to prevent it from occurring, but also succeeded in marking the party's platform with an anti–Wilmot Proviso stamp. Interest in forming a coalition with the Free Soilers was more widespread among the Whigs, who had not held the governorship in eight years. Following the resignation of the Whig nominee for governor, John Owen, Whigs reconvened and nominated Littlejohn as their standard bearer as well.

86. The contemporary claim that Pittsfield went Free Soil in the elections of 1849 and 1850 is not accurate. Although individual Free Soilers were victorious, both elections were two-party contests in which the third party failed to nominate its own ticket. *Washtenaw Whig*, April 4, 1849; *Michigan Argus*, April 3, 1850; Pittsfield Township Records, April 2, 1849, April 1, 1850, in Pittsfield Township Office. See also Formisano, *Birth of Mass Political Parties*, 216.

87. Nathan M. Thomas to *Michigan Liberty Press*, January 3, 1849, Erastus Hussey to Nathan M. Thomas, January 10, 1849, both in Thomas Papers.

Littlejohn's Democratic past offended many Whigs, however, and because many of them either failed to vote, or cast ballots for the Democratic nominee, John Barry, the Democrats again carried the day.[88] The *Washtenaw Whig* trumpeted the free-soil elements of this ticket and with greater ardor than the local Whig press had displayed in several years, beseeched its readers to get out the vote. The county's Whig convention not only endorsed free-soil principles, but called slavery in the District of Columbia a "national reproach" and urged its abolition there. With local Whigs embracing the Free Soil platform and state Whigs accepting the Free Soil candidate for governor, the Free Soilers or "Free Democracy" of Washtenaw County returned these favors by endorsing the Whig nominees for the state legislature. And although this coalition procured a lower percentage of the vote than the combined Whig and Free Soil percentages of 1848, it still proved victorious in Washtenaw County (Table 19).[89]

In the wake of the disappointing statewide outcome in this election, the Free Soil Party in Michigan went into further decline, partially as a result of failing to nominate its own members and instead endorsing candidates of free-soil persuasion nominated by other parties. Free Soilers in Ann Arbor pursued the coalition strategy in the April township races and openly united with the Democrats for the posts of supervisor and justice of the peace. For the remaining eleven contested offices, Free Soilers offered only four of their own nominations, and otherwise endorsed those Whig and Democratic nominees who met their approval. The four Free Soil nominees did not fare as well as had their party's nominees from the previous year; their votes ranged from 98 to 183 and their proportion from 13.6 percent to 24.5 percent, with a composite of 18.3 percent. While Ann Arbor Free Soilers would certainly boast that one of their own, Sumner Hicks, now occupied the township's top post, some may have questioned whether Hicks was more of a Free Soiler or a Democrat. Though Hicks remained with the antislavery party through 1853, by 1856, after the Free Soil party had been incorporated into the Republican party, Hicks, a former Libertyite, chose to stay with the Democrats.[90]

88. Smith, *Liberty and Free Soil Parties,* 198–204; Seavoy, "Republican Party in Michigan," 350–58; *Washtenaw Whig,* July 4, 18, September 26, 1849; Nathan M. Thomas to R. McBratney, November 9, 1849, in Thomas Papers.

89. *Washtenaw Whig,* September 26, October 10, 31, 1849; *Michigan Argus,* November 21, 1849.

90. Ann Arbor Township Minutes, April 7, 1845, April 6, 1846, April 1, 1850, April 4, 1853; *Washtenaw Whig,* April 3, 1850; *Michigan Argus,* April 11, 1856.

In May of 1850, county Free Soilers again refrained from nominating their own candidates for a special election to select delegates to a state constitutional convention. Despite a report that local Whigs were "straining every nerve" to have the county Free Soilers unite with them, the third party instead endorsed four Whigs and four Democrats already nominated by their respective parties. Consequently, the four Whigs and four Democrats who had failed to obtain Free Soil endorsement formed their own ticket. The returns of the election were not favorable to the Free Soil–endorsed candidates, as only two of the eight—both Democrats—were selected as delegates. Some townships—most notably Bridgewater, Dexter, Lima, Lyndon, Manchester, and Scio—revealed a strong animosity toward the Free Soil–backed candidates; in others—Ann Arbor, Augusta, Salem, Pittsfield, and Webster—the Free Soil–backed candidates did better than those supported by either party or by the anti–Free Soil coalition. The results from these eleven townships suggest that notwithstanding the virtual moribundity of the Free Soil Party, antislavery politics remained—as the Congress debated the various proposals that were later incorporated into the Compromise of 1850—a trenchant issue among many voters. On the other hand, in the towns of Freedom, Lodi, Northfield, Sharon, Superior, Sylvan, and York, the votes were generally cast along Whig/Democrat lines, while no pattern was discernible for Saline and Ypsilanti (Table 20).[91]

Michigan Free Soilers held two conventions in 1850. In May a small rally in Marshall voiced its opposition to the Compromise of 1850, and in September the party nominated candidates for the fall election. The party's weakness was exhibited by its failure to nominate candidates for state supreme court justice and attorney general; one leader complained that he was unable to find suitable candidates for any statewide office. In Washtenaw County, Free Soilers did worse at the polls than any antislavery party since 1840. Their statewide candidates obtained only 5 percent of the vote, and their candidates for the legislature and county office 2 percent or less (Table 21). But Free Soilers could take some pleasure in knowing that their votes helped to defeat two Democratic nominees for Congress who were closely aligned with Lewis Cass. Washtenaw Free Soilers were particularly incensed by the passage of the Fugitive Slave Law and labeled it "an outrage upon the rights of citizens, repugnant to every principle of justice, dishonorable to the nation." Accordingly, they focused

91. *Michigan Argus,* April 17, May 8, 22, 1850; *Washtenaw Whig,* March 27, April 3, May 1, 8, 1850.

their wrath upon Alexander W. Buel, who represented Washtenaw in Congress and had voted for this law. At their convention in October, Free Soilers acknowledged that while they were "opposed to uniting with any other political party," they felt it their obligation to "defeat this tool of tyranny and oppression," and they tacitly gave their approval to Buel's Whig opponent, Ebenezer J. Penniman, without mentioning the latter by name. Penniman, who opposed the Fugitive Slave Law and the extension of slavery into the federal territories, soundly defeated Buel. In Washtenaw County, Buel received only 41.4 percent of the vote, and the fact that he ran almost 250 votes behind the rest of his party's ticket there suggests that many Democrats opposed his positions on slavery-related issues.[92]

Voters also considered the question of black male suffrage at this election. The issue had been debated by delegates to the 1835 constitutional convention but was easily defeated. The Liberty Party endorsed black suffrage in subsequent years, and the idea had other proponents. Foremost among them, of course, was Michigan's small African American community, whose organizations—such as the Colored Vigilant Committee of the City of Detroit—petitioned the legislature for the right to vote. In December 1841, "a full meeting of the colored people of Washtenaw County" went further, arguing that "as our fathers fought side by side with the white man for natural liberty, we are entitled to all the benefits of the revolutionary contest." Ann Arbor's *Michigan State Journal* first endorsed black suffrage in December 1842—according to the *Signal of Liberty*, it was the first nonabolitionist paper in Michigan to do so— and during the editorial tenure of George Corselius, essays advocating this measure appeared in the paper frequently. The Ypsilanti *Sentinel,* the county's other Whig paper, also supported this reform, although editor Charles Woodruff wanted to proceed more cautiously than Corselius.[93] Some Washtenaw residents submitted petitions to the Michigan legislature calling for an end to

---

92. Smith, *Liberty and Free Soil Parties,* 205–208; Seavoy, "Republican Party in Michigan," 358–60; *Washtenaw Whig,* October 16, 1850; *Michigan Argus,* November 13, 1850. Democrats throughout Buel's district reportedly campaigned against him because of his support for the Fugitive Slave Law, while in Jonesville, Hillsdale County, Buel was burned in effigy following a campaign stop there. Roger L. Rosentreter, "Michigan and the Compromise of 1850," *Old Northwest,* VI (Summer 1980), 163–64, 171–72.

93. *Signal of Liberty,* January 19, December 12, 1842, January 23, October 9, 1843, November 28, 1846; *Michigan State Journal,* May 15, 1845, March 18, April 15, May 6, 1846; Ypsilanti *Sentinel,* March 18, September 2, 1846.

racial exclusion with respect to voting, and several of the county's legislators—Whig James M. Edmunds and Democrats Norton R. Ramsdell and Samuel Denton—either issued legislative reports or introduced bills favoring black male suffrage.[94]

Despite the optimism of the Ypsilanti *Sentinel* in 1846—that if the question were submitted to the electorate, "it would be nearly unanimously decided in the affirmative"—delegates to the 1850 Michigan constitutional convention were overwhelmingly hostile to recognizing this right for black males. Nevertheless, they agreed to submit the question to the electorate in a referendum separate from ratification of the new constitution. The constitution was approved by a large majority, but only 28.5 percent of the state's voters endorsed the suffrage referendum. That 24 percent fewer people cast ballots on this separate amendment than voted for members of Congress suggests that many voters were either confused or apathetic regarding black male suffrage. Lower participation on this referendum was also the rule in Washtenaw County; in Ann Arbor, only 70.5 percent of the voters who cast ballots for Congress voted on the suffrage question; countywide, the figure was 72.0 percent. The reception to this measure was more positive in Washtenaw County, though, than it was statewide, as 42.2 percent of the county's voters approved it. In Ann Arbor black male suffrage was overwhelmingly victorious, 402 to 159 (71.2 percent). Although the long-time advocacy of the change by abolitionists, along with its endorsement by political elites and major party newspapers, may account for some of its local success, the issue was ignored by Ann Arbor's newspaper editors in the weeks prior to the referendum. One oblique reference in the *Michigan Argus* suggests that the *Washtenaw Whig* favored black male suffrage prior to the constitutional convention, but the *Whig* said nothing about the proposal immediately before the November election. Following the election, however, the *Argus* reported that the success of the referendum in Ann Arbor occurred because of a bargain struck between Whigs and Free Soilers, "by which the whigs agreed to vote for the extension of the right of suffrage to colored persons, if the Abolitionists would vote for the whig nominee for Congress."[95]

94. *Michigan State Journal,* February 1, 1843, May 14, 1845, March 18, 1846; *Signal of Liberty,* November 6, 1843, September 29, 1845.

95. Ypsilanti *Sentinel,* March 18, 1846; Ronald P. Formisano, "The Edge of Caste: Colored Suffrage in Michigan, 1827–1861," *Michigan History,* LVI (Spring 1972), 19–41; *Michigan Argus,* May 1, 22, November 6, 13, 1850; *Washtenaw Whig,* October 23, 30, 1850. At 42.2 percent, Washtenaw County ranked sixth among the state's 35 counties in the support it gave to black male

Although the majority of Free Soilers, like their Liberty Party predecessors, appear to have favored suffrage for African American males, not all did. Sensitivity to this minority who opposed black male suffrage is reflected in the fact that the party never endorsed this issue at any of its conventions. Prior to the Michigan constitutional convention, moreover, the editor of the *Argus* reported that some Free Soilers had communicated to him that they were opposed to black male suffrage "without proper and just qualification, one that would protect against the abusers of the right," because they believed "that it would be an injury to the negro to give him such a privilege before he was prepared to exercise it properly." Although such comments about Free Soilers may have been motivated by the *Argus* editor's own fears of black suffrage, they were not without foundation. Flavius Littlejohn, the Free Soil nominee for governor in 1849, had, while a member of the legislature in 1843, issued a report against recognizing black male suffrage, arguing that it would lead to "marital amalgamation" and cause Michigan to "become the hiding place of numerous refugee slaves." There is no evidence to suggest that Littlejohn changed his views when he became a Free Soiler; indeed, he shortly returned to the Democratic Party, was elected to the legislature under that party's banner in 1854, and served as the Democratic nominee for Michigan's Third Congressional District in 1856.[96]

These coalitions with the Whigs in 1848, 1849, and 1850, along with the belief of many Americans that the Compromise of 1850 was the definitive solution to the controversy over slavery in the territories, resulted in an eviscerated Free Soil Party in 1851. Michigan lacked a Free Soil newspaper once the *Peninsular Freeman* expired in early 1851. The moribund state of the party was lampooned by the Jackson *American Citizen* in 1851 when it announced that the

suffrage. Minus the strong support in Ann Arbor, however, only 36.1 percent (972 of 2,696) of the county's voters endorsed this issue. Returns from the county's other townships are available only for Sylvan and Manchester, where the proposal received 40.9 percent (45 of 110) and 21.5 percent (38 of 177) of the votes, respectively. County Canvassers' Statements of Votes, December 19, 1850, in State Archives of Michigan; Sylvan Township Records, October 5, 1850, in Bentley Library; Manchester Township Minutes, November 1850, in Manchester Town Hall.

96. *Michigan Argus*, May 1, 1850; *Signal of Liberty*, January 30, 1843; Seavoy, "Republican Party in Michigan," 375 n. 36; *Michigan Argus*, September 12, 1856; Richard H. Sewell, "Slavery, Race, and the Free Soil Party, 1848–1854," in *Crusaders and Compromisers: Essays on the Relationship of the Antislavery Struggle to the Antebellum Party System*, ed. Alan M. Kraut (Westport, Conn., 1983), 101–24. For Littlejohn's hostility to antislavery in 1845, see Jessie Ethelyn Sexton, *Congregationalism, Slavery, and the Civil War* (Lansing, 1966), 10.

Free Soilers *"as a party,* are now beggarded in credit and honor—almost as entirely destitute of self-respect as they are of the respect of others." Their agenda was "now to be found only in old newspaper files; it is not spoken of by friend or foe as alive [*sic*] thing." Enthusiasm for abolition, according to the *Citizen,* had also waned: "We have no more lectures about the immediate abolition of slavery, and very little about the phraseology of the 'paramount idea.'" Ann Arbor's Free Soilers failed to organize for the 1851 and 1852 township races, and in the gubernatorial election of 1851, Michigan's Free Soilers did not nominate a candidate. Many third-party adherents may have voted for Democrat Robert McClelland, who occasionally mouthed Free Soil pieties. In other states, the party had either diminished or ceased to exist altogether. But despite the party's languishing condition, national Free Soil leaders assembled in Cleveland in September 1851 and made preparations to mount a presidential campaign the following year.[97]

In Michigan, preparations for the fall 1852 campaign commenced the preceding winter. In March, Francis Denison of Kalamazoo lamented: "We have so long neglected to convene that we hardly know the latitude that we are in." He believed , however, that Free Soilers could be invigorated at the state convention planned for June. Denison observed that during the preceding three years, Free Soilers throughout the North had elected twenty-three members to the United States House of Representatives, had sent four senators to the Capitol, and had held the balance of power in several states, which successes "should urge us to renewed organized effort." Following a national convention in Pittsburgh in August, the Michigan Free Soil Party—now renamed the Free Democrats—commenced publishing a paper in Detroit and reconvened in Ann Arbor in September, where they were addressed by Joshua Giddings, an Ohio congressman who had himself defected from the Whigs to the Free Soilers in 1848. At the Ann Arbor conference, delegates ratified the platform and nominations of the Pittsburgh gathering and sought to "take such measures as may be deemed best for the perfection of our state organization." Later that month in Kalamazoo, the Free Democrats nominated a full state ticket. Washtenaw's Free Democrats were far less willing to forge coalitions in this election than they had been previously: they endorsed former Libertyite Hor-

97. *Peninsular Freeman,* February 4, 1851; *American Citizen* quoted in *Michigan Argus,* April 30, 1851; Seavoy, "Republican Party in Michigan," 359–61; Smith, *Liberty and Free Soil Parties,* 206–207; Formisano, *Birth of Mass Political Parties,* 210–11; Sewell, *Ballots for Freedom,* 230–31, 239–42.

ace Carpenter, a Whig nominee for the legislature, but rejected a joint candidate for Congress, selecting instead longtime temperance devotee Samuel W. Dexter. Members of this party also exhibited considerably greater energy than they had in previous campaigns. By early September, Ann Arbor activists sent the names of ninety-five subscribers—"with pay"—to the *Michigan Free Democrat.* Free Democrat enthusiasm often surpassed the Whigs', as many members of the latter party throughout the country were dispirited by their candidate, Winfield Scott. This lethargy showed in Ann Arbor, where, according to the *Michigan Argus,* impromptu Free Democrat rallies were as large as Whig festivities that enjoyed advance notice.

Free Democrats expectedly lost the election, and although they performed considerably better than in 1850, their percentage of the vote remained significantly below the 1848 figures. Nevertheless, the party, now largely purged of its Barnburner elements, was actually more akin to the old Liberty Party. John P. Hale—the Libertyite nominee in 1848 prior to the formation of the Free Soil Party—was the Free Democrat standard bearer, and the party's platform denounced slavery more strongly than the 1848 Buffalo manifesto had done. Compared with the Liberty Party, the Free Democrats of 1852 achieved better electoral results, receiving 8.7 percent of the Michigan vote and 11.0 percent of the Washtenaw County vote. The enthusiasm of the resurrected party was manifested by the call for a state convention to meet in early January 1853. The following April at the Washtenaw County township and city elections, the Free Democrats fielded candidates in at least six of the county's polities; in Ann Arbor city and Lodi, the party obtained nearly a fifth of the vote (Tables 22 and 32). With many believing that the Whig Party as a national institution was disintegrating, some Free Democrats anticipated that their party would fill that void.[98]

Because of changes in Michigan's 1850 constitution, after 1851 statewide elections were no longer held in odd-numbered years. Events following the 1852 election forced vast changes upon the political scene in Michigan and the nation—changes that resulted in the demise of both the Whig and Free Democratic Parties. The emergence of Michigan's Republican Party has been

---

98. F. Denison to Ransom Dunn, March 8, 1852, in Ransom Dunn Papers, Bentley Library; Smith, *Liberty and Free Soil Parties,* 246; Erastus Hussey to Nathan Thomas, August 21, 1852, in Thomas Papers; *Washtenaw Whig,* August 25, November 24, 1852; *Michigan Free Democrat,* September 7, December 29, 1852; *Michigan Argus,* September 29, October 6, 1852; Smith, *Liberty and Free Soil Parties,* 254; Sewell, *Ballots for Freedom,* 244–46, 250–51.

detailed elsewhere and is beyond the scope of this study. It is not my intention to delineate the extent to which temperance, nativism, disillusionment with the existing parties, opposition to Stephen Douglas' bill that organized the Nebraska Territory and repealed the Missouri Compromise, hostility to the South, and other factors led to the creation of the Republican Party in 1854. Although the Free Democrats and Whigs had discussed joining forces eleven months prior to the November 1854 election, their eventual merger was sometimes tortuous. Fusion did not appear inevitable to Free Democrats following the announcement of Douglas' Nebraska bill in January 1854, as the third party convened in February and nominated a full ticket for the fall balloting. The Free Democratic platform was unobjectionable to most Whig leaders, and the convention delegates placed a few Whigs on the statewide ticket, but distrust kept the parties from coalescing. Some Free Democrats clung to the conviction that the Whigs would inevitably rally to their ticket. Whigs, on the other hand, refused to recognize the Free Democrat nominations, and argued that their own party members would accept a fusion movement only if the nominations were independent. Behind-the-scenes negotiations continued for several months, and by early June, Free Democrats were finally reconciled to an independent fusion movement "irrespective of existing political organizations." In Kalamazoo on June 21, at the Free Democrat convention originally called to protest the repeal of the Missouri Compromise, delegates issued a call for a fusion convention to meet in Jackson on July 6 and agreed "willingly [to] surrender our distinctive organization" and to withdraw their ticket nominated the previous February should the fusion platform prove satisfactory.[99]

In Washtenaw County, protest against the introduction of the Nebraska Act appeared first in Dexter village, where in early February citizens held a public meeting and circulated "remonstrances." The following month the "Friends of Freedom, without distinction of Party," assembled in Sharon to protest the actions of the Fillmore and Pierce administrations, and in particular to object to the introduction of slavery into territories in which it had been prohibited by the Missouri Compromise. Although the *Washtenaw Whig* asked Ann Arbor Whigs in mid-February to emulate the village of Dexter's example, nothing occurred until politicos considered nominations for the

---

99. Formisano, *Birth of Mass Political Parties*, 217–42; Seavoy, "Republican Party in Michigan," 362–66; William E. Gienapp, *The Origins of the Republican Party, 1852–1856* (New York, 1987), 103–106; Detroit *Daily Democrat*, June 1, 1854; *Washtenaw Whig*, June 28, 1854.

April city election. At a meeting of the Ann Arbor city Whigs, Donald McIntyre announced that some of the Democratic nominees for city office had "avowed their determination" to make the repeal of the Missouri Compromise a "test at the coming election," and "he for one was willing to accept the issue." McIntyre urged that all who were opposed to this Democratic effort "should act in unison," and he proposed that this assembly of Whigs adjourn in favor of a "meeting of citizens irrespective of former party associations, for the nomination of candidates for city officers." This convention shortly reconvened, passed a resolution calling upon all who were opposed to the repeal of the Missouri Compromise to unite their forces for the city election, and consequently nominated "the citizens' Anti-Nebraska Ticket for city officers."[100]

The *Michigan Argus* immediately recognized the significance of this gathering. In a short piece entitled "Fusion," its editor reported that both Whigs and Free Democrats were on this ticket, and proclaimed: "This is a virtual dissolution of the Whig Party, as far as this city is concerned, and a fusion of the Whigs and Free Soilers." Although the fusionists won ten of fifteen offices in the election, no one in Washtenaw County was yet calling the new coalition permanent. The Free Democrats maintained their hold on township government in Salem and ran competitively in Saline. And despite the convention of the "Friends of Freedom, without distinction of Party" in Sharon, township elections there were tripartisan as well. In fact, Stephen B. McCracken, the

100. *Washtenaw Whig*, February 15, 1854; Detroit *Daily Democrat*, March 30, 1854; *Washtenaw Whig*, March 29, 1854. Ronald P. Formisano inaccurately characterizes this electoral ticket by failing to mention its anti-Nebraska character and citing only the editorial remarks of Stephen B. McCracken—that these candidates were the "friends and supporters of our educational system in all its phases." Although McCracken served as secretary to both meetings, and notwithstanding his comment in the *Whig* that he "urged in private conversation the very course that was pursued," McCracken in his editorial endorsement said nothing that echoed Donald McIntyre's insistence that national issues were at stake in this election. McCracken's reluctance to say anything on Nebraska may have been the result of what he later admitted was his antipathy to the emerging Republican Party. Although he supported the new party throughout the 1854 campaign, he sold the *Washtenaw Whig* following the election and subsequently edited papers that supported the American Party candidacy of Millard Fillmore in 1856 and the Democratic candidacy of Stephen Douglas in 1860. Formisano, *Birth of Mass Political Parties*, 237; *Michigan Argus*, July 18, August 1, 1856, June 22, 1860. See also *Michigan Argus*, April 6, 1854, which reprints an editorial from the Whig Ypsilanti *Sentinel* rebuking Ann Arbor's Whigs for dissolving their old party and forming a new one in order to make the "Nebraska Bill" the "ground of action" and thus to "test the sense of the public on that question."

editor of the *Washtenaw Whig*, who later claimed that he was never won over to fusion, listed the victors of the county's municipal elections as either Whig, Democrat, or Free Democrat and mentioned nothing about any fusionist activities elsewhere in the county. In early June the *Whig* doubted whether a fusion ticket would be agreed upon for the fall campaign. Three weeks later, however, in the midst of the widespread enthusiasm for the coming July 6 fusion convention, McCracken disingenuously announced, "We claim to have been one of the first to urge a union of all lovers of freedom against the encroachments of the slave power, and against the high handed measures and corrupt tendencies of the present National and State administrations."[101]

Although the Republican triumph in November put an end to thirteen years of Democratic rule in Michigan and was one of the first victories of the incipient fusion movement that was spreading throughout the North during the early to mid-1850s, most contemporary observers concluded that the party platform in Michigan was "too steep" to bring success in other states. Despite a brief discussion of economic issues, the bulk of the document was preoccupied with slavery, condemning it as a "great moral, social, and political evil," and urging its abolition in the District of Columbia, the repeal of the Fugitive Slave Law and the Kansas-Nebraska Act, the prohibition of slavery in all territories, and a pledge to defend nonslaveholding settlers in the territories from the depredations of slaveholders. More strident in these pronouncements than some Free Democratic platforms, and hosting on its statewide ticket long-time abolitionists Seymour B. Treadwell for land office commissioner and Erastus Hussey for state senator from Battle Creek, the new Republican Party convinced some abolitionists that they had at last succeeded in converting Michigan to their principles. Such was the conclusion of former MSASS president Charles H. Stewart. Congratulating Treadwell shortly after his electoral victory, Stewart reminisced about the old days when he and Treadwell preached abolition in log cabins before crowds of a half dozen. Stewart viewed the Republican sweep as a victory of their "one idea."[102] Indeed, Michigan's first Re-

101. *Michigan Argus*, March 30, April 6, 1854; *Washtenaw Whig*, April 5, June 7, 28, 1854.

102. *Washtenaw Whig*, July 12, 1854; Charles H. Stewart to S. B. Treadwell, January 2, 1855, in Treadwell Papers. The Ypsilanti *Sentinel*, which remained skeptical about the fusion movement, complained before this election that Treadwell "is without the slightest change of his politics or principles, a candidate for whom the suffrage of Whigs is asked—nay demanded" (quoted in *Washtenaw Whig*, September 6, 1854). After the election, Governor Kinsley Bingham appointed Theodore Foster to be a member of the Board of Control for the House of Correction for Juvenile

publican legislature nullified the Fugitive Slave Law and passed resolutions urging Congress to abolish slavery in the District of Columbia and the territories. And although failing to pass any legislation granting suffrage to African American males, the Republican legislatures of the mid-to-late 1850s came much closer to accomplishing this objective than had their predecessors.[103]

Although the Republican Party stood squarely against the expansion of slavery into the territories and was solidly opposed to the "slave power's" influence in national councils, in Washtenaw County sentiment favoring abolition was now generally deemphasized in the political arena. Concern for the rights of African Americans, enslaved or free, was also virtually absent from the new party's resolutions and newspapers. Garrisonian abolitionist Aaron M. Powell complained in 1856 that "Free Soil, or *Republicanism*, has nearly swallowed up the Abolitionists of [Ypsilanti] and a great many other places," and charged that the "influence of the Republican party, time-serving as it is, is among the worst with which we have to contend." Antislavery zeal had been more pronounced in the Whig *Michigan State Journal* of the previous decade; in 1856, the Republican *Ann Arbor Journal* blasted abolitionists William Lloyd Garrison, Henry Ward Beecher, and Charles C. Burleigh as "disunionists." The distance between the Republicans and preceding antislavery parties on the questions of race and slavery is perhaps best exhibited in the remarks of Ann Arbor *Journal* editor Ezra Seaman regarding Abraham Lincoln following his electoral victory in 1860: "We believe him to be a National Republican of the Henry Clay school, and no abolitionist. . . . He has declared himself distinctly opposed to negro suffrage, and we have faith that he is not afflctd [*sic*] with any . . . delusive theory that the African race are either intellectually or morally equal to the European, or capable of being made equal by education."[104]

Offenders, of which Foster afterward became superintendent. Foster also served as editor of the Lansing *State Republican* for two years during the 1860s. Willis H. Miller, ed., "Theodore Foster Writes from Lansing," *Michigan History*, XXXV (September 1951), 314–15.

103. Formisano, *Birth of Mass Political Parties*, 255; Formisano, "Edge of Caste," 35–39; Maurice Dickson Ndukwu, "Antislavery in Michigan: A Study of Its Origin, Development, and Expression from Territorial Period to 1860" (Ph.D. dissertation, Michigan State University, 1979), 223–26.

104. *Liberator* (Boston), January 25, 1856 (see November 20, December 18, 1857, for a debate among Michigan Garrisonians regarding the weakening of their movement in the wake of the rise of the Republican Party); Ann Arbor *Journal*, February 13, 1856, November 14, 1860. During the Civil War, the Ann Arbor *Peninsular Courier and Family Visitant* was more favorable to anti-

Although some white southerners, as we saw in chapter 5, suspected that colonization was tied to abolitionism, abolitionists in Washtenaw County generally remained aloof from this effort. To be sure, there were exceptions. For example, Chandler Carter of Manchester, who chaired the Liberty Party in his township as well as two Washtenaw County Liberty conventions during the mid-1840s, contributed money to the American Colonization Society in 1859. On the other hand, both the *Michigan Freeman* and the *Signal of Liberty* condemned colonization as an effort calculated to strengthen slavery. The *Signal* satirized this endeavor by calling the underground railroad "Successful Colonization," and announced that "the abolitionists will soon outdo the Colonizationists in colonizing the free people of color, and more emphatically, 'with their own consent.'" But perhaps the most telling evidence of the antipathy of abolitionists to colonization is revealed in the fact that only nine of the forty-nine Washtenaw County proponents of colonization whom I have identified could be linked to antislavery activity—mostly petition signers and Free Soilers. In contrast to the temperance and benevolence causes in Washtenaw County, which enjoyed enthusiastic support from some abolitionists, colonization was generally shunned by the antislavery rank and file—suggesting that their views and those of the leadership were alike on the issue.[105]

Despite editorial endorsements of colonization by George Corselius during the early 1830s, and approval from the *Michigan Argus* and the *Michigan State Journal* later in the decade, there was no known colonization activity in Washtenaw County until 1847, when the Ypsilanti *Sentinel* printed an announcement for a colonization meeting. (O. J. Tennis, who issued the call for this meeting, pronounced that this cause "like every other good work, has its vio-

---

slavery; on one occasion the *Journal* called the *Courier* a "miserable little croaking abolition sheet." Ann Arbor *Journal*, February 11, 1863, quoted in Doll, *History of the Newspapers of Ann Arbor*, 61.

105. On Carter: *Signal of Liberty*, September 29, 1845, March 27, October 16, 1847; *True Democrat*, September 28, 1848; *African Repository*, XXXV (February 1859), 63. For anticolonization editorials: *Michigan Freeman*, October 23, 1839; *Signal of Liberty*, August 4, September 1, 1841. For supporters of colonization: Ypsilanti *Sentinel*, May 23, 1847; *True Democrat*, March 28, 1848; *African Repository*, XXII (November 1846), 360, XXIII (October 1847), 322, XXIV (May 1848), 160, XXXIII (September 1857), 288, XXXIV (June 1858), 192, XXXV (February 1859), 63. Incidentally, 6 abolitionists who supported colonization were also active in the temperance movement. Overall, 13 of the 49 colonizationists were traced to temperance, and 7—6 of whom were temperance activists—were correlated with a cause of the benevolent empire.

lent opposers, with their supposed objections, such as 'an institution of the South to perpetuate slavery'—objections in themselves untenable.") The following spring, colonizationists organized a society in Ann Arbor, although there is no record of its meeting subsequently. The ephemeral characteristics of this cause probably arose from the fact that colonization lacked the passionate and committed supporters of temperance, benevolence, and abolition. Even activists undoubtedly recognized the impossibility of ever expatriating all of the country's free African Americans—let alone the slave population. And in contrast to Tuscaloosa, there was no lingering fear among Washtenaw County whites that the local slave population might be corrupted unless free blacks were deported. In the late 1850s, however, American Colonization Society agents found a number of Washtenaw County residents who were willing to contribute money, indicating that some support for this cause was present, even if it was not fervent.[106]

Washtenaw County's African Americans felt more passion regarding colonization. Those present at a meeting of the county's "colored people" announced in 1842 that they were "inflexibly opposed to all Colonization whatever, whether American or Foreign." Some others, though, were not as dismissive of Liberian emigration. In 1851, interested "colored persons" called for a meeting "to take into consideration the propriety of sending an agent to Liberia to collect facts regarding that country." Seven months later Dennis Washington, an African American and an Ann Arbor resident of seven years, placed an advertisement in the *Michigan Argus* announcing his intention to emigrate to Liberia. There he expected to "enjoy the immunities of a freedom vouchsafed by a government organized and controlled by a People of his own Color," and he believed that his circumstances and those of his family "would be very much enhanced pecuniarily, as well as socially." Although he had sufficient means to pay for his own passage, he sought to raise $150 to meet the expenses of transporting his family. In 1854, though, Washington still remained in Ann Arbor. He may have lost faith in colonization, as that year he pledged an undisclosed sum to Stephen S. and Abby Kelley Foster, who were laboring on behalf of the Garrisonian—and staunchly anticolonizationist—

106. *Michigan Argus,* August 13, 1835; *Michigan State Journal,* November 9, 1837; Ypsilanti *Sentinel,* June 23, 1847; *True Democrat,* March 28, 1848; *Michigan Argus,* March 29, May 17, 1848, February 28, 1849, November 10, 1852; *African Repository,* XXXIII (September 1857), 288, XXXIV (June 1858), 192, XXXV (February 1859), 63.

Michigan Anti-Slavery Society. Yet interest in the cause continued among the county's blacks, as six years later, a Mr. Truss of Ypsilanti announced his intention of emigrating to Liberia.[107]

Unfortunately, social data on Washtenaw County's colonizationists are sparse. Only twenty-five of the forty-nine identified colonizationists were found on the 1850 census, where their mean real estate holding was $3,016 (median $1,800). Both the average and median age in 1850 was 42 for the twenty-six colonizationists with discernible ages. The occupations of thirty-one colonizationists were ascertained, however, of whom the majority (thirteen) were professionals (including five clergy, three professors, and two attorneys), ten farmers, five artisans, two shopkeepers/proprietors, and one laborer.

Even though the abolitionist movement in Michigan diminished considerably following the demise of the Liberty Party and the MSASS in 1848 and 1849, it made a mild recovery during the mid-to-late 1850s among Garrisonians. In 1840 the American Anti-Slavery Society had fractured over political action and what it meant to be an abolitionist. One wing, led by William Lloyd Garrison, denied that abolitionists were obliged to vote for antislavery political candidates and opposed the formation of an independent political party. This faction instead favored a broad platform denoting a true abolitionist as anyone who believed slavery to be a sin and embraced black equality. Garrison's opponents, led by Lewis Tappan, endorsed political action but were divided regarding the utility of a third party. More to the point, though, the anti-Garrisonian wing of the American Anti-Slavery Society was repulsed by its adversaries' abrasive denunciations of churches and by their various other radicalisms, including advocacy of women's rights, antisabbatarianism, nonresistance, and Christian anarchism. The Garrisonians retained control of the American

107. *Signal of Liberty*, January 19, 1842; *Michigan Argus*, July 30, 1851, February 25, 1852; Notebook No. 3, p. 8, in Harriet DeGarmo Fuller Papers, Clements Library; *African Repository*, XXXVII (February 1861), 47. During the antebellum years, Michigan newspapers paid scant attention to any activism among the state's few African Americans. Besides the 1842 meeting, the only other contemporary report came from a Detroit Free Soil paper, which pithily noted that "the colored citizens of Ann Arbor . . . have organized an 'Anti-slavery Vigilance Association.'" Presumably this organization aimed to protect its members from slave catchers who had been empowered by the Fugitive Slave Act of 1850. *Peninsular Freeman*, February 4, 1851.

Anti-Slavery Society, while the Tappanites formed the American and Foreign Anti-Slavery Society.[108]

After the MSASS, which was initially an auxiliary of the American Anti-Slavery Society, severed its ties with that body in 1841, most abolitionists in Michigan either wound up in the Liberty Party or ceased being active in secular antislavery activity. As mentioned earlier, not all abolitionists flocked to the Libertyite banner, as a number continued to believe that moral suasion was the best strategy. After the strong presence of moral suasionists—and at least one Garrisonian—at the January 1844 MSASS meeting, Theodore Foster mentioned the Garrisonians in his columns a few times. On those few occasions, he showed little evidence of antagonism toward these opponents of political abolition. In fact, although acknowledging his disagreements with Garrison, Foster wrote of this veteran of abolitionism with admiration. Of course Foster could afford to view Garrison this way, as there were too few Garrisonians in Michigan to challenge the Liberty Party. As Foster reported in June 1844: "There is a great unanimity of views among genuine Abolitionists in this state in support of the Liberty party. But there are a small portion of them who are Friends or Non-Resistants, who do not vote, and of course disapprove of the political movement." On the other hand, Foster reminded his readers that the Garrisonians had "no contention" with the Liberty Party in the West, and he reprinted one piece from the *Liberator,* which argued that Garrisonianism was not as necessary in the western states since the people there were not as "priest-ridden."[109]

Many of the members of Michigan's earliest abolition society—formed by Hicksite Quakers in Lenawee County in 1832—never embraced political abolitionism, and they formed the nucleus of Michigan's Garrisonian resurgence of the 1850s. The most prominent male among this cohort was Thomas Chan-

108. Dillon, *Abolitionists,* 113–26; Stewart, *Holy Warriors,* 92–95; Aileen S. Kraditor, *Means and Ends in American Abolitionism: Garrison and his Critics on Strategy and Tactics, 1834–1850* (New York, 1967).

109. *Signal of Liberty,* April 28, May 12, 1841, February 5, 12, 26, May 27, June 17, 1844. Although there were some exceptions—one of the vice-presidents of the American Anti-Slavery Society in 1845 was Zephaniah Platt, formerly the Whig attorney general of Michigan, and Thomas Chandler of Lenawee County, who was chosen a manager of the society in 1841—Garrisonianism was scarcely present in Michigan during the 1840s. *Ibid.,* May 19, 1845; Douglas Andrew Gamble, "Moral Suasion in the West: Garrisonian Abolitionism, 1831–1861" (Ph.D. dissertation, Ohio State University, 1973), iv, 221, 292, 297, 311–12.

dler, the brother of Elizabeth Margaret Chandler. Active in abolitionism since the early 1830s, he became a vice-president of the Garrisonian-dominated Western Anti-Slavery Society, based in Salem, Ohio, in 1850. Garrisonian agents began visiting Michigan in 1852, and by the fall of 1853, Henry C. Wright, Parker Pillsbury, Stephen S. Foster, Abby Kelley Foster, James W. Walker, and Giles Stebbins had toured the state. In October 1853, abolitionists assembled in Adrian to form the Michigan Anti-Slavery Society (MASS). It differed from the MSASS most notably by permitting women to serve as officers: Vice-Presidents Emeline DeGarmo of Ypsilanti and Harriet De-Garmo Fuller of Plymouth were its highest-ranking women, and they were joined by several others who served on the executive committee and as the executive secretary.

MASS resolutions were far more strident than those of the Free Soil Party and surpassed many of the Liberty Party's pronouncements of the previous decade. They denounced white supremacy; condemned as "thoroughly corrupt, and fit only to be trodden in the dust" all laws, sects, parties, and governments that "recognize the right of man to hold property in man"; agreed that all who rejected immediate emancipation "stand condemned out of their own mouths, as destitute of moral principle"; and charged that the "strength of the Slave Power" was not in the South but in "Northern cowardice, servility, conservatism—in Northern religious fellowship and cooperation—in Northern party alliance and subserviency— . . . in hatred of the free people of color—and in a general lack of manhood, moral principle, and regard for Liberty." Six years later, this body praised John Brown's raid at Harpers Ferry, Virginia, as "an act of humanity and heroism of so divine a character as that the memory of the brave men who attempted it will be held in admiration by American posterity when the name and fame of Lafayette and Kosciusko shall have been long forgotten." Cyrus Fuller, president of this body in 1854, possibly best expressed the sentiments of other members when he wrote: "I think the Garrisonian Movement is the soul and body of all the movements of the day." Many Free Soilers, though, had nothing but contempt for Garrisonians, and during the visit of Abby Kelley Foster and Stephen S. Foster to Detroit in 1853, the city's Free Soil organ, the Detroit *Free Democrat*, excoriated the couple's lectures.[110]

110. Dillon, "Elizabeth Chandler"; Carlisle G. Dickinson, "A Profile of Hicksite Quakerism in Michigan," *Quaker History*, LIX (Autumn 1970), 106–12; American Anti-Slavery Society, *Annual Report*, II (1835), 85; *Report of the Proceedings of the Anti-Slavery State Convention*, 4; William Lloyd Garrison to Helen E. Garrison, October 15, 17, 1853, in Ruchames, ed., *Letters of William*

Garrisonian agents visited Ann Arbor and Ypsilanti throughout the 1850s; local newspapers noted the presence of Abby Kelley Foster, James W. Walker, Lucy Stone, Parker Pillsbury, Charles L. Remond, Sarah P. Remond, and Wendell Phillips.[111] Garrison himself visited Ann Arbor and Ypsilanti in 1853 prior to the organization of the MASS. Preceding Garrison in each place were Abby Kelley Foster and Stephen S. Foster, who "considerably stirred up" Ann Arbor, which Garrison described as "full of sectarianism and pro-slavery." There is little surviving evidence regarding Garrisonianism in Washtenaw County, but it does not appear that these radical abolitionists succeeded in converting many residents. Aaron M. Powell wrote in 1856 that a recent Garrisonian convention in Ypsilanti "was but thinly attended, and not very much interest manifested." There were a few notable Washtenaw Garrisonians, however. During Garrison's sojourn in Ann Arbor, he stayed with Richard Glasier, a Quaker who later served on the MASS executive committee and occasionally lectured in the state. In 1856, Glasier was assaulted by vegetable projectiles while visiting Pontiac. His meeting there was disrupted by rowdies, and he escaped violence by having a group of women escort him from the lecture hall. In addition to Emeline DeGarmo, Ypsilanti was the home of Samuel D. Moore, who also served several times on the MASS executive committee. Moore was earnestly committed to nonresistance and in January 1856 placed the following notice in the Ypsilanti *Sentinel:* "Know all men (and women too) by this, that as the State of Michigan thro' the General Government is pledged to protect and sustain the unrighteous system of chattel slavery, that I hereby refuse to pay of my own free will and consent, all the taxes for the support and maintenance of said State and National Government." The *Michigan Argus,* which flippantly reported Moore's manifesto as a curiosity in 1856, was annoyed by his "Annual Protest" the following year and asked, "Why don't Mr. Moore emigrate to Canada?" In 1858, Moore reiterated his complaint and advised editor Elihu Pond to go to Canada.[112]

Lloyd Garrison, IV, 269, 273, respectively (see also 265 n. 8); Gamble, "Moral Suasion," 373, 381, 382, 397, 401, 402, 422–23; *Liberator,* November 11, December 2, 1853; *National Anti-Slavery Standard* (New York), December 3, 1859; Cyrus Fuller to Thomas Chandler, October 22, 1854, in Elizabeth Chandler Papers, Bentley Library; Dorothy Sterling, *Ahead of Her Time: Abby Kelley and the Politics of Antislavery* (New York, 1991), 289. The Harriet DeGarmo Fuller Papers, Clements Library, richly document the meetings of the Michigan Anti-Slavery Society.

111. *Washtenaw Whig,* October 4, 1853; Detroit *Daily Democrat,* February 9, 1854; *Michigan Argus,* March 2, 1855, December 12, 1856; *Local News and Advertiser,* September 29, October 6, 1857.

112. *Liberator,* November 11, December 2, 1853; William Lloyd Garrison to Helen E. Garrison, October 10, 1853, in Ruchames, ed., *Letters of William Lloyd Garrison,* IV, 262; *Annual Report*

Perhaps the most noteworthy Garrisonian activity in Washtenaw County occurred between 1857 and 1861, much of it centered around the enthusiasms of Giles Stebbins, an occasional resident of Ann Arbor who in addition to Garrisonian abolitionism was a devotee of temperance and spiritualism. His lectures at the Free Church—the precursor to Ann Arbor's Unitarian society—were often announced in local newspapers, and he was probably the impetus behind the large gathering of men and women who designated themselves as the "Friends of Progress" in Ann Arbor in September 1859. This assemblage of Garrisonians, temperance proponents, spiritualists, ex-Hicksite Quakers, freethinkers, and women's rights advocates attracted visitors from several states, including abolitionist Henry C. Wright and former Ann Arborite George W. Clarke, now living in New York; other well-known radicals sent letters regretting their inability to be present. Whereas previous gatherings of abolitionists in Ann Arbor had often invoked Christianity in their condemnations of slavery, these enthusiasts resolved it to be their duty to resist all laws that sustained slavery "whether such laws purport to come from God or man, or whether found in the Bible or the Constitution, or any other record," and "never to worship any being as God, that councils us to be subject to the 'powers that be' in Church or State . . . or enjoins submission to a law that sanctions slave hunting or the rendition of fugitive slaves."[113]

The "Friends of Progress" convened without incident. In January 1861, however, some Ann Arborites, aroused by the secession crisis, greeted a two-day convention of the "Friends of Freedom in Michigan," organized by Stebbins, with violent hostility. Although Parker Pillsbury had previously lectured unmolested in Ann Arbor both as an abolitionist and as the invited guest of the University of Michigan's Student Lecture Association, some residents were

---

Presented to the American Anti-Slavery Society (New York, 1856), 74; *Liberator,* January 25, March 14, 1856; Ypsilanti *Sentinel* quoted in *Michigan Argus,* January 25, 1856; *Michigan Argus,* January 23, 1857, January 29, 1858; *Liberator,* February 29, 1856. Regarding Moore's abolitionist activity, see *National Anti-Slavery Standard,* July 16, 1866. Both Moore and Glasier were singled out by Parker Pillsbury as being among the leading Garrisonians in Michigan; *Liberator,* October 23, 1857 (see also December 18, 1857).

113. Ann Arbor *Journal,* February 2, August 17, October 5, 1859, June 20, September 12, 1860, January 16, March 27, 1861; *Local News and Advertiser,* September 27, 1859. See also Giles Badger Stebbins, *Upward Steps of Seventy Years* (New York, 1890). Regarding a similar meeting held in Battle Creek, see *Liberator,* October 23, November 20, December 18, 1857; on this group's New York connection, see Christopher Densmore, "After the Separation," in Hugh Barbour, *et al.,* eds., *Quaker Crosscurrents: Three Hundred Years of Friends in the New York Yearly Meetings* (Syracuse, N.Y., 1995), 134–35.

greatly incensed by handbills that announced his presence at the convention under the headline "No Union with Slaveholders, Religiously or Politically." At the first session of this conference, Josephine Griffing of Ohio was hissed by the audience. Later that day, during Pillsbury's remarks, the hostile crowd reportedly forced the abolitionists to flee the Free Church through the windows, after which the mob vandalized the church. The Friends of Freedom nevertheless assembled on the following day at the despoiled church, where Pillsbury "eloquently defended his Christian character by 'returning good for evil.'" Stebbins also spoke. He blamed the preceding day's riot on the advance notice in the *Michigan Argus,* which had labeled the meeting a celebration of the dissolution of the Union, regretted "that our city could not have escaped" the disgrace of hosting this gathering, and called Pillsbury and Griffing "a couple of raving, crazy fanatics of the Garrison Phillips school" and Stebbins "a nominal resident of the same stripe." Both the Ann Arbor *Journal* and the *Michigan Argus* condemned the mob action, although they were more denunciatory of Pillsbury, whose speech they pronounced treasonous. Local word had it that University of Michigan students were responsible for the riot. Resolutions from students of the literary and law departments, however, censured the rioters and countered that "the greater portion of the students present" were committed to "see that order was maintained and the right of free speech vindicated"; the few students "who disgraced themselves by engaging in the riot were assisted by a rabble no way connected with the University." The legacy of this riot persisted for over a year, and local officials took extreme precautions to ensure that a similar melee did not erupt when Wendell Phillips addressed the Student Lecture Association in April 1862.[114]

Although women figured more prominently in Garrisonian abolitionism of the 1850s, they had participated in abolitionist activities in Michigan since the 1830s. As we saw earlier, the state's first antislavery society was formed in 1832 through the instrumentality of Elizabeth Margaret Chandler in Lenawee

114. *Local News and Advertiser,* October 6, 1857; Ann Arbor *Journal,* November 2, 1859, January 23, 30, February 13, 1861; *Michigan Argus,* January 25, February 1, 15, 1861; *National Anti-Slavery Standard,* February 9, 1861; Stebbins, *Upward Steps,* 214; George S. May, "Parker Pillsbury and Wendell Phillips in Ann Arbor," *Michigan History,* XXXIII (June 1949), 155–61, in which May understates abolitionist support in Ann Arbor. Phillips' previous engagement before the Student Lecture Association passed without incident. *Michigan Argus,* December 12, 1856.

County. Later that decade, the all-male MSASS leadership encouraged women to form their own societies.[115] The extent of female antislavery activism in the 1830s is most notably demonstrated by the fact that throughout the North, women signed and circulated many of the petitions during that decade's petition campaign. Washtenaw County women, however, are conspicuously absent on the extant antislavery petitions submitted to the Twenty-fifth, Twenty-sixth, and Twenty-seventh Congresses, as Isabella Cowlary is the only female name among the 237 petition signers found at the National Archives. Significantly, her signature was crossed out on both petitions in which it appeared (the texts of some of the extant Washtenaw petitions—particularly those of the 1840s—declare that the signers are "legal voters"). But following the organization of the Liberty Party and the concurrent declining use of moral suasion in favor of electoral politics, the state abolition society ceased encouraging women's activity. The public role of abolitionist women diminished considerably, and Michigan's male-dominated antislavery press devoted even less space to women's involvement in the movement.[116]

One notable exception to this trend was exhibited in an announcement for an Oakland County antislavery convention in Pontiac. Despite its condemnation of some contemporary gender customs, the announcement indicated that female abolitionists ought to focus their activism on the emancipation of female slaves. "Abolitionists," it claimed, "are not of that bigoted class of beings who would sink the female sex into a mere appendage of humanity, and deprive them of all opportunity of manifesting their sympathy and regard for the millions of their own sex who are down-trodden and degraded beyond descrip-

115. Dillon, "Elizabeth Chandler," 491; *Report of the Proceedings of the Anti-Slavery State Convention*, 13; *American Freeman*, July 2, 1839.

116. Gerda Lerner, "The Political Activities of Antislavery Women," in *The Majority Finds Its Past: Placing Women in History*, ed. Gerda Lerner (New York, 1979), 112–28; Deborah Bingham Van Broekhoven, "'Let Your Names Be Enrolled': Method and Ideology in Women's Antislavery Petitioning," in Jean Fagan Yellin and John C. Van Horne, eds., *The Abolitionist Sisterhood: Women's Political Culture in Antebellum America* (Ithaca, 1994), 179–99; Judith Wellman, "Women and Radical Reform in Antebellum Upstate New York: A Profile of Grassroots Female Abolitionists," in Mabel E. Deutrich and Virginia C. Purdy, eds., *Clio Was a Woman: Studies in the History of American Women* (Washington, D.C., 1980), 113–27, 52 inhabitants of [Saline] (HR25A-H1.7); 44 citizens of [Saline] (HR25A-H1.8). Hewitt, *Women's Activism*, 120, 127, reports that antislavery women in Rochester, New York, who were allied with the men in the Liberty Party—which women Hewitt classifies as "perfectionist"—"retreated from antislavery activity entirely" during the 1840s. See also Ginzberg, *Women and the Work of Benevolence*, 88, 91.

tion." After the meeting was postponed, a second announcement suggested an auxiliary role for women in the abolitionist struggle: "Ladies, will _you_ meet with us? . . . Come then to the meeting and cheer us on, and nerve our arms in assisting to bring back the country to a just sense of the necessity of purifying it of this Heaven-doomed curse of slavery. . . . 'Your tears may rust the captive's chain' and your silent prayer accelerate the happy period when 'every yoke shall be broken.'" The fact that the published minutes of the gathering failed to report whether women accepted the challenge suggests that even the male abolitionists of Oakland County regarded female participation in the movement as extraneous.[117]

During the mid-1840s, however, as enthusiasts of the Liberty Party became increasingly discouraged at their prospects for electoral success, male abolitionist leaders again publicly advocated the participation of women in the movement. A principal focal point of this encouragement was the commencement of the _Star of Freedom_, published by Jane Van Fleet briefly in 1845 in Niles, Michigan. At a meeting in February 1845, the Michigan Liberty Party passed a resolution in support of Van Fleet's newspaper. Like the male abolitionists in Oakland County who wanted their female allies to labor for the freedom of female slaves, these abolitionist delegates encouraged separate, sex-segregated spheres with respect to the _Star of Freedom_: "And especially do we entreat that the ladies of Michigan will sustain their sister in her work of love."[118] Later that year, a correspondent to the _Signal of Liberty_ acknowledged that women's antislavery activity had diminished during the 1840s, and called upon them for renewed participation:

> Say not that it is man's business to destroy slavery. I know man ought to do it— he should have done it a long time ago, but he has been recreant to his duty. Now let woman speak, and it shall be done. You are aware of the extent of your influence. I have frequently observed that antislavery sentiments are much oftener cherished by females than by the other sex. Their sympathies for the oppressed are generally deeper and lasting; and were they sufficiently firm in their advocacy of man's 'inalienable rights,' the result would be most happy and beneficial.

117. _Signal of Liberty_, May 23, July 18, August 29, 1842. At the Michigan Liberty convention in Ann Arbor that fall, women were invited to "cheer and animate the meeting by their presence"; _ibid._, October 17, 24, 1842.

118. _Signal of Liberty_, February 17, April 28, 1845; _History of Berrien and Van Buren Counties_ (Philadelphia, 1880), 137. There are no known copies of the _Star of Freedom_ in existence.

Much of the success that has hitherto attended the antislavery cause is owing to the efforts of woman. May we not hope that those efforts will be redoubled?[119]

The following year, women's antislavery activity was repeatedly "redoubled." In June 1846, the Young Men's Liberty Association of Michigan rejoiced that women were "becoming so extensively interested in the Liberty cause" and hailed "their cooperation as a bright omen of the slave's more speedy deliverance from his bondage." Evidently, much of the increased activity among women followed a series of lectures presented by the slave refugee Henry Bibb. Immediately following each of Bibb's presentations, Seymour Treadwell would appeal to the women of the audience to form their own antislavery society. One of the earliest places to organize was in the Liberty Party stronghold of Salem, where women established a society of thirty-two members and pledged to raise money to help Bibb publish his slave narrative. During 1846 and 1847, according to the *Signal of Liberty*, other female antislavery societies emerged throughout the state. The MSASS executive committee was pleased and, in a circular addressing female antislavery, encouraged autonomy from male abolitionist bodies: "As to the plans and manner of perfecting your organizations, we are disposed to leave them entirely to yourselves, as they must vary under varying circumstances." Women ought not be shaken "by the idle taunt" of those who "enquire what can a woman do in a cause so interwoven in the political framework of society." Recognizing the influence of women among men, the committee hoped that they could use moral suasion to revolutionize the way men looked at slavery: "We know that it is not in your province or duty to enter that arena and war amid the din and strife of contending political parties. Yours is a purer sphere—one that might enjoy an angel's sympathies and powers, to move amid the tender, sacred chords of benevolent feeling in others' hearts and by the mild, yet firm and constant presentation of soul-stirring truth, impel to action."[120]

Nevertheless, Theodore Foster of the *Signal*, like other newspaper editors in both Washtenaw and Tuscaloosa Counties, provided less coverage to the creation of women's voluntary associations than to men's. The existence of the Female Anti-Slavery Society of Webster and Scio—the latter town being Foster's own residence—is revealed only through a letter from W. A. Bronson to

119. *Signal of Liberty*, August 11, 1845.

120. *Ibid.*, June 13, 20, July 4, 11, 25, September 5, 26, November 7, 1846, September 13, 1847. See also Henry Bibb's letter "To the Anti-Slavery Ladies of Michigan," *ibid.*, January 2, 1847.

the *Signal* thanking the women for donating a box of clothing "for the benefit of the colored people of Marshall." The presence of a similar body in Ann Arbor can be confirmed only by a notice in a village newspaper charging that "several of the most zealous and leading members" of this association "make slaves of their hired help, refusing to treat them as equals" or permit them "to sit at the same table as themselves."[121]

Some antislavery women believed that their male colleagues viewed oppression too narrowly. This fact permits us to digress briefly on the small yet significant women's suffrage movement in Michigan—which cause was entirely absent in Alabama. In the *Signal of Liberty*, Maria Celestia of Grand Rapids urged recognition of women's right to vote, and B. F. C. of Ottawa County complained that families spent far more in educating their sons than their daughters, which resulted in arrogant twelve-year-old males believing that they knew more than a mature woman: "So long as domestic slavery is venerated as one of our household gods, we have little reason to believe that African slavery will receive the condemnation it deserves from the professed friends of freedom." Notwithstanding the publication of these essays in the *Signal*, Theodore Foster poked fun at abolitionists who endorsed feminism. To William Lloyd Garrison's contention that "all women are in a state of abject slavery to men" and deserve "an equality with men *in all respects*," Foster responded: "It unfortunately happens, however, that the fair sex are very slow to perceive or acknowledge their own wretched situation." Foster used a similar logic to point out the excesses of former Ann Arbor resident George W. Clarke, who had explained his position during a long mutual stagecoach ride in 1846:

> Friend Clarke is a radical in about everything. Among his other peculiarities, he
> is a "Woman's Rights Man" of the strongest kind, being an advocate of the abso-
> lute equality of the condition of the sexes. . . . But though friend Clarke showed
> great perseverance and logic, we thought he was rather unsuccessful in making
> converts. The gentlemen had no notion of having their wives taken away from
> the nursery to sit on juries or on the judge's seat, or even to vote; and as to the
> ladies, we must say we thought they turned the cold shoulder to their warm-
> hearted advocate. —We could not avoid the conclusion *that they were not dis-*

---

121. *Ibid.*, January 29, 1848; *True Democrat*, August 20, 1846. This comment appeared in the *True Democrat* during its espousal of the Democratic Party—two years before becoming a Free Soil print.

posed to accept their liberty even if it were offered to them! But friend Clarke consoled himself with a belief that "a better time is coming, girls."

Over the next ten years, Foster changed his mind. By 1856 he had concluded that women deserved the right to vote, and he predicted that by the middle of the twentieth century, "female suffrage will generally prevail in the United States." Nevertheless, the slow conversion of this political outcast to women's suffrage underlines the extent to which this question was deemed radical by many contemporaries who were active in politics.[122]

Some reform-minded papers in Michigan were more favorable than the *Signal* to female suffrage. The *Michigan Temperance Journal and Washingtonian* hoped that if women voted in liquor-licensing elections, liquor retailers would finally close, and George Corselius of the *Michigan State Journal* fully endorsed female suffrage: "We know of no reason why women should not vote as well as men; and there appears to be some strong grounds of principle and expediency why they should. Who knows but what it is the means appointed by Divine Providence for bringing public affairs up to the level of humanity and justice." A number of Michigan legislators were also sympathetic to women's suffrage. As early as 1841, Gurdon C. Leech of Macomb County called for the suffrage of unmarried women with a freehold of at least $250, but the house of representatives voted down the bill, 10–31. Eight years later, the Special Senate Committee on the General Revision of the Constitution favored women's suffrage as did several delegates to Michigan's 1850 constitutional convention, and in subsequent years, the legislature received petitions calling for recognition of this right.[123]

In 1848 the cause of women's rights gained widespread publicity from the convention in Seneca Falls, New York, in July. Prior to this meeting in Seneca Falls, though, the question of the rights of woman—not merely her "sphere"— had been discussed at the Ypsilanti Literary Association in January, when L. D. Norris lectured on "Woman's Influence and Woman's Rights." That No-

122. *Signal of Liberty,* May 12, 1841, March 9, April 13, July 4, 1846; Theodore Foster, "Miscellaneous Thoughts" (from 1856), 62–70, in Foster Papers. See also Blanche Glassman Hersh, *The Slavery of Sex: Feminist-Abolitionists in America* (Urbana, Ill., 1978); Ellen DuBois, "Women's Rights and Abolitionism: The Nature of the Connection," in *Antislavery Reconsidered: New Perspectives on the Abolitionists,* ed. Lewis Perry and Michael Fellman (Baton Rouge, 1979), 238–51.

123. *Michigan Temperance Journal and Washingtonian,* April 15, 1846; *Michigan State Journal,* May 6, 1846; Virginia Ann Paganelli Caruso, "A History of Woman Suffrage in Michigan" (Ph.D. dissertation, Michigan State University, 1986), 12, 19–21, 26–31.

vember the *Washtenaw Whig* conceded a few points to the growing movement: "[women] are made too dependent upon the men—so much so, that when that dependence fails them, and they are obliged to resort to their own hands for support, their wages are kept down so low as to oblige some of them . . . to resort to *surer* and *baser* means of support. We know not why ten hours' hard work of a woman should not be entitled to as much pay as ten hours' no harder work by a man." The *Whig* added that if women voted, town meetings would be more orderly and immoral politicians would no longer be elected, but the paper was not sure whether women should exercise suffrage on all occasions. Nevertheless, it concluded that "modesty, propriety and good sense should regulate this matter, rather than law." A subsequent change of editors resulted in the *Whig*'s being less friendly to women's rights. A year and a half later, editor S. S. Shoff ridiculed a feminist gathering in Ohio as a precursor to a time when women would conduct political campaigns and serve in the legislature while men would be "left at home to look after the *baby* and to superintend the mysteries of the nursery and the kitchen."[124]

Although there is no record of Washtenaw County women forming any local association favoring the recognition of greater rights for women, this omission does not mean that the issue was not discussed. Nationally known feminists Abby Kelley Foster and Lucy Stone lectured in Ann Arbor on abolition and women's rights, as did Giles Stebbins at the Friends of Progress gathering in 1859.[125] Further evidence that this topic was discussed locally is found in the manifesto of Ann Arbor women who in 1853 protested the condition of the town's sidewalks. The authors insisted that "we are no woman's rights women" but nonetheless asserted that "we have the same right to the franchise of sidewalks as our opposites have, and therefore may be allowed to publicly express a preference in regard to them." In an essay in the *Michigan Argus*, "Ellen" noted that "Much is being said now a days about 'Woman's Rights.'" Like her fellow residents who agitated for better sidewalks, Ellen did not favor this reform in its entirety, contending that "man holds a political sway; woman a moral one." In her mind, women—"though differing as they do in certain respects"—were equal to men regarding natural rights and the intellect. The use of a woman's intellect, however, ought not to be devoted to governmental matters, but to be-

124. Ypsilanti *Sentinel,* January 26, 1848; *Washtenaw Whig,* November 29, 1848, May 8, 1850.

125. *Washtenaw Whig,* October 4, 1853; *Michigan Argus,* March 2, 1855; Ann Arbor *Journal,* October 5, 1859. See also *Washtenaw Whig,* December 18, 1850.

ing "keepers at home" and conceiving charitable acts. That women's rights was a distasteful subject among some men was revealed later in the decade when the University of Michigan's regents discussed whether to admit women to the school. The Detroit *Free Press* claimed that the proposal might as well have been introduced by the enemies of the university, as it was based upon the "prevalent ideas of woman's rights" and presumed "that the state has provided certain privileges to males which are denied to females, and that this is an evil calling for a remedy." The *Free Press* stressed that the "natural sphere of man and woman" was different and called upon the state to build separate high schools and colleges for women. Not all prints were hostile to women's rights, though; the Ann Arbor *Journal* in 1860 reprinted a lengthy essay from the *Michigan Farmer* advocating equal suffrage for women.[126]

The religious thrust of many abolitionists has been cited often in this chapter. Seymour Treadwell acknowledged in 1840 that a number of readers had complained that the *Michigan Freeman* often seemed to be a religious rather than an abolitionist paper. Later that decade, the state Liberty convention voted to "utterly repudiate the atheistic principle that all is fair in politics" and contended "that we are under the same obligation to vote conscientiously as we are to pray conscientiously." Years after the demise of the Liberty Party, Theodore Foster privately reminisced that its members had been "mostly moral and religious men, but little influenced by ambitious views, and for these it required no great sacrifice to make the question of human rights the paramount one in their political faith."[127] But while the bulk of the Liberty Party may have been religiously committed people, most church members did not belong to the Liberty Party. Some abolitionists refused to participate with the third party— a few, with any political party—and endeavored to promote antislavery from within their churches. Many Christians, however, resisted all efforts to classify slavery as a sin, and believed that abolitionists disrupted the tranquility of their churches. More so than benevolence and temperance, slavery and aboli-

126. *Washtenaw Whig*, April 20, 1853; *Michigan Argus*, March 16, 1855; Detroit *Free Press* quoted in *Michigan Argus*, July 9, 1858 (see also Ann Arbor *Journal*, August 18, 1858); Ann Arbor *Journal*, May 23, 1860.

127. *Michigan Freeman*, April 8, 1840; *Signal of Liberty*, July 3, 1847; Foster, "Liberty Party," 76–77.

tion were topics of contention and causes of schism in many of Washtenaw
County's churches.

The foremost advocates of abolition were often ministers. The *Michigan
Freeman* authorized "all Ministers of the Gospel, Postmasters, and official
members of any Christian Church" to serve as agents and to procure subscriptions for the paper. J. M. Williams explained in 1840 that there was among the
clergy in Michigan "little of that cringeing vassalage to Southern influence
which exists in other states." Of the forty-nine evangelical ministers with
whom he was acquainted, "all, with one or two exceptions, at least in the presence of abolitionists, profess friendship to our cause." Theodore Foster likewise acknowledged that "the clergy have furnished more than their numerical
proportion of the whole body of Abolitionists" and that their talent added
much to the party. In a memoir, he claimed that the public usually forgave
ministers for their activity in the Liberty Party because of its moralistic bent:
"They found that they could vote for its candidates without incurring the reproach of being political intriguers; and among members of their respective
congregations they exerted, for their support of the party, a permanent and
most effective influence." Later, the Jackson *Patriot* condemned those members of the clergy who, arguing that slavery was contrary to the "higher law" of
God, encouraged their flocks to violate the Fugitive Slave Law. Of course,
some ministers opposed the abolitionists: in 1840, Guy Beckley reported that
three ministers in Northville countered him publicly. More often, however,
abolitionists complained that ministers mouthed antislavery niceties but were
not converted to immediate abolition. As Beckley and Foster wrote to James
G. Birney, "We find that a large share of the leading clergy are ready enough to
concede that slavery in general, or in the abstract is a bad thing—very bad—
but in certain circumstances, practised with good intentions, it is justifiable, or
excusable. In this way their hearers are kept easy, and the edge of antislavery
truth is taken off."[128]

The Jackson *Patriot* absolved Episcopalian ministers from the charge of advocating "the 'higher law' doctrine" but asserted that among New School Presbyterians, Congregationalists, Methodists, and Baptists were "ministers who
advise their congregations to boldly violate the law." Although there is no evi-

128. *Michigan Freeman*, October 23, 1839, February 12, 1840; *Signal of Liberty*, October 9, 1843;
Foster, "Liberty Party," 21; *Jackson Patriot* quoted in *Michigan Argus*, November 27, 1850; Guy
Beckley and Theodore Foster to James G. Birney, December 19, 1843, in Dumond, ed., *Birney
Letters*, II, 764.

dence that any of these denominations' ministers urged such actions in Washtenaw County, many of their members endeavored to have their churches take a tougher line against slavery. Washtenaw's Presbyterians—virtually all of whom were New Schoolers—generally agreed that slavery was wrong, but they were divided regarding the proper course to take. Two years following the Presbyterian schism into New School and Old School churches, the New School General Assembly—which had most of its churches in the North and, as a body, was more favorable to antislavery than the Old Schoolers—delegated the slavery question to the synods, presbyteries, and local churches. Thus, in 1839, Washtenaw Presbyterians commenced a long and sometimes painful debate regarding the course that the church ought to pursue with respect to slavery. At the church in Webster, Theodore Foster and Jacob Doremus proposed in 1839 that the congregation's Articles of Practice be amended to state "that slavery is a sin against God which ought to be immediately repented of and forsaken" and that slaveholders would not be "received into this church or addmitted [*sic*] to its communion." Although a number of abolitionists worshiped at this church, it took them a year and a half to convince the rest of the congregation to endorse this measure. Not long afterward, the Salem Presbyterian Church adopted similar resolutions.

Of course, it was unlikely that any slaveholder would venture as far North as these remote townships to partake of Christian communion, and certainly the local abolitionists knew it. Nevertheless, they regarded these measures as major steps in the war against slavery. The resolutions not only labeled slavery a sin, but also—in prohibiting slaveholders from communion—elevated the degree of its sinfulness to the heinous level of adultery, stealing, swearing, physical violence, and Sabbath desecration. The resolutions would thus assist in purifying the church from evil. As fourteen members of the Lodi Presbyterian Church argued in their effort to have their congregation recognize the sinfulness of slavery, it was the "solemn duty of the members of the church of Christ, to preserve its purity; and not only to bear testimony against all evil, but in order to render the influence of that testimony effectual, to make use of those powers which they possess to carry it in to practical operation." Further, many abolitionists believed that American churches were, in the words of James Birney, the "Bulwarks of American Slavery," whose refusal to condemn slavery made it impossible to persuade slaveholders that the possession of human chattel was a sin; according to Guy Beckley, "the American churches as a body, interposed themselves as a bulwark and a defence between slaveholder

and public opinion." Church-oriented abolitionists believed that passing resolutions on the local level was only the first step. Having other local churches
and national church bodies condemn slavery would collectively strike a lethal
blow to the peculiar institution. Thus Theodore Foster's praise for the resolutions of the Salem church: "Should every church in the Free States adopt the
same course, slavery would be annihilated immediately." Naturally, not all
church members embraced this strategy. A month following the Webster
church's new standard with respect to slavery, a member revealed that he would
no longer attend services because the pastor, Charles G. Clarke, had publicly
announced "that he would never knowingly administer the Lord's supper to a
slaveholder"—which this angry member believed to be "an unchristian
spirit."[129]

The Washtenaw Presbytery also condemned slavery but, as a body, proved
reluctant to take the same steps as the Webster and Salem churches. In February 1839, the presbytery resolved that "American slavery is an enormous sin
exposing our country to the just judgements of God, and calling on the part of
all guilty in it for immediate repentance," and it exhorted Christians to "bear
their decided testimony against this sin in every Christian way." The following
year, though, the body refused to petition the Presbyterian General Assembly
to alter the church constitution so as to exclude from communion those "who
are guilty of voluntarily holding their fellowmen in bondage." The presbytery
conceded that slaveholders ought to be excluded but argued that doing so
would "seriously embarrass brethren" in the South who were laboring to eliminate slavery. Naturally, some members of the presbytery were displeased with
this decision. One of them was Theodore Foster, who ridiculed the premise of
"voluntary slaveholding" as being the logical equivalent of "voluntary horse
stealing."[130]

129. Records of the First United Church of Christ, Webster Township, October 25, November 8, 1839, February 14, March 24, 1841, in Bentley Library; *Signal of Liberty*, April 28, May 5, November 3, 1841, February 5, 1844; undated petition to the Lodi Presbyterian Church, in "Histories
of Churches in Washtenaw Presbytery," James Dubuar Papers, Bentley Library; Marsden, *Evangelical Mind*, 98–101, 119. When the Washtenaw Baptist Association voted to deny fellowship to
slaveholders, Foster praised the action as he did the Salem resolutions: if American Christians
followed the example of the Washtenaw Association, slavery would "soon be numbered among
the things that were"; *Signal of Liberty*, June 27, 1842. By 1847, however, Foster was convinced that
emancipation would only occur through "Legislative-Authority" and not through "any amount
of Ecclesiastical action"; *Signal of Liberty*, August 21, 1847.

130. Minutes of the Washtenaw Presbytery, February 7, 1839, February 12, 13, 1840 (pp. 60–61,
91, 95–96), in Bentley Library; *Signal of Liberty*, November 3, 1841.

In 1844 the Washtenaw Presbytery reiterated its previous position on the sinfulness of slavery, adding that its "removal" should be accomplished not with "carnal weapons" but through "truth and love." Other resolutions revealed that slavery was causing more contention than ever before. For example, the Presbytery rebuked abolitionists who were trying to "make this a question of angry strife and division in our churches," and it expressed disapproval of the efforts by some "to make the ministers of the Gospel political partizans on this subject." Charles G. Clarke lamented the discord arising from this question, as he feared the conflict over "ultra-Abolitionism" would shortly divide churches. In any case, the Washtenaw Presbytery's condemnation of abolitionist tactics did not stop abolitionists from demanding harsher condemnations of slavery. Following another set of resolutions in 1845, the presbytery in 1846 finally consented to petition the General Assembly to enumerate slavery as a sin.

After abolitionists obtained this victory, the topic was not discussed at Washtenaw Presbytery meetings until 1856, when the body submitted to the General Assembly another memorial denouncing slavery.[131] Despite this quiescence regarding slavery on the part of the Washtenaw Presbytery, individual churches in the county continued to find slavery a troublesome issue. Especially contentious was the Lodi Presbyterian Church. In the late 1840s or early 1850s, eight male and six female members petitioned the church to "forever bar the slaveholder and the apologist of slaveholding from fellowship and communion" and from the congregation's pulpit. Their remonstrance was not granted, and in 1853 one of the petitioners, Eli Benton, was charged by the session with "breach of covenant"—specifically for failing to provide the ministry with sufficient financial support. Although Benton continued to attend the church and to fulfill his other obligations under the church's covenant—and had, over the years, made substantial financial contributions to the church—he was at the time of his trial sending money to the Free Presbyterian Church, a schismatic denomination committed to nonfellowship with slaveholders. During Benton's trial, one witness testified that when he approached Benton to obtain a yearly subscription for the support of the ministry, Benton proclaimed, "I am an antislavery man," and committed only one dollar. Another witness reported that Benton had explained his withholding money: "he thought that this church did not take the stand on slavery that they ought and also Mr. Benton

131. Minutes of the Washtenaw Presbytery, May 14, 1844, February 11, 1845, February 10, 1846, February 12, 1856; Charles G. Clarke to AHMS, July 1, 1844, in AHMS Papers. On the role slavery played in the deliberations of the Michigan Synod, see Vander Velde, "Synod of Michigan and Movements for Social Reform," 52–70.

thought that the meetinghouse had been withheld from antislavery lecturers." Although the accusations against Benton express nothing specific regarding his ardent abolitionism, it is clear that his antislavery activity was on trial. The church had never before tried a member for failure to subscribe sufficient money, and one member who reproached Benton for "operating against the interests of this church" explained that Benton's "course was occasioning a division in the church calculated to divert from the interests of religion." After a trial lasting more than three weeks the charges against Benton were sustained, although one of the church's elders, Darius S. Wood—a longtime activist in the Liberty and Free Soil Parties—dissented.

Following this disciplinary action, Benton transferred his membership to the Ann Arbor Congregational Church, which had just approved a resolution similar to the one that Benton had urged the Lodi Presbyterians to adopt. More significant for the Lodi church, though, was that twenty-two others— including ten of the petitioners—transferred their membership to the antislavery-friendly Ann Arbor Congregational Church. The small Lodi church was mortally wounded by this exodus of members who proved willing to travel several miles distant to worship. Eight months following Benton's trial, Lodi's Presbyterian elders voted unanimously to dismiss their pastor, the Reverend Justin Marsh, because some members with "extreme views on the subject of slavery have become opposed to him and the church, and . . . have either left the church or withheld their support." Possibly turned off by this tumultuous state of affairs, twenty-four additional members obtained letters of dismission to join a new church in Lodi in December 1854. Three years later, the Lodi Presbyterian Church dissolved.[132]

Many abolitionists in Ann Arbor were either Presbyterians or Congregationalists who worshiped at the Presbyterian church. But because the church's early records are missing, we cannot know what battles may have raged among its members over slavery. As noted earlier, the MSASS first met at this church, and although the church subsequently denied the abolitionists the use of the

132. "Trial of Eli Benton," August 4–29, 1853, in Dubuar Papers; Records of the First Presbyterian Church of Lodi, May 7, 1853, April 23, December 17, 1854, December 27, 1857, in Bentley Library; Clerk's Record, 1847–1916, of the First Congregational Church of Ann Arbor, in Bentley Library, 406; "Catalogue of the Members of the Church," Records of the Lodi Presbyterian Church, 1839–1857, in Bentley Library. On Darius S. Wood, see *Signal of Liberty*, September 5, 1842, February 20, October 30, 1843, August 26, 1844, September 29, 1845; *Washtenaw Whig*, October 16, 1850; Lodi Township Minutes, April 5, 1853, in Lodi Township Hall.

building, the ban was not permanent. By 1841 antislavery meetings were again conducted there, and the pastor at the time, John P. Cleaveland, was one of Michigan's leading abolitionists. But evidently a majority of the Presbyterian leaders in Ann Arbor resisted taking a sufficiently strong position against slavery—one of the grievances cited by those who broke from the Presbyterians to form the Ann Arbor Congregational Church in 1847. The Washtenaw Presbytery partly attributed its reluctance to take a firmer stand to the existence of a small yet significant southern wing of the church. Achieving a consensus on slavery satisfactory to both wings was a continual challenge to New School Presbyterian leaders, as many of the denomination's northern members were committed to immediate emancipation. Congregationalists were not constrained in this manner, both because there were few Congregational churches in the South and because their system of church government vested policy making in the local churches. Therefore, northern Congregationalists feared no denominational backlash from their abolitionist campaigns.[133]

As mentioned in chapter 2, during the 1850s Congregationalists in Michigan and in Ann Arbor distanced themselves from national benevolent societies that they felt were unwilling to condemn slavery. Six and a half years after its creation, the Ann Arbor Congregational Church enacted resolutions similar to the ones passed by the Webster and Salem churches in 1841 but added the conditions of excluding from their pulpit and communion the ministers and members of churches that, in their estimation, sustained slavery, as well as "all others who may be properly regarded as advocates or apologists for such sinners." Likewise, in 1843 the Congregationalist General Association of Michigan commenced passing resolutions condemning slavery from both a religious and a secular viewpoint. In addition to endorsing the Refugee Home Society—which worked to provide "homes and religious instruction in Canada, for the refugees from Southern slavery"—and to reiterating the sinfulness of slavery, the General Association lamented the repeal of the Missouri Compromise; approved of the settlement of northerners in Kansas and Nebraska "to preserve them from the grasp of Slaveholders"; later pledged "our sympathies, our prayers, and our support" to the settlers in Kansas who were threatened by "armed bands from a neighboring state"; condemned the "cowardly and brutal

---

133. *Signal of Liberty,* October 6, 1841; Goodrich, *First Presbyterian Church of Ann Arbor;* Calvin O. Davis, *A History of the Congregational Church in Ann Arbor, 1847 to 1947* (Ann Arbor, 1947), 1, 7; Andrew Ten Brook, "Sketches of the Early History of Ann Arbor," in Andrew Ten Brook Papers, Bentley Library (typescript), 72; Howard, *Conscience and Slavery,* xii.

attack" upon Senator Charles Sumner; censured the Fugitive Slave Law and the federal government for imprisoning resisters to that law; and deprecated the "Slave Power's" "bold, arrogant, and reckless efforts to secure the control and direction of our national government."[134]

It was among the Methodists that the slavery issue proved most divisive. With its episcopal form of church government, all matters of policy, doctrine, and rules for discipline in the Methodist Episcopal Church were enacted at the state and General Conference level, not by individual congregations. During the early to mid-nineteenth century, the Methodist Episcopal Church was America's largest denomination, with adherents widely spread throughout the North and South. Thus, even more than the New School Presbyterians, the Methodist Episcopal leadership was adamant in not allowing slavery to become a divisive force in the church, despite the antislavery teachings of the denomination's founder, John Wesley. But as we saw in chapter 5, the issue eventually disrupted the church, and the Methodists split into northern and southern denominations in 1844. Prior to this split, many members of the church hierarchy in Michigan had come to despise the abolitionists and used every effort to repudiate or silence them. Initially, though, the state's Methodist leadership did not display antagonism toward abolitionists. James Gilruth, presiding elder of the Detroit District from 1832 to 1836 and frequently a Washtenaw County resident, reportedly looked favorably on abolitionism. At the formation of the Michigan Conference in 1836, abolitionists considered pushing for a firm stand against slavery but decided against it, recognizing that their minority status precluded them from obtaining "a report favorable to anti-slavery," and because "those who differed from them were not oppressive or arbitrary in their course."

Antislavery Methodists did not attempt any action in 1837 either, but they

134. Minutes of the First Congregational Church of Ann Arbor, October 27, 1853, Bentley Library; *Minutes of the General Association of Michigan at Their Meeting in Grass Lake, Sept. 1843* (Marshall, 1843), 6; *Minutes of the General Association of Michigan at their Meeting in Dexter, Sept. 1846*, 15; *Minutes of the General Association of Michigan at Their Meeting in Ann Arbor, May 30, 1848* (Jackson, 1848), 6; *Minutes of the General Association of Michigan at Their Meeting in Kalamazoo, May 28, 1850* (Detroit, 1850), 8; *Minutes of the General Association of Michigan at Their Meeting in Clinton, May 27, 1851* (Detroit, 1851), 6–7; *Minutes of the General Association of Michigan at Their Meeting in Ann Arbor, May 31, 1853* (Detroit, 1853), 14–15; *Minutes of the General Association of Michigan at Their Meeting in Detroit, May 30, 1854*, 14; *Minutes of the General Association of Michigan at Their Meeting in Kalamazoo, May 29th, 1855* (Adrian, 1855), 10; *Minutes of the General Association of Michigan at Their Meeting in Jackson, May 27, 1856* (Detroit, 1856), 11–12; *Minutes of the*

were optimistic that abolitionist sentiment would grow and that positive action could be taken in the future. Thus slavery opponents were surprised in 1838 when the Michigan Conference passed resolutions condemning abolitionists on the ground that their activities were "prejudicial to the interests of the Church." Henceforth it was the duty of conference members to "refrain from agitating the Church, by forming abolition societies in or out of the church, or by attending Methodist abolition conventions." *Zion's Watchman*, a Methodist antislavery publication, was denigrated as "anti-methodistical in its general course," and the conference not only urged its members not to "patronize or circulate it," but also announced that preachers would hereafter be subject to church discipline if they should support such nonapproved periodicals. In response, abolitionists prepared an address to be presented at the following year's conference in Ann Arbor. But that gathering further rebuked abolitionists by voting 75–1 against endorsing a measure authorized by the New England Conference to prohibit all Methodists from engaging in the slave trade.

Recounting these actions a decade later, William M. Sullivan explained to Lucius Matlack that prior to the conference's action, a few Methodist ministers in Michigan "professed to be abolitionists, and blustered a little in its support." Following the 1838 resolutions, though, "the anti-abolition screws were brought to bear upon them, and they basely submitted, and that has been the last of abolition in this body of ministers." Not only did the Methodist hierarchy apply pressure upon its members to abstain from the abolitionist struggle, but some of the Methodist laity also urged their abolitionist co-religionists to reconsider their commitment to antislavery. Among Sullivan's relatives, only his father encouraged his antislavery activism. Sullivan wrote that when he visited his wife's relatives in Washtenaw County in 1838, "they with tears remonstrated me to desist from laboring in behalf of the slave." These implorings left Sullivan "with a sad heart." Shortly afterward, "I found a letter from my relatives in Ohio remonstrating in the same manner, begging by all that's filial towards relatives to desist. This was still more trying."[135]

Undaunted, Methodist abolitionists met first at Plainfield, Oakland

---

General Association of Michigan at Their Meeting in Adrian, May 20, 1858; Minutes of the General Association of Michigan at Their Meeting in Detroit, May 19, 1859 (Adrian, 1859), 9.

135. Macmillan, *Methodist Church in Michigan*, 106–15, 136; Lucius Matlack, *The History of American Slavery and Methodism, from 1780 to 1849: and History of the Wesleyan Methodist Connection of America* (New York, 1849), 193, 197–99; William M. Sullivan to Thomas Chandler, December 24, 1838, quoted in Kooker, "Antislavery," 282.

County, in December 1838, and then a month later at Medina, Lenawee County. In Sharon Township, these dissenters formed the Methodist State Anti-Slavery Society on February 9, 1839, and employed a lecturer who, during the following year, delivered two hundred lectures arguing for "the claims of the enslaved before the Methodist people in this State" and was instrumental in forming local auxiliaries.[136] Many of these abolitionists continued with the Methodist Episcopal Church and hoped to change its policies, but others, according to Sullivan, grew "weary of the proscriptions which they were compelled to bear" from what seemed to be an increasingly authoritarian church government. Some withdrew from the Methodists to join other denominations, while others "stood alone for many months, without the aids in the maintenance of their Christian character." Large-scale secessions commenced following the 1839 session of the Michigan Conference, which refused to ordain preachers Marcus Swift and Samuel Bebens as elders due to their well-known abolitionist activities; in the Northville/Farmington area of Oakland County, where these preachers were well respected, thirty Methodists were sufficiently outraged to request letters of dismission. In February 1841, eighty Methodists in western Wayne County withdrew from the Methodist Episcopal Church, and during the following year, they formally organized themselves into a church they termed "Wesleyan Methodist." Shortly afterward, an indeterminate number of Methodists in Salem and Saline Townships seceded, and thirty members of the church in Manchester signed a manifesto requesting letters of dismission from the Methodist Episcopal Church, "believing after due and prayerful deliberation that we can satisfy our consciences and discharge our christian duties more to our satisfaction by a *union* with the Wesleyan Methodist Church."

At about this time, many Methodists throughout the northern states took similar actions. In November 1842, three leading Methodist abolitionists in the Northeast announced their defection from the Methodist Episcopal body and called for the numerous secessionists in the North to unite and form a new Methodist denomination unshackled by slavery. Though many secessionists were weary of being constantly repudiated by Methodist Episcopal leaders,

136. William M. Sullivan to Thomas Chandler, December 24, 1838, cited in Kooker, "Antislavery," 281–82; Matlack, *History of American Slavery*, 198–99. The Methodist State Antislavery Society held quarterly meetings in 1839 in Saline and Ann Arbor, and an annual meeting the following year in Saline, while an auxiliary was active in Sharon. *Ibid.*, 199; *Michigan Freeman*, March 18, 1840, November 27, 1839.

many were also motivated by the spirit of "come-outerism." For religious-minded abolitionists, this concept—inspired by the biblical injunction of Revelation 18:4: "Come out of her [Babylon], my people, that ye be not partakers of her sins"—required that they divorce themselves from slavery-contaminated organizations lest they too be culpable. Such sentiment was obvious to a Universalist observer, who recorded the following upon the formal organization of a Wesleyan Methodist Church in Ann Arbor in 1843: "Quite a respectable portion of the [Methodist Episcopal] members, becoming convinced that she is a slaveholding and a slavery defending church, and that as long as the [*sic*] remained in her communion, they virtually countenanced and fellowshipped this sin against God, formed the magnanimous resolution that they would come out of her, that they might not 'be partakers of her sins, and receive of her plagues.'"

Not everyone who joined the Wesleyan denomination came to it from the Methodist Episcopal Church. Some antislavery Christians joined the new church solely for its strong position against slavery. According to the Washtenaw Presbytery, an elder of the Bridgewater Presbyterian Church in 1842 seemed anxious to dissolve his congregation, after which he joined the Wesleyan Methodists. Two members of the Pittsfield Wesleyan Church may have belonged solely because of its position against slavery, as they transferred their memberships to the Ann Arbor Congregational Church—a body that was presumably more to their geographic or theological taste—immediately after the latter church adopted its antislavery resolutions in 1853. And a come-outer spirit was plainly evident among fourteen members of the Lodi Presbyterian Church, who urged the other members of their congregation to "dissolve all connection with those churches and ecclesiastical bodies, who in any way fellowship or countenance the sin of slaveholding, for the plain reason, that Christ cannot approve of it." Eventually, as we saw, this zeal—and the reaction to it—led to the dissolution of the Lodi church.[137]

137. Matlack, *History of American Slavery*, 303–306; Macmillan, *Methodist Church in Michigan*, 139; Petition to the Methodist Episcopal Preacher of the Saline Circuit, March 14, 1842, in Bentley Library; Mathews, *Slavery and Methodism*, 229–33; McKivigan, *War Against Proslavery Religion*, 84–85; Chris Padgett, "Hearing the Antislavery Rank-and-File: The Wesleyan Methodist Schism of 1843," *Journal of the Early Republic*, XII (Spring 1992), 63–84; *Primitive Expounder*, I (August 26, 1843), 89; Minutes of the Washtenaw Presbytery, September 27, 1842, in Bentley Library; Records of the First Congregational Church of Ann Arbor, October 27, 1853, in Bentley Library; Petition of the Lodi Presbyterian Church, in "Histories of Churches in Washtenaw

Come-outerism, however, was not universal among even the most committed abolitionists. Although Theodore Foster had only the highest praise for the Wesleyan Methodists, he was "not prepared to give advice" when a reader asked him whether it was right to support the Methodists when they knowingly employed ministers who taught that slavery was a divine institution: "The question of withdrawing from church fellowship embraces a great variety of considerations of the most serious import, concerning which each must judge for himself." For many who eventually embraced the Wesleyan Methodist Church, or who "came out" of any other denomination, the decision was often long and painful. Guy Beckley's departure from the Methodist Episcopal Church was undoubtedly a case in point. As early as 1839, he was endeavoring to spread abolitionism among Michigan's Methodists, but met with resistance. In June 1841, Beckley denied rumors that he had departed from the Methodist Episcopal Church; he claimed that he would do so only when he was convinced that the denomination was impervious to change. In January 1842, he was named president of the Michigan Wesleyan Anti-Slavery Society. But even though this body denounced the Methodist Episcopal Church for tolerating slavery and condemned the church's Missionary Society for its connections with slaveholders, its members resolved not to secede, proclaiming instead that it was "the imperative duty of all who love the church and desire its prosperity to seek by all 'wise and prudent means' its purification."

The Michigan Wesleyan Anti-Slavery Society did challenge the Methodist hierarchy on several points—for example, by urging abolitionists to withhold all money from the Missionary Society. It also proclaimed that unless the Michigan Conference rescinded its antiabolitionist resolutions, abolitionists would not "sanction the members of that body as ministers of the Gospel." In subsequent months, the *Signal of Liberty* occasionally attacked the Methodist Episcopal Church's position on slavery and openly sympathized with the emerging Wesleyan denomination. These repeated assaults eventually elicited feverish responses from John Scotford and Bradford Frazee, both Methodist Episcopal ministers. After an extended correspondence between Beckley and both preachers, Frazee brought charges against Beckley of "slander, falsehood, and inveighing against the discipline of the M. E. Church." At the church trial on July 20, 1843, defending himself before a tribunal of ministers, Beckley ex-

---

Presbytery," Dubuar Papers. A more radical group was encountered by Rev. D. R. Dixon, who labored for three months as an agent of the ATS in Jackson and Washtenaw Counties in 1843. He simply identified them as "a new sect, called the 'Come-outers,' who reject the ministry and ordinances." ATS (New York) *Annual Report*, XIX (1844), 67.

pressed his hope "that the church would reform on the subject of slavery, and that secessions and divisions were utterly uncalled for," and he argued that the trial was instituted only because of his abolitionist activities. Beckley was acquitted of all charges, but his experience evidently left him cold toward the church to which he had devoted twenty years of his life. Ten days later, he and twenty other Ann Arbor Methodists seceded and formed a local Wesleyan Methodist Church.[138]

Following the exit of the Wesleyan Methodists—which diluted abolitionist sentiment in the main body of Methodism—and the schism of Northern and Southern Methodists in 1844, Methodist Episcopal leaders no longer had reason to stifle the remaining abolitionists within their denomination. Thus much of the impetus for joining the Wesleyan Methodists was removed, particularly among moderate abolitionists, and the Wesleyan sect's growth slowed. Evidence of the Methodist Episcopal Church's new tolerance of abolition may be seen in the example of James V. Watson, who by 1847 was publishing the *Family Favorite*, a sheet openly friendly to abolition, in Adrian. After converting this newspaper into a temperance magazine in December 1849 and serving as its editor for a year, Watson formed the *Michigan Christian Advocate*, which although a private venture, served the state's Methodists. He soon folded this paper and became the editor of a denominational publication, the Chicago *Northwest Christian Advocate*, which served Methodists throughout the Old Northwest. Both of these Methodist prints were fiercely antislavery. Further evidence of Methodism's changed attitude toward slavery was seen at the annual meetings of the Michigan Conference, where antislavery sentiment erupted following the Compromise of 1850. In 1851, the conference condemned the Fugitive Slave Law and urged nonviolent disobedience to it. Later conference sessions passed resolutions bemoaning the repeal of the Missouri Compromise, expressing solidarity with northern settlers in Kansas, and—in 1858—demanding that slavery be "denounced and destroyed" the same as "idolatry, adultery and intemperance." And although the Church still had some slaveholder members in the border states, in 1856 the Michigan Conference petitioned the General Conference to prohibit slaveholding among lay members as well as the clergy.[139]

138. *Signal of Liberty*, November 7, 1842, October 9, 1843, June 30, 1841, January 19, 1842, July 31, 1843; *Michigan Freeman*, December 25, 1839; Kephart, "Voice for Freedom," 121–34; Macmillan, *Methodist Church in Michigan*, 160–62.

139. McKivigan, *War Against Proslavery Religion*, 85–87; *Family Favorite*, May 24, 1849 (this paper was subtitled "Devoted to Christianity, Education, Temperance, Antislavery, Foreign and

The American Baptists also had differences on slavery that, in 1845, resulted in a national division. But the autonomy of Baptist congregations prevented the institutional attempts to suppress abolitionism that occurred among the Methodists. Thus, to a *Signal of Liberty* correspondent's complaint in 1841 that the actions of the Baptist Triennial Convention were "illustrative of Northern servility to Southern domination in ecclesiastical matters," Theodore Foster countered that such was not the rule in Michigan: "The Baptists of this state have excluded slaveholders from communion of their churches. In this respect, we believe they are in advance of other denominations." This testimony was seconded by the executive committee of the Michigan State Anti-Slavery Society, which in February 1842 reported that while only "some individual churches of other denominations" had "formally withdrawn from slaveholders the fellowship of their churches," most of Michigan's Baptist Associations had already taken this step. Four months later, when the Washtenaw Baptist Association debated whether and how to condemn slavery, some delegates demurred on the grounds that resolutions condemning slavery were of a "political character" and encouraged the union of church and state. Any objections of this sort were overcome by the majority, and the association shortly issued a circular letter that thundered against slavery, contending that

> it insults God by defacing his image in his creature, man, and brings him to the level of the brutes, makes him a thing, a mere chattel, strips him of his liberty, robs him of the avails of his labor, takes from him his wife and children, [and] withholds the key of [religious] knowledge. . . . Let the cause of the oppressor and the oppressed be the burden of your prayers before the mercy seat—think about it, talk about it, weep about it, and in every reasonable way disfellowship it, and to all its abettors and defenders show no fellowship.

The following October, the Michigan Baptist Convention voted to "have no fellowship for the humanity-debasing and God-dishonoring system." In subsequent years, the state convention, like the state's other Protestant faiths, condemned actions of the federal government that its members believed further entrenched slavery.[140]

Domestic News, Agriculture, Commerce, and the Markets"); *Family Favorite and Temperance Journal,* I (December 1850), 284; Wesley Norton, "The Methodist Episcopal Church in Michigan and the Politics of Slavery: 1850–1860," *Michigan History,* XLVIII (September 1964), 193–213; Macmillan, *Methodist Church in Michigan,* 181–83, 213.

140. *Signal of Liberty,* October 20, November 24, 1841, February 16, June 13, 27, 1842; *Michigan Christian Herald,* November 1, 1845; Judson LeRoy Day II, *The Baptists of Michigan and the Civil*

Not all Baptists were pleased with their church's position on slavery. One such individual was Timothy W. Hunt of Lodi, whose political identity evolved from Whig during the mid-1840s to Free Democrat by 1853 to supporting the 1856 presidential candidacy of the Liberty League's Gerrit Smith, for whom Hunt served as one of Michigan's electors. In February 1854, Hunt presented a list of antislavery resolutions to the leaders of the Saline Baptist Church, of which he was a deacon; a month later, they were "rejected as *uncalled* for" by a vote of five to two. Shortly afterward Hunt quit attending church. In September, a church committee visited him, and was informed "that he cannot nor will not walk with the Church because they with their minister are Pro Slavery." Aggrieved of these charges, which the church voted upon as being "untrue," the leaders accused Hunt of neglecting his position as deacon and failing to "fulfill his covenant obligations to this church." Nevertheless, Hunt and the church were soon reconciled. Hunt admitted that the only thing keeping him from attending was the lack of a pronouncement on slavery, and "after a lengthy conversation," he accepted the church's reasoning that the resolutions he had presented amounted to "a political list." At this point, the church passed a resolution condemning slavery as "wicked in the sight of God" and proclaiming that it would not fellowship "any supporters of this evil." Immediately thereafter, Hunt announced that he "would again resume his travail with the church."[141]

Matters at the Saline Baptist Church did not long remain quiet. Six months later, the church called upon George Moor to explain his absence from meetings. According to the minutes, Moor accused "the Church of acting Hypocritically in passing a resolution upon the subject of slavery last September, as he says for the purpose of getting Brother Hunt to resume his [travail] with the church. And thus having lost his confidence in the church on account of their moral dishonesty," Moor concluded that "he could not [travail] with the

---

War (Lansing, 1965), 8–9; Waid, *Centennial History of the Michigan Baptist Convention*, 33–34, 44. Theodore Foster—or possibly Guy Beckley—praised the Washtenaw Association's resolutions as "rich and valuable," especially "when contrasted with the cowardly and time-serving resolutions of the Michigan Conference of the Michigan Episcopal Church"; *Signal of Liberty*, June 27, 1842.

141. *Michigan State Journal*, September 7, 1841; *History of Washtenaw County*, 253 (Hunt was the Whig candidate for Washtenaw County coroner in 1844, 1845, and 1846); Lodi Township Minutes, April 5, 1853; *Michigan Argus*, November 28, 1856; Records of the First Baptist Church of Saline, February 11, March 11, September 3, 15, 1854, in Bentley Library. Hunt was one of only three Washtenaw County voters who cast ballots for Gerrit Smith in 1856; statewide, Smith received only 150 votes. *Michigan Argus*, November 28, December 5, 1856.

church." Meanwhile, Hunt had again absented himself. Although he still expressed satisfaction with the resolutions of the preceding September, he explained that he could no longer fellowship with the church because it accepted contributions earmarked for the American Baptist Missionary Union. Hunt wanted all of the church's missionary donations—rather than a portion—submitted to the unquestionably abolitionist American Baptist Free Mission Society. In the end, neither Hunt nor Moor was reconciled to the church, and both were excluded from fellowship.[142]

The Free Will Baptists were far fewer in Michigan than the regular Baptists, but their opposition to slavery was more pronounced. Although only two of the Washtenaw County Free Will Baptists were linked with an antislavery society or political party, Free Will Baptists in Salem, Pittsfield, Ypsilanti, Saline, Webster, and—after 1855—Manchester may have constituted key elements in antislavery organizations. The denomination had long favored antislavery principles. It had embraced immediate emancipation in 1834 and had ordained African American males as ministers as early as 1827; by the 1840s, Free Will Baptist conventions and newspapers urged members to vote for antislavery candidates.[143] The Michigan Association of Free Will Baptists endorsed political abolitionism even before the Michigan State Anti-Slavery Society: its members resolved in 1839 that it was "the duty of Christians and Christian ministers to oppose slavery at the ballot box[,] in the desk, and by publick lecture." Two years later, however, delegates voted to preface the resolution with "in our opinion" and to omit all the words after *slavery*. Although efforts to overturn this softened amendment failed, the Michigan Association's responses to slavery and the slave-extension issues of the 1840s and 1850s were more strident than those of Michigan's other Protestant denominations. During these years, the association condemned the Mexican War, contending that it was being fought to extend slavery; called for the repeal of the Fugitive Slave Law and pressed northern legislatures to mandate severe penalties for all

142. Records of the First Baptist Church of Saline, December 1, 1854, March 17, April 7, May 4, 1855; McKivigan, *War Against Proslavery Religion,* 88–89.

143. Records of the Michigan Association of the Free Will Baptists, August 23, 1839, June 12, 1840, June 11, 1852, in Bentley Library; English, comp., "History of Manchester Township"; Records of the Free Will Baptists of Manchester, in Bentley Library; *History of Washtenaw County,* 611; Coe Hayne, *Baptist Trail-Makers in Michigan* (Philadelphia, 1936), 89–90; McKivigan, *War Against Proslavery Religion,* 28, 43–44, 148, 162–63. The churches in Ypsilanti, Saline, and Webster were formed in the early 1830s and may have been defunct by the commencement of antislavery activity, as they are not mentioned in the Records of the Michigan Association.

within their borders who assisted in its execution; urged the abolition of slavery in the territories and the District of Columbia; and exhorted the federal government to use military force to protect the rights of free-state settlers in Kansas. In 1853 the clerk of the Van Buren Quarterly Meeting wrote that it was "almost universally acknowledged" that Free Will Baptists were

> uncompromisingly and unflinchingly opposed to American slavery, and that this question is maintained at the ballot box. I hesitate not to say that a large majority of the voters, connected with this Quarterly Meeting are bold to vote against slavery. Every minister among us licensed or ordained regards it as a part of his business to preach against it, and then to vote as he preaches. There are some churches in the Quarterly Meeting of whom it would be safe to say that every voter votes against slavery. Two of our churches are situated in towns which gave a majority vote last fall against it, and Free Will Baptists have done at least their share to bring about this result. Still some vote with one or the other of the old political parties, at times at least. . . . From information received from other parts of the State, we are authorized to say that the above is a fair representation of our cause in the other Quarterly Meetings. The slave has no more true and earnest friends than in our ministry and membership in Michigan.[144]

Universalists were even fewer in Michigan, but small congregations were present in Manchester, Ann Arbor, and Ypsilanti; their organ, the *Primitive Expounder*, was published in Ann Arbor from 1843 to 1844 and 1846 to 1848. The *Expounder* often contained antislavery essays and frequently argued that Universalism and abolitionism were common causes. One writer explained to Theodore Foster that Foster could not "be a *consistent* Abolitionist till he becomes a Universalist." But despite a "Protest Against American Slavery" signed by 304 American Universalist ministers in 1846, and the several Universalists in Washtenaw County who were active abolitionists, there is no evidence indicating that any of this denomination's churches in Michigan, or its larger Central Association of Universalists, ever took official positions on slavery or abolitionism. And similarly, Washtenaw County's Catholic, Episcopal, and Lutheran churches are not known to have acted on these questions.[145]

144. Records of the Michigan Association of Free Will Baptists, August 23, 1839, June 11, 1841, June 11, 1847, June 11, 1852, June 21, 1854, June 8, 1855; Hayne, *Baptist Trail-Makers in Michigan*, 106. This denomination was also praised in the *Signal of Liberty*, July 28, 1841.

145. Annetta English, "The Universalist Church," in Palmer, comp., "A History of Manchester Township"; *Primitive Expounder*, I (July 15, 1843), 42, I (July 29, 1843), 55, I (August 12, 1843), 74, II (January 23, 1845), 76, III (May 7, 1846), 183, V (January 13, 1848), 45, V (November 16, 1848),

⌒⌒

When considering the rank-and-file of Washtenaw County's antislavery advocates, a few observations ought to be made about the petitions submitted by
abolitionists to the United States Congress and about the petitioners themselves. That Congress refused to hear these petitions did not discourage abolitionists for long, as they could now proclaim southern slaveholders sought to
take away the constitutional rights of anyone who dared opposed them—an
argument that resonated powerfully among many Northerners, including
those who were not abolitionists. Indeed, many who signed petitions were
merely sympathetic to antislavery, hostile to the South, or displeased with the
gag rule. James Brewer Stewart has noted that many antislavery petitions
"were drawn up so that all people suspicious of Southern institutions, not just
committed immediatists, could sign them."[146] How many earnest and activist
abolitionists, then, were found among the signers of Washtenaw County's
antislavery petitions? Did those who attached their names to petitions calling
for an end to slavery in the federal territories and the District of Columbia, the
abolition of the interstate slave trade, the diplomatic recognition of Haiti, the
rescinding of the congressional gag rule, the rejection of Texas annexation, and
the further admission of slave states into the Union actually place a high prior-
ity on these positions?

Although committed abolitionists dedicated themselves to faithfully circulating these petitions, the surviving evidence indicates that not all petition
signers threw their hearts into the cause. For example, some names affixed to
petitions protesting Texas annexation or the gag rule were absent from petitions—circulated simultaneously—that urged the repeal of all laws that implicated the federal government with slavery. A total of 369 antislavery petition
signers were identified from sources located in two places: 141 names published
in the *Michigan Argus* in 1837 were copied off a petition to be forwarded to
Washington, D.C., and 237 names located on manuscript petitions were sent
to the 25th, 26th, and 27th Congresses (tabled between 1838 and 1842), which
have since been deposited in the National Archives (nine individuals were
found on both the published petition and the manuscript ones). Only 111 of

396, VI (November 29, 1849), 366. On Universalism in Michigan, see N. Gordon Thomas, *The
Millennial Impulse in Michigan, 1830–1860: The Second Coming in the Third New England* (Lewiston, N.Y., 1989), 34–51.

    146. Stewart, *Holy Warriors*, 82; see also Barnes, *Antislavery Impulse*, 132, 136–37.

these 369 signers (30.1 percent) had antislavery sentiments that showed up elsewhere, such as participation in the Liberty or Free Soil Parties, the Michigan State Anti-Slavery Society, Garrisonian abolitionism, a subscription to the *Signal of Liberty,* or public protests of the U.S. congressional gag rule in 1842. Although a sizeable minority of petition signers were active in the antislavery movement, the majority seem to have confined their antislavery sentiments to the petition. Nor did this majority of petition signers express much interest in other reform causes described in earlier chapters. Only 85 of these petitioners were linked to the temperance movement, and 25 to the benevolent empire. Two hundred and twenty-two of the 369 (60.2 percent) could not be linked to any other reform activity.[147] The possibility exists that these petitioners were dutiful abolitionists whose names did not survive in other extant sources, but it is more likely that the majority of petitioners did not define their lives by the antebellum reform impulse. Notwithstanding the limited activism evidenced by most petition signers, I have considered their profile in conjunction with others whose antislavery conviction seemed more certain.

As with Washtenaw's temperance activists, only about a third of the county's abolitionists and Free Soilers could be linked to a church. Also as with temperance, Presbyterians and Congregationalists—whose churches, as noted in chapter 2, often coalesced in Michigan during the early to mid-

147. The extent to which these petitioners' names appeared in other extant antislavery sources varied according to the petition's date and township of origin. For example, 249 Washtenaw County residents signed petitions sent to the Twenty-fifth or Twenty-sixth Congresses (1837–41), including the petition published in the *Michigan Argus,* March 2, 1837. Of this group, only 57 (22.9 percent) were linked to other antislavery causes or activities. Those petitions sent to the Twenty-seventh Congress (1841–43) contained 134 names, of whom 65 (48.5 percent) were traced to other antislavery causes or activities. The higher figure, though, is weighted by the high abolitionist presence on the petitions collected in Ann Arbor in 1841. Of the 56 Ann Arbor petitions, 41 (73.2 percent) were linked to the Michigan State Anti-Slavery Society, the Liberty or Free Soil Parties, subscribed to the *Signal of Liberty,* or publicly protested the U.S. Congressional gag rule in 1842. In contrast, of the petitioners to the Twenty-seventh congress from Saline (15) and Sharon and Manchester (63), the names of only 5 (3.3 percent) and 19 (30.2 percent, respectively, appeared in other sources linking them to antislavery. Ann Arbor petitioners clearly focused upon the local abolitionist community. Comparing the number of petitioners in Sharon and Manchester with the Liberty Party returns for these townships, however, it is evident that activists in both places went beyond the Liberty Party's community in pursuit of signatures (Tables 10 through 20). On the other hand, subscribers to the *Signal of Liberty*—to be discussed later— were more likely to be linked to other forms of antislavery activity; 157 of 323 (48.6 percent) and only 146 of 323 (45.2 percent) did not show up in antislavery, temperance, or benevolence sources.

nineteenth century—were the largest denominational segment of antislavery, constituting almost half of those abolitionists with identifiable church linkages. Regular Methodists were not as well represented among abolitionists as in the temperance ranks, but their religious cousins, the Wesleyan Methodists, were almost as common in the antislavery columns as the Episcopalians, a denomination with a more numerous membership. Few Baptists were traced to the movement during the 1830s, but they were more common during the 1840s. Again, as with the temperance cause in Washtenaw and Tuscaloosa Counties, abolition commenced among Presbyterians and then spread to the Methodists and Baptists during the 1840s (Table 33).

An examination of the antislavery rank-and-file also confirms the contemporary observation that most abolitionists came from the Whig Party. Of the 131 Liberty Party members of Washtenaw County whose prior political affiliation was traceable, 118 (90.1 percent) were former Whigs, and only 13 (9.9 percent) were former Democrats. But of course, party affiliation for some mid-nineteenth-century voters fluctuated. Thus, of the 353 Washtenaw County individuals who were linked to the Liberty Party, 11 subsequently went to the Democrats. Of the 29 Liberty Party members who publicly announced in 1844 their intention to vote for Henry Clay, 4 were again linked to the Whigs following the 1844 election, and only 1 was subsequently traced to the Liberty Party; in addition to these individuals, 9 other Libertyites were later found in the Whig ranks. Whigs were also well represented among abolitionists of the 1830s. Of the 83 individuals traced to abolition prior to formation of the Liberty Party, the party affiliation was found for 52 of these activists. Only 2 Democrats were located in this group, as against 36 Whigs—19 of whom were later found in the Liberty ranks, while 1 was subsequently a Free Soiler—and 14 were connected with the Liberty Party but had no discernible prior party affiliation. A similar pattern was present among the 241 signers of county petitions submitted to the 25th and 26th Congresses and the petition published in the *Michigan Argus* in 1837. The names of only 117 individuals could be correlated with a political party affiliation, of whom 15 were Democrats, 88 Whigs—19 and 1 of whom subsequently affiliated with the Liberty and Free Soil Parties, respectively—13 Libertyites, and 1 Free Soiler who could not be linked to any prior political affiliation. The petitions to the 27th Congress were submitted after the creation of the Liberty party, and describing the political affiliations of these signers is less complicated. Of these 134 petitioners, 87 were linked to a political party, of whom 53 were Libertyites, 2 were Free Soilers who could not be traced to the Liberty Party, 23 were Whigs, and 9 were Democrats. Antislavery sympathizers and former Liberty Party members, however, constituted the largest segment of the Free Soilers. Among the 138 Washtenaw individuals linked to the latter party, 82 had a traceable prior political affiliation, of whom 49, 18, and 15 were former Libertyites, Whigs, and Democrats, respectively. The long-standing antislavery proclivities of these Free Soilers are also evident in that over half—71 of the 138—were linked to the Liberty Party, the MSASS, the 1842 Ann Arbor protest of the congressional gag rule, antislavery petitions, the efforts within a church to declare slavery a sin, or the subscription list of the *Signal of Liberty*.[148]

Similar to Washtenaw County's temperance community, the vast majority of abolitionists, Free Soilers, and petitioners from all cohorts with ascertainable places of birth were from the North—86.1 percent were born in New York or New England—and were more likely to hail from these regions than was the case with the control group of south-central Michigan officeholders described in chapter 4:

Place of Birth	Number
New England (Mass. 66, Vt. 55, Conn. 50, N.H. 15, R.I. 2)	188
New York	251
Other Middle States (N.J. 12, Penn. 10)	22
Old Northwest (Mich. 1, Ohio 2)	3
South (Va. 1, Md. 2, Ky. 1)	4
Foreign (England 21, Ireland 7, Germany 6, Canada 5, Scotland 2)	41
Total	509

But in contrast to Washtenaw County's temperance and benevolence movements, antislavery was less likely to draw its constituency from the ranks of shopkeepers/proprietors and professionals who resided in the county's villages and towns and was more apt to attract farmers and artisans. Similar to the earliest manifestations of the temperance movement in Washtenaw County, though, the abolitionists active in the cause prior to the formation of the Liberty Party were the wealthiest of the persons who became active in the

148. Regarding sources of political party affiliation, see n. 92 in chap. 4 herein. On the prior political ties of Free Soilers, see n. 83 this chap.

movement and the ones most likely to hold a professional occupation. Of the 83 members of this cohort, an occupation could be attached to 44, of whom 14 (31.8 percent) were professionals (including 9 clergy and 2 newspaper editors), followed by farmers (12, or 27.3 percent), artisans (10, or 22.7 percent), those who were found on the 1850 census but for whom no occupation was listed (4, or 9.1 percent), shopkeepers/proprietors (3, or 6.8 percent), and no occupation (1, or 2.3 percent). The real-estate holdings of 32 were ascertainable from the 1850 census, the median and mean holdings being $2,000 and $2,505, respectively. A different profile results when we examine all the signers of the anti-slavery petitions. Because Washtenaw's abolitionists circulated petitions in the towns and countryside, the occupational profile of these signers better reflected the county's rural character. The occupations of only 154 of the 369 signers could be found, of whom half (77, or 50.0 percent) were farmers, followed by artisans (34, or 22.1 percent), shopkeepers/proprietors (18, or 11.7 percent), professionals (17, or 11.0 percent), nothing listed on census (5, or 3.2 percent), clerks (2, or 1.3 percent), and no occupation (1, or 0.6 percent). The median and mean real estate holdings were $1,600 and $3,043, for the 135 petition signers located on the 1850 census.

Although antislavery petitioners—considered collectively—formed the largest cohort, it is without question that those active in the Liberty Party constituted the largest portion (353) of engaged abolitionists. More so than the petitioners, Liberty Party members were identified from throughout the county—often as candidates for county and township office—and not only through lists of people present at abolitionist gatherings, which almost always occurred in villages. Of the 213 who were linked to an occupation, almost half (105, or 49.3 percent) were farmers, followed by artisans (54, or 25.3 percent), professionals (25, or 11.7 percent—including 10 clergy, 9 physicians, and 3 attorneys), nothing listed on census (11, or 5.2 percent), shopkeepers/proprietors (12, or 5.6 percent), clerks (3, or 1.4 percent), laborers and no occupation (1 each, or 0.5 percent). The median and mean real-wealth holdings of the 195 subjects found on the 1850 census were $1,500 and $2,341. Subscribers to the *Signal of Liberty* displayed a similar profile. As with the subscribers to the *Michigan Temperance Herald* described in chapter 4, or the petitioners considered in this chapter, there is no guarantee that all of Washtenaw County's 323 subscribers to the *Signal*—only one of whom was a woman, while five were African American males—were ardent abolitionists.[149] It is likely that some subscrib-

---

149. In "Great Majority," 341, I counted only those individuals—310—who lived in Wash-

ers were antislavery Whigs or Democrats or apolitical moral suasionists, and took the paper because it was the only one in Michigan dedicated to abolition. A few individuals must have subscribed merely to keep a watchful eye on the machinations of a rival political party. Notwithstanding these caveats, the majority of the 154 Washtenaw County subscribers whose political party affiliation could be determined were Liberty Party members (112, or 72.7 percent), followed by 17 Free Soilers who were never identified as Libertyites, 12 Democrats, 11 Whigs, and 2 persons who were active in a small nativist party in Ann Arbor during the mid-1840s.[150] The MSASS executive committee argued that regular readership of the *Signal* created a positive effect upon antislavery commitment: "The weekly return of antislavery intelligence to the fireside of the citizen is admirably calculated to produce a permanent impression upon his mind, and to excite a continued interest in the subject. It is not too much to say, that no intelligent man can be a constant reader of a well conducted antislavery paper, without an abiding conviction of the great truths of the antislavery enterprise."[151] And since both the Liberty Party's voter turnout and the number of *Signal of Liberty* subscribers declined after 1846—about the time that the list was created—it is likely that many of the names on this list were among the most devoted rank-and-file Libertyites in Michigan.

Of the 243 Washtenaw County male subscribers whose occupation could be found, the largest segment were farmers (117, or 48.1 percent), followed by artisans (74, or 30.5 percent), professionals (24, or 9.9 percent, including 8 physicians, 6 clergy, and 6 attorneys), shopkeepers/proprietors (12, or 4.9 percent), nothing listed on the census (8, or 3.3 percent), laborers (4, or 1.6 percent), clerks and other (2 each, or 0.8 percent each). Although almost a fourth of the 1,375 subscribers came from Washtenaw County, as did the majority of the *Signal*'s advertising, the paper was well received throughout the state's lower four tiers of counties due to an aggressive network of agents who solicited subscrip-

tenaw County at the time they subscribed to the *Signal of Liberty*, as Washtenaw County residents. In the present work, I also include those who at one time lived in the county but subsequently relocated elsewhere.

150. All of these party linkages were based upon post-1840 political affiliations. In addition to these individuals, 28 subscribers were traced to other forms of antislavery activity—including petition signing; of these, 6 had political links to the Whigs, Democrats, or Nativists of the 1840s. Furthermore, of those *Signal of Liberty* subscribers for whom no political affiliation could be determined during the life of the Liberty Party, 17 were traced to the Whig party prior to 1841, and 5 subscribers were found among the Democrats before 1841. The *Signal of Liberty* subscription list is in the Foster Papers.

151. *Signal of Liberty*, February 16, 1842.

tions. The rural character of abolitionism is even more pronounced when we look at the occupational profile of *Signal* subscribers throughout the state. Of the 870 Michigan subscribers—including those from Washtenaw County—whose occupations could be ascertained, a considerable majority (527, or 60.6 percent) were farmers, followed by artisans (181, or 20.8 percent), professionals (74, or 8.5 percent, including 30 physicians, 25 clergy, and 12 attorneys), shop-keepers/proprietors (40, or 4.6 percent), laborers (16, or 1.8 percent), no occupations listed in the census (15, or 1.7 percent), clerks (8, or 0.9 percent), and other (7, or 0.8 percent). Two entries (0.2 percent), were illegible. With the exception of the disproportionately low representation of laborers, the occupational profile of this cohort of abolitionists mirrored that of the adult male work force in Michigan in 1850: farmers, 60.3 percent; artisans, 16.4 percent; laborers, 15.3 percent; professionals, 4.2 percent; shopkeepers/proprietors, 2.7 percent; and other, 1.1 percent. The mean real estate holdings of 227 Washtenaw and 824 statewide white male subscribers to the *Signal of Liberty* were $1,910 and $1,670, respectively (medians of both, $1,000)—both of which were higher than the respective mean household real estate holdings in 1850 of the population at large, $1,485 and $1,048.[152]

These occupational findings accord with the understanding that contemporaries had of the antislavery movement in Michigan. Theodore Foster's assertion of the Liberty Party's strong clerical voice seems to be borne out; indeed, the 3.0 percent of the Michigan subscribers with identifiable occupations who were members of the clergy was far in excess of the 0.5 percent of the statewide occupational profile of the adult male population. But more important is the large number of farmers found among *Signal* subscribers. Foster reported in his paper that "the great majority of our subscribers are farmers, and have expected to pay their subscriptions as soon as they dispose of their crops."[153] This fact should not be surprising, given that 92.7 percent of Michigan's 1850 population lived on farms or in towns of fewer than 2,500—a boundary used often to distinguish "urban" from "rural" (84.7 percent of the national population,

152. There were 1,267 individual subscribers to the *Signal of Liberty* in Michigan. See Quist, "Great Majority," 333 n. 13. The mean real-estate holdings for Michigan were calculated from *Statistics of the State of Michigan, Compiled from the Census of 1850*, 158, 159, 170, 171; the state's occupational profile was compiled from De Bow, *Seventh Census*, 902–903.

153. De Bow, *Seventh Census*, 902–903; *Signal of Liberty*, September 11, 1843. Foster offered no insights, however, on the similarly large number of physicians among his subscribers. Regarding the rural dimensions of antislavery in Michigan, see Quist, "Great Majority."

and 80.1 percent of the northern population in 1850 were also rural). The rural character of abolitionism, however, is a point that has occasionally eluded scholars of the movement's constituency, as they have sometimes utilized sources generated in urban locales, and then concluded that artisans made up the core of abolitionism. Nevertheless, viewing Liberty Party activists and *Signal* subscribers in Ann Arbor village—which with a population of 4,025 was Michigan's second largest population center in 1850—shows that the urban antislavery constituency in Michigan was similarly dominated by artisans. Of the 88 Ann Arbor village subscribers for whom an occupation could be found, 53 (60.2 percent) were artisans, followed by professionals (13, or 14.8 percent), shopkeepers/proprietors (10, or 11.4 percent), nothing listed on census (5, or 5.7 percent), farmers (4, or 4.5 percent), clerks, laborers and other (1 each, or 1.1 percent); of the 43 Ann Arbor village Liberty Party activists who could be linked to an occupation, the largest portion again was artisans (20, or 46.5 percent), followed by professionals (10, or 23.3 percent), farmers (5, or 11.6 percent), shopkeepers/proprietors (3, or 7.0 percent), laborers and nothing listed on census (2 each, or 4.7 percent), and no occupation (1, or 2.3 percent).[154]

Protestors of the congressional gag rule who assembled in Ann Arbor in 1842 were mostly from Ann Arbor and its immediate rural environs and thus had an occupational profile similar to that of the Ann Arbor subscribers to the *Signal of Liberty*. The occupations of only 40 of the 66 members of this latter

---

154. *Historical Statistics of the United States: Colonial Times to 1970* (Washington, D.C., 1975), 12, 22, 29; *Michigan Argus*, August 21, 1850. For other studies of the abolitionist rank and file, see David Donald, "Toward a Reconsideration of Abolitionists," in his *Lincoln Reconsidered: Essays on the Civil War Era* (New York, 1956), 19–36; Robert Allen Skotheim, "A Note on Historical Method: David Donald's 'Toward a Reconsideration of Abolitionists,'" *Journal of Southern History*, XXV (August 1959), 356–65; Gerald Sorin, "The Historical Theory of Political Radicalism: Michigan Abolitionists as a Test Case" (M. A. Thesis, Wayne State University, 1964); Gerald Sorin, *The New York Abolitionists: A Case Study of Political Radicalism* (Westport, Conn., 1971); Leonard Richards, *"Gentlemen of Property and Standing": Anti-Abolitionist Mobs in Jacksonian America* (New York, 1970); John Jentz, "The Antislavery Constituency in Jacksonian New York City," *Civil War History*, XXVII (June 1981), 101–22; Edward Magdol, *The Antislavery Rank and File: A Social Profile of the Abolitionists' Constituency* (Westport, Conn., 1986); Alan M. Kraut, "The Liberty Men of New York: Political Abolitionism in New York State" (Ph.D. dissertation, Cornell University, 1975), 307–61; Alan M. Kraut, "The Forgotten Reformers: A Profile of Third Party Abolitionists in Antebellum New York," *Antislavery Reconsidered*, ed. Perry and Fellman, 119–48; Hewitt, *Women's Activism*, 266–73; Debra Gold Hansen, *Strained Sisterhood: Gender and Class in the Boston Female Anti-Slavery Society* (Amherst, Mass., 1993), 64–92. I have further developed my argument regarding the antislavery constituency in Quist, "Great Majority."

group were ascertained, of whom artisans (16, or 40 percent) were foremost, followed by farmers (12, or 30 percent), professionals (5, or 12.5 percent), shop-keepers/proprietors (4, or 10 percent), and no occupation (2, or 5.0 percent), and clerk (1, or 2.5 percent). In contrast, Washtenaw County Free Soilers were similar to the countywide Liberty Party with respect to occupation, as the largest portion again was farmers (48 of 111, or 43.2 percent), followed by arti-sans (35, or 31.5 percent), professionals (16, or 14.4 percent), shopkeepers/pro-prietors (7, or 6.3 percent), nothing listed on census and clerk (2 each, or 1.8 per-cent), and no occupation (1, or 0.9 percent). The gag rule protestors were slightly less wealthy than the Free Soilers; the mean property holding for the former was $1,906 (median $1,000; thirty-two subjects were found on the 1850 federal census), while for the latter it was $2,454 (median $1,250; 102 subjects).

Exactly why the antislavery message was best received by farmers and arti-sans is difficult, if not impossible, to determine conclusively. This fact is espe-cially significant when we recall that the temperance movements and evangeli-cal benevolence in both Washtenaw and Tuscaloosa Counties were usually dominated by professionals. Perhaps part of the explanation lies in the fact that the sources used to identify many abolitionists—a newspaper subscription list and a partially reconstructed roster of Liberty candidates for county and town-ship office—better register the rural support for reform than they do any other sources. Without question, few Michiganders would have explained their po-sition on abolition as a function of their occupation.

Nevertheless, this concentration of antislavery support among artisans and farmers merits some consideration. Theodore Foster's comment that the "most influential citizens" of northern cities resisted abolitionism because they "were connected with slaveholders, by ties of business, consanguinity, or friendship" was assuredly less true for the small towns of Michigan than it was for the large cities of the northeast.[155] Of course, the fact that farmers and artisans were the two largest occupational categories in Michigan undeniably contributed to the shape of the antislavery constituency. But the strong antislavery sentiment among farmers and artisans may also have reflected recognition by members of these groups, who lived by the sweat of their brow, that slavery demeaned their own labor. And the fact that most abolitionists in Michigan were either farm-ers or artisans certainly shaped abolitionist rhetoric—for example, in aboli-tionist vituperations against the Slave Power. One writer warned northerners

155. Theodore Foster, "Liberty Party," 67.

that southern slaveholders aspired eventually to enslave free state workers: "It seems unreasonable to suppose that slaveholding principles should recognize the right of laborers to possess any share in the administration of government. . . . The leading trait in their system of policy, as avowed by their most prominent statesmen, is, that *all laborers ought to be slaves.*" It was undoubtedly this laboring constituency that Theodore Foster had in mind when he inserted the following remarks in the *Signal of Liberty:*

> We showed, last week, that at the South, all laborers, throughout the earth, are accounted and denominated slaves. Another principle naturally follows close upon that, which is, that *laborers ought not to have any voice in making or executing the laws.* . . . If these slaveholders could legislate for Michigan, they would deprive of the privilege of voting, and of holding office . . . all who "depend upon their daily labor for their subsistence," viz: All the agriculturists who have not property enough to live without work. . . . The whole government of the state would then be in the hands of the members of the learned professions . . . and of such other individuals as might be able to live without manual labor. . . . Upon this principle, six thousand men would legislate for the whole state, while more than fifty thousand would be deprived of all political privileges. . . . Such are the principles by which the laboring classes in the slave states are governed, and these same principles the slaveholding statesmen would rejoice to see bringing into subjection, and grinding down to slavery, the free working men of Michigan, and of all the free states. . . . It is not strange that, having such feelings toward the freemen of the North, they should treat their petitions with contempt and scorn. What right have slaves to petition? What do laboring men know about public affairs?[156]

Abolitionists were also more likely than the population at large, and even than most temperance cohorts, to send their children to school—suggesting that abolitionists, as well as temperance and benevolence activists in both Washtenaw and Tuscaloosa Counties, were more receptive to the growth of the market than was the population at large:[157]

156. *Signal of Liberty,* February 2, 1842, May 19, 1841. For other expressions of this theme, see *ibid.,* May 26, June 2, 1841, May 16, 1842, June 12, September 18, 1843, December 9, 1844, April 7, 1845, September 26, 1846, and Williston H. Lofton, "Abolition and Labor," *Journal of Negro History,* XXXIII (July 1948), 249–83.

157. Through the examination of aggregate-level data—rather than individual-level data as has been done in this study—Vernon L. Volpe argues that in the townships where the Liberty

Antislavery cohort	Children 5–19 of parents in cohort, 1850	# children in school, 1850	Percent
1836–40 (pre-Liberty)	64	54	84.4
1837–42 petition signers	293	261	89.1
Liberty Party activists	365	324	88.8
1842 gag rule protestors	68	59	86.8
Signal of Liberty subscribers (whites)	422	369	87.4
Non-Liberty abolitionists, 1841–48	29	25	86.2
Free Soilers	202	182	90.1
Non–Free Soil abolitionists, 1850–60	10	8	80.0
Female abolitionists	25	21	84.0
Afr.-American abolitionists	20	3	15.0
All white male abolitionists and antislavery petitioners	898	785	87.4

The importance of education appeared frequently in Michigan's antislavery rhetoric. Indeed, Michigan abolitionists considered "the diffusion of education among all classes" to be integral to their agenda and announced at the Liberty Party state convention in 1843 that education "will most effectively promote the interests of free-labor and thereby advance the prosperity of the country." Theodore Foster further insisted that the advancement of common schools worked to promote well-being. "The interests of every man requires that all his fellow citizens should be able to read and write, keep accounts and understand geography," Foster claimed. Additionally, he maintained that Massachusetts was prosperous because "knowledge is generally diffused there"; South Carolina, on the other hand, was a "savage nation" and its workers "stupid, indolent creatures" because only "the rich are well educated." Abolitionists in Oakland County agreed that the institution of slavery stood op-

Party was most successful, the party's members retreated from the expansion of the market. Volpe, *Forlorn Hope*, esp. 56–79.

posed to the spread of common schools, and caused higher illiteracy, even among the southern free population.[158]

Another significant contrast between abolitionists and temperance enthusiasts is in their years of birth. Whereas the median ages of the various temperance cohorts in 1850 ranged from thirty-five to fifty-four, the median and mean age of abolitionists fell within a narrower spectrum:

Antislavery cohort	White males in cohort	# with known age	Median age	Median yr. of birth
1836–1840 (pre-Liberty)	83	37	45	1805
1837–1842 petition signers	368	139	46	1804
Liberty Party activists	353	201	43	1807
1842 gag rule protestors	66	34	41	1809
Signal of Liberty subscribers	317	225	42	1808
Non-Liberty abolitionists, 1841–48	46	12	47.5	1802
Free Soilers	138	104	42	1808
Non–Free Soil abolitionists, 1850–60	22	14	38	1812
White male abolitionists and antislavery petitioners, all	999	422	43	1807
Female abolitionists	27	15	34	1816
African American abolitionists	9	9	38	1812

When compared with a control group of adult white males in Michigan in 1850, the similarity of ages among all Washtenaw County abolitionist groups dominated by white males—and among *Signal of Liberty* subscribers—becomes even more striking (Table 34). In 1850 the largest ten-year age interval among all adult white males in Michigan was for those between twenty and twenty-nine; succeeding age groups decreased in number by an interval of about 8 percent. Abolitionists, on the other hand were underrepresented among men in their twenties and peaked in the forty to forty-nine age bracket—although they were most clustered between the ages of thirty-five and forty-five. And notwithstanding that the number of abolitionists decreased significantly in the two succeeding age groups, men aged fifty and

158. *Signal of Liberty,* February 20, April 10, March 27, 1843, October 20, 1845.

above nonetheless constituted a larger percentage of the abolitionist population than they did of the state population.

Given that they had more time to accumulate wealth, the greater ages of abolitionists were undoubtedly part of the reason they owned more property than
the population at large and had few laborers in their ranks; many of those classified on the census as "laborer" may have been young men who had not yet acquired enough capital to purchase a farm or the tools with which to commence
a trade. But it is also important that a number of other scholars, primarily investigating abolitionists of the 1830s, have found that these earlier opponents
of slavery were united by an age cohort not substantially different from that of
Signal of Liberty subscribers a decade later. For example, David Donald, who
authored the first serious examination of the antislavery rank-and-file, recognized that most of his subjects were born between 1790 and 1810; Lewis Perry
noted that many of the Garrisonian abolitionists were born between 1795 and
1805; a majority of Edward Magdol's subjects were born between the late 1790s
and the mid-1810s; and James McElroy revealed that his abolitionists dated
their births between 1790 and 1820. Analyzing abolitionism from the 1840s,
both Alan M. Kraut and Chris Padgett discovered that most of their subjects
were born from 1800 to 1820.[159]

This age cohort around which these abolitionists were centered is highly
significant, as it suggests that belief in abolitionism was a generational phenomenon. "Common experience precipitates common perceptions and out-
looks," Arthur M. Schlesinger Jr. observed. "People tend to be shaped
throughout their lives by the events and ideals dominating the time when they
arrived at political consciousness."[160] Naturally, the question most difficult to
answer is what events and ideals may have shaped Americans born during the

159. Donald, "Toward a Reconsideration of Abolitionists," 26–27; Lewis Perry, *Radical Abo-
litionism: Anarchy and the Government of God in Antislavery Thought* (Ithaca, 1973), 33; Magdol,
Antislavery Rank and File, 64; James L. McElroy, "Social Control and Romantic Reform: The
Case of Rochester, New York," *New York History*, LVIII (January 1977), 17–46; Kraut, "Liberty
Men of New York," 339, 353; Padgett, "Hearing the Antislavery Rank-and-File," 75. Boston's female abolitionists identified by Debra Gold Hansen had an average age of 33 in 1835, while James
M. McPherson, who did not specify when his abolitionists were active in the movement, found
that their median year of birth was 1805. Hansen, *Strained Sisterhood*, 66; McPherson, *Ordeal by
Fire*, 47–48. Allen P. Stouffer, *The Light of Nature and the Law of God: Antislavery in Ontario, 1833–
1877* (Baton Rouge, 1992), 172, 174, discovered a birth cohort for abolitionists in Canada similar to
the one identified here.

160. Arthur M. Schlesinger Jr., *The Cycles of American History* (Boston, 1986), 29–30.

early national period to cause a significant minority of them to embrace abolitionism. If individuals develop their values and ideology during the formative years of adolescence and young adulthood—as a number of scholars have suggested—then it is likely that the world views of many individual abolitionists were shaped by the revivals of the Second Great Awakening. As we have seen repeatedly throughout this chapter, the rhetoric of abolitionists was frequently interwoven with evangelical language, and they were often more successful in having their churches accept antislavery resolutions than in convincing the major political parties to do the same. Of course, revivals were present throughout America during the early nineteenth century, and most people who were touched by the revival—particularly white southerners—did not subsequently endorse abolitionism. Nevertheless, a number of studies have demonstrated close ties between abolitionism and revivalism, suggesting that while revivalism did not necessarily lead to abolitionism, the crusade against slavery found fertile soil among northerners—most notably those with roots in New England and New York—whose religious and social awareness had been aroused through a conversion.[161]

But beyond sharing this generational affinity, abolitionists failed to recruit many supporters who were born after the mid-1810s. Of course, the Liberty Party's lack of success may have made it seem a futile enterprise to those who were awakening to political consciousness during the 1840s. But it may also be significant that revivalism was waning at this time. Justin Marsh, a Presbyterian pastor in Augusta Township, conducted many revivals throughout the 1830s and early 1840s. In 1845, however, he was alarmed over declining interest in religion: "The dearth of revivals in our whole nation is at present most distressing. It seems that the number in our churches that have been excommunicated, & those that have been removed from earth, is greater than the number of those who have been added. The same it appears is general fact in all evangelical denominations." Others similarly sounded the alarm. Between 1847 and 1849 the Baptist *Michigan Christian Herald* constantly bemoaned the pau-

161. Regarding the formation of one's belief-system during youth, see *ibid.*, 29–30, and Lois Banner, "Religion and Reform in the Early Republic: The Role of Youth," *American Quarterly*, XXV (Winter 1971), 677–95. On revivalism and reform, see Gilbert Barnes, *Antislavery Impulse;* Cross, *Burned-Over District;* Thomas, "Romantic Reform in America," 656–81; McElroy, "Social Control and Romantic Reform," 17–46; Paul Johnson, *Shopkeepers' Millennium;* and John L. Hammond, *The Politics of Benevolence: Revival Religion and American Voting Behavior* (Norwood, N.J., 1979).

city of revivals in both the state and the nation, and the Webster Presbyterian Church reported with some concern in 1853 that it had been eight years since the last revival. The decrease in the number of revivals after the early 1840s was not a lamentation peculiar to contemporary Michigan commentators; it has also been observed by twentieth-century scholars investigating New York and New England.[162] One reason the growth of abolitionism may have slowed during the mid-to-late 1840s is that revivalism had run its course and therefore could not prick the social conscience of the rising generation.

In this chapter we have seen how abolitionism in Washtenaw County evolved, as did temperance, from favoring moral suasion to seeking its objectives through the ballot box. Abolitionists sometimes worked within political parties and churches, but they almost always failed to convert these organizations into abolition societies. Nevertheless, even before the sectionalist controversy over Texas, they succeeded in softening the Democrats' and Whigs' hostility to antislavery—even if much of this change in attitude was due to the dynamics of party politics rather than to any increased compassion for American slaves—and they convinced many nonabolitionist churches to accept the sinfulness of slavery. As with temperance and benevolence, sources on the activity of Washtenaw women in antislavery are scarce. Notwithstanding this paucity, it appears that the abolitionist activism of a few women led them to reconsider the relations between the sexes. Farmers made up the largest segment

162. Justin Marsh to AHMS, March 18, 1845, in AHMS Papers; *Michigan Christian Herald,* January 4–June 7, 1847, *passim,* August 30, 1847, November 8, 1847-February 18, 1848, *passim,* July 14, 1848, January 19, 26, 1849; *Primitive Expounder,* November 4, 1847; "Narrative of the State of Religion in the Church of Webster—to the Presbytery of Washtenaw," February 1, 1853, in "Histories of Churches in Washtenaw Presbytery," Dubuar Papers; Samuel W. Dike, "A Study of New England Revivals," *American Journal of Sociology,* XV (November 1909), 361–78; Cross, *Burned-Over District,* 268–70, 274, 354; Hewitt, *Women's Activism,* 127; Randolph A. Roth, *The Democratic Dilemma: Religion, Reform, and the Social Order in the Connecticut River Valley of Vermont, 1791–1850* (Cambridge, Eng., 1987), 219; Curtis Johnson, *Islands of Holiness,* 74–75, 183; Maffly-Kipp, *Religion and Society in Frontier California,* 41–42. Although Timothy L. Smith, *Revivalism and Social Reform in Mid-Nineteenth-Century America,* 45–62, does not maintain that the frequency of revivals increased during the 1840s, he nevertheless asserts that revivalism gained greater legitimacy in American churches between 1840 and 1857. And although they are not generally considered to be "evangelical"—and thus possibly not as deeply influenced by the revivals of the Second Great Awakening—51 of the 63 (81.0 percent) Indiana Quaker abolitionists identified by Thomas Hamm *et al.* were born between 1792 and 1821; Thomas D. Hamm *et al.,* "Moral Choices: Two Indiana Quaker Communities and the Abolition Movement," *Indiana Magazine of History,* LXXXVII (June 1991), 138, 140, 154.

of the abolitionist constituency in Michigan, although in the larger villages, such as Ann Arbor, the cause was dominated by artisans—in contrast to temperance and benevolence, where professionals and shopkeepers/proprietors were predominant. On the whole, abolitionists owned more real wealth than the population at large and were neither poor outcasts nor a displaced elite. Similar to benevolence and temperance activists in both Tuscaloosa and Washtenaw Counties, abolitionists welcomed the market economy, as the overwhelming majority sent their children to school. These correlates should not, of course, be equated with motivation, but they do let us know in what quarters the abolitionist message best resonated.

Despite the comfortable lives led by many of Washtenaw County's abolitionists, and notwithstanding their minor successes within religious and political circles, their passion for antislavery caused a few to act in ways that undoubtedly complicated their lives or even made them outcasts in their own communities. Eli Benton, Timothy Hunt, and Guy Beckley, all of whom had devoted their time, talents, and wealth to their respective Presbyterian, Baptist, and Methodist churches, followed their antislavery convictions rather than remain tied to what they believed were proslavery institutions. The remonstrances and tears showered upon William M. Sullivan by his Methodist relatives were doubtless experienced by other abolitionists. Leaving one's political party was probably not as traumatic, but when Seymour Treadwell noted that Whigs and Democrats were "wedded" to their parties by a thousand *"endearing* and almost indissoluble ties," he recognized that more was at stake in political party membership than simply ideological conviction. Many abolitionist gatherings—meetings of the Liberty Party, the state antislavery society, come-outer denominations, the Monthly Concert of Prayer for the Enslaved, their separate Independence Day celebrations, and even perhaps the underground railroad—certainly provided a sense of community for individuals who held a radically different vision of America from that of most of their contemporaries.

Conclusion

Writing in 1841, an unidentified author asked the readers of the *Signal of Liberty* whether in the slaveholding states there was ever assembled "a state or county convention for the purpose of promoting any interest not directly connected with slavery?"[1] To be sure, white Tuscaloosans took extraordinary measures to safeguard the peculiar institution. They passed laws regulating slave activities, rang a bell every evening to remind everyone that all slaves were required to be in their quarters, created slave patrols, formed a vigilance society that publicly protested and forcibly halted the distribution of antislavery publications, and indicted a New York abolitionist *in absentia.* It would be difficult to argue, however, that all of Tuscaloosa County's temperance and benevolence activity was explicitly directed toward the perpetuation of slavery. It is true that reform efforts in Tuscaloosa were occasionally aimed at the local slave community, but these pursuits—particularly those of the temperance, Bible, tract, and Sunday-school societies among Tuscaloosa's African Americans—constituted only a small portion of reformist activities. Most reform enterprises were directed toward whites, and there is little evidence to suggest that white Tuscaloosans viewed them with suspicion.

But perhaps most significant is the fact that abolitionists shared many reformist ideals with the whites of Tuscaloosa County. Theodore Foster's articles on evangelical benevolence in the *Signal of Liberty* often criticized national societies for their complicity with slavery and denounced white southerners for refusing to extend Bibles, tracts, and Sunday schools to the slave community, but he shared with many white Tuscaloosans the conviction that the fate of America lay in such benevolent projects. Many of Washtenaw County's lead-

1. *Signal of Liberty,* September 1, 1841.

ing proponents of Bibles, tracts, and Sunday schools were also abolitionists, and many among Tuscaloosa's slaveholders were also proponents of these evangelical pursuits. This fundamental similarity between northern and southern reform has too often been obscured in the historiography of the subject. A classic work in this field, Louis Filler's *Crusade Against Slavery*, labels antislavery as the "central hub of reform." It is understandable that one could reach this conclusion after looking solely at the northern manifestations of reform. Yet if a scholar examined reform in the South and ignored important activities in the North, then he or she could reasonably conclude that reform—particularly temperance and evangelical benevolence—was the domain of slaveholders.

The similarities between the two counties' temperance movements are striking. Not only were slaveholders and abolitionists each disproportionately active in temperance, but the evolution of the cause in both counties proceeded in a like fashion. Temperance commenced in both places as an upper-class affair that, through moral suasion, called only for the end of hard-liquor consumption; by the late 1830s, temperance devotees in Tuscaloosa and Washtenaw adopted total abstinence and tried to halt the legal sale of liquor. They reverted to moral suasion during the early 1840s and embraced first the cause of the Washingtonians and later the regalia of the Sons of Temperance. Washtenaw County commenced a series of local-option referendums in 1845, while Tuscaloosa town and Northport enacted $1,000-license laws in 1851 and flirted with various high-license laws for the remainder of the decade. During the 1850s temperance partisans in both states rallied for legislatively sanctioned prohibition. Although prohibitionists were more successful in Michigan than in Alabama, activism on behalf of the "Alabama Law" was nevertheless considerable. And following the failure of statewide prohibition in Michigan and the unsuccessful local-option campaign in Alabama, antebellum temperance went into another of its recurrent periods of moribundity. The parallel development of the temperance movement in both states underlines how this cause was a national effort and suggests that enthusiasts in both states closely monitored temperance activities elsewhere. Additionally, the rank and file of temperance and benevolence in both counties showed—through their occupations, wealth, and willingness to send their children to school—a strong affinity for the growth of the market economy.[2]

2. Filler, *Crusade Against Slavery*, xiii. See also William E. Gienapp, "Abolitionism and the Nature of Antebellum Reform," in *Courage and Conscience: Black and White Abolitionists in Boston*, ed. Donald M. Jacobs (Bloomington, Ind., 1993), 21–46.

Although not specifically addressed in this study, the spirit of reform was also present in both Alabama and Michigan with respect to the construction of asylums for the mentally ill, the growth of public education, and the abolition of capital punishment. During the 1850s, Tuscaloosa became the site for the Alabama Asylum for the Insane, and Michigan's analogous institution was established in Kalamazoo.[3] In both states promoters of education succeeded in instituting professional superintendence over public schools and endeavored to have teachers incorporate new instructional methods into the classroom. Although Alabama lagged behind Michigan in educational reform—partially because the southern state was harder hit by the depression of 1837—state legislators attempted to remedy some of the deficiencies with the Public Schools Act of 1854 and the Public Schools Amendments Act of 1856. Michigan was the first state in the Union to abolish capital punishment for first degree murder in 1846. This cause was less popular in Alabama, but it was not absent. Tuscaloosan Benjamin F. Porter, a member of the Alabama House of Representatives, succeeded in bringing the question up for a vote in the house in 1846, only to have it overwhelmingly defeated, 15–64.[4]

3. *Independent Monitor*, July 15, 1853, June 25, 1857; *Tuscaloosa Observer*, July 10, 1861; Basil Manly Diary No. 5, July 14, 1853; Thornton, *Politics and Power*, 302; Bill L. Weaver, "Establishing and Organizing the Alabama Insane Hospital, 1846–1861," *Alabama Review*, XLVIII (July 1995), 219–32; Dunbar and May, *Michigan*, 529; David J. Rothman, *The Discovery of the Asylum: Social Order and Disorder in the New Republic* (Boston, 1971). For further local sentiment regarding asylums, see *Alabama State Intelligencer*, June 1, 1833; *Flag of the Union*, November 8, 1837, June 20, 1838, January 23, 1839; *State Journal and Flag of the Union*, June 19, 1846; *Independent Monitor*, May 28, 1845, January 28, July 8, 1846, January 4, 1849; *Michigan Argus*, April 10, 1844; *Signal of Liberty*, October 16, 1847.

4. Thornton, *Politics and Power*, 293–95, 300–302, 304; Hunt, "Organizing a New South"; Dunbar and May, *Michigan*, 329–38; Edward W. Bennett, "The Reasons for Michigan's Abolition of Capital Punishment," *Michigan History*, LXII (November–December 1978), 42–55; *Independent Monitor*, January 28, 1846; Benjamin F. Porter, *Argument of Benjamin F. Porter. In Support of a Bill, Introduced by Him, in the House of Representatives of Alabama, to Abrogate the Punishment of Death* (Tuscaloosa, 1846). Paul M. Pruitt Jr., "An Antebellum Law Reformer: Passages in the Life of Benjamin F. Porter," *Gulf Coast Historical Review*, XI (Fall 1995), 22–58, provides a complete account of Porter's effort to abolish the death penalty in Alabama. Louis P. Masur, *Rites of Execution: Capital Punishment and the Transformation of American Culture, 1776–1865* (New York, 1989), analyzes the northern opposition to capital punishment but has little to say regarding the South, while Philip English Mackey, "Edward Livingston and the Origins of the Movement to Abolish Capital Punishment in America," *Louisiana History*, XVI (Spring 1975), 146–66, is only slightly more helpful.

Of course, these similarities can be pushed too far. Clearly there were essential differences in each county's reform climate. Foremost was the complete absence of the abolition movement in Tuscaloosa and its active presence in Washtenaw, which is underlined in the ways that colonization was denounced in both places—by some Michigan abolitionists as proslavery and by some Alabama slaveholders as abolitionist. Obviously the failure to eliminate capital punishment in Alabama stands in stark contrast to the movement's success in Michigan. The differences between the two counties extended to other reform causes as well. In some ways, women's rights made more headway in Alabama than in Michigan—for instance, during the 1850s, the Alabama legislature enacted a law that guaranteed separate estates to married women. But whereas in Michigan the question of women's suffrage was openly, if often derisively, discussed, there is no evidence that it was ever publicly and seriously debated in Tuscaloosa County.[5] And although women participated in reform in both counties, there were some differences here as well. True, Tuscaloosa's women who governed the Female Benevolent Society did so without any apparent male oversight; their case demonstrates that southern white women from slaveholding households sometimes created and managed their own voluntary associations. But despite John Warren's urging in the *Crystal Fount* that Alabama women form their own temperance societies, the evidence strongly indicates that female-operated bodies were more common in Michigan. While women in both places attended male-dominated temperance meetings and taught Sunday school, Washtenaw women took a more active role in the circulation of Bibles and tracts and were more likely to superintend their own societies. This lesser participation of Tuscaloosa County women implies that gender roles were more circumscribed in the southern locale. Notwithstanding the differing public roles of Tuscaloosa and Washtenaw women in reform efforts, how these dissimilarities affected reform objectives and ideology—if at all—is not clear. In any case, there is no evidence that antebellum women activists in either county moved from benevolence or temperance into protofeminist advocacy, and only a few isolated suggestions that antislavery activism caused women to reexamine their subordinate position with respect to men.

5. Thornton, *Politics and Power,* 471; Ellen Carol DuBois, *Feminism and Suffrage: The Emergence of an Independent Women's Movement in America, 1848–1869* (Ithaca, 1978), 41–42; Peggy A. Rabkin, "The Origins of Law Reform: The Social Significance of the Nineteenth-Century Certification Movement and Its Contribution to the Passage of the Early Married Women's Property Acts," *Buffalo Law Review,* XXIV (Spring 1975), 683–760.

The reception of Tuscaloosa and Washtenaw County residents to Fourierism also differed. Though we have not considered this subject heretofore, it merits a brief consideration. Notwithstanding that fewer Americans participated in communitarian ventures than in the other causes discussed in this study, the antebellum years were a period of communitarian activity in the North—both secular and religious—that was unequaled in the United States until the 1960s. Fourierist societies were of the secular variety. Based upon the teachings of Charles Fourier, a native of France, Fourierism was popularized in America by Albert Brisbane and Horace Greeley. Fourier was troubled by the class conflict, mean-spiritedness, and disorder of a competitive market economy, and he sought to implement a peaceful but radical restructuring of economic and social relationships by constructing ideal communities based upon scientific laws of unity that he had discovered. Each commune, or "phalanx," would be centered around a "phalanstery," or dwelling of the phalanx's 1,620 residents—although no American phalanx ever achieved Fourier's ideal size. Not only did phalanxes strive toward social harmony, but they also aimed to be economically self-sufficient and to provide social and cultural fulfillment for all their members. The successful operation of these phalanxes, Fourierists believed, would thus provide compelling evidence to the remainder of society of the inadequacy of conventional social and economic arrangements, and thus promote the complete reconstruction of society upon the basis of cooperation rather than competition.[6]

Fourierism was not only discussed in Washtenaw County between 1842 and 1846, but a number of residents were active in the "Washtenaw Phalanx"—a voluntary association promotive of Fourierism that was not, in this case, a residential cooperative—and assisted in the establishment of the Alphadelphia commune in Kalamazoo County. Although the Whig *Michigan State Journal* was especially favorable toward Fourierism, this cause also enjoyed support from some Democrats. While T. N. Caulkins, editor of the Ann Arbor *Democratic Herald,* rejoiced in the political victories of his party, he gloried "still more in the triumphs of Fourierists and the principles of Association, for the reason that we are confident that a Fourier Association will prove to be the perfection of political democracy." Caulkins tried to make this form of communitarianism palatable to the members of his party by explaining that when Fourierism was fully implemented, it would no longer be necessary to rely upon the

6. Carl J. Guarneri, *The Utopian Alternative: Fourierism in Nineteenth-Century America* (Ithaca, 1991).

state and federal governments to construct internal improvements—which governmental support the Democratic Party of the 1830s and 1840s opposed. On the other hand, Theodore Foster of the *Signal of Liberty* did not expect Fourieristic associations to become the new order of society, as he believed that under Fourierism, the *"depraved heart"* of humanity would encourage "a portion of the community to prey on the rest"—that is, individuals who preferred idleness would attempt to live off other people's labor. Nevertheless, a number of abolitionists—Sabin Felch, Converse J. Garland, and antislavery Whig George Corselius, for example—were active in the Washtenaw Phalanx. The most enthusiastic proponent of Fourierism in Washtenaw County, though, was the Universalist *Primitive Expounder,* which paper moved from Ann Arbor to Alphadelphia upon the establishment of that phalanx in 1844. Although this commune was disintegrating by 1846 and finally dissolved in 1848—thus effectively ending any further discussion of Fourierism in Washtenaw County's newspapers—the cause was nevertheless celebrated frequently for almost four years in Ann Arbor. Although there were a few ventures in the South—Frances Wright's Nashoba colony existed briefly in Tennessee during the 1820s, and a predominantly French commune of Fourierists was present in Texas in the mid-1850s—the reception in the slave states to communitarianism was cooler than it was in the North. Accordingly, aside from the reprinting—without comment—of a Fourierist essay from the New York *Tribune* in the *Independent Monitor* in 1842, the issue was never publicly broached in Tuscaloosa.[7]

Ann Arborites were undoubtedly exceptional in their enthusiasm for Fourierism. Although this cause was discussed throughout the North, and notwithstanding the fact that phalanxes were found in many states, participation

7. *Democratic Herald,* November 16, 1842; *Signal of Liberty,* June 19, 1843; Thomas, *Millenarian Impulse in Michigan,* 42–51; John Humphrey Noyes, *History of American Socialisms* (Philadelphia, 1870), 388–96; A. D. P. Van Buren, "The Alphadelphia Association: Its History in Comstock, Kalamazoo County," *Michigan Pioneer and Historical Collections,* V (1882), 406–12; *Independent Monitor,* June 1, 1842; Carl J. Guarneri, "Two Utopian Socialist Plans for Emancipation in Antebellum Louisiana," *Louisiana History,* XXIV (Winter 1983), 5–24; Guarneri, *Utopian Alternative,* 261–67, 328–32; Tyler, *Freedom's Ferment,* 206–11. On Fourierism in Washtenaw County, see *Michigan State Journal,* June 1, August 10, 17, September 14, 28, November 23, 1842, January 25, February 22, March 8, 22, May 3, 10, November 15, 29, 1843, April 3, 10, December 25, 1844, February 12, May 21, 1845, April 29, 1846; *Democratic Herald,* November 30, December 7, 1842; *Michigan Argus,* May 10, 17, 31, 1843, April 3, December 18, 1844, May 27, 1846; *Signal of Liberty,* May 22, June 5, 1843, April 8, 1844, February 3, 1845; *Ypsilanti Sentinel,* May 14, 1845, May 27, 1846; *Primitive Expounder,* June 24, 1843–May 25, 1844, *passim,* March 26, 1846.

in this "critical-utopian socialism"—Karl Marx and Friedrich Engels' pejorative from their *Communist Manifesto*—was never as widespread in the North as was temperance, benevolence, or abolition. The unwillingness of Tuscaloosans and other white southerners to consider women's suffrage and Fourierism was undoubtedly because they apprehended these radical efforts to be associated with abolitionism, as well as the ferment of what they perceived to be a turbulent northern society overwhelmed by class conflict, which many white southerners had grown to fear and despise. As the *Independent Monitor* commented in 1846, "The prosperity of the North, so much boasted, seems not to engross the attention of all who reside there. A band of restless visionaries are always in motion, to draw off the masses from their true interests, and to embitter them against the established order of things. At periods, slavery is so terrible in their imaginations, that they almost swear never to eat or sleep until it is banished from the Union." These sentiments were echoed in a speech by Alabama Governor John Winston at Huntsville in 1855, where he explained why he differed with the Know-Nothing Party: "He did not like the source from which the Know Nothing platform sprung—the land where Federalism, Abolitionism, Mormonism, Spiritual Rappings, and other heretical isms originated." And earlier that year, when the *Dallas Gazette* ridiculed prospective gubernatorial candidate R. A. Baker as "the representative of all the humbug *isms* that can get a footing in the state," the paper tellingly added: "All he has to do, or his friends for him, is to mount the woman's rights platform, embrace Fourierism, and then he will be a candidate *as is a candidate*."[8]

Of course, hostility to these causes and other reforms was not peculiar to the South. Some Washtenaw County residents took exception to benevolence, temperance, and abolition. Nor were threats of violence toward abolitionists restricted to the Deep South. Indeed, Tuscaloosa County's vigilance society was more orderly than some of Michigan's antiabolitionists. In chapter 6, we saw that Ann Arbor's Presbyterians and Methodists, as well as the officials responsible for the Washtenaw County courthouse, denied the abolitionists the use of their buildings in 1838, as they feared antiabolitionist violence—which in fact erupted at an antislavery meeting at the Ann Arbor Free Church in 1861.

8. Thornton, *Politics and Power,* 210–11, 221, 229; *Independent Monitor,* February 18, 1846; Huntsville *Democrat,* July 26, 1855; *Dallas Gazette* (Cahaba, Ala.), February 16, 1855. Alabama voters did not consider Know-Nothingism to be as heretical as Winston suggested it was, as this nativist party's candidate, George Shortridge, received 30,639 (42.0 percent) of the votes in the 1855 state gubernatorial race. See the discussion herein associated with n. 104, chap. 3.

Most of the violence against abolitionists in Michigan, however, occurred during the late 1830s, when abolitionists reported that such acts prevented them from speaking in Kalamazoo, Pontiac, Bellevue, and other places.[9] And as detailed in chapter 4, some Washtenaw residents were not above using intimidation to counter prohibitionist forces.

Sometimes the reform impulse was the subject of ridicule and parody in Washtenaw County. In 1838 the *Michigan Argus* published the mock minutes of the "tee-totalist starvation society of Ann Arbor" that would "forever hereafter, use nothing but moonshine," and the following year, an essayist for the *Michigan State Journal* derided the officiousness of contemporary activists by announcing the creation of "A New Society Called the Self-Examining Society of the County of Washtenaw, Mich." He explained: "If the members of some of our societies, would take half the pains to examine their own faults, that they do to hunt up others, how much more like Christians they would be? How much more happy and peaceable would be the condition of every community and neighborhood? And were a society of self-examination once instituted, in our land, and become of so much interest as other societies, it is evident that there would be less running to and fro, or members standing in corners of the streets, marketplaces, and uppermost seats in the synagogues, thanking God that they are not like other men." The writer further lampooned the constituency of reform associations—and implicitly sustained findings that have been detailed in this study with respect to the organizations active during the 1830s—by declaring that "the members of this society shall not be selected out of the aristocracy of wealth, nor made up of the popular part of the community."[10]

Although hostility to prohibition grew in Ann Arbor and Tuscaloosa as this cause became stronger after the mid-1840s, in both counties opposition to benevolence and temperance had generally expired by this time, as had antagonism toward abolitionism in Washtenaw County. During the 1840s, abolitionism in Washtenaw County gained greater respectability through the activities of the Liberty Party and the regular publication of the *Signal of Liberty*. In addition to the disappearance of threats and violence by hostile antiabolitionists, antislaveryites were also no longer dismissed by mainstream political newspa-

9. Nathan Thomas to Jesse Thomas, December 29, 1837, in Thomas Papers; *State Journal,* February 23, 1837; *American Freeman,* August 13, 1839; *Michigan Freeman,* December 18, 1839, February 12, 1840.

10. *Michigan Argus,* January 4, 18, 1838; *Michigan State Journal,* September 11, 1839.

pers as they had been during the 1830s. Whigs now treated the cause of anti-slavery—if not the Liberty Party—even more delicately, realizing that they could not win elections without the support of moderate abolitionists. Democrats likewise no longer greeted abolitionists with the ridicule they provided during the late 1830s, for fear of arousing abolitionist animosity and encouraging some moderate antislaveryites to vote with the Whigs. By 1845 the *Michigan Argus* may have reflected the changing sentiments of some of the party faithful when it announced that it supported Texas annexation only if it would not enlarge the domain of slavery. Most significantly, nearly three-fourths of Ann Arbor voters endorsed suffrage for African American males in 1850, when only slightly more than a fourth of the state's voters did likewise. In short, the continued presence of abolitionism in Washtenaw County resulted in an increased toleration—if not total acceptance—of antislavery ideas, and may have similarly created a wider field of political and social dissent in which other social innovations, such as Fourierism and women's rights, could be more readily discussed. But to reiterate, both communitarianism and female suffrage were considered radical throughout most of the country; in neither Washtenaw nor Tuscaloosa County were multitudes eagerly embracing these causes. While it is undoubtedly true that some white southerners feared that any reform more radical than temperance was too closely linked to abolition and were thus unreceptive or hostile to it, it is also true that the greater intellectual ferment in Washtenaw County—rather than merely a deeper conservatism in Tuscaloosa County—partly accounts for the counties' different receptions to these two radical causes.

Despite their important differences, the similarities between Washtenaw and Tuscaloosa Counties with respect to antebellum reform are also important. During the antebellum years, more people participated in or in some way encountered temperance and evangelical benevolence than Fourierism, women's rights, and even abolitionism. In both counties, proponents of benevolence not only desired to provide people with the means to salvation; they also endeavored to transform the morals of Americans and to remove the barriers that they believed created social problems, hindered the development of human potential, and ultimately stood in the way of economic progress. Temperance devotees also promoted similar goals. These two reforms, as well as abolition, were advanced by individuals who identified closely—though at times elusively—with the growth of American towns and cities, education, and the market economy.

Appendix

Tables 1–34

1. Tuscaloosa County Population, 1820–1860
2. Slaveholding in Tuscaloosa County, 1830–1860
3. Church Buildings and Church Seats, Tuscaloosa County and Alabama, 1850
4. Church Buildings and Church Seats, Washtenaw County and Michigan, 1850
5. Places of Birth for Tuscaloosa County Male Heads of Household, 1850
6. Tavern Licenses in Tuscaloosa County, 1820–1832
7. Religious Affiliation of Tuscaloosa County Temperance Activists by Temperance Cohort and Denomination
8. Washtenaw County Township Votes on License and No License, 1845–1850
9. Religious Affiliation of Washtenaw County Temperance Activists by Temperance Cohort and Denomination
10. Washtenaw County Election Returns, 1840 Presidential
11. Washtenaw County Election Returns, 1841 Gubernatorial
12. Washtenaw County Election Returns, 1842 State Senate
13. Washtenaw County Election Returns, 1843 Gubernatorial
14. Washtenaw County Election Returns, 1844 Presidential
15. Washtenaw County Election Returns, 1845 Gubernatorial
16. Washtenaw County Election Returns, 1846 Congressional
17. Washtenaw County Election Returns, 1847 Gubernatorial
18. Washtenaw County Election Returns, 1848 Presidential
19. Washtenaw County Election Returns, 1849 Gubernatorial

20. Washtenaw County Election Returns, 1850 Delegates to the State Constitutional Convention

21. Washtenaw County Election Returns, 1850 State Treasurer

22. Washtenaw County Election Returns, 1852 Presidential

23. Washtenaw County Township Election Returns, 1841

24. Washtenaw County Township Election Returns, 1842

25. Washtenaw County Township Election Returns, 1843

26. Washtenaw County Township Election Returns, 1844

27. Washtenaw County Township Election Returns, 1845

28. Washtenaw County Township Election Returns, 1846

29. Washtenaw County Township Election Returns, 1847

30. Washtenaw County Township Election Returns, 1848

31. Washtenaw County Township Election Returns, 1849

32. Washtenaw County Township Election Returns, 1853

33. Religious Affiliation of Washtenaw County Abolitionists by Cohort and Denomination

34. Ages of Washtenaw County White Male Abolitionists (Including Free Soilers and Petition Signers) and Michigan Subscribers to the *Signal of Liberty*

Table 1. Tuscaloosa County Population, 1820–1860

Year	Total population	Tuscaloosa Co. rank among Ala. counties, total pop.	# of slaves	Tuscaloosa Co. rank among Ala. counties, # of slaves	% of pop. slave	% of Ala. pop. slave	Tuscaloosa Co. rank among Ala. counties, % of pop. slave	# of counties in Ala.
1820	8,229	5	2,335	6	28.4	32.7	16	23
1827	12,800	6	4,151	9	32.8	37.4	19	
1830	13,646	6	4,793	12	35.1	37.8	24	36
1838	18,579	13	7,146	15	38.5	42.7	24	49
1840	16,583	15	6,552	NA	39.5	42.9	NA	49
1844	16,994		NA		NA	42.4		50
1850	18,056	17	7,477	19	41.4	45.4	27	52
1855	19,389	NA	8,530	NA	44.0	NA	NA	
1860	23,200	18	10,145	16	43.7	45.1	21	52

Note: The slavery figures for 1838 include both slaves and free blacks.

Sources: Compiled from the following: *Fifth Census; or, Enumeration of the Inhabitants of the United States, 1830* (Washington, D.C., 1832), 22–23, 98–101; *Compendium of the Enumeration of the Inhabitants and Statistics of the United States, as Obtained at the Department of State, from the Returns of the Sixth Census . . .* (Washington, D.C., 1841), 52–55; J. D. B. De Bow, *The Seventh Census of the United States: 1850* (Washington, D.C., 1853), 421; *Population of the United States in 1860: Compiled from the Original Returns of the Eighth Census, Under the Direction of the Secretary of the Interior, by Joseph C. G. Kennedy, Superintendent of the Census* (Washington, D.C., 1864), 8; *Huntsville Democrat,* December 14, 1827; *Independent Monitor,* January 29, 1841, December 18, 1844; Alabama State Manuscript Census for Tuscaloosa County, 1855, ADAH.

TABLE 2. SLAVEHOLDING IN TUSCALOOSA COUNTY, 1830–1860

Year	Total slaveholders	Total households	% households with slaves	Median slaveholding*	Mean slaveholding*	# slaveholders with 25 or more slaves	Largest slaveholding
1830	590	1,481	39.8	4	8.1	41	101
1840	674	1,799	37.5	5	9.7	47	113
1850	672	1,897	35.4	6	11.1	54	274
1855	741	2,055	36.1	6	11.5	68	336
1860	815	2,939	27.7	4	12.5	98	248

*Figures in these two columns do not include households without slaves.

Sources: 1830 federal manuscript census returns for Tuscaloosa County, Alabama; 1840 federal manuscript census for Tuscaloosa County, Alabama; Population and slave schedules of the 1850 census, Tuscaloosa County, Alabama; Population schedule of the 1860 census, Tuscaloosa County, Alabama; Alabama state manuscript census for Tuscaloosa County, 1855; Louis Herzberg, "Negro Slavery in Tuscaloosa County, Alabama, 1818–1865" (M.A. thesis, University of Alabama, 1955), 100, 102, 103, 104, 106, 108, 110, 127, 128, 129, 132, 133, 134, 138. The data for 1820 are not available.

Table 3. Church Buildings and Church Seats, Tuscaloosa County and Alabama, 1850

Denomination	Church buildings in Tuscaloosa Co.	Church seats in Tuscaloosa Co.	% of church seats in Tuscaloosa Co.	Church buildings in Ala.	Church seats in Ala.	% of church seats in Ala.
Baptist	22	12,000	40.7	579	189,980	43.2
Total Methodist	19	11,200	38.0	577	169,025	38.4
Methodist Episcopal	18					
Methodist Protestant	1					
Total Presbyterian	11	5,500	18.6	162	58,805	13.4
Old School Presbyterian	5					
Cumberland Presbyterian	6					
Episcopal	1	800	2.7	17	6,920	1.6
Roman Catholic				5	5,200	1.2
Christian (Disciples of Christ)				17	4,050	0.9
Smaller denominations (Free, Lutheran, Union, Unitarian, Universalist, and "Minor Sects")				16	5,625	1.3
Totals	53	29,500	100.0	1,373	439,605	100.0

Sources: Social schedule of the 1850 census, Tuscaloosa County, ADAH; De Bow, *Seventh Census*, 435–38.

Table 4. Church Buildings and Church Seats, Washtenaw County and Michigan, 1850

Denomination	Church buildings in Washtenaw Co.	Church seats in Washtenaw Co.	% of church seats in Washtenaw Co.	Church buildings in Mich.	Church seats in Mich.	% of church seats in Mich.
Methodist	10	4,275	25.9	119	33,885	28.2
Total Presbyterian	7	2,800	17.0	72	22,530	18.8
New School Presbyterian	5	2,200	13.3	44	16,122	13.4
Roman Catholic	6	1,930	11.7	66	17,865	14.9
Baptist	4	1,900	11.5	29	10,500	8.7
Congregational	3	825	5.0	25	8,425	7.0
Episcopal	1	700	4.2	1	700	0.6
Free	3	625	3.8	12	3,205	2.7
Lutheran	2	400	2.4	7	1,360	1.1

German Methodist	1	300	1.8			
Old School Presbyterian*	1	250	1.5			
Wesleyan Methodist	1	200	1.2			
Friends	1	100	0.6	7	1,400	1.2
Smaller denominations (Christian, Dutch Reformed, Moravian, Union, and "Minor Sects")				17	4,125	3.4
Totals	45	16,505	99.9	399	120,117	100.0

*The social schedule's designation of the Presbyterian church in Augusta Township as Old School may be erroneous because the Stoney Creek Presbyterian church—the only known Presbyterian congregation in that polity—was associated with the New School–based Washtenaw Presbytery.

Sources: Washtenaw County figures are from the social schedule of the 1850 census, Washtenaw County, Bentley Library. These figures differ slightly from those found in De Bow, Seventh Census, 908–12, which is also the source of the statewide figures.

Place of Birth	#	%
Southern States		
South Carolina	514	
Alabama	291	
Georgia	291	
North Carolina	248	
Tennessee	108	
Virginia	106	
Kentucky	36	
Maryland	11	
Mississippi	4	
Total	1,609	93.4
Northern States		
New York	13	
Pennsylvania	12	
Massachusetts	10	
New Jersey	5	

Connecticut	4	
Other North	10	
Total	54	3.1
Foreign		
Ireland	18	
England	8	
Scotland	8	
Germany	6	
Other foreign	3	
Total	43	2.5
No Place of Birth Listed	3	0.2
Unknown	14	0.8
Totals	1,723	100.0

Source: Compiled from the 1850 federal manuscript census, Tuscaloosa County, Alabama.

TABLE 6. TAVERN LICENSES IN TUSCALOOSA COUNTY, 1820–1832

Year	To operate tavern, Tuscaloosa town		To sell liquor, Tuscaloosa town		To operate tavern, Tuscaloosa town, w/o selling spirits		To operate tavern, rural Tuscaloosa Co.*		To sell liquor, rural Tuscaloosa Co.		To keep tavern, location unspecified		Total liquor licenses**
	No. licenses granted	Cost per license ($)	No. licenses granted	Cost per license ($)	No. licenses granted	Cost per license ($)	No. licenses granted	Cost per license ($)	No. licenses granted	Cost per license ($)	No. licenses granted	Cost per license ($)	
1820	1	10	1	10			1	10			1	10	4
1823	0	20	3	10			5	5					8
1824	2	20	5	10			13	5					20
1825	3	20	9	10			6	5					18
1826	2	20	18	10	1	15	10	5	1	10			31
1827	3	20	7	15			6	5	4	10			20
1828	4	20	9	15			4	5					17
1829	3	20	10	15			5	5					18
1830	4	20	6	15			9	5					19
1831	3	20	6	15	1	10	5	5					14
1832	6	20	5	15			5	5					16

*For rural Tuscaloosa County prior to 1826, the docket does not distinguish a license to keep a tavern from a license to sell liquor.

**Assumes that a license to operate a tavern is also a license to sell spirits.

Source: Tuscaloosa County Tavern License Docket, 1818–1832, Tuscaloosa County Courthouse. See also James Benson Sellers, The Prohibition Movement in Alabama, 1702–1943 (Chapel Hill, 1943), 30.

$$\text{T{\small ABLE} 7. R{\small ELIGIOUS} A{\small FFILIATION} of T{\small USCALOOSA} C{\small OUNTY} T{\small EMPERANCE} A{\small CTIVISTS}}$$
$$\text{by T{\small EMPERANCE} C{\small OHORT} and D{\small ENOMINATION}}$$

	Tuscaloosa Temperance Society, 1829–40	Young Men's Total Abstinence Society, 1839–40	Alabama Total Abstinence Society, 1843	Sons of Temperance, 1846–59	All Tuscaloosa temperance activists*
Baptists	8	3	7	23	46
Catholics	0	0	2	0	3
Episcopalians	0	2	3	7	11
Methodists	10	6	16	16	44
Presbyterians	16	4	4	8	30
Cumberland Presbyterians	0	0	0	2	2
Totals	34	15	32	56	136
Total temperance activists in cohort	45	54	104	136	330

*The column on the right includes a number of temperance partisans who did not belong to any of the other cohorts. Additionally, many temperance activists belonged to more than one cohort. This column, therefore, does not represent the summation of the columns to its left.

Sources: Most temperance activists were identified from Tuscaloosa newspapers. Church affiliations were gathered from the sources cited in chapter 1, n. 47.

TABLE 8. Washtenaw County Township Votes on License and No License, 1845–1850

	1845				1846			
	No license	License	% No license	% Turnout*	No license	License	% No license	% Turnout*
Ann Arbor Village**	125	88	58.7	NA				
Ann Arbor	325	200	61.9	67	390	38	91.1	60
Augusta	No license majority; twp. records do not give count							
Bridgewater								
Dexter								
Freedom								
Lima								
Lodi								
Lyndon								
Manchester	71	52	57.7	50	68	96	41.5	75
Northfield								
Pittsfield	No license won; *Signal* did not give count				96	10	90.6	NA
Salem	No license won; *Signal* did not give count							
Saline					No license won by 26 votes (no other figures given)			
Scio	121	137	46.9	NA				
Sharon	No license won; *Signal* did not give count							
Superior								
Sylvan	52	72	41.9	100				
Webster	81	26	75.7	71	71	7	91.0	64
York								
Ypsilanti	179	146	55.1	100	62	71	46.6	32

	1847				1848			
	No license	License	% No license	% Turnout*	No license	License	% No license	% Turnout*
Ann Arbor Village	198	215	47.9		134	136	49.6	
Ann Arbor	347	314	52.5	83	384	51	88.3	55
Augusta								
Bridgewater					12	44	21.4	71
Dexter								
Freedom								
Lima								
Lodi								
Lyndon								
Manchester	120	84	58.8	87	104	57	64.6	89
Northfield								
Pittsfield	72	32	69.2	83	50	61	45.0	74
Salem								
Saline								
Scio	137	114	54.6	90	License won by 20 votes (no other figures given)			
Sharon								
Superior								
Sylvan	89	63	58.6	89	26	76	25.5	66
Webster					No license won (no figures given)			
York								
Ypsilanti	27	23	54.0	11	111	84	56.9	40

TABLE 8 (*continued*). WASHTENAW COUNTY TOWNSHIP VOTES ON LICENSE AND NO LICENSE, 1845–1850

	1849			1850			
	No license	License	% No license	% Turnout*	No license	License	% No license	% Turnout*
Ann Arbor Village	197	211	48.3		169	121	58.3	
Ann Arbor	425	30	93.4	57	86	3	96.6	12
Augusta								
Bridgewater	No license won by 11 votes (only figure given)				11	67	14.1	NA
Dexter								
Freedom								
Lima								
Lodi								
Lyndon								
Manchester	53	99	34.9	68	51	94	35.2	77
Northfield								
Pittsfield	81	27	75.0	59	19	45	29.7	39

Salem				
Saline				
Scio	146	95	60.6	87
Sharon				
Superior				
Sylvan				
Webster	44	1	97.8	56
York	191	96	66.6	57
Ypsilanti	244	20		52

*Percentage of voters who participated in both the selection of township officers and the license/no license referendum.

**Ann Arbor Village elections on the license/no license referendum occurred in May or July separately from the township election.

Sources: Record Book of the Ann Arbor Village Council, 1834–1845, and Record Book of the Ann Arbor Village/City Council, 1847–1858, Michigan Historical Collections, Bentley Historical Library, University of Michigan; Ann Arbor Township Records, Ann Arbor Township Hall; Bridgewater Township Records, Bridgewater Township Clerk; Manchester Township Records, Manchester Township Hall; Pittsfield Township Records, Pittsfield Township Hall; Scio Township Records, Scio Township Hall; Sylvan Township Records, Bentley Library; Webster Township Records, Webster Township Clerk; Ypsilanti Township Records, Bentley Library; *Signal of Liberty*, April 14, 1845.

TABLE 9. RELIGIOUS AFFILIATION OF WASHTENAW COUNTY TEMPERANCE ACTIVISTS BY TEMPERANCE COHORT AND DENOMINATION

	1829–34	1835–40	1838 subscribers	1841–46	Sons of Temperance	1851–60	All temperance activists*
Baptists	2	7	26	6	5	6	51
Free Will Baptists	0	0	0	0	0	0	0
Catholics	0	0	0	0	4	0	4
Episcopalians	2	2	5	1	10	11	29
Congregationalists	4	6	12	5	8	10	35
Presbyterians	11	24	53	15	7	15	106
Methodists	4	7	14	9	4	15	46
Wesleyan Methodists	0	1	2	3	0	3	6
Unitarians	0	0	0	0	0	2	2
Universalists	1	1	2	2	1	4	9
Swedenborgians	1	1	0	0	0	0	1
Spiritualists	0	1	1	0	0	1	2
Totals	25	50	115	41	39	67	291
Total temperance activists in cohort	39	205	264	106	269	124	988

*Includes a number of temperance partisans who did not belong to any of the listed cohorts. Additionally, many temperance activists belonged to more than one cohort. This column, therefore, does not represent the summation of the columns to its left.

Sources: Most of the above individuals were identified as temperance activists from Washtenaw County newspapers and manuscript sources cited in the footnotes. A few church affiliations were also culled from newspapers, as well as the following sources: *History of Washtenaw County, Michigan* (Chicago, 1881); AHMS Papers, Bentley Library; ASSU Papers, Samford University Library, Birmingham, Alabama (microfilm); Jane Palmer, "A History of Manchester Township," typescript, Manchester Township Library; *Articles of Faith and Covenant, Adapted by the First Presbyterian Church of Ann Arbor* (Ann Arbor, 1841); Francis L. D. Goodrich, *Historical Facts Concerning the First Presbyterian Church of Ann Arbor* (Ann Arbor, 1961); Ann Arbor Methodist Episcopal Directory, Moses Boylan Papers, Bentley Library. The following church records were also consulted at the Bentley Library: St. Andrew's Episcopal Church, Ann Arbor; St. Luke's Episcopal Church, Ypsilanti; First Baptist Church of Ann Arbor; First Baptist Church of Saline; First Baptist Church of Manchester; Manchester Free Will Baptist Church; First Baptist Church of Chelsea (Sylvan); First Congregational Church of Ann Arbor; First Congregational Church of Chelsea; First Congregational Church of Salem; Minutes of the Washtenaw Presbytery; First Presbyterian Church of Lodi; First Presbyterian Church of Stoney Creek (Augusta); First United Church of Christ, Webster Township; First Presbyterian Church of Ypsilanti; First United Methodist Church of Ann Arbor; First United Methodist Church of Ypsilanti. The records of St. John the Baptist Catholic Church, Ypsilanti; St. Patrick's Catholic Church, Northfield; St. Thomas the Apostle Catholic Church, Ann Arbor; and the First Baptist Church of Ypsilanti were examined at their respective meetinghouses.

TABLE 10. WASHTENAW COUNTY ELECTION RETURNS, 1840 PRESIDENTIAL

	Whig	%	Democrat	%	Liberty	%	Total votes
Ann Arbor	327	51.7	285	45.0	21	3.3	633
Augusta	74	61.2	47	38.8	0	0.0	121
Bridgewater	100	48.8	104	50.7	1	0.5	205
Dexter	60	43.2	79	56.8	0	0.0	139
Freedom	60	36.1	106	63.9	0	0.0	166
Lima	109	49.3	112	50.7	0	0.0	221
Lodi	100	52.4	90	47.1	1	0.5	191
Lyndon	42	51.9	38	46.9	1	1.2	81
Manchester	126	55.5	101	44.5	0	0.0	227
Northfield	65	33.3	129	66.2	1	0.5	195
Pittsfield	142	68.3	59	28.4	7	3.4	208
Salem	137	50.4	124	45.6	11	4.0	272
Saline	178	62.7	106	37.3	0	0.0	284
Scio	167	54.6	131	42.8	8	2.6	306
Sharon	85	57.0	63	42.3	1	0.7	149
Superior	138	56.3	107	43.7	0	0.0	245
Sylvan	69	60.5	41	36.0	4	3.5	114
Webster	94	58.0	68	42.0	0	0.0	162
York	125	53.0	111	47.0	0	0.0	236
Ypsilanti	329	67.3	156	31.9	4	0.8	489
Totals	2,527	54.4	2,057	44.3	60	1.3	4,644

Source: Records of Elections and Archives Division, Department of State, State of Michigan, Lansing.

Table 11. Washtenaw County Election Returns, 1841 Gubernatorial

	Whig	%	Democrat	%	Liberty	%	Total votes
Ann Arbor	240	42.4	277	48.9	49	8.7	566
Augusta	35	43.2	36	44.4	10	12.3	81
Bridgewater	66	38.4	99	57.6	7	4.1	172
Dexter	37	35.6	67	64.4	0	0.0	104
Freedom	42	35.9	75	64.1	0	0.0	117
Lima	75	39.1	117	60.9	0	0.0	192
Lodi	82	47.1	88	50.6	4	2.3	174
Lyndon	19	26.0	54	74.0	0	0.0	73
Manchester	74	39.2	102	54.0	13	6.9	189
Northfield	35	22.6	116	74.8	4	2.6	155
Pittsfield	79	50.0	62	39.2	17	10.8	158
Salem	62	27.3	106	46.7	59	26.0	227
Saline	129	53.1	109	44.9	5	2.1	243
Scio	107	42.8	123	49.2	20	8.0	250
Sharon	60	47.6	57	45.2	9	7.1	126
Superior	102	46.6	117	53.4	0	0.0	219
Sylvan	23	20.0	67	58.3	25	21.7	115
Webster	49	37.4	70	53.4	12	9.2	131
York	93	50.5	91	49.5	0	0.0	184
Ypsilanti	250	55.8	179	40.0	19	4.2	448
Totals	1,659	42.3	2,012	51.3	253	6.4	3,924

Source: Records of Elections and Archives Division, Department of State, State of Michigan, Lansing.

TABLE 12. WASHTENAW COUNTY ELECTION RETURNS, 1842 STATE SENATE

	Whig	%	Democrat	%	Liberty	%	Total votes
Ann Arbor	277	49.5	231	41.3	52	9.3	560
Augusta							
Bridgewater							
Dexter							
Freedom							
Lima					6		NA
Lodi							
Lyndon							
Manchester							
Northfield							
Pittsfield							

Salem							
Saline					22		NA
Scio							
Sharon							
Superior							
Sylvan							
Webster	60	51.7	42	36.2	14	12.1	116
York							
Ypsilanti							
Totals	1,589	43.2	1,781	48.4	306	8.3	3,676

Note: Two seats in the state senate were contested in the 1842 election, and the above totals are the mean vote for the candidates of each party.

Sources: Michigan State Journal, November 9, 1842; *Signal of Liberty*, November 14, 21, 1842; Webster Township Minutes, in possession of Webster Township Clerk.

	Whig	%	Democrat	%	Liberty	%	Total votes
Ann Arbor	298	48.5	235	38.2	82	13.3	615
Augusta	14	20.0	35	50.0	21	30.0	70
Bridgewater	70	38.9	97	53.9	13	7.2	180
Dexter	41	39.0	64	61.0	0	0.0	105
Freedom	35	37.2	59	62.8	0	0.0	94
Lima	74	44.8	82	49.7	9	5.5	165
Lodi	64	41.3	80	51.6	11	7.1	155
Lyndon	24	40.0	35	58.3	1	1.7	60
Manchester	83	40.1	120	58.0	4	1.9	207
Northfield	35	24.8	104	73.8	2	1.4	141
Pittsfield	86	49.7	73	42.2	14	8.1	173
Salem	58	29.6	87	44.4	51	26.0	196
Saline	143	52.0	114	41.5	18	6.5	275
Scio	107	44.8	113	47.3	19	7.9	239
Sharon	46	47.9	49	51.0	1	1.0	96
Superior	66	39.8	100	60.2	0	0.0	166
Sylvan	33	30.8	57	53.3	17	15.9	107
Webster	57	47.9	48	40.3	14	11.8	119
York	102	50.0	96	47.1	6	2.9	204
Ypsilanti	248	52.7	195	41.4	28	5.9	471
Totals	1,684	43.9	1,843	48.0	311	8.1	3,838

Source: Signal of Liberty, November 20, 1843.

TABLE 14. WASHTENAW COUNTY ELECTION RETURNS, 1844 PRESIDENTIAL

	Whig	%	Democrat	%	Liberty	%	Total votes
Ann Arbor	369	45.4	345	42.3	98	12.1	812
Augusta	54	44.3	52	42.6	16	13.1	122
Bridgewater	88	39.6	112	50.5	22	9.9	222
Dexter	55	37.9	90	62.1	0	0.0	145
Freedom	55	31.3	119	67.6	2	1.1	176
Lima	100	46.3	106	49.1	10	4.6	216
Lodi	101	49.0	96	46.6	9	4.4	206
Lyndon	48	41.7	66	57.4	1	0.9	115
Manchester	115	44.7	137	53.3	5	1.9	257
Northfield	58	26.2	153	69.2	10	4.5	221
Pittsfield	110	47.8	96	41.7	24	10.4	230
Salem	98	34.8	123	43.6	61	21.6	282
Saline	180	52.0	138	39.9	28	8.1	346
Scio	143	43.1	165	49.7	24	7.2	332
Sharon	84	55.6	60	39.7	7	4.6	151
Superior	112	43.9	137	53.7	6	2.4	255
Sylvan	68	40.7	83	49.7	16	9.6	167
Webster	95	55.9	61	35.9	14	8.2	170
York	120	44.1	143	52.6	9	3.3	272
Ypsilanti	296	50.3	268	45.6	24	4.1	588
Totals	2,349	44.4	2,550	48.2	386	7.3	5,285

Source: Michigan State Journal, November 20, 1844.

TABLE 15. WASHTENAW COUNTY ELECTION RETURNS, 1845 GUBERNATORIAL

	Whig	%	Democrat	%	Liberty	%	Total votes
Ann Arbor	277	45.6	240	39.5	90	14.8	607
Augusta							
Bridgewater							
Dexter							
Freedom							
Lima							
Lodi							
Lyndon							
Manchester							
Northfield							
Pittsfield							
Salem	64	34.0	64	34.0	60	31.9	188
Saline							
Scio							
Sharon							
Superior							
Sylvan							
Webster	74	63.8	32	27.6	10	8.6	116
York							
Ypsilanti							
Totals	2,005	49.3	1,759	43.2	305	7.5	4,069

Sources: Signal of Liberty, November 10, 24, 1845; Webster Township Minutes, in possession of Webster Township Clerk.

TABLE 16. WASHTENAW COUNTY ELECTION RETURNS, 1846 CONGRESSIONAL

	Whig	%	Democrat	%	Liberty	%	Total votes
Ann Arbor	435	60.3	222	30.8	64	8.9	721
Augusta	35	45.5	32	41.6	10	13.0	77
Bridgewater	65	38.5	96	56.8	8	4.7	169
Dexter	11	13.4	71	86.6	0	0.0	82
Freedom	33	36.3	58	63.7	0	0.0	91
Lima	84	61.8	50	36.8	2	1.5	136
Lodi	89	53.0	70	41.7	9	5.4	168
Lyndon	26	40.6	38	59.4	0	0.0	64
Manchester	75	39.1	105	54.7	12	6.3	192
Northfield	43	31.2	91	65.9	4	2.9	138
Pittsfield	102	62.6	49	30.1	12	7.4	163
Salem	48	26.8	58	32.4	73	40.8	179
Saline	140	53.8	98	37.7	22	8.5	260
Scio	97	43.7	111	50.0	14	6.3	222
Sharon	57	46.0	58	46.8	9	7.3	124
Superior	78	55.3	63	44.7	0	0.0	141
Sylvan	52	39.4	69	52.3	11	8.3	132
Webster	74	51.7	59	41.3	10	7.0	143
York	80	43.5	101	54.9	3	1.6	184
Ypsilanti	229	57.3	158	39.5	13	3.3	400
Totals	1,853	48.9	1,657	43.8	276	7.3	3,786

Source: Records of Elections and Archives Division, Department of State, State of Michigan, Lansing.

TABLE 17. WASHTENAW COUNTY ELECTION RETURNS, 1847 GUBERNATORIAL

	Whig	%	Democrat	%	Liberty	%	Total votes
Ann Arbor	368	47.5	335	43.2	72	9.3	775
Augusta	36	37.9	48	50.5	11	11.6	95
Bridgewater	61	33.9	112	62.2	7	3.9	180
Dexter	33	40.2	49	59.8	0	0.0	82
Freedom	35	36.8	60	63.2	0	0.0	95
Lima	81	64.8	41	32.8	3	2.4	125
Lodi	69	44.2	78	50.0	9	5.8	156
Lyndon	23	42.6	30	55.6	1	1.9	54
Manchester	61	33.9	106	58.9	13	7.2	180
Northfield	48	35.6	87	64.4	0	0.0	135
Pittsfield	82	54.3	54	35.8	15	9.9	151
Salem	43	23.6	75	41.2	64	35.2	182
Saline	134	51.7	110	42.5	15	5.8	259
Scio	88	40.4	111	50.9	19	8.7	218
Sharon	57	49.1	55	47.4	4	3.4	116
Superior	104	58.1	75	41.9	0	0.0	179
Sylvan	54	40.9	70	53.0	8	6.1	132
Webster	57	52.8	37	34.3	14	13.0	108
York	80	41.9	111	58.1	0	0.0	191
Ypsilanti	292	57.3	205	40.2	13	2.5	510
Totals	1,806	46.0	1,849	47.1	268	6.8	3,923

Source: Signal of Liberty, December 4, 1847.

TABLE 18. WASHTENAW COUNTY ELECTION RETURNS, 1848 PRESIDENTIAL

	Whig	%	Democrat	%	Free Soil	%	Total votes
Ann Arbor	352	38.7	326	35.8	232	25.5	910
Augusta	44	33.3	53	40.2	35	26.5	132
Bridgewater	64	34.6	94	50.8	27	14.6	185
Dexter	53	46.1	57	49.6	5	4.3	115
Freedom	22	15.6	92	65.2	27	19.1	141
Lima	84	50.3	58	34.7	25	15.0	167
Lodi	63	35.6	66	37.3	48	27.1	177
Lyndon	40	36.4	56	50.9	14	12.7	110
Manchester	87	36.3	99	41.3	54	22.5	240
Northfield	56	29.5	113	59.5	21	11.1	190
Pittsfield	89	42.4	58	27.6	63	30.0	210
Salem	69	27.2	83	32.7	102	40.2	254
Saline	161	47.8	120	35.6	56	16.6	337
Scio	127	42.1	127	42.1	48	15.9	302
Sharon	68	42.2	59	36.6	34	21.1	161
Superior	113	47.7	114	48.1	10	4.2	237
Sylvan	53	34.9	66	43.4	33	21.7	152
Webster	85	49.7	61	35.7	25	14.6	171
York	105	46.3	100	44.1	22	9.7	227
Ypsilanti	294	48.2	279	45.7	37	6.1	610
Totals	2,029	40.4	2,081	41.4	918	18.3	5,028

Source: True Democrat, November 23, 1848.

TABLE 19. WASHTENAW COUNTY ELECTION RETURNS, 1849 GUBERNATORIAL

	Whig/Free Soil	%	Democrat	%	Total votes
Ann Arbor	413	56.7	315	43.3	728
Augusta	42	66.7	21	33.3	63
Bridgewater	65	42.8	87	57.2	152
Dexter	40	44.9	49	55.1	89
Freedom	29	35.4	53	64.6	82
Lima	86	65.6	45	34.4	131
Lodi	80	53.0	71	47.0	151
Lyndon	31	38.8	49	61.3	80
Manchester	91	45.0	111	55.0	202
Northfield	56	34.1	108	65.9	164
Pittsfield	131	67.9	62	32.1	193
Salem	119	59.5	81	40.5	200
Saline	137	53.9	117	46.1	254
Scio	110	51.6	103	48.4	213
Sharon	62	48.4	66	51.6	128
Superior	80	52.3	73	47.7	153
Sylvan	59	49.6	60	50.4	119
Webster	62	50.8	60	49.2	122
York	65	39.4	100	60.6	165
Ypsilanti	248	50.6	242	49.4	490
Totals	2,006	51.7	1,873	48.3	3,879

Source: *Michigan Argus*, November 21, 1849.

TABLE 20. WASHTENAW COUNTY ELECTION RETURNS,
1850 DELEGATES TO THE STATE CONSTITUTIONAL CONVENTION

	James Kingsley *	Daniel Hixson *	E. M. Skinner *	Beriah King	T. H. Marsh	Earl P. Gardiner *	M. O'Brien *	P. Staring *
Ann Arbor	321	171	261	253	157	200	187	267
Augusta	21	12	24	23	14	13	13	23
Bridgewater	71	118	67	67	96	118	117	67
Dexter	3	76	4	4	77	77	73	4
Freedom	64	64	64	65	59	65	64	66
Lima	47	111	44	45	69	112	112	82
Lodi	63	65	63	62	62	64	64	61
Lyndon	1	32	1	1	32	32	32	1
Manchester	26	101	25	27	93	101	99	23
Northfield	95	84	64	67	72	74	107	91
Pittsfield	58	32	65	55	28	38	5	53
Salem	101	61	100	100	58	62	60	99
Saline	67	73	69	24	135	69	66	67
Scio	108	134	96	114	134	142	120	98
Sharon	47	45	44	45	37	43	42	45
Superior	47	52	47	49	34	56	49	51
Sylvan	48	59	47	48	46	58	59	53
Webster	41	18	44	48	26	24	30	55
York	51	50	50	50	45	50	50	50
Ypsilanti	139	176	292	140	123	178	97	124
Totals	1,419	1,534	1,471	1,287	1,397	1,576	1,446	1,380

Table 20 (continued). Washtenaw County Election Returns, 1850 Delegates to the State Constitutional Convention

	Dwight Webb	Z. C. Brown	W. S. Carr *	Darius Pierce	J. M. Edmunds *	George Renwick	S. W. Bowers *	B. W. Waite *
Ann Arbor	275	295	200	177	206	305	297	210
Augusta	20	20	11	11	9	20	20	11
Bridgewater	12	13	62	60	59	14	13	62
Dexter	1	0	73	73	73	0	0	73
Freedom	14	18	18	17	18	18	18	17
Lima	23	27	83	88	87	23	25	92
Lodi	44	45	47	47	46	44	43	47
Lyndon	4	4	35	35	35	4	4	35
Manchester	22	20	90	90	90	21	19	90
Northfield	29	31	31	29	30	31	30	30
Pittsfield	81	85	60	43	39	81	78	63
Salem	68	69	30	29	40	66	66	30
Saline	23	111	101	103	130	101	101	103
Scio	63	74	113	98	111	75	70	111
Sharon	31	33	28	29	30	31	26	30
Superior	53	61	61	60	62	55	66	63
Sylvan	29	40	55	58	49	40	40	51
Webster	60	61	36	29	33	61	59	27
York	45	41	46	46	40	46	45	46
Ypsilanti	75	206	235	199	338	242	201	236
Totals	972	1,254	1,415	1,321	1,525	1,278	1,221	1,427

*Source: Michigan Argus, May 8, 1850. Some of the column totals listed in the Argus differ from those presented here.
Candidates in regular type are Democrats. Candidates in italics are Whigs. **Candidates in bold are Free Soil–endorsed candidates.**

TABLE 21. WASHTENAW COUNTY ELECTION RETURNS, 1850 STATE TREASURER

	Whig	%	Democrat	%	Free Soil	%	Total votes
Ann Arbor	389	48.1	321	39.7	98	12.1	808
Augusta							
Bridgewater							
Dexter							
Freedom							
Lima							
Lodi							
Lyndon							
Manchester					6		
Northfield							
Pittsfield							
Salem							
Saline							
Scio							
Sharon							
Superior							
Sylvan							
Webster	75	54.0	53	38.1	11	7.9	139
York							
Ypsilanti							
Totals	2,219	48.5	2,122	46.4	232	5.1	4,573

Sources: Michigan Argus, November 6, 13, 1850; Webster Township Minutes, in possession of Webster Township Clerk; Manchester Township Minutes, Manchester Township Hall.

TABLE 22. WASHTENAW COUNTY ELECTION RETURNS, 1852 PRESIDENTIAL

	Whig	%	Democrat	%	Free Soil	%	Total votes
Ann Arbor City	210	36.0	300	51.4	74	12.7	584
Ann Arbor	138	46.0	118	39.3	44	14.7	300
Augusta	51	33.6	54	35.5	47	30.9	152
Bridgewater	80	36.9	126	58.1	11	5.1	217
Dexter	54	33.5	101	62.7	6	3.7	161
Freedom	56	28.1	137	68.8	6	3.0	199
Lima	76	43.2	67	38.1	33	18.8	176
Lodi	76	33.8	112	49.8	37	16.4	225
Lyndon	50	40.7	68	55.3	5	4.1	123
Manchester	114	43.0	122	46.0	29	10.9	265
Northfield	70	32.1	138	63.3	10	4.6	218
Pittsfield	108	51.7	76	36.4	25	12.0	209
Salem	71	27.5	106	41.1	81	31.4	258
Saline	166	45.2	148	40.3	53	14.4	367
Scio	156	47.6	146	44.5	26	7.9	328
Sharon	76	45.8	78	47.0	12	7.2	166
Superior	116	47.5	127	52.0	1	0.4	244
Sylvan	72	40.4	79	44.4	27	15.2	178
Webster	93	47.4	81	41.3	22	11.2	196
York	133	44.8	149	50.2	15	5.1	297
Ypsilanti	308	49.8	271	43.9	39	6.3	618
Totals	2,274	41.5	2,604	47.5	603	11.0	5,481

Source: Washtenaw Whig, November 24, 1852.

TABLE 23. WASHTENAW COUNTY TOWNSHIP ELECTION RETURNS, 1841

	Total votes	Liberty votes	%
Ann Arbor	551	50	9.1
Augusta			
Bridgewater			
Dexter			
Freedom			
Lima			
Lodi			
Lyndon			
Manchester	no Liberty ticket		
Northfield			
Pittsfield	no Liberty ticket		

TABLE 23 (*continued*). WASHTENAW COUNTY TOWNSHIP ELECTION RETURNS, 1841

	Total votes	Liberty votes	%
Salem	202	42	20.8
Saline			
Scio	NA	19	
Sharon			
Superior			
Sylvan	no Liberty ticket		
Webster	no Liberty ticket		
York			
Ypsilanti	no Liberty ticket		

Note: Party affiliations of non-Liberty candidates in township elections are sometimes difficult to determine; occasionally, Liberty Party tickets faced a single opposition ticket, as Whigs and Democrats frequently put aside partisan differences for township elections. Thus, only the Liberty Party (and after 1848, Free Soil or Free Democrat) vote percentage is shown in Tables 23 through 32.

Sources: Michigan State Journal, April 6, 1841; *Signal of Liberty*, April 28, 1841, May 2, 1842; Ypsilanti Township Election Book, Bentley Library; Sylvan Township Records, Bentley Library; Pittsfield Township Records, Bentley Library and Pittsfield Township Hall; Webster Township Minutes, in possession of Webster Township Clerk; Manchester Township Minutes, Manchester Town Hall.

TABLE 24. WASHTENAW COUNTY TOWNSHIP ELECTION RETURNS, 1842

	Total votes	Liberty	%
Ann Arbor	539	72	13.4
Augusta			
Bridgewater	NA	20	
Dexter			
Freedom			
Lima			
Lodi	NA	18	
Lyndon			
Manchester	179	30	16.8
Northfield			
Pittsfield	153	28	18.3
Salem	NA	69	
Saline			
Scio	NA	15	
Sharon			
Superior			
Sylvan	102	28	27.5
Webster	120	15	12.5
York			
Ypsilanti	319	35	11.0

Sources: Signal of Liberty, April 6, 13, 25, May 2, 1842; township minutes as cited in Table 23.

Table 25. Washtenaw County Township Election Returns, 1843

	Total votes	Liberty	%
Ann Arbor	542	64	11.8
Augusta			
Bridgewater			
Dexter			
Freedom			
Lima			
Lodi			
Lyndon			
Manchester	no Liberty ticket (all of the Liberty votes of the previous year went to the Whigs)		
Northfield			
Pittsfield			
Salem	158	64	40.5
Saline	NA		
Scio		24	
Sharon			
Superior			
Sylvan	104	18	17.3
Webster	116	13	11.2
York			
Ypsilanti	no Liberty ticket		

Sources: Michigan State Journal, April 5, 1843; *Signal of Liberty*, April 10, 1843; April 15, 1844 (Salem figures for 1843 extrapolated from these latter two sources); township minutes as cited in Table 23.

TABLE 26. WASHTENAW COUNTY ELECTION RETURNS, 1844

	Total votes	Liberty	%	
Ann Arbor	640	95	14.8	
Augusta				
Bridgewater				
Dexter				
Freedom				
Lima				
Lodi				
Lyndon				
Manchester	221	17	7.7	
Northfield				
Pittsfield	NA	18		
Salem	230	83	36.1	(Whig 43, Democrat 104)
Saline				
Scio	267	30	11.2	
Sharon				
Superior				
Sylvan	no Liberty ticket			
Webster	133	16	12.0	
York				
Ypsilanti	487	18	3.7	

Sources: Scio Township Minutes, Scio Township Hall; *Signal of Liberty,* April 8, 15, 1844; township minutes as cited in Table 23.

TABLE 27. Washtenaw County Township Election Returns, 1845

	Total votes	Liberty	%
Ann Arbor	785	108	13.8
Augusta			
Bridgewater			
Dexter			
Freedom			
Lima			
Lodi			
Lyndon			
Manchester	226	8	3.5
Northfield			
Pittsfield			
Salem	NA	79	(The Liberty ticket was "lacking a few votes of a majority.")
Saline			
Scio			
Sharon			
Superior			
Sylvan	no Liberty ticket		
Webster	149	15	10.1
York			
Ypsilanti	333	45	13.5

Sources: Ann Arbor Township Election Returns, Ann Arbor Township Hall; *Signal of Liberty*, April 14, 1845; township minutes as cited in Table 23.

TABLE 28. WASHTENAW COUNTY TOWNSHIP ELECTION RETURNS, 1846

	Total votes	Liberty	%
Ann Arbor*	713	69	9.7
Augusta			
Bridgewater			
Dexter			
Freedom			
Lima			
Lodi			
Lyndon			
Manchester	219	7	3.2
Northfield			
Pittsfield			
Salem	"The entire Liberty ticket was elected, excepting for three offices."		
Saline			
Scio			
Sharon			
Superior			
Sylvan	no Liberty ticket		
Webster	124	14	11.3
York			
Ypsilanti	no Liberty ticket		

*In Ann Arbor, a nativist party also ran a ticket. The non-Liberty parties received the following votes: Whig 312 (43.8%), Democrat 262 (36.8%), Nativist 69 (9.7%).

Sources: Signal of Liberty, April 13, 1846; township minutes as cited in Table 23.

TABLE 29. WASHTENAW COUNTY TOWNSHIP ELECTION RETURNS, 1847

	Total votes	Liberty	%
Ann Arbor	789	77	9.8
Augusta			
Bridgewater			
Dexter			
Freedom			
Lima			
Lodi			
Lyndon			
Manchester	237	8	3.4
Northfield			
Pittsfield	125	12	9.6
Salem	156	92	59.0 (no Whig ticket was run)
Saline			
Scio	no Liberty ticket		
Sharon			
Superior			
Sylvan	no Liberty ticket		
Webster	no Liberty ticket		
York			
Ypsilanti	443	26	5.9

Sources: Signal of Liberty, April 10, 1847; township minutes as cited in Table 23.

TABLE 30. WASHTENAW COUNTY TOWNSHIP ELECTION RETURNS, 1848

	Total votes	Liberty	%
Ann Arbor	794	50	6.3
Augusta	no Liberty ticket		
Bridgewater	no Liberty ticket		
Dexter			
Freedom	no Liberty ticket		
Lima			
Lodi			
Lyndon			
Manchester	no Liberty ticket		
Northfield			
Pittsfield	150	14	9.3
Salem			
Saline			
Scio	no Liberty ticket		
Sharon			
Superior			
Sylvan	no Liberty ticket		
Webster	no Liberty ticket		
York			
Ypsilanti	no Liberty ticket		

Sources: Ann Arbor Township Election Returns, Ann Arbor Township Hall; Freedom Township Minutes, Freedom Township Hall; Bridgewater Township Minutes, in possession of Bridgewater Township Clerk; Scio Township Minutes, Scio Township Hall; other township minutes as cited in Table 23.

TABLE 31. WASHTENAW COUNTY TOWNSHIP ELECTION RETURNS, 1849

	Total votes	Free Soil	%
Ann Arbor	777	226	29.1
Augusta			
Bridgewater			
Dexter			
Freedom	no Free Soil ticket		
Lima			
Lodi			
Lyndon			
Manchester	225	40	17.8
Northfield			
Pittsfield	no Free Soil ticket		
Salem			
Saline			
Scio	273	21	7.7
Sharon			
Superior			
Sylvan	no Free Soil ticket		
Webster	no Free Soil ticket		
York			
Ypsilanti	no Free Soil ticket		

Note: The Ann Arbor figure constitutes the average for those races that the Free Soilers contested with independent nominations, and does not include those races in which Free Soilers supported a candidate who also enjoyed another party's nomination.

Sources: Township minutes as cited in Tables 23 and 30.

TABLE 32. WASHTENAW COUNTY TOWNSHIP ELECTION RETURNS, 1853

	Total votes	Free Democrat	%
Ann Arbor	257	29	11.3
Ann Arbor City	514	100	19.5
Augusta			
Bridgewater			
Dexter			
Freedom	no Free Democrat ticket		
Lima			
Lodi	191	38	19.9
Lyndon			
Manchester	235	36	15.3
Northfield			
Pittsfield	no Free Democrat ticket		
Salem			
Saline			
Scio	292	20	6.8
Sharon			
Superior			
Sylvan	no Free Democrat ticket		
Webster	no Free Democrat ticket		
York			
Ypsilanti	515	16	3.1

Sources: Washtenaw Whig, April 6, 1853; Lodi Township Minutes, Lodi Township Hall; township minutes as cited in Tables 23 and 30.

TABLE 33. RELIGIOUS AFFILIATION OF WASHTENAW COUNTY ABOLITIONISTS BY COHORT AND DENOMINATION

	Antislavery Cohort				
	1836–1840 (pre–Liberty)	Petition signers 1837–42	Liberty Party activists	1842 gag-rule protestors	*Signal of Liberty* subscribers
Baptists	0	24	23	2	14
Free Will Baptists	0	1	1	0	0
Catholics	0	0	0	0	2
Episcopalians	2	5	6	2	15
Congregationalists	10	21	34	5	25
Presbyterians	28	37	58	9	25
Methodists	2	14	15	4	15
Wesleyan Methodists	3	13	15	7	9
Quakers	0	0	0	0	1
Unitarians	0	0	0	0	0
Universalists	0	2	7	1	7
Swedenborgians	0	0	0	0	0
Spiritualists	1	0	1	0	0
Totals	46	117	160	30	113
Total antislavery activists in cohort	83	369	353	66	323

TABLE 34. AGES OF WASHTENAW COUNTY WHITE MALE ABOLITIONISTS (INCLUDING FREE SOILERS AND PETITION SIGNERS) AND MICHIGAN SUBSCRIBERS TO THE *SIGNAL OF LIBERTY*

Age Group	Washtenaw County abolitionists	%	*Signal* subscribers	%	Michigan adult white males %
20–24	10		11		
25–29	25	7.3	54	7.9	35.9
30–34	56		113		
35–39	86	29.5	155	32.8	27.9
40–44	86		149		
45–49	82	34.9	135	34.7	19.2
50–54	58		79		
55–59	27	17.7	55	16.4	10.3
60–64	20		30		
65–69	19	8.1	26	6.8	4.8
70–74	5		5		
75–79	5	2.1	2	0.9	1.6
80–84	2		2		
85–89	0	0.4	2	0.5	0.3
Totals	481	100.0	818	100.0	100.0

Sources: De Bow, *Seventh Census*, 882–83; 1850 federal manuscript census; see Table 33.

	Non–Liberty abolitionists, 1841–48	Free Soilers	Non–Free Soil abolitionists, 1850–60	Female abolitionists	African American abolitionists	All Washtenaw anti-slavery activists and petitioners
Baptists	1	5	2	1	2	55
Free Will Baptists	0	1	0	0	0	3
Catholics	0	0	0	0	0	2
Episcopalians	0	4	0	0	1	27
Congregationalists	3	13	6	5	0	60
Presbyterians	3	11	2	2	0	108
Methodists	2	13	1	0	0	41
Wesleyan Methodists	4	4	0	0	1	23
Quakers	0	0	4	1	0	4
Unitarians	0	0	0	0	0	0
Universalists	3	4	0	0	0	14
Swedenborgians	0	1	0	0	0	1
Spiritualists	0	0	2	0	0	2
Totals	16	56	17	9	4	340
Total antislavery activists in cohort	46	138	28	27	9	1,035

Sources: Most of the above individuals were identified as antislavery activists from Washtenaw County newspapers and from the *Signal of Liberty* subscription list, Theodore Foster Papers, Bentley Library. Regarding church affiliations, see Table 9.

BIBLIOGRAPHY

UNPUBLISHED PRIMARY SOURCES

Church Records

Alabama Department of Archives and History, Montgomery

Alabama Presbytery, Cumberland Presbyterian Church, 1825–1867. Records.
Synod of Alabama, 1837–1849. Records.

Michigan Historical Collections, Bentley Historical Library, University of Michigan

First Baptist Church of Ann Arbor. Records.
First Baptist Church of Chelsea (Sylvan). Records.
First Baptist Church of Manchester. Records.
First Baptist Church of Saline. Records.
First Congregational Church of Ann Arbor. Records.
First Congregational Church of Chelsea (Sylvan). Records.
First Congregational Church of Lima. Records.
First Congregational Church of Salem. Records.
First Presbyterian Church of Lodi. Records.
First Presbyterian Church of Stoney Creek (Augusta). Records.
First Presbyterian Church of Ypsilanti. Records.
First United Church of Christ, Webster Township. Records.
First United Methodist Church of Ann Arbor. Records.
First United Methodist Church of Ypsilanti. Records.
Free Will Baptist Church of Manchester. Records.
Michigan Association of Free Will Baptists. Records.
Moses Boylan Papers. Ann Arbor Methodist Episcopal Directory.
St. Andrew's Episcopal Church, Ann Arbor. Records.

St. Luke's Episcopal Church, Ypsilanti. Records.
Washtenaw Presbytery. Minutes.

Special Collections, Samford University, Birmingham, Alabama

Gilgal Baptist Church, Tuscaloosa County. Records.
Grant's Creek Baptist Church, Fosters, Alabama. Records.
Liberty Baptist Church, Tuscaloosa County. Records.

W. S. Hoole Special Collections Library, University of Alabama

Bethabera Baptist Church (filed as Bone Camp Methodist Church), Tuscaloosa
    County. Records.
Bethany Baptist Church, Tuscaloosa County. Records.
Big Creek Baptist Church, Tuscaloosa County. Records.
Dunn's Creek Baptist Church, Tuscaloosa County. Records.

The following records remain in the possession of their respective churches:
Christ Episcopal Church, Tuscaloosa. Records.
First Baptist Church of Tuscaloosa. Records.
First Baptist Church of Ypsilanti, 1854–1871. Records.
First Presbyterian Church of Tuscaloosa. Records. Minutes of the Teachers' As-
    sociation of the Tuscaloosa Union Sunday School.
St. John the Baptist Catholic Church, Ypsilanti. Records.
St. John's Catholic Church, Tuscaloosa. Records.
St. Patrick's Catholic Church, Northfield. Records.
St. Thomas the Apostle Catholic Church, Ann Arbor. Records.

Municipal and Other Manuscript Government Records

Alabama Department of Archives and History, Montgomery, Alabama

Alabama state census, 1855, Tuscaloosa County.
Population schedule of the 1830 census, Tuscaloosa County, Alabama.
Population schedule of the 1840 census, Tuscaloosa County, Alabama.
Population schedule of the 1850 census, Tuscaloosa County, Alabama.
Population schedule of the 1860 census, Tuscaloosa County, Alabama.
Slave schedule of the 1850 census, Tuscaloosa County, Alabama.
Social schedule of the 1850 census, Tuscaloosa County, Alabama.

Tuscaloosa County Courthouse, Tuscaloosa, Alabama

Circuit Court Records, 1824–1855.
Tuscaloosa County Tavern License Docket, 1818–1832.

Michigan Historical Collections, Bentley Historical Library, University of Michigan

Agricultural schedule of the 1850 census, Washtenaw County, Michigan.
Population schedule of the 1850 census, Washtenaw County, Michigan.
Social schedule of the 1850 census, Washtenaw County, Michigan.
Ann Arbor Village Council. Record book. 1834–1845.
Ann Arbor Village and City Council. Record Book. 1847–1861.
Dexter Township. Poll list, 1840.
Manchester Township. Poll list, 1840.
Northfield Township. Poll list, 1840.
Pittsfield Township. Records.
Saline Township. Poll list, 1840.
Sylvan Township. Poll list (1840) and Records.
Webster Township. Poll list, 1840.
York Township. Poll list, 1852.
Ypsilanti Township. Records.

The following Washtenaw County records remain in the custody of their respective township clerks:

Ann Arbor Township. Poll list (1840) and Records.
Bridgewater Township. Records.
Freedom Township. Records.
Lodi Township. Records.
Manchester Township. Records.
Pittsfield Township. Records.
Scio Township. Records.
Webster Township. Records.

Records of Elections and Archives Division, Department of State, Lansing, Michigan

County Canvassers' Statements of Votes for County, State, and Federal Offices.

Washtenaw County Courthouse, Ann Arbor, Michigan

Washtenaw County Circuit Court Calendars, 1832–1860.
Washtenaw County District Court Journal, April 4, 1843–December 23, 1846.

National Archives, Washington, D.C.

Records of the U.S. House of Representatives, Record Group 233. 25th Congress–27th Congress. Petitions and Memorials Referred to Committees.

Manuscript Collections

American Bible Society Archives, New York

 Agent Papers.

Auburn University Archives, Auburn, Alabama

 Porter, Benjamin F. Papers.

Alabama Department of Archives and History, Montgomery, Alabama

 Blue, Matthew P. Papers.
 Meek, A. B. Diary.
 Searcy, James T. Papers.

Library of Congress, Washington, D.C.

 American Colonization Society Papers.

Michigan Historical Collections, Bentley Historical Library, University of Michigan

 American Home Missionary Society. Papers.
 Ann Arbor Temperance Society. Minutes.
 Chandler, Elizabeth. Papers.
 Clarke, George W. Papers.
 College Temperance Society. Records.
 Collins, Judson D. Papers.
 Davis, Lorenzo. Papers.
 Dubuar, James. Papers.
 Dunn, Ransom. Papers.
 Foster, Theodore. Papers.
 Kooker, Arthur Raymond. Papers.
 Pattengill Family. Papers.
 Phoenix Division No. 79, Sons of Temperance. Records.
 Ten Brook, Andrew. Papers.
 Thomas, Nathan Macy. Papers.
 Treadwell, Seymour Boughton. Papers.

Special Collections, Samford University, Birmingham, Alabama

 Papers of the American Home Missionary Society (microfilm).
 Papers of the American Sunday School Union (microfilm).

William L. Clements Library, University of Michigan

> Birney, James Gillespie. Papers.
> Fuller, Harriet DeGarmo. Papers.

W. S. Hoole Special Collections Library, University of Alabama

> Anderson, James Austin. Papers.
> Manly Family. Papers.
> Tuscaloosa Female Benevolent Society. Records.
> Tuscaloosa Scrapbook No. 5, "On the History of Tuscaloosa."

Published Primary Sources

Alabama and Michigan Newspapers

(Alabama newspapers—Tuscaloosa unless otherwise noted)

> *Alabama Baptist* (Marion)
> *Alabama Baptist Advocate* (Marion)
> *Alabama Intelligencer and State Rights Expositor*
> *Alabama Sentinel*
> *Alabama State Intelligencer*
> *Alabama State Sentinel* (Selma)
> *American Mirror*
> *Crystal Fount*
> *Daily Alabama Journal* (Montgomery)
> *Daily Montgomery Journal*
> *Dallas Gazette* (Cahaba)
> *Democratic Gazette*
> *Democratic Mentor*
> *Democratic Watchtower* (Talladega)
> *Flag of the Union*
> Huntsville *Democrat*
> *Independent Monitor*
> *Jones Valley Times* (Elyton)
> Montgomery *Advertiser*
> *South Western Baptist* (Marion, Montgomery, and Tuskegee)
> *Spirit of the Age*
> *State Journal and Flag of the Union*
> *State Rights Expositor and Spirit of the Age*

Tuscaloosa *Chronicle*
Tuscaloosa *Inquirer*
Tuscaloosa *Observer*
Tuscumbia *Telegraph*
Tuskaloosa *Whig*
Universalist Herald (Notasulga)

(Michigan newspapers—Ann Arbor unless otherwise noted)

American Freeman (Jackson)
Ann Arbor *American*
Ann Arbor *Journal*
B'Hoys' Eagle
Democratic Herald
Detroit *Daily Advertiser*
Detroit *Daily Democrat*
Detroit *Free Press*
Emigrant
Family Favorite (Adrian)
Local News and Advertiser
Michigan Argus
Michigan Christian Herald (Detroit)
Michigan Emigrant
Michigan Free Democrat (Detroit)
Michigan Freeman (Jackson)
Michigan Liberty Press (Battle Creek)
Michigan State Journal
Michigan Temperance Journal and Washingtonian (Jackson)
Michigan Times
Michigan Whig
Michigan Whig and Washtenaw Democrat
Monroe *Times*
Peninsular Freeman (Detroit)
Primitive Expounder
Signal of Liberty
State Journal
True Democrat
Washtenaw Whig
Western Emigrant
Young Men's Temperance Journal and Advocate of Temperance (Detroit)
Ypsilanti *Sentinel*

Other Newspapers, Periodicals

African Repository (Washington, D.C.)

American Anti-Slavery Society *Annual Report* (New York)

American Baptist Home Mission Society *Annual Report* (New York)

American Bible Society *Annual Report* (New York)

American Temperance Magazine and Sons of Temperance Offering (New York)

American Tract Society (Boston) *Annual Report*

American Tract Society (New York) *Annual Report*

Anti-Masonic Herald and Lancaster (Pa.) Weekly Courier

Family Favorite and Temperance Journal (Adrian)

Journal of Humanity, and Herald of the American Temperance Society (Andover, Mass.)

Journal of the American Temperance Union (Philadelphia)

Liberator (Boston)

National Anti-Slavery Standard (New York)

Temperance Banner (Penfield, Ga.)

Published Church Minutes

(Alabama Baptist State Convention)

Minutes of the Sixth Anniversary of the Alabama Baptist State Convention. Montgomery, 1829.

Minutes of the Eleventh Anniversary of the Baptist State Convention, in Alabama, Held at Salem Meeting House, Near Greensborough. Tuscaloosa, 1834.

Minutes of the Thirteenth Anniversary of the Alabama Baptist State Convention, Held at Fellowship Meeting House, Wilcox County, Alabama. Commencing on Saturday, November 12th, 1836. Tuscaloosa, 1836.

Minutes of the Fourteenth Anniversary of the Baptist State Convention of Alabama, Held at Enon Meeting House, Madison County. Tuscaloosa, 1837.

Minutes of the Sixteenth Anniversary of the Baptist State Convention of Alabama, Held at Oakmulgee Meeting House, Perry County, Commencing on Saturday, Nov. 9, 1839. Tuscaloosa, 1839.

Minutes of the Seventeenth Anniversary of the Baptist State Convention of Alabama, Held at Salem, Greene County, Alabama. Tuscaloosa, 1840.

Minutes of the Eighteenth Anniversary of the Baptist State Convention, of Alabama. N.p., 1841[?].

Minutes of the Nineteenth Anniversary of the Baptist State Convention of Alabama. N.p., 1842[?].

Journal of the Proceedings of the Baptist State Convention in Alabama at Its Twentieth Anniversary at Marion, Perry County, Commencing on Saturday, November 16, 1844. N.p., 1844[?].

Minutes of the Twenty-first Anniversary of the Alabama Baptist State Convention. N.p., 1845[?].

Minutes of the Twenty-second Anniversary of the Alabama Baptist State Convention, Marion, Perry County, November 14–17, 1846. N.p., 1846[?].

Minutes of the Alabama Baptist State Convention, 1847. N.p., 1847[?].

Minutes of the Alabama Baptist State Convention, 1848. N.p., 1848[?].

Minutes of the Alabama Baptist State Convention, 1849. N.p., 1849[?].

Minutes of the Thirty-third Annual Session of the Alabama Baptist Association, Held in the Providence Church, Dallas Co., Ala., October 8th to 11th, 1852. Montgomery, 1852.

Minutes of the Thirty-first Anniversary of the Alabama Baptist State Convention, Held at Marion, Perry County. Marion, 1854.

Minutes of the Thirty-fourth Anniversary of the Alabama Baptist State Convention, Held at Marion. Tuskegee, Alabama, 1857.

(Tuscaloosa Baptist Association)

Minutes of the Eleventh Annual Session of the Tuscaloosa Baptist Association, Held at the Gilgal Meeting-House, Tuscaloosa County, Alabama. Tuscaloosa, 1843.

Minutes of the Twelfth Annual Session of the Tuscaloosa Baptist Association, Held at Spring Hill Meeting House, Tuscaloosa County, from the 14th to the 17th of September 1844. Tuscaloosa, 1844.

Minutes of the Fourteenth Annual Session of the Tuscaloosa Baptist Association. Tuscaloosa, 1846.

Minutes of the Fifteenth Annual Session of the Tuscaloosa Baptist Association, Held at Hopewell Meeting-House, Tuscaloosa County, Alabama. Tuscaloosa, 1847.

Minutes of the Sixteenth Annual Session of the Tuscaloosa Baptist Association, Held at Concord Meeting-House, Fayette County, Alabama. Tuscaloosa, 1848.

Minutes of the Seventeenth Annual Session of the Tuscaloosa Baptist Association, Held at the Mt. Moriah Meeting-House, Bibb Co., Ala. Tuscaloosa, 1849.

Minutes of the Eighteenth Annual Session of the Tuscaloosa Baptist Association, Held at the Friendship Meeting-House, Tuscaloosa County, Alabama. Tuscaloosa, 1850.

Minutes of the Twenty-first Annual Session of the Tuscaloosa Baptist Association, Held at the Hepzibah Meeting House, Tuscaloosa Co., Ala., from the 17th to 20th Sept., 1853. Tuscaloosa, 1853.

Minutes of the Twenty-Second Annual Session of the Tuscaloosa Baptist Association. Tuscaloosa, 1854.

Minutes of the Twenty-Fourth Annual Session of the Tuscaloosa Baptist Association. Tuscaloosa, 1856.

Minutes of the Twenty-Fifth Annual Session of the Tuskaloosa Baptist Association. Tuscaloosa, 1857.

(Alabama Conference of the Methodist Episcopal Church)

Minutes of the Alabama Conference of the M. E. Church, South, Held at Talladega, Ala., December 13th, 1854, Together with the Annual Sermon, Preached Before the Conference by A. M. Mitchell, D.D. Montgomery, 1855.

Minutes of the Alabama Conference of the Methodist Episcopal Church, South, Held in Eutaw, Alabama, December 5, 1855, Together with the Annual Sermon, Preached Before the Conference by Phil P. Heely, D.D. Montgomery, 1856.

(General Association of Michigan [Congregationalist])

Minutes of the General Association of Michigan at Their Meeting in Grass Lake, Sept. 1843. Marshall, 1843.

Minutes of the General Association of Michigan at Their Meeting at Marshall, Sept. 1844. Marshall, 1844.

Minutes of the General Association of Michigan at Their Meeting in Dexter, Sept. 1846. Detroit, 1846.

Minutes of the General Association of Michigan at Their Meeting in Ann Arbor, May 30, 1848. Jackson, 1848.

Minutes of the General Association of Michigan at Their Meeting in Kalamazoo, May 28, 1850. Detroit, 1850.

Minutes of the General Association of Michigan at Their Meeting in Clinton, May 27, 1851. Detroit, 1851.

Minutes of the General Association of Michigan at Their Meeting in Ann Arbor, May 31, 1853. Detroit, 1853.

Minutes of the General Association of Michigan at Their Meeting in Detroit, May 30th, 1854. Ann Arbor, 1854.

Minutes of the General Association of Michigan at Their Meeting in Kalamazoo, May 29th, 1855. Adrian, 1855.

Minutes of the General Association of Michigan at Their Meeting in Jackson, May 27, 1856. Detroit, 1856.

Minutes of the General Association of Michigan at Their Meeting in Adrian, May 20, 1858. Adrian, 1858.

Minutes of the General Association of Michigan at Their Meeting in Detroit, May 19, 1859. Adrian, 1859.

Government Documents

Alabama

Acts of the Seventh Biennial Session of the General Assembly of Alabama. Montgomery, 1860.

Acts Passed at the Eighth Annual Session of the General Assembly of the State of Alabama. Tuscaloosa, 1827.

Acts Passed at the Tenth Annual Session of the General Assembly of the State of Alabama. Tuscaloosa, 1829.

Acts Passed at the Thirteenth Annual Session of the General Assembly of the State of Alabama. Tuscaloosa, 1832.

Acts Passed at the Extra and Annual Sessions of the General Assembly of the State of Alabama. Tuscaloosa, 1832.

Clay, C. C., compiler. *Digest of the Laws of the State of Alabama.* Tuscaloosa, 1843.

Ormond, John J., Arthur P. Bagby, and George Goldwaite, comps.. *The Code of Alabama.* Montgomery, 1852.

Michigan

Acts of the Legislature of Michigan Passed at the Annual Session of 1845. Detroit, 1845.

Acts of the Legislature of the State of Michigan Passed at the Annual Session of 1849. Lansing, 1849.

Documents Accompanying the Journal of the House of Representatives of the State of Michigan, at the Annual Session of 1840. Volume II. Detroit, 1840.

The Revised Statutes of the State of Michigan, Passed and Approved May 18, 1846. Detroit, 1846.

Statistics of the State of Michigan, Compiled from the Census of 1850, Taken by Authority of the United States. Condensed for Publication by the Secretary of State of the State of Michigan. Lansing, 1851.

Statistics of the State of Michigan, Compiled from the Census of 1860, Taken by Authority of the United States. Lansing, 1861.

United States

Compendium of the Enumeration of the Inhabitants and Statistics of the United States, as Obtained from the Department of State, from the Returns of the Sixth Census. Washington, D.C., 1841.

Compendium of the Ninth Census. Washington, D.C., 1872.

Congressional Globe. 25th Cong., 2d Sess., Vol. VI.

De Bow, J. D. B. *The Seventh Census of the United States: 1850.* Washington, D.C., 1853.

————. *Statistical View of the United States . . . Being a Compendium of the Seventh Census.* Washington, D.C., 1854.

Fifth Census; or, Enumeration of the Inhabitants of the United States. 1830. Washington, D.C., 1832.

Historical Statistics of the United States: Colonial Times to 1970. Washington, D.C., 1975.

Population of the United States in 1860: Compiled from the Original Returns of the Eighth Census. Washington, D.C., 1864.

Statistics of the United States (Including Mortality, Property, & C.) in 1860: Compiled from the . . . Eighth Census. Washington, D.C., 1866.

Decisions of the Alabama Supreme Court

The Intendant and Council of the Town of Marion v. *Chandler.* 6 Alabama Reports, 899–904 (1844).

The Mayor, & c. of Mobile v. *Rouse.* 8 Alabama Reports 515–517 (1845).

Harris v. *The Intendant and Council of Livingston,* 28 Alabama Reports 577–580 (1856).

Ex Parte James T. Burnett, 30 Alabama Reports 461–470 (1858).

Pickens Adm'r. v. *Pickens' Distributees,* 35 Alabama Reports 442–452 (1860).

Decisions of the Michigan Supreme Court

The People v. *Thomas Gallagher,* 4 Michigan 244–285 (1856).

John J. Ortman, plaintiff in error v. *William B. Greenman* et al., *defendants in error,* 4 Michigan 291–294 (1856).

Other Published Primary Sources

Annual Report Presented to the American Anti-Slavery Society. New York, 1856.

Articles of Faith and Covenant, Adopted by the First Presbyterian Church of Ann Arbor. Ann Arbor, 1841.

Blue, M[atthew] P., *et al. City Directory and History of Montgomery, with a Summary of Events in That History, Calendarically Arranged.* Montgomery, 1878.

Burnham, W. Dean. *Presidential Ballots, 1836–1892.* Baltimore, 1955.

Cole, Maurice, ed. *Voices from the Wilderness.* Ann Arbor, 1961.

Dumond, Dwight L., ed. *Letters of James Gillespie Birney.* 2 vols. New York, 1938.

The First Annual Report of the Michigan Sunday School Union Society. Detroit, 1832.

Garrett, William. *Reminiscences of Public Men in Alabama, for Thirty Years.* Atlanta, 1872.

Haviland, Laura S. *A Woman's Life-Work: Labors and Experiences of Laura S. Haviland.* Cincinnati, 1882.

History of Berrien and Van Buren Counties. Philadelphia, 1880.

Hoole, W. Stanley, ed. "Elyton, Alabama, and the Connecticut Asylum: The Letters of William H. Ely, 1820–1821." *Alabama Review,* III (January 1950), 36–69.

Hubbs, G. Ward, ed. *Rowdy Tales from Early Alabama: The Humor of John Gorman Barr.* University, Ala., 1981.

Lincecum, Gideon. "Autobiography of Gideon Lincecum." *Publications of the Mississippi Historical Society,* VIII (1904), 443–519.

Little, George. *Memoirs of George Little.* Tuscaloosa, 1924.

Lyell, Charles. *A Second Visit to the United States of North America.* 2 vols. New York, 1849.

Matlack, Lucius. *The History of American Slavery and Methodism, from 1780 to 1849: and History of the Wesleyan Methodist Connection of America.* New York, 1849.

Maxwell, James Robert. *Autobiography of James Robert Maxwell of Tuskaloosa, Alabama.* New York, 1926.

Maxwell, Thomas. "Mobile and Tuscaloosa, 1836–1837." *Alabama University Monthly,* I (February 1874), 53–58.

Mayhew, Ira. *Popular Education for the Use of Parents and Teachers, and for Young Persons of Both Sexes.* New York, 1850.

Merrill, Walter M., and Louis Ruchames, editors. *The Letters of William Lloyd Garrison.* 6 vols. Cambridge, Mass., 1971–81.

Miller, Stephen F. *The Bench and Bar in Georgia: Memoirs and Sketches.* 2 vols. Philadelphia, 1858.

Miller, Willis H., ed. "Theodore R. Foster Writes from Lansing." *Michigan History,* XXXV (September 1951), 314–30.

Pierson, George Wilson, ed. *Tocqueville in America.* Gloucester, Mass., 1969.

Pilcher, Elijah H. *Protestantism in Michigan: Being a Special History of the Methodist Episcopal Church.* Detroit, 1878.

Porter, Kirk H., and Donald Bruce Johnson, comps. *National Party Platforms, 1840–1960.* Urbana, Ill., 1961.

Powell, E. A. "Fifty-five Years in West Alabama." (1886–1889; rpr. *Alabama Historical Quarterly,* IV [Winter 1942], 459–639.)

Proceedings of the Young Men's State Temperance Convention, Held at Ann Arbor, January 20, 1836. Detroit, 1836.

Report of the Meeting of the Michigan State Anti-Slavery Society, June 28th, 1837, Being the First Annual Meeting. Detroit, 1837.

Report of the Proceedings of the Anti-Slavery State Convention Held at Ann Arbor, Michigan, the Tenth and Eleventh of November, 1836. Detroit, 1836.

Smith, William Russell. *Reminiscences of a Long Life: Historical, Political, Personal and Literary.* Washington, D.C., 1889.

Stebbins, Giles Badger. *Upward Steps of Seventy Years.* New York, 1890.

Sweet, William Warren, ed. *The Congregationalists: A Collection of Source Materials.* Chicago, 1939. Vol. III of Sweet, ed., *Religion on the American Frontier, 1783–1850.* 4 vols.

Thompson, O. C. "Observations and Experiences in Michigan Forty Years Ago." *Michigan Pioneer and Historical Collections,* I (1877), 395–402.

Townes, S. A. *The History of Marion, Sketches of Life, & c. in Perry County, Alabama.* Marion, Ala., 1844.

Warner, Robert M. "A Document of Pioneer Michigan Life: A Letter from Ann Arbor." *Michigan History,* XL (June 1956), 212–24.

Weld, Theodore Dwight. *American Slavery As It Is: Testimony of a Thousand Witnesses.* New York, 1839.

West, Anson. *A History of Methodism in Alabama.* Nashville, 1893.

Williams, Clanton W., ed. "Extracts from the Records of the City of Montgomery, Alabama, 1820–1821." *Alabama Review,* I (April 1948), 136–37.

SECONDARY SOURCES

Abzug, Robert H. *Cosmos Crumbling: American Reform and the Religious Imagination.* New York, 1994.

Alexander, Ruth M. " 'We Are Engaged as a Band of Sisters': Class and Domesticity in the Washingtonian Temperance Movement, 1840–1850." *Journal of American History,* LXXV (December 1988), 763–85.

Alexander, Thomas B., *et al.* "The Basis of Alabama's Antebellum Two-Party System," *Alabama Review,* XIX (October 1966), 243–76.

———. "Who Were the Alabama Whigs?" *Alabama Review,* XVI (January 1963), 5–19.

Amos, Harriet E. *Cotton City: Urban Development in Antebellum Mobile.* University, Ala., 1985.

Anbinder, Tyler. *Nativism and Slavery: The Northern Know Nothings and the Politics of the 1850s.* New York, 1992.

Ashworth, John. *"Agrarians" and "Aristocrats": Party Political Ideology in the United States, 1837–1846.* 1983; rpr. Cambridge, Eng., 1987.

Atack, Jeremy, and Fred Bateman. "Yankee Farming and Settlement in the Old Northwest: A Comparative Analysis." In *Essays on the Economy of the Old Northwest,* edited by David C. Klingaman and Richard K. Vedder. Athens, Ohio, 1987.

Bailey, David T. *Shadow on the Church: Southwestern Evangelical Religion and the Issue of Slavery, 1783–1860.* Ithaca, 1985.

Baker, Robert Andrew. *Relations Between Northern and Southern Baptists.* [Fort Worth], 1948.

Bancroft, Frederic. "The Early Antislavery Movement and African Colonization." In *Frederic Bancroft, Historian,* edited by Jacob Cook. Norman, Okla., 1957.

Banner, Lois. "Religion and Reform in the Early Republic: The Role of Youth." *American Quarterly,* XXV (Winter 1971), 677–95.

———. "Religious Benevolence as Social Control: A Critique of an Interpretation." *Journal of American History,* LX (June 1973), 23–41.

Barnes, Gilbert Hobbs. *The Antislavery Impulse, 1830–1844.* New York, 1933.

Barnes, William Wright. *The Southern Baptist Convention, 1845–1953.* Nashville, 1954.

Bateman, Fred, and James D. Foust. "A Sample of Rural Households Selected from the 1860 Manuscript Censuses." *Agricultural History,* XLVIII (January 1974), 75–93.

Beakes, Samuel W. *Past and Present of Washtenaw County, Michigan.* Chicago, 1906.

Bellows, Barbara L. *Benevolence Among Slaveholders: Assisting the Poor in Charleston, 1670–1860.* Baton Rouge, 1993.

Benson, T. Lloyd. "Entrepreneurialism in Late Antebellum Indiana and Mississippi." Paper presented April 16, 1993, to the eighty-sixth annual meeting of the Organization of American Historians, Anaheim, California.

Benson, Theodore Lloyd. "Planters and Hoosiers: The Development of Sectional Society in Antebellum Alabama and Mississippi." Ph.D. dissertation, University of Virginia, 1990.

Berg, Barbara J. *The Remembered Gate: Origins of American Feminism: The Woman and the City, 1800–1860.* New York, 1978.

Biographical Directory of the United States Congress, 1774–1989. Washington, D.C., 1989.

Birney, William. *James G. Birney and His Times.* New York, 1890.

Blanks, W. D. "Corrective Church Discipline in the Presbyterian Churches of the Nineteenth Century South." *Journal of Presbyterian History,* XLIV (June 1966), 89–105.

Blocker, Jack S. Jr. *American Temperance Movements: Cycles of Reform.* Boston, 1988.

Blue, Frederick J. *The Free Soilers: Third Party Politics, 1848–1854.* Urbana, Ill., 1973.

Blumin, Stuart M. *The Emergence of the Middle Class: Social Experience in the American City, 1760–1900.* Cambridge, Eng., 1989.

Bode, Frederick A. "The Formation of Evangelical Communities in Middle Georgia: Twiggs County, 1820–1861." *Journal of Southern History,* LX (November 1994), 711–48.

———. "A Common Sphere: White Evangelicals and Gender in Antebellum Georgia." *Georgia Historical Quarterly,* LXXIX (Winter 1995), 775–809.

Bodo, John R. *The Protestant Clergy and Public Issues, 1812–1848.* Princeton, 1954.

Boles, John B. "Evangelical Protestantism in the Old South: From Religious Dissent to Cultural Dominance." In *Religion in the Old South,* edited by Charles Reagan Wilson. Jackson, Miss., 1985.

Boles, John B., ed. *Masters and Slaves in the House of the Lord: Race and Religion in the American South, 1740–1870.* Lexington, Ky., 1988.

Bordin, Ruth. *Washtenaw County: An Illustrated History.* Northridge, Calif., 1988.

Boucher, Morris Raymond. "Factors in the History of Tuscaloosa, Alabama, 1816–1846." M. A. thesis, University of Alabama, 1947.

Boyd, Charles E. *At Liberty on Bear Creek, 1835–1985: A 150th Anniversary of Liberty Baptist Church, Hagler, Alabama.* Birmingham, Ala., 1984.

Boyd, Minnie Clare. *Alabama in the Fifties: A Social Study.* New York, 1931.

Boyer, Paul. *Urban Masses and Moral Order in America, 1820–1920.* Cambridge, Mass., 1978.

Boylan, Anne. *Sunday School: The Formation of an American Institution, 1790–1880.* New Haven, 1988.

Brown, Richard D. *Modernization: The Transformation of American Life, 1600–1865.* New York, 1976.

Bruce, Dickson. *And They All Sang Hallelujah: Plain-Folk Camp-Meeting Religion, 1800–1845.* Knoxville, Tenn., 1974.

Brunger, Ronald A. "The Ladies Aid Societies in Michigan Methodism." *Methodist History*, V (January 1967), 31–48.

Butler, Diana Hochstedt. "The Church and American Destiny: Evangelical Episcopalians and Voluntary Societies in Antebellum America." *Religion and American Culture*, IV (Summer 1994), 193–219.

Carlson, Douglas Wiley. "Temperance Reform in the Cotton Kingdom." Ph.D. dissertation, University of Illinois, 1982.

————. "The Ideology of Southern Temperance." Paper presented at the eleventh annual meeting of the Society for Historians of the Early American Republic, Charlottesville, Va., July 1989.

Caruso, Virginia Ann Paganelli. "A History of Woman Suffrage in Michigan." Ph.D. dissertation, Michigan State University, 1986.

Carwardine, Richard J. *Evangelicals and Politics in Antebellum America.* New Haven, 1993.

Cash, W. J. *The Mind of the South.* New York, 1941.

Cashin, Joan E. *A Family Venture: Men and Women on the Southern Frontier.* Baltimore, 1991.

Charnley, Jeffrey G. "'Swords into Plowshares,' a Hope Unfulfilled: Michigan Opposition to the Mexican War, 1846–1848." *Old Northwest*, VIII (Fall 1982), 199–222.

Chute, William J. *Damn Yankee! The First Career of Frederick A. P. Barnard.* Port Washington, N.Y., 1978.

Clark, Norman H. *Deliver Us from Evil: An Interpretation of American Prohibition.* New York, 1976.

Clinton, Matthew William. *Tuscaloosa, Alabama: Its Early Days, 1816–1865.* Tuscaloosa, 1958.

Colburn, Harvey C. *The Story of Ypsilanti.* Ypsilanti, 1923.

Cole, Arthur C. *The Irrepressible Conflict: 1850–1865.* New York, 1934.

Cole, Charles C. Jr. *The Social Ideas of the Northern Evangelists, 1826–1860.* New York, 1954.

Comin, John, and Harold F. Fredsell. *History of the Presbyterian Church in Michigan.* Ann Arbor, 1950.

Commager, Henry Steele, ed. *The Era of Reform, 1830–1860.* Princeton, 1960.

Cornelius, Janet Duitsman. *"When I Can Read My Title Clear": Literacy, Slavery, and Religion in the Antebellum South.* Columbia, S. C., 1991.

Cross, Whitney. *The Burned-Over District: The Social and Intellectual History of Enthusiastic Religion in Western New York, 1800–1850.* Ithaca, 1950.

Curry, Leonard P. "Urbanization and Urbanism in the Old South: A Comparative View." *Journal of Southern History,* XL (February 1974), 43–60.

Dannenbaum, Jed. *Drink and Disorder: Temperance Reform in Cincinnati from the Washingtonian Revival to the WCTU.* Urbana, Ill., 1984.

Davis, Calvin O. *A History of the Congregational Church in Ann Arbor, 1847 to 1947.* Ann Arbor, 1947.

Davis, David Brion, ed. *Ante-Bellum Reform.* New York, 1967.

Day, Judson LeRoy II. *The Baptists of Michigan and the Civil War.* Lansing, 1965.

Degler, Carl N. *Place over Time: The Continuity of Southern Distinctiveness.* Baton Rouge, 1977.

Densmore, Christopher. "After the Separation." In *Quaker Crosscurrents: Three Hundred Years of Friends in the New York Yearly Meetings,* edited by Hugh Barbour *et al.* Syracuse, N.Y., 1995.

Dickinson, Carlisle G. "A Profile of Hicksite Quakerism in Michigan." *Quaker History,* LIX (Autumn 1970), 106–12.

Dike, Samuel W. "A Study of New England Revivals." *American Journal of Sociology,* XV (November 1909), 361–78.

Dillon, Merton L. "Elizabeth Chandler and the Spread of Antislavery Sentiment to Michigan." *Michigan History,* XXXIX (December 1955), 481–94.

———. *The Abolitionists: The Growth of a Dissenting Minority.* DeKalb, Ill., 1974.

Doan, Ruth Alden. "Race and Revivalism in *The Southern Christian Advocate.*" Paper presented at the thirteenth annual meeting of the Society for Historians of the Early American Republic, Madison, Wisc., July 1991.

Doll, Louis William. *The History of Saint Thomas Parish, Ann Arbor.* Ann Arbor, 1941.

———. *A History of the Newspapers of Ann Arbor, 1829–1920.* Detroit, 1959.

Donald, David. "Toward a Reconsideration of Abolitionists." In *Lincoln Reconsidered: Essays on the Civil War Era.* New York, 1956.

Donnelly, Walter A., ed. *The University of Michigan: An Encyclopedic Survey.* Ann Arbor, 1958.

Dorman, Lewy. *Party Politics in Alabama from 1850 through 1860.* Wetumpka, Ala., 1935.

Doster, James F. "Tuscaloosa Historians." *Alabama Review,* XXVII (April 1974), 83–100.

Doyle, Don Harrison. *The Social Origins of a Frontier Community: Jacksonville, Illinois, 1825–1870.* Urbana, Ill., 1978.

Drury, Clifford Merrill. *William Anderson Scott: "No Ordinary Man."* Glendale, Calif., 1967.

DuBois, Ellen. "Women's Rights and Abolitionism: The Nature of the Connection." In *Antislavery Reconsidered: New Perspectives on the Abolitionists,* edited by Lewis Perry and Michael Fellman. Baton Rouge, 1979.

Dumond, Dwight Lowell. *Antislavery: The Crusade for Freedom in America.* Ann Arbor, 1961.

Dunbar, Willis F., and George S. May. *Michigan: A History of the Wolverine State.* Rev. ed., Grand Rapids, 1980.

Dupre, Daniel. "Barbecues and Pledges: Electioneering and the Rise of Democratic Politics in Antebellum Alabama." *Journal of Southern History,* LX (August 1994), 479–512.

————. "Liberty and Order on the Cotton Frontier: Madison County, Alabama, 1800–1840." Ph.D. dissertation, Brandeis University, 1991.

Dvorak, Katherine L. *An African-American Exodus: The Segregation of the Southern Churches.* Brooklyn, N.Y., 1991.

Eaton, Clement. *The Freedom-of-Thought Struggle in the Old South.* New York, 1964.

Egerton, Douglas R. "'Its Origin Is Not a Little Curious': A New Look at the American Colonization Society." *Journal of the Early Republic,* V (Winter 1985), 463–80.

Ellison, Rhoda Coleman. *A Checklist of Alabama Imprints, 1807–1870.* University, Ala., 1946.

————. *History and Bibliography of Alabama Newspapers in the Nineteenth Century.* University, Ala., 1954.

English, Annetta, compiler. "History of Manchester Township." Typescript, 1930. Copy at Manchester (Mich.) Area Library.

Eslinger, Ellen. "Antebellum Liquor Reform in Lexington, Virginia: The Story of a Small Southern Town." *Virginia Magazine of History and Biography,* XCIX (April 1991), 163–86.

Fahey, David M. "Who Joined the Sons of Temperance? Livelihood and Age in the Black Book and Minutes, Phoenix Division, Dexter, Michigan, 1848–1851." *Old Northwest,* XI (Fall–Winter 1985–86), 221–26.

Faust, Drew Gilpin. "The Peculiar South Revisited: White Society, Culture, and Politics in the Antebellum Period, 1800–1860." In *Interpreting Southern History:*

Historiographical Essays in Honor of Sanford W. Higginbotham, edited by John B. Boles and Evelyn Thomas Nolen. Baton Rouge, 1987.

Filler, Louis. *The Crusade Against Slavery, 1830–1860.* New York, 1960.

Filler, Louis, ed. *Abolition and Social Justice in the Era of Reform.* New York, 1972.

Fladeland, Betty. *James Gillespie Birney: Slaveholder to Abolitionist.* Ithaca, 1955.

Flynt, J. Wayne. "Alabama." In *Religion in the Southern States: A Historical Survey,* edited by Samuel S. Hill. Macon, Ga., 1983.

Foner, Eric. *Free Soil, Free Labor, Free Men: The Ideology of the Republican Party Before the Civil War.* New York, 1970.

Formisano, Ronald P. *The Birth of Mass Political Parties: Michigan, 1827–1861.* Princeton, 1971.

———. "The Edge of Caste: Colored Suffrage in Michigan, 1827–1861." *Michigan History,* LVI (Spring 1972), 19–41.

Foster, Charles I. *An Errand of Mercy: The Evangelical United Front, 1790–1837.* Chapel Hill, 1960.

Foster, Henry B. *History of the Tuscaloosa County Baptist Association.* Tuscaloosa, 1934.

Fox-Genovese, Elizabeth. *Within the Plantation Household: Black and White Women of the Old South.* Chapel Hill, 1988.

Fredrickson, George M. *The Black Image in the White Mind: The Debate on Afro-American Character and Destiny, 1817–1914.* New York, 1971.

Friedman, Jean E. *The Enclosed Garden: Women and Community in the Evangelical South.* Chapel Hill, 1985.

Friedman, Lawrence J. "Purifying the White Man's Country: The American Colonization Society Reconsidered." *Societas,* VI (Winter 1976), 1–24.

———. "Pious Fellowship and Modernity: A Psychosocial Interpretation." In *Crusaders and Compromisers: Essays on the Relationship of the Antislavery Struggle to the Antebellum Party System,* edited by Alan M. Kraut. Westport, Conn., 1983.

Fulton, John. *Memoirs of Frederick A. P. Barnard.* New York, 1896.

Gamble, Douglas Andrew. "Moral Suasion in the West: Garrisonian Abolitionism, 1831–1861." Ph.D. dissertation, Ohio State University, 1973.

Gara, Larry. *The Liberty Line: The Legend of the Underground Railroad.* Lexington, Ky., 1961.

———. "Slavery and the Slave Power: A Crucial Distinction." *Civil War History,* XV (March 1969), 5–18.

Garrison, Wendell Phillips, and Francis Jackson Garrison. *William Lloyd Garrison, 1805–1879: The Story of His Life Told by His Children.* New York, 1885.

Genovese, Eugene D. *The Political Economy of Slavery: Studies in the Economy and Society of the Slave South.* 1965; rpr. New York, 1967.

———. *Roll, Jordan, Roll: The World the Slaves Made.* New York, 1974.

———. *The Slaveholder's Dilemma: Freedom and Progress in Southern Conservative Thought, 1820–1860.* Columbia, S.C., 1992.

Gienapp, William E. "Abolitionism and the Nature of Antebellum Reform." In *Courage and Conscience: Black and White Abolitionists in Boston,* edited by Donald M. Jacobs. Bloomington, Ind., 1993.

――――. *The Origins of the Republican Party, 1852–1856.* New York, 1987.

Ginzberg, Lori D. *Women and the Work of Benevolence: Morality, Politics, and Class in the Nineteenth-Century United States.* New Haven, 1990.

Glynn, Robert L. *"How Firm a Foundation": A History of the First Black Church in Tuscaloosa County, Alabama.* Tuscaloosa, 1976.

Goodrich, Francis L. D. *Historical Facts Concerning the First Presbyterian Church of Ann Arbor.* Ann Arbor, 1961.

Goodykoontz, Colin Brummitt. *Home Missions on the American Frontier.* Caldwell, Idaho, 1939.

Govan, Thomas. "Americans Below the Potomac." In *The Southerner as American,* edited by Charles Grier Sellers Jr. Chapel Hill, 1960.

Green, Fletcher M. "Democracy in the Old South." *Journal of Southern History,* XII (February 1946), 3–23.

Griffin, Clifford S. "Religious Benevolence as Social Control." *Mississippi Valley Historical Review,* XLIV (December 1957), 423–44.

――――. *Their Brothers' Keepers: Moral Stewardship in the United States, 1800–1865.* New Brunswick, N.J., 1960.

――――. *The Ferment of Reform, 1830–1860.* New York, 1967.

Gusfield, Joseph R. *Symbolic Crusade: Status Politics and the American Temperance Movement.* Urbana, Ill., 1963.

Hamm, Thomas D., *et al.* "Moral Choices: Two Indiana Quaker Communities and the Abolition Movement." *Indiana Magazine of History,* LXXXVII (June 1991), 117–54.

Hammond, John L. *The Politics of Benevolence: Revival Religion and American Voting Behavior.* Norwood, N.J., 1979.

Hanley, Mark Y. *Beyond a Christian Commonwealth: The Protestant Quarrel with the American Republic, 1830–1860.* Chapel Hill, 1994.

Hansen, Debra Gold. *Strained Sisterhood: Gender and Class in the Boston Female Anti-Slavery Society.* Amherst, Mass., 1993.

Hardy, James D. Jr., and Robert B. Robinson. "A Peculiarity of the Peculiar Institution: An Alabama Case." *Alabama Review,* XLV (January 1992), 18–25.

Hatch, Nathan O. *The Democratization of American Christianity.* New Haven, 1989.

Hersh, Blanche Glassman. *The Slavery of Sex: Feminist-Abolitionists in America.* Urbana, Ill., 1978.

Herzberg, Louis. "Negro Slavery in Tuscaloosa County, Alabama, 1818–1865." M. A. thesis, University of Alabama, 1955.

Hewitt, Nancy A. *Women's Activism and Social Change: Rochester, New York, 1822–1872.* Ithaca, 1984.

Higginbotham, R. Don. "The Martial Spirit in the Antebellum South: Some Further Speculations in a National Context." *Journal of Southern History,* LVIII (February 1992), 3–26.

Hindus, Michael "Black Justice Under White Law: Criminal Prosecutions of Blacks in Antebellum South Carolina." *Journal of American History,* LXIII (December 1976), 575–99.

History of Washtenaw County, Michigan; Together with Sketches of its Cities, Villages, and Townships, Educational, Religious, Civil, Military, and Political History; Portraits of Prominent Persons, and Biographies of Representative Citizens. Chicago, 1881.

Holifield, E. Brooks. *The Gentlemen Theologians: American Theology and Southern Culture, 1795–1860.* Durham, N. C., 1978.

Hood, Fred J. *Reformed America: The Middle and Southern States, 1783–1837.* University, Ala., 1980.

Howard, Victor B. *Conscience and Slavery: The Evangelistic Calvinist Domestic Missions, 1837–1861.* Kent, Ohio, 1990.

Howe, Daniel Walker. *The Political Culture of the American Whigs.* Chicago, 1979.

———. "Religion and Politics in the Antebellum North." In *Religion and American Politics: From the Colonial Period to the 1980s,* edited by Mark A. Noll. New York, 1990.

———. "The Evangelical Movement and Political Culture in the North During the Second Party System." *Journal of American History,* LXXVII (March 1991), 1216–39.

Hubbs, G. Ward. *Tuscaloosa: Portrait of an Alabama County.* Northridge, Calif., 1987.

Hugins, Walter, ed., *The Reform Impulse, 1825–1850.* New York, 1972.

Hunt, Robert Eno. "Organizing a New South: Education Reformers in Antebellum Alabama, 1840–1860." Ph.D. dissertation, University of Missouri, 1988.

Jack, Theodore H. *Sectionalism and Party Politics in Alabama, 1819–1842.* Menasha, Wisc., 1919.

Jentz, John Barkley. "Artisans, Evangelicals, and the City: A Social History of Abolition and Labor Reform in Jacksonian New York." Ph.D. dissertation, City University of New York, 1977.

———. "The Antislavery Constituency in Jacksonian New York City." *Civil War History,* XXVII (June 1981), 101–22.

John, Richard R. "Taking Sabbatarianism Seriously: The Postal System, the Sabbath, and the Transformation of American Political Culture." *Journal of the Early Republic,* X (Winter 1990), 517–67.

Johnson, Charles A. *The Frontier Camp Meeting: Religion's Harvest Time.* Dallas, Texas, 1955.

Johnson, Curtis D. *Islands of Holiness: Rural Religion in Upstate New York, 1790–1860.* Ithaca, 1989.

Johnson, Paul E. *A Shopkeepers' Millennium: Society and Revivals in Rochester, New York, 1815–1837.* New York, 1978.

Kaestle, Carl F. *Pillars of the Republic: Common Schools and American Society, 1780–1860*. New York, 1983.

Katz, Michael B. *In the Shadow of the Poorhouse: A Social History of Welfare in America*. New York, 1986.

Kephart, John Edgar. "A Voice for Freedom: The *Signal of Liberty*, 1841–1848." Ph.D. dissertation, University of Michigan, 1960.

Kerr, Norwood Allen. "The Mississippi Colonization Society (1831–1860)." *Journal of Mississippi History*, XLIII (February 1981), 1–30.

Knight, J. Steven Jr. "Discontent, Disunity, and Dissent in the Antebellum South: Virginia as a Test Case, 1844–1846." *Virginia Magazine of History and Biography*, LXXXI (October 1973), 437–56.

Kohl, Lawrence Frederick. "The Concept of Social Control and the History of Jacksonian America." *Journal of the Early Republic*, V (Spring 1985), 21–34.

———. *The Politics of Individualism: Parties and the American Character in the Jacksonian Era*. New York, 1989.

Kolchin, Peter. *American Slavery, 1619–1877*. New York, 1993.

———. *First Freedom: The Responses of Alabama's Blacks to Emancipation and Reconstruction*. Westport, Conn., 1972.

Kooker, Arthur Raymond. "The Antislavery Movement in Michigan, 1796–1840: A Study of Humanitarianism on an American Frontier." Ph.D. dissertation, University of Michigan, 1941.

Kraditor, Aileen S. *Means and Ends in American Abolitionism: Garrison and His Critics on Strategy and Tactics, 1834–1850*. New York, 1967.

Kraut, Alan M. "The Liberty Men of New York: Political Abolitionism in New York State." Ph.D. dissertation, Cornell University, 1975.

———. "The Forgotten Reformers: A Profile of Third Party Abolitionists in Antebellum New York." In *Antislavery Reconsidered: New Perspectives on the Abolitionists*, edited by Lewis Perry and Michael Fellman. Baton Rouge, 1979.

Krout, John A. *The Origins of Prohibition*. New York, 1925.

Kuhns, Frederick Irving. "The Breakup of the Plan of Union in Michigan." *Michigan History*, XXXII (June 1948), 157–80.

———. *The American Home Missionary Society in Relation to the Antislavery Controversy in the Old Northwest*. Billings, Mont., 1959.

Kuykendall, John W. *Southern Enterprize: The Work of National Evangelical Societies in the Antebellum South*. Westport, Conn., 1982.

Lamb, Robert Paul. "James G. Birney and the Road to Abolitionism." *Alabama Review*, XLVII (April 1994), 83–134.

Lambert, Byron Cecil. "The Rise of the Anti-mission Baptists: Sources and Leaders, 1800–1840." Ph.D. dissertation, University of Chicago, 1957.

Lebsock, Suzanne. *The Free Women of Petersburg: Status and Culture in a Southern Town, 1784–1860*. New York, 1984.

Lender, Mark Edward, and James Kirby Martin. *Drinking in America: A History.* Rev. ed. New York, 1987.

Levine, Lawrence W. *Black Culture and Black Consciousness: Afro-American Folk Thought from Slavery to Freedom.* New York, 1977.

Lewis, W. David. "The Reformer as Conservative: Protestant Counter-Subversion in the Early Republic." In *The Development of an American Culture,* edited by Stanley Coben and Lorman Ratner. Englewood Cliffs, N.J., 1970.

Lofton, Williston H. "Abolition and Labor." *Journal of Negro History,* XXXIII (July 1948), 249–83.

Loveland, Anne C. *Southern Evangelicals and the Social Order, 1800–1860.* Baton Rouge, 1980.

McDaid, William. "Kinsley S. Bingham and the Republican Ideology of Antislavery, 1847–1855." *Michigan Historical Review,* XVI (Fall 1990), 43–73.

McDaniel, Antonio. "Extreme Mortality in Nineteenth-Century Africa: The Case of Liberian Immigrants." *Demography,* XXIX (November 1992), 581–94.

McDonald, Forrest, and Grady McWhiney. "The South from Self-Sufficiency to Peonage: An Interpretation." *American Historical Review,* LXXXV (December 1980), 1095–1118.

McEachlin, Archibald Bruce. *The History of Tuscaloosa, 1816–1880.* 1880; rpr. University, Ala., 1977.

McElroy, James L. "Social Control and Romantic Reform: The Case of Rochester, New York." *New York History,* LVIII (January 1977), 17–46.

McGraw, Marie Tyler. "Richmond Free Blacks and African Colonization, 1816–1832." *Journal of American Studies,* XXI (August 1987), 207–24.

McKenzie, Robert. "Newspapers and Newspaper Men During Tuscaloosa's Capital Period, 1826–1846." *Alabama Historical Quarterly,* XLIV (Fall–Winter 1982), 187–201.

McKivigan, John R. "The Antislavery 'Comeouter' Sects: A Neglected Dimension of the Abolitionist Movement." *Civil War History,* XXVI (June 1980), 142–60.

———. *The War Against Proslavery Religion: Abolitionism and the Northern Churches, 1830–1865.* Ithaca, 1984.

Macmillan, Margaret Burnham. *The Methodist Church in Michigan: The Nineteenth Century.* Grand Rapids, 1967.

McPherson, James M. *Ordeal by Fire: The Civil War and Reconstruction.* Second ed. New York, 1992.

———. "Antebellum Southern Exceptionalism: A New Look at an Old Question." *Civil War History,* XXIX (September 1983), 230–44.

Maffly-Kipp, Laurie F. *Religion and Society in Frontier California.* New Haven, 1994.

Magdol, Edward. *The Antislavery Rank and File: A Social Profile of the Abolitionists' Constituency.* Westport, Conn., 1986.

Marsden, George M. *The Evangelical Mind and the New School Presbyterian Experience:*

A Case Study of Thought and Theology in Nineteenth-Century America. New Haven, 1970.

Marwil, Jonathan. *A History of Ann Arbor.* Ann Arbor, 1987.

Massie, Larry, and Keith A. Owens. "Michigan's Railroad to Freedom." Ann Arbor *News,* July 12, 1987, pp. F1-F2.

Mathews, Donald G. *Slavery and Methodism: A Chapter in American Morality, 1780–1845.* Princeton, 1965.

———. "The Second Great Awakening as an Organizing Process, 1780–1830: An Hypothesis." *American Quarterly,* XXI (Spring 1969), 23–43.

———. "Charles Colcock Jones and the Southern Evangelical Crusade to Form a Biracial Community." *Journal of Southern History,* XLI (August 1975), 299–320.

———. *Religion in the Old South.* Chicago, 1977.

Matijasic, Thomas D. "The African Colonization Movement and Ohio's Protestant Community." *Phylon,* XLVI (Spring 1985), 16–24.

———. "Whig Support for African Colonization: Ohio as a Test Case." *Mid-America,* LXVI (May–July 1984), 79–91.

May, George S. "Parker Pillsbury and Wendell Phillips in Ann Arbor." *Michigan History,* XXXIII (June 1949), 155–61.

May, Henry F. *The Enlightenment in America.* New York, 1976.

Mayfield, John. *Rehearsal for Republicanism: Free Soil and the Politics of Antislavery.* Port Washington, N.Y., 1980.

Miller, Douglas T. *The Birth of Modern America, 1820–1850.* New York, 1970.

Miller, Floyd J. *The Search for a Black Nationality: Black Emigration and Colonization, 1787–1863.* Urbana, Ill., 1975.

Miller, Perry. *The Life of the Mind in America from the Revolution to the Civil War.* New York, 1965.

Mills, Gary B. "Miscegenation and the Free Negro in Antebellum 'Anglo' Alabama: A Reexamination of Southern Race Relations." *Journal of American History,* LXVIII (June 1981), 16–34.

Mintz, Steven. *Moralists and Modernizers: America's Pre–Civil War Reformers.* Baltimore, 1995.

Miyakawa, T. Scott. *Protestants and Pioneers: Individualism and Conformity on the American Frontier.* Chicago, 1964.

Mooney, Chase H. *William H. Crawford, 1772–1834.* Lexington, Ky., 1974.

Murphy, Teresa Anne. *Ten Hours' Labor: Religion, Reform, and Gender in Early New England.* Ithaca, 1991.

Murray, Andrew E. "Bright Delusion: Presbyterians and African Colonization." *Journal of Presbyterian History,* LVIII (Fall 1980), 224–37.

Murray, Gail S. "Within the Bounds of Race and Class: Female Benevolence in the Old South." *South Carolina Magazine of History,* XCVI (January 1995), 54–70.

Musser, Necia Ann. "Home Missionaries on the Michigan Frontier: A Calendar of the Michigan Letters of the American Home Missionary Society, 1825–1846." Ph.D. dissertation, University of Michigan, 1967.

Nation, Richard F. "Primitive Baptists and the Anti-Missionary Movement." Seminar paper, University of Michigan, 1990.

Ndukwu, Maurice Dickson. "Antislavery in Michigan: A Study of Its Origin, Development, and Expression from Territorial Period to 1860." Ph.D. dissertation, Michigan State University, 1979.

Nord, Paul. "Religious Reading and Readers in Antebellum America." *Journal of the Early Republic*, XV (Summer 1995), 241–72.

Norton, Clark F. "Early Michigan Supreme Court Decisions on the Liquor Question." *Michigan History*, XXVIII (January-March 1944), 41–66.

Norton, Wesley. "The Methodist Episcopal Church in Michigan and the Politics of Slavery: 1850–1860." *Michigan History*, XLVIII (September 1964), 193–213.

Noyes, John Humphrey. *History of American Socialisms*. Philadelphia, 1870.

Oakes, James. *The Ruling Race: A History of American Slaveholders*. New York, 1982.

————. *Slavery and Freedom: An Interpretation of the Old South*. New York, 1990.

Owen, Thomas McAdory. *History of Alabama and Dictionary of Alabama Biography*. 4 vols.; Chicago, 1921.

Owens, Keith A. "Tracking Down Local Stations." Ann Arbor *News*, July 12, 1987, pp. F1-F2.

Owsley, Frank L. "The Irrepressible Conflict." In Twelve Southerners, *I'll Take My Stand: The South and the Agrarian Tradition*. New York, 1930.

Owsley, Frank L., and Harriet C. Owsley. "The Economic Basis of Society in the Late Ante-Bellum South." *Journal of Southern History*, VI (February 1940), 24–45.

Padgett, Chris. "Hearing the Antislavery Rank-and-File: The Wesleyan Methodist Schism of 1843." *Journal of the Early Republic*, XII (Spring 1992), 63–84.

Palmer, Jane, compiler. "A History of Manchester Township." Typescript, 1964, in Bentley Library.

Pease, Jane H., and William H. Pease. *Ladies, Women, and Wenches: Choice and Constraint in Antebellum Charleston and Boston*. Chapel Hill, 1990.

Pease, William H., and Jane H. Pease. *The Web of Progress: Private Values and Public Styles in Boston and Charleston, 1828–1843*. New York, 1985.

Peckham, Howard H. *The Making of the University of Michigan*. Ann Arbor, 1967.

Pessen, Edward. "How Different from Each Other Were the Antebellum North and South?" *American Historical Review*, LXXXV (December 1980), 1119–49.

Petersen, Svend. *A Statistical History of the American Presidential Elections*. Westport, Conn., 1981.

Phillips, Ulrich B. *Life and Labor in the Old South*. Boston, 1929.

Pioneers of Tuscaloosa County, Alabama Prior to 1830. Tuscaloosa, 1981.

Porch, Luther Quentin. *History of the First Baptist Church, Tuscaloosa, Alabama, 1818–1968*. Tuscaloosa, 1968.

Portrait and Biographical Album of Washtenaw County, Michigan. Chicago, 1891.

Posey, Walter Brownlow. *Frontier Mission: A History of Religion West of the Southern Appalachians to 1861.* Lexington, Ky., 1966.

Post, Albert. *Popular Freethought in America, 1825–1850.* New York, 1943.

Potter, David M. *The Impending Crisis, 1848–1861.* New York, 1976.

Pruitt, Paul M. Jr. "The Education of Julia Tutwiler: Background to a Life of Reform." *Alabama Review,* XLVI (July 1993), 199–226.

———. "An Antebellum Law Reformer: Passages in the Life of Benjamin F. Porter." *Gulf Coast Historical Review,* XI (Fall 1995), 22–58.

Putnam, Mary B. *The Baptists and Slavery, 1840–1845.* Ann Arbor, 1913.

Quist, John W. "Social and Moral Reform in the Old North and the Old South: Washtenaw County, Michigan, and Tuscaloosa County, Alabama, 1820–1860." Ph.D. dissertation, University of Michigan, 1992.

———. " 'The Great Majority of Our Subscribers Are Farmers': The Michigan Abolitionist Constituency of the 1840s." *Journal of the Early Republic,* XIV (Fall 1994), 325–58.

———. "Slaveholding Operatives of the Benevolent Empire: Bible, Tract, and Sunday School Societies in Antebellum Tuscaloosa County, Alabama." *Journal of Southern History,* LXII (August 1996), 481–526.

Rabkin, Peggy A. "The Origins of Law Reform: The Social Significance of the Nineteenth-Century Codification Movement and Its Contribution to the Passage of the Early Married Women's Property Acts." *Buffalo Law Review,* XXIV (Spring, 1975), 683–760.

Raboteau, Albert J. *Slave Religion: The "Invisible Institution" in the Antebellum South.* New York, 1978.

Rainard, R. Lyn. "An Analysis of Membership in Temperance Organizations in Antebellum Virginia." Paper presented April 13, 1991, at the eighty-fourth annual meeting of the Organization of American Historians, Louisville, Kentucky.

Ratner, Lorman, ed. *Pre–Civil War Reform: The Variety of Principles and Programs.* Englewood Cliffs, N.J., 1967.

Rayback, Joseph G. *Free Soil: The Election of 1848.* Lexington, Ky., 1970.

Richards, Leonard L. *"Gentlemen of Property and Standing": Anti-Abolition Mobs in Jacksonian America.* New York, 1970.

Riley, B. F. *History of the Baptists of Alabama: From the Time of their First Occupation of Alabama in 1808, Until 1894.* Birmingham, Ala., 1895.

Robins, Roger. "Vernacular American Landscape: Methodists, Camp Meetings, and Social Respectability." *Religion and American Culture,* IV (Summer 1994), 165–91.

Rogin, Leo. *The Introduction of Farm Machinery in Its Relation to the Productivity of Labor in the Agriculture of the United States During the Nineteenth Century.* Berkeley, Calif., 1931.

Rorabaugh, W. J. *The Alcoholic Republic: An American Tradition.* New York, 1979.

————. "The Sons of Temperance in Antebellum Jasper County." *Georgia Historical Quarterly,* LXIV (Fall 1980), 263–79.

————. "Prohibition as Progress: New York State's License Elections, 1846." *Journal of Social History,* XIV (Spring 1981), 425–43.

Rose, Gregory. "South Central Michigan Yankees." *Michigan History,* LXX (March–April 1986), 32–39.

Rosentreter, Roger L. "Michigan and the Compromise of 1850." *Old Northwest,* VI (Summer 1980), 153–173.

Roth, Randolph A. *The Democratic Dilemma: Religion, Reform, and the Social Order in the Connecticut River Valley of Vermont, 1791–1850.* Cambridge, Eng., 1987.

Ryan, Mary P. *Cradle of the Middle Class: The Family in Oneida County, New York, 1790–1865.* Cambridge, Eng., 1981.

Schlesinger, Arthur M. Jr. *The Cycles of American History.* Boston, 1986.

Schultz, Stanley K. "Temperance Reform in the Antebellum South: Social Control and Urban Order." *South Atlantic Quarterly,* LXXXIII (Summer 1984), 323–39.

Seavoy, Ronald E. "The Organization of the Republican Party in Michigan, 1846–1854." *Old Northwest,* VI (Winter 1980–81), 343–76.

Sellers, Charles Grier Jr. "The Travail of Slavery." In *The Southerner as American,* edited by Charles Grier Sellers Jr. Chapel Hill, 1960.

Sellers, James Benson. *The Prohibition Movement in Alabama, from 1702 to 1943.* Chapel Hill, 1943.

————. *Slavery in Alabama.* University, Ala., 1950.

————. *History of the University of Alabama.* University, Ala., 1953.

————. *The First Methodist Church of Tuscaloosa, Alabama, 1818–1968.* Tuscaloosa, 1968.

————. "Free Negroes of Tuscaloosa County Before the Thirteenth Amendment," *Alabama Review,* XXIII (April 1970), 110–27.

Sewell, Richard H. *Ballots for Freedom: Antislavery Politics in the United States, 1837–1860.* New York, 1976.

————. "Slavery, Race, and the Free Soil Party, 1848–1854." In *Crusaders and Compromisers: Essays on the Relationship of the Antislavery Struggle to the Antebellum Party System,* edited by Alan M. Kraut. Westport, Conn., 1983.

Sexton, Jessie Ethelyn. *Congregationalism, Slavery, and the Civil War.* Lansing, 1966.

Shields, Johanna Nichol. "A Social History of Antebellum Alabama Writers." *Alabama Review,* XXXIX (July 1989), 163–91.

Singleton, Gregory H. "Protestant Voluntary Organizations and the Shaping of Victorian America." *American Quarterly,* XXV (December 1975), 549–60.

Skotheim, Robert Allen. "A Note on Historical Method: David Donald's 'Toward a Reconsideration of Abolitionists.'" *Journal of Southern History,* XXVII (August 1959), 356–65.

Slavcheff, Peter Donald. "The Temperate Republic: Liquor Control in Michigan, 1800–1860." Ph.D. dissertation, Wayne State University, 1987.

Smith, Theodore Clarke. *The Liberty and Free Soil Parties in the Northwest.* New York, 1897.

Smith, Timothy L. *Revivalism and Social Reform in Mid-Nineteenth-Century America.* New York, 1980.

Smith-Rosenberg, Carroll. *Religion and the Rise of the American City: The New York City Mission Movement, 1812–1870.* Ithaca, 1971.

Snay, Mitchell. *Gospel of Disunion: Religion and Separatism in the Antebellum South.* Cambridge, Eng., 1993.

Sonne, Niels Henry. *Liberal Kentucky, 1780–1828.* New York, 1939.

Sorin, Gerald. "The Historical Theory of Political Radicalism: Michigan Abolitionists as a Test Case." M. A. thesis, Wayne State University, 1964.

———. *The New York Abolitionists: A Case Study of Political Radicalism.* Westport, Conn., 1971.

Staudenraus, P. J. *The African Colonization Movement, 1816–1865.* New York, 1961.

Sterling, Dorothy. *Ahead of Her Time: Abby Kelley and the Politics of Antislavery.* New York, 1991.

Stewart, James Brewer. *Holy Warriors: The Abolitionists and American Slavery.* Rev. ed. New York, 1996.

Stouffer, Allen P. *The Light of Nature and the Law of God: Antislavery in Ontario, 1833–1877.* Baton Rouge, 1992.

Streeter, Floyd Benjamin. *Political Parties in Michigan, 1837–1860.* Lansing, 1918.

Streifford, David M. "The American Colonization Society: An Application of Republican Ideology to Early Antebellum Reform." *Journal of Southern History,* XLV (May 1979), 201–20.

Taber, Morris C. "New England Influence in South Central Michigan." *Michigan History,* XLV (December 1961), 305–36.

Tap, Bruce. "'The Evils of Intemperance Are Universally Conceded': The Temperance Debate in Early Grand Rapids." *Michigan Historical Review,* XIX (Spring 1993), 17–45.

Thomas, George M. *Revivalism and Cultural Change: Christianity, Nation Building, and the Market in the Nineteenth-Century United States.* Chicago, 1989.

Thomas, John L. "Romantic Reform in America, 1815–1865." *American Quarterly,* XVII (Winter 1965), 656–81.

Thomas, N. Gordon. *The Millennial Impulse in Michigan, 1830–1860: The Second Coming in the Third New England.* Lewiston, N.Y., 1989.

Thornton, J. Mills III. *Politics and Power in a Slave Society: Alabama, 1800–1860.* Baton Rouge, 1978.

———. "The Ethic of Subsistence and the Origins of Southern Secession." *Tennessee Historical Quarterly,* XLVIII (Summer 1989), 67–85.

Topetzes, James Gregory. "Foundations of Partisanship in the Presidential Election of 1840: Washtenaw County, Michigan." Senior honors thesis, University of Michigan, 1990.

Trowbridge, M. E. D. *History of Baptists in Michigan.* Published by the Michigan Baptist State Convention. N.p., 1909.

Tyler, Alice Felt. *Freedom's Ferment: Phases of American Social History from the Colonial Period to the Outbreak of the Civil War.* Minneapolis, 1944.

Tyrrell, Ian R. *Sobering Up: From Temperance to Prohibition in Antebellum America, 1800–1860.* Westport, Conn., 1979.

———. "Women and Temperance in Antebellum America." *Civil War History,* XXVIII (June 1982), 128–152.

———. "Drink and Temperance in the Antebellum South: An Overview and Interpretation." *Journal of Southern History,* XLVIII (November 1982), 485–510.

Valois, Karl Eric. "To Revolutionize the World: The American Tract Society and the Regeneration of the Republic, 1825–1877." Ph.D. dissertation, University of Connecticut, 1994.

Van Broekhoven, Deborah Bingham. "'Let Your Names Be Enrolled': Method and Ideology in Women's Antislavery Petitioning." In *The Abolitionist Sisterhood: Women's Political Culture in Antebellum America,* edited by Jean Fagan Yellin and John C. Van Horne. Ithaca, 1994.

Vander Velde, L. G. "The Synod of Michigan and Movements for Social Reform, 1834–1869." *Church History,* V (March 1936), 52–70.

Vaughn, William Preston. *The Antimasonic Party in the United States, 1826–1843.* Lexington, Ky., 1983.

Volpe, Vernon L. *Forlorn Hope of Freedom: The Liberty Party in the Old Northwest, 1838–1848.* Kent, Ohio, 1990.

Waid, George H. *Centennial History of the Michigan Baptist Convention.* Lansing, 1936.

Waldrep, Christopher. "The Making of a Border State Society: James McReady, the Great Revival, and the Prosecution of Profanity in Kentucky." *American Historical Review,* XCIX (June 1994), 767–84.

Walters, Ronald G. *American Reformers, 1815–1860.* Rev. ed. New York, 1997.

Way, Peter. "Evil Humors and Ardent Spirits: The Rough Culture of Canal Construction Workers." *Journal of American History,* LXXIX (March 1993), 1397–1429.

Wellman, Judith. "Women and Radical Reform in Antebellum Upstate New York: A Profile of Grassroots Female Abolitionists." In *Clio Was a Woman: Studies in the History of American Women,* edited by Mabel E. Deutrich and Virginia C. Purdy. Washington, D.C., 1980.

Welter, Rush. *The Mind of America, 1820–1860.* New York, 1975.

Wilentz, Sean. *Chants Democratic: New York City and the Rise of the American Working Class, 1788–1850.* New York, 1984.

Wilson, Harold. "Basil Manly, Apologist for Slavocracy." *Alabama Review*, XV (January 1962), 38–53.

Wolfe, Suzanne Rau. *The University of Alabama: A Pictorial History*. University, Ala., 1983.

Wosh, Peter J. "Bibles, Benevolence, and Emerging Bureaucracy: The Persistence of the American Bible Society, 1816–1890." Ph.D. dissertation, New York University, 1988.

———. *Spreading the Word: The Bible Business in Nineteenth-Century America*. Ithaca, 1994.

Wyatt-Brown, Bertram. *Lewis Tappan and the Evangelical War Against Slavery*, Cleveland, 1969.

———. "The Antimission Movement in the Jacksonian South: A Study in Regional Folk Culture." *Journal of Southern History*, XXXVI (November 1970), 501–29.

———. "Prelude to Abolitionism: Sabbatarian Politics and the Rise of the Second Party System." *Journal of American History*, LVIII (September 1971), 316–41.

———. "Religion and the 'Civilizing Process' in the Early American South, 1600–1860." In *Religion and American Politics: From the Colonial Period to the 1980s*, edited by Mark A. Noll. New York, 1990.

Index

Abel, William A., 373
ABHMS. *See* American Baptist Home Missionary Society
Abolitionism: 354–461; and benevolence, 122, 130, 137, 145–51, 440, 444; and church affiliation, 447–48, Table 33; and Fourierism, 467; and religion, 429–45; and temperance, 263, 288, 294–98, 300–301; white Tuscaloosan attitudes toward, 304, 306–14. *See also* American Anti-Slavery Society; Antiabolition; Baptists; Beckley, Guy; Benevolence activists; Congregationalists; Democratic Party; Foster, Theodore; Free Soil Party; Garrisonian abolitionism; Liberty Party; Methodists; Michigan Anti-Slavery Society; Michigan State Anti-Slavery Society; Moral suasion; Presbyterians; Social profile; Treadwell, Seymour B.; Whig Party; Washtenaw County Anti-Slavery Society; Women
ABS. *See* American Bible Society
Abzug, Robert, 3
ACS. *See* American Colonization Society
Activists' social profile. *See* Social profile
Adams, Henry, 71
Adams, John Quincy, 362, 377
Adrian, Mich., 9, 296, 419
African Americans: attitudes toward colonization, 334–36; male suffrage among, 406–408; revival participation, 28. *See also* Free blacks
Agnew, John Holmes, 131

AHMS. *See* American Home Missionary Society
Alabama, male occupations in, 332n
Alabama Agricultural Society. *See* Alabama State Agricultural Society
Alabama Annual Conference (Methodists), 350
Alabama Asylum for the Insane, 210, 464
Alabama Baptist Bible Society, 38–40, 44, 70
Alabama Baptist State Convention, 96, 182, 183, 190, 216, 230, 233, 341, 343–44
Alabama Bible Society, 70–71, 72, 74, 76, 79, 113, 314, 321, 323
Alabama Central Sunday School Union. *See* Central Alabama Sunday School Union
Alabama Colonization Society, 321–27
Alabama Law, 213–16, 463
Alabama State Agricultural Society, 74, 178
Alabama State Bible Society. *See* Alabama Bible Society
Alabama State Colonization Society, 333–34
Alabama State Sabbath Convention, 321
Alabama State Temperance Society, 177–78, 182, 213, 311, 313
Alabama Supreme Court. *See* Supreme Court of Alabama
Alabama Synod, 351
Alabama Total Abstinence Society, 177–78, 187–89, 196, 223–25, 233n
Alcohol consumption, decline of, 168–69, 190, 191, 216–17, 301–302

Alcohol regulation, 166, 170; targeting Tusca-
    loosa slaves, 306–307
Allen, John, 139, 237, 238
Alphadelphia Association, 253n, 466–67
American and Foreign Anti-Slavery Society,
    418
American and Foreign Bible Society, 40, 44,
    132
American Anti-Slavery Society, 359, 361, 368,
    372, 417–18
American Baptist Board of Foreign Missions,
    38, 40, 132, 149
American Baptist Foreign Missionary Soci-
    ety, 341
American Baptist Free Mission Society, 149,
    444
American Baptist Home Missionary Soci-
    ety, 119n, 127–28, 132, 140, 149, 341–42,
    344, 346
American Baptist Missionary Union, 132, 149,
    444
American Bible Society: 32–36, 45, 90n, 64,
    103, 111, 114, 116, 121, 122, 132, 143, 147, 148,
    152, 352; and Baptists, 37–41, and Method-
    ists, 37, 152n; and Presbyterians, 37. *See also*
    Bible circulation; Social profile
American Board of Commissioners for For-
    eign Missions, 132, 148
American Colonization Society, 315–18, 320,
    322, 327, 329, 333–36
American Education Society, 124
American Home Missionary Society: and
    slavery, 132; in Tuscaloosa County and the
    South, 125n; 107, 109, 112, 118, 124–29, 141,
    143, 236, 237, 244
American Missionary Association: 126, 132
American Party, 11, 140. *See also* Know-
    Nothing Party; Nativism
American Sunday School Union: 47–69, 77,
    93, 100, 103, 107, 118, 119, 121, 132, 133, 146,
    152; Methodist resistance to, 94–95, 119–
    20; regular Baptist support of, 95–97
American Temperance Society, 156n
American Tract Society: 36, 38, 41–47, 81, 90,
    94, 103, 108, 114, 116, 117, 121, 122, 138, 146,

149, 152, 162n, 326, 440n; and Alabama
    Baptists, 44–45; and slavery, 153. *See also*
    Social profile; Tract circulation
American Tract Society (Boston), 81n, 117n,
    121
Andrew, James O., 349
Ann Arbor, Mich., 9, 11, 107, 109, 110, 119, 126,
    131, 132, 139, 144, 150, 236, 245, 248, 254, 255,
    257, 261, 262, 265, 267, 268, 270, 275, 279,
    280, 282, 285, 293, 364, 372, 374, 377, 378,
    379, 381, 382, 393, 395, 402, 404, 405, 407,
    420, 426, 434, 435, 439, 445
Ann Arbor Anti-Slavery Society, 361–62
Ann Arbor Bible Society, 115, 121, 143
Ann Arbor Brewery, 243
Ann Arbor Circuit (Methodists), 293
Ann Arbor City Bible Society, 147n
Ann Arbor City Temperance Society, 278
Ann Arbor Female Tract Society, 116, 142–43
Ann Arbor Society for the Promotion of Tem-
    perance, 237, 239, 284
Ann Arbor Temperance Society, 147n, 238
Ann Arbor Total Abstinence Society, 147n,
    247–49
Ann Arbor village: distinction from Ann
    Arbor Township, 9n, 290; male occupa-
    tions in, 289
Antiabolition, 106, 212, 308–14, 356–58, 468–
    69
Anticatholicism. *See* Catholicism
Anticlericalism, 22
Anti-Electioneering Association, 158–59
Antimasonic Party, 296n. *See also* Anti-
    masonry
Antimasonry, 30, 104, 194–95, 237, 238–39, 260
Antimission Baptists. *See* Baptists
Anti-Slavery Vigilance Association, 417n
Arnold, Orrin, 399–400
ASSU. *See* American Sunday School Union
ATS. *See* American Tract Society
Augusta Township, Mich., 126, 141, 142, 143,
    250, 281, 293, 405, 459

Bacon, William, 113
Bagby, Arthur, 172–73, 324

Bagley, Amasa, 109

Baker, Robert A., 215, 468

Baldwin County, Ala., 320, 323, 329n

Baptist Board of Foreign Missions. *See* American Baptist Board of Foreign Missions

Baptist Female Sewing Society, 83n

Baptist Missionary Convention of the State of New York, 127

Baptist Missionary Society of Tuscaloosa County, 31, 99, 323

Baptists: and abolition, 364, 442–45; and benevolence, 31, 36, 37–41, 43–46 *passim,* 50–56 *passim,* 63, 70–71, 78, 80, 81, 95, 96–100, 103, 119, 120, 123, 127, 128, 129, 132, 139, 140, 145, 149, 150, 341–42, 444; and plantation mission 341–49; and revivalism, 27, 28, 108, 110; and sectionalism, 341–43; and slavery, 430, 432n; and temperance, 169, 209, 230, 232–33, 250, 261, 291–92; Antimission, 5n, 12, 13n, 97–100, 119, 233n; Free Will, 12, 262, 293, 444–45

Barnard, Frederick Augustus Porter, 199–200

Barnburner Democrats, 397–99

Barnes, Gilbert Hobbs, 120–21

Barnum, George, 250

Barr, John Gorman, 82, 195, 197, 200

Barry, John S., 252, 404

Battle, Alfred, 46n, 74n, 313, 331–32

Baughman, J. A., 114

Baylor, Robert E. B., 324

Beach, John, 109

Bebens, Samuel, 438

Beckley, Guy: 148n, 371, 374–75, 377, 380, 382, 398, 430, 431, 443n, 460, 440; and come-outerism, 440; and underground railroad, 381; on Liberty Party platform expansion, 394–96; on Sons of Temperance, 263; on temperance, 252; on Texas annexation, 388n; property attacked by antiprohibitionists, 255

Bellevue, Mich., 469

Belser, James E., 187

Benevolence: 19–154; and women, 80–89, 142–45; and sectionalism, 40–41, 46, 56, 93–94, 341–42; and the South, 51, 54–56; as a solution to social disorder, 77–80, 133–42; economic depression's impact on, 34, 42, 48, 112–13; opposition to, 89–100, 113; support from industrialists, 73–75. *See also* Benevolence activists; Bible circulation; Sabbath observance; Slaveholding; Social profile; Sunday schools; Tract circulation

Benevolence activists: as abolitionists, 122, 130, 137, 145–51; as temperance supporters, 35, 39, 45, 51, 52, 60, 63, 106, 112, 128, 130, 133, 140, 146, 147n, 150

Benevolent Society of the University of Alabama, 43–44

Benton, Eli, 433–34, 460

Benton County (Ala.) Temperance Society, 182

Bestor, Daniel P., 174

Bibb, Henry, 381, 382, 425

Bible circulation, 32–42, 47, 48, 91, 111–16, 340–41. *See also* Alabama Bible Society; American and Foreign Bible Society; American Bible Society; Ann Arbor Bible Society; Madison County Bible Society; Michigan Bible Society; Social profile; Tuscaloosa Bible Society; Tuskaloosa Association Baptist Bible Society; Tuskaloosa Baptist Bible Society; Washtenaw County Bible Society

Bible Society of Michigan. *See* Michigan Bible Society

Big Sandy Creek, Ala., 349

Bingham, Kinsley S., 400n, 413n

Birney, James Gillespie, 47n, 93, 311, 317–21, 327–28, 368, 370, 381, 388n, 390, 393–96 *passim,* 430, 431

Black Warrior River, 9, 10, 161

Blair, R., 307

Blevins, George P., 200, 231

Blount, Robert P., 63n

Blue laws. *See* Sabbath observance

Booth, John, 119n

Boucher, Joshua, 349

Boylan, Anne M., 48, 138

Branch, Israel, 239, 284

Brewill, Charles, 255

Bridgewater Township, Mich., 269, 405, 439
Bronson, N. A., 256, 282
Bronson, W. A., 425
Brookshire, Ervin E., 191n
Brown, Belah, 373
Browne, Newbern Hobbs, 63n
Bruce, Dickson D. Jr., 25
Brumby, Richard T., 61–62, 200, 308
Buck, David, 314
Buel, Alexander 405
Buffalo, N.Y.: Free Soil convention in, 397–99; Sabbath convention in, 129
Burgess, Celia, 335–336
Burke, Thomas J., 212, 233n
Burned-over district, 105
Burns, Willis, 43

Cadets of Temperance, 194, 263
Cahaba, Ala., 32, 79, 216
Caldwell, John S., 63n
Camp meetings. *See* Revivalism
Canada: missionary work among slave refugees in, 150–51
Capital punishment: movement to abolish, 464–65
Carpenter, Horace, 409–10
Carpenter, J., 296
Carroll, Edenborough, 336
Carroll, Nancy, 336
Carson League, 269–70
Carter, Chandler, 415
Carthage, Ala., 161n
Cary, Samuel F., 264
Catholicism: evangelical fear of, 104, 115, 137, 139–40, 152
Catholics: 12; and abolition, 445; and temperance, 232, 291; behavior offensive to evangelicals, 130. *See also* German Catholics; Irish Catholics
Caulkins, T. N., 466–67
Celestia, Maria, 426
Central Alabama Sunday School Union, 78, 79, 80
Central Association of Universalists, 445
Chandler, Elizabeth Margaret, 359, 419

Chandler, John, 147n
Chandler, Thomas, 418–19
Chandler, Zachariah, 268
Chase, W. L., 43
Chelsea, Mich., 143. *See also* Sylvan Township
Childress, James L., 59n
Chipman, Samuel, 250, 251
Christiancy, Isaac P., 268
Church affiliation, 12–13n, Tables 3 and 4
Circus: evangelical opposition to, 25, 107
Clark, Charlotte, 336
Clark, Frederick, 336
Clark, Lincoln, 35, 47n, 60n, 331, 335–36
Clarke, Charles G., 105, 108, 110, 112, 114, 118, 121, 137, 141, 142, 237, 238, 244, 432, 433
Clarke, George W., 292, 421, 426–27
Cleaveland, John P., 117n, 121, 146, 296, 435
Clinton, Mich., 261
Clintonville, Mich., 142
Cobb, Nicholas Hamner, 35, 47n
Colclazer, Henry, 114
Colgin, William R., 63n
College Temperance Society, 296n
Collier, Henry W., 35, 46n, 47n, 52, 63n, 74–75, 80, 95, 177–78, 187, 203, 219n, 313, 322, 331, 334, 335
Colonization, 288, 314–37, 255, 415–17, 465
Colored Total Abstinence Society, 338
Colored Vigilant Committee of the City of Detroit, 406
Colporteurs, 37, 42–43, 44, 47, 70, 114, 116, 117, 121, 138, 146, 147n
Comegys, Edward F., 178
Come-outerism, 377, 439–40
Common schools, 2, 45, 60, 61, 63, 122, 148, 177, 178, 311, 456, 457, 464
Communitarianism. *See* Fourierism
Comstock, Oliver, 136, 137, 251
Congregationalist General Association of Michigan, 131n, 149, 151, 293, 435
Congregationalists: 125–26; and abolition, 434–36; and benevolence, 103, 122, 123, 125, 126, 132, 141, 146, 149, 151, 152, 435; and Presbyterians, 103; and revivalism, 111; and slavery, 430; and temperance, 244; 262, 291–93;

Tuscaloosa County presence of, 12. *See also* Ladies' Sewing Society; Plan of Union

Conscience Whigs, 397

Cook, J. B., 42

Cook, R. S., 44

Corning, Alexander, 128

Corselius, George: 135, 238, 239, 240, 243, 257, 389, 406; and Fourierism, 467; as an antislavery Whig, 391–93; defection to Free Soilers, 393n; on antiabolition, 356–57; on colonization, 355–56, 415; on women's suffrage, 427

Cowlary, Isabella, 423

Cowles, John S., 361

Cowles, Martin H., 255, 373

Cox, Thomas W., 53, 54–55, 57, 77, 93, 100

Craigham, Daniel, 161

Crane, W. Carey, 42

Crary, Isaac, 362

Crawford, William, 90

Creighton, Samuel, 381

Cribbs, Harvey, 198

Croom, Isaac, 35, 47n

Cross, Whitney, 132

Cumberland Presbyterians. *See* Presbyterians

Cunningham, Robert M., 46n

Curtis, Thomas F., 78, 346–47

Dagg, John L., 38

Dallas County, Ala., 351

Dancing: evangelical opposition to, 25, 107, 142

Davenport, John G., 23, 304

Davidson, Robert, 255

Davis, Lorenzo, 243, 244n, 251, 272, 275

Davis, Nicholas, 167n

Dearing, James H., 52, 178

DeForest, A., 272

DeGarmo, Emeline, 419, 420

Deism. *See* Rationalism

Deland, William R., 372

Democratic Party: and abolition, 357–58, 360–61, 363–65, 386, 388n, 389–90, 397, 448–49; and benevolence, 59–61; and colonization, 331; and Fourierism, 466–67, and Free Soil, 399–400, 402–406; and prohibition, 260, 267–68, 271, 274, 275–76; and temperance, 175–79, 249, 294–95, 298; constituency of, 105

Denison, Francis, 409

Dent, Henry, 336

Denton, Samuel, 361, 407

Detroit, Mich., 9, 126, 146n, 151, 247, 267, 269, 406

Detroit Presbytery, 236

DeVotie, James H., 39, 345

Dexter, Samuel W., 104, 237, 238, 260, 410

Dexter Township, Mich., 105, 269, 275, 405

Dexter village, 11, 105, 108, 112, 116, 118, 119, 126, 128, 130, 141, 237, 238, 248, 252n, 256, 262, 264–66, 282, 285, 362, 381, 382, 411

Dexter Anti-Slavery Society, 361

Dexter Female Tract Society, 116, 142–43

Dixboro, Mich. *See* Panama, Mich.

Dixon, David R., 117, 121, 440n

Doctrinal and Tract Society, 132

Dodson, Reuben, 43, 98, 345

Donald, David, 458

Doremus, Jacob, 431

Doty, Samuel R., 402

Dow, Neal, 273

Duffee, Mathew, 205

Duffield, George, 146n, 370

Dunlap, James Madison, 59n

Dunlap, Sarah H., 59n

Duties of Masters, 45, 149

Earnest, William S., 214

Edmunds, James M., 407

Electioneering, 158–59, 161, 164, 166–68

Ellis, Harrison W., 336, 351n

Ely, William H., 21, 156

Elyton, Ala., 211

Emerson, Edward B., 244

Emmons, Halmer H., 256

Episcopalians: and abolition, 430, 445; and benevolence, 46, 63, 89, 102, 122, 123; and colonization, 316, 326, 330; and temperance, 232, 291, 294

Eutaw, Ala., 211n

Factory children, Sunday school for, 64–65

Factory in Tuscaloosa, 84

Fairfield, Mich., 119n

Farmington, Mich., 296

Farmington Anti-Slavery Society, 359

Fayette County (Ala.) Temperance Society, 182

Fayetteville, Ala., 198

Felch, Alpheus, 280

Felch, Sabin, 467

Female Anti-Slavery Society of Ann Arbor, 426

Female Anti-Slavery Society of Webster and Scio, 425

Female Baptist Missionary Society of Tuscaloosa, 31, 81

Female Benevolent Societies (Mich.), 143

Female Benevolent Society (Augusta), 143

Female Benevolent Society (Lima), 143

Female Benevolent Society (Mobile), 162n

Female Benevolent Society (Tuscaloosa), 83–89, 311n

Female Home Missionary Society, 143

Female Missionary Association, 143

Female tract societies, 116

Filler, Louis, 462

Finnell, Colin, 99

Fiquet, Charles J., 312–13, 351–52

Fontaine, Benjamin B., 47n, 63n, 167n, 324

Foote, C. C., 151

Foster, Abby Kelley, 416, 419, 420, 428

Foster, Gustavus L., 128

Foster, James, 39, 63n

Foster, Joshua H., 80

Foster, Robert S., 38, 39, 49–50, 78, 314

Foster, Samuel W., 396, 398n

Foster, Stephen S., 419

Foster, Theodore: 147, 375–76, 418, 443n, 445, 454, 462; and underground railroad, 381; as antislavery officer, 359; appointed as *Signal of Liberty* editor, 374–75; appointed to state government post, 413n; on antislavery Whigs, 393; on come-outerism, 440; on common schools, 456; on denying communion to slaveholders, 431–32, 442; on female antislavery, 425–26; on female temperance, 283; on Fourierism, 467; on Liberty Party platform expansion, 393–96; on prohibition, 256, 259; on religious thrust of the Liberty Party, 429–30; on the Slave Power, 386, 455; on women's rights, 426–27; property attacked by antiprohibitionists, 255; resignation as *Signal of Liberty* editor, 396–97; Sabbatarian sympathies of, 130

Foster's Settlement, Ala., 49, 194, 344

Fourierism, 253n, 466–67

Fowler, W. H., 217, 219

Franklin County, Ala., 323

Frazee, Bradford, 440

Free blacks (Ala.), 306, 307, 334–336

Free Church, 421–22

Free Democrat Party, 409–13. *See also* Free Soil Party

Free Mission Society, 132

Free Presbyterian Church, 433

Free Soil Party: 397–413, 434, 447; and prohibition, 268; and temperance, 294–96, 297–98; on the Slave Power, 386; prior political affiliations, 448–49; social profile, 454

Free Will Baptists. *See* Baptists

Freedom Township, Mich., 105, 269, 405

Friends of Freedom in Michigan, 421–22

Friends of Progress, 421, 428

Friends of Sabbath Instruction and Moral and Religious Improvement, 121, 147n

Fuller, Cyrus, 419

Fuller, Edward L., 116n

Fuller, Harriet DeGarmo, 419

Gambling: 22; evangelical opposition to, 25, 29, 31, 107

Gardiner, Earl P., 261, 262, 298, 361, 364, 390n

Garland, Converse J., 467

Garland forgery, 388n

Garland, Landon C., 74n, 85, 311n

Garrett, William, 187, 331

Garrison, William Lloyd, 315, 368, 420, 426

Garrisonian abolitionism, 297, 376, 414, 416–22, 447

Garvin, J. S., 219

Gayle, John, 167n, 233n

General Association of Michigan. *See* Congregationalist General Association of Michigan

German Catholics, 105, 115

Giddings, Joshua, 377, 409

Gilruth, James, 436

Glasier, Richard, 420

Goodwin, Justus, 246

Gore, A. S., 183–85, 221

Grand Rapids, Mich., 9, 385

Grant's Creek, Ala., 78, 210

Grant's Creek Sunday School, 49–50

Grant's Creek Temperance Society, 182

Greene County, Ala., 26, 28, 174, 199n, 349

Greensboro, 91

Griffin, Clifford S., 3, 71, 121

Griffing, Josephine, 422

Gurney, Chester, 382

Gusfield, Joseph R., 220, 228

Hale, Samuel A., 27, 174–81 *passim*

Hamilton, Hiram S., 128

Hardshell Baptists. *See* Baptists [Antimission]

Hargrove, Daniel Jones, 63n

Hargrove, Dudley, 349

Harris, J., 349

Haviland, Laura, 381n

Hawkins, Olney, 270n

Haynes, C. E., 215

Henry, W. E., 161

Herrick, J. F., 44

Hicks, Sumner, 402, 404

Hicksites. *See* Quakers

Hill, Oliver, 141, 143

Hillhouse, James, 91

Hills, James W., 267

Hitchcock, Henry, 47n

Hobart, Jane Louisa, 144

Hobart, L. Smith, 144

Hodges, John A., 39, 59n

Hogan, Alexander Perry, 46n

Holbert, J., 314

Holcombe, A. J., 39, 175, 202

Holifield, R. C., 215

Holley, Myron, 368

Home for the Friendless, 144

Home missions, 124–28

Hopkins, Arthur F., 74n, 190, 321–22, 324–25

Howard, Jacob, 383

Hubbard, David, 95n

Humphrey, Luther, 367–68

Hunker Democrats, 397

Hunt, Timothy W., 149, 443–44, 460

Huntington, Backus W., 233n

Huntsville, Ala., 11, 91, 93, 162n, 327

Huron River, 142, 248

Hussey, Erastus, 397–99, 401, 403, 413

Hyde, Alonzo, 257, 282

Independence Day celebrations, 92, 95, 106, 120, 143, 145, 147n, 150, 156, 165, 189, 190, 237, 238, 248, 250, 251n, 281, 326, 382, 461

Industrialists: support for benevolence, 73–75

Inge, R. S., 189

Irish Catholics, 105, 115

Irish, Mary A., 144

Jackson, Mich., 145, 150, 278, 385, 393, 398, 399

Jackson County, Mich., 106, 117, 145, 250, 378

Jackson County Anti-Slavery Society, 369–70

Jefferson County, Ala., 26, 230

Jemison, Robert, 333

Jewett, George W., 385–86

Johnson, J. J., 186

Johnston, David, 323

Jones, Fernando, 283

Jones, S. W., 336

Jones, William, 107, 108, 129, 237

Jonesboro, Ala., 198

Kain, John, 34, 35

Kalamazoo, Mich., 9, 469

Kanouse, John G., 110, 244

Keener, John Christian, 28–29

Kennon, Robert Lewis, 31, 47n, 161, 322–23, 324

Kidder, Hollis Coudy, 59n

King, George P., 128

Kingsley, Mrs. Jennab, 144
Kingsley, William, 131
Kinney, Munnis, 130, 131, 134, 146, 247, 253n
Know-Nothing Party, 178, 216, 468. *See also*
  American Party; Nativism
Kohl, Lawrence Frederick, 59–60
Kraut, Alan, 458
Kuykendall, John W., 20, 153

Lacy, Joseph, 39
Ladd, Thomas M., 373
Ladies' Aid Society (Ann Arbor), 143
Ladies' Aid Society (Webster), 143
Ladies' Benevolent Society, 82, 83
Ladies Fair, 82
Ladies' Sewing Society, 144–45, 262
Ladies' Temperance Society (Ann Arbor), 283
Ladies' Temperance Society (Dexter), 282
Ladies' Total Abstinence Society (Dexter),
  256
Ladies' Total Abstinence Society of Ann
  Arbor, 282
Lane, Marcus, 113
Lansing, Francis M., 146
Lauderdale County, Ala., 323
Lawrence County, Ala., 323
Lawrence, D. C., 400n
Lawrence, Edwin, 358
Lawrence, N. P., 219
Lawrence, William H., 219
Leach, Sewell Jones, 60n, 74n
Leavitt, Joshua, 380
Leech, Gurdon C., 427
Legal suasion. *See* Alcohol regulation; Liquor
  licensing; Prohibition
Lenawee County, Mich., 119n, 418, 438
Lenawee County Anti-Slavery Society, 359
Leoni, Mich., 250
Lesuer, David, 255
Lesuer, Erastus, 255
Liberty Baptist Association, 217
Liberty League, 443
Liberty Party: 366–99, 402, 409, 434; and
  Democrats, 389–90, 392; and Garrisonian
  abolitionism, 417–19; and prohibition,

260; and temperance, 249, 255–56, 294–98,
  376; and Whigs, 11, 371–74, 377, 386–93;
  and women, 423–26; creation of, 366–74;
  debates regarding platform expansion,
  393–96; Free Soil Party merger, 397–99,
  401; members' other political affiliations,
  448–49; Michigan State Anti-Slavery
  Society endorsement of, 375–77; religious
  thrust of, 429–30, 452–53; social profile of,
  447–60
Lima Township, Mich., 110, 126, 128, 141, 390,
  405
Lincecum, Gideon, 24n
Lipscomb, Abner, 324, 326
Liquor laws: enforcement of, 277–80
Liquor licensing, 202–209, 239–43, 246–47,
  249, 251–60, 265, Tables 6 and 8
Little, George, 63–64
Littlejohn, Flavius J., 403, 408
Livingston (Ala.) Temperance Society, 182
Livingston County, Mich., 110, 117
Local option, 202–209, 254–60
Lockwood, Clark, 130–31, 262
Lodi Township, Mich., 126, 244, 405, 431, 433–
  34, 439, 443
Lowell, Mich., 142
Lumsden, D. F., 294
Lundy, Benjamin, 304
Lutherans, 12, 445
Lyell, Charles, 190, 351
Lyndon Township, Mich., 269, 405
Lyons, Jonathan, 69, 352

Macomb County, Mich., 119
Macomb County Bible Society, 112n
Maddin, Thomas, 98
Madison County, Ala., 323
Madison County Bible Society, 33
Magdol, Edward, 458
Maine Law, 208–209, 212–13, 216, 235, 265,
  267–77, 279, 293
Male occupations: in Alabama, 332n; in Ann
  Arbor village, 289; in Michigan, 289; in
  Tuscaloosa (town), 73; in Tuscaloosa
  County, 73n

Manchester Lyceum, 361
Manchester Township, Mich., 108, 110, 126, 141, 380, 402, 405, 415, 447n
Manchester village, Mich., 127, 128, 132, 262, 267, 382, 445
Manly, Basil: and benevolence, 35, 45, 47n, 53–54, 63n, 80, 95, 153; and colonization, 331, 332; and high license, 204, 207n; and sectionalism, 312–13, 341–43; defends Sons of Temperance, 232–33, 261; conversion of, 340; on Antimission Baptists, 99–100n; on plantation mission, 343–45, 347; on revivalism, 28–29; on slavery, 320–22; on temperance at the University of Alabama, 199–202
Mann, Solomon, 131
Manning, Thomas, 50, 98, 351–52
Marion, Ala., 202–203
Marion Temperance Society, 182
Marr, William M., 323, 324
Marsh, Justin, 141, 142, 250, 281, 434, 459
Marshall, Mich., 247, 394, 405, 426
Martha Washington Temperance Society, 282
Martin, Joshua L., 60n, 61, 331
Martin, Peter, 60n
Martin, William B., 233n
Masonry, 30, 107, 192, 193, 194, 210, 232, 239, 263
MASS. *See* Michigan Anti-Slavery Society
Matlack, Lucius, 437
Maxwell, Thomas, 73n
May, Pleasant H., 178, 308
Mayhew, Ira, 135n
McAlpin, R. C., 156
McClelland, Robert M., 268, 403, 409
McCollum, David T., 255
McConnell, Felix Grundy, 187–88, 233n
McCracken, Stephen B., 271–72, 412–13
McCullough, Louis, 307–308
McElroy, James, 458
McFarlane, Dugald, 158n
McGown, Henry, 233n
McGuire, H. M., 161
McGuire, W. W., 161
McIntyre, Donald, 276, 412

McMath's, Ala., 194
Mead, Amos, 372n
Mears, John A., 191
Mechanics' Temperance Society, 281
Medina, Mich., 438
Meek, Alexander B., 178, 233n, 308–309, 311, 318, 319n
Meek, John, 164, 303
Meek, Samuel Mills, 33, 47n, 52, 63n, 167–68, 313–14, 323, 324
Methodist Book Concern, 95n
Methodist Episcopal Church. *See* Methodists
Methodist Episcopal Tract Society Auxiliary, 43, 81
Methodist Protestant Church, 52
Methodist State Anti-Slavery Society, 438
Methodists: and abolition, 364, 436–41; and benevolence, 31, 33, 34, 35, 37, 43, 46, 50, 52, 63, 81, 89, 94–96, 101, 103, 119–20, 122, 123, 126, 129, 131, 132, 137, 150, 440; and plantation mission, 348–50; and revivalism, 26, 28–29, 109, 110–11; and sectionalism, 349, 441; and slavery, 349, 430; and temperance, 160, 161, 169, 195, 230, 232, 250, 251, 262, 276, 292–93; Wesleyan, 12, 438–41
Mexican-American War, 396n
Michigan: male occupations in, 289; real property holdings in, 290; school attendance in, 124
Michigan Annual Conference of the Methodist Episcopal Church, 119–20, 131, 132, 293, 436–38, 440–41, 443n
Michigan Anti-Slavery Society, 417, 419–20
Michigan Association of Free Will Baptists, 293, 444
Michigan Baptist State Convention, 127, 139, 140, 442
Michigan Bible Society, 113, 121
Michigan Central Railroad, 129–31
Michigan Education Society, 124
Michigan Freeman, 372, 374
Michigan Home Missionary Society, 143
Michigan Liberty Press, 397
Michigan State Anti-Slavery Society, 146, 148n, 296, 297, 358, 360, 362, 364, 366–69,

371–76, 380, 383, 394, 396, 396–97, 401, 403, 413, 417, 419, 423, 425, 434, 442, 444, 447, 451

Michigan State Temperance Alliance, 278

Michigan State Temperance Society, 146, 242, 246, 248, 251, 252, 254, 259, 266, 267, 271, 276, 282, 296

Michigan Sunday School Union, 118, 121, 137, 140

Michigan Supreme Court. *See* Supreme Court of Michigan

Michigan Synod, 146n, 433n

Michigan Temperance Herald, 284–85, 297

Michigan Total Abstinence Society, 244

Michigan Wesleyan Anti-Slavery Society, 151n, 440

Mill Creek Temperance Society, 238, 281

Miller, Perry, 23

Miller, Stephen F., 179, 188, 190, 191, 203, 331

Mills, Simeon, 236

Minor, Henry, 63n

Mission to the slaves. *See* Plantation mission

Missionary Society of the Methodist Episcopal Church, 151n

Mississippi: local option law in, 209

Mobile, Ala., 9, 162n, 319, 327

Monroe, James, 355

Monroe, Mich., 135n, 247

Monroe Presbytery, 139

Montgomery, Ala., 10, 32n, 93, 178, 192, 215, 333

Monthly Concert for the Enslaved, 381

Moody, Washington, 73n

Moor, George, 443–44

Moore, David, 324

Moore, Gabriel, 47n

Moore, Samuel D., 420

Moral suasion: and abolition, 366–68, 376; and temperance, 170, 180, 189, 240, 243, 245, 249, 250, 252, 256

Mosely, Charles, 147n, 373

Mowry, Israel, 402

MSASS. *See* Michigan State Anti-Slavery Society

Muller, A. A., 82

Murphy, John, 47n

National Methodist Missionary Society, 127n, 440

Nativism, 140, 271, 411. *See also* American Party; Catholicism; Know-Nothing Party

New England. *See* Yankee origins

New Lexington, Ala., 217

New School Presbyterians. *See* Presbyterians

New York. *See* Yankee origins

Nicks, A. Q., 214

Niles, Mich., 424

No license. *See* Liquor licensing

Norment, James M., 188–89, 192, 196, 229, 303

Norris, L. D., 235–36, 427

North Tuscaloosa Temperance Society, 182

Northeast and Southwest Alabama Railroad, 178, 210, 212

Northfield Township, Mich., 105, 115, 270, 381, 382, 405

Northport, Ala., 77, 194, 204–205, 463

Northrup, Henry Horatio, 141

Oakland County, Mich., 142, 401, 423, 437, 456

Odd Fellows, 84, 192, 194, 210, 232, 261n, 262, 263

Old School Presbyterians. *See* Presbyterians

Oliver, Samuel C., 35, 47n

O'Neil, L. W., 307–308

Ormond, John J., 47n, 331, 333, 334

Ortman, John J., 270n

Osgood, L. W., 252

Osgood, Thaddeus, 251n

Overby, Basil H., 203n

Owen, John, 308, 403

Owen, Thomas, 313

Packard, Benjamin, 236

Padgett, Chris, 458

Page, William, 108, 111, 142, 236

Paine, Thomas, 23

Panama, Mich., 118

Panama Temperance Society, 238

Parks, J. A., 147n

Parsons, Harriett, 118

Parsons, Roswell, 373

Payson, Albert L., 107, 108, 119–20, 136, 142

Peabody, Charles, 138

Pease, John Morris, 334n

Peck, Elisha Wolsey, 323, 331, 335

Penniman, Ebineezer, 405

Perry, Lewis, 458

Perry, Sion L., 324

Peters, Thomas M., 60n

Petitioning: and retailing of alcohol, 171–74, 180, 181, 182, 183, 189, 198–99, 202, 208, 214–15, 217, 235, 246–47, and Sabbatarian legislation, 129–30; and slavery, 357–58, 360, 362–63, 382–83, 423, 446–47, 448

Phelan, Joseph, 35, 47n

Philips, George, 47n

Philips, Wendell, 420, 422

Philomathic Society, 318

Phoenix Division, Sons of Temperance (Dexter), 262, 264–66, 281, 286

Pickens, Israel, 47n, 79

Pickens, Samuel, 47n

Pillsbury, Parker, 419, 420, 421–22

Pinney, John B., 329, 335–36

Pittsfield Township, Mich., 118, 146, 244, 257, 374, 376, 380, 402, 403n, 405, 439, 444

Place of birth. *See* Southern origins; Yankee origins

Plainfield, Mich., 437

Plan of Union, 125–26, 132, 291

Plantation mission, 339–52

Planters' culture, 153, 227

Platt, Ezra H., 121

Platt, Zephaniah, 418n

Plymouth, Mich., 255

Polk, Josiah, 318–19, 322

Pond, Elihu, 271, 273, 275, 298, 420

Pontiac, Mich., 109, 357, 393, 423, 469

Poor whites: and the benevolence message, 36, 48–49, 64–71, 79, 82, 84, 136, 143–45, 151; and the temperance message, 183, 189, 243, 252

Porter, A. L., 371

Porter, Benjamin F., 189, 313, 464

Powell, Aaron M., 414, 420

Powell, R., 261

Power, Nathan, 296, 401

Presbyterians: and abolition, 360, 364, 431–35; and benevolence, 37, 42, 46, 50–62 *passim*, 64, 65, 68, 69, 89, 91, 94, 95, 103, 112, 117–137 *passim*, 146, 152; and Congregationalists, 103, 122, 125–26, 131–32, 143, 146, 244, 291, 292, 434–35, 447–48; and plantation mission, 350–52; and revivalism, 26, 27, 108–11; and temperance, 169, 185, 230, 232, 238, 239, 244, 247, 250, 262, 291–93; Cumberland, 12, 26, 103n; New School, 12, 125–26, 430–31, 435, 436; Old School, 12, 103, 125–26, 431; schism, 125–26

Priest, Erastus, 240

Primitive Baptists. *See* Baptists [Antimission]

Prohibition: Alabama efforts, 171–75, 202–209, 212–18; Michigan efforts, 239–43, 246–47, 248–49, 251–60, 285; opposition to, 175, 180, 216, 217–18, 255, 269, 280. *See also* Liquor licensing; Temperance

Quakers: 460n; Hicksite, 359, 418, 421

Racial mixing: white evangelical fears of, 77

Ramsdell, Norton R., 253n, 407

Rationalism, 22–23, 163, 231

Ready, Aaron, 313

Reddins, Randolph, 70–71

Reed, John B., 64

Reed, Susan W. Childress, 59n

Reform: confluence of different efforts, 51, 60–61, 63, 106, 120–22, 145–51, 248, 250, 296, 323, 332, 415; opposition to, 89–100, 106, 113, 159–63, 180, 255, 469. *See also* Antiabolition; Prohibition

Refugee Home Society, 151

Remond, Charles L., 420

Remond, Sarah P., 420

Republican Party: and prohibition, 271, 275–76; and temperance, 294–95; emergence of, 140, 410–14; on the Slave Power, 386

Revivalism: and temperance, 169–70; behavioral impact of, 27, 29; Democratic endorsement, 26–27; in Alabama, 23–31,

90; in Michigan, 106, 107–11, 119, 459–60;
    Whig endorsement, 27
Rice, Samuel F., 167, 218n
Richardson, A. W., 195
Richardson, Warfield Creath, 178, 193–94
Rives, George W., 192
Robertson, A., 219
Root, Henry, 108, 244
Rorabaugh, W. J., 220, 228
Rose, Gregory, 300

Sabbath observance: and Democrats, 130;
    evangelical promotion of, 32, 91, 107, 122,
    128–31, 133–34, 142; and Whigs, 129–30
Sabbath School Concert, 94
Sabbath schools. *See* Sunday schools
Saffold, Reuben, 324
Salem Township, Mich., 126, 128, 143,
    270, 374, 379, 381, 395, 405, 435, 444,
    425, 431–32
Saline Township, Mich., 110, 127, 132, 149,
    262, 282, 293, 380, 405, 438n, 443, 444
Sanford, J. H., 136
Sawyer, Franklin, 386
Sayre, William, 93
Schlesinger, Arthur M. Jr., 458
Scio Liberty Association, 147n
Scio Township, Mich., 119, 248, 256, 364n, 374,
    380, 402, 405
Scotford, John, 440
Seaman, Ezra, 414
Searcy, Reuben, 60n
Second Great Awakening, 459–60
Secret societies: opposition to, 263–64
Selma, Ala., 198–99, 212–13
Sharon Township, Mich., 382, 405, 411–12,
    438, 447n
Shaw, Luther, 112
Sheldon, E. M., 117n
Shepard, Mrs., 283
Shepherd, Simpson, 53
Shoff, S. S., 258, 428
Shortridge, George D., 178, 216, 468n
Signal of Liberty, 374–75, 396–97, 450–53
Simpson, Thomas, 355

Sims, B. G., 323
Sink, Philip L., 35, 36, 57
Skepticism. *See* Rationalism
Slade, Marmaduke J., 313
Slade, William, 362
Slave Power, 377, 384–86, 396, 401, 414, 436,
    454–55
Slaveholding: among benevolence enthusi-
    asts, 46, 59, 62; among Female Benevolent
    Society contributors, 88; among Sunday-
    school students' households, 68; among
    temperance enthusiasts, 221–23, 227;
    among Tuscaloosa County residents, 88,
    Table 2; among Tuscaloosa town residents,
    88; and benevolence, 71, 101
Slavery: and reform, 337–38, 462; and temper-
    ance, 337–38; defense of, 85; efforts to con-
    trol, 305–308
Smart, J. S., 276
Smith, Gerrit, 148, 370, 443
Snow, Henry Adams, 179, 310, 331
Social profile: abolitionists and Free Soilers,
    446–60; American Bible Society and
    American Tract Society activists, (Ala.)
    45–46, (Mich.) 122–23; colonization activ-
    ists, (Ala.) 323–26, (Mich.) 329–32, 417;
    Female Benevolent Society contributors,
    85–89; Sunday-school activists, (Ala.) 58–
    62, (Mich.) 123–24; Sunday-school stu-
    dents, (Ala.) 63–69; temperance activists,
    (Ala.) 221–29, 231–32, (Mich.) 284–91
Society of the State of Alabama for the Pro-
    motion of Temperance. *See* Alabama State
    Temperance Society
Sons of Malta, 84
Sons of Temperance: 166n, 186, 463; and aboli-
    tionists, 263; and Baptists, 232; in Ala-
    bama, 82, 192–99, 201–202, 206, 209–12,
    216, 220, 224–27, 228, 229, 230; in Michi-
    gan, 147n, 260–67, 285–88, 290
Southern Baptist Convention, 341–42, 346
Southern origins: of Alabama colonization-
    ists, 326, 330–31; of Alabama settlers, 8; of
    Alabama Sunday school activists, 59; of
    Alabama temperance activists, 228; of

Female Benevolent Society contributors, 86; of Tuscaloosa male heads of household, 228, Table 5

Spencer, Grove, 133–34, 292

Sprague, William, 400n

Star of Freedom, 424

Stebbins, Giles, 419, 421–22, 428

Stewart, Alvan, 363, 365, 368, 370

Stewart, Charles H., 296, 377, 413

Stewart, James Brewer, 446

Stiteler, J. B., 212

Stone, Lucy, 420, 428

Stoney Creek, Mich. *See* Augusta Township, Mich.

Student Lecture Association, 421–22

Sturgis, Columbus Franklin, 80, 95, 353

Sullivan, William M., 151, 380, 437, 461

Sunday mail controversy. *See* Sabbath observance

Sunday schools: 47–69, 78, 80, 91, 106, 118–20, 123–24, 133, 136–37, 138, 142, 248, 250, 340–41. *See also* American Sunday School Union; Central Alabama Sunday School Union; Grant's Creek Sunday School; Michigan Sunday School Union; Slaveholding; Social profile; Tuscaloosa Sunday School Union; Tuscaloosa Union Sunday School; Washtenaw County Sunday School Union

Superior Township, Mich., 112, 118, 142, 270, 382, 405

Supreme Court of Alabama: and liquor licensing, 203–204, 213, 218

Supreme Court of Michigan: and Maine Law, 270, 274–75

Swift, Marcus, 438

Sykes, Abraham, 364

Sylvan Township, Mich., 108, 126, 147n, 244, 250, 402, 405

Talladega, Ala., 210

Talladega Temperance Society, 182

Tappan, Henry P., 279

Tavern licenses, 163–64, Table 6

Taylor, John M., 324

Teetotalism. *See* Total abstinence

Temperance: 145–46, 155–302; and church affiliation, 231–32, 290–91, Tables 7 and 9; and political parties, 294–99; and recidivism, 233; and respectability, 169, and slaves, 337–39; opposition to, 89–90, 106; in southern states, 5n. *See also* Abolitionism; Alabama State Temperance Society; Alabama Total Abstinence Society; Baptists; Benevolence activists; Congregationalists; Democratic Party; Liberty Party; Liquor licensing; Methodists; Michigan State Temperance Society; Moral suasion; Presbyterians; Prohibition; Slaveholding; Slavery; Social profile; Sons of Temperance; Total abstinence; Tuscaloosa Temperance Society; Washingtonians; Washtenaw County Temperance Society; Whig Party; Women

Temperance activists: as abolitionists, 294–98, 300–301. *See also* Benevolence activists

Temperance Society of the University of Alabama, 181n

Temperance Society of Ypsilanti. *See* Ypsilanti Temperance Society

Ten Brook, Andrew, 131

Ten Islands Baptist Association, 217

Tennis, O. J., 415

Terry, Nathaniel, 187

Theater: evangelical opposition to, 25, 29, 107

Thom, A. E., 333

Thomas, Nathan, 361–62, 403

Thompson, Oren C., 109, 121, 133, 141

Tocqueville, Alexis de, 109

Total abstinence, 169, 176, 180, 180–85, 219, 235, 239, 243–45, 247–50, 276, 463. *See also* Alabama Total Abstinence Society; Ann Arbor Total Abstinence Society; Colored Total Abstinence Society; Ladies' Total Abstinence Society (Dexter); Ladies' Total Abstinence Society of Ann Arbor; Michigan Total Abstinence Society; Tuscaloosa Total Abstinence Society; Washtenaw County Total Abstinence Society;

Young Men's Total Abstinence Society; Ypsilanti Total Abstinence Society

Townships in Michigan, 258n

Townson, Calvin, 373

Tract circulation, 47, 48, 340–41. *See also* American Tract Society; Ann Arbor Female Tract Society; Benevolent Society of the University of Alabama; Dexter Female Tract Society; Doctrinal and Tract Society; Female Tract Societies; Methodist Episcopal Tract Society Auxiliary; Social profile

Treadwell, Seymour B., 369–72, 376, 382, 384, 403, 413, 425, 429, 460

True Democrat, 399–400

Truss, Mr., 417

Turner, J. W., 204n

Tuscaloosa (town): frontier conditions in, 21–22; male occupations in, 73; population of, 9, 76n; real property holdings in, 226–27; school attendance in, 75–76; slaveholding in, 88

Tuscaloosa Baptist Association, 96, 167, 230, 345, 347

Tuscaloosa Bible Society, 74, 313

Tuscaloosa Classical and Scientific School, 179

Tuscaloosa County, Ala.: geography, 8; residents' origins, 228; male occupations in, 73n; political characteristics of, 11; population of, 8, Table 1; racial composition of, 8, Table 1; real property holdings in, 226; religious characteristics of, 12, Table 3; school attendance in, 75–76; slaveholding in, 88, 228, Table 2

Tuscaloosa Female Academy, 178

Tuscaloosa Maternal Association, 83

Tuscaloosa Presbytery, 350

Tuscaloosa Society for the Promotion of Temperance. *See* Tuscaloosa Temperance Society

Tuscaloosa Sunday School Union, 52–55 *passim,* 94

Tuscaloosa Temperance Society, 159–83 *passim,* 196, 216, 221–25, 228, 313, 323, 337

Tuscaloosa Total Abstinence Society, 183–84, 186

Tuscaloosa Union Sunday School, 53, 54, 57–69 *passim,* 72–73, 76, 81, 313, 323, 336

Tuskaloosa Association Baptist Bible Society, 40

Tuskaloosa Baptist Bible Society, 39–40, 81

Tutwiler, Henry, 317–18, 320, 324, 327, 329, 340

Twiss, John S., 147n

Tyler, Alice Felt, 3

Tyrrell, Ian, 220, 228

Underground railroad, 381, 415

Union Missionary Society, 150–51

Union Sabbath School Missionary Society, 95, 96

Unitarians, 421

Universalists: and abolition, 439, 445; and benevolence, 136; and Fourierism, 467; and temperance, 250, 294n, Michigan presence, 12

University of Alabama: 210, 312, 318; and alcohol regulation, 205–206, 217; enrollment of, 10; student benevolence activity at, 43–44; student temperance activity at, 181n, 194, 199–202, 216

University of Michigan: and alcohol regulation, 258, 278–79; enrollment of, 10; female admission to, 429; faculty benevolence activity at, 131; fraternities at, 261; student temperance activity at, 296n

University of Virginia, 202

Van Dyke, T. Nixon, 63n, 323, 342, 326

Van Fleet, Jane, 424

Van Hoose, Azor, 209

Vaughan, Albert J., 324

Vaughn, Mary, 198

Voorhies, William C. 121

Walker, Erasmus, 91–92, 167n

Walker, James W., 419, 420

Walker, Richard W., 214

Walker, Robert L., 94

Wallace, Harriette, 82, 195, 197

Wallace, James B., 60n, 68n

Walters, Ronald G., 3

Warren, John, 198, 199, 204–214 *passim,* 219, 229, 338

Washington, Dennis, 415

Washington, Lewis, 382

Washingtonian Temperance Society of Medina, 252

Washingtonian Total Abstinence Society of the State of Alabama. *See* Alabama Total Abstinence Society

Washingtonians: 166n, 463; in Alabama, 186–88, 191, 223; in Michigan, 250–53, 282, 283, 285

Washtenaw Baptist Association, 432n, 442, 443n

Washtenaw County, Mich.: political characteristics of, 11–12; population of, 8; racial composition of, 8; real property holdings in, 123, 290; religious characteristics of, 12, Table 4; school attendance in, 124

Washtenaw County Anti-Slavery Society, 358, 363, 364, 367, 373

Washtenaw County Bible Society, 111–12, 114–15, 118, 121, 141, 146, 147n, 373

Washtenaw County Board of Supervisors, 274, 280

Washtenaw County Sunday School Union, 112, 118, 121, 147n

Washtenaw County Temperance Society, 112, 146, 147n, 238, 241, 281

Washtenaw County Total Abstinence Society, 245, 246n

Washtenaw Phalanx, 467

Washtenaw Presbytery, 108, 129, 145, 293, 433, 435

Watson, James V., 441

Wayne County, Mich., 108, 110, 255

Weed, Ira M., 107, 109, 112, 121, 240, 244

Webster Township, Mich., 110, 114, 126, 130, 141, 146, 244, 253n, 293, 380, 381, 402, 405, 431–32, 435, 444, 460

Webster/Scio Anti-Slavery Society, 359

Wesleyan Methodists. *See* Methodists

West, Anson, 26, 28

West, Nathaniel, 376

Western Anti-Slavery Society, 419

Wheedon, Daniel B., 131

Whig Party: and abolition, 357–58, 360–61, 365, 371–73, 377, 386–93, 395, 397, 448–49; and benevolence, 21, 35, 39, 59, 61, 62, 63, 71, 79, 100, 129, 130, 133, 154; and colonization, 331; and Free Soil, 399–400, 402–406, 407–13; and prohibition, 267–68; and temperance, 177, 247, 249, 294–95, 299; collapse of, 410–413

White, John, 324

Whitfield, Benjamin, 32, 314, 345

Whitfield, Newton L., 211–12, 231

Willas, Thomas, 151

Williams, J. M., 430

Williams, John D., 39

Williams, Ransom G., 309

Williams, William H., 49–55 *passim,* 94, 96, 323

Wines, W. W., 147n

Winston, John A. , 214, 215, 468

Wisconsin Law, 266, 301

Wisc, Henry A., 179

Withers, Jones M., 60n

Witherspoon, Reverend, 335

Women: abolitionist activism among, 422–26; benevolence activism among, 81–89, 115, 116–17, 142–45; colonization activism among, 322; direct action among, 282–83; temperance activism among, 165, 195–99, 242, 280–84, 465

Women's rights, 199, 421, 465

Women's suffrage, 426–29, 468

Wood, Darius S., 434

Wood, George W., 357

Woodbridge, William, 246

Woodbury, Silas, 108, 141

Woodruff, Charles, 254, 262, 263, 406

Woodruff, David, 42, 47n, 60n, 331

Woodruff, Milford, 57, 233n

Woods, Alva, 52, 53, 95n

Wright, Henry C., 419, 421

Wyatt-Brown, Bertram, 97

Yankee origins: of Michigan abolitionists,
    449; of Michigan benevolence activists,
    122–23; of Michigan settlers, 8, 103, 299–
    300; of Michigan temperance activists,
    299–300
York Township, Mich., 244, 405
Yorkville (Ala.) Temperance Society,
    182
Young America, 229
Young Men's Association, 276
Young Men's Christian Association, 84
Young Men's Liberty Association of Michi-
    gan, 425

Young Men's Temperance Association, 244
Young Men's Total Abstinence Society (Tus-
    caloosa), 177–78, 180–83, 212n, 222–25, 228
Young Men's Total Abstinence Society of
    Clinton, 182
Ypsilanti, Mich., 9, 107, 108, 109, 110, 113, 126,
    127, 133, 136, 137, 236, 240, 248, 249, 252, 254,
    262, 266, 269, 270, 276, 285, 293, 380, 381,
    382, 402, 405, 420, 444, 445
Ypsilanti Literary Association, 427
Ypsilanti Temperance Society, 237, 238, 244,
    292
Ypsilanti Total Abstinence Society, 278